EXPLORING MICROSOFT® OFFICE 2000 PROFESSIONAL

Volume I

Robert T. Grauer / Maryann Barber

University of Miami

Prentice Hall, Upper Saddle River, New Jersey 07458

Executive Editor: Alex von Rosenberg
Managing Editor: Susan Rifkin
Editorial Assistant: Jennifer Surich
Director of Strategic Marketing: Nancy Evans
Production Manager: Gail Steier
Production Editor: Greg Hubit
Project Manager: Lynne Breitfeller
Senior Manufacturing Supervisor: Paul Smolenski
Manufacturing Coordinator: Dawn-Marie Reisner
Manufacturing Manager: Vincent Scelta
Design Manager: Patricia Smythe
Cover Design: Marjory Dressler
Composition: GTS Graphics

ISBN 0-13-014996-9

Prentice-Hall International (UK) Limited, London
Prentice-Hall of Australia Pty. Limited, Sydney
Prentice-Hall Canada Inc., Toronto
Prentice-Hall Hispanoamericana, S.A., Mexico
Prentice-Hall of India Private Limited, New Delhi
Prentice-Hall of Japan, Inc., Tokyo
Editora Prentice-Hall do Brasil, Ltda., Rio de Janeiro

Printed in the United States of America

10   9   8   7   6   5   4

CONTENTS

PREFACE   XI

PREREQUISITES: ESSENTIALS OF WINDOWS 95/98

EXPLORING MICROSOFT® WORD 2000

4

ADVANCED FEATURES: OUTLINES, TABLES, STYLES, AND SECTIONS   155

EXPLORING MICROSOFT® EXCEL 2000

1

INTRODUCTION TO MICROSOFT® EXCEL: WHAT IS A SPREADSHEET?   1

2

GAINING PROFICIENCY: COPYING, FORMATTING, AND ISOLATING ASSUMPTIONS   41

3

SPREADSHEETS IN DECISION MAKING: WHAT IF?   85

4

GRAPHS AND CHARTS: DELIVERING A MESSAGE   137

EXPLORING MICROSOFT® ACCESS 2000

EXPLORING MICROSOFT® POWERPOINT 2000

INTERNET EXPLORER 5.0

GETTING STARTED: ESSENTIAL COMPUTING CONCEPTS

INDEX

To Marion—my wife, my lover, and my best friend
—Robert Grauer

To my Mother and Father—for all their love and support
these many years
—Maryann Barber

PREFACE

We are proud to announce the fourth edition of the *Exploring Windows* series in conjunction with Microsoft® Office 2000. The series has expanded in two important ways—recognition by the ***Microsoft Office User Specialist (MOUS)*** program, and a significantly expanded Web site at ***www.prenhall.com/grauer***. The Web site provides password-protected solutions for instructors and online study guides (Companion Web sites) for students. Practice files and PowerPoint lectures are available for both student and instructor. The site also contains information about Microsoft Certification, CD-based tutorials for use with the series, and SkillCheck® assessment software.

The organization of the series is essentially unchanged. There are separate titles for each application—*Word 2000, Excel 2000, Access 2000,* and *PowerPoint 2000,* a book on *Windows® 98,* and eventually, *Windows® 2000.* There are also four combined texts—*Exploring Microsoft Office Professional, Volumes I* and *II, Exploring Microsoft Office Proficient Certification Edition,* and *Brief Office. Volume I* is a unique combination of applications and concepts for the introductory computer course. It covers all four Office applications and includes supporting material on Windows 95/98, Internet Explorer, and Essential Computing Concepts. The modules for Word and Excel satisfy the requirements for proficient certification. The *Proficient Certification Edition* extends the coverage of Access and PowerPoint from *Volume I* to meet the certification requirements, but (because of length) deletes the units on Internet Explorer and Essential Computing Concepts that are found in *Volume I. Volume II* includes the advanced features in all four applications and extends certification to the expert level. *Brief Office* is intended to get the reader "up and running," without concern for certification requirements.

The Internet and World Wide Web are integrated throughout the series. Students learn Office applications as before, and in addition are sent to the Web as appropriate for supplementary exercises. The sections on Object Linking and Embedding, for example, not only draw on resources within Microsoft Office, but on the Web as well. Students are directed to search the Web for information, and then download resources for inclusion in Office documents. The icon at the left of this paragraph appears throughout the text whenever there is a Web reference.

The *Exploring Windows* series is part of the Prentice Hall custom-binding (*Right PHit*) program, enabling instructors to create their own texts by selecting modules from *Volume I,* the *Proficient Certification Edition,* and/or *Brief Office* to suit the needs of a specific course. An instructor could, for example, create a custom text consisting of the proficient modules in Word and Excel, coupled with the brief modules for Access and PowerPoint. Instructors can also take advantage of our *ValuePack program* to shrink-wrap multiple books together at a substantial saving for the student. A ValuePack is ideal in courses that require complete coverage of multiple applications.

Instructors will want to obtain the *Instructor's Resource CD* from their Prentice Hall representative. The CD contains the student data disks, solutions to all exercises in machine-readable format, PowerPoint lectures, and the Instructor Manuals themselves in Word format. The CD also has a Windows-based test generator. Please visit us on the Web at ***www.prenhall.com/grauer*** for additional information.

FEATURES AND BENEFITS

Exploring Microsoft Office Volume I is written for the novice and assumes no previous knowledge of the operating system. A 64-page prerequisites section introduces the reader to the essentials of Windows 95/98/NT and emphasizes the file operations he or she will need.

Our text emphasizes the benefits of the common user interface, which pertains to all applications in Office 2000. Individuals already familiar with one Office application are encouraged to leverage what they already know to learn a new application more quickly.

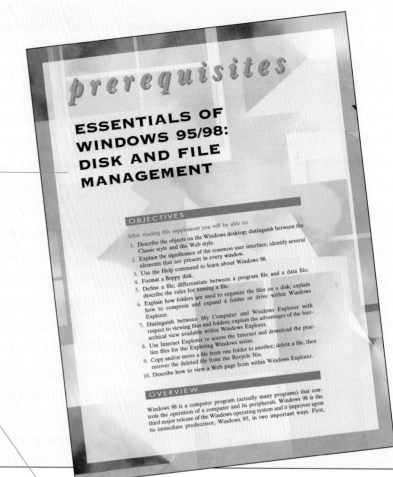

Figure 13 Microsoft Office 2000

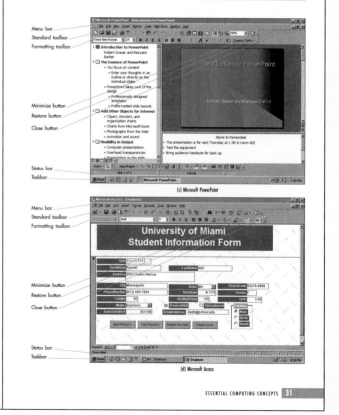

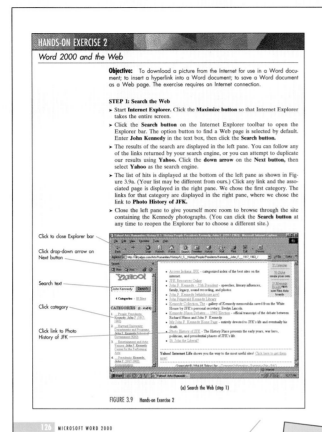

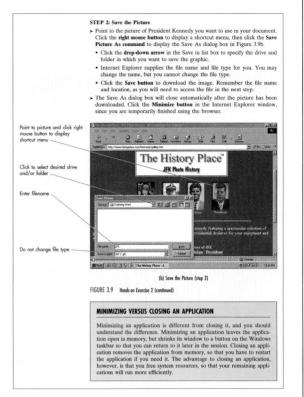

A total of 45 in-depth tutorials (hands-on exercises) guide the reader at the computer and are illustrated with large, full-color, screen captures that are clear and easy to read. This exercise shows the reader how to download resources from the Web for inclusion in a Word document.

A unique 48-page section acquaints the student with essential computing concepts that pertain to the PC as well as the mainframe. The reader learns about the CPU memory, auxiliary storage, input and output devices, operating systems, and application software.

Computer World's Annual Pre-Inventory Sale

When: **June 21, 1999**
             8:00AM - 10:00PM

Where: **13640 South Dixie Highway**

Computer World

Computers
Printers
Fax/Modems
CD-ROM drives
Sound Systems
Software
Etc.

Pre-Inventory Sale

Sales Associate: Bianca Costo

FIGURE 3.13   Inserting Objects (Exercise 1)

♥ ♥ ♥ ♥ ♥ ♥ ♥ ♥ ♥ ♥ ♥ ♥ ♥ ♥ ♥

Valentine's Day
We'll serenade your sweetheart
Call 284-LOVE

♥ ♥ ♥ ♥ ♥ ♥ ♥ ♥ ♥ ♥ ♥ ♥ ♥ ♥ ♥

STUDENT COMPUTER LAB
Fall Semester Hours

🕘AM - 🕛PM

FIGURE 3.14   Exploring TrueType (Exercise 2)

Every chapter contains a large number of practice exercises that review the material and expose the student to a wide range of different documents. These exercises are taken from Chapter 3 in Word.

Every chapter also contains a number of less-structured case studies to challenge the student. The Web icon appears throughout the text whenever the student is directed to the World Wide Web as a source of additional material.

CASE STUDIES

The United States of America

What is the total population of the United States? What is its area? Can you name the 13 original states or the last five states admitted to the Union? Do you know the 10 states with the highest population or the five largest states in terms of area? Which states have the highest population density (people per square mile)?

The answers to these and other questions can be obtained from the United States database that is available on the data disk. The key to the assignment is to use the Top Values property within a query that limits the number of records returned in the dynaset. Use the database to create several reports that you think will be of interest to the class.

The Super Bowl

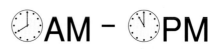

How many times has the NFC won the Super Bowl? When was the last time the AFC won? What was the largest margin of victory? What was the closest game? What is the most points scored by two teams in one game? How many times have the Miami Dolphins appeared? How many times did they win? Use the data in the Super Bowl database to create a trivia sheet on the Super Bowl, then incorporate your analysis into a letter addressed to NBC Sports. Convince them you are a super fan and that you merit two tickets to next year's game. Go to the home page of the National Football League (www.nfl.com) to obtain score(s) from the most recent game(s) to update our table if necessary.

Mail Merge

A mail merge takes the tedium out of sending form letters, as it creates the same letter many times, changing the name, address, and other information as appropriate from letter to letter. The form letter is created in a word processor (e.g., Microsoft Word), but the data file may be taken from an Access table or query. Use the Our Students database as the basis for two different form letters sent to two different groups of students. The first letter is to congratulate students on the Dean's list (GPA of 3.50 or higher). The second letter is a warning to students on academic probation (GPA of less than 2.00).

Compacting versus Compressing

An Access database becomes fragmented, and thus unnecessarily large, as objects (e.g., reports and forms) are modified or deleted. It is important, therefore, to periodically compact a database to reduce its size (enabling you to back it up on a floppy disk). Choose a database with multiple objects; e.g., the Our Students database used in this chapter. Use the Windows Explorer to record the file size of the database as it presently exists. Start Access, open the database, pull down the Tools menu and select Database Utilities to compact the database, then record the size of the database after compacting. You can also compress a compacted database (using a standard Windows utility such as WinZip) to further reduce your requirement for disk storage. Summarize your findings in a short report to your instructor. Try compacting and compressing at least two different databases to better appreciate these techniques.

The *Exploring Windows* series is a unique combination of concepts as well as hands-on exercises. Chapter 1 in each section starts with the basics of the application and assumes no previous knowledge on the part of the reader.

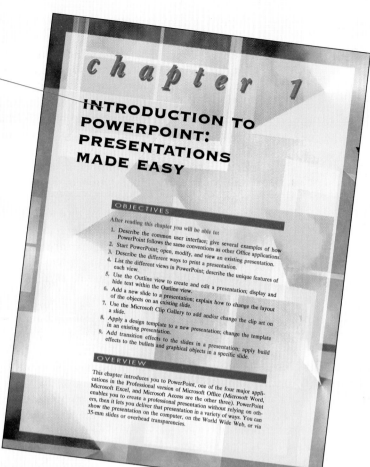

Knowledge of search engines is essential in order to use the Internet effectively. This example from Chapter 2 in the Internet Explorer section shows the importance of using multiple engines for the same query.

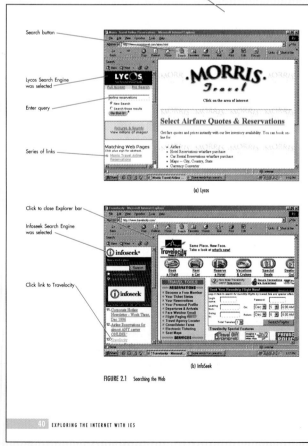

(a) Lycos

(b) InfoSeek

FIGURE 2.1 Searching the Web

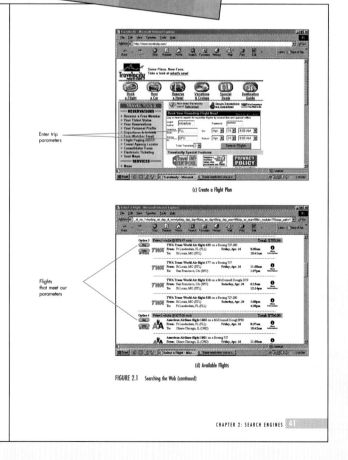

(c) Create a Flight Plan

(d) Available Flights

FIGURE 2.1 Searching the Web (continued)

Acknowledgments

We want to thank the many individuals who have helped to bring this project to fruition. We are especially grateful to Nancy Evans and PJ Boardman, who continue to offer inspiration and guidance. Alex von Rosenberg, executive editor at Prentice Hall, has provided new leadership in extending the series to Office 2000. Nancy Welcher did an absolutely incredible job on our Web site. Susan Rifkin coordinated the myriad details of production and the certification process. Greg Christofferson was instrumental in the acquisition of supporting software. Lynne Breitfeller was the project manager. Paul Smolenski was senior manufacturing supervisor. Greg Hubit has been masterful as the external production editor for every book in the series. Cecil Yarbrough did an outstanding job in checking the manuscript for technical accuracy. Jennifer Surich was the editorial assistant. Leanne Nieglos was the supplements editor. Cindy Stevens, Karen Vignare, and Michael Olmstead wrote the Instructor Manuals. Patricia Smythe developed the innovative and attractive design. We also want to acknowledge our reviewers who, through their comments and constructive criticism, greatly improved the series.

Lynne Band, Middlesex Community College
Don Belle, Central Piedmont Community College
Stuart P. Brian, Holy Family College
Carl M. Briggs, Indiana University School of Business
Kimberly Chambers, Scottsdale Community College
Alok Charturvedi, Purdue University
Jerry Chin, Southwest Missouri State University
Dean Combellick, Scottsdale Community College
Cody Copeland, Johnson County Community College
Larry S. Corman, Fort Lewis College
Janis Cox, Tri-County Technical College
Martin Crossland, Southwest Missouri State University
Paul E. Daurelle, Western Piedmont Community College
David Douglas, University of Arkansas
Carlotta Eaton, Radford University
Judith M. Fitspatrick, Gulf Coast Community College
Raymond Frost, Central Connecticut State University
Midge Gerber, Southwestern Oklahoma State University
James Gips, Boston College
Vernon Griffin, Austin Community College
Michael Hassett, Fort Hays State University
Wanda D. Heller, Seminole Community College
Bonnie Homan, San Francisco State University
Ernie Ivey, Polk Community College
Mike Kelly, Community College of Rhode Island
Jane King, Everett Community College
Rose M. Laird, Northern Virginia Community College

John Lesson, University of Central Florida
David B. Meinert, Southwest Missouri State University
Bill Morse, DeVry Institute of Technology
Alan Moltz, Naugatuck Valley Technical Community College
Kim Montney, Kellogg Community College
Kevin Pauli, University of Nebraska
Mary McKenry Percival, University of Miami
Delores Pusins, Hillsborough Community College
Gale E. Rand, College Misericordia
Judith Rice, Santa Fe Community College
David Rinehard, Lansing Community College
Marilyn Salas, Scottsdale Community College
John Shepherd, Duquesne University
Barbara Sherman, Buffalo State College
Robert Spear, Prince George's Community College
Michael Stewardson, San Jacinto College—North
Helen Stoloff, Hudson Valley Community College
Margaret Thomas, Ohio University
Mike Thomas, Indiana University School of Business
Suzanne Tomlinson, Iowa State University
Karen Tracey, Central Connecticut State University
Sally Visci, Lorain County Community College
David Weiner, University of San Francisco
Connie Wells, Georgia State University
Wallace John Whistance-Smith, Ryerson Polytechnic University
Jack Zeller, Kirkwood Community College

A final word of thanks to the unnamed students at the University of Miami, who make it all worthwhile. Most of all, thanks to you, our readers, for choosing this book. Please feel free to contact us with any comments and suggestions.

Robert T. Grauer
rgrauer@sba.miami.edu
www.bus.miami.edu/~rgrauer
www.prenhall.com/grauer

Maryann Barber
mbarber@sba.bus.miami.edu
www.bus.miami.edu/~mbarber

prerequisites

ESSENTIALS OF WINDOWS 95/98: DISK AND FILE MANAGEMENT

OBJECTIVES

After reading this supplement you will be able to:

1. Describe the objects on the Windows desktop; distinguish between the Classic style and the Web style.
2. Explain the significance of the common user interface; identify several elements that are present in every window.
3. Use the Help command to learn about Windows 98.
4. Format a floppy disk.
5. Define a file; differentiate between a program file and a data file; describe the rules for naming a file.
6. Explain how folders are used to organize the files on a disk; explain how to compress and expand a folder or drive within Windows Explorer.
7. Distinguish between My Computer and Windows Explorer with respect to viewing files and folders; explain the advantages of the hierarchical view available within Windows Explorer.
8. Use Internet Explorer to access the Internet and download the practice files for the Exploring Windows series.
9. Copy and/or move a file from one folder to another; delete a file, then recover the deleted file from the Recycle Bin.
10. Describe how to view a Web page from within Windows Explorer.

OVERVIEW

Windows 98 is a computer program (actually many programs) that controls the operation of a computer and its peripherals. Windows 98 is the third major release of the Windows operating system and it improves upon its immediate predecessor, Windows 95, in two important ways. First, there are many enhancements "under the surface" that make the PC run more efficiently. Second, Windows 98 brings the Internet to the desktop. Unlike Windows 95, however, Windows 98 has two distinct interfaces, a "Classic Style" and a "Web Style." The Classic style works identically to Windows 95, and thus we have titled this section, "Essentials of Windows 95/98" in that the Classic Style applies to both operating systems.

We begin with a discussion of the Windows desktop and describe the common user interface and consistent command structure that is present in every Windows application. We identify the basic components of a window and discuss how to execute commands and supply information through different elements in a dialog box. We introduce you to My Computer, an icon on the Windows desktop, and show you how to use My Computer to access the various components of your system. We also describe how to access the Help command.

The supplement focuses, however, on disk and file management. We present the basic definitions of a file and a folder, then describe how to use My Computer to look for a specific file or folder. We introduce Windows Explorer, which provides a more efficient way of finding data on your system, then show you how to move or copy a file from one folder to another. We discuss other basic operations such as renaming and deleting a file. We also describe how to recover a deleted file (if necessary) from the Recycle Bin.

There are also four hands-on exercises that enable you to apply the conceptual discussion in the text at the computer. The exercises refer to a set of practice files (known as a data disk) that we have created for you. You can obtain the practice files from our Web site (www.prenhall.com/grauer) or from a local area network if your professor has downloaded the files for you.

WINDOWS NT VERSUS WINDOWS 98

The computer you purchase for home use will have Windows 98. The computer you use at school or the office, however, will most likely have **Windows NT**, a more secure version of Windows that is intended for networked environments. This is significant to system personnel, but transparent to the user because Windows NT 5.0 (which will be called **Windows 2000**) has the same user interface as Windows 98. There are subtle differences, but for the most part, the screens are identical, and thus you will be able to use this text with either operating system.

THE DESKTOP

All versions of Windows create a working environment for your computer that parallels the working environment at home or in an office. You work at a desk. Windows operations take place on the *desktop.* There are physical objects on a desk such as folders, a dictionary, a calculator, or a phone. The computer equivalents of those objects appear as *icons* (pictorial symbols) on the desktop. Each object on a real desk has attributes (properties) such as size, weight, and color. In similar fashion, Windows assigns properties to every object on its desktop. And just as you can move the objects on a real desk, you can rearrange the objects on the Windows desktop.

Figure 1 displays three different versions of the **Windows 98** desktop. Figures 1a and 1b illustrate the desktop when Windows 98 is first installed on a new computer. These desktops have only a few objects and are similar to the desk in a new office, just after you move in. Figure 1a is displayed in the **Classic style,** which for all practical purposes is identical to the **Windows 95** desktop. Figure 1b

Click icon to select it;
double click icon to open it —

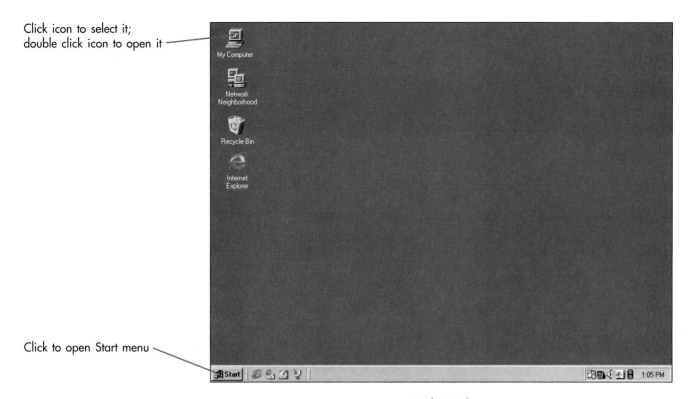

(a) Classic Style

Click to open Start menu —

Point to icon to select it;
click icon to open it —

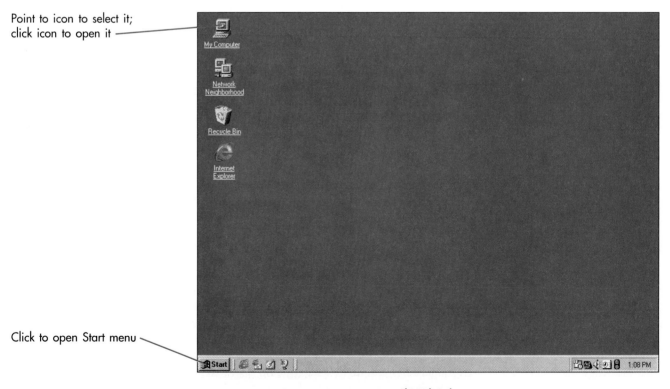

(b) Web Style

Click to open Start menu —

FIGURE 1   The Different Faces of Windows 98

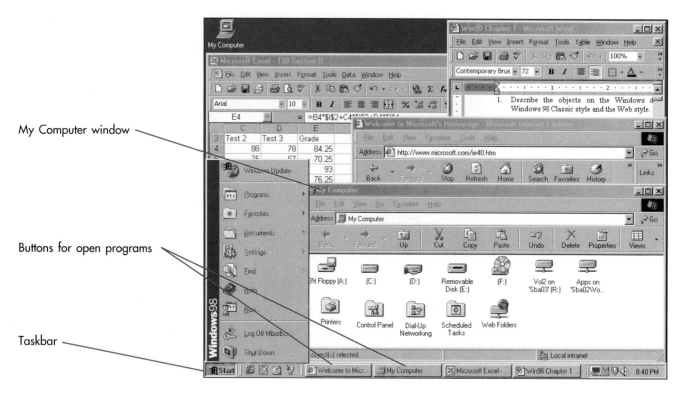

My Computer window

Buttons for open programs

Taskbar

(c) A Working Desktop

FIGURE 1   The Different Faces of Windows 98 (continued)

is displayed in the **Web style,** which is new to Windows 98. The icons on a Web style desktop are underlined and function identically to the hyperlinks within a browser such as Internet Explorer or Netscape Communicator.

The styles differ in visual appearance and in the way the icons work. In the Classic style, you click an icon to select it (mouse operations are described on page 10), and you double click the icon to open it. In the Web style, however, you point to an icon to select it, and you click the icon to open it. These operations mimic those of a Web browser—hence the term, "Web style." (It is a misnomer of sorts, in that the Web style has nothing to do with the Web per se, as you are not necessarily connected to the Internet nor are you viewing any Web pages.) You can display your desktop in either style by setting the appropriate option through the View menu in My Computer, as will be described later in a hands-on exercise. The choice depends entirely on personal preference.

Do not be concerned if your desktop is different from ours. Your real desk is arranged differently from those of your friends, and so your Windows desktop will also be different. What is important is that you recognize the capabilities inherent in Windows 98, as illustrated in Figure 1. Thus, it is the simplicity of the desktops in Figures 1a and 1b that helps you to focus on what is important. The **Start button,** as its name suggests, is where you begin. Click the Start button and you see a menu that lets you start any program installed on your computer. Starting a program opens a window on the desktop and from there you go to work.

Look now at Figure 1c, which displays an entirely different desktop, one with four open windows, that is similar to a desk in the middle of a working day. Each window in Figure 1c displays a program that is currently in use. The ability to run several programs at the same time is known as **multitasking,** and it is a major benefit of the Windows environment. Multitasking enables you to run a word processor in one window, create a spreadsheet in a second window, surf the Internet in a third window, play a game in a fourth window, and so on. You can work in a program as long as you want, then change to a different program by clicking its program.

You can also change from one program to another by using the taskbar at the bottom of the desktop. The *taskbar* contains a button for each open program, and it enables you to switch back and forth between those programs by clicking the appropriate button. The taskbars in Figures 1a and 1b do not contain any buttons (other than the Start button) since there are no open applications. The taskbar in Figure 1c, however, contains four additional buttons, one for each open program.

The icons on the desktop in Figures 1a and 1b are used to access programs or other functions in Windows 98. The *My Computer* icon is the most basic, and it enables you to view the devices on your system. Open My Computer in either Figure 1a or 1b, for example, and you see the objects in the My Computer window of Figure 1c. The contents of the My Computer window depend on the hardware of the specific computer system. Our system, for example, has one floppy drive, two hard (fixed) disks, a removable disk (an Iomega Zip drive), a CD-ROM, and access to two network drives. The My Computer window also contains the Control Panel, Printers, Dial-Up Networking, Web Folders, and Scheduled Tasks folders, which allow access to functions that control other elements in the environment on your computer. (These capabilities are not used by beginners and are generally "off limits" in a lab environment, and thus are not discussed further.)

The other icons on the desktop in Figures 1a and 1b are also noteworthy. *Network Neighborhood* extends your view of the computer to include the accessible drives on the network to which your machine is attached, if indeed it is part of a network. (You will not see this icon if you are not connected to a network.) The *Recycle Bin* allows you to restore a file that was previously deleted. The Internet Explorer icon starts *Internet Explorer,* the Web browser that is built into Windows 98. Indeed, the single biggest difference between Windows 98 and its predecessor, Windows 95, is the tight integration with the Internet and the World Wide Web.

THE COMMON USER INTERFACE

All Windows applications share a *common user interface* and possess a consistent command structure. This is a critically important concept and one of the most significant benefits of the Windows environment, as it provides a sense of familiarity from one application to the next. In essence, every Windows application follows the same conventions and works essentially the same way. Thus, once you learn the basic concepts and techniques in one application, you can apply that knowledge to every other application. The next several pages present this material, after which you will have an opportunity to practice in a hands-on exercise.

Anatomy of a Window

Figure 2 displays a typical window and labels its essential elements. Figure 2a displays the window in the Classic style. Figure 2b shows the identical window using the Web style. Regardless of the style, each window has a title bar, a minimize button, a maximize or restore button, and a close button. Other elements, which may or may not be visible, include a horizontal and/or vertical scroll bar, a menu bar, a status bar, and one or more toolbars. A window may also contain additional objects (icons) that pertain specifically to the programs or data associated with that window.

Title bar

Menu bar

Toolbars

Minimize button

Maximize button

Close button

Status bar

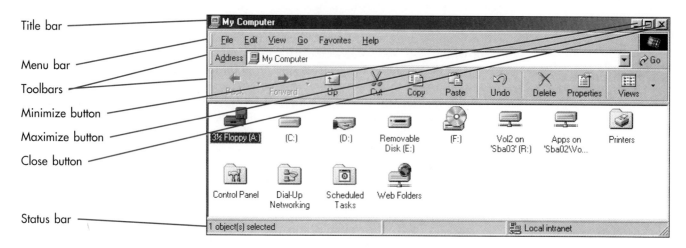

(a) Classic Style

Title bar

Menu bar

Toolbars

Minimize button

Maximize button

Close button

Status bar

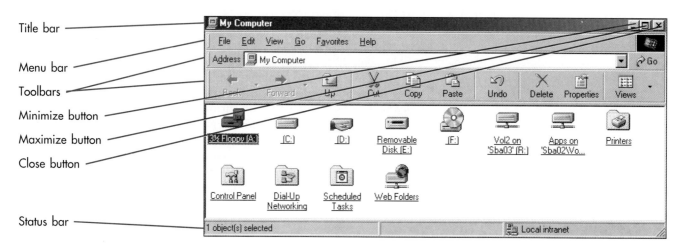

(b) Web Style

FIGURE 2   Anatomy of a Window

The *title bar* appears at the top of the window and displays the name of the window; for example, My Computer in both Figures 2a and 2b. The icon at the extreme left of the title bar provides access to a control menu that lets you select operations relevant to the window such as moving it or sizing it. The *minimize button* shrinks the window to a button on the taskbar, but leaves the application in memory. The *maximize button* enlarges the window so that it takes up the entire desktop. The *restore button* (not shown in Figure 2) appears instead of the maximize button after a window has been maximized, and restores the window to its previous size. The *close button* closes the window and removes it from memory and the desktop.

The *menu bar* appears immediately below the title bar and provides access to pull-down menus (as discussed later). Two toolbars, the *Address bar* and *Standard Buttons bar,* appear below the menu bar. The *status bar* at the bottom of the window displays information about the window as a whole or about a selected object within a window.

A *vertical* (or *horizontal*) *scroll bar* appears at the right (or bottom) border of a window when its contents are not completely visible and provides access to the unseen areas. Scroll bars do not appear in Figure 2 since all of the objects in the window are visible at the same time.

Moving and Sizing a Window

A window can be sized or moved on the desktop through appropriate actions with the mouse. To *size a window,* point to any border (the mouse pointer changes to a double arrow), then drag the border in the direction you want to go—inward to shrink the window or outward to enlarge it. You can also drag a corner (instead of a border) to change both dimensions at the same time. To *move a window* while retaining its current size, click and drag the title bar to a new position on the desktop.

Pull-down Menus

The menu bar provides access to *pull-down menus* that enable you to execute commands within an application (program). A pull-down menu is accessed by clicking the menu name or by pressing the Alt key plus the underlined letter in the menu name; for example, press Alt+V to pull down the View menu. Three pull-down menus associated with My Computer are shown in Figure 3.

Commands within a menu are executed by clicking the command or by typing the underlined letter (for example, C to execute the Close command in the File menu) once the menu has been pulled down. Alternatively, you can bypass the menu entirely if you know the equivalent keystrokes shown to the right of the command in the menu (e.g., Ctrl+X, Ctrl+C, or Ctrl+V to cut, copy, or paste as shown within the Edit menu). A *dimmed command* (e.g., the Paste command in the Edit menu) means the command is not currently executable, and that some additional action has to be taken for the command to become available.

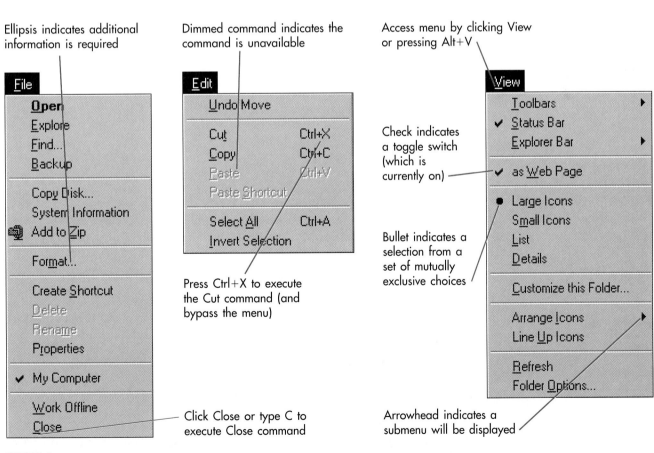

FIGURE 3   Pull-down Menus

An *ellipsis* (...) following a command indicates that additional information is required to execute the command; for example, selection of the Format command in the File menu requires the user to specify additional information about the formatting process. This information is entered into a dialog box (discussed in the next section) which appears immediately after the command has been selected.

A *check* next to a command indicates a toggle switch, whereby the command is either on or off. There is a check next to the Status Bar command in the View menu of Figure 3, which means the command is in effect (and thus the status bar will be displayed). Click the Status Bar command, and the check disappears, which suppresses the display of the status bar. Click the command a second time, and the check reappears, as does the status bar in the associated window.

A *bullet* next to an item (e.g., Large Icons in Figure 3c) indicates a selection from a set of mutually exclusive choices. Click another option within the group (e.g., Small Icons), and the bullet will disappear from the previous selection (Large Icons) and appear next to the new selection (Small Icons).

An *arrowhead* after a command (e.g., the Arrange Icons command in the View menu) indicates that a *submenu* (also known as a cascaded menu) will be displayed with additional menu options.

Dialog Boxes

A *dialog box* appears when additional information is needed to execute a command. The Format command, for example, requires information about which drive to format and the type of formatting desired.

Option (radio) buttons indicate mutually exclusive choices, one of which must be chosen; for example, one of three Format Type options in Figure 4a. Click a button to select an option, which automatically deselects the previously selected option.

Check boxes are used instead of option buttons if the choices are not mutually exclusive or if an option is not required. Multiple boxes can be checked as in Figure 4a, or no boxes may be checked as in Figure 4b. Individual options are selected and cleared by clicking the appropriate check box.

A *text box* is used to enter descriptive information—for example, Bob's Disk in Figure 4a. A flashing vertical bar (an I-beam) appears within the text box when the text box is active, to mark the insertion point for the text you will enter.

A *list box* displays some or all of the available choices, any one of which is selected by clicking the desired item. A *drop-down list box,* such as the Capacity list box in Figure 4a, conserves space by showing only the current selection. Click the arrow of a drop-down list box to display the list of available options. An *open list box,* such as those in Figure 4b, displays multiple choices at one time. (A scroll bar appears within an open list box if all of the choices are not visible and provides access to the hidden choices.)

A *tabbed dialog box* provides multiple sets of options. The dialog box in Figure 4c, for example, has six tabs, each with its own set of options. Click a tab (the Web tab is currently selected) to display the associated options.

The *Help button* (a question mark at the right end of the title bar) provides help for any item in the dialog box. Click the button, then click the item in the dialog box for which you want additional information. The close button (the X at the extreme right of the title bar) closes the dialog box.

All dialog boxes also contain one or more *command buttons,* the function of which is generally apparent from the button's name. The Start button, in Figure 4a, for example, initiates the formatting process. The OK command button in Figure 4b accepts the settings and closes the dialog box. The Cancel button does just the opposite, and ignores (cancels) any changes made to the settings, then closes the dialog box without further action.

Drop-down list box shows current selection (click arrow to see list of available options)

Start button begins formatting (executes command)

Option buttons indicate mutually exclusive choices

Text box is used to enter descriptive information

Check boxes indicate choices that are not mutually exclusive

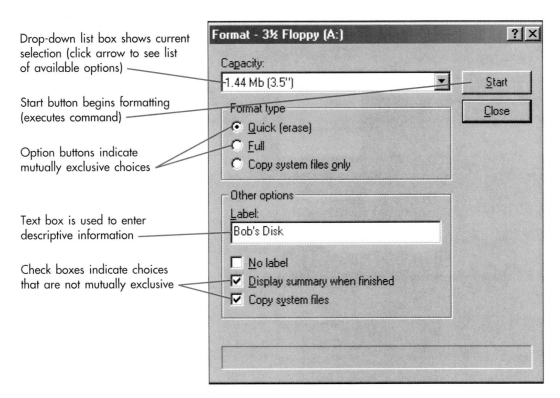

(a) Option Boxes and Check Boxes

Open list box displays multiple options

Scroll bar indicates that not all choices are visible

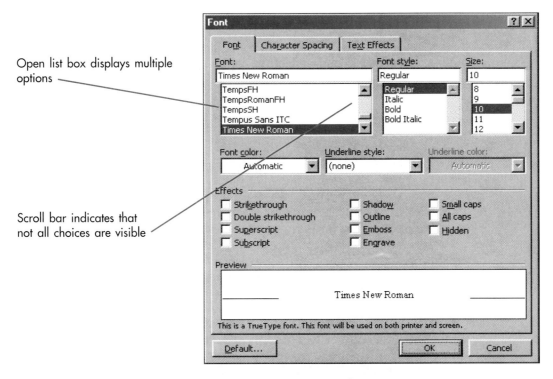

(b) List Boxes

FIGURE 4   Dialog Boxes

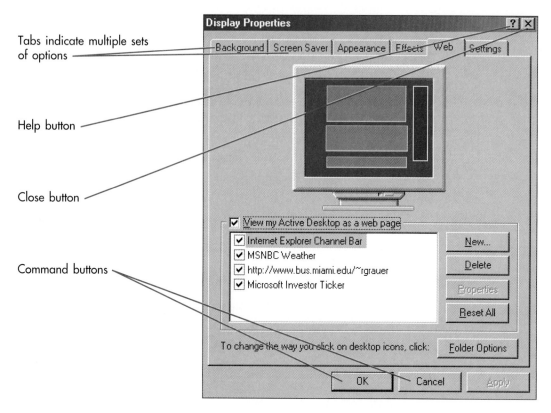

Tabs indicate multiple sets of options

Help button

Close button

Command buttons

(c) Tabbed Dialog Box

FIGURE 4   Dialog Boxes (continued)

THE MOUSE

The mouse is indispensable to Windows and is referenced continually in the hands-on exercises throughout the text. There are five basic operations with which you must become familiar:

- To **point** to an object, move the mouse pointer onto the object.
- To **click** an object, point to it, then press and release the left mouse button.
- To **right click** an object, point to the object, then press and release the right mouse button.
- To **double click** an object, point to it, then quickly click the left button twice in succession.
- To **drag** an object, move the pointer to the object, then press and hold the left button while you move the mouse to a new position.

The mouse is a pointing device—move the mouse on your desk and the **mouse pointer,** typically a small arrowhead, moves on the monitor. The mouse pointer assumes different shapes according to the location of the pointer or the nature of the current action. You will see a double arrow when you change the size of a window, an I-beam as you insert text, a hand to jump from one help topic to the next, or a circle with a line through it to indicate that an attempted action is invalid.

The mouse pointer will also change to an hourglass to indicate Windows is processing your command, and that no further commands may be issued until the action is completed. The more powerful your computer, the less frequently the hourglass will appear.

The Mouse versus the Keyboard

Almost every command in Windows can be executed in different ways, using either the mouse or the keyboard. Most people start with the mouse and add keyboard shortcuts as they become more proficient. There is no right or wrong technique, just different techniques, and the one you choose depends entirely on personal preference in a specific situation. If, for example, your hands are already on the keyboard, it is faster to use the keyboard equivalent. Other times, your hand will be on the mouse and that will be the fastest way. Toolbars provide still other ways to execute common commands.

In the beginning, you may wonder why there are so many different ways to do the same thing, but you will eventually recognize the many options as part of Windows' charm. It is not necessary to memorize anything, nor should you even try; just be flexible and willing to experiment. The more you practice, the faster all of this will become second nature to you.

THE HELP COMMAND

Windows 98 includes extensive documentation with detailed information about virtually every area in Windows. It is accessed through the ***Help command*** on the Start menu, which provides three different ways to search for information.

The ***Contents tab*** in Figure 5a is analogous to the table of contents in an ordinary book. The topics are listed in the left pane, and the information for the selected topic is displayed in the right pane. The list of topics can be displayed in varying amounts of detail, by opening and closing the various book icons that appear.

A closed book (e.g., Troubleshooting) indicates that there are subtopics that can be seen by opening (clicking) the book. An open book (e.g., How the Screen Looks) indicates that all of the subtopics are visible. (You can click an open book to close it and gain additional space in the left pane.) A question mark (e.g., Set up a screen saver) indicates the actual topic, the contents of which are displayed in the right side of the screen. An underlined entry (e.g., Related Topics) indicates a hyperlink, which you can click to display additional information. You can also print the information in the right pane by pulling down the Options menu and selecting the Print command.

The ***Index tab*** in Figure 5b is analogous to the index of an ordinary book. You enter the first several letters of the topic to look up (e.g., Internet), choose a topic from the resulting list, and then click the Display button to view the information in the right pane. The underlined entries represent hyperlinks, which you can click to display additional topics. And, as in the Contents window, you can print the information in the right pane by pulling down the Options menu and selecting the Print command.

The ***Search tab*** (not shown in Figure 5) contains a more extensive listing of entries than does the Index tab. It lets you enter a specific word or phrase, then it returns every topic containing that word or phrase.

GET HELP ONLINE

The Windows 98 Help file is a powerful tool, but it may not have the answer to every question. Click the Start button, click Help to display the Windows Help dialog box, then click the Web Help button on the toolbar. Click the link to Support online and you will be connected to the Microsoft technical support site, where you can search the Microsoft Knowledge base.

Index tab

Search tab

Open book indicates that
subtopics are listed; click to
close book and hide subtopics

Selected topic; contents
displayed in right pane

Hyperlink; click to display
additional information

Click to open book and
see list of subtopics

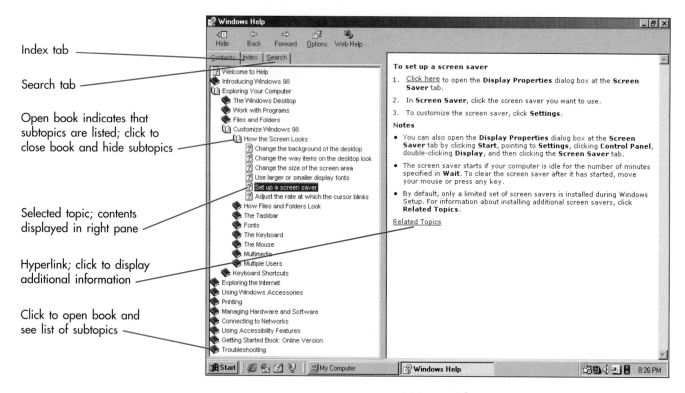

(a) Contents Tab

Enter topic

Click specific topic

Click specific topic

Click display

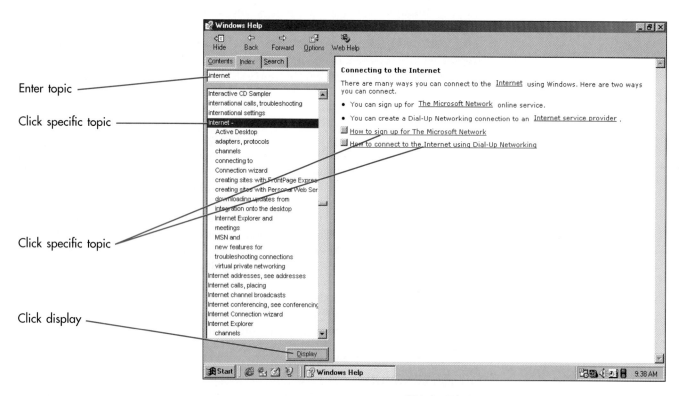

(b) Index Tab

FIGURE 5   The Help Command

STARTING YOUR COMPUTER

The number and location of the on/off switches depend on the nature and manufacturer of the devices connected to the computer. The easiest possible setup is when all components of the system are plugged into a surge protector, in which case only a single switch has to be turned on. In any event, turn on the monitor, printer, and system unit. Note, too, that newcomers to computing often forget that the floppy drive should be empty prior to starting a computer. This ensures that the system starts by reading files from the hard disk (which contains the Windows files) as opposed to a floppy disk (which does not).

STEP 2: Customize My Computer

➤ Pull down the **View menu,** then click (or point to) the **Toolbars command** to display a cascaded menu as shown in Figure 6b. If necessary, check the commands for the **Standard Buttons** and **Address Bar,** and clear the commands for Links and Text Labels.

➤ If necessary, pull down the **View menu** a second time to make or verify the selections in Figure 6b. (You have to pull down the menu each time you choose a different command.)

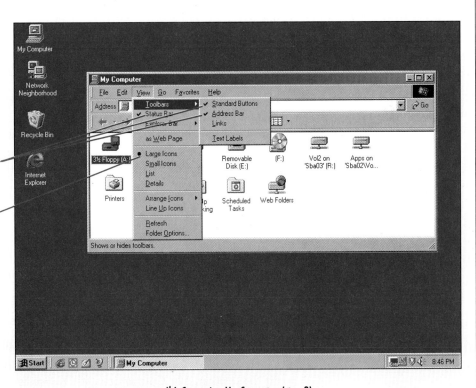

Status Bar, Standard Buttons, and Address Bar are checked

Large Icons is selected

(b) Customize My Computer (step 2)

FIGURE 6   Hands-on Exercise 1 (continued)

- The **Status Bar command** should be checked. The Status Bar command functions as a toggle switch. Click the command, and the status bar is displayed; click the command a second time, and the status bar disappears.
- **Large Icons** should be selected as the current view. (The Large Icons view is one of four mutually exclusive views in My Computer.)

➤ Pull down the **View menu** once again, click (or point to) the **Explorer Bar command** and verify that none of the options are checked. Each option functions as a toggle switch; i.e., click an option to check it, and click it a second time to remove the check.

➤ Pull down the **View menu** a final time. Click (or point to) the **Arrange Icons command** and (if necessary) click the **AutoArrange command** so that a check appears. Click outside the menu (or press the **Esc key**) if the command is already checked.

DESIGNATING THE DEVICES ON A SYSTEM

The first (usually only) floppy drive is always designated as drive A. (A second floppy drive, if it were present, would be drive B.) The first (often only) hard disk on a system is always drive C, whether or not there are one or two floppy drives. A system with one floppy drive and one hard disk (today's most common configuration) will contain icons for drive A and drive C. Additional hard drives (if any) and/or the CD-ROM are labeled from D on.

STEP 3: Move and Size a Window

➤ Click the **maximize button** so that the My Computer window expands to fill the entire screen. Click the **restore button** (which replaces the maximize button and is not shown in Figure 6c) to return the window to its previous size.

➤ Pull down the **View menu** and click **Details.** (Alternatively, you can click the **Down Arrow** for the **Views button** on the toolbar and select **Details** from the resulting menu.)

➤ Move and size the My Computer window on your desktop to match the display in Figure 6c.

- To change the width or height of the window, click and drag a border (the mouse pointer changes to a double arrow) in the direction you want to go. Thus you drag the border inward to shrink the window or drag it outward to enlarge it.
- To change the width and height at the same time, click and drag a corner rather than a border.
- To change the position of the window, click and drag the title bar.

➤ Click the **minimize button** to shrink the My Computer window to a button on the taskbar. My Computer is still active in memory although its window is no longer visible.

➤ Click the **My Computer button** on the taskbar to reopen the window.

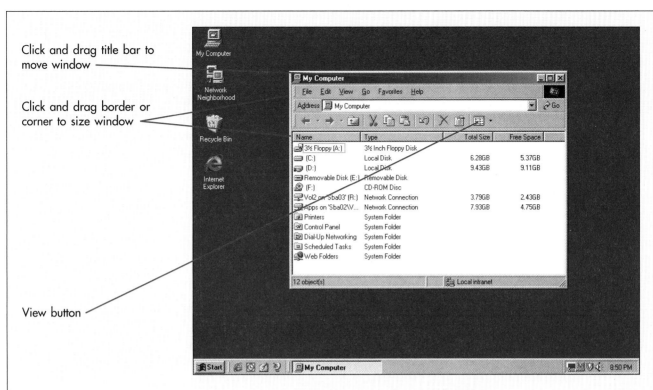

Click and drag title bar to move window

Click and drag border or corner to size window

View button

(c) Move and Size a Window (step 3)

FIGURE 6   Hands-on Exercise 1 (continued)

MINIMIZING VERSUS CLOSING AN APPLICATION

Minimizing an application leaves the application open in memory and available at the click of the taskbar button. Closing it, however, removes the application from memory, which also causes it to disappear from the taskbar. The advantage of minimizing an application is that you can return to the application immediately. The disadvantage is that leaving too many applications open will degrade the performance of your system.

STEP 4: Format a Floppy Disk

➤ Place a floppy disk in drive A. The formatting process erases anything that is on the disk, so be sure that you do not need anything on the disk.

➤ The way you select drive A and display the Format dialog box depends on the style in effect. Thus:

- In the Classic style, click (do not double click) the icon for **drive A,** then pull down the **File menu** and click the **Format command.**

- In the Web style, point to (do not click) the icon for **drive A,** then pull down the **File menu** and click the **Format command.**

- In either style, right click the icon for **drive A** to select it and display a context-sensitive menu, then click the **Format command.**

➤ Move the Format dialog box by clicking and dragging its **title bar** so that the display on your desktop matches ours. Set the formatting parameters as shown in Figure 6d:

- Set the **Capacity** to match the floppy disk you purchased (1.44MB for a high-density disk and 720KB for a double-density disk).

- Click the **Full option button** to choose a full format, which checks a disk for errors as it is formatted. This option is worth the extra time as compared to a quick format; the latter erases the files on a previously formatted disk but does not check for errors.

- Click the **Label text box** if it's empty or click and drag over the existing label if there is an entry. Enter a new label (containing up to 11 characters) such as **Bob's Disk.**

- Click the **Start command button** to begin the formatting operation. This will take a minute or two. You can see the progress of the formatting process at the bottom of the dialog box.

➤ After the formatting process is complete, you will see the Format Results message box. Read the information, then click the **Close command button** to close the informational dialog box.

➤ Click the **close button** to close the Format dialog box. Save the formatted disk for use with various exercises later in the text.

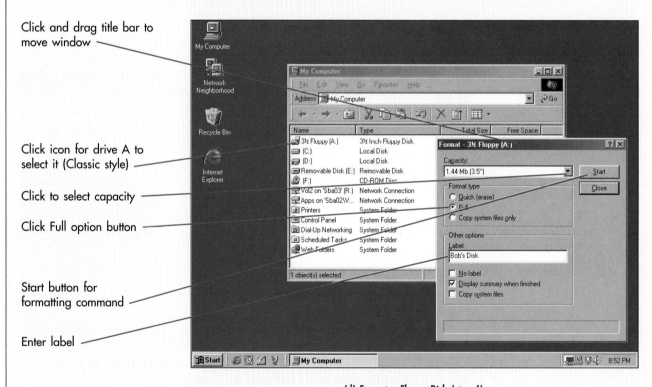

Click and drag title bar to move window

Click icon for drive A to select it (Classic style)

Click to select capacity

Click Full option button

Start button for formatting command

Enter label

(d) Format a Floppy Disk (step 4)

FIGURE 6   Hands-on Exercise 1 (continued)

THE HELP BUTTON

The Help button (a question mark) appears in the title bar of almost every dialog box. Click the question mark, then click the item you want information about (which then appears in a pop-up window). To print the contents of the pop-up window, click the right mouse button inside the window, and click Print Topic. Click outside the pop-up window to close the window and continue working.

STEP 5: Change the Style

➤ Pull down the **View menu** and click the **Folder Options command** to display the Folder Options dialog box in Figure 6e. Click the **General tab,** click the option button for **Web style,** then click **OK** to accept the settings and close the Folder Options dialog box.

➤ The icons in the My Computer window should be underlined because you have changed to the Web style. Click the icon for **drive A** to view the contents of the floppy disk. The contents of the Address bar change to reflect drive A. The disk is empty, so you do not see any files.

➤ Close the My Computer window. Click the (underlined) **My Computer icon** on the desktop to open My Computer. You click (rather than double click) the icon to open it because you are in the Web style.

➤ Close My Computer.

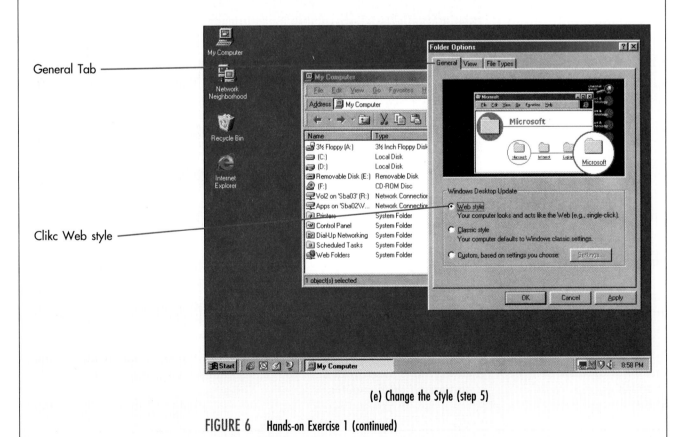

General Tab

Clikc Web style

(e) Change the Style (step 5)

FIGURE 6   Hands-on Exercise 1 (continued)

STEP 6: The Help Command

➤ Click the **Start button** on the taskbar, then click the **Help command** to display the Help window in Figure 6f. Do not be concerned if the size or position of your window is different from ours.

➤ Click the **Index tab,** then click in the text box to enter the desired topic. Type **Web st** (the first letters in "Web style," the topic you are searching for). Note that when you enter the last letter, the Help window displays "Web style folders" in the list of topics.

➤ Click (select) **Web style mouse selection,** then click the **Display button** to view the information in Figure 6f. Read the instructions carefully.

➤ Pull down the **Options menu** and click the **Print command** to display the Print dialog box. Click **OK** to print the selected page.

➤ Click the **close button** to close the Help window.

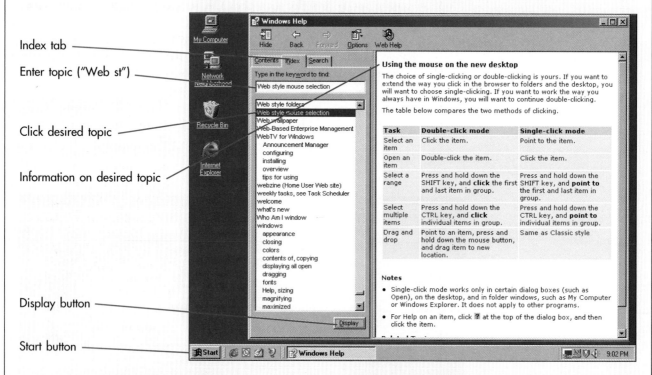

Index tab

Enter topic ("Web st")

Click desired topic

Information on desired topic

Display button

Start button

(f) The Help Command (step 6)

FIGURE 6   Hands-on Exercise 1 (continued)

STEP 7: Shut Down the Computer

➤ Click the **Start button,** click the **Shut Down command** to display the Shut Down Windows dialog box, and if necessary, click the option button to shut down the computer.

➤ Click the **Yes command button,** then wait as Windows gets ready to shut down your system. Wait until you see another screen indicating that it is OK to turn off the computer.

FILES AND FOLDERS

A *file* is a set of instructions or data that has been given a name and stored on disk. There are two basic types of files, program files and data files. Microsoft Word and Microsoft Excel are examples of program files. The documents and workbooks created by these programs are examples of data files.

A *program file* is an executable file because it contains instructions that tell the computer what to do. A *data file* is not executable and can be used only in conjunction with a specific program. As a student, you execute (run) program files, then you use those programs to create and/or modify the associated data files.

Every file must have a *file name* so that it can be identified. The file name may contain up to 255 characters and may include spaces and other punctuation. (This is very different from the rules that existed under MS-DOS, which limited file names to eight characters followed by an optional three-character extension.) Long file names permit descriptive entries such as *Term Paper for Western Civilization* (as opposed to *TPWCIV* that would be required under MS-DOS).

Files are stored in *folders* to better organize the hundreds (often thousands) of files on a hard disk. A Windows folder is similar in concept to a manila folder in a filing cabinet into which you put one or more documents (files) that are somehow related to each other. An office worker stores his or her documents in manila folders. In Windows, you store your files (documents) in electronic folders on disk.

Folders are the keys to the Windows storage system. Some folders are created automatically; for example, the installation of a program such as Microsoft Office automatically creates one or more folders to hold the various program files. Other folders are created by the user to hold the documents he or she creates. You could, for example, create one folder for your word processing documents and a second folder for your spreadsheets. Alternatively, you can create a folder to hold all of your work for a specific class, which may contain a combination of word processing documents and spreadsheets. Anything at all can go into a folder—program files, data files, even other folders.

Figure 7 displays a My Computer window for a folder containing six documents. Figure 7a shows the folder in the Classic style whereas Figure 7b shows it in the Web style. The choice between the two is one of personal preference and has to do with the action of the mouse. In the Classic style, you click an icon to select it, and you double click the icon to open it. In the Web style, you point to an icon to select it, and you click the icon to open it. (These operations mimic those of a Web browser.)

Regardless of the style in effect, the name of the folder (Homework) appears in the title bar next to the icon of an open folder. The minimize, maximize, and close buttons appear at the right of the title bar. A menu bar with six pull-down menus appears below the title bar. The Address bar appears below the menu bar and the toolbar appears below that. As with any toolbar, you can point to any button to display a ScreenTip that is indicative of the button's function. A status bar appears at the bottom of both windows, indicating that the Homework folder contains six objects (documents) and that the total file size is 333KB.

The Homework folder in both Figures 7a and 7b is displayed in *Details view,* one of four views available in My Computer. (The other views are Large Icons, Small Icons, and List view. The choice of view depends on your personal preference.) The Details view contains the maximum amount of information for each file and is used more frequently than the other views. It shows the file size, the type of file, and the date and time the file was last modified. The Details view also displays a small icon to the left of each file name that represents the application that is associated with the file. The Views button is the easiest way to switch from one view to another.

Name of folder

Menu bar

Address bar

Tool bar

Views button

Icon indicates associated application

Status bar

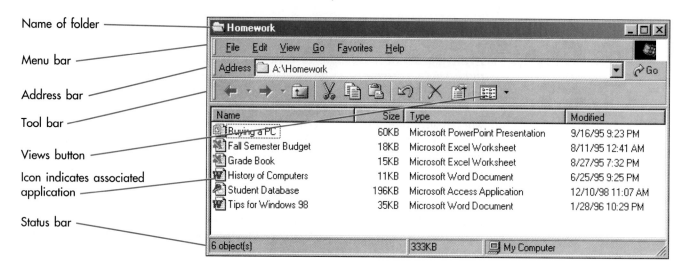

(a) Classic Style

Type column

Web Style has underlined icons

Icon indicates a Word document

Number of objects in window

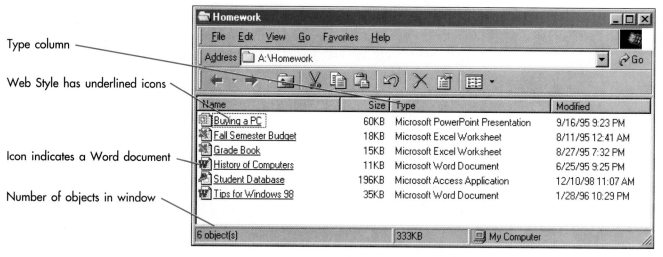

(b) Web Style

FIGURE 7   The Homework Folder

CLASSIC STYLE OR WEB STYLE

The Classic style and Web style are very different from one another, but neither style is a "better" style. The choice is one of personal preference, and depends on how you want to view the desktop and how you want to open its objects, by double clicking or clicking, respectively. We encourage you to experiment with both styles, and indeed, we find ourselves switching back and forth between the two. Use the Folder Options command in the View menu to change the style.

File Type

Every data file has a specific *file type* that is determined by the application used to create the file. One way to recognize the file type is to examine the Type column in the Details view as shown in Figure 7a. The History of Computers file, for example, is a Microsoft Word document. The Grade Book is a Microsoft Excel worksheet.

You can also determine the file type (or associated application) in any view by examining the application icon displayed next to the file name. Look carefully at the icon next to the History of Computers document in Figure 7a or 7b, for example, and you will recognize the icon for Microsoft Word. The application icon is recognized more easily in Large Icons view, as shown in Figure 8. Each application in Microsoft Office has a distinct icon.

Still another way to determine the file type is through a three-character *extension,* which is appended to the file name, but which is not shown in Figure 7. (A period separates the file name from the extension.) Each application has a unique extension that is automatically assigned to the file name when the file is created. DOC and XLS, for example, are the extensions for Microsoft Word and Excel, respectively. The extension may be suppressed or displayed according to an option in the View menu, but is better left suppressed.

My Computer

My Computer enables you to browse through the various folders on your system so that you can locate a document and go to work. Let's assume that you're looking for your term paper on the History of Computers, which you began yesterday, and which you saved in a folder called Homework.

My Computer can be used to locate the Homework file, and as indicated earlier, you can use either the Classic style in Figure 8a or the Web style in Figure 8b. The concepts are identical, but there are differences in the appearance of the icons (they are underlined in the Web style) and in the way the commands are executed. One other difference is that the Classic style opens a new window for each open folder, whereas the Web style uses a single window throughout the process.

In the Classic style in Figure 8a, you begin by double clicking the My Computer icon on the desktop to open the My Computer window, which in turn displays the devices on your system. Next, you double click the icon for drive C to open a second window that displays the folders on drive C. From there, you double click the icon for the Homework folder to open a third window containing the documents in the Homework folder. Once in the Homework folder, you can double click the icon of an existing document, which starts the associated application and opens the document, enabling you to begin work.

The Web style in Figure 8b follows the same sequence, but has you click rather than double click. Equally important, it uses a single window throughout the process as opposed to the multiple windows in the Classic style. You begin by clicking the My Computer icon on the desktop to display the contents of My Computer, which includes an icon for drive C. Then you click the icon for drive C, which in turn lets you click the Homework folder, from which you can click the icon for the data file to start the associated application and open the document. Note, too, the back arrow on the toolbar in Figure 8b, which is active throughout the Web style. You can click the back arrow to return to the previous folder (drive C in this example), just as you can click the back arrow on a Web browser to return to the previous Web page.

Double click My Computer icon

Double click icon for Drive C

Double click icon for
Homework folder

Double click to start Excel and
open Grade Book file

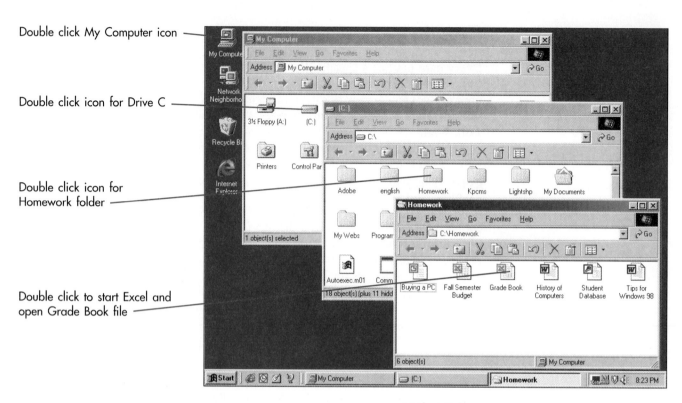

(a) Classic Style

Click to open My computer

Click Back arrow to
return to previous folder

Click to start Excel and
open Grade Book file

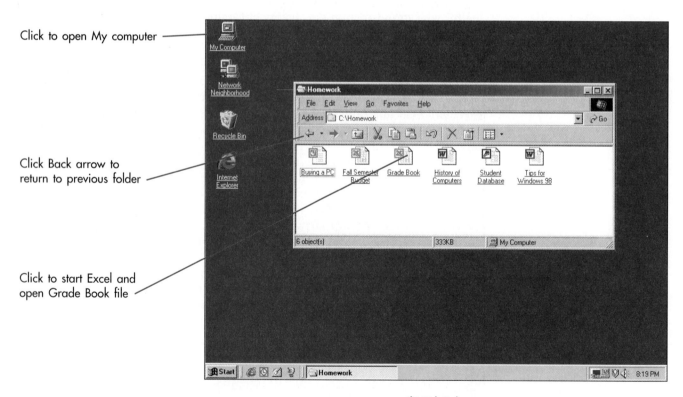

(b) Web Style

FIGURE 8   Browsing My Computer

The Exploring Windows Home Page

Objective: To download a file from the Web to a PC using the Classic and/or Web style. The exercise requires a formatted floppy disk and access to the Internet. Use Figure 9 as a guide in the exercise.

STEP 1: Start Internet Explorer

➤ Start Internet Explorer by clicking its icon on the desktop. If necessary, click the **maximize button** so that Internet Explorer takes the entire desktop.

➤ Enter the address of the site you want to visit:

- Pull down the **File menu,** click the **Open command** to display the Open dialog box, and enter **www.prenhall.com/grauer** (the http:// is assumed). Click **OK.**

- *Or, c*lick in the **Address bar** below the toolbar, which automatically selects the current address (so that whatever you type replaces the current address). Enter the address of the site, **www.prenhall.com/grauer** (the http:// is assumed). Press **Enter.**

➤ You should see the Exploring Windows series home page as shown in Figure 9a. Click the book for **Office 2000,** which takes you to the Office 2000 home page. Click the **Student Resources link** (at the top of the window) to go to the Student Resources page.

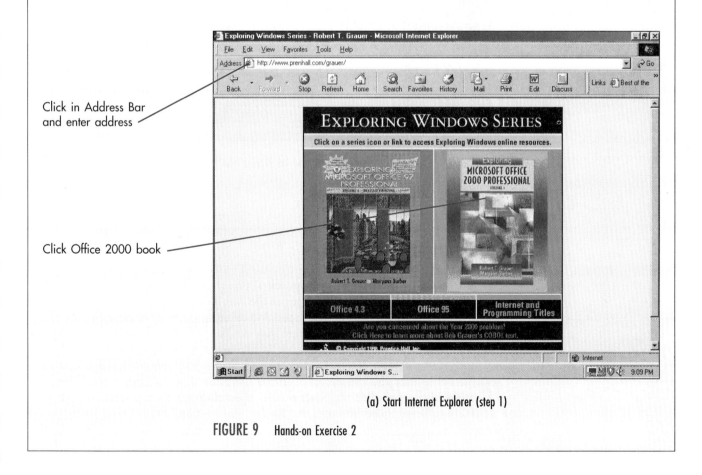

Click in Address Bar and enter address

Click Office 2000 book

(a) Start Internet Explorer (step 1)

FIGURE 9   Hands-on Exercise 2

STEP 2: Download the Practice Files

➤ Click the link to **Student Data Disk** (in the left frame), then scroll down the page until you see Windows 98 Prerequisites. Click the indicated link to download the student data disk as shown in Figure 9b.

➤ You will see the File Download dialog box asking what you want to do. The option button to save this program to disk is selected. Click **OK.** The Save As dialog box appears.

➤ Place a formatted floppy disk in drive A, click the **drop-down arrow** on the Save in list box, and select (click) **drive A.** Click **Save** to begin downloading the file.

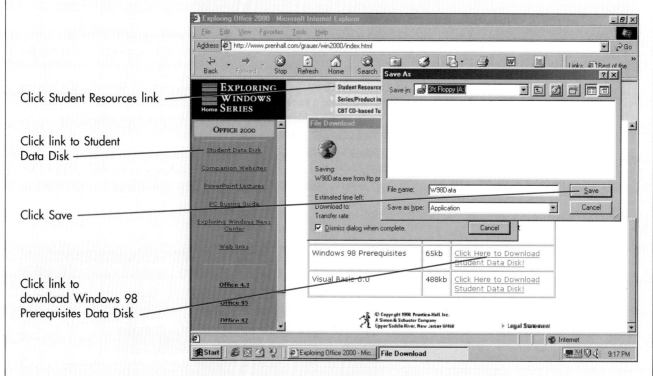

Click Student Resources link

Click link to Student Data Disk

Click Save

Click link to download Windows 98 Prerequisites Data Disk

(b) Download the Practice Files (step 2)

FIGURE 9   Hands-on Exercise 2 (continued)

REMEMBER THE LOCATION

It's easy to download a file from the Web. The only tricky part, if any, is remembering where you have saved the file. This exercise is written for a laboratory setting, and thus we specified drive A as the destination, so that you will have the file on a floppy disk at the end of the exercise. If you have your own computer, however, it's faster to save the file to the desktop or in a temporary folder on drive C. Just remember where you save the file so that you can access it after it has been downloaded. And, if you really lose a file, click the Start button, then click the Find command. Use Help to learn more about searching for files on your PC.

➤ The File Download window will reappear on your screen and show you the status of the downloading operation. Be patient as this may take a few minutes.

➤ The File Download window will close automatically when the downloading is complete. If necessary, click **Close** when you see the dialog box indicating that the download is complete. Close Internet Explorer.

STEP 3: Classic Style or Web Style

➤ The instructions for opening My Computer and installing the practice files vary slightly, depending on which style is in effect on your desktop.

- In the Classic style you click an icon to select it, and you double click the icon to open it.

- In the Web style you point to an icon to select it, and you click the icon to open it. These operations mimic those of a Web browser—hence the term "Web style."

➤ You can switch from one style to the other using **My Computer.** Pull down the **View menu,** click the **Folder Options command,** then click the **General tab.** Select the option button for **Web style** or **Classic style** as desired, then click **OK** to accept the settings and close the Folder Options dialog box.

➤ Go to **step 4** or **step 6,** depending on which style is in effect on your desktop. You might even want to do the exercise both ways, in order to determine which style you prefer.

TO CLICK OR DOUBLE CLICK

The choice between Web style and Classic style is personal and depends on how you want to open a document, by clicking or double clicking, respectively. One way to change from one style to the other is to point to the desktop, click the right mouse button to display a context-sensitive menu, then click the Properties command to open the Display Properties dialog box. Click the Web tab, click the Folder Options command button, click Yes when prompted whether to view the folder options, then choose the style you want.

STEP 4: Install the Practice Files in Classic Style

➤ Double click the **My Computer icon** on the desktop to open the My Computer window. Double click the icon for **drive A** to open a second window as shown in Figure 9c. The size and/or position of these windows on your desktop may differ from ours; the second window, for example, may appear directly on top of the existing window.

➤ Double click the **W98Data icon** to install the data disk. You will see a dialog box thanking you for selecting the Exploring Windows series. Click **OK** when you have finished reading the dialog box to continue the installation and display the WinZip Self-Extractor dialog box in Figure 9c.

➤ Check that the Unzip To Folder text box specifies **A:\\,** which will extract the files to the floppy disk. (You can enter a different drive and/or folder if you prefer.)

➤ Click the **Unzip button** to extract (uncompress) the practice files and copy them onto the designated drive. Click **OK** after you see the message indicating that the files have been unzipped successfully. Close the WinZip dialog box.

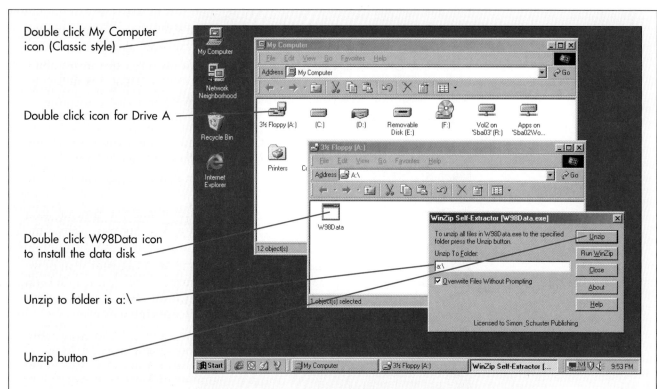

Double click My Computer icon (Classic style)

Double click icon for Drive A

Double click W98Data icon to install the data disk

Unzip to folder is a:\

Unzip button

(c) Install the Practice Files in Classic Style (step 4)

FIGURE 9   Hands-on Exercise 2 (continued)

CUSTOMIZE MY COMPUTER

You can customize the My Computer window regardless of whether you choose the Classic style or Web style. Pull down the View menu, click the Toolbars command to display a cascaded menu, then check the commands for the Standard Buttons and Address Bar, and clear the commands for Links and Text Labels. Pull down the View menu a second time and select (click) the desired view. Pull down the View menu a final time, click the Arrange Icons command, and (if necessary) click the AutoArrange command so that a check appears. Click outside the menu (or press the Esc key) if the command is already checked.

STEP 5: Delete the Compressed File in Classic Style

➤ The practice files have been extracted to drive A and should appear in the drive A window. If you do not see the files, pull down the **View menu** and click the **Refresh command.**

➤ You should see a total of six files in the drive A window. Five of these are the practice files on the data disk; the sixth is the original file that you downloaded earlier.

➤ If necessary, pull down the **View menu** and click **Details** (or click the **Views button** repeatedly) to change to the Details view. Your display should match Figure 9d.

➤ Select (click) the **W98Data icon.** Pull down the **File menu** and click the **Delete command** or click the **Delete button** on the toolbar. Click **Yes** when asked to confirm the deletion. The ie4datadisk file disappears from the drive A window.

➤ Go to **step 8** to complete this exercise; that is, you can skip steps 6 and 7, which illustrate the Web style.

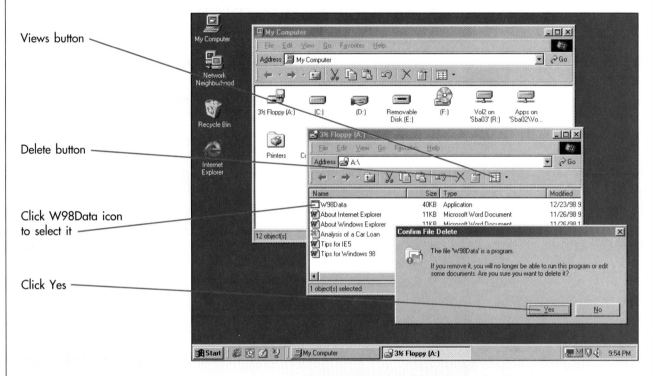

(d) Delete the Compressed File in Classic Style (step 5)

FIGURE 9   Hands-on Exercise 2 (continued)

ONE WINDOW OR MANY

The Classic style opens a new window every time you open a new drive or folder using My Computer, which can quickly lead to a cluttered desktop. You can, however, customize the Classic style to display the objects in a single window. Pull down the View menu, click the Folder Options command, click the option button for Custom based on the settings you choose, then click the Settings command button to display the Custom Settings dialog box. Click the option button in the Browse folders area to open each folder in the same window, click OK to close the Custom Settings dialog box, then click OK to close the Folder Options dialog box.

STEP 6: Install the Practice Files in Web Style

➤ Click the **My Computer icon** on the desktop to open the My Computer window, then click the icon for **drive A** within My Computer. Click the **W98Data icon** to install the data disk.

➤ You will see a dialog box thanking you for selecting the Exploring Windows series. Click **OK** when you have finished reading the dialog box to continue the installation and display the WinZip Self-Extractor dialog box in Figure 9e.

➤ Check that the Unzip To Folder text box specifies **A:**, which will extract the files to the floppy disk. (You can enter a different drive and/or folder if you prefer.)

➤ Click the **Unzip button** to extract the practice files and copy them onto the designated drive. Click **OK** after you see the message indicating that the files have been unzipped successfully. Close the WinZip dialog box.

➤ The practice files have been extracted to drive A and should appear in the drive A window. If you do not see the files, pull down the **View menu** and click the **Refresh command.**

➤ Pull down the **View menu.** Toggle the command **as Web Page** on or off as you prefer. The command is off in Figure 9e.

Click My Computer icon (Web style) ——

Click W98Data icon to install the data disk ——

Unzip to folder is a:\——

Click OK ——

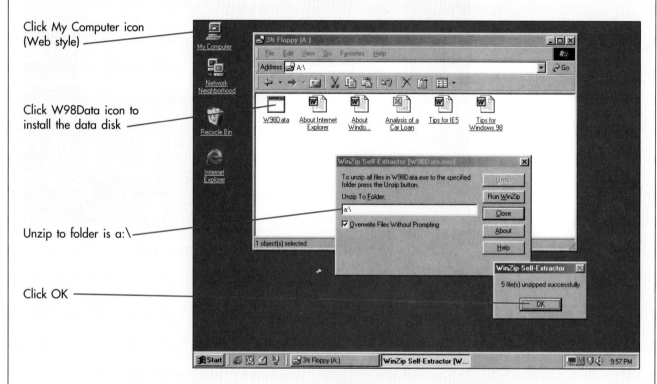

(e) Install the Practice Files in Web Style (step 6)

FIGURE 9   Hands-on Exercise 2 (continued)

THE BACK AND FORWARD BUTTONS IN MY COMPUTER

The Web style is so named because it follows the conventions of a Web browser. Unlike the Classic style, which displays a separate window for each drive or folder, the Web style uses a single window throughout. Thus, you can click the Back button on the My Computer toolbar to return to a previous folder. In similar fashion you can click the Forward button from a previously viewed folder to go to the next folder.

STEP 7: Delete the Compressed File in Web Style

➤ You should see a total of six files in the drive A window. Five of these are the practice files on the data disk; the sixth is the original file that you downloaded earlier.

➤ If necessary, pull down the **View menu** and click **Details** to change to the Details view in Figure 9f so that your display matches ours.

➤ Point to the **W98Data icon,** which in turn selects the file. Pull down the **File menu** and click the **Delete command** or click the **Delete button** on the toolbar. Click **Yes** when asked to confirm the deletion. The W98Data file disappears from the drive A window.

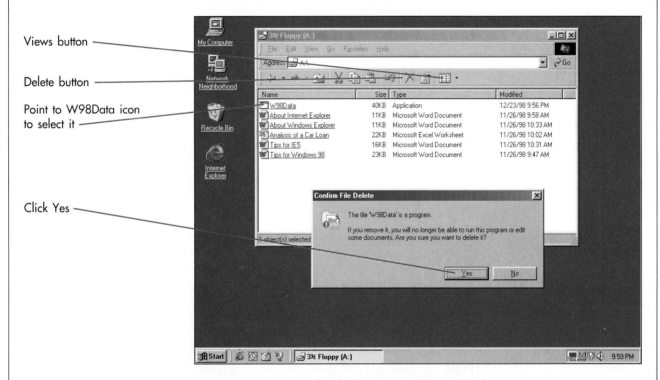

Views button ——

Delete button ——

Point to W98Data icon to select it ——

Click Yes ——

(f) Delete the Compressed File in Web Style (step 7)

FIGURE 9   Hands-on Exercise 2 (continued)

CHANGE THE VIEW

The contents of drive A are displayed in the Details view, one of four views available in My Computer. Details view displays the maximum amount of information for each file and is our general preference. You can, however, click the Views button on the My Computer toolbar to cycle through the other views (Large Icons, Small Icons, and List). You can also pull down the View menu and toggle the As Web Page command on, which will display additional information in the My Computer window.

STEP 8: Modify a File

➤ It doesn't matter whether you are in the Web style or the Classic style. (Our figure displays the Web style.) What is important, however, is that you have successfully downloaded the practice files.

➤ Open the **About Internet Explorer** document:

  • Click the icon in Web style.

  • Double click the document icon in Classic style.

➤ If necessary, maximize the window for Microsoft Word. (The document will open in the WordPad accessory if Microsoft Word is not installed on your machine.)

➤ Read the document, then click inside the document window and press **Ctrl+End** to move to the end of the document. Add the sentence shown in Figure 9g followed by your name.

➤ Pull down the **File menu,** click **Print,** then click **OK** to print the document and prove to your instructor that you did the exercise. Pull down the **File menu** and click **Exit** to close the application. Click **Yes** if prompted whether to save the file.

➤ Exit Windows if you do not want to continue with the next exercise at this time.

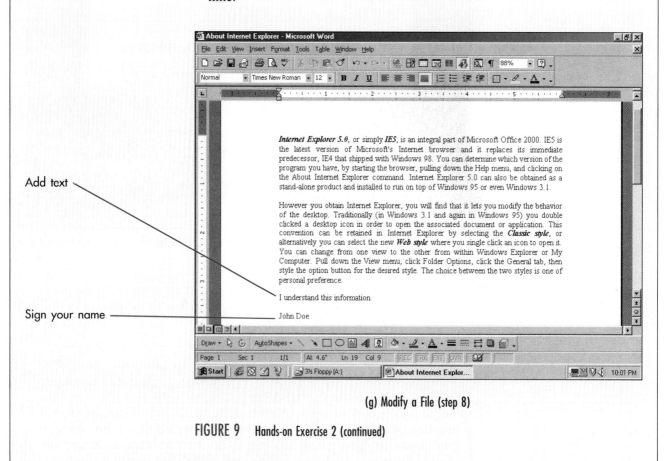

(g) Modify a File (step 8)

FIGURE 9   Hands-on Exercise 2 (continued)

There are two programs that manage the files and folders on your system, My Computer and Windows Explorer. My Computer is intuitive, but less efficient, as you have to open each folder in succession. Windows Explorer is more sophisticated, as it provides a hierarchical view of the entire system in a single window. A beginner might prefer My Computer whereas a more experienced user will most likely opt for Windows Explorer.

Assume, for example, that you are taking four classes this semester, and that you are using the computer in each course. You've created a separate folder to hold the work for each class and have stored the contents of all four folders on a single floppy disk. Assume further that you need to retrieve your third English assignment so that you can modify the assignment, then submit the revised version to your instructor.

Figure 10 illustrates how *Windows Explorer* could be used to locate your assignment. As with My Computer, you can display Windows Explorer in either the Classic style or the Web style. The concepts are identical, but there are differences in the appearance of the icons (they are underlined in the Web style) and in the way the commands are executed. The choice is one of personal preference and you can switch back and forth between the two. (Pull down the View menu and click the Folder Options command to change from one style to the other.)

The Explorer window in both Figure 10a and Figure 10b is divided into two panes. The left pane contains a tree diagram (or hierarchical view) of the entire system showing all drives and, optionally, the folders in each drive. The right pane shows the contents of the active (open) drive or folder. Only one object (a drive or folder) can be active in the left pane, and its contents are displayed automatically in the right pane.

Look carefully at the icon for the English folder in the left pane of either figure. The folder is open, whereas the icon for every other folder is closed. The open folder indicates that the English folder is the active folder. (The name of the active folder also appears in the title bar of Windows Explorer and in the address bar on the toolbar.) The contents of the active folder (three Word documents in this example) are displayed in the right pane. The right pane is displayed in Details view, but could just as easily have been displayed in another view (e.g., Large or Small Icons).

As indicated, only one folder can be open (active) at a time in the left pane. Thus, to see the contents of a different folder such as Accounting, you would open (click on) the Accounting folder, which automatically closes the English folder. The contents of the Accounting folder would then appear in the right pane.

Look carefully at the tree structure in either Figure 10a or Figure 10b and note that it contains an icon for Internet Explorer, which when selected, starts Internet Explorer and displays a Web page in the contents pane of Windows Explorer. Thus you can use Windows Explorer to view Web pages, and conversely, you can use Internet Explorer to view documents and/or folders that are stored locally.

ORGANIZE YOUR WORK

Organize your folder in ways that make sense to you, such as a separate folder for every class you are taking. You can also create folders within folders; for example, a correspondence folder may contain two folders of its own, one for business correspondence and one for personal letters.

Name of active folder

Minus indicates object is
expanded

Selected folder

Contents of selected folder

Plus signs indicate drives
are collapsed

Icon for Internet Explorer

Click to display Web page
in right pane

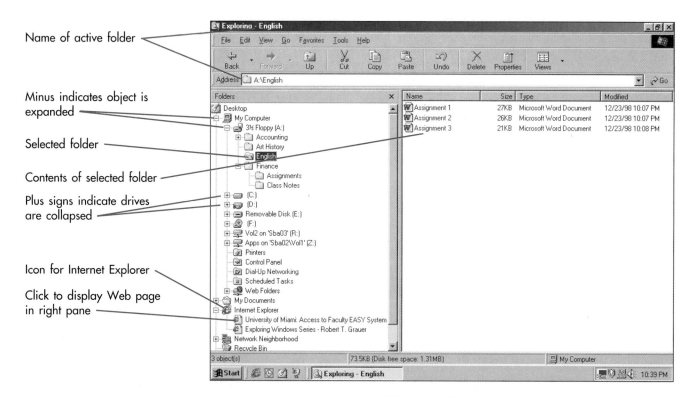

(a) Classic Style (Details view)

Name of active folder

Selected folder

Click minus to collapse folder

Contents of selected folder

Click plus to expand drive

Icon for Internet Explorer

Click to display Web page
in right pane

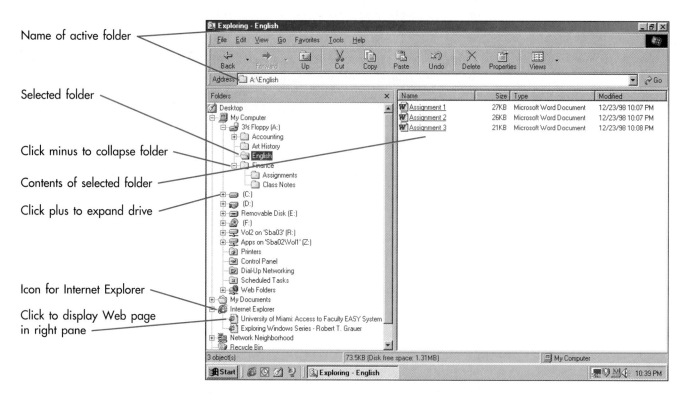

(b) Web Style (Details view)

FIGURE 10   Windows Explorer

Expanding and Collapsing a Drive

The tree diagram in Windows Explorer displays the devices on your system in hierarchical fashion. The desktop is always at the top of the hierarchy, and it contains various icons such as My Computer, the Recycle Bin, Internet Explorer, and Network Neighborhood. My Computer in turn contains the various drives that are accessible from your system, each of which contains folders, which in turn contain documents and/or additional folders. Each *icon* may be *expanded* or *collapsed* by clicking the plus or minus sign, respectively. Click either sign to toggle to the other. Clicking a plus sign, for example, expands the drive, then displays a minus sign next to the drive to indicate that its subordinates are visible.

Return to either Figure 10a or 10b and look at the icon next to My Computer. It is a minus sign (as opposed to a plus sign), and it indicates that My Computer has been expanded to show the devices on the system. There is also a minus sign next to the icon for drive A to indicate that it too has been expanded to show the folders on the disk. There is also a minus sign next to the Internet Explorer icon, which displays the Web sites that were visited in this session. Note, however, the plus sign next to drives C and D, indicating that these parts of the tree are currently collapsed and thus their subordinates (in this case, folders) are not visible.

A folder may contain additional folders, and thus individual folders may also be expanded or collapsed. The minus sign next to the Finance folder, for example, indicates that the folder has been expanded and contains two additional folders, for Assignments and Class Notes, respectively. The plus sign next to the Accounting folder, however, indicates the opposite; that is, the folder is collapsed and its subordinate folders are not currently visible. A folder with neither a plus or minus sign, such as Art History, does not contain additional folders and cannot be expanded or collapsed.

The hierarchical view within Windows Explorer, and the ability to expand and collapse the various folders on a system, enables the user to quickly locate a specific file or folder. If, for example, you wanted to see the contents of the Art History folder, all you would do is click its icon in the left pane, which automatically changes the display in the right pane to show the documents in that folder.

Windows Explorer is ideal for moving or copying files from one folder or drive to another. You simply select (open) the folder that contains the files, use the scroll bar in the left pane (if necessary) so that the destination folder is visible, then click and drag the files from the right pane to the destination folder. Windows Explorer is a powerful tool, but it takes practice to master. It's time for another hands-on exercise in which we use Windows Explorer to copy the practice files from a network drive to a floppy disk. (The exercise assumes that your instructor has placed our files on your local area network.)

THE DOCUMENT, NOT THE APPLICATION

Windows 98 is document oriented, meaning that you are able to think in terms of the document rather than the application that created it. You can still open a document in traditional fashion, by starting the application that created the document, then using the File Open command in that program to retrieve the document. It's often easier, however, to open the document from within My Computer (or Windows Explorer) by clicking its icon in Web view, or double clicking the icon in Classic view. Windows then starts the application and opens the data file. In other words, you can open a document without explicitly starting the application.

The Practice Files (via a local area network)

Objective: To use Windows Explorer to copy the practice files from a network drive to a floppy disk. The exercise requires a formatted floppy disk and access to a local area network. Use Figure 11 as a guide in the exercise.

CONVERGENCE OF THE EXPLORERS

Windows Explorer and Internet Explorer are separate programs, but each includes some functionality of the other. You can use Windows Explorer to display a Web page by clicking the Internet Explorer icon within the tree structure in the left pane. Conversely, you can use Internet Explorer to display a local drive, document, or folder. Start Internet Explorer in the usual fashion, click in the Address bar, then enter the appropriate address such as C: to display the contents of drive C.

STEP 1: Start Windows Explorer

➤ Click the **Start button,** click (or point to) the **Programs command,** then click **Windows Explorer** to start this program. Click the **maximize button.**

➤ Make or verify the following selections using the **View menu** as shown in Figure 11a. You have to pull down the **View menu** each time you choose a different command.

Status Bar should be selected

Large Icons should be selected

Standard Buttons, Address Bar, and Text Labels should be selected

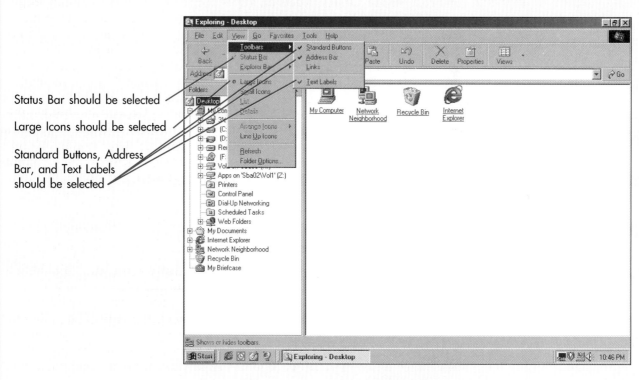

(a) Start Windows Explorer (step 1)

FIGURE 11   Hands-on Exercise 3

- The **Standard Buttons, Address Bar,** and **Text Labels** should be checked.
- The **Status Bar command** should be checked.
- The **Large Icons view** should be selected.

➤ Click (select) the **Desktop icon** in the left pane to display the contents of the desktop in the right pane. Our desktop contains icons for My Computer, Network Neighborhood, the Recycle Bin, and Internet Explorer.

➤ Your desktop may have different icons from ours, but your screen should otherwise match the one in Figure 11a, given that you are in Web style.

CLASSIC STYLE OR WEB STYLE

Which do you prefer, Coke or Pepsi? They are both good, and the choice is one of personal preference. So it is with Classic style and Web style. They are different, but neither is clearly better than the other, and indeed we find ourselves switching between the two. This exercise is written for the Classic style.

STEP 2: Change to Classic Style (if necessary)

➤ You can skip this step if your desktop is already in Classic style. Pull down the **View menu,** click the **Folder Options command** to display the Folder Options dialog box, then click the **General tab** as shown in Figure 11b.

➤ Click the **Classic style option button,** then click **OK** to accept this setting and close the Folder Options dialog box. The icons within Windows Explorer should be displayed in Classic style.

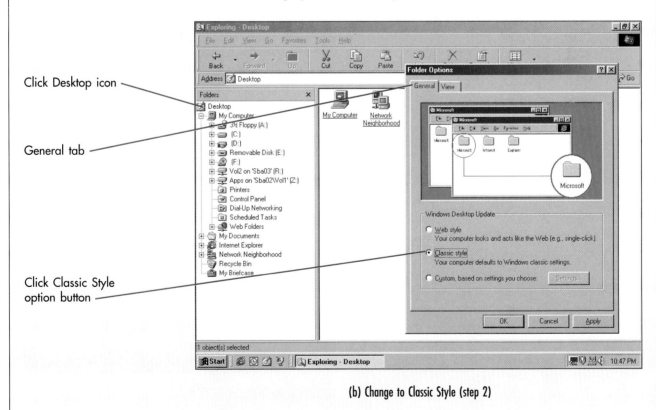

Click Desktop icon

General tab

Click Classic Style option button

(b) Change to Classic Style (step 2)

FIGURE 11   Hands-on Exercise 3 (continued)

FILE EXTENSIONS

Long-time DOS users remember a three-character extension at the end of a file name to indicate the file type; for example, DOC or XLS to indicate a Word document or Excel workbook, respectively. The extensions are displayed or hidden according to the option you choose through the View menu of Windows Explorer. Pull down the View menu, click the Folder Options command to display the Folder Options dialog box, click the View tab, then check (or clear) the box to hide (or show) file extensions for known file types. Click OK to accept the setting and exit the dialog box.

STEP 3: Collapse the Individual Drives

➤ Click the **minus** (or the **plus**) **sign** next to My Computer to collapse (or expand) My Computer. Toggle the signs back and forth a few times for practice. End with a minus sign next to My Computer.

➤ Place a formatted floppy disk in drive A. Click the drive icon next to **drive A** to select the drive and display its contents in the right pane as shown in Figure 11c. The disk does not contain any files, and hence the right pane is empty.

➤ Click the **plus sign** next to drive A. The plus sign disappears, as drive A does not have any folders.

➤ Click the **sign** next to the other drives to toggle back and forth between expanding and collapsing the individual drives on your system. End this step with every drive collapsed; that is, there should be a **plus sign** next to every drive except drive A, as shown in Figure 11c.

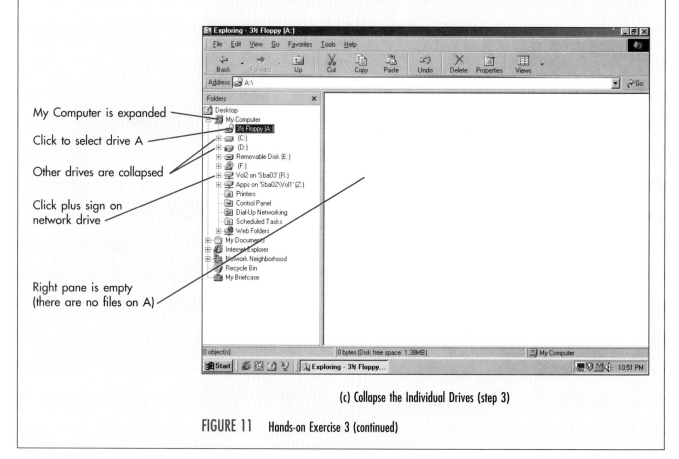

(c) Collapse the Individual Drives (step 3)

FIGURE 11   Hands-on Exercise 3 (continued)

THE PLUS AND MINUS SIGNS

Any drive, be it local or on the network, may be expanded or collapsed to display or hide its folders. A minus sign indicates that the drive has been expanded and that its folders are visible. A plus sign indicates the reverse; that is, the device is collapsed and its folders are not visible. Click either sign to toggle to the other. Clicking a plus sign, for example, expands the drive, then displays a minus sign next to the drive to indicate that the folders are visible. Clicking a minus sign has the reverse effect; that is, it collapses the drive, hiding its folders.

STEP 4: Select the Network Drive

➤ Click the **plus sign** for the network drive that contains the files you are to copy (e.g., **drive R** in Figure 11d). Select (click) the **Exploring Windows 98 folder** to open this folder.

➤ You may need to expand other folders on the network drive (such as the Datadisk folder on our network) as per instructions from your professor. Note the following:

- The Exploring Windows 98 folder is highlighted in the left pane, its icon has changed to an open folder, and its contents are displayed in the right pane.

- The status bar indicates that the folder contains five objects and the total file size is 82.5KB.

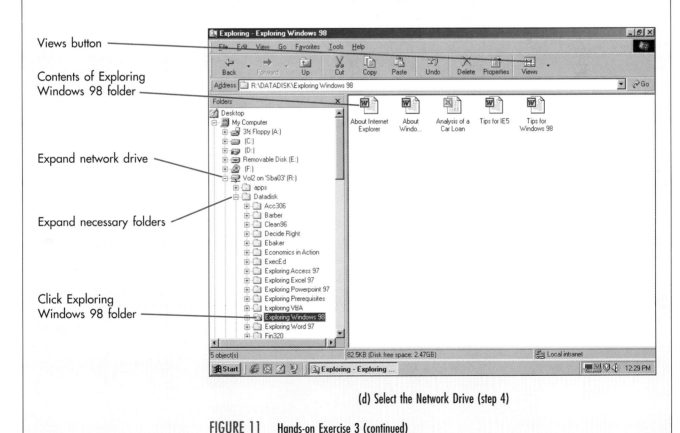

Views button

Contents of Exploring
Windows 98 folder

Expand network drive

Expand necessary folders

Click Exploring
Windows 98 folder

(d) Select the Network Drive (step 4)

FIGURE 11   Hands-on Exercise 3 (continued)

➤ Click the icon next to any other folder to select the folder, which in turn de-selects the Exploring Windows 98 folder. (Only one folder in the left pane can be active at a time.)

➤ Reselect (click) the **Exploring Windows 98 folder,** and its contents are again visible in the right pane.

➤ Pull down the **View menu** and select **Details** (or click the arrow on the **Views button** on the toolbar to display the different views, then **Details**). This enables you to see the file sizes of the individual files.

SORT BY NAME, DATE, FILE TYPE, OR SIZE

The files within a folder can be displayed in ascending or descending sequence by name, date modified, file type, or size. Change to the Details view. Select the desired folder in the left pane, then click the desired column heading in the right pane; click size, for example, to display the contents of the selected folder according to the size of the individual files. Click the column heading a second time to reverse the sequence—that is, to switch from ascending to descending, and vice versa.

STEP 5: Copy the Individual Files

➤ Select (click) the file called **About Windows Explorer,** which highlights the file as shown in Figure 11e. The Exploring Windows 98 folder is no longer highlighted because a different object has been selected. The folder is still open, however, and its contents are displayed in the right pane.

➤ Click and drag the selected file in the right pane to the **drive A icon** in the left pane:

• You will see the ⊘ symbol as you drag the file until you reach a suitable destination (e.g., until you point to the icon for drive A). The ⊘ symbol will change to a plus sign when the icon for drive A is highlighted, indicating that the file can be copied successfully.

• Release the mouse to complete the copy operation. You will see a pop-up window, which indicates the status of the copy operation. This may take several seconds depending on the size of the file.

➤ Select (click) the file **Tips for Windows 98,** which automatically deselects the previously selected file (About Windows Explorer). Copy the selected file to drive A by dragging its icon from the right pane to the drive A icon in the left pane.

➤ Copy the three remaining files to drive A as well. (You can select multiple files at the same time by pressing and holding the **Ctrl key** as you click each file in turn. Point to any of the selected files, then click and drag the files as a group.)

➤ Select (click) **drive A** in the left pane, which in turn displays the contents of the floppy disk in the right pane. You should see the five files you have copied to drive A.

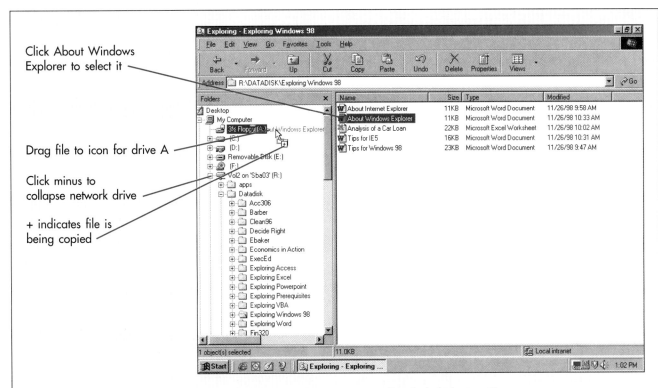

Click About Windows
Explorer to select it

Drag file to icon for drive A

Click minus to
collapse network drive

+ indicates file is
being copied

(e) Copy the Individual Files (step 5)

FIGURE 11   Hands-on Exercise 3 (continued)

SELECT MULTIPLE FILES

Selecting (clicking) one file automatically deselects the previously selected file. You can, however, select multiple files by pressing and holding the Ctrl key as you click each file in succession. You can also select multiple files that are adjacent to one another by using the Shift key; that is, click the icon of the first file, then press and hold the Shift key as you click the icon of the last file. You can also select every file in a folder through the Select All command in the Edit menu (or by clicking in the right pane and pressing Ctrl+A). The same commands work in the Web style, except that you hover over an icon (point to it and pause) rather than click it; for example, point to the first file, then press the Ctrl key as you hover over each subsequent file that you want to select.

STEP 6: Display a Web Page

➤ This step requires an Internet connection. Click the **minus sign** next to the network drive to collapse that drive. Click the **minus sign** next to any other expanded drive so that the left pane in Windows Explorer is similar to Figure 11f.

➤ Click the **Internet Explorer icon** to start Internet Explorer and display the starting page for your configuration. Click in the Address bar near the top of the window. Type **www.prenhall.com/grauer** to go to the *Exploring Windows* home page.

➤ Look closely at the icons on the toolbar, which have changed to reflect the tools associated with viewing a Web page.

➤ Click the **Back button** to return to drive A, which was the previously displayed item in Windows Explorer. The icons on the toolbar return to those associated with a folder.

➤ Click the **Forward button** to return to the Web page. The icons on the toolbar change back to those associated with the Internet.

➤ Close Windows Explorer. Shut down the computer if you do not want to continue with the next exercise at this time.

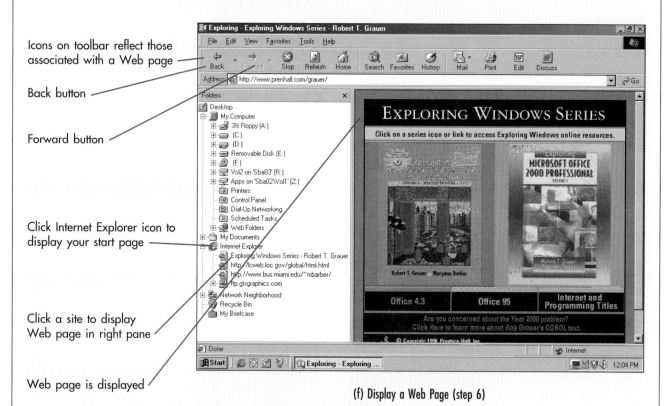

Icons on toolbar reflect those associated with a Web page

Back button

Forward button

Click Internet Explorer icon to display your start page

Click a site to display Web page in right pane

Web page is displayed

(f) Display a Web Page (step 6)

FIGURE 11   Hands-on Exercise 3 (continued)

THE SMART TOOLBAR

The toolbar in Windows Explorer recognizes whether you are viewing a Web page or a set of files and folders, and changes accordingly. The icons that are displayed when viewing a Web page are identical to those in Internet Explorer and include the Search, History, Favorites, and buttons that show various sets of Internet links. The buttons that are displayed when viewing a file or folder include the Undo, Delete, and Views buttons that are used in file management. Both sets of icons include the Back button to return to the previous object.

THE BASICS OF FILE MANAGEMENT

As you grow to depend on the computer, you will create a variety of files in applications such as Microsoft Word or Excel. Learning how to manage those files is one of the most important skills you can acquire. The purpose of Hands-on Exercises 2 and 3 was to give you a set of files with which to practice. That way, when you have your own files, you will be comfortable executing the various file management commands you will need on a daily basis. Accordingly, we discuss the basic commands you will use, then present another hands-on exercise in which you apply those commands.

Moving and Copying a File

Moving and copying a file from one location to another is the essence of file management. It is accomplished most easily by clicking and dragging the file icon from the source drive or folder to the destination drive or folder, within Windows Explorer. There is a subtlety, however, in that the result of dragging a file (i.e., whether the file is moved or copied) depends on whether the source and destination are on the same or different drives. Dragging a file from one folder to another folder on the same drive moves the file. Dragging a file to a folder on a different drive copies the file. The same rules apply to dragging a folder, where the folder and every file in it are moved or copied as per the rules for an individual file.

This process is not as arbitrary as it may seem. Windows assumes that if you drag an object (a file or folder) to a different drive (e.g., from drive C to drive A), you want the object to appear in both places. Hence, the default action when you click and drag an object to a different drive is to copy the object. You can, however, override the default and move the object by pressing and holding the Shift key as you drag.

Windows also assumes that you do not want two copies of an object on the same drive, as that would result in wasted disk space. Thus, the default action when you click and drag an object to a different folder on the same drive is to move the object. You can override the default and copy the object by pressing and holding the Ctrl key as you drag.

You don't have to remember these conventions, however. Just click and drag with the right mouse button and you will be presented with a context-sensitive menu asking whether to move or copy the files. It's not as complicated as it sounds, and you get a chance to practice in the hands-on exercise, which follows shortly.

Deleting a File

The ***Delete command*** deletes (removes) a file from a disk. The command can be executed in different ways, most easily by selecting a file, then pressing the Del key. Even after a file is deleted, however, you can usually get it back because it is not physically deleted from the hard disk, but moved instead to the Recycle Bin from where it can be recovered.

The ***Recycle Bin*** is a special folder that contains all files that were previously deleted from any hard disk on your system. Think of the Recycle Bin as similar to the wastebasket in your room. You throw out (delete) a report by tossing it into a wastebasket. The report is gone (deleted) from your desk, but you can still get it back by taking it out of the wastebasket as long as the basket wasn't emptied. The Recycle Bin works the same way. Files are not deleted from the hard disk per se, but moved instead to the Recycle Bin from where they can be restored to their original location.

The Recycle Bin will eventually run out of space, in which case the files that have been in the Recycle Bin the longest are deleted to make room for additional files. Accordingly, once a file is removed from the Recycle Bin, it can no longer be restored, as it has been physically deleted from the hard disk. Note, too, that the protection afforded by the Recycle Bin does not extend to files deleted from a floppy disk. Such files can be recovered, but only through utility programs outside of Windows 98.

Backup

It's not a question of *if* it will happen, but *when*—hard disks die, files are lost, or viruses may infect a system. It has happened to us and it will happen to you, but you can prepare for the inevitable by creating adequate backup *before* the problem occurs. The essence of a *backup strategy* is to decide which files to back up, how often to do the backup, and where to keep the backup. Once you decide on a strategy, follow it, and follow it faithfully!

Our strategy is very simple—back up what you can't afford to lose, do so on a daily basis, and store the backup away from your computer. You need not copy every file, every day. Instead, copy just the files that changed during the current session. Realize, too, that it is much more important to back up your data files than your program files. You can always reinstall the application from the original disks or CD, or if necessary, go to the vendor for another copy of an application. You, however, are the only one who has a copy of the term paper that is due tomorrow.

We cannot overemphasize the importance of adequate backup and urge you to copy your data files to floppy disks and store those disks away from your computer. You might also want to write-protect your backup disks so that you cannot accidentally erase a file. It takes only a few minutes, but you will thank us, when (not if) you lose an important file and wish you had another copy.

Write-protection

A floppy disk is normally *write-enabled* (the square hole is covered with the movable tab) so that you can change the contents of the disk. Thus, you can create (save) new files to a write-enabled disk and/or edit or delete existing files. Occasionally, however, you may want to *write-protect* a floppy disk (by sliding the tab to expose the square hole) so that its contents cannot be modified. This is typically done with a backup disk where you want to prevent the accidental deletion of a file and/or the threat of virus infection.

Our Next Exercise

As we have indicated throughout this supplement, the ability to move and copy files is of paramount importance. The only way to master these skills is through practice, and so we offer our next exercise in which you execute various commands for file management.

The exercise begins with the floppy disk containing the five practice files in drive A. We ask you to create two folders on drive A (step 1) and to move the various files into these folders (step 2). Next, you copy a folder from drive A to drive C (step 3), modify one of the files in the folder on drive C (step 4), then copy the modified file back to drive A (step 5). We ask you to delete a file in step 6, then recover it from the Recycle Bin in step 7. We also show you how to write-protect a floppy disk in step 8. Disk and file management is a critical skill, and you will want to master the exercise in its entirety. There is a lot to do, so let's get started.

Windows Explorer

Objective: Use Windows Explorer to move, copy, and delete a file. Use Figure 12, which was done using the Classic style, as a guide.

STEP 1: Create a New Folder

➤ Start Windows Explorer. Place the floppy disk from Hands-on Exercise 2 or 3 in drive A. Select (click) the icon for **drive A** in the left pane of the Explorer window. Drive A should contain the files shown in Figure 12a.

➤ You will create two folders on drive A, using two different techniques:

- Point to a blank area anywhere in the **right pane,** click the **right mouse button** to display a context-sensitive menu, click (or point to) the **New command,** then click **Folder** as the type of object to create. The icon for a new folder will appear with the name of the folder (New Folder) highlighted. Type **Computing 101** to change the name of the folder. Press **Enter.**

- Click the icon for **drive A** once again. Pull down the **File menu,** click (or point to) the **New command,** and click **Folder** as the type of object to create. Type **IE Documents** to change the name of the folder. Press **Enter.** The right pane should now contain five documents and two folders.

➤ Pull down the **View menu.** Click (or point to) the **Arrange Icons command** to display a submenu, then click the **By Name command.**

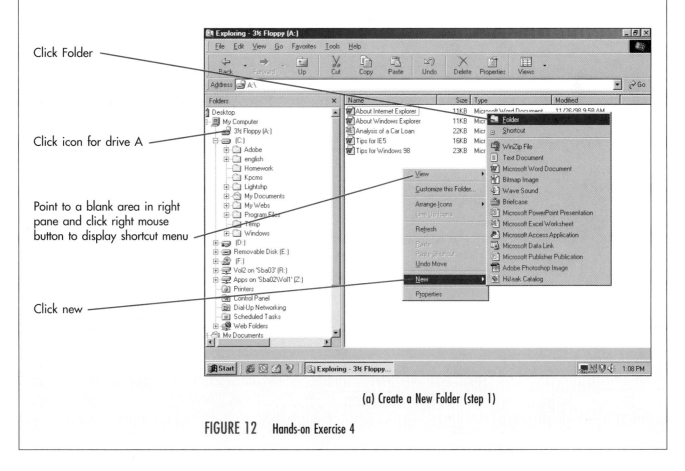

Click Folder

Click icon for drive A

Point to a blank area in right pane and click right mouse button to display shortcut menu

Click new

(a) Create a New Folder (step 1)

FIGURE 12 Hands-on Exercise 4

RENAME COMMAND

Every file or folder is assigned a name at the time it is created, but you may want to change that name at some point in the future. Point to a file or a folder, then click the right mouse button to display a menu with commands pertaining to the object. Click the Rename command. The name of the file or folder will be highlighted with the insertion point (a flashing vertical line) positioned at the end of the name. Enter a new name to replace the selected name, or click anywhere within the name to change the insertion point and edit the name.

STEP 2: Move a File

➤ Pull down the **View** menu and click **Refresh.** Click the **plus sign** next to drive A to expand the drive as shown in Figure 12b. Note the following:

• The left pane shows that drive A is selected. The right pane displays the contents of drive A (the selected object in the left pane). The folders are shown first and appear in alphabetical order. The file names are displayed after the folders and are also in alphabetical order.

• There is a minus sign next to the icon for drive A in the left pane, indicating that it has been expanded and that its folders are visible. Thus, the folder names also appear under drive A in the left pane.

➤ Click and drag the icon for **About Windows Explorer** from the right pane to the **Computing 101 folder** in the left pane to move the file into that folder.

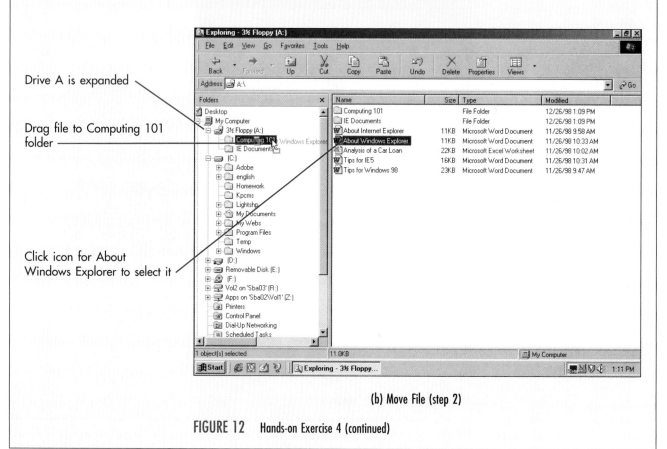

(b) Move File (step 2)

FIGURE 12   Hands-on Exercise 4 (continued)

➤ Click and drag the **Tips for Windows 98 icon** and the **Analysis of a Car Loan icon** to the **Computing 101 folder** in similar fashion.

➤ Click the **Computing 101 icon** in the left pane to select the folder and display its contents in the right pane. You should see the three files.

➤ Click the icon for **drive A** in the left pane, then click and drag the remaining files, **About Internet Explorer** and **Tips for IE5,** to the **IE Documents folder.**

RIGHT CLICK AND DRAG

The result of dragging a file with the left mouse button depends on whether the source and destination folders are on the same or different drives. Dragging a file to a folder on a different drive copies the file. Dragging the file to a folder on the same drive moves the file. If you find this hard to remember, click and drag with the right mouse button to display a shortcut menu asking whether you want to copy or move the file. This simple tip can save you from making a careless (and potentially serious) error.

STEP 3: Copy a Folder

➤ If necessary, click the **plus sign** next to the icon for drive C to expand the drive and display its folders as shown in Figure 12c.

➤ Do *not* click the icon for drive C, as drive A is to remain selected. (You can expand or collapse an object without selecting it.)

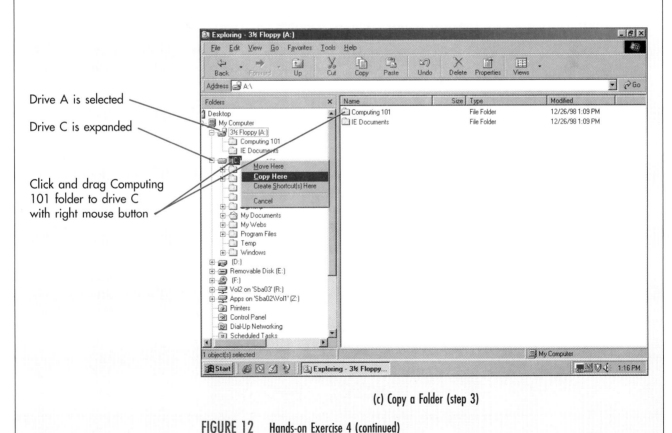

Drive A is selected

Drive C is expanded

Click and drag Computing 101 folder to drive C with right mouse button

(c) Copy a Folder (step 3)

FIGURE 12   Hands-on Exercise 4 (continued)

➤ Point to the **Computing 101 folder** in either pane, click the **right mouse button,** and drag the folder to the icon for **drive C** in the left pane, then release the mouse to display a shortcut menu. Click the **Copy Here command.**

- You may see a Copy files dialog box as the individual files within the folder are copied from drive A to drive C.

- If you see the Confirm Folder Replace dialog box, it means that the previous student forgot to delete the Computing 101 folder when he or she did this exercise. Click the **Yes to All button** so that the files on your floppy disk will replace the previous versions on drive C.

➤ Please remember to **delete** the Computing 101 folder on drive C, when you get to step 9 at the end of the exercise.

CUSTOMIZE WINDOWS EXPLORER

Increase or decrease the size of the left pane within Windows Explorer by dragging the vertical line separating the left and right panes in the appropriate direction. You can also drag the right border of the various column headings (Name, Size, Type, and Modified) in the right pane to increase or decrease the width of the column and see more or less information in that column. And best of all, you can click any column heading to display the contents of the selected folder in sequence by that column. Click the heading a second time, and the sequence changes from ascending to descending and vice versa.

STEP 4: Modify a Document

➤ Click the **Computing 101 folder** on drive C to make this folder the active folder and display its contents in the right pane. Open the **About Windows Explorer** document:

- Double click the document icon in Classic style.

- Click the icon in Web style.

➤ Do not be concerned if the size and/or position of the Microsoft Word window is different from ours. All that matters is that you see the document. If necessary, click inside the document window, then press **Ctrl+End** to move to the end of the document.

➤ Add the sentence shown in Figure 12d followed by your name. Pull down the **File menu** and click **Save** to save the modified file (or click the **Save button** on the Standard toolbar). Pull down the **File menu** and click **Exit** to exit from Microsoft Word.

➤ Pull down the **View menu** in Windows Explorer and click **Refresh** (or press the **F5 key**) to update the contents of the right pane. The date and time associated with the About Windows Explorer file has been changed to indicate that the file has just been modified.

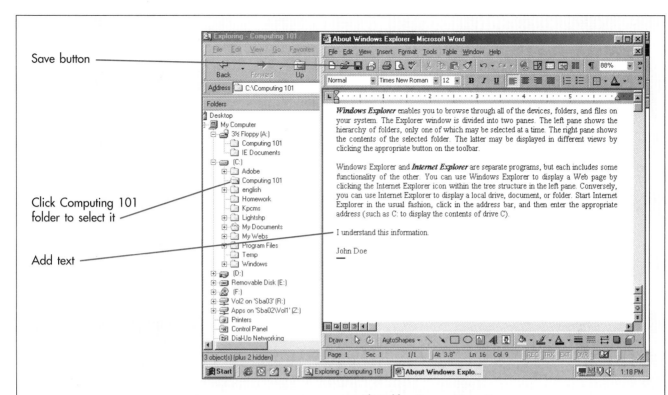

Save button

Click Computing 101 folder to select it

Add text

(d) Modify a Document (step 4)

FIGURE 12   Hands-on Exercise 4 (continued)

KEYBOARD SHORTCUTS

Most people begin with the mouse, but add keyboard shortcuts as they become more proficient. Ctrl+B, Ctrl+I, and Ctrl+U are shortcuts to boldface, italicize, and underline, respectively. Ctrl+X (the X is supposed to remind you of a pair of scissors), Ctrl+C, and Ctrl+V correspond to Cut, Copy, and Paste, respectively. Ctrl+Home and Ctrl+End move to the beginning or end of a document. These shortcuts are not unique to Microsoft Word, but are recognized in virtually every Windows application.

STEP 5: Copy (Back Up) a File

➤ Verify that the **Computing 101 folder** on drive C is the active folder as denoted by the open folder icon. Click and drag the icon for the **About Windows Explorer** file from the right pane to the **Computing 101 folder** on **drive A** in the left pane.

➤ You will see the message in Figure 12e, indicating that the folder (drive A) already contains a file called About Windows Explorer and asking whether you want to replace the existing file. Click **Yes** because you want to replace the previous version of the file on drive A with the updated version from drive C.

➤ You have just backed up the file; in other words, you have created a copy of the file on drive C on the disk in drive A. Thus, you can use the floppy disk to restore the file on drive C should anything happen to it. We cannot overemphasize the importance of adequate backup!

Click and drag About Windows Explorer file to Computing 101 folder on drive A

Computing 101 folder on drive C is selected

Click Yes

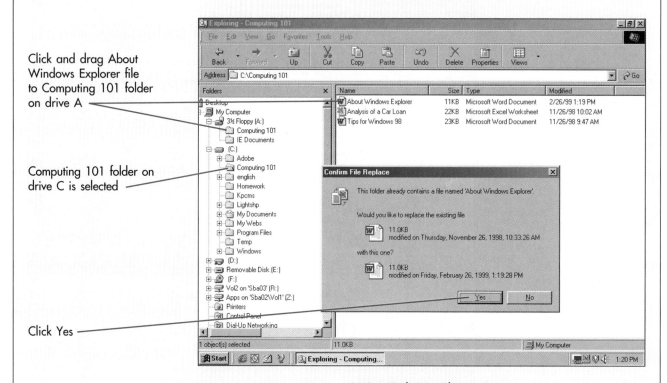

(e) Copy (Back Up) a File (step 5)

FIGURE 12   Hands-on Exercise 4 (continued)

COPYING FROM ONE FLOPPY DISK TO ANOTHER

You've learned how to copy a file from drive C to drive A, or from drive A to drive C, but how do you copy a file from one floppy disk to another? It's easy when you know how. Place the first floppy disk in drive A, select drive A in the left pane of the Explorer window, then copy the file from the right pane to a temporary folder on drive C in the left pane. Remove the first floppy disk, and replace it with the second. Select the temporary folder on drive C in the left pane, then click and drag the file from the right pane to the floppy disk in the left pane.

STEP 6: Delete a Folder

➤ Select (click) the **Computing 101 folder** on drive C in the left pane. Pull down the **File menu** and click **Delete** (or press the **Del key**).

➤ You will see the dialog box in Figure 12f asking whether you are sure you want to delete the folder (i.e., send the folder and its contents to the Recycle Bin). Note the green recycle logo within the box, which implies that you will be able to restore the file.

➤ Click **Yes** to delete the folder. The folder disappears from drive C. Pull down the **Edit menu.** Click **Undo Delete.**

➤ The deletion is cancelled and the folder reappears in the left pane. If you don't see the folder, pull down the **View menu** and click the **Refresh command.**

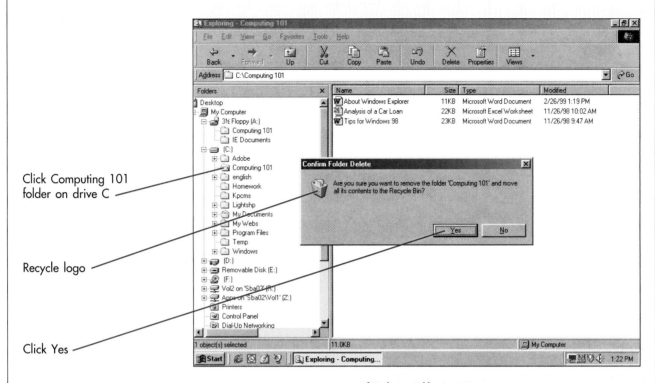

(f) Delete a Folder (step 6)

FIGURE 12 Hands-on Exercise 4 (continued)

THE UNDO COMMAND

The Undo command is present not only in application programs such as Word or Excel, but in Windows Explorer as well. You can use the command to undelete a file if it is executed immediately (within a few commands) after the Delete command. To execute the Undo command, right click anywhere in the right pane to display a shortcut menu, then select the Undo action. You can also pull down the Edit menu and click Undo to reverse (undo) the last command. Some operations cannot be undone (in which case the command will be dimmed), but Undo is always worth a try.

STEP 7: The Recycle Bin

➤ The Recycle Bin can also be used to recover a deleted file provided that the network administrator has not disabled this function.

➤ If necessary, select the **Computing 101 folder** on drive C in the left pane. Select (click) the **About Windows Explorer** file in the right pane. Press the **Del key,** then click **Yes** when asked whether to send the file to the Recycle Bin.

➤ Click the **down arrow** in the vertical scroll bar in the left pane until you see the icon for the **Recycle Bin.** (You can also open the Recycle Bin from the desktop.) Click the icon to make the Recycle Bin the active folder and display its contents in the right pane.

➤ The Recycle Bin contains all files that have been previously deleted from drive C, and hence you will see a different set of files than those displayed in Figure 12g. Pull down the **View menu,** click (or point to) **Arrange Icons,** then click **By Delete Date** to display the files in this sequence.

➤ Click in the **right pane.** Press **Ctrl+End** or scroll to the bottom of the window. Point to the **About Windows Explorer** file, click the **right mouse button** to display the shortcut menu in Figure 12g, then click **Restore.**

➤ The file disappears from the Recycle Bin because it has been returned to the Computing 101 folder. You can open the Computing 101 folder on drive C to confirm that the file has been restored.

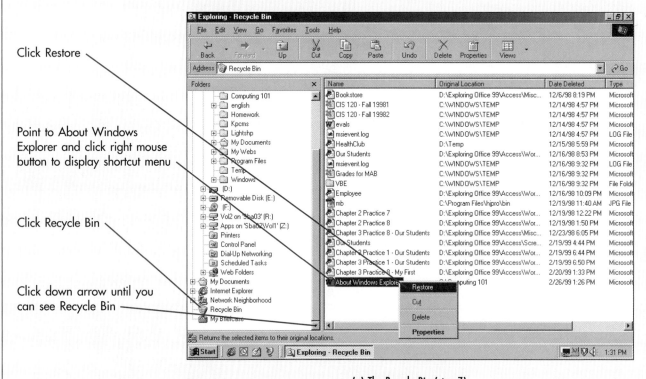

Click Restore

Point to About Windows Explorer and click right mouse button to display shortcut menu

Click Recycle Bin

Click down arrow until you can see Recycle Bin

(g) The Recycle Bin (step 7)

FIGURE 12   Hands-on Exercise 4 (continued)

THE SHOW DESKTOP BUTTON

The Show Desktop button on the taskbar enables you to minimize all open windows with a single click. The button functions as a toggle switch. Click it once and all windows are minimized. Click it a second time and the open windows are restored to their position on the desktop. If you do not see the Show Desktop button, right click a blank area of the taskbar to display a context-sensitive menu, click Toolbars, then check the Quick Launch toolbar, which contains the Show Desktop button.

STEP 8: Write-protect a Floppy Disk

➤ You can write-protect a floppy disk so that its contents cannot be modified. Remove the floppy disk from drive A, then move the built-in tab on the disk so that the square hole on the disk is open. The disk is now write-protected.

➤ If necessary, expand drive A in the left pane, select the **Computing 101 folder,** select the **Analysis of a Car Loan document** in the right pane, then press the **Del key.** Click **Yes** when asked whether to delete the file.

➤ You will see the message in Figure 12h indicating that the file cannot be deleted because the disk is write-protected. Click **OK.** Remove the write-protection by moving the built-in tab to cover the square hole.

➤ Repeat the procedure to delete the **Analysis of a Car Loan document.** Click **Yes** in response to the confirmation message asking whether you want to delete the file. Note, however, the icon that appears in this dialog box is a red exclamation point, rather than a recycle emblem, indicating you cannot (easily) recover a deleted file from a floppy disk.

➤ The file disappears from the right pane indicating it has been deleted. The Computing 101 folder on drive A should contain only two files.

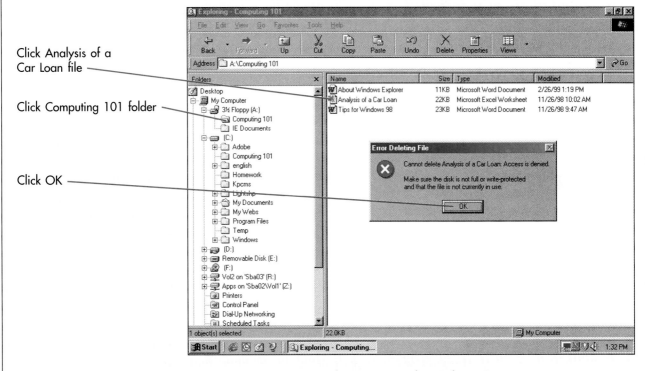

Click Analysis of a Car Loan file

Click Computing 101 folder

Click OK

(h) Write-protect a Floppy Disk (step 8)

FIGURE 12   Hands-on Exercise 4 (continued)

STEP 9: Complete the Exercise

➤ Delete the **Computing 101 folder** on drive C as a courtesy to the next student in the Computer Lab.

➤ Exit Windows Explorer. Welcome to Windows 98!

Windows 98 is a computer program (actually many programs) that controls the operation of your computer and its peripherals. It is the third major release of the Windows operating system, following Windows 3.1 and Windows 95.

All Windows operations take place on the desktop, which is displayed in either the Classic style or the Web style. The choice between the two is one of personal preference. The Classic style is virtually identical to the Windows 95 desktop and requires you to click an icon to select it, and double click the icon to open it. The Web style uses underlined icons that function identically to the hyperlinks in a browser; thus you point to an icon to select it, and click the icon to open it.

All Windows applications share a common user interface and possess a consistent command structure. Every window on the desktop contains the same basic elements, which include a title bar, a minimize button, a maximize or restore button, and a close button. Other elements that may be present include a menu bar, vertical and/or horizontal scroll bars, a status bar, and a toolbar. All windows may be moved and sized.

Multitasking is a major benefit of the Windows environment as it enables you to run several programs at the same time. The taskbar contains a button for each open program and enables you to switch back and forth between those programs by clicking the appropriate button.

The mouse is essential to Windows and has five basic actions: pointing, clicking, right clicking, double clicking, and dragging. The mouse pointer assumes different shapes according to the nature of the current action.

A dialog box supplies information needed to execute a command. Option buttons indicate mutually exclusive choices, one of which must be chosen. Check boxes are used if the choices are not mutually exclusive or if an option is not required. A text box supplies descriptive information. A (drop-down or open) list box displays multiple choices, any of which may be selected. A tabbed dialog box provides access to multiple sets of options.

The Help command on the Start menu provides access to detailed information about Windows 98. You can search for information three ways—through the Contents, Index, and Find tabs. You can also go to the Microsoft Web site, where you have access to the Windows Knowledge Base of current information.

A floppy disk must be formatted before it can store data. Formatting is accomplished through the Format command within the My Computer window. My Computer enables you to browse the disk drives and other devices attached to your system. My Computer is present on every desktop, but its contents depend on your specific configuration.

A file is a set of data or set of instructions that has been given a name and stored on disk. There are two basic types of files—program files and data files. A program file is an executable file, whereas a data file can be used only in conjunction with a specific program. Every file has a file name and a file type. The file name can be up to 255 characters in length and may include spaces.

Files are stored in folders to better organize the hundreds (or thousands) of files on a disk. A folder may contain program files, data files, and/or other folders. There are two basic ways to search through the folders on your system—My Computer and Windows Explorer. My Computer is intuitive but less efficient than Windows Explorer, as you have to open each folder in succession. Windows Explorer is more sophisticated as it provides a hierarchical view of the entire system.

Windows Explorer is divided into two panes. The left pane displays all of the devices and, optionally, the folders on each device. The right pane shows the contents of the active (open) drive or folder. Only one drive or folder can be active in the left pane. Any device, be it local or on the network, may be expanded or collapsed to display or hide its folders. A minus sign indicates that the drive has been expanded and that its folders are visible. A plus sign indicates the reverse; that is, the device is collapsed and its folders are not visible.

The result of dragging a file (or folder) from one location to another depends on whether the source and destination folders are on the same or different drives. Dragging the file to a folder on the same drive moves the file. Dragging the file to a folder on a different drive copies the file. It's easier, therefore, to click and drag with the right mouse button to display a menu from which you can select the desired operation.

The Delete command deletes (removes) a file from a disk. A file deleted from a hard disk can be restored from the Recycle Bin. This is not true, however, for files that are deleted from a floppy disk.

The choice between Web style and Classic style is strictly one of personal preference and depends on how you want to open a document, by clicking or double clicking, respectively. The Folder Options command in the View menu of My Computer or Windows Explorer enables you to switch from one style to the other.

KEY WORDS AND CONCEPTS

Backup strategy	Folder	Rename a file
Check box	Format command	Restore a file
Classic style	Help command	Restore button
Close button	Horizontal scroll bar	Search tab
Collapsed icon	Index tab	Smart toolbar
Command button	Internet Explorer	Start button
Common user interface	List box	Status bar
Contents tab	Maximize button	Tabbed dialog box
Copy a file	Menu bar	Taskbar
Data file	Minimize button	Text box
Delete a file	Mouse operations	Title bar
Desktop	Move a file	Vertical scroll bar
Dialog box	Multitasking	Web style
Dimmed command	My Computer	Windows 2000
Drop-down list box	Network Neighborhood	Windows 95
Expanded icon	Option button	Windows 98
Extension	Program file	Windows NT
File	Pull-down menu	Windows Explorer
File name	Radio button	Write-enabled
File type	Recycle Bin	Write-protected

1. What is the significance of a faded (dimmed) command in a pull-down menu?
   (a) The command is not currently accessible
   (b) A dialog box will appear if the command is selected
   (c) A Help window will appear if the command is selected
   (d) There are no equivalent keystrokes for the particular command

2. Which of the following is true regarding a dialog box?
   (a) Option buttons indicate mutually exclusive choices
   (b) Check boxes imply that multiple options may be selected
   (c) Both (a) and (b)
   (d) Neither (a) nor (b)

3. Which of the following is the first step in sizing a window?
   (a) Point to the title bar
   (b) Pull down the View menu to display the toolbar
   (c) Point to any corner or border
   (d) Pull down the View menu and change to large icons

4. Which of the following is the first step in moving a window?
   (a) Point to the title bar
   (b) Pull down the View menu to display the toolbar
   (c) Point to any corner or border
   (d) Pull down the View menu and change to large icons

5. How do you exit Windows?
   (a) Click the Start button, then click the Shut Down command
   (b) Right click the Start button, then click the Shut Down command
   (c) Click the End button, then click the Shut Down command
   (d) Right click the End button, then click the Shut Down command

6. How do you open My Computer?
   (a) Double click the My Computer icon in the Windows 98 Classic style
   (b) Click the My Computer icon in the Windows 98 Web style
   (c) Both (a) and (b)
   (d) Neither (a) nor (b)

7. Which button appears immediately after a window has been maximized?
   (a) The close button
   (b) The restore button
   (c) The maximize button
   (d) All of the above

8. What happens to a window that has been minimized?
   (a) The window is still visible but it no longer has a minimize button
   (b) The window shrinks to a button on the taskbar
   (c) The window is closed and the application is removed from memory
   (d) The window is still open but the application has been removed from memory

9. What is the significance of three dots next to a command in a pull-down menu?
   (a) The command is not currently accessible
   (b) A dialog box will appear if the command is selected
   (c) A Help window will appear if the command is selected
   (d) There are no equivalent keystrokes for the particular command

10. The Recycle Bin enables you to restore a file that was deleted from:
    (a) Drive A
    (b) Drive C
    (c) Both (a) and (b)
    (d) Neither (a) nor (b)

11. The left pane of Windows Explorer may contain:
    (a) One or more folders with a plus sign
    (b) One or more folders with a minus sign
    (c) Both (a) and (b)
    (d) Neither (a) nor (b)

12. Which of the following was suggested as essential to a backup strategy?
    (a) Back up all program files at the end of every session
    (b) Store backup files at another location
    (c) Both (a) and (b)
    (d) Neither (a) nor (b)

13. Which of the following is true regarding a disk that has been write protected?
    (a) Existing files cannot be modified or erased
    (b) A new file cannot be added to the disk
    (c) Both (a) and (b)
    (d) Neither (a) nor (b)

14. How do you open a file from within My Computer or Windows Explorer?
    (a) Click the file icon if you are in the Classic style
    (b) Double click the file icon if you are in the Web style
    (c) Both (a) and (b)
    (d) Neither (a) nor (b)

15. How do you change from the Web style to the Classic style?
    (a) Open My Computer, pull down the View menu, click Options, click the General tab, and specify Classic style
    (b) Open Windows Explorer, pull down the View menu, click Folder Options, click the General tab, and specify Classic style
    (c) Both (a) and (b)
    (d) Neither (a) nor (b)

Answers

1. a	**6.** c	**11.** c
2. c	**7.** b	**12.** b
3. c	**8.** b	**13.** c
4. a	**9.** b	**14.** d
5. a	**10.** b	**15.** c

1. **My Computer:** Figure 13 displays a document that was created using the WordPad program, a simple word processor that is included in Windows 98. You can do the exercise using WordPad, or alternatively you can use Microsoft Word. Our directions are for WordPad:

   a. Open My Computer. Pull down the View menu and switch to the Details view. Size the window as necessary.

   b. Press Alt+Print Screen to copy the My Computer window to the clipboard.

   c. Click the Start menu, click Programs, click Accessories, then click Word-Pad to open the word processor. Maximize the window.

   d. Pull down the Edit menu. Click the Paste command to copy the contents of the clipboard to the document you are about to create. The My Computer window should be pasted into your document.

   e. Click below the graphic, press Ctrl+End to move to the end of your document. Press the enter key three times (to leave three blank lines).

   f. Type a modified form of the memo in Figure 13 so that it conforms to your configuration. Type just as you would on a regular typewriter except do not press the enter key at the end of a line as the program will automatically wrap from one line to the next. If you make a mistake, just press the backspace key to erase the last character, and continue typing.

   g. Finish the memo and sign your name. Pull down the File menu, click the Print command, then click OK in the dialog box to print the document.

2. **Windows Explorer:** Prove to your instructor that you have completed the four hands-on exercises by capturing a screen similar to Figure 14 that displays the contents of the floppy disk at the end of the exercise. Follow these instructions to create the document in Figure 14 on page 60:

   a. Do the hands-on exercises as described in the text. Place the floppy disk used in the exercise in drive A, and select the Computing 101 folder to display its contents in the right pane of Windows Explorer. If necessary, change to Details view.

   b. Press the Print Screen key to copy the screen to the clipboard (an area of memory that is available to every Windows application).

   c. Click the Start button, click Programs, click Accessories, then click Paint to open the Paint accessory. If necessary, click the maximize button so that the Paint window takes the entire desktop.

   d. Pull down the Edit menu. Click Paste to copy the screen from the clipboard to the drawing. Click Yes if you are asked to enlarge the bitmap.

   e. Click the text tool (the capital A), then click and drag in the drawing area to create a dotted rectangle that will contain the message to your instructor. Type the text indicating that you did your homework. (If necessary, pull down the View menu and check the command for the Text toolbar. This enables you to change the font and/or point size). Click outside the text to deselect it.

   f. Pull down the File menu and click the Page Setup command to display the Page Setup dialog box. Click the Landscape option button. Change the margins to one inch all around. Click OK.

   g. Pull down the File menu a second time. Click Print. Click OK.

   h. Exit Paint. You do not have to save the file. Submit the document to your instructor.

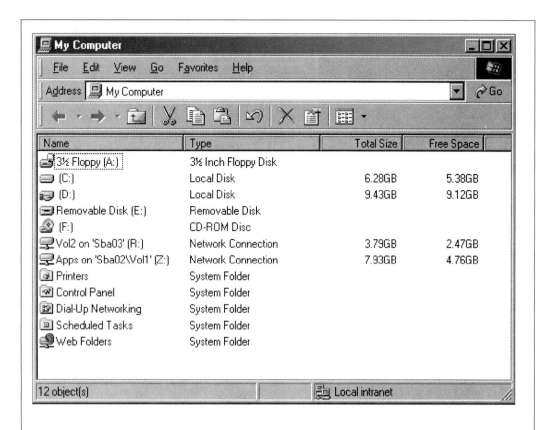

Dear Professor,

Please find above the contents of My Computer (displayed in the Classic style) as it exists on my computer system. As you can see, I have one floppy drive, labeled drive A, and two hard drives, labeled C and D. There are 5.38Gb free on drive C and 9.12Gb free on drive D. I still have a lot of free space left. I have a high-capacity removable disk drive (drive E) and a CD-ROM drive (drive F). In addition to my local drives, I have access to two network drives, drives R and Z.

I enjoyed reading the chapter and I look forward to learning more about the Active Desktop and Internet Explorer.

Sincerely,

Eric Simon

FIGURE 13   My Computer (Exercise 1)

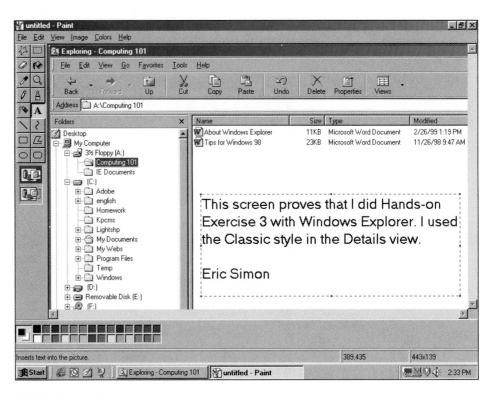

FIGURE 14 Windows Explorer (Exercise 2)

3. Companion Web Sites: Each book in the *Exploring Microsoft® Office 2000* series is accompanied by an online study guide or Companion Web site as shown in Figure 15. Start Internet Explorer and go to the Exploring Windows home page at www.prenhall.com/grauer. Click the book to Office 2000, click the Companion Web site link at the top of the screen, then choose the appropriate text (e.g., *Exploring Microsoft Office Professional Volume I*) and chapter within the text (e.g., *Essentials of Windows 95/98*).

Each study guide contains a series of short-answer exercises (multiple-choice, true/false, and matching) to review the material in the chapter. You can take practice quizzes by yourself and/or e-mail the results to your instructor. You can try the essay questions for additional practice and engage in online chat sessions. We hope you will find the online guide to be a valuable resource.

4. Organize Your Work: A folder may contain documents, programs, or other folders. The My Classes folder in Figure 16, for example, contains five folders, one folder for each class you are taking this semester, and in similar fashion, the Correspondence folder contains two additional folders according to the type of correspondence. We use folders in this fashion to organize our work, and we suggest you do likewise. The best way to practice with folders is on a floppy disk, as was done in Figure 16. Accordingly:

   a. Format a floppy disk or alternatively, use the floppy disk you have been using throughout the chapter.

   b. Create a Correspondence folder. Create a Business and Personal folder within the Correspondence folder as shown in Figure 16.

   c. Create a My Courses folder. Create a separate folder for each course you are taking within the My Courses folder as shown in Figure 16.

   d. Use the technique described in problem 2 to capture the screen shown in Figure 16. Add your name to the captured screen, and then submit it to your instructor as proof that you have done the exercise.

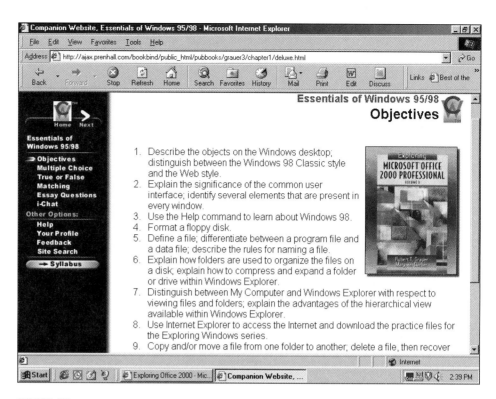

FIGURE 15 Companion Web Sites (Exercise 3)

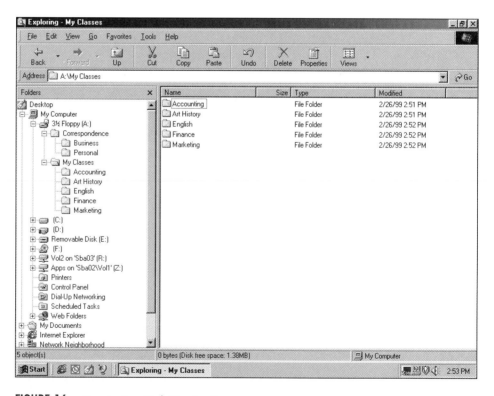

FIGURE 16 Organize Your Work (Exercise 4)

5. View Folders as a Web Page: Windows 98 enables you to view a folder as a Web page, as shown in Figure 17. Start Windows Explorer, collapse all of the drives on your system, select the My Computer icon, then pull down the View menu and click the As Web Page command. Click the Views button to cycle through the different views until your screen matches ours. Use the Folder Options command in the Views menu to experiment with additional ways to view the folders on your system. Summarize your option of this feature in a brief note to your instructor.

FIGURE 17   View Folders as a Web Page (Exercise 5)

6. Discover Windows 98: This exercise requires the Windows 98 CD. The opening screen in Windows 98 displays a Welcome window that invites you to take a discovery tour of Windows 98. (If you do not see the Welcome window, click the Start button, click Run, enter C:\windows\welcome in the Open text box, and press enter.) Click the option to discover Windows 98, which in turn displays the screen in Figure 18. Take a tour of Windows 98, then summarize the highlights in a short note to your instructor.

7. Implement a Screen Saver: A screen saver is a program that protects your monitor by producing a constantly changing pattern after a designated period of inactivity. This is not something you can do in a laboratory setting, but it is well worth doing on your own machine.

Point to a blank area of the desktop, click the right mouse button to display a context-sensitive menu, then click the Properties command to open the Display Properties dialog box in Figure 19. Click the Screen Saver tab, click the down arrow in the Screen Saver list box and select Scrolling Marquee. Click the Settings command button, enter the text and other options for your message, then click OK to close the Options dialog box. Click OK a second time to close the Display Properties dialog box.

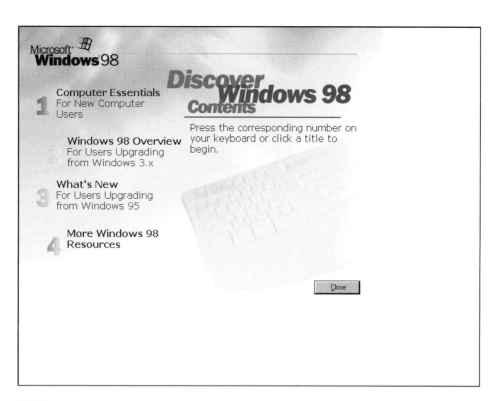

FIGURE 18   Discover Windows 98 (Exercise 6)

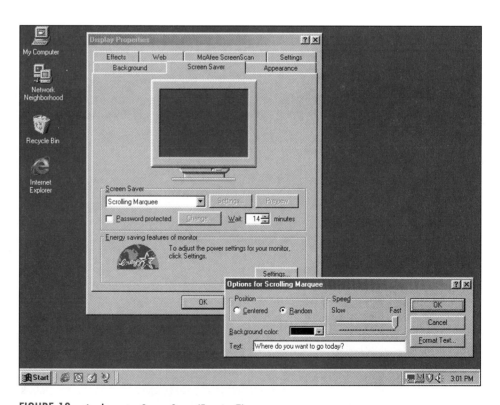

FIGURE 19   Implement a Screen Saver (Exercise 7)

Planning for Disaster

Do you have a backup strategy? Do you even know what a backup strategy is? You had better learn, because sooner or later you will wish you had one. You will erase a file, be unable to read from a floppy disk, or worse yet suffer a hardware failure in which you are unable to access the hard drive. The problem always seems to occur the night before an assignment is due. The ultimate disaster is the disappearance of your computer, by theft or natural disaster. Describe, in 250 words or less, the backup strategy you plan to implement in conjunction with your work in this class.

The Boot Disk

We don't want to give you undue cause for concern, but there is a real possibility that the hard drive on your machine will fail some time in the future and hence you will be unable to start your system. Should that occur, you will want to have a boot (startup) disk at your disposal to start the system from the floppy drive in order to access your hard drive. Use the Help command to learn how to create a startup disk, then follow the instructions if you haven't yet created one. Put the disk in a safe place. We hope you never have to use it, but you should be prepared.

File Compression

You've learned your lesson and have come to appreciate the importance of backing up all of your data files. The problem is that you work with large documents that exceed the 1.44MB capacity of a floppy disk. Accordingly, you might want to consider the acquisition of a file compression program to facilitate copying large documents to a floppy disk in order to transport your documents to and from school, home, or work. You can download an evaluation copy of the popular WinZip program at www.winzip.com. Investigate the subject of file compression, then submit a summary of your findings to your instructor.

The Threat of Virus Infection

A computer virus is an actively infectious program that attaches itself to other programs and alters the way a computer works. Some viruses do nothing more than display an annoying message at an inopportune time. Most, however, are more harmful, and in the worst case, erase all files on the disk. When is a computer subject to infection by a virus? What precautions does your school or university take against the threat of virus infection in its computer lab? What precautions, if any, do you take at home? What is the difference between the scan function in an antivirus program versus leaving the antivirus program active in memory? Can you feel confident that your machine will not be infected if you faithfully use a state-of-the-art antivirus program that was purchased in January 1997?

chapter 1

MICROSOFT® WORD 2000: WHAT WILL WORD PROCESSING DO FOR ME?

OBJECTIVES

After reading this chapter you will be able to:

1. Define word wrap; differentiate between a hard and a soft return.
2. Distinguish between the insert and overtype modes.
3. Describe the elements on the Microsoft Word screen.
4. Create, save, retrieve, edit, and print a simple document.
5. Check a document for spelling; describe the function of the custom dictionary.
6. Describe the AutoCorrect and AutoText features; explain how either feature can be used to create a personal shorthand.
7. Use the thesaurus to look up synonyms and antonyms.
8. Explain the objectives and limitations of the grammar check; customize the grammar check for business or casual writing.
9. Differentiate between the Save and Save As commands; describe various backup options that can be selected.

OVERVIEW

Have you ever produced what you thought was the perfect term paper only to discover that you omitted a sentence or misspelled a word, or that the paper was three pages too short or one page too long? Wouldn't it be nice to make the necessary changes, and then be able to reprint the entire paper with the touch of a key? Welcome to the world of word processing, where you are no longer stuck with having to retype anything. Instead, you retrieve your work from disk, display it on the monitor and revise it as necessary, then print it at any time, in draft or final form.

This chapter provides a broad-based introduction to word processing in general and Microsoft Word in particular. We begin by presenting (or perhaps reviewing) the essential concepts of a word processor, then show you how these concepts are implemented in Word. We show you how to create a document, how to save it on disk, then retrieve the document you just created. We introduce you to the spell check and thesaurus, two essential tools in any word processor. We also present the grammar check as a convenient way of finding a variety of errors but remind you there is no substitute for carefully proofreading the final document.

THE BASICS OF WORD PROCESSING

All word processors adhere to certain basic concepts that must be understood if you are to use the programs effectively. The next several pages introduce ideas that are applicable to any word processor (and which you may already know). We follow the conceptual material with a hands-on exercise that enables you to apply what you have learned.

The Insertion Point

The *insertion point* is a flashing vertical line that marks the place where text will be entered. The insertion point is always at the beginning of a new document, but it can be moved anywhere within an existing document. If, for example, you wanted to add text to the end of a document, you would move the insertion point to the end of the document, then begin typing.

Word Wrap

A newcomer to word processing has one major transition to make from a typewriter, and it is an absolutely critical adjustment. Whereas a typist returns the carriage at the end of every line, just the opposite is true of a word processor. One types continually *without* pressing the enter key at the end of a line because the word processor automatically wraps text from one line to the next. This concept is known as *word wrap* and is illustrated in Figure 1.1.

The word *primitive* does not fit on the current line in Figure 1.1a, and is automatically shifted to the next line, *without* the user having to press the enter key. The user continues to enter the document, with additional words being wrapped to subsequent lines as necessary. The only time you use the enter key is at the end of a paragraph, or when you want the insertion point to move to the next line and the end of the current line doesn't reach the right margin.

Word wrap is closely associated with another concept, that of hard and soft returns. A *hard return* is created by the user when he or she presses the enter key at the end of a paragraph; a *soft return* is created by the word processor as it wraps text from one line to the next. The locations of the soft returns change automatically as a document is edited (e.g., as text is inserted or deleted, or as margins or fonts are changed). The locations of the hard returns can be changed only by the user, who must intentionally insert or delete each hard return.

There are two hard returns in Figure 1.1b, one at the end of each paragraph. There are also six soft returns in the first paragraph (one at the end of every line except the last) and three soft returns in the second paragraph. Now suppose the margins in the document are made smaller (that is, the line is made longer) as shown in Figure 1.1c. The number of soft returns drops to four and two (in the first and second paragraphs, respectively) as more text fits on a line and fewer lines are needed. The revised document still contains the two original hard returns, one at the end of each paragraph.

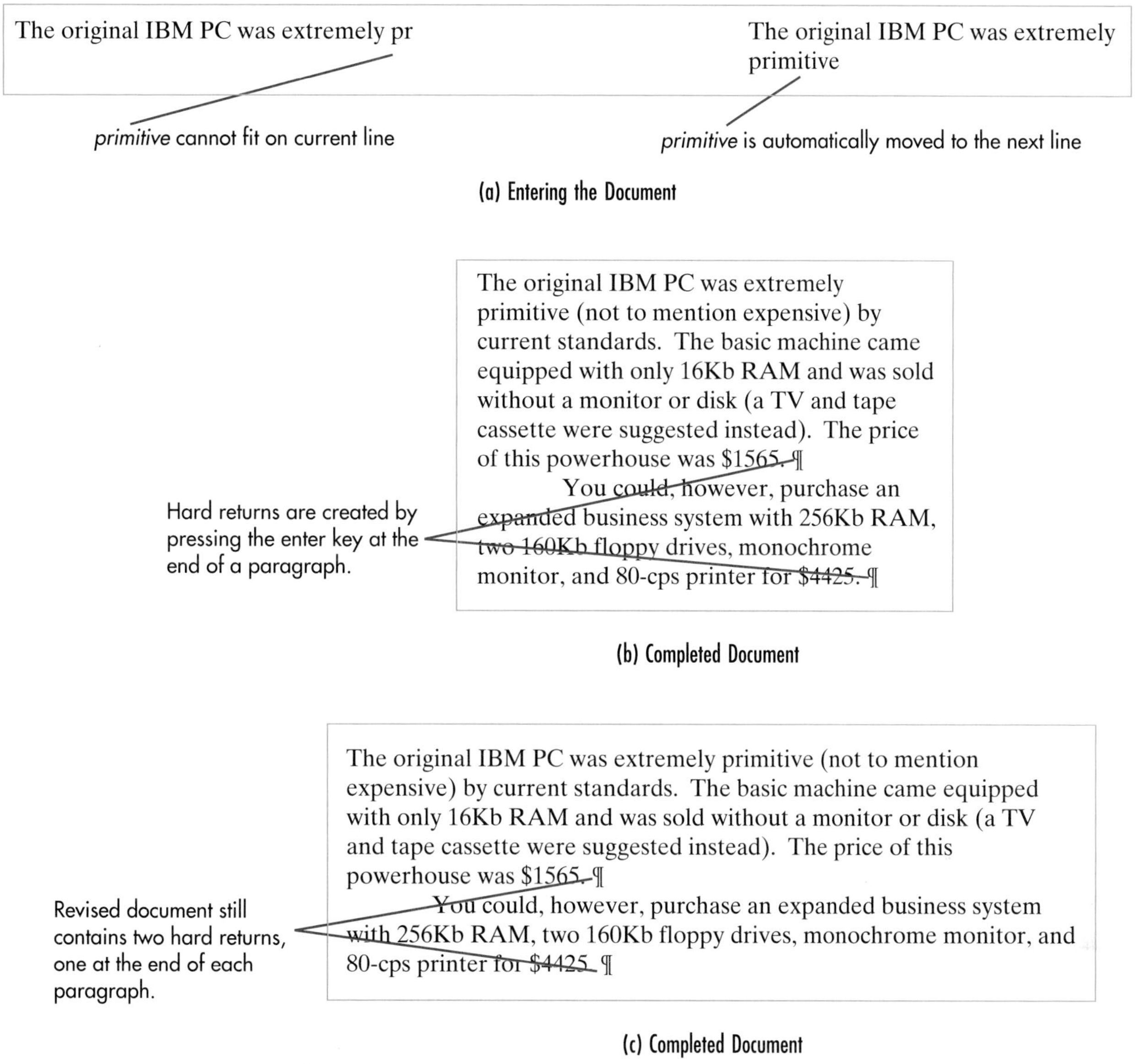

The original IBM PC was extremely pr

primitive cannot fit on current line

The original IBM PC was extremely
primitive

primitive is automatically moved to the next line

(a) Entering the Document

The original IBM PC was extremely
primitive (not to mention expensive) by
current standards. The basic machine came
equipped with only 16Kb RAM and was sold
without a monitor or disk (a TV and tape
cassette were suggested instead). The price
of this powerhouse was $1565. ¶
        You could, however, purchase an
expanded business system with 256Kb RAM,
two 160Kb floppy drives, monochrome
monitor, and 80-cps printer for $4425. ¶

Hard returns are created by
pressing the enter key at the
end of a paragraph.

(b) Completed Document

The original IBM PC was extremely primitive (not to mention
expensive) by current standards. The basic machine came equipped
with only 16Kb RAM and was sold without a monitor or disk (a TV
and tape cassette were suggested instead). The price of this
powerhouse was $1565. ¶
        You could, however, purchase an expanded business system
with 256Kb RAM, two 160Kb floppy drives, monochrome monitor, and
80-cps printer for $4425. ¶

Revised document still
contains two hard returns,
one at the end of each
paragraph.

(c) Completed Document

FIGURE 1.1   Word Wrap

Toggle Switches

Suppose you sat down at the keyboard and typed an entire sentence without pressing the Shift key; the sentence would be in all lowercase letters. Then you pressed
the Caps Lock key and retyped the sentence, again without pressing the Shift key.
This time the sentence would be in all uppercase letters. You could repeat the
process as often as you like. Each time you pressed the Caps Lock key, the sentence would switch from lowercase to uppercase and vice versa.

        The point of this exercise is to introduce the concept of a ***toggle switch,*** a
device that causes the computer to alternate between two states. The Caps Lock
key is an example of a toggle switch. Each time you press it, newly typed text will
change from uppercase to lowercase and back again. We will see several other
examples of toggle switches as we proceed in our discussion of word processing.

Insert versus Overtype

Microsoft Word is always in one of two modes, **insert** or **overtype**, and uses a toggle switch (the Ins key) to alternate between the two. Press the Ins key once and you switch from insert to overtype. Press the Ins key a second time and you go from overtype back to insert. Text that is entered into a document during the insert mode moves existing text to the right to accommodate the characters being added. Text entered from the overtype mode replaces (overtypes) existing text. Regardless of which mode you are in, text is always entered or replaced immediately to the right of the insertion point.

The insert mode is best when you enter text for the first time, but either mode can be used to make corrections. The insert mode is the better choice when the correction requires you to add new text; the overtype mode is easier when you are substituting one or more character(s) for another. The difference is illustrated in Figure 1.2.

Figure 1.2a displays the text as it was originally entered, with two misspellings. The letters *se* have been omitted from the word *insert,* and an *x* has been erroneously typed instead of an *r* in the word *overtype.* The insert mode is used in Figure 1.2b to add the missing letters, which in turn moves the rest of the line to the right. The overtype mode is used in Figure 1.2c to replace the *x* with an *r.*

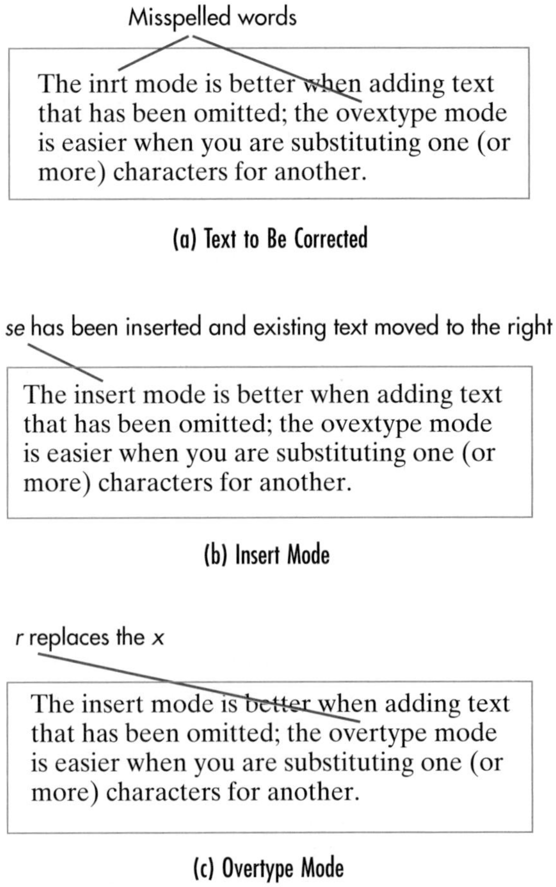

Misspelled words

The inrt mode is better when adding text that has been omitted; the ovextype mode is easier when you are substituting one (or more) characters for another.

(a) Text to Be Corrected

se has been inserted and existing text moved to the right

The insert mode is better when adding text that has been omitted; the ovextype mode is easier when you are substituting one (or more) characters for another.

(b) Insert Mode

r replaces the x

The insert mode is better when adding text that has been omitted; the overtype mode is easier when you are substituting one (or more) characters for another.

(c) Overtype Mode

FIGURE 1.2   Insert and Overtype Modes

Deleting Text

The backspace and Del keys delete one character immediately to the left or right of the insertion point, respectively. The choice between them depends on when you need to erase a character(s). The backspace key is easier if you want to delete a character immediately after typing it. The Del key is preferable during subsequent editing.

You can delete several characters at one time by selecting (dragging the mouse over) the characters to be deleted, then pressing the Del key. And finally, you can delete and replace text in one operation by selecting the text to be replaced and then typing the new text in its place.

LEARN TO TYPE

The ultimate limitation of any word processor is the speed at which you enter data; hence the ability to type quickly is invaluable. Learning how to type is easy, especially with the availability of computer-based typing programs. As little as a half hour a day for a couple of weeks will have you up to speed, and if you do any significant amount of writing at all, the investment will pay off many times.

INTRODUCTION TO MICROSOFT WORD

We used Microsoft Word to write this book, as can be inferred from the screen in Figure 1.3. Your screen will be different from ours in many ways. You will not have the same document nor is it likely that you will customize Word in exactly the same way. You should, however, be able to recognize the basic elements that are found in the Microsoft Word window that is open on the desktop.

There are actually two open windows in Figure 1.3—an application window for Microsoft Word and a document window for the specific document on which you are working. The application window has its own Minimize, Maximize (or Restore) and Close buttons. The document window has only a Close button. There is, however, only one title bar that appears at the top of the application window and it reflects the application (Microsoft Word) as well as the document name (Word Chapter 1). A menu bar appears immediately below the title bar. Vertical and horizontal scroll bars appear at the right and bottom of the document window. The Windows taskbar appears at the bottom of the screen and shows the open applications.

Microsoft Word is also part of the Microsoft Office suite of applications, and thus shares additional features with Excel, Access, and PowerPoint, that are also part of the Office suite. *Toolbars* provide immediate access to common commands and appear immediately below the menu bar. The toolbars can be displayed or hidden using the Toolbars command in the View menu.

The *Standard toolbar* contains buttons corresponding to the most basic commands in Word—for example, opening a file or printing a document. The icon on the button is intended to be indicative of its function (e.g., a printer to indicate the Print command). You can also point to the button to display a *ScreenTip* showing the name of the button. The *Formatting toolbar* appears under the Standard toolbar and provides access to common formatting operations such as boldface, italics, or underlining.

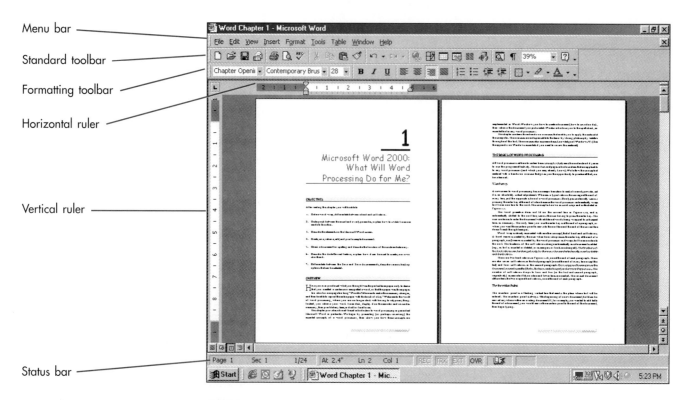

Menu bar

Standard toolbar

Formatting toolbar

Horizontal ruler

Vertical ruler

Status bar

FIGURE 1.3   Microsoft Word

The toolbars may appear overwhelming at first, but there is absolutely no need to memorize what the individual buttons do. That will come with time. We suggest, however, that you will have a better appreciation for the various buttons if you consider them in groups, according to their general function, as shown in Figure 1.4a. Note, too, that many of the commands in the pull-down menus are displayed with an image that corresponds to a button on a toolbar.

The ***horizontal ruler*** is displayed underneath the toolbars and enables you to change margins, tabs, and/or indents for all or part of a document. A ***vertical ruler*** shows the vertical position of text on the page and can be used to change the top or bottom margins.

The ***status bar*** at the bottom of the document window displays the location of the insertion point (or information about the command being executed.) The status bar also shows the status (settings) of various indicators—for example, OVR to show that Word is in the overtype, as opposed to the insert, mode.

CHANGES IN OFFICE 2000

Office 2000 implements one very significant change over previous versions in that it displays a series of short menus that contain only basic commands. The bottom of each menu has a double arrow that you can click to display the additional commands. Each time you execute a command it is added to the menu, and conversely, Word will remove commands from a menu if they are not used after a period of time. You can, however, display the full menus through the Customize command in the Tools menu by clearing the check boxes associated with personalized menus and toolbars.

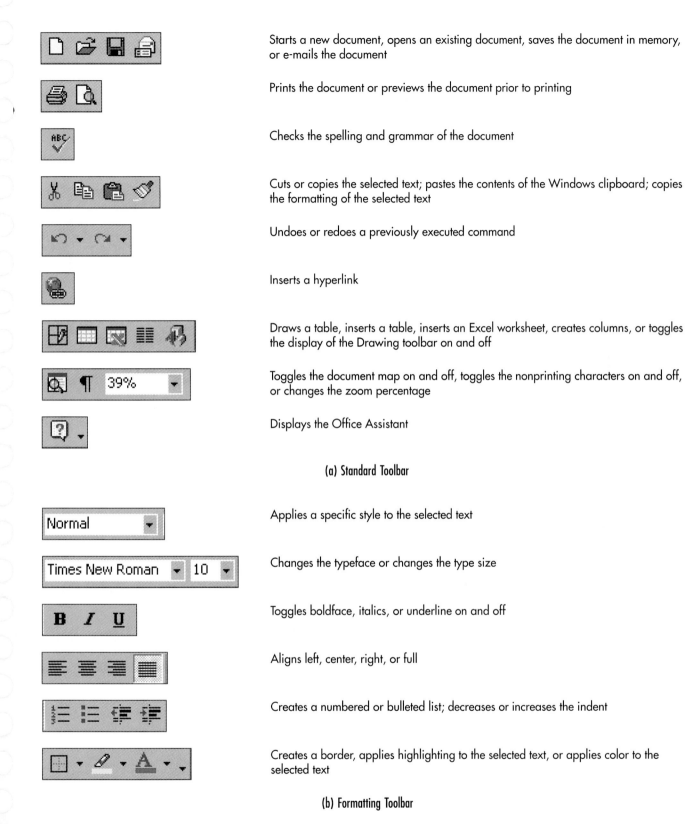

Starts a new document, opens an existing document, saves the document in memory, or e-mails the document

Prints the document or previews the document prior to printing

Checks the spelling and grammar of the document

Cuts or copies the selected text; pastes the contents of the Windows clipboard; copies the formatting of the selected text

Undoes or redoes a previously executed command

Inserts a hyperlink

Draws a table, inserts a table, inserts an Excel worksheet, creates columns, or toggles the display of the Drawing toolbar on and off

Toggles the document map on and off, toggles the nonprinting characters on and off, or changes the zoom percentage

Displays the Office Assistant

(a) Standard Toolbar

Applies a specific style to the selected text

Changes the typeface or changes the type size

Toggles boldface, italics, or underline on and off

Aligns left, center, right, or full

Creates a numbered or bulleted list; decreases or increases the indent

Creates a border, applies highlighting to the selected text, or applies color to the selected text

(b) Formatting Toolbar

FIGURE 1.4   Toolbars

The *File Menu* is a critically important menu in virtually every Windows application. It contains the Save and Open commands to save a document on disk, then subsequently retrieve (open) that document at a later time. The File Menu also contains the *Print command* to print a document, the *Close command* to close the current document but continue working in the application, and the *Exit command* to quit the application altogether.

The *Save command* copies the document that you are working on (i.e., the document that is currently in memory) to disk. The command functions differently the first time it is executed for a new document, in that it displays the Save As dialog box as shown in Figure 1.5a. The dialog box requires you to specify the name of the document, the drive (and an optional folder) in which the document is stored, and its file type. All subsequent executions of the command will save the document under the assigned name, each time replacing the previously saved version with the new version.

The *file name* (e.g., My First Document) can contain up to 255 characters including spaces, commas, and/or periods. (Periods are discouraged, however, since they are too easily confused with DOS extensions.) The Save In list box is used to select the drive (which is not visible in Figure 1.5a) and the optional folder (e.g., Exploring Word). The *Places Bar* provides a shortcut to any of its folders without having to search through the Save In list box. Click the Desktop icon, for example, and the file is saved automatically on the Windows desktop. The *file type* defaults to a Word 2000 document. You can, however, choose a different format such as Word 95 to maintain compatibility with earlier versions of Microsoft Word. You can also save any Word document as a Web page (or HTML document).

The *Open command* is the opposite of the Save command as it brings a copy of an existing document into memory, enabling you to work with that document. The Open command displays the Open dialog box in which you specify the file name, the drive (and optionally the folder) that contains the file, and the file type. Microsoft Word will then list all files of that type on the designated drive (and folder), enabling you to open the file you want. The Save and Open commands work in conjunction with one another. The Save As dialog box in Figure 1.5a, for example, saves the file My First Document in the Exploring Word folder. The Open dialog box in Figure 1.5b loads that file into memory so that you can work with the file, after which you can save the revised file for use at a later time.

The toolbars in the Save As and Open dialog boxes have several buttons in common that facilitate the execution of either command. The Views button lets you display the files in either dialog box in one of four different views. The Details view (in Figure 1.5a) shows the file size as well as the date and time a file was last modified. The Preview view (in Figure 1.5b) shows the beginning of a document, without having to open the document. The List view displays only the file names, and thus lets you see more files at one time. The Properties view shows information about the document including the date of creation and number of revisions.

SORT BY NAME, DATE, OR FILE SIZE

The files in the Save As and Open dialog boxes can be displayed in ascending or descending sequence by name, date modified, or size. Change to the Details view, then click the heading of the desired column; e.g., click the Modified column to list the files according to the date they were last changed. Click the column heading a second time to reverse the sequence.

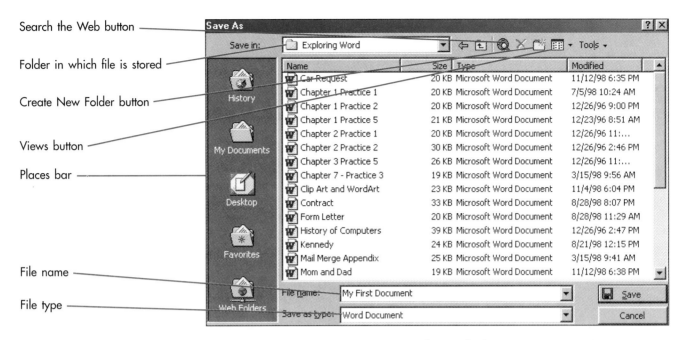

Search the Web button

Folder in which file is stored

Create New Folder button

Views button

Places bar

File name

File type

(a) Save As Dialog Box (details view)

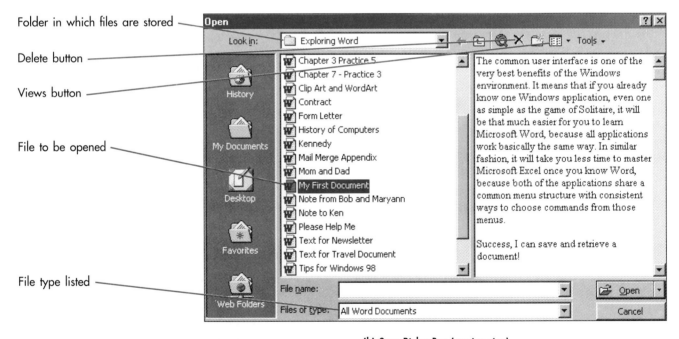

Folder in which files are stored

Delete button

Views button

File to be opened

File type listed

(b) Open Dialog Box (preview view)

FIGURE 1.5   The Save and Open Commands

LEARNING BY DOING

Every chapter contains a series of hands-on exercises that enable you to apply what you learn at the computer. The exercises in this chapter are linked to one another in that you create a simple document in exercise one, then open and edit that document in exercise two. The ability to save and open a document is critical, and you do not want to spend an inordinate amount of time entering text unless you are confident in your ability to retrieve it later.

My First Document

Objective: To start Microsoft Word in order to create, save, and print a simple document; to execute commands via the toolbar or from pull-down menus. Use Figure 1.6 as a guide in doing the exercise.

STEP 1: The Windows Desktop

➤ Turn on the computer and all of its peripherals. The floppy drive should be empty prior to starting your machine. This ensures that the system starts from the hard disk, which contains the Windows files, as opposed to a floppy disk, which does not.

➤ Your system will take a minute or so to get started, after which you should see the Windows desktop in Figure 1.6a. Do not be concerned if the appearance of your desktop is different from ours.

➤ You may see additional objects on the desktop in Windows 95 and/or the active desktop content in Windows 98. It doesn't matter which operating system you are using because Office 2000 runs equally well under both Windows 95 and Windows 98 (as well as Windows NT).

➤ You may see a Welcome to Windows 95/Windows 98 dialog box with command buttons to take a tour of the operating system. If so, click the appropriate button(s) or close the dialog box.

Start button

(a) The Windows Desktop (step 1)

FIGURE 1.6   Hands-on Exercise 1

STEP 2: Obtain the Practice Files

➤ We have created a series of practice files (also called a "data disk") for you to use throughout the text. Your instructor will make these files available to you in a variety of ways:

- The files may be on a network drive, in which case you use Windows Explorer to copy the files from the network to a floppy disk.

- There may be an actual "data disk" that you are to check out from the lab in order to use the Copy Disk command to duplicate the disk.

➤ You can also download the files from our Web site provided you have an Internet connection. Start Internet Explorer, then go to the Exploring Windows home page at **www.prenhall.com/grauer.**

- Click the book for **Office 2000,** which takes you to the Office 2000 home page. Click the **Student Resources tab** (at the top of the window) to go to the Student Resources page as shown in Figure 1.6b.

- Click the link to **Student Data Disk** (in the left frame), then scroll down the page until you can select Word 2000. Click the link to download the student data disk.

- You will see the File Download dialog box asking what you want to do. The option button to save this program to disk is selected. Click **OK.** The Save As dialog box appears.

- Click the down arrow in the Save In list box to enter the drive and folder where you want to save the file. It's best to save the file to the Windows desktop or to a temporary folder on drive C.

- Double click the file after it has been downloaded to your PC, then follow the onscreen instructions.

➤ Check with your instructor for additional information.

Click tab to go to
Student Resources page

Click here for student
data disk

Click here for Companion
Web site (see problem 8 at
the end of the chapter)

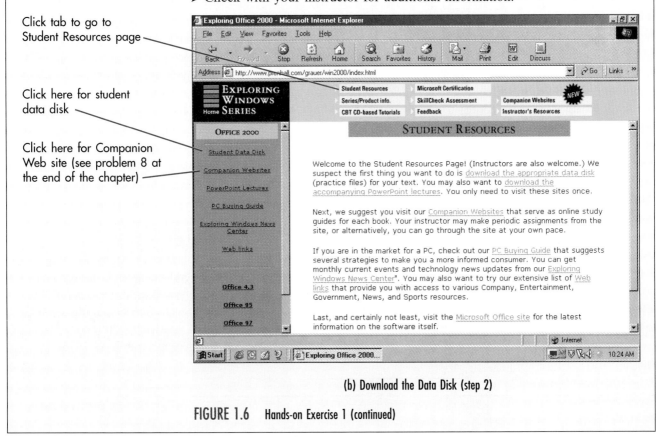

(b) Download the Data Disk (step 2)

FIGURE 1.6   Hands-on Exercise 1 (continued)

STEP 3: Start Microsoft Word

➤ Click the **Start button** to display the Start menu. Click (or point to) the **Programs menu,** then click **Microsoft Word 2000** to start the program.

➤ Click and drag the Office Assistant out of the way. (The Office Assistant is illustrated in step 6 of this exercise.)

➤ If necessary, click the **Maximize button** in the application window so that Word takes the entire desktop as shown in Figure 1.6c.

➤ Do not be concerned if your screen is different from ours as we include a troubleshooting section immediately following this exercise.

Click OK

Click and drag Office Assistant out of way

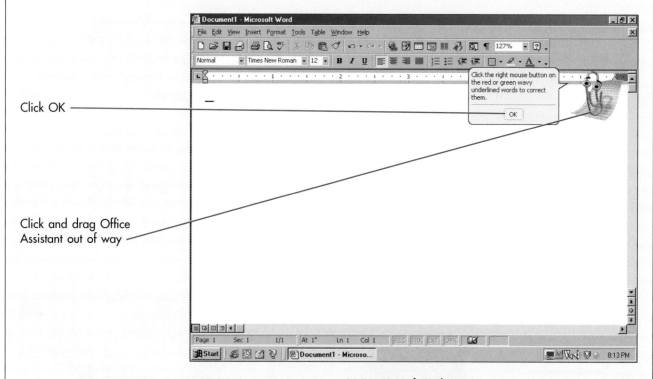

(c) Start Microsoft Word (step 3)

FIGURE 1.6 Hands-on Exercise 1 (continued)

ABOUT THE ASSISTANT

The Assistant is very powerful and hence you want to experiment with various ways to use it. To ask a question, click the Assistant's icon to toggle its balloon on or off. To change the way in which the Assistant works, click the Options tab within this balloon and experiment with the various check boxes to see their effects. If you find the Assistant distracting, click and drag the character out of the way or hide it altogether by pulling down the Help menu and clicking the Hide Office Assistant command. Pull down the Help menu and click the Show Office Assistant command to return the Assistant to the desktop.

STEP 4: Create the Document

➤ Create the document in Figure 1.6d. Type just as you would on a typewriter with one exception; do *not* press the enter key at the end of a line because Word will automatically wrap text from one line to the next.

➤ Press the **enter key** at the end of the paragraph.

➤ You may see a red or green wavy line to indicate spelling or grammatical errors respectively. Both features are discussed later in the chapter.

➤ Point to the red wavy line (if any), click the **right mouse button** to display a list of suggested corrections, then click (select) the appropriate substitution.

➤ Ignore the green wavy line (if any).

Office Assistant

Enter text

Press enter key at end of paragraph

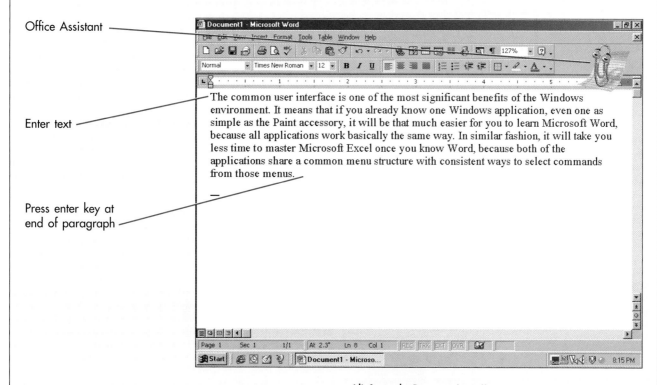

(d) Create the Document (step 4)

SEPARATE THE TOOLBARS

Office 2000 displays the Standard and Formatting toolbars on the same row to save space within the application window. The result is that only a limited number of buttons are visible on each toolbar, and hence you may need to click the double arrow (More Buttons) tool at the end of the toolbar to view additional buttons. You can, however, separate the toolbars. Pull down the Tools menu, click the Customize command, click the Options tab, then clear the check box that has the toolbars share one row.

STEP 5: Save the Document

➤ Pull down the **File menu** and click **Save** (or click the **Save button** on the Standard toolbar). You should see the Save As dialog box in Figure 1.6e.

➤ If necessary, click the **drop-down arrow** on the View button and select the **Details View,** so that the display on your monitor matches our figure.

➤ To save the file:

- Click the **drop-down arrow** on the Save In list box.

- Click the appropriate drive, e.g., drive C or drive Λ, depending on whether or not you installed the data disk on your hard drive.

- Double click the **Exploring Word folder,** to make it the active folder (the folder in which you will save the document).

- Click and drag over the default entry in the File name text box. Type **My First Document** as the name of your document. (A DOC extension will be added automatically when the file is saved to indicate that this is a Word document.)

- Click **Save** or press the **enter key.** The title bar changes to reflect the document name.

➤ Add your name at the end of the document, then click the **Save button** on the Standard toolbar to save the document with the revision. This time the Save As dialog box does not appear, since Word already knows the name of the document.

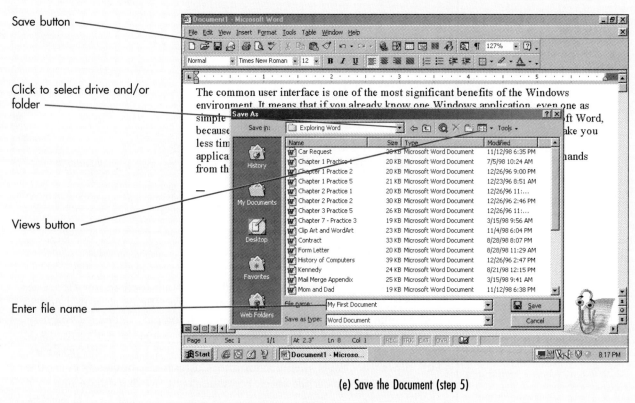

(e) Save the Document (step 5)

FIGURE 1.6 Hands-on Exercise 1 (continued)

STEP 6: The Office Assistant

➤ If necessary, pull down the **Help menu** and click the command to **Show the Office Assistant.** You may see a different character than the one we have selected.

➤ Click the Assistant, enter the question, **How do I print?** as shown in Figure 1.6f, then click the **Search button** to look for the answer. The size of the Assistant's balloon expands as the Assistant suggests several topics that may be appropriate.

➤ Click the topic, **Print a document** which in turn displays a Help window that contains links to various topics, each with detailed information. Click the Office Assistant to hide the balloon (or drag the Assistant out of the way).

➤ Click any of the links in the Help window to read the information. You can print the contents of any topic by clicking the **Print button** in the Help window. Close the Help window when you are finished.

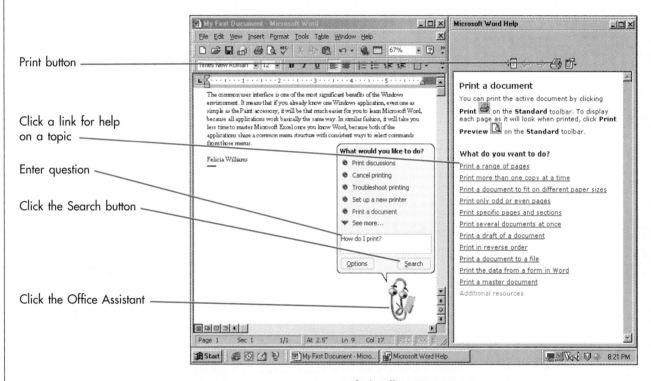

Print button

Click a link for help on a topic

Enter question

Click the Search button

Click the Office Assistant

(f) The Office Assistant (step 6)

FIGURE 1.6   Hands-on Exercise 1 (continued)

TIP OF THE DAY

You can set the Office Assistant to greet you with a "tip of the day" each time you start Word. Click the Microsoft Word Help button (or press the F1 key) to display the Assistant, then click the Options button to display the Office Assistant dialog box. Click the Options tab, then check the Show the Tip of the Day at Startup box and click OK. The next time you start Microsoft Word, you will be greeted by the Assistant, who will offer you the tip of the day.

STEP 7: Print the Document

➤ You can print the document in one of two ways:

- Pull down the **File menu.** Click **Print** to display the dialog box of Figure 1.6g. Click the **OK command button** to print the document.

- Click the **Print button** on the Standard toolbar to print the document immediately without displaying the Print dialog box.

Print button

Click OK to print the file

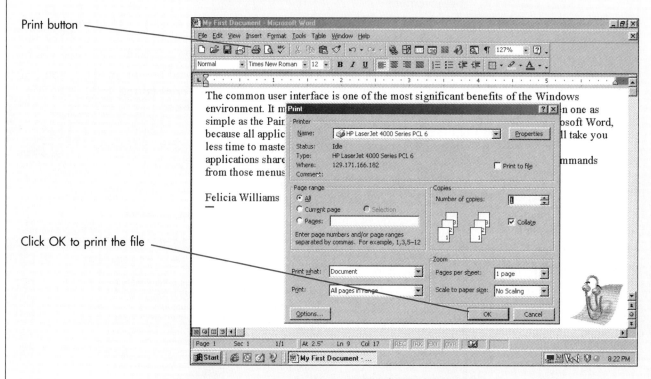

(g) Print the Document (step 7)

FIGURE 1.6   Hands-on Exercise 1 (continued)

ABOUT MICROSOFT WORD

Pull down the Help menu and click About Microsoft Word to display the specific release number and other licensing information, including the product ID. This help screen also contains two very useful command buttons, System Information and Technical Support. The first button displays information about the hardware installed on your system, including the amount of memory and available space on the hard drive. The Technical Support button provides telephone numbers for technical assistance.

STEP 8: Close the Document

➤ Pull down the **File menu.** Click **Close** to close this document but remain in Word. If you don't see the Close command, click the double arrow at the bottom of the menu. Click **Yes** if prompted to save the document.

➤ Pull down the **File menu** a second time. Click **Exit** to close Word if you do not want to continue with the next exercise at this time.

TROUBLESHOOTING

We trust that you completed the hands-on exercise without difficulty, and that you were able to create, save, and print the document in the exercise. There is, however, considerable flexibility in the way you do the exercise in that you can display different toolbars and menus, and/or execute commands in a variety of ways. This section describes various ways in which you can customize Microsoft Word, and in so doing, will help you to troubleshoot future exercises.

Figure 1.7 displays two different views of the same document. Your screen may not match either figure, and indeed, there is no requirement that it should. You should, however, be aware of different options so that you can develop preferences of your own. Consider:

- Figure 1.7a uses the default settings of short menus (note the double arrow at the bottom of the menu to display additional commands) and a shared row for the Standard and Formatting toolbars. Figure 1.7b displays the full menu and displays the toolbars on separate rows. We prefer the latter settings, which are set through the Customize command in the Tools menu.

- Figure 1.7a shows the Office Assistant (but drags it out of the way) whereas Figure 1.7b hides it. We find the Assistant distracting, and display it only when necessary by pressing the F1 key. You can also use the appropriate option in the Help menu to hide or show the Assistant and/or you can right click the Assistant to hide it.

- Figure 1.7a displays the document in the *Normal view* whereas Figure 1.7b uses the *Print Layout view.* The Normal view is simpler, but the Print Layout view more closely resembles the printed page as it displays top and bottom margins, headers and footers, graphic elements in their exact position, a vertical ruler, and other elements not seen in the Normal view. We alternate between the two. Note, too, that you can change the magnification in either view to make the text larger or smaller.

- Figure 1.7a displays the ¶ and other nonprinting symbols whereas they are hidden in Figure 1.7b. We prefer the cleaner screen without the symbols, but on occasion display the symbols if there is a problem in formatting a document. The *Show/Hide ¶ button* toggles the symbols on or off.

- Figure 1.7b displays an additional toolbar, the Drawing toolbar, at the bottom of the screen. Microsoft Word has more than 20 toolbars that are suppressed or displayed through the Toolbars command in the View menu. Note, too, that you can change the position of any visible toolbar by dragging its move handle (the parallel lines) at the left of the toolbar.

THE MOUSE VERSUS THE KEYBOARD

Almost every command in Office can be executed in different ways, using either the mouse or the keyboard. Most people start with the mouse and add keyboard shortcuts as they become more proficient. There is no right or wrong technique, just different techniques, and the one you choose depends entirely on personal preference in a specific situation. If, for example, your hands are already on the keyboard, it is faster to use the keyboard equivalent. Other times, your hand will be on the mouse and that will be the fastest way.

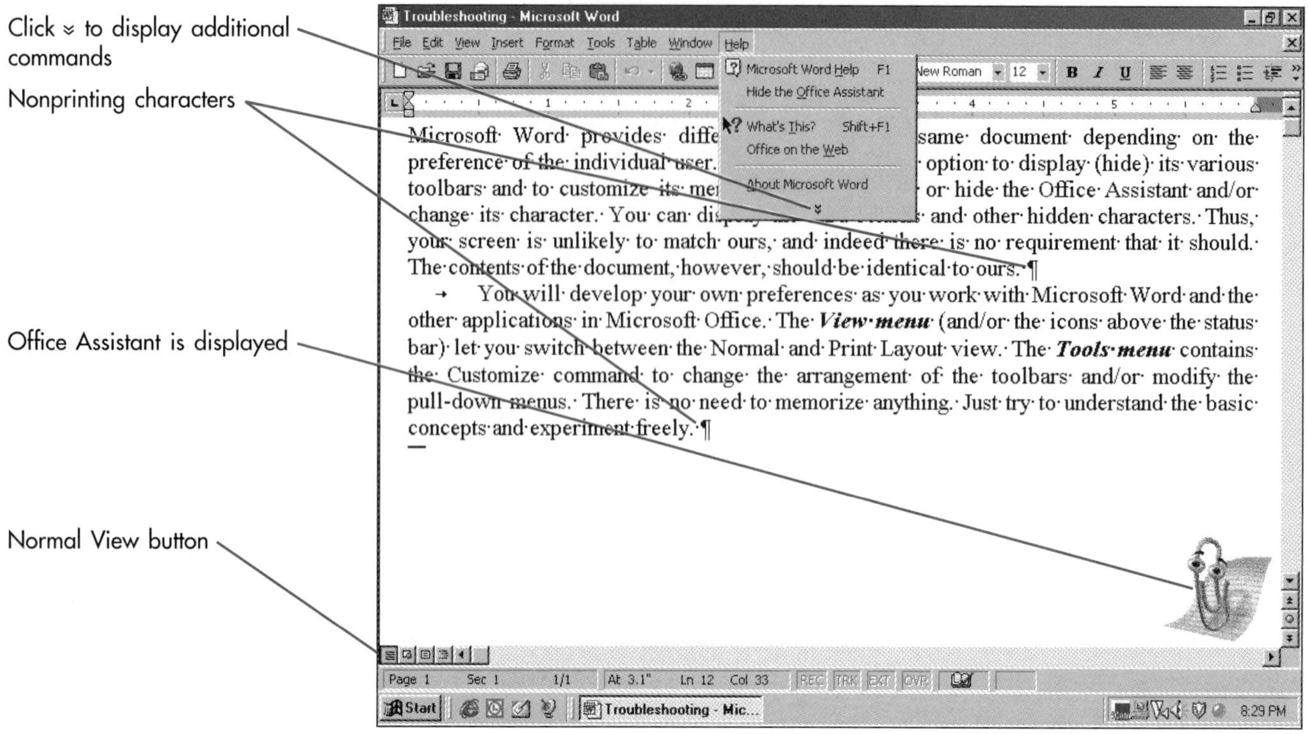
Click » to display additional commands
Nonprinting characters
Office Assistant is displayed
Normal View button
Troubleshooting - Microsoft Word

(a) Normal View

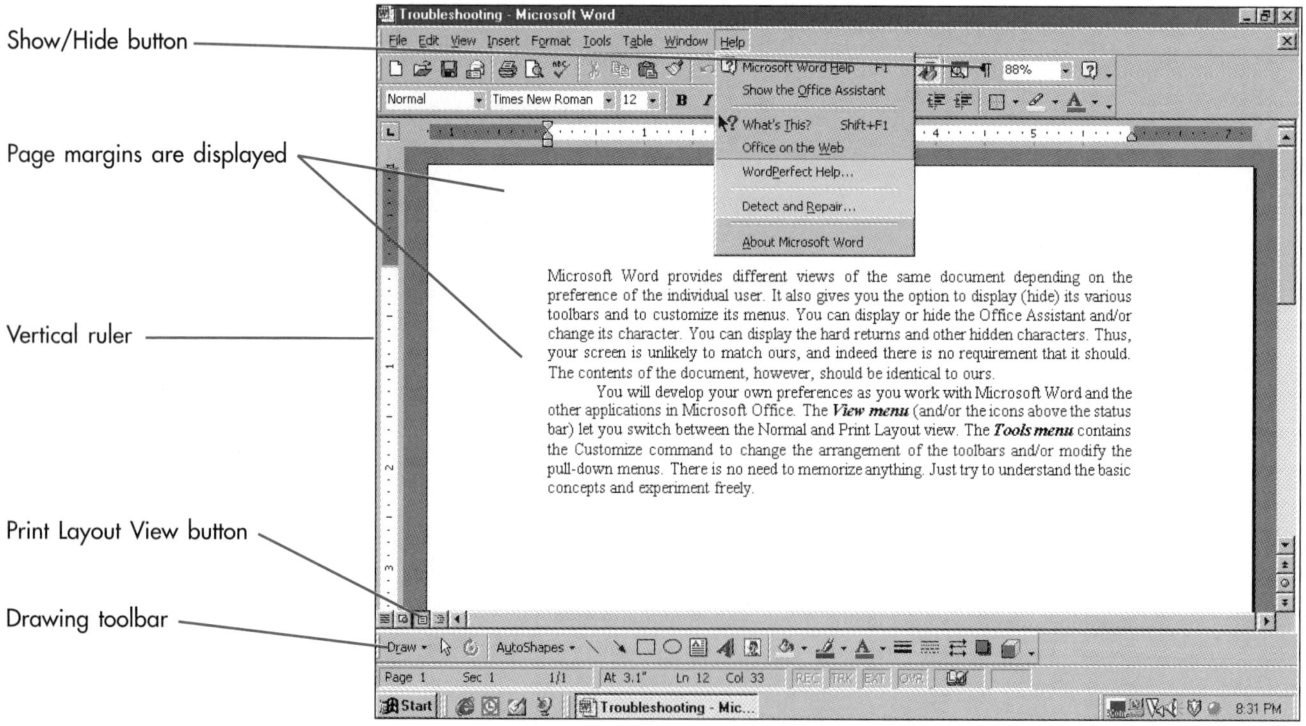
Show/Hide button
Page margins are displayed
Vertical ruler
Print Layout View button
Drawing toolbar
Troubleshooting - Microsoft Word

(b) Print Layout View

FIGURE 1.7 Troubleshooting

Modifying an Existing Document

Objective: To open an existing document, revise it, and save the revision; to use the Undo and Help commands. Use Figure 1.8 as a guide in doing the exercise.

STEP 1: Open an Existing Document

➤ Start Microsoft Word. Click and drag the Assistant out of the way if it appears.

➤ Pull down the **File menu** and click **Open** (or click the **Open button** on the Standard toolbar). You should see a dialog box similar to the one in Figure 1.8a.

➤ To open a file:

• If necessary, click the **drop-down arrow** on the View button and change to the **Details view.** Click and drag the vertical border between columns to increase (or decrease) the size of a column.

• Click the drop-down arrow on the Look In list box.

• Click the appropriate drive; for example, drive C or drive A.

• Double click the **Exploring Word folder** to make it the active folder (the folder from which you will open the document).

• Click the **down arrow** on the vertical scroll bar in the Name list box, then scroll until you can select the **My First Document** from the first exercise. Click the **Open command button** to open the file.

➤ Your document should appear on the screen.

Click to select drive/folder

View button

Select file

Click to scroll through
filenames

Drag Office Assistant out of
way

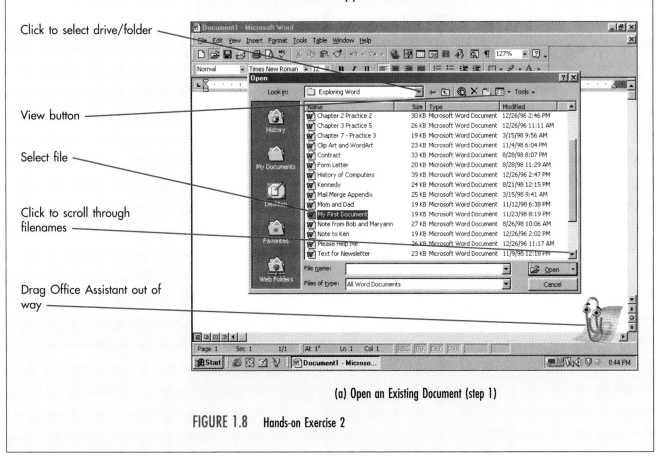

(a) Open an Existing Document (step 1)

FIGURE 1.8   Hands-on Exercise 2

STEP 2: Troubleshooting

➤ Modify the settings within Word so that the document on your screen matches Figure 1.8b.

- To separate the Standard and Formatting toolbars, pull down the **Tools menu,** click **Customize,** click the **Options tab,** then clear the check box that indicates the Standard and Formatting toolbars should share the same row.

- To display the complete menus, pull down the **Tools menu,** click **Customize,** click the **Options tab,** then clear the **Menus show recently used commands** check box.

- To change to the Normal view, pull down the **View menu** and click **Normal** (or click the **Normal View** button at the bottom of the window).

- To change the amount of text that is visible on the screen, click the drop-down arrow on the **Zoom box** on the Standard toolbar and select **Page Width.**

- To display (hide) the ruler, pull down the **View menu** and toggle the **Ruler command** on or off. End with the ruler on. (If you don't see the Ruler command, click the double arrow at the bottom of the menu, or use the Options command in the Tools menu to display the complete menus.)

➤ Click the **Show/Hide ¶ button** to display or hide the hard returns as you see fit. The button functions as a toggle switch.

➤ There may still be subtle differences between your screen and ours, depending on the resolution of your monitor. These variations, if any, need not concern you as long as you are able to complete the exercise.

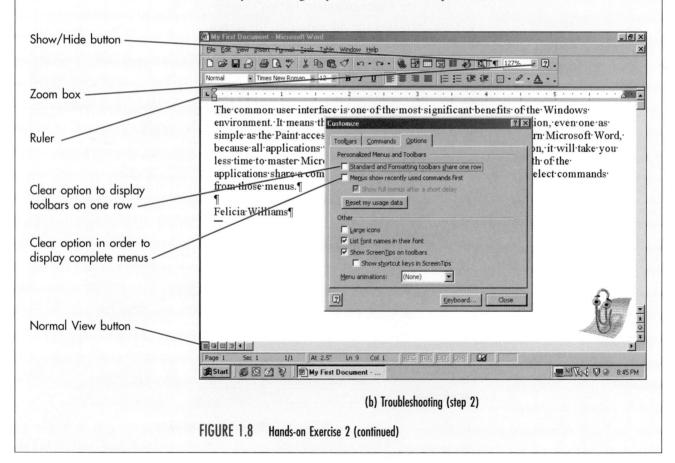

Show/Hide button

Zoom box

Ruler

Clear option to display toolbars on one row

Clear option in order to display complete menus

Normal View button

(b) Troubleshooting (step 2)

FIGURE 1.8   Hands-on Exercise 2 (continued)

STEP 3: Modify the Document

➤ Press **Ctrl+End** to move to the end of the document. Press the **up arrow key** once or twice until the insertion point is on a blank line above your name. If necessary, press the **enter key** once (or twice) to add additional blank line(s).

➤ Add the sentence, **Success, I can save and retrieve a document!,** as shown in Figure 1.8c.

➤ Make the following additional modifications to practice editing:

  • Change the phrase *most significant* to **very best.**

  • Change *Paint accessory* to **game of Solitaire.**

  • Change the word *select* to **choose.**

➤ Use the **Ins key** to switch between insert and overtype modes as necessary. (You can also double click the **OVR indicator** on the status bar to toggle between the insert and overtype modes.)

➤ Pull down the **File menu** and click **Save,** or click the **Save button.**

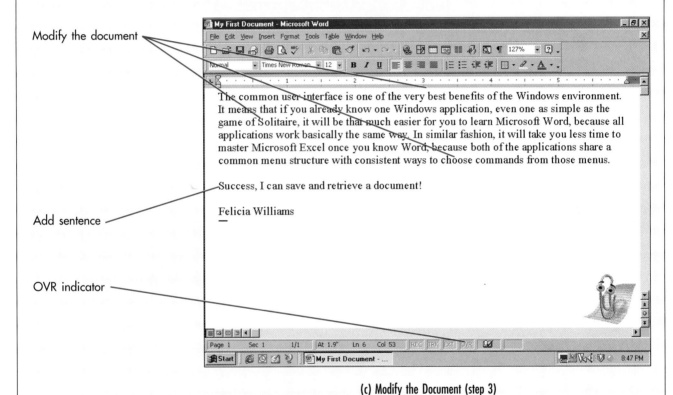

(c) Modify the Document (step 3)

FIGURE 1.8   Hands-on Exercise 2 (continued)

MOVING WITHIN A DOCUMENT

Press Ctrl+Home and Ctrl+End to move to the beginning and end of a document, respectively. You can also press the Home or End key to move to the beginning or end of a line. These shortcuts work not just in Word, but in any Office application, and are worth remembering as they allow your hands to remain on the keyboard as you type.

STEP 4: Deleting Text

➤ Press and hold the left mouse button as you drag the mouse over the phrase, **even one as simple as the game of Solitaire,** as shown in Figure 1.8d.

➤ Press the **Del** key to delete the selected text from the document. Pull down the **Edit menu** and click the **Undo command** (or click the **Undo button** on the Standard toolbar) to reverse (undo) the last command. The deleted text should be returned to your document.

➤ Pull down the **Edit menu** a second time and click the **Redo command** (or click the **Redo button**) to repeat the Delete command.

➤ Click the **Save button** on the Standard toolbar to save the revised document a final time.

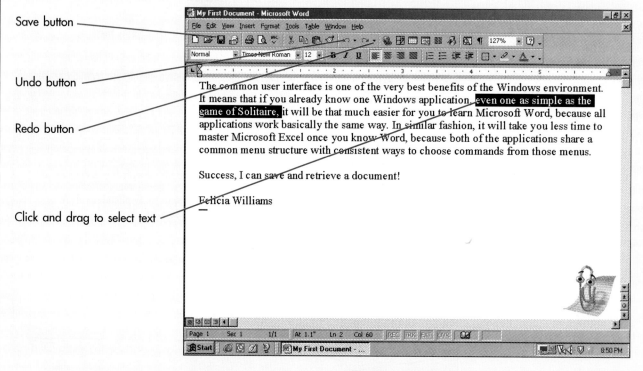

Save button

Undo button

Redo button

Click and drag to select text

(d) Deleting Text (step 4)

FIGURE 1.8   Hands-on Exercise 2 (continued)

THE UNDO AND REDO COMMANDS

Click the drop-down arrow next to the Undo button to display a list of your previous actions, then click the action you want to undo which also undoes all of the preceding commands. Undoing the fifth command in the list, for example, will also undo the preceding four commands. The Redo command works in reverse and cancels the last Undo command.

STEP 5: The Office Assistant

➤ Click the **Office Assistant** to display the balloon. Enter a question such as **How do I get help,** then click the **Search button.** The Assistant returns a list of topics that it considers potential answers. Click any topic you think is appropriate (we chose **How to get started with Word 2000**) to open the Help window as shown in Figure 1.8e.

➤ Click the link to **printed and online resources that are available.** Read the information, then click the **Print button** in the Help window to print this topic.

➤ Use the **Contents, Answer Wizard,** and/or **Index tabs** to search through the available help. Close the Help window when you have finished.

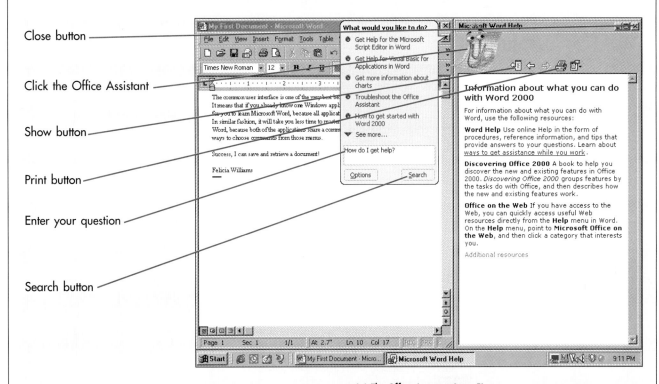

Close button

Click the Office Assistant

Show button

Print button

Enter your question

Search button

(e) The Office Assistant (step 5)

FIGURE 1.8   Hands-on Exercise 2 (continued)

CHOOSE YOUR OWN ASSISTANT

You can choose your own personal assistant from one of several available candidates. If necessary, press the F1 key to display the Assistant, click the Options button to display the Office Assistant dialog box, then click the Gallery tab where you choose your character. (The Office 2000 CD is required in order to select some of the other characters.) Some assistants are more animated (distracting) than others. The Office logo is the most passive, while Rocky is quite animated. Experiment with the various check boxes on the Options tab to see the effects on the Assistant.

STEP 6: E-mail Your Document

➤ You should check with your professor before attempting this step.

➤ Click the **E-mail button** on the Standard toolbar to display a screen similar to Figure 1.8f. The text of your document is entered automatically into the body of the e-mail message.

➤ Enter your professor's e-mail address in the To text box. The document title is automatically entered in the Subject line. Press the **Tab key** to move to the body of the message. Type a short note above the inserted document to your professor, then click the **Send a Copy button** to mail the message.

➤ The e-mail window closes and you are back in Microsoft Word. The introductory text has been added to the document. Pull down the **File menu.** Click **Close** to close the document (there is no need to save the document).

➤ Pull down the **File menu.** Click **Exit** if you do not want to continue with the next exercise at this time.

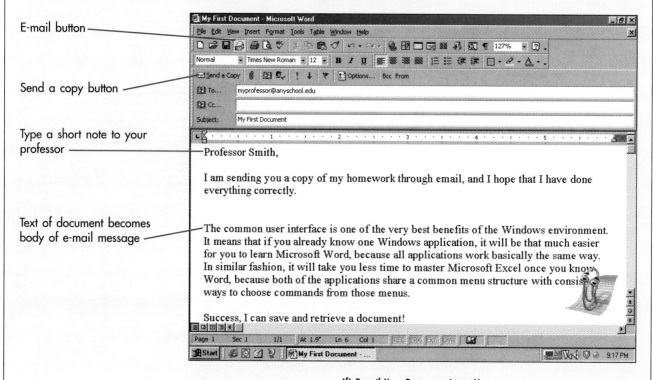

(f) E-mail Your Document (step 6)

FIGURE 1.8   Hands-on Exercise 2 (continued)

DOCUMENT PROPERTIES

Prove to your instructor how hard you've worked by printing various statistics about your document including the number of revisions and the total editing time. Pull down the File menu, click the Print command to display the Print dialog box, click the drop-down arrow in the Print What list box, select Document properties, then click OK. You can view the information (without printing) by pulling down the File menu, clicking the Properties command, then selecting the Statistics tab.

There is simply no excuse to misspell a word, since the *spell check* is an integral part of Microsoft Word. (The spell check is also available for every other application in the Microsoft Office.) Spelling errors make your work look sloppy and discourage the reader before he or she has read what you had to say. They can cost you a job, a grade, a lucrative contract, or an award you deserve.

The spell check can be set to automatically check a document as text is entered, or it can be called explicitly by clicking the Spelling and Grammar button on the Standard toolbar. The spell check compares each word in a document to the entries in a built-in dictionary, then flags any word that is in the document, but not in the built-in dictionary, as an error.

The dictionary included with Microsoft Office is limited to standard English and does not include many proper names, acronyms, abbreviations, or specialized terms, and hence, the use of any such item is considered a misspelling. You can, however, add such words to a *custom dictionary* so that they will not be flagged in the future. The spell check will inform you of repeated words and irregular capitalization. It cannot, however, flag properly spelled words that are used improperly, and thus cannot tell you that *Two bee or knot too be* is not the answer.

The capabilities of the spell check are illustrated in conjunction with Figure 1.9a. Microsoft Word will indicate the errors as you type by underlining them in red. Alternatively, you can click the Spelling and Grammar button on the Standard toolbar at any time to move through the entire document. The spell check will then go through the document and return the errors one at a time, offering several options for each mistake. You can change the misspelled word to one of the alternatives suggested by Word, leave the word as is, or add the word to a custom dictionary.

The first error is the word *embarassing*, with Word's suggestion(s) for correction displayed in the list box in Figure 1.9b. To accept the highlighted suggestion, click the Change command button and the substitution will be made automatically in the document. To accept an alternative suggestion, click the desired word, then click the Change command button. Alternatively, you can click the AutoCorrect button to correct the mistake in the current document, and, in addition, automatically correct the same mistake in any future document.

The spell check detects both irregular capitalization and duplicated words, as shown in Figures 1.9c and 1.9d, respectively. The last error, *Grauer,* is not a misspelling per se, but a proper noun not found in the standard dictionary. No correction is required and the appropriate action is to ignore the word (taking no further action)—or better yet, add it to the custom dictionary so that it will not be flagged in future sessions.

A spell check will catch embarassing mistakes, iRregular capitalization, and duplicate words words. It will also flag proper nouns, for example Robert Grauer, but you can add these terms to a custom dictionary. It will not notice properly spelled words that are used incorrectly; for example, too bee or knot to be are not the answer.

(a) The Text

FIGURE 1.9   The Spell Check

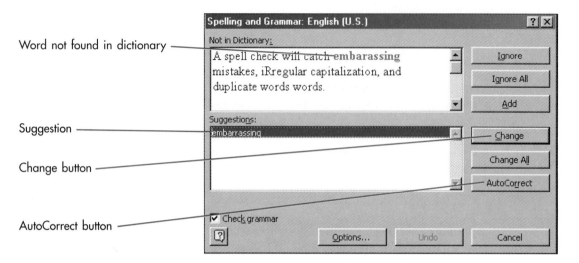

Word not found in dictionary

Suggestion

Change button

AutoCorrect button

(b) Ordinary Misspelling

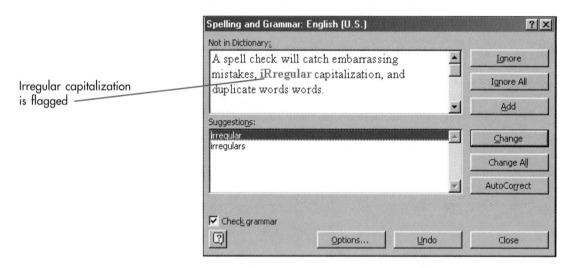

Irregular capitalization is flagged

(c) Irregular Capitalization

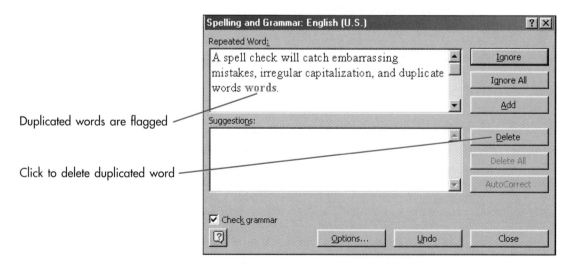

Duplicated words are flagged

Click to delete duplicated word

(d) Duplicated Word

FIGURE 1.9   The Spell Check (continued)

AutoCorrect and AutoText

The *AutoCorrect* feature corrects mistakes as they are made without any effort on your part. It makes you a better typist. If, for example, you typed *teh* instead of *the,* Word would change the spelling without even telling you. Word will also change *adn* to *and, i* to *I,* and occu*r*ence to occu*rr*ence. All of this is accomplished through a predefined table of common mistakes that Word uses to make substitutions whenever it encounters an entry in the table. You can add additional items to the table to include the frequent errors you make. You can also use the feature to define your own shorthand—for example, cis for Computer Information Systems as shown in Figure 1.10a.

The AutoCorrect feature will also correct mistakes in capitalization; for example, it will capitalize the first letter in a sentence, recognize that MIami should be Miami, and capitalize the days of the week. It's even smart enough to correct the accidental use of the Caps Lock key, and it will toggle the key off!

The *AutoText* feature is similar in concept to AutoCorrect in that both substitute a predefined item for a specific character string. The difference is that the substitution occurs automatically with the AutoCorrect entry, whereas you have to take deliberate action for the AutoText substitution to take place. AutoText entries can also include significantly more text, formatting, and even clip art.

Microsoft Word includes a host of predefined AutoText entries. And as with the AutoCorrect feature, you can define additional entries of your own. (You may, however, not be able to do this in a computer lab environment.) The entry in Figure 1.10b is named "signature" and once created, it is available to all Word documents. To insert an AutoText entry into a new document, just type the first several letters in the AutoText name (signature in our example), then press the enter key when Word displays a ScreenTip containing the text of the entry.

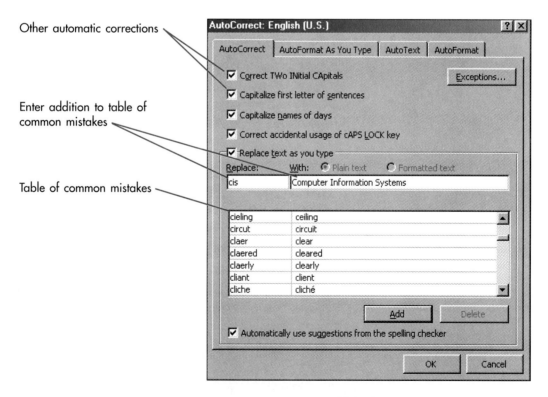

(a) AutoCorrect

FIGURE 1.10   AutoCorrect and AutoText

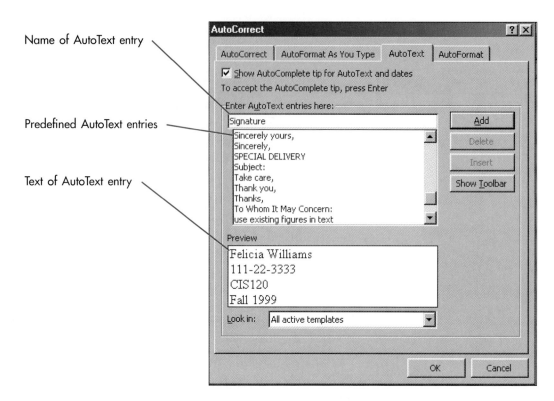

Name of AutoText entry

Predefined AutoText entries

Text of AutoText entry

(b) AutoText

FIGURE 1.10   AutoCorrect and AutoText (continued)

THESAURUS

The ***thesaurus*** helps you to avoid repetition and polish your writing. The thesaurus is called from the Language command in the Tools menu. You position the cursor at the appropriate word within the document, then invoke the thesaurus and follow your instincts. The thesaurus recognizes multiple meanings and forms of a word (for example, adjective, noun, and verb) as in Figure 1.11a. Click a meaning, then double click a synonym to produce additional choices as in Figure 1.11b. You can explore further alternatives by selecting a synonym or antonym and clicking the Look Up button. We show antonyms in Figure 1.11c.

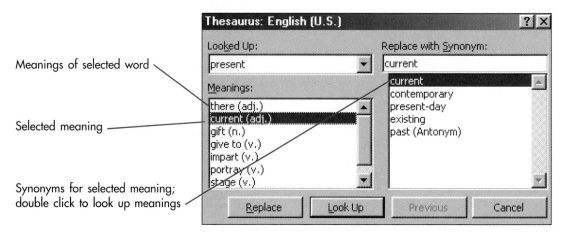

Meanings of selected word

Selected meaning

Synonyms for selected meaning;
double click to look up meanings

(a) Initial Word

FIGURE 1.11   The Thesaurus

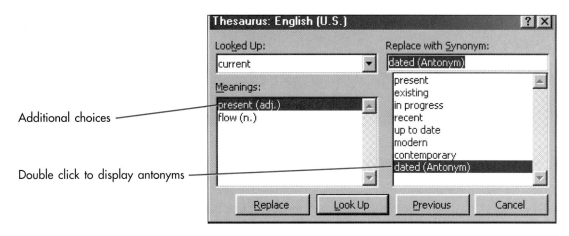

Additional choices

Double click to display antonyms

(b) Additional Choices

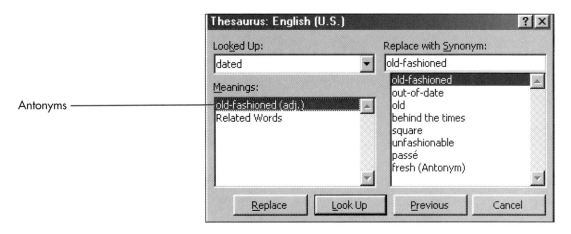

Antonyms

(c) Antonyms

FIGURE 1.11   The Thesaurus (continued)

GRAMMAR CHECK

The ***grammar check*** attempts to catch mistakes in punctuation, writing style, and word usage by comparing strings of text within a document to a series of predefined rules. As with the spell check, errors are brought to the screen where you can accept the suggested correction and make the replacement automatically, or more often, edit the selected text and make your own changes.

You can also ask the grammar check to explain the rule it is attempting to enforce. Unlike the spell check, the grammar check is subjective, and what seems appropriate to you may be objectionable to someone else. Indeed, the grammar check is quite flexible, and can be set to check for different writing styles; that is, you can implement one set of rules to check a business letter and a different set of rules for casual writing. Many times, however, you will find that the English language is just too complex for the grammar check to detect every error, although it will find many errors.

The grammar check caught the inconsistency between subject and verb in Figure 1.12a and suggested the appropriate correction (am instead of are). In Figure 1.12b, it suggested the elimination of the superfluous comma. These examples show the grammar check at its best, but it is often more subjective and less capable. It detected the error in Figure 1.12c, for example, but suggested an inappropriate correction, "to complicate" as opposed to "too complicated". Suffice it to say, that there is no substitute for carefully proofreading every document.

Inconsistency between subject and verb is detected

Suggested correction

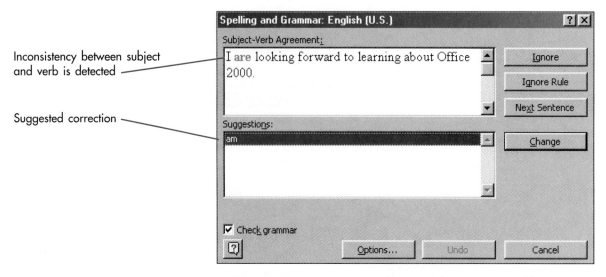

(a) Inconsistent Verb

Two commas are detected

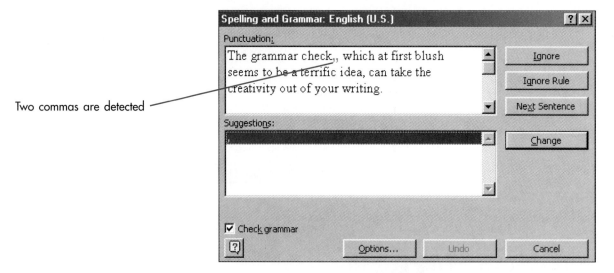

(b) Doubled Punctuation

Suggestion is inappropriate

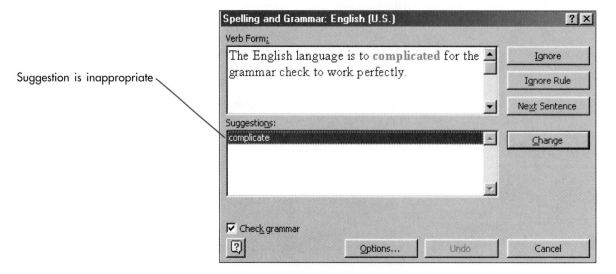

(c) Limitation

FIGURE 1.12   The Grammar Check

SAVE COMMAND

The Save command was used in the first two exercises. The Save As command will be introduced in the next exercise as a very useful alternative. We also introduce you to different backup options. We believe that now, when you are first starting to learn about word processing, is the time to develop good working habits.

You already know that the Save command copies the document currently being edited (the document in memory) to disk. The initial execution of the command requires you to assign a file name and to specify the drive and folder in which the file is to be stored. All subsequent executions of the Save command save the document under the original name, replacing the previously saved version with the new one.

The *Save As command* saves another copy of a document under a different name (and/or a different file type), and is useful when you want to retain a copy of the original document. The Save As command provides you with two copies of a document. The original document is kept on disk under its original name. A copy of the document is saved on disk under a new name and remains in memory. All subsequent editing is done on the new document.

We cannot overemphasize the importance of periodically saving a document, so that if something does go wrong, you won't lose all of your work. Nothing is more frustrating than to lose two hours of effort, due to an unexpected program crash or to a temporary loss of power. Save your work frequently, at least once every 15 minutes. Pull down the File menu and click Save, or click the Save button on the Standard toolbar. Do it!

QUIT WITHOUT SAVING

There will be times when you do not want to save the changes to a document, such as when you have edited it beyond recognition and wish you had never started. Pull down the File menu and click the Close command, then click No in response to the message asking whether you want to save the changes to the document. Pull down the File menu and reopen the file (it should be the first file in the list of most recently edited documents), then start over from the beginning.

Backup Options

Microsoft Word offers several different *backup* options. We believe the two most important options are to create a backup copy in conjunction with every save command, and to periodically (and automatically) save a document. Both options are implemented in step 3 in the next hands-on exercise.

Figure 1.13 illustrates the option to create a backup copy of the document every time a Save command is executed. Assume, for example, that you have created the simple document, *The fox jumped over the fence* and saved it under the name "Fox". Assume further that you edit the document to read, *The quick brown fox jumped over the fence,* and that you saved it a second time. The second save command changes the name of the original document from "Fox" to "Backup of Fox", then saves the current contents of memory as "Fox". In other words, the disk now contains two versions of the document: the current version "Fox" and the most recent previous version "Backup of Fox".

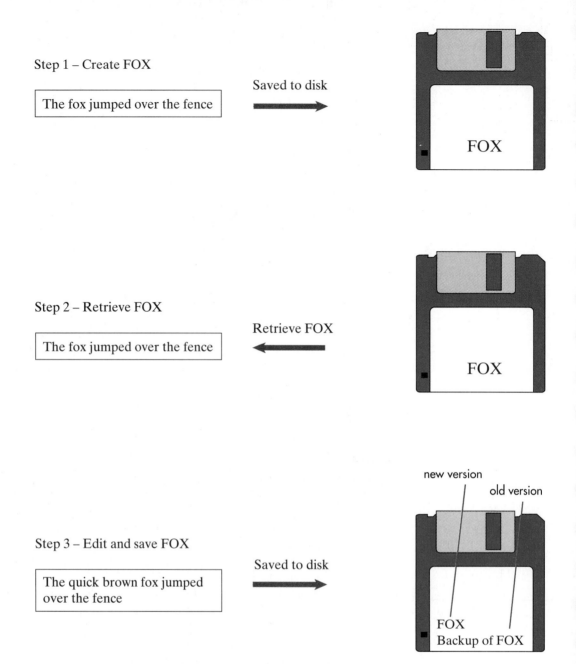

Step 1 – Create FOX

The fox jumped over the fence

Saved to disk

FOX

Step 2 – Retrieve FOX

The fox jumped over the fence

Retrieve FOX

FOX

Step 3 – Edit and save FOX

The quick brown fox jumped over the fence

Saved to disk

new version

old version

FOX
Backup of FOX

FIGURE 1.13   Backup Procedures

The cycle goes on indefinitely, with "Fox" always containing the current version, and "Backup of Fox" the most recent previous version. Thus if you revise and save the document a third time, "Fox" will contain the latest revision while "Backup of Fox" would contain the previous version alluding to the quick brown fox. The original (first) version of the document disappears entirely since only two versions are kept.

The contents of "Fox" and "Backup of Fox" are different, but the existence of the latter enables you to retrieve the previous version if you inadvertently edit beyond repair or accidentally erase the current "Fox" version. Should this occur (and it will), you can always retrieve its predecessor and at least salvage your work prior to the last save operation.

Objective: To open an existing document, check it for spelling, then use the Save As command to save the document under a different file name. Use Figure 1.14 as a guide in the exercise.

STEP 1: Preview a Document

➤ Start Microsoft Word. Pull down the **Help menu.** Click the command to **Hide** the **Office Assistant.**

➤ Pull down the **File menu** and click **Open** (or click the **Open button** on the Standard toolbar). You should see a dialog box similar to the one in Figure 1.14a.

➤ Select the appropriate drive, drive C or drive A, depending on the location of your data. Double click the **Exploring Word folder** to make it the active folder (the folder from which you will open the document).

➤ Scroll in the Name list box until you can select (click) the **Try the Spell Check** document. Click the **drop-down arrow** on the **Views button** and click **Preview** to preview the document as shown in Figure 1.14a.

➤ Click the **Open command button** to open the file. Your document should appear on the screen.

Open button

Click to select drive and/or folder

Views button

Click and drag scroll box to scroll through filenames

Click file name

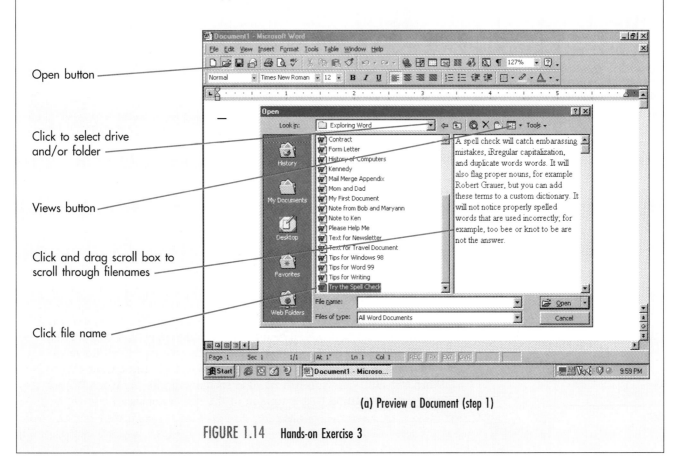

(a) Preview a Document (step 1)

FIGURE 1.14   Hands-on Exercise 3

STEP 2: The Save As Command

➤ Pull down the **File menu.** Click **Save As** to produce the dialog box in Figure 1.14b.

➤ Enter **Modified Spell Check** as the name of the new document. (A file name may contain up to 255 characters, and blanks are permitted.) Click the **Save command button.**

➤ There are now two identical copies of the file on disk: Try the Spell Check, which we supplied, and Modified Spell Check, which you just created. The title bar shows the latter name as it is the document in memory.

Enter new file name

Click here to change file type for compatibility with Word 95

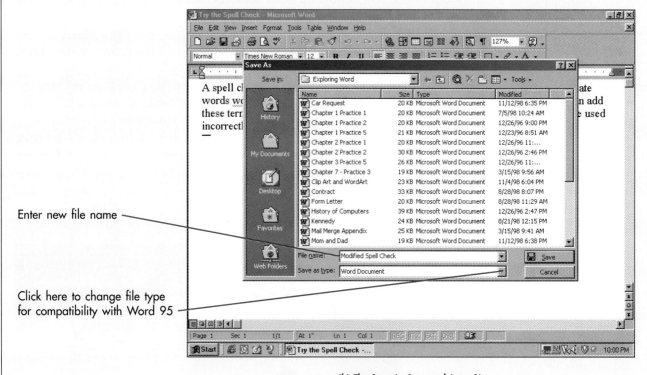

(b) The Save As Command (step 2)

FIGURE 1.14   Hands-on Exercise 3 (continued)

DIFFERENT FILE TYPES

The file format for Word 2000 is compatible with Word 97, but incompatible with earlier versions such as Word 95. The newer releases can open a document that was created using the older program (Word 95), but the reverse is not true; that is, you cannot open a document that was created in Word 2000 in Word 95 unless you change the file type. Pull down the File menu, click the Save As command, then specify the earlier (Word 6.0/Word 95) file type. You will be able to read the file in Word 95, but will lose any formatting that is unique to the newer release.

STEP 3: Create a Backup Copy

➤ Pull down the **Tools menu.** Click **Options.** Click the **Save tab** to display the dialog box of Figure 1.14c.

➤ Click the first check box to choose **Always create backup copy.**

➤ Set the other options as you see fit; for example, you can specify that the document be saved automatically every 10–15 minutes. Click **OK.**

Title bar reflects new name

Select Always create backup copy

Save tab

Select to AutoSave the document

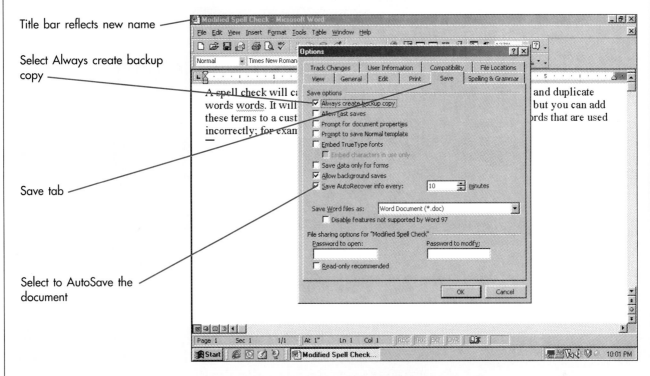

(c) Create a Backup Copy (step 3)

FIGURE 1.14   Hands-on Exercise 3 (continued)

STEP 4: The Spell Check

➤ If necessary, press **Ctrl+Home** to move to the beginning of the document. Click the **Spelling and Grammar button** on the Standard toolbar to check the document.

➤ "Embarassing" is flagged as the first misspelling as shown in Figure 1.14d. Click the **Change button** to accept the suggested spelling.

➤ "iRregular" is flagged as an example of irregular capitalization. Click the **Change button** to accept the suggested correction.

➤ Continue checking the document, which displays misspellings and other irregularities one at a time. Click the appropriate command button as each mistake is found.

• Click the **Delete button** to remove the duplicated word.

• Click the **Ignore button** to accept Grauer (or click the **Add button** to add Grauer to the custom dictionary).

➤ The last sentence is flagged because of a grammatical error and is discussed in the next step.

Spelling and Grammar button —

Misspelled word is detected —

Suggested correction —

Change button —

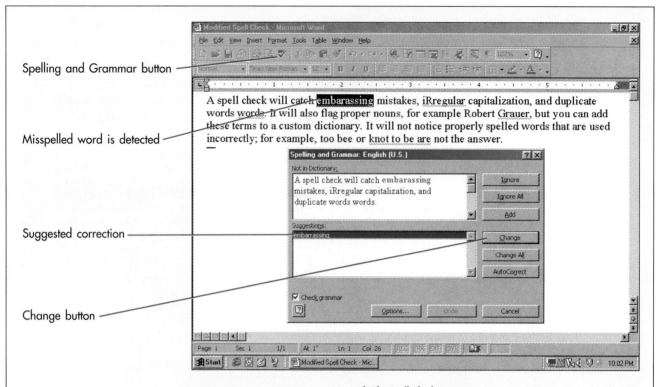

(d) The Spell Check (step 4)

FIGURE 1.14   Hands-on Exercise 3 (continued)

AUTOMATIC SPELLING AND GRAMMAR CHECKING

Red and green wavy lines may appear throughout a document to indicate spelling and grammatical errors, respectively. Point to any underlined word, then click the right mouse button to display a context-sensitive help menu with suggested corrections. To enable (disable) these options, pull down the Tools menu, click the Options command, click the Spelling and Grammar tab, and check (clear) the options to check spelling (or grammar) as you type.

STEP 5: The Grammar Check

➤ The last sentence, "Two bee or knot to be is not the answer", should be flagged as an error, as shown in Figure 1.14e. If this is not the case:

- Pull down the **Tools menu,** click **Options,** then click the **Spelling and Grammar tab.**

- Check the box to **Check Grammar with Spelling,** then click the button to **Recheck document.** Click **Yes** when told that the spelling and grammar check will be reset, then click **OK** to close the Options dialog box.

- Press **Ctrl+Home** to return to the beginning of the document, then click the **Spelling and Grammar button** to recheck the document.

➤ Click the **Office Assistant button** in the Spelling and Grammar dialog box.

Grammatical error is flagged

Explanation of grammatical error

Office Assistant button

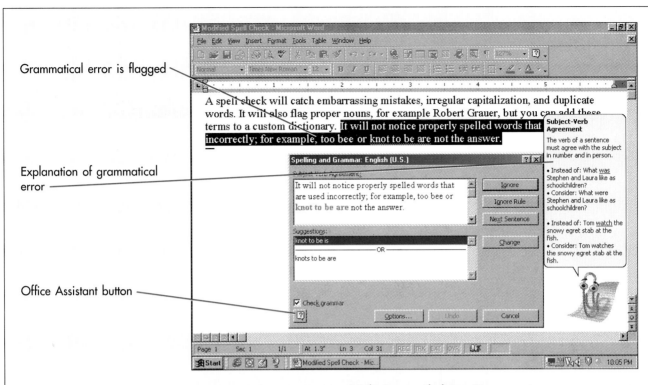

(e) The Grammar Check (step 5)

FIGURE 1.14   Hands-on Exercise 3 (continued)

> The Office Assistant will appear, indicating that there needs to be number agreement between subject and verb. Hide the Office Assistant after you have read the explanation.
> Click **Ignore** to reject the suggestion. Click **OK** when you see the dialog box, indicating the spelling and grammar check is complete.

CHECK SPELLING ONLY

The grammar check is invoked by default in conjunction with the spell check. You can, however, check the spelling of a document without checking its grammar. Pull down the Tools menu, click Options to display the Options dialog box, then click the Spelling and Grammar tab. Clear the box to check grammar with spelling, then click OK to accept the change and close the dialog box.

STEP 6: The Thesaurus

> Select (click) the word *incorrectly*, which appears on the last line of your document as shown in Figure 1.14f.
> Pull down the **Tools menu,** click **Language,** then click **Thesaurus** to display synonyms for the word you selected.
> Select (click) *inaccurately*, the synonym you will use in place of the original word. Click the **Replace button** to make the change automatically.

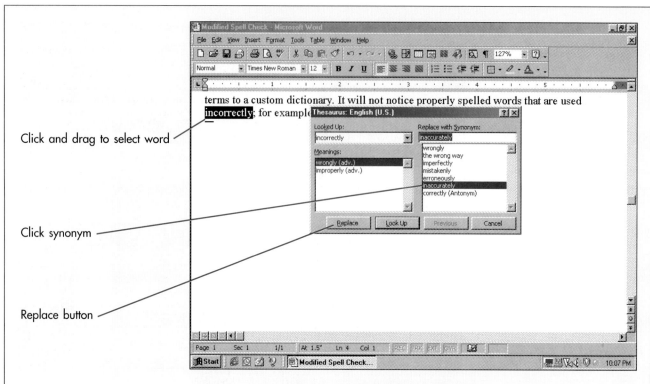

Click and drag to select word

Click synonym

Replace button

(f) The Thesaurus (step 6)

FIGURE 1.14   Hands-on Exercise 3 (continued)

STEP 7: AutoCorrect

➤ Press **Ctrl+Home** to move to the beginning of the document.

➤ Type the *misspelled* phrase **Teh Spell Check was used to check this document.**
Try to look at the monitor as you type to see the AutoCorrect feature in
action; Word will correct the misspelling and change *Teh* to *The*.

➤ If you did not see the correction being made, click the arrow next to the Undo
command on the Standard toolbar and undo the last several actions. Click
the arrow next to the Redo command and redo the corrections.

➤ Pull down the **Tools menu** and click the **AutoCorrect command** to display the
AutoCorrect dialog box. If necessary, click the AutoCorrect tab to view the
list of predefined corrections.

➤ The first several entries in the list pertain to symbols. Type (c), for example,
and you see the © symbol. Type :) or :(and you see a happy and sad face,
respectively. Click **Cancel** to close the dialog box.

CREATE YOUR OWN SHORTHAND

Use AutoCorrect to expand abbreviations such as "usa" for United States
of America. Pull down the Tools menu, click AutoCorrect, type the abbreviation in the Replace text box and the expanded entry in the With text
box. Click the Add command button, then click OK to exit the dialog box
and return to the document. The next time you type usa in a document,
it will automatically be expanded to United States of America.

STEP 8: Create an AutoText Entry

➤ Press **Ctrl+End** to move to the end of the document. Press the **enter key** twice. Enter your name, social security number, and class.

➤ Click and drag to select the information you just entered. Pull down the **Insert menu,** select the **AutoText command,** then select **AutoText** to display the AutoCorrect dialog box in Figure 1.14g.

➤ Your name (Felicia Williams in our example) is suggested automatically as the name of the AutoText entry. Click the **Add button.**

➤ To test the entry, you can delete your name and other information, then use the AutoText feature. Your name and other information should still be highlighted. Press the **Del key** to delete the information.

➤ Type the first few letters of your name and watch the screen as you do. You should see a ScreenTip containing your name and other information. Press the **enter key** or the **F3 key** when you see the ScreenTip.

➤ Save the document. Print the document for your instructor. Exit Word.

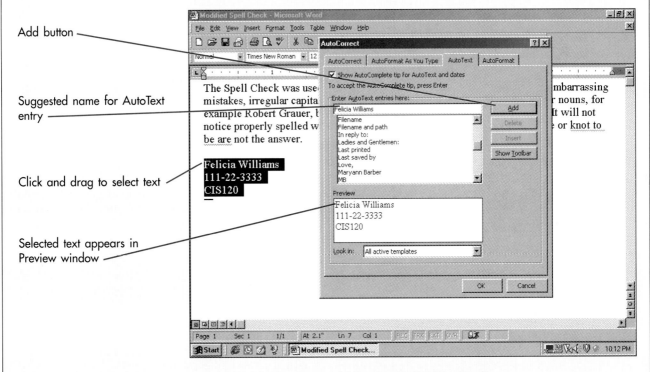

(g) Create an AutoText Entry (step 8)

FIGURE 1.14   Hands-on Exercise 3 (continued)

THE AUTOTEXT TOOLBAR

Point to any visible toolbar, click the right mouse button to display a context-sensitive menu, then click AutoText to display the AutoText toolbar. The AutoText toolbar groups the various AutoText entries into categories, making it easier to select the proper entry. Click the down arrow on the All Entries button to display the various categories, click a category, then select the entry you want to insert into the document.

SUMMARY

The chapter provided a broad-based introduction to word processing in general and to Microsoft Word in particular. Help is available from many sources. You can use the Help menu or the Office Assistant as you can in any Office application. You can also go to the Microsoft Web site to obtain more recent, and often more detailed, information.

Microsoft Word is always in one of two modes, insert or overtype; the choice between the two depends on the desired editing. The insertion point marks the place within a document where text is added or replaced.

The enter key is pressed at the end of a paragraph, but not at the end of a line because Word automatically wraps text from one line to the next. A hard return is created by the user when he or she presses the enter key; a soft return is created by Word as it wraps text and begins a new line.

The Save and Open commands work in conjunction with one another. The Save command copies the document in memory to disk under its existing name. The Open command retrieves a previously saved document. The Save As command saves the document under a different name and is useful when you want to retain a copy of the current document prior to all changes.

A spell check compares the words in a document to those in a standard and/or custom dictionary and offers suggestions to correct the mistakes it finds. It will detect misspellings, duplicated phrases, and/or irregular capitalization, but will not flag properly spelled words that are used incorrectly.

The AutoCorrect feature corrects predefined spelling errors and/or mistakes in capitalization, automatically, as the words are entered. The AutoText feature is similar in concept except that it can contain longer entries that include formatting and clip art. Either feature can be used to create a personal shorthand to expand abbreviations as they are typed.

The thesaurus suggests synonyms and/or antonyms. It can also recognize multiple forms of a word (noun, verb, and adjective) and offer suggestions for each. The grammar check searches for mistakes in punctuation, writing style, and word usage by comparing strings of text within a document to a series of predefined rules.

KEY WORDS AND CONCEPTS

AutoCorrect	Insert mode	Soft return
AutoText	Insertion point	Spell check
Backup	Normal view	Standard toolbar
Close command	Office Assistant	Status bar
Custom dictionary	Open command	Text box
Exit command	Overtype mode	Thesaurus
File menu	Places Bar	Toggle switch
File name	Print command	Toolbar
File type	Print Layout view	Undo command
Formatting toolbar	Save As command	Vertical ruler
Grammar check	Save command	View menu
Hard return	ScreenTip	Word wrap
Horizontal ruler	Show/Hide ¶ button	

1. When entering text within a document, the enter key is normally pressed at the end of every:
   (a) Line
   (b) Sentence
   (c) Paragraph
   (d) All of the above

2. Which menu contains the commands to save the current document, or to open a previously saved document?
   (a) The Tools menu
   (b) The File menu
   (c) The View menu
   (d) The Edit menu

3. How do you execute the Print command?
   (a) Click the Print button on the standard toolbar
   (b) Pull down the File menu, then click the Print command
   (c) Use the appropriate keyboard shortcut
   (d) All of the above

4. The Open command:
   (a) Brings a document from disk into memory
   (b) Brings a document from disk into memory, then erases the document on disk
   (c) Stores the document in memory on disk
   (d) Stores the document in memory on disk, then erases the document from memory

5. The Save command:
   (a) Brings a document from disk into memory
   (b) Brings a document from disk into memory, then erases the document on disk
   (c) Stores the document in memory on disk
   (d) Stores the document in memory on disk, then erases the document from memory

6. What is the easiest way to change the phrase, *revenues, profits, gross margin,* to read *revenues, profits, and gross margin?*
   (a) Use the insert mode, position the cursor before the *g* in *gross,* then type the word *and* followed by a space
   (b) Use the insert mode, position the cursor after the *g* in *gross,* then type the word *and* followed by a space
   (c) Use the overtype mode, position the cursor before the *g* in *gross,* then type the word *and* followed by a space
   (d) Use the overtype mode, position the cursor after the *g* in *gross,* then type the word *and* followed by a space

7. A document has been entered into Word with a given set of margins, which are subsequently changed. What can you say about the number of hard and soft returns before and after the change in margins?
   (a) The number of hard returns is the same, but the number and/or position of the soft returns is different
   (b) The number of soft returns is the same, but the number and/or position of the hard returns is different
   (c) The number and position of both hard and soft returns is unchanged
   (d) The number and position of both hard and soft returns is different

8. Which of the following will be detected by the spell check?
   (a) Duplicate words
   (b) Irregular capitalization
   (c) Both (a) and (b)
   (d) Neither (a) nor (b)

9. Which of the following is likely to be found in a custom dictionary?
   (a) Proper names
   (b) Words related to the user's particular application
   (c) Acronyms created by the user for his or her application
   (d) All of the above

10. Ted and Sally both use Word but on different computers. Both have written a letter to Dr. Joel Stutz and have run a spell check on their respective documents. Ted's program flags *Stutz* as a misspelling, whereas Sally's accepts it as written. Why?
    (a) The situation is impossible; that is, if they use identical word processing programs they should get identical results
    (b) Ted has added *Stutz* to his custom dictionary
    (c) Sally has added *Stutz* to her custom dictionary
    (d) All of the above reasons are equally likely as a cause of the problem

11. The spell check will do all of the following *except*:
    (a) Flag properly spelled words used incorrectly
    (b) Identify misspelled words
    (c) Accept (as correctly spelled) words found in the custom dictionary
    (d) Suggest alternatives to misspellings it identifies

12. The AutoCorrect feature will:
    (a) Correct errors in capitalization as they occur during typing
    (b) Expand user-defined abbreviations as the entries are typed
    (c) Both (a) and (b)
    (d) Neither (a) nor (b)

13. When does the Save As dialog box appear?
    (a) The first time a file is saved using either the Save or Save As commands
    (b) Every time a file is saved by clicking the Save button on the Standard toolbar
    (c) Both (a) and (b)
    (d) Neither (a) nor (b)

14. Which of the following is true about the thesaurus?
    (a) It recognizes different forms of a word; for example, a noun and a verb
    (b) It provides antonyms as well as synonyms
    (c) Both (a) and (b)
    (d) Neither (a) nor (b)

15. The grammar check:
    (a) Implements different rules for casual and business writing
    (b) Will detect all subtleties in the English language
    (c) Is always run in conjunction with a spell check
    (d) All of the above

ANSWERS

1. c	**6.** a	**11.** a
2. b	**7.** a	**12.** c
3. d	**8.** c	**13.** a
4. a	**9.** d	**14.** c
5. c	**10.** c	**15.** a

PRACTICE WITH MICROSOFT WORD

1. Retrieve the *Chapter1 Practice 1* document shown in Figure 1.15 from the Exploring Word folder, then make the following changes:

   a. Select the text *Your name* and replace it with your name.

   b. Replace *May 31, 1999* with the current date.

   c. Insert the phrase *one or* in line 2 so that the text reads *. . . one or more characters than currently exist.*

   d. Delete the word *And* from sentence four in line 5, then change the w in *when* to a capital letter to begin the sentence.

   e. Change the phrase *most efficient* to *best.*

   f. Place the insertion point at the end of sentence 2, make sure you are in the insert mode, then add the following sentence: *The insert mode adds characters at the insertion point while moving existing text to the right in order to make room for the new text.*

   g. Place the insertion point at the end of the last sentence, press the enter key twice in a row, then enter the following text: *There are several keys that function as toggle switches of which you should be aware. The Caps Lock key toggles between upper- and lowercase letters, and the Num Lock key alternates between typing numbers and using the arrow keys.*

   h. Save the revised document, then print it and submit it to your instructor.

2. Select-Then-Do: Formatting is not covered until Chapter 2, but we think you are ready to try your hand at basic formatting now. Most formatting operations are done in the context of select-then-do as described in the document in Figure 1.16. You select the text you want to format, then you execute the appropriate formatting command, most easily by clicking the appropriate button on the Formatting toolbar. The function of each button should be apparent from its icon, but you can simply point to a button to display a ScreenTip that is indicative of the button's function.

To: Your name

From: Robert Grauer and Maryann Barber

Subject: Microsoft® Word 2000

Date: May 31, 1999

This is just a short note to help you get acquainted with the insertion and replacement modes in Word for Windows. When the editing to be done results in more characters than currently exist, you want to be in the insertion mode when making the change. On the other hand, when the editing to be done contains the same or fewer characters, the replacement mode is best. And when replacing characters, it is most efficient to use the mouse to select the characters to be deleted and then just type the new characters; the selected characters are automatically deleted and the new characters typed take their place.

FIGURE 1.15   Editing Text (Exercise 1)

An unformatted version of the document in Figure 1.16 exists on the data disk as *Chapter1 Practice 2.* Open the document, then format it to match the completed version in Figure 1.16. Just select the text to format, then click the appropriate button. We changed type size in the original document to 24 points for the title and 12 points for text in the document itself. Be sure to add your name and date as shown in the figure, then submit the completed document to your instructor.

3. Your Background: Write a short description of your computer background similar to the document in Figure 1.17. The document should be in the form of a note from student to instructor that describes your background and should mention any previous knowledge of computers you have, prior computer courses you have taken, your objectives for this course, and so on. Indicate whether you own a PC, whether you have access to one at work, and/or whether you are considering purchase. Include any other information about yourself and/or your computer-related background.

Place your name somewhere in the document in boldface italics. We would also like you to use boldface and italics to emphasize the components of any computer system you describe. Use any font or point size you like. Note, too, the last paragraph, which asks you to print the summary statistics for the document when you submit the assignment to your instructor. (Use the tip on Document Properties on page 25 to print the total editing time and other information about your document.)

4. The Cover Page: Create a cover page that you can use for your assignments this semester. Your cover page should be similar to the one in Figure 1.18 with respect to content and should include the title of the assignment, your name, course information, and date. The formatting is up to you. Print the completed cover page and submit it to your instructor for inclusion in a class contest to judge the most innovative design.

Select-Then-Do

Many operations in Word are executed as select-then-do operations. You first select a block of text, and then you issue a command that will affect the selected text. You may select the text in many different ways, the most basic of which is to click and drag over the desired characters. You may also take one of many shortcuts, which include double clicking on a word, pressing Ctrl as you click a sentence, and triple clicking on a paragraph.

Once text is selected, you may then delete it, **boldface** or *italicize* it, or even change its color. You may move it or copy it to another location in the same or a different document. You can highlight it, underline, or even check its spelling. Then, depending on whether or not you like what you have done, you may undo it, redo it, and/or repeat it on subsequently selected text.

Jessica Kinzer
March 1, 1999

FIGURE 1.16   Select-Then-Do (Exercise 2)

The Computer and Me

My name is Jessica Kinzer and I am a complete novice when it comes to computers. I did not take a computer course in high school and this is my first semester at the University of Miami. My family does not own a computer, nor have I had the opportunity to use one at work. So when it comes to beginners, I am a beginner's beginner. I am looking forward to taking this course, as I have heard that it will truly make me computer literate. I know that I desperately need computer skills not only when I enter the job market, to but to survive my four years here as well. I am looking forward to learning Word, Excel, and PowerPoint and I hope that I can pick up some Internet skills as well.

I did not buy a computer before I came to school as I wanted to see what type of system I would be using for my classes. After my first few weeks in class, I think that I would like to buy a 400 *MZ Pentium II* machine with *64MB RAM* and a *10 GB hard drive*. I would like a *DVD CD-ROM* and a *sound card* (with *speakers*, of course). I also would like to get a high-speed *modem* and a *laser printer*. Now, if only I had the money.

This document did not take long at all to create as you can see by the summary statistics that are printed on the next page. I think that I will really enjoy this class.

Jessica Kinzer
March 2, 1999

FIGURE 1.17   Your Computer Background (Exercise 3)

Exploring Word Assignment

Jessica Kinzer
CIS 120
March 2, 1999

FIGURE 1.18 The Cover Page (Exercise 4)

5. Proofing a Document: Figure 1.19 contains the draft version of the *Chapter 1 Practice 5* document contained on the data disk.

   a. Proofread the document and circle any mistakes in spelling, grammar, capitalization, or punctuation.

   b. Open the document in Word and run the spell check. Did Word catch any mistakes you missed? Did you find any errors that were missed by the program?

   c. Use the thesaurus to come up with alternative words for *document,* which appears entirely too often within the paragraph.

   d. Run the grammar check on the revised document. Did the program catch any grammatical errors you missed? Did you find any mistakes that were missed by the program?

   e. Add a short paragraph with your opinion of the spelling and grammar check.

   f. Add your name to the revised document, save it, print it, and submit the completed document to your instructor.

6. Webster Online: Figure 1.20 shows our favorite online dictionary. We have erased the address, however, or else the problem would be too easy. Thus, you have to search the Web to look for our dictionary or its equivalent. Once you locate a dictionary, enter the word you want to look up (*oxymoron,* for example), then press the Look Up Word button to display the definition in Figure 1.21. This is truly an interactive dictionary because most words in it are created as hyperlinks, which in turn will lead you to other definitions. Use the dictionary to look up the meaning of the word *palindrome.* How many examples of oxymorons and palindromes can you think of?

The Grammar Check

All documents should be thoroughly proofed before they be printed and distributed. This means that documents, at a minimum should be spell cheked, grammar cheked,, and proof read by the author. A documents that has spelling errors and/or grammatical errors makes the Author look unprofessional and illiterate and their is nothing worse than allowing a first impression too be won that makes you appear slopy and disinterested, and a document full or of misteakes will do exactly that. Alot of people do not realize how damaging a bad first impression could be, and documents full of misteakes has cost people opportunities that they trained and prepared many years for.

Microsoft Word includes an automated grammar check that will detect many, but certainly not all, errors as the previous paragraph demonstrates. Unlike the spell check, the grammar check is subjective, and what seems appropriate to you may be objectionable to someone else. The English language is just to complicated for the grammar check to detect every error, or even most errors. Hence, there is no substitute for carefully proof reading a document your self. Hence there is no substitute for carefully proof reading a document your self.

FIGURE 1.19   Proofing a Document (Exercise 5)

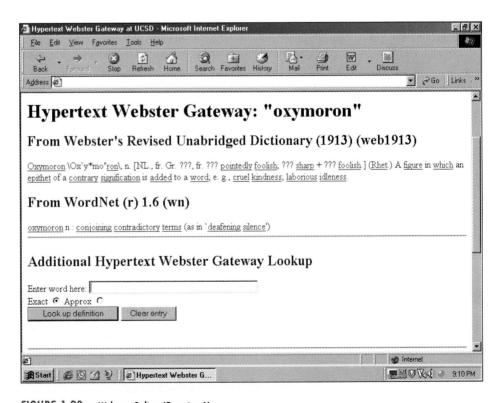

FIGURE 1.20   Webster Online (Exercise 6)

Companion Web Sites

A Companion Web site (or online study guide) accompanies each book in the *Exploring Microsoft Office 2000* series. Go to the Exploring Windows home page at www.prenhall.com/grauer, click the book to Office 2000, and click the Companion Web site tab at the top of the screen. Choose the appropriate text (Exploring Word 2000) and the chapter within the text (e.g., Chapter 1).

Each chapter contains a series of short-answer exercises (multiple-choice, true/false, and matching) to review the material in the chapter. You can take practice quizzes by yourself and/or e-mail the results to your instructor. You can try the essay questions for additional practice and engage in online chat sessions. We hope you will find the online guide to be a valuable resource.

It's a Mess

Newcomers to word processing quickly learn the concept of word wrap and the distinction between hard and soft returns. This lesson was lost, however, on your friend who created the *Please Help Me* document on the data disk. The first several sentences were entered without any hard returns at all, whereas the opposite problem exists toward the end of the document. This is a good friend, and her paper is due in one hour. Please help.

Planning for Disaster

Do you have a backup strategy? Do you even know what a backup strategy is? You should learn, because sooner or later you will wish you had one. You will erase a file, be unable to read from a floppy disk, or worse yet suffer a hardware failure in which you are unable to access the hard drive. The problem always seems to occur the night before an assignment is due. The ultimate disaster is the disappearance of your computer, by theft or natural disaster (e.g., Hurricane Andrew). Describe in 250 words or less the backup strategy you plan to implement in conjunction with your work in this class.

A Letter Home

You really like this course and want very much to have your own computer, but you're strapped for cash and have decided to ask your parents for help. Write a one-page letter describing the advantages of having your own system and how it will help you in school. Tell your parents what the system will cost, and that you can save money by buying through the mail. Describe the configuration you intend to buy (don't forget to include the price of software) and then provide prices from at least three different companies. Cut out the advertisements and include them in your letter. Bring your material to class and compare your research with that of your classmates.

Computer Magazines

A subscription to a computer magazine should be given serious consideration if you intend to stay abreast in a rapidly changing field. The reviews on new products are especially helpful and you will appreciate the advertisements should you need to buy. Go to the library or a newsstand and obtain a magazine that appeals to you, then write a brief review of the magazine for class. Devote at least one paragraph to an article or other item you found useful.

A Junior Year Abroad

How lucky can you get? You are spending the second half of your junior year in Paris. The problem is you will have to submit your work in French, and the English version of Microsoft Word won't do. Is there a foreign-language version available? What about the dictionary and thesaurus? How do you enter the accented characters, which occur so frequently? You are leaving in two months, so you'd better get busy. What are your options? *Bon voyage!*

The Writer's Reference

The chapter discussed the use of a spell check, thesaurus, and grammar check, but many other resources are available. The Web contains a host of sites with additional resources that are invaluable to the writer. You can find Shakespeare online, as well as Bartlett's quotations. You can also find Webster's dictionary as well as a dictionary of acronyms. One way to find these resources is to click the Search button in Internet Explorer, then scroll down the page to the Writer's Reference section. You can also go to the address directly (home.microsoft.com/access. allinone.asp). Explore one or more of these resources, then write a short note to your instructor to summarize your findings.

Microsoft Online

Help for Microsoft Word is available from a variety of sources. You can consult the Office Assistant, or you can pull down the Help menu to display the Help Contents and Index. Both techniques were illustrated in the chapter. In addition, you can go to the Microsoft Web site to obtain more recent, and often more detailed, information. You will find the answers to the most frequently asked questions and you can access the same knowledge base used by Microsoft support engineers. Experiment with various sources of help, then submit a summary of your findings to your instructor. Try to differentiate among the various techniques and suggest the most appropriate use for each.

Changing Menus and Toolbars

Office 2000 implements one very significant change over previous versions of Office in that it displays a series of short menus that contain only basic commands. The additional commands are made visible by clicking the double arrow that appears at the bottom of the menu. New commands are added to the menu as they are used, and conversely, other commands are removed if they are not used. A similar strategy is followed for the Standard and Formatting toolbars that are displayed on a single row, and thus do not show all of the buttons at one time. The intent is to simplify Office 2000 for the new user by limiting the number of commands that are visible. The consequence, however, is that the individual is not exposed to new commands, and hence may not use Office to its full potential. Which set of menus do you prefer? How do you switch from one set to the other?

chapter 2

GAINING PROFICIENCY: EDITING AND FORMATTING

OBJECTIVES

After reading this chapter you will be able to:

1. Define the select-then-do methodology; describe several shortcuts with the mouse and/or the keyboard to select text.

2. Move and copy text within a document; distinguish between the Windows clipboard and the Office clipboard.

3. Use the Find, Replace, and Go To commands to substitute one character string for another.

4. Define scrolling; scroll to the beginning and end of a document.

5. Distinguish between the Normal and Print Layout views; state how to change the view and/or magnification of a document.

6. Define typography; distinguish between a serif and a sans serif typeface; use the Format Font command to change the font and/or type size.

7. Use the Format Paragraph command to change line spacing, alignment, tabs, and indents, and to control pagination.

8. Use the Borders and Shading command to box and shade text.

9. Describe the Undo and Redo commands and how they are related to one another.

10. Use the Page Setup command to change the margins and/or orientation; differentiate between a soft and a hard page break.

11. Enter and edit text in columns; change the column structure of a document through section formatting.

OVERVIEW

The previous chapter taught you the basics of Microsoft Word and enabled you to create and print a simple document. The present chapter significantly extends your capabilities, by presenting a variety of commands to change the contents and appearance of a document. These operations are known as editing and formatting, respectively.

You will learn how to move and copy text within a document and how to find and replace one character string with another. You will also learn the basics of typography and be able to switch between the different fonts included within Windows. You will be able to change alignment, indentation, line spacing, margins, and page orientation. All of these commands are used in three hands-on exercises, which require your participation at the computer, and which are the very essence of the chapter.

As you read the chapter, realize that there are many different ways to accomplish the same task and that it would be impossible to cover them all. Our approach is to present the overall concepts and suggest the ways we think are most appropriate at the time we introduce the material. We also offer numerous shortcuts in the form of boxed tips that appear throughout the chapter and urge you to explore further on your own. It is not necessary for you to memorize anything as online help is always available. Be flexible and willing to experiment.

WRITE NOW, EDIT LATER

You write a sentence, then change it, and change it again, and one hour later you've produced a single paragraph. It happens to every writer—you stare at a blank screen and flashing cursor and are unable to write. The best solution is to brainstorm and write down anything that pops into your head, and to keep on writing. Don't worry about typos or spelling errors because you can fix them later. Above all, resist the temptation to continually edit the few words you've written because overediting will drain the life out of what you are writing. The important thing is to get your ideas on paper.

SELECT-THEN-DO

Many operations in Word take place within the context of a **select-then-do** methodology; that is, you select a block of text, then you execute the command to operate on that text. The most basic way to select text is by dragging the mouse; that is, click at the beginning of the selection, press and hold the left mouse button as you move to the end of the selection, then release the mouse.

There are, however, a variety of shortcuts to facilitate the process; for example, double click anywhere within a word to select the word, or press the Ctrl key and click the mouse anywhere within a sentence to select the sentence. Additional shortcuts are presented in each of the hands-on exercises, at which point you will have many opportunities to practice selecting text.

Selected text is affected by any subsequent operation; for example, clicking the Bold or Italic button changes the selected text to boldface or italics, respectively. You can also drag the selected text to a new location, press the Del key to erase the selected text, or execute any other editing or formatting command. The text continues to be selected until you click elsewhere in the document.

INSERT THE DATE AND TIME

Most documents include the date and time they were created. Pull down the Insert menu, select the Date and Time command to display the Date and Time dialog box, then choose a format. Check the box to update the date automatically if you want your document to reflect the date on which it is opened or clear the box to retain the date on which the document was created. See exercise seven at the end of the chapter.

MOVING AND COPYING TEXT

The ability to move and/or copy text is essential in order to develop any degree of proficiency in editing. A move operation removes the text from its current location and places it elsewhere in the same (or even a different) document; a copy operation retains the text in its present location and places a duplicate elsewhere. Either operation can be accomplished using the Windows clipboard and a combination of the *Cut, Copy,* and *Paste commands.*

The *Windows clipboard* is a temporary storage area available to any Windows application. Selected text is cut or copied from a document and placed onto the clipboard from where it can be pasted to a new location(s). A move requires that you select the text and execute a Cut command to remove the text from the document and place it on the clipboard. You then move the insertion point to the new location and paste the text from the clipboard into that location. A copy operation necessitates the same steps except that a Copy command is executed rather than a cut, leaving the selected text in its original location as well as placing a copy on the clipboard.

The Cut, Copy, and Paste commands are found in the Edit menu, or alternatively, can be executed by clicking the appropriate buttons on the Standard toolbar. The contents of the Windows clipboard are replaced by each subsequent Cut or Copy command, but are unaffected by the Paste command. The contents of the clipboard can be pasted into multiple locations in the same or different documents.

Office 2000 introduces its own clipboard that enables you to collect and paste multiple items. The *Office clipboard* differs from the Windows clipboard in that the contents of each successive Copy command are added to the clipboard. Thus, you could copy the first paragraph of a document to the Office clipboard, then copy (add) a bulleted list in the middle of the document to the Office clipboard, and finally copy (add) the last paragraph (three items in all) to the Office clipboard. You could then go to another place in the document or to a different document altogether, and paste the contents of the Office clipboard (three separate items) with a single command.

Selected text is copied automatically to the Office clipboard regardless of whether you use the Copy command in the Edit menu, the Copy button on the Standard toolbar, or the Ctrl+C shortcut. You must, however, use the Clipboard toolbar to paste items from the Office clipboard into a document.

UNDO, REDO, AND REPEAT COMMANDS

The *Undo command* was introduced in Chapter 1, but it is repeated here because it is so valuable. The command is executed from the Edit menu or by clicking the Undo button on the Standard toolbar. Word enables you to undo multiple changes to a document. You just click the down arrow next to the Undo button on the Standard toolbar to display a reverse-order list of your previous commands, then you click the command you want to undo, which also undoes all of the preceding commands. Undoing the fifth command in the list, for example, will also undo the preceding four commands.

The *Redo command* redoes (reverses) the last command that was undone. As with the Undo command, the Redo command redoes all of the previous commands prior to the command you select. Redoing the fifth command in the list, for example, will also redo the preceding four commands. The Undo and Redo commands work in conjunction with one another; that is, every time a command is undone it can be redone at a later time. The *Repeat command* does what its name implies and repeats the last action or command. It is executed from the Edit menu.

The Find, Replace, and Go To commands share a common dialog box with different tabs for each command as shown in Figure 2.1. The **Find command** locates one or more occurrences of specific text (e.g., a word or phrase). The **Replace command** goes one step further in that it locates the text, and then enables you to optionally replace (one or more occurrences of) that text with different text. The **Go To command** goes directly to a specific place (e.g., a specific page) in the document.

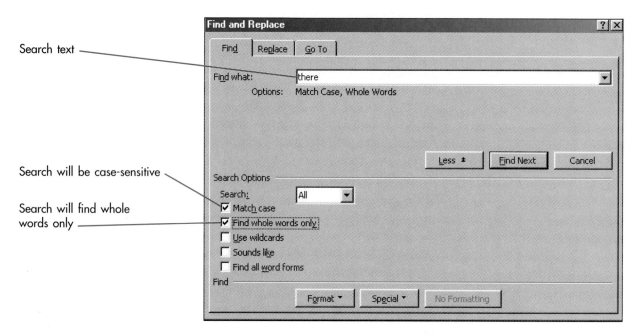

(a) Find Command

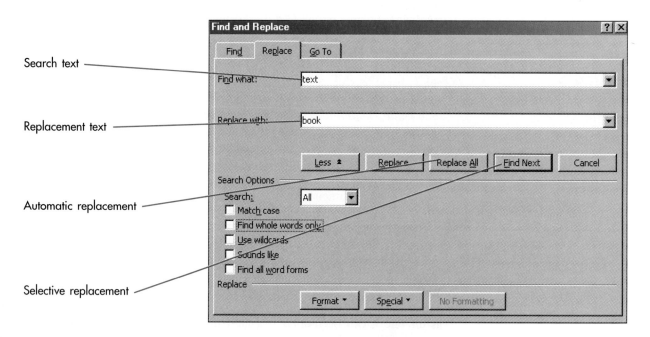

(b) Replace Command

FIGURE 2.1   The Find, Replace, Go To Commands

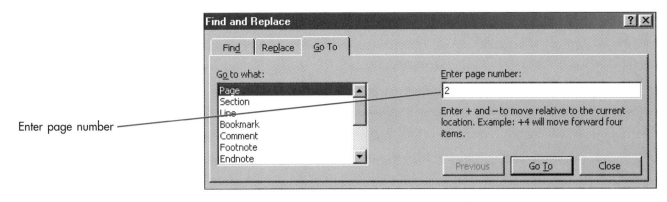

Enter page number

(c) Go To Command

FIGURE 2.1 The Find, Replace, and Go To Commands (continued)

The search in both the Find and Replace commands is case-sensitive or case-insensitive. A **case-sensitive search** (where Match Case is selected as in Figure 2.1a) matches not only the text, but also the use of upper- and lowercase letters. Thus, *There* is different from *there*, and a search on one will not identify the other. A **case-insensitive search** (where Match Case is *not* as selected in Figure 2.1b) is just the opposite and finds both *There* and *there*. A search may also specify **whole words only** to identify *there*, but not *therefore* or *thereby*. And finally, the search and replacement text can also specify different numbers of characters; for example, you could replace *16* with *sixteen*.

The Replace command in Figure 2.1b implements either **selective replacement,** which lets you examine each occurrence of the character string in context and decide whether to replace it, or **automatic replacement,** where the substitution is made automatically. Selective replacement is implemented by clicking the Find Next command button, then clicking (or not clicking) the Replace button to make the substitution. Automatic replacement (through the entire document) is implemented by clicking the Replace All button. This often produces unintended consequences and is not recommended; for example, if you substitute the word *text* for *book*, the phrase *text book* would become *text text,* which is not what you had in mind.

The Find and Replace commands can include formatting and/or special characters. You can, for example, change all italicized text to boldface, or you can change five consecutive spaces to a tab character. You can also use special characters in the character string such as the "any character" (consisting of ^?). For example, to find all four-letter words that begin with "f" and end with "l" (such as *fall, fill,* or *fail*), search for f^?^?l. (The question mark stands for any character, just like a wild card in a card game.) You can also search for all forms of a word; for example, if you specify *am*, it will also find *is* and *are*. You can even search for a word based on how it sounds. When searching for *Marion*, for example, check the Sounds Like check box, and the search will find both *Marion* and *Marian.*

SCROLLING

Scrolling occurs when a document is too large to be seen in its entirety. Figure 2.2a displays a large printed document, only part of which is visible on the screen as illustrated in Figure 2.2b. In order to see a different portion of the document, you need to scroll, whereby new lines will be brought into view as the old lines disappear.

To: Our Students
From: Robert Grauer and Maryann Barber

Welcome to the wonderful world of word processing and desktop publishing. Over the next several chapters we will build a foundation in the basics of Microsoft Word, then teach you to format specialized documents, create professional looking tables and charts, publish well-designed newsletters, and create Web pages. Before you know it, you will be a word processing and desktop publishing wizard!

The first chapter presented the basics of word processing and showed you how to create a simple document. You learned how to insert, replace, and/or delete text. This chapter will teach you about fonts and special effects (such as **boldfacing** and *italicizing*) and how to use them effectively — how too little is better than too much.

You will go on to experiment with margins, tab stops, line spacing, and justification, learning first to format simple documents and then going on to longer, more complex ones. It is with the latter that we explore headers and footers, page numbering, widows and orphans (yes, we really did mean widows and orphans). It is here that we bring in graphics, working with newspaper-type columns, and the elements of a good page design. And without question, we will introduce the tools that make life so much easier (and your writing so much more impressive) — the Spell Check, Grammar Check, Thesaurus, and Styles.

If you are wondering what all these things are, read on in the text and proceed with the hands-on exercises. We will show you how to create a simple newsletter, and then improve it by adding graphics, fonts, and WordArt. You will create a simple calendar using the Tables feature, and then create more intricate forms that will rival anything you have seen. You will learn how to create a résumé with your beginner's skills, and then make it look like so much more with your intermediate (even advanced) skills. You will learn how to download resources from the Internet and how to create your own Web page. Last, but not least, run a mail merge to produce the cover letters that will accompany your resume as it is mailed to companies across the United States (and even the world).

It is up to you to practice for it is only through working at the computer, that you will learn what you need to know. Experiment and don't be afraid to make mistakes. Practice and practice some more.

Our goal is for you to learn and to enjoy what you are learning. We have great confidence in you, and in our ability to help you discover what you can do. Visit the home page for the Exploring Windows series. You can also send us e-mail. Bob's address is rgrauer@sba.miam.edu. Maryann's address is mbarber@sba.miami.edu. As you read the last sentence, notice that Word 2000 is Web-enabled and that the Internet and e-mail references appear as hyperlinks in this document. Thus, you can click the address of our home page from within Word, then view the page immediately, provided you have an Internet connection. You can also click the e-mail address to open your mail program, provided it has been configured correctly.

We look forward to hearing from you and hope that you will like our textbook. You are about to embark on a wonderful journey toward computer literacy. Be patient and inquisitive.

(a) Printed Document

FIGURE 2.2   Scrolling

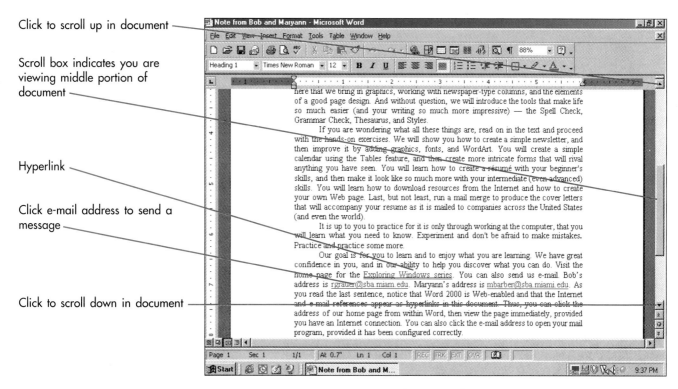

Click to scroll up in document

Scroll box indicates you are viewing middle portion of document

Hyperlink

Click e-mail address to send a message

Click to scroll down in document

(b) Screen Display

FIGURE 2.2   Scrolling (continued)

Scrolling comes about automatically as you reach the bottom of the screen. Entering a new line of text, clicking on the down arrow within the scroll bar, or pressing the down arrow key brings a new line into view at the bottom of the screen and simultaneously removes a line at the top. (The process is reversed at the top of the screen.)

Scrolling can be done with either the mouse or the keyboard. Scrolling with the mouse (e.g., clicking the down arrow in the scroll bar) changes what is displayed on the screen, but does not move the insertion point, so that you must click the mouse after scrolling prior to entering the text at the new location. Scrolling with the keyboard, however (e.g., pressing Ctrl+Home or Ctrl+End to move to the beginning or end of a document, respectively), changes what is displayed on the screen as well as the location of the insertion point, and you can begin typing immediately.

Scrolling occurs most often in a vertical direction as shown in Figure 2.2. It can also occur horizontally, when the length of a line in a document exceeds the number of characters that can be displayed horizontally on the screen.

IT'S WEB-ENABLED

Every document in Office 2000 is Web-enabled, which means that Internet and e-mail references appear as hyperlinks within a document. Thus you can click the address of any Web page from within Word to display the page, provided you have an Internet connection. You can also click the e-mail address to open your mail program, provided it has been configured correctly.

The *View menu* provides different views of a document. Each view can be displayed at different magnifications, which in turn determine the amount of scrolling necessary to see remote parts of a document.

The *Normal view* is the default view and it provides the fastest way to enter text. The *Print Layout* view more closely resembles the printed document and displays the top and bottom margins, headers and footers, page numbers, graphics, and other features that do not appear in the Normal view. The Normal view tends to be faster because Word spends less time formatting the display.

The *Zoom command* displays the document on the screen at different magnifications; for example, 75%, 100%, or 200%. (The Zoom command does not affect the size of the text on the printed page.) A Zoom percentage (magnification) of 100% displays the document in the approximate size of the text on the printed page. You can increase the percentage to 200% to make the characters appear larger. You can also decrease the magnification to 75% to see more of the document at one time.

Word will automatically determine the magnification if you select one of four additional Zoom options—Page Width, Text Width, Whole Page, or Many Pages (Whole Page and Many Pages are available only in the Print Layout view). Figure 2.3a, for example, displays a two-page document in Print Layout view. Figure 2.3b shows the corresponding settings in the Zoom command. (The 37% magnification is determined automatically once you specify the number of pages as shown in the figure.)

Zoom button

Two pages are displayed

Print Layout View button

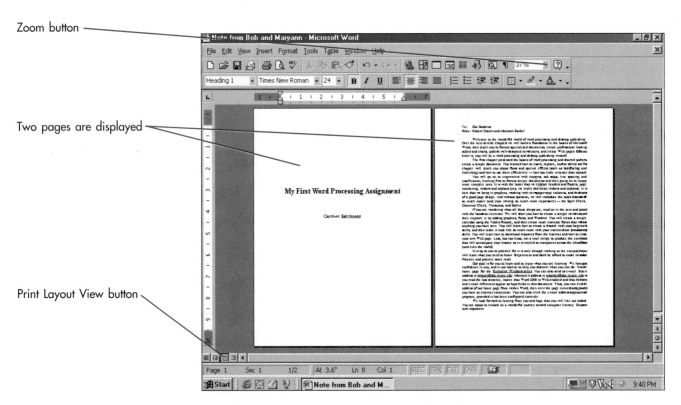

(a) Page Layout View

FIGURE 2.3   View Menu and Zoom Command

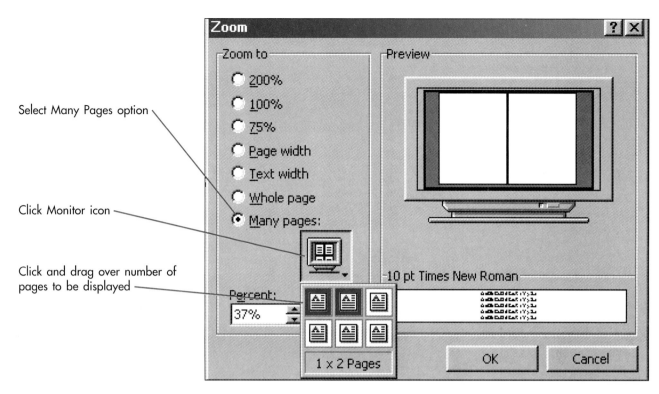

Select Many Pages option

Click Monitor icon

Click and drag over number of pages to be displayed

(b) Zoom Command

FIGURE 2.3   View Menu and Zoom Command (continued)

HANDS-ON EXERCISE 1

Editing a Document

Objective: To edit an existing document; to change the view and magnification of a document; to scroll through a document. To use the Find and Replace commands; to move and copy text using the clipboard and the drag-and-drop facility. Use Figure 2.4 as a guide in the exercise.

STEP 1: The View Menu

➤ Start Word as described in the hands-on exercises from Chapter 1. Pull down the **File menu** and click **Open** (or click the **Open button** on the toolbar).

- Click the **drop-down arrow** on the Look In list box. Click the appropriate drive, drive C or drive A, depending on the location of your data.

- Double click the **Exploring Word folder** to make it the active folder (the folder in which you will save the document).

- Scroll in the Name list box (if necessary) until you can click the **Note from Bob and Maryann** to select this document. Double click the **document icon** or click the **Open command button** to open the file.

➤ The document should appear on the screen as shown in Figure 2.4a.

➤ Change to the Print Layout view at Page Width magnification:

- Pull down the **View menu** and click **Print Layout** (or click the **Print Layout View button** above the status bar) as shown in Figure 2.4a.

- Click the **down arrow** in the Zoom box to change to **Page Width.**

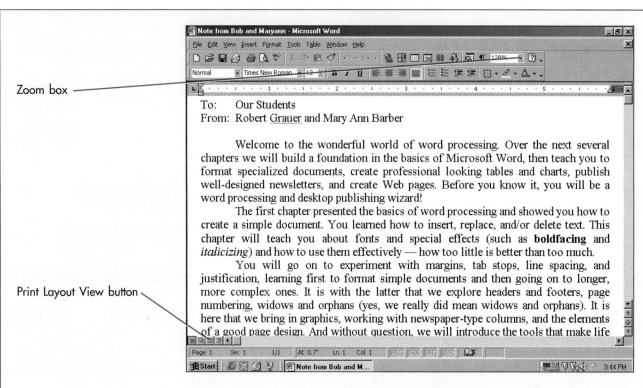

Zoom box

Print Layout View button

To: Our Students
From: Robert Grauer and Mary Ann Barber

Welcome to the wonderful world of word processing. Over the next several chapters we will build a foundation in the basics of Microsoft Word, then teach you to format specialized documents, create professional looking tables and charts, publish well-designed newsletters, and create Web pages. Before you know it, you will be a word processing and desktop publishing wizard!

The first chapter presented the basics of word processing and showed you how to create a simple document. You learned how to insert, replace, and/or delete text. This chapter will teach you about fonts and special effects (such as **boldfacing** and *italicizing*) and how to use them effectively — how too little is better than too much.

You will go on to experiment with margins, tab stops, line spacing, and justification, learning first to format simple documents and then going on to longer, more complex ones. It is with the latter that we explore headers and footers, page numbering, widows and orphans (yes, we really did mean widows and orphans). It is here that we bring in graphics, working with newspaper-type columns, and the elements of a good page design. And without question, we will introduce the tools that make life

(a) The View Menu (step 1)

FIGURE 2.4   Hands-on Exercise 1

➤ Click and drag the mouse to select the phrase **Our Students,** which appears at the beginning of the document. Type your name to replace the selected text.

➤ Pull down the **File menu,** click the **Save As** command, then save the document as **Modified Note.** (This creates a second copy of the document.)

CREATE A BACKUP COPY

Microsoft Word enables you to automatically create a backup copy of a document in conjunction with the Save command. Pull down the Tools menu, click the Options button, click the Save tab, then check the box to always create a backup copy. The next time you save the file, the previously saved version is renamed "Backup of document" after which the document in memory is saved as the current version. In other words, the disk will contain the two most recent versions of the document.

STEP 2: Scrolling

➤ Click and drag the **scroll box** within the vertical scroll bar to scroll to the end of the document as shown in Figure 2.4b. Click immediately before the period at the end of the last sentence.

➤ Type a **comma** and a space, then insert the phrase **but most of all, enjoy.**

➤ Drag the **scroll box** to the top of the scroll bar to get back to the beginning of the document. Click immediately before the period ending the first sentence, press the **space bar,** then add the phrase **and desktop publishing.**

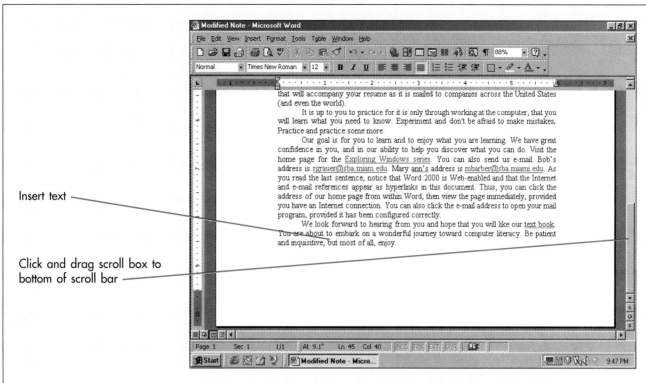

Insert text

Click and drag scroll box to bottom of scroll bar

(b) Scrolling (step 2)

FIGURE 2.4   Hands-on Exercise 1 (continued)

THE MOUSE AND THE SCROLL BAR

Scroll quickly through a document by clicking above or below the scroll box to scroll up or down an entire screen. Move to the top, bottom, or an approximate position within a document by dragging the scroll box to the corresponding position in the scroll bar; for example, dragging the scroll box to the middle of the bar moves the mouse pointer to the middle of the document. Scrolling with the mouse does not change the location of the insertion point, however, and thus you must click the mouse at the new location prior to entering text at that location.

STEP 3: The Replace Command

➤ Press **Ctrl+Home** to move to the beginning of the document. Pull down the **Edit menu.** Click **Replace** to produce the dialog box of Figure 2.4c. Click the **More button** to display the available options.

- Type **text** in the Find what text box.
- Press the **Tab key.** Type **book** in the Replace with text box.

➤ Click the **Find Next button** to find the first occurrence of the word *text*. The dialog box remains on the screen and the first occurrence of *text* is selected. This is *not* an appropriate substitution; that is, you should not substitute *book* for *text* at this point.

➤ Click the **Find Next button** to move to the next occurrence without making the replacement. This time the substitution is appropriate.

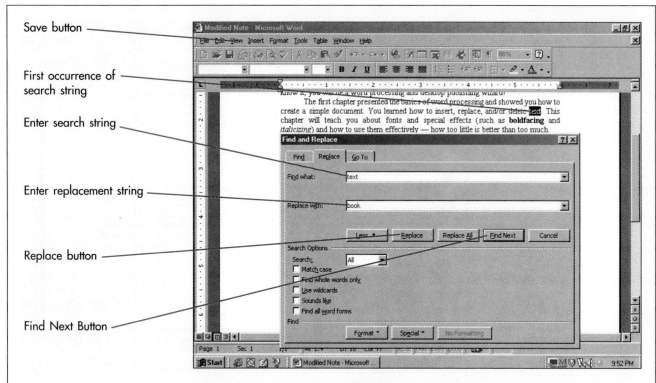

Save button

First occurrence of search string

Enter search string

Enter replacement string

Replace button

Find Next Button

(c) The Replace Command (step 3)

FIGURE 2.4   Hands-on Exercise 1 (continued)

➤ Click **Replace** to make the change and automatically move to the next occurrence where the substitution is again inappropriate. Click **Find Next** a final time. Word will indicate that it has finished searching the document. Click **OK.**

➤ Change the Find and Replace strings to **Mary Ann** and **Maryann,** respectively. Click the **Replace All** button to make the substitution globally without confirmation. Word will indicate that it has finished searching and that two replacements were made. Click **OK.**

➤ Click the **Close command button** to close the dialog box. Click the **Save button** to save the document. Scroll through the document to review your changes.

SCROLLING WITH THE KEYBOARD

Press Ctrl+Home and Ctrl+End to move to the beginning and end of a document, respectively. Press Home and End to move to the beginning and end of a line. Press PgUp or PgDn to scroll one screen in the indicated direction. The advantage of scrolling via the keyboard (instead of the mouse) is that the location of the insertion point changes automatically and you can begin typing immediately.

STEP 4: The Windows Clipboard

➤ Press **PgDn** to scroll toward the end of the document until you come to the paragraph beginning **It is up to you.** Select the sentence **Practice and practice some more** by dragging the mouse over the sentence. (Be sure to include the period.) The sentence will be selected as shown in Figure 2.4d.

➤ Pull down the **Edit menu** and click the **Copy command** or click the **Copy button** on the Standard toolbar.

➤ Press **Ctrl+End** to scroll to the end of the document. Press the **space bar.** Pull down the **Edit menu** and click the **Paste command** (or click the **Paste button** on the Standard toolbar).

➤ Move the insertion point to the end of the first paragraph (following the exclamation point after the word *wizard*). Press the **space bar.** Click the **Paste button** on the Standard toolbar to paste the sentence a second time.

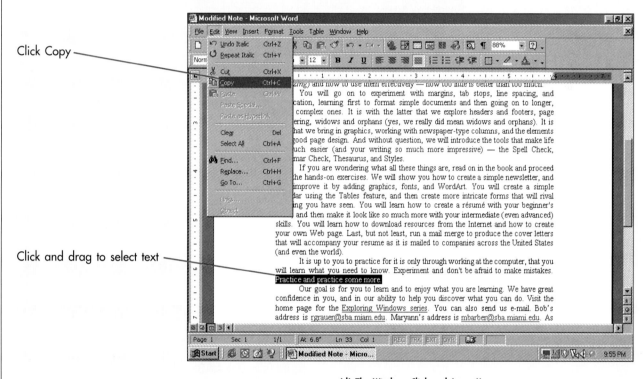

Click Copy

Click and drag to select text

(d) The Windows Clipboard (step 4)

FIGURE 2.4   Hands-on Exercise 1 (continued)

CUT, COPY, AND PASTE

Ctrl+X, Ctrl+C, and Ctrl+V are keyboard shortcuts to cut, copy, and paste, respectively. (The shortcuts are easier to remember when you realize that the operative letters X, C, and V are next to each other at the bottom left side of the keyboard.) You can also use the Cut, Copy, and Paste buttons on the Standard toolbar.

STEP 5: The Office Clipboard

➤ Pull down the **View menu,** click (or point to) the **Toolbars command,** then click **Clipboard** to display the Clipboard toolbar as shown in Figure 2.4e.

➤ Scroll down in the document until you can click and drag to select the two sentences that indicate you can send us e-mail, and that contain our e-mail addresses. Click the **Copy button** to copy these sentences to the Office clipboard, which now contains the icons for two Word documents.

➤ Press **Ctrl+End** to move to the end of the document, press **enter** to begin a new paragraph, and press the **Tab key** to indent the paragraph. Click the **Paste All button** on the Office clipboard to paste both items at the end of the document. (You may have to add a space between the two sentences.)

➤ Close the Clipboard toolbar.

Office Toolbar

Paste All button

Two different selections have been copied

Screen tip is displayed when you point to icon

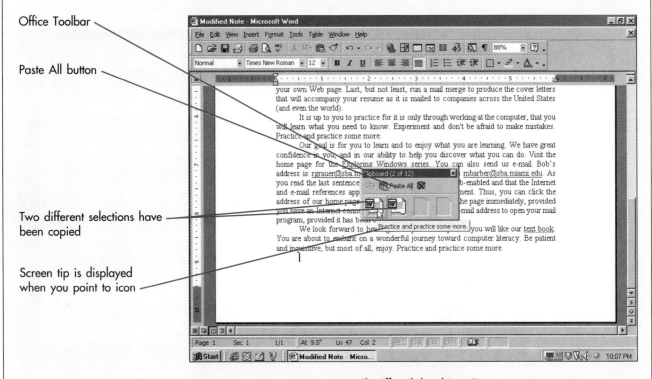

(e) The Office Clipboard (step 5)

FIGURE 2.4   Hands-on Exercise 1 (continued)

TWO DIFFERENT CLIPBOARDS

The Office clipboard is different from the Windows clipboard. Each successive copy operation adds an object to the Office clipboard (up to a maximum of 12 objects), whereas it replaces the contents of the Windows clipboard. Execution of the Paste command (via the Edit menu, Paste button, or Ctrl+V shortcut) pastes the contents of the Windows clipboard or the last item on the Office clipboard. The Office clipboard, however, lets you paste multiple objects. Note, too, that clearing the Office clipboard also clears the Windows clipboard.

STEP 6: Undo and Redo Commands

➤ Click the **drop-down arrow** next to the Undo button to display the previously executed actions as in Figure 2.4f. The list of actions corresponds to the editing commands you have issued since the start of the exercise. (Your list will be different from ours if you deviated from any instructions in the hands-on exercise.)

➤ Click **Paste** (the first command on the list) to undo the last editing command; the sentence asking you to send us e-mail disappears from the last paragraph.

➤ Click the **Undo** button a second time and the sentence, Practice and practice some more, disappears from the end of the first paragraph.

➤ Click the remaining steps on the undo list to retrace your steps through the exercise one command at a time. Alternatively, you can scroll to the bottom of the list and click the last command, which automatically undoes all of the preceding commands.

➤ Either way, when the undo list is empty, you will have the document as it existed at the start of the exercise.

➤ Click the **drop-down arrow** for the Redo command to display the list of commands you have undone.

➤ Click each command in sequence (or click the command at the bottom of the list) and you will restore the document.

➤ Save the document.

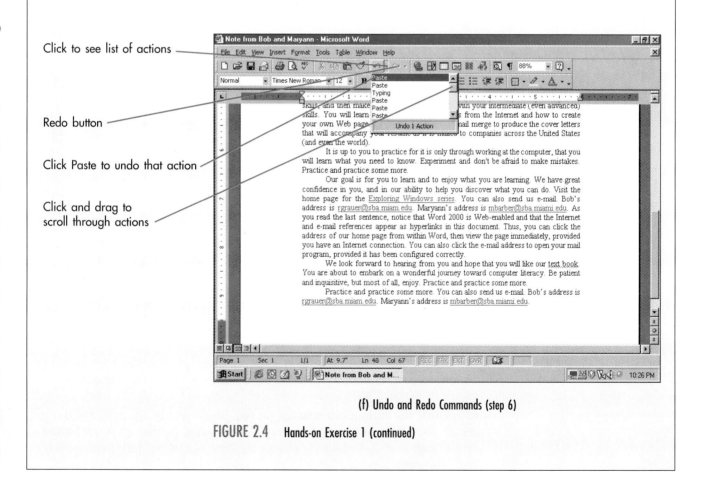

Click to see list of actions

Redo button

Click Paste to undo that action

Click and drag to
scroll through actions

(f) Undo and Redo Commands (step 6)

FIGURE 2.4   Hands-on Exercise 1 (continued)

STEP 7: Drag and Drop

➤ Click and drag to select the phrase **format specialized documents** (including the comma and space) as shown in Figure 2.4g, then drag the phrase to its new location immediately before the word *and*. (A dotted vertical bar appears as you drag the text, to indicate its new location.)

➤ Release the mouse button to complete the move.

➤ Click the **drop-down arrow** for the Undo command; click **Move** to undo the move.

➤ To copy the selected text to the same location (instead of moving it), press and hold the **Ctrl key** as you drag the text to its new location. (A plus sign appears as you drag the text, to indicate it is being copied rather than moved.)

➤ Practice the drag-and-drop procedure several times until you are confident you can move and copy with precision.

➤ Click anywhere in the document to deselect the text. Save the document.

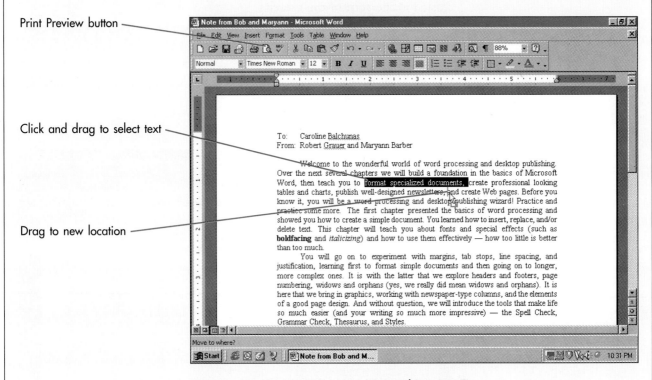

Print Preview button

Click and drag to select text

Drag to new location

(g) Drag and Drop (step 7)

FIGURE 2.4   Hands-on Exercise 1 (continued)

STEP 8: The Print Preview Command

➤ Pull down the **File menu** and click **Print Preview** (or click the **Print Preview button** on the Standard toolbar). You should see your entire document as shown in Figure 2.4h.

➤ Check that the entire document fits on one page—that is, check that you can see all three lines in the last paragraph. If not, click the **Shrink to Fit button** on the toolbar to automatically change the font size in the document to force it on one page.

Shrink to Fit button

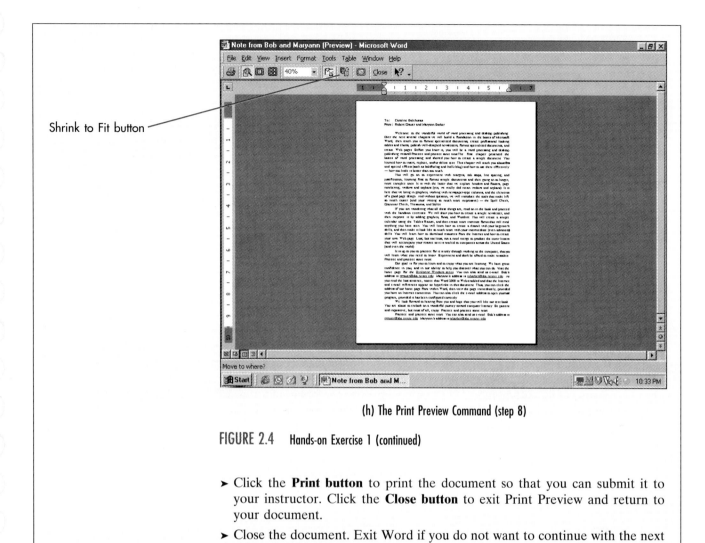

(h) The Print Preview Command (step 8)

FIGURE 2.4   Hands-on Exercise 1 (continued)

> Click the **Print button** to print the document so that you can submit it to your instructor. Click the **Close button** to exit Print Preview and return to your document.

> Close the document. Exit Word if you do not want to continue with the next exercise at this time.

TYPOGRAPHY

Typography is the process of selecting typefaces, type styles, and type sizes. The importance of these decisions is obvious, for the ultimate success of any document depends greatly on its appearance. Type should reinforce the message without calling attention to itself and should be consistent with the information you want to convey.

Typeface

A ***typeface*** or ***font*** is a complete set of characters (upper- and lowercase letters, numbers, punctuation marks, and special symbols). Figure 2.5 illustrates three typefaces—***Times New Roman, Arial,*** and ***Courier New***—that are supplied with Windows, and which in turn are accessible from any Windows application.

A definitive characteristic of any typeface is the presence or absence of tiny cross lines that end the main strokes of each letter. A ***serif*** typeface has these lines. A ***sans serif*** typeface (*sans* from the French for *without*) does not. Times New Roman and Courier New are examples of a serif typeface. Arial is a sans serif typeface.

Typography is the process of selecting typefaces, type styles, and type sizes. A serif typeface has tiny cross strokes that end the main strokes of each letter. A sans serif typeface does not have these strokes. Serif typefaces are typically used with large amounts of text. Sans serif typefaces are used for headings and limited amounts of text. A proportional typeface allocates space in accordance with the width of each character and is what you are used to seeing. A monospaced typeface uses the same amount of space for every character. A well-designed document will limit the number of typefaces so as not to overwhelm the reader.

(a) Times New Roman (serif and proportional)

Typography is the process of selecting typefaces, type styles, and type sizes. A serif typeface has tiny cross strokes that end the main strokes of each letter. A sans serif typeface does not have these strokes. Serif typefaces are typically used with large amounts of text. Sans serif typefaces are used for headings and limited amounts of text. A proportional typeface allocates space in accordance with the width of each character and is what you are used to seeing. A monospaced typeface uses the same amount of space for every character. A well-designed document will limit the number of typefaces so as not to overwhelm the reader.

(b) Arial (sans serif and proportional)

```
Typography is the process of selecting typefaces, type styles,
and type sizes. A serif typeface has tiny cross strokes that end
the main strokes of each letter. A sans serif typeface does not
have these strokes. Serif typefaces are typically used with large
amounts of text. Sans serif typefaces are used for headings and
limited amounts of text. A proportional typeface allocates space
in accordance with the width of each character and is what you
are used to seeing. A monospaced typeface uses the same amount of
space for every character. A well-designed document will limit
the number of typefaces so as not to overwhelm the reader.
```

(c) Courier New (serif and monospaced)

FIGURE 2.5   Typefaces

Serifs help the eye to connect one letter with the next and are generally used with large amounts of text. This book, for example, is set in a serif typeface. A sans serif typeface is more effective with smaller amounts of text and appears in headlines, corporate logos, airport signs, and so on.

A second characteristic of a typeface is whether it is monospaced or proportional. A **monospaced typeface** (e.g., Courier New) uses the same amount of space for every character regardless of its width. A **proportional typeface** (e.g., Times New Roman or Arial) allocates space according to the width of the character. Monospaced fonts are used in tables and financial projections where text must be precisely lined up, one character underneath the other. Proportional typefaces create a more professional appearance and are appropriate for most documents. Any typeface can be set in different **type styles** (such as regular, **bold,** or *italic*).

TYPOGRAPHY TIP—USE RESTRAINT

More is not better, especially in the case of too many typefaces and styles, which produce cluttered documents that impress no one. Try to limit yourself to a maximum of two typefaces per document, but choose multiple sizes and/or styles within those typefaces. Use boldface or italics for emphasis; but do so in moderation, because if you emphasize too many elements, the effect is lost.

Type Size

Type size is a vertical measurement and is specified in points. One **point** is equal to $\frac{1}{72}$ of an inch; that is, there are 72 points to the inch. The measurement is made from the top of the tallest letter in a character set (for example, an uppercase T) to the bottom of the lowest letter (for example, a lowercase y). Most documents are set in 10 or 12 point type. Newspaper columns may be set as small as 8 point type, but that is the smallest type size you should consider. Conversely, type sizes of 14 points or higher are ineffective for large amounts of text.

Figure 2.6 shows the same phrase set in varying type sizes. Some typefaces appear larger (smaller) than others even though they may be set in the same point size. The type in Figure 2.6a, for example, looks smaller than the corresponding type in Figure 2.6b even though both are set in the same point size. Note, too, that you can vary the type size of a specific font within a document for emphasis. The eye needs at least two points to distinguish between different type sizes.

Format Font Command

The **Format Font command** gives you complete control over the typeface, size, and style of the text in a document. Executing the command before entering text will set the format of the text you type from that point on. You can also use the command to change the font of existing text by selecting the text, then executing the command. Either way, you will see the dialog box in Figure 2.7, in which you specify the font (typeface), style, and point size.

You can choose any of the special effects (e.g., ~~strikethrough~~ or SMALL CAPS) and/or change the underline options (whether or not spaces are to be underlined). You can even change the color of the text on the monitor, but you need a color printer for the printed document. (The Character Spacing and Text Effects tabs produce different sets of options in which you control the spacing and appearance of the characters and are beyond the scope of our discussion.)

This is Arial 8 point type

This is Arial 10 point type

This is Arial 12 point type

This is Arial 18 point type

This is Arial 24 point type

This is Arial 30 point type

(a) Sans Serif Typeface

This is Times New Roman 8 point type

This is Times New Roman 10 point type

This is Times New Roman 12 point type

This is Times New Roman 18 point type

This is Times New Roman 24 point type

This is Times New Roman 30 point

(b) Serif Typeface

FIGURE 2.6   Type Size

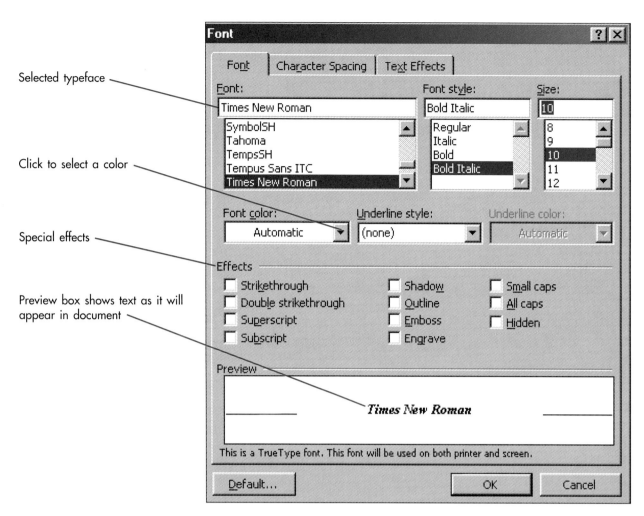

Selected typeface

Click to select a color

Special effects

Preview box shows text as it will
appear in document

FIGURE 2.7 Format Font Command

The Preview box shows the text as it will appear in the document. The message at the bottom of the dialog box indicates that Times New Roman is a TrueType font and that the same font will be used on both the screen and the monitor. TrueType fonts ensure that your document is truly WYSIWYG (What You See Is What You Get) because the fonts you see on the monitor will be identical to those in the printed document.

PAGE SETUP COMMAND

The *Page Setup command* in the File menu lets you change margins, paper size, orientation, paper source, and/or layout. All parameters are accessed from the dialog box in Figure 2.8 by clicking the appropriate tab within the dialog box.

The default margins are indicated in Figure 2.8a and are one inch on the top and bottom of the page, and one and a quarter inches on the left and right. You can change any (or all) of these settings by entering a new value in the appropriate text box, either by typing it explicitly or clicking the up/down arrow. All of the settings in the Page Setup command apply to the whole document regardless of the position of the insertion point. (Different settings for any option in the Page Setup dialog box can be established for different parts of a document by creating sections. Sections also affect column formatting, as discussed later in the chapter.)

Margin tab

Enter new value to change setting

Click to change setting

Preview box

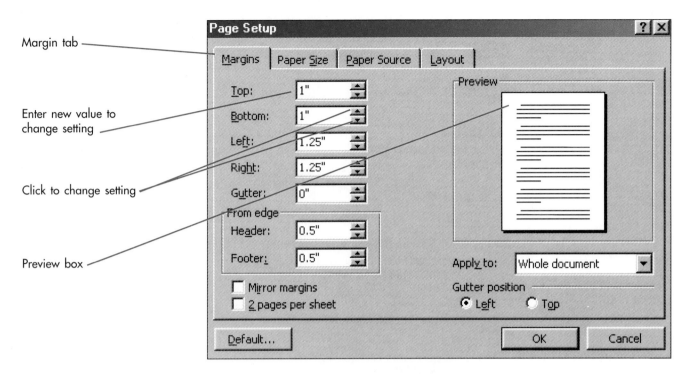

(a) Margins

Paper Size tab

Preview box

Click to select orientation

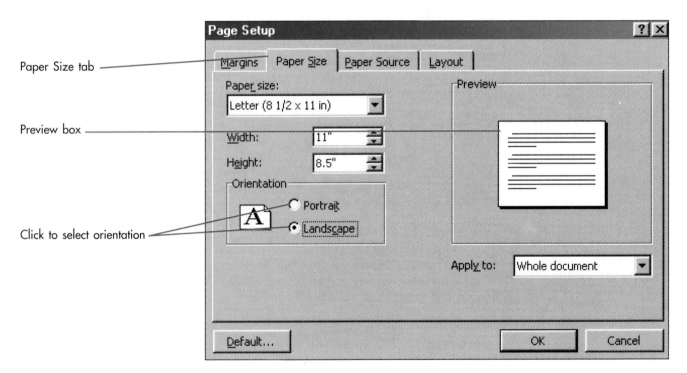

(b) Size and Orientation

FIGURE 2.8   Page Setup Command

The Paper Size tab within the Page Setup command enables you to change the orientation of a page as shown in Figure 2.8b. *Portrait orientation* is the default. *Landscape orientation* flips the page 90 degrees so that its dimensions are 11 × 8½ rather than the other way around. Note, too, the Preview area in both Figures 2.8a and 2.8b, which shows how the document will appear with the selected parameters.

The Paper Source tab is used to specify which tray should be used on printers with multiple trays, and is helpful when you want to load different types of paper simultaneously. The Layout tab is used to specify options for headers and footers (text that appears at the top or bottom of each page in a document), and/or to change the vertical alignment of text on the page.

Page Breaks

One of the first concepts you learned was that of word wrap, whereby Word inserts a soft return at the end of a line in order to begin a new line. The number and/or location of the soft returns change automatically as you add or delete text within a document. Soft returns are very different from the hard returns inserted by the user, whose number and location remain constant.

In much the same way, Word creates a *soft page break* to go to the top of a new page when text no longer fits on the current page. And just as you can insert a hard return to start a new paragraph, you can insert a *hard page break* to force any part of a document to begin on a new page. A hard page break is inserted into a document using the Break command in the Insert menu or more easily through the Ctrl+enter keyboard shortcut. (You can prevent the occurrence of awkward page breaks through the Format Paragraph command as described later in the chapter.)

AN EXERCISE IN DESIGN

The following exercise has you retrieve an existing document from the set of practice files, then experiment with various typefaces, type styles, and point sizes. The original document uses a monospaced (typewriter style) font, without boldface or italics, and you are asked to improve its appearance. The first step directs you to save the document under a new name so that you can always return to the original if necessary.

There is no right and wrong with respect to design, and you are free to choose any combination of fonts that appeals to you. The exercise takes you through various formatting options but lets you make the final decision. It does, however, ask you to print the final document and submit it to your instructor. Experiment freely and print multiple versions with different designs.

IMPOSE A TIME LIMIT

A word processor is supposed to save time and make you more productive. It will do exactly that, provided you use the word processor for its primary purpose—writing and editing. It is all too easy, however, to lose sight of that objective and spend too much time formatting the document. Concentrate on the content of your document rather than its appearance. Impose a time limit on the amount of time you will spend on formatting. End the session when the limit is reached.

Objective: To experiment with character formatting; to change fonts and to use boldface and italics; to copy formatting with the format painter; to insert a page break and see different views of a document. Use Figure 2.9 as a guide in the exercise.

STEP 1: Open the Existing Document

➤ Start Word. Pull down the **File menu** and click **Open** (or click the **Open button** on the toolbar). To open a file:

- Click the **drop-down arrow** on the Look In list box. Click the appropriate drive, drive C or drive A, depending on the location of your data.
- Double click the **Exploring Word folder** to make it the active folder (the folder in which you will open and save the document).
- Scroll in the **Open list box** (if necessary) until you can click **Tips for Writing** to select this document.

➤ Double click the **document icon** or click the **Open command button** to open the file.

➤ Pull down the **File menu.** Click the **Save As command** to save the document as **Modified Tips.**

➤ Pull down the **View menu** and click **Normal** (or click the **Normal View button** above the status bar).

➤ Set the magnification (zoom) to **Page Width.**

SELECTING TEXT

The selection bar, a blank column at the far left of the document window, makes it easy to select a line, paragraph, or the entire document. To select a line, move the mouse pointer to the selection bar, point to the line and click the left mouse button. To select a paragraph, move the mouse pointer to the selection bar, point to any line in the paragraph, and double click the mouse. To select the entire document, move the mouse pointer to the selection bar and press the Ctrl key while you click the mouse.

STEP 2: The Right Mouse Button

➤ Select the first tip as shown in Figure 2.9a. Point to the selected text and click the **right mouse button** to display a context-sensitive or shortcut menu.

➤ Click outside the menu to close the menu without executing a command.

➤ Press the **Ctrl key** as you click the selection bar to select the entire document, then click the **right mouse button** to display the shortcut menu.

➤ Click **Font** to execute the Format Font command.

Open button

Selection bar

Point to selected text and click right mouse button to display shortcut menu

Normal View button

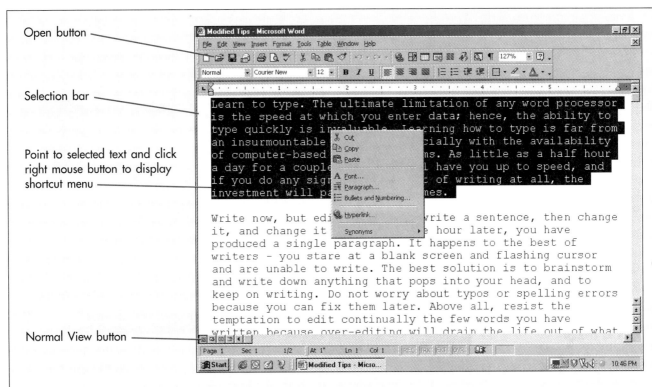

(a) The Right Mouse Button (step 2)

FIGURE 2.9   Hands-on Exercise 2

STEP 3: The Format Font Command

➤ Click the **down arrow** on the Font list box of Figure 2.9b to scroll through the available fonts. Select a different font, such as Times New Roman.

➤ Click the **down arrow** in the Font Size list box to choose a point size.

➤ Click **OK** to change the font and point size for the selected text.

➤ Pull down the **Edit menu** and click **Undo** (or click the **Undo button** on the Standard toolbar) to return to the original font.

➤ Experiment with different fonts and/or different point sizes until you are satisfied with the selection. We chose 12 point Times New Roman.

FIND AND REPLACE FORMATTING

The Replace command enables you to replace formatting as well as text. To replace any text set in bold with the same text in italics, pull down the Edit menu, and click the Replace command. Click the Find what text box, but do *not* enter any text. Click the More button to expand the dialog box. Click the Format command button, click Font, click Bold in the Font Style list, and click OK. Click the Replace with text box and again do *not* enter any text. Click the Format command button, click Font, click Italic in the Font Style list, and click OK. Click the Find Next or Replace All command button to do selective or automatic replacement. Use a similar technique to replace one font with another.

Undo button

Click to scroll through
available fonts

Click to scroll through
available font sizes

Click to change
underlining options

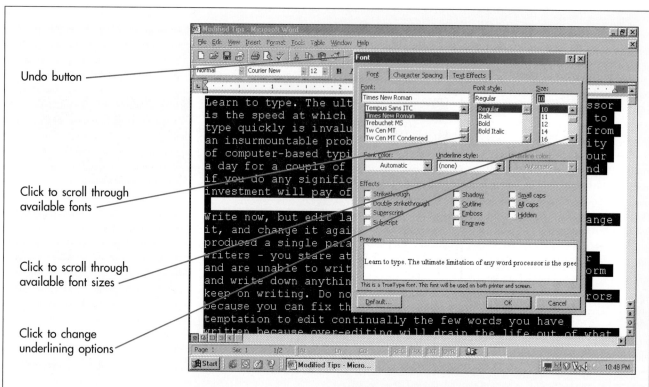

(b) The Format Command (step 3)

FIGURE 2.9   Hands-on Exercise 2 (continued)

STEP 4: Boldface and Italics

➤ Select the sentence **Learn to type** at the beginning of the document.

➤ Click the **Italic button** on the Formatting toolbar to italicize the selected phrase, which will remain selected after the italics take effect.

➤ Click the **Bold button** to boldface the selected text. The text is now in bold italic.

➤ Experiment with different styles (bold, italics, underlining, or bold italic) until you are satisfied. The Italic, Bold, and Underline buttons function as toggle switches; that is, clicking the Italic button when text is already italicized returns the text to normal.

➤ Save the document

UNDERLINING TEXT

Underlining is less popular than it was, but Word provides a complete range of underlining options. Select the text to underline, pull down the Format menu, click Font to display the Font dialog box, and click the Font tab if necessary. Click the down arrow on the Underline Style list box to choose the type of underlining you want. You can choose whether to underline the words only (i.e., the underline does not appear in the space between words). You can also choose the type of line you want—solid, dashed, thick, or thin.

STEP 5: The Format Painter

➤ Click anywhere within the sentence Learn to Type. **Double click** the **Format Painter button** on the Standard toolbar. The mouse pointer changes to a paintbrush as shown in Figure 2.9c.

➤ Drag the mouse pointer over the next title, **Write now, but edit later,** and release the mouse. The formatting from the original sentence (bold italic as shown in Figure 2.9c) has been applied to this sentence as well.

➤ Drag the mouse pointer (in the shape of a paintbrush) over the remaining titles (the first sentence in each paragraph) to copy the formatting.

➤ Click the **Format Painter button** after you have painted the title of the last tip to turn the feature off.

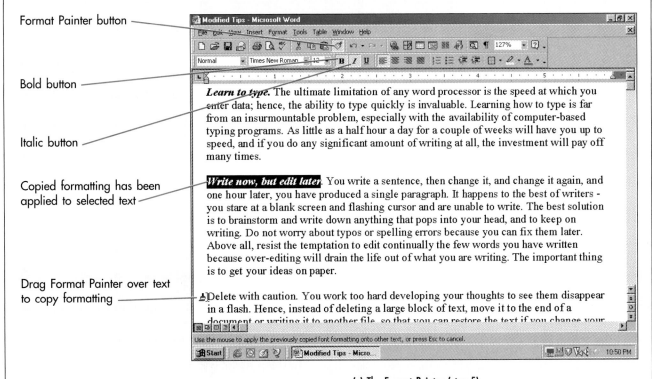

Format Painter button

Bold button

Italic button

Copied formatting has been applied to selected text

Drag Format Painter over text to copy formatting

(c) The Format Painter (step 5)

FIGURE 2.9   Hands-on Exercise 2 (continued)

THE FORMAT PAINTER

The Format Painter copies the formatting of the selected text to other places in a document. Select the text with the formatting you want to copy, then click or double click the Format Painter button on the Standard toolbar. Clicking the button will paint only one selection. Double clicking the button will paint multiple selections until the feature is turned off by again clicking the Format Painter button. Either way, the mouse pointer changes to a paintbrush, which you can drag over text to give it the identical formatting characteristics as the original selection.

STEP 6: Change Margins

➤ Press **Ctrl+End** to move to the end of the document as shown in Figure 2.9d. You will see a dotted line indicating a soft page break. (If you do not see the page break, it means that your document fits on one page because you used a different font and/or a smaller point size. We used 12 point Times New Roman.)

➤ Pull down the **File menu.** Click **Page Setup.** Click the **Margins tab** if necessary. Change the bottom margin to **.75** inch. Check that these settings apply to the **Whole Document.** Click **OK.**

➤ The page break disappears because more text fits on the page.

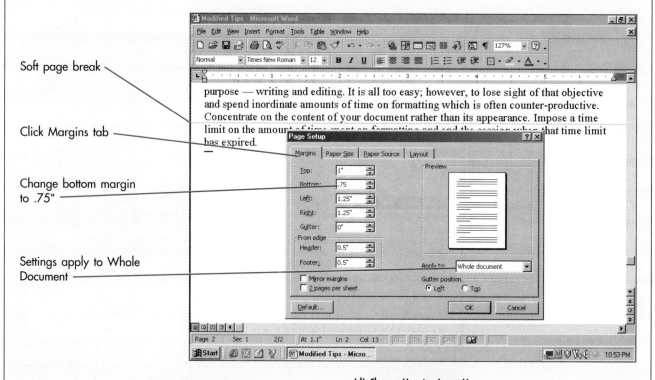

Soft page break

Click Margins tab

Change bottom margin to .75"

Settings apply to Whole Document

(d) Change Margins (step 6)

FIGURE 2.9   Hands-on Exercise 2 (continued)

DIALOG BOX SHORTCUTS

You can use keyboard shortcuts to select options in a dialog box. Press Tab (Shift+Tab) to move forward (backward) from one field or command button to the next. Press Alt plus the underlined letter to move directly to a field or command button. Press enter to activate the selected command button. Press Esc to exit the dialog box without taking action. Press the space bar to toggle check boxes on or off. Press the down arrow to open a drop-down list box once the list has been accessed, then press the up or down arrow to move between options in a list box.

STEP 7: Create the Title Page

➤ Press **Ctrl+Home** to move to the beginning of the document. Press **enter** three or four times to add a few blank lines.

➤ Press **Ctrl+enter** to insert a hard page break. You will see the words "Page Break" in the middle of a dotted line as shown in Figure 2.9e.

➤ Press the **up arrow key** three times. Enter the title **Tips for Writing.** Select the title, and format it in a larger point size, such as 24 points.

➤ Enter your name on the next line and format it in a different point size, such as 14 points. Select both the title and your name as shown in the figure. Click the **Center button** on the Formatting toolbar. Save the document.

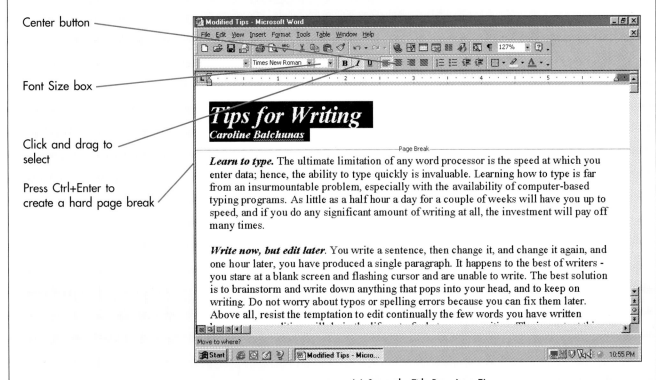

Center button

Font Size box

Click and drag to select

Press Ctrl+Enter to create a hard page break

(e) Create the Title Page (step 7)

FIGURE 2.9   Hands-on Exercise 2 (continued)

DOUBLE CLICK AND TYPE

Creating a title page is a breeze if you take advantage of the (double) click and type feature in Word 2000. Pull down the View menu and change to the Print Layout view, then look closely at the mouse pointer and notice the horizontal lines that surround the I-beam shape. Double click anywhere on the page and you can begin typing immediately at that location, without having to type several blank lines, or set tabs. The feature does not work in the Normal view or in a document that has columns. To enable (disable) the feature, pull down the Tools menu, click the Options command, click the Edit tab, then check (clear) the Enable Click and Type check box.

STEP 8: The Completed Document

➤ Pull down the **View menu** and click **Print Layout** (or click the **Print Layout button** above the status bar).

➤ Click the **Zoom Control arrow** on the Standard toolbar and select **Two Pages.** Release the mouse to view the completed document in Figure 2.9f. You may want to add additional blank lines at the top of the title page to move the title further down on the page.

➤ Save the document a final time. Exit Word if you do not want to continue with the next exercise at this time.

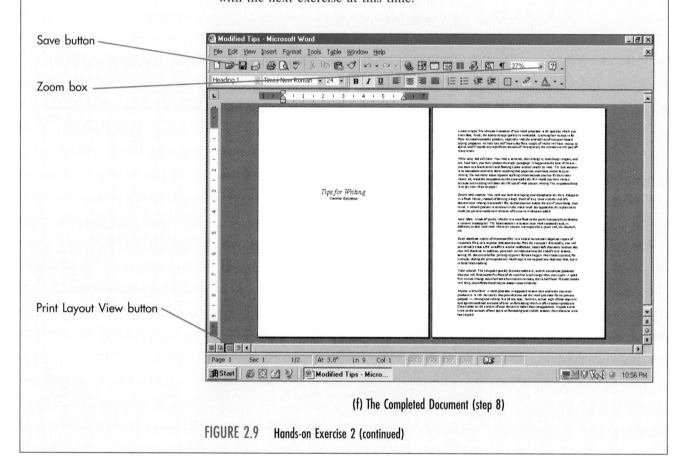

Save button

Zoom box

Print Layout View button

(f) The Completed Document (step 8)

FIGURE 2.9   Hands-on Exercise 2 (continued)

PARAGRAPH FORMATTING

A change in typography is only one way to alter the appearance of a document. You can also change the alignment, indentation, tab stops, or line spacing for any paragraph(s) within the document. You can control the pagination and prevent the occurrence of awkward page breaks by specifying that an entire paragraph has to appear on the same page, or that a one-line paragraph (e.g., a heading) should appear on the same page as the next paragraph. You can include borders or shading for added emphasis around selected paragraphs.

All of these features are implemented at the paragraph level and affect all selected paragraphs. If no paragraphs are selected, the commands affect the entire current paragraph (the paragraph containing the insertion point), regardless of the position of the insertion point when the command is executed.

Alignment

Text can be aligned in four different ways as shown in Figure 2.10. It may be justified (flush left/flush right), left aligned (flush left with a ragged right margin), right aligned (flush right with a ragged left margin), or centered within the margins (ragged left and right).

Left aligned text is perhaps the easiest to read. The first letters of each line align with each other, helping the eye to find the beginning of each line. The lines themselves are of irregular length. There is uniform spacing between words, and the ragged margin on the right adds white space to the text, giving it a lighter and more informal look.

Justified text produces lines of equal length, with the spacing between words adjusted to align at the margins. It may be more difficult to read than text that is left aligned because of the uneven (sometimes excessive) word spacing and/or the greater number of hyphenated words needed to justify the lines.

Type that is centered or right aligned is restricted to limited amounts of text where the effect is more important than the ease of reading. Centered text, for example, appears frequently on wedding invitations, poems, or formal announcements. Right aligned text is used with figure captions and short headlines.

Indents

Individual paragraphs can be indented so that they appear to have different margins from the rest of a document. Indentation is established at the paragraph level; thus different indentation can be in effect for different paragraphs. One paragraph may be indented from the left margin only, another from the right margin only, and a third from both the left and right margins. The first line of any paragraph may be indented differently from the rest of the paragraph. And finally, a paragraph may be set with no indentation at all, so that it aligns on the left and right margins.

The indentation of a paragraph is determined by three settings: the *left indent,* the *right indent,* and a *special indent* (if any). There are two types of special indentation, first line and hanging, as will be explained shortly. The left and right indents are set to zero by default, as is the special indent, and produce a paragraph with no indentation at all as shown in Figure 2.11a. Positive values for the left and right indents offset the paragraph from both margins as shown in Figure 2.11b.

The *first line indent* (Figure 2.11c) affects only the first line in the paragraph and is implemented by pressing the Tab key at the beginning of the paragraph. A *hanging indent* (Figure 2.11d) sets the first line of a paragraph at the left indent and indents the remaining lines according to the amount specified. Hanging indents are often used with bulleted or numbered lists.

INDENTS VERSUS MARGINS

Indents measure the distance between the text and the margins. Margins mark the distance from the text to the edge of the page. Indents are determined at the paragraph level, whereas margins are established at the section (document) level. The left and right margins are set (by default) to 1.25 inches each; the left and right indents default to zero. The first line indent is measured from the setting of the left indent.

We, the people of the United States, in order to form a more perfect Union, establish justice, insure domestic tranquillity, provide for the common defense, promote the general welfare, and secure the blessings of liberty to ourselves and our posterity, do ordain and establish this Constitution for the United States of America.

(a) Justified (flush left/flush right)

We, the people of the United States, in order to form a more perfect Union, establish justice, insure domestic tranquillity, provide for the common defense, promote the general welfare, and secure the blessings of liberty to ourselves and our posterity, do ordain and establish this Constitution for the United States of America.

(b) Left Aligned (flush left/ragged right)

We, the people of the United States, in order to form a more perfect Union, establish justice, insure domestic tranquillity, provide for the common defense, promote the general welfare, and secure the blessings of liberty to ourselves and our posterity, do ordain and establish this Constitution for the United States of America.

(c) Right Aligned (ragged left/flush right)

We, the people of the United States, in order to form a more perfect Union, establish justice, insure domestic tranquillity, provide for the common defense, promote the general welfare, and secure the blessings of liberty to ourselves and our posterity, do ordain and establish this Constitution for the United States of America.

(d) Centered (ragged left/ragged right)

FIGURE 2.10   Alignment

The left and right indents are defined as the distance between the text and the left and right margins, respectively. Both parameters are set to zero in this paragraph and so the text aligns on both margins. Different indentation can be applied to different paragraphs in the same document.

(a) No Indents

Positive values for the left and right indents offset a paragraph from the rest of a document and are often used for long quotations. This paragraph has left and right indents of one-half inch each. Different indentation can be applied to different paragraphs in the same document.

(b) Left and Right Indents

A first line indent affects only the first line in the paragraph and is implemented by pressing the Tab key at the beginning of the paragraph. The remainder of the paragraph is aligned at the left margin (or the left indent if it differs from the left margin) as can be seen from this example. Different indentation can be applied to different paragraphs in the same document.

(c) First Line Indent

A hanging indent sets the first line of a paragraph at the left indent and indents the remaining lines according to the amount specified. Hanging indents are often used with bulleted or numbered lists. Different indentation can be applied to different paragraphs in the same document.

(d) Hanging (Special) Indent

FIGURE 2.11   Indents

Tabs

Anyone who has used a typewriter is familiar with the function of the Tab key; that is, press Tab and the insertion point moves to the next *tab stop* (a measured position to align text at a specific place). The Tab key is much more powerful in Word as you can choose from four different types of tab stops (left, center, right, and decimal). You can also specify a *leader character,* typically dots or hyphens, to draw the reader's eye across the page. Tabs are often used to create columns of text within a document.

The default tab stops are set every ½ inch and are left aligned, but you can change the alignment and/or position with the Format Tabs command. Figure 2.12 illustrates a dot leader in combination with a right tab to produce a Table of Contents. The default tab stops have been cleared in Figure 2.12a, in favor of a single right tab at 5.5 inches. The option button for a dot leader has also been checked. The resulting document is shown in Figure 2.12b.

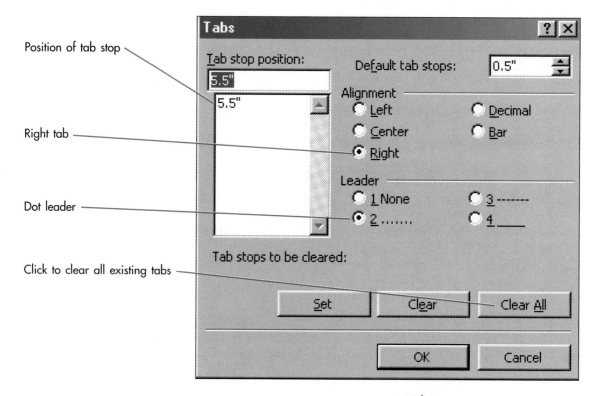

(a) Tab Stops

Right tab with dot leader

(b) Table of Contents

FIGURE 2.12   Tabs

Hyphenation

Hyphenation gives a document a more professional look by eliminating excessive gaps of white space. It is especially useful in narrow columns and/or justified text. Hyphenation is implemented through the Language command in the Tools menu. You can choose to hyphenate a document automatically, in which case the hyphens are inserted as the document is created. (Microsoft Word will automatically rehyphenate the document to adjust for subsequent changes in editing.)

You can also hyphenate a document manually, to have Word prompt you prior to inserting each hyphen. Manual hyphenation does not, however, adjust for changes that affect the line breaks, and so it should be done only after the document is complete. And finally, you can fine-tune the use of hyphenation by preventing a hyphenated word from breaking if it falls at the end of a line. This is done by inserting a ***nonbreaking hyphen*** (press Ctrl+Shift+Hyphen) when the word is typed initially.

Line Spacing

Line spacing determines the space between the lines in a paragraph. Word provides complete flexibility and enables you to select any multiple of line spacing (single, double, line and a half, and so on). You can also specify line spacing in terms of points (there are 72 points per inch).

Line spacing is set at the paragraph level through the Format Paragraph command, which sets the spacing within a paragraph. The command also enables you to add extra spacing before the first line in a paragraph or after the last line. (Either technique is preferable to the common practice of single spacing the paragraphs within a document, then adding a blank line between paragraphs.)

FORMAT PARAGRAPH COMMAND

The ***Format Paragraph command*** is used to specify the alignment, indentation, line spacing, and pagination for the selected paragraph(s). As indicated, all of these features are implemented at the paragraph level and affect all selected paragraphs. If no paragraphs are selected, the command affects the entire current paragraph (the paragraph containing the insertion point).

The Format Paragraph command is illustrated in Figure 2.13. The Indents and Spacing tab in Figure 2.13a calls for a hanging indent, line spacing of 1.5 lines, and justified alignment. The preview area within the dialog box enables you to see how the paragraph will appear within the document.

The Line and Page Breaks tab in Figure 2.13b illustrates an entirely different set of parameters in which you control the pagination within a document. The check boxes in Figure 2.13b enable you to prevent the occurrence of awkward soft page breaks that detract from the appearance of a document.

You might, for example, want to prevent widows and orphans, terms used to describe isolated lines that seem out of place. A *widow* refers to the last line of a paragraph appearing by itself at the top of a page. An *orphan* is the first line of a paragraph appearing by itself at the bottom of a page.

You can also impose additional controls by clicking one or more check boxes. Use the Keep Lines Together option to prevent a soft page break from occurring within a paragraph and ensure that the entire paragraph appears on the same page. (The paragraph is moved to the top of the next page if it doesn't fit on the bottom of the current page.) Use the Keep with Next option to prevent a soft page break between the two paragraphs. This option is typically used to keep a heading (a one-line paragraph) with its associated text in the next paragraph.

Indents and Spacing tab

Full justification

Hanging indent

Preview of paragraph formatting selected

1½ line spacing

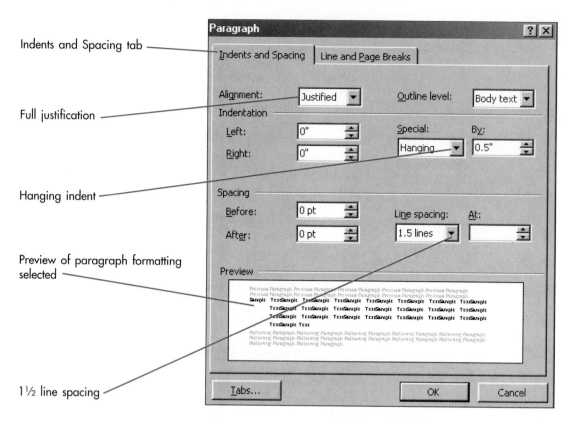

(a) Indents and Spacing

Line and Page Breaks tab

Options to control soft page breaks

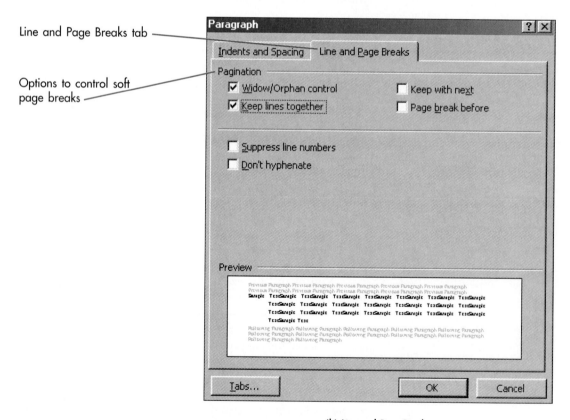

(b) Line and Page Breaks

FIGURE 2.13   Format Paragraph Command

Borders and Shading

The **Borders and Shading command** puts the finishing touches on a document and is illustrated in Figure 2.14. The command is applied to selected text within a paragraph or to the entire paragraph if no text is selected. Thus, you can create boxed and/or shaded text as well as place horizontal or vertical lines around a paragraph. You can choose from several different line styles in any color (assuming you have a color printer). You can place a uniform border around a paragraph (choose Box), or you can choose a shadow effect with thicker lines at the right and bottom. You can also apply lines to selected sides of a paragraph(s) by selecting a line style, then clicking the desired sides as appropriate.

Shading is implemented independently of the border. Clear (no shading) is the default. Solid (100%) shading creates a solid box where the text is turned white so you can read it. Shading of 10 or 20 percent is generally most effective to add emphasis to the selected paragraph. The Borders and Shading command is implemented on the paragraph level and affects the entire paragraph—either the current or selected paragraph(s).

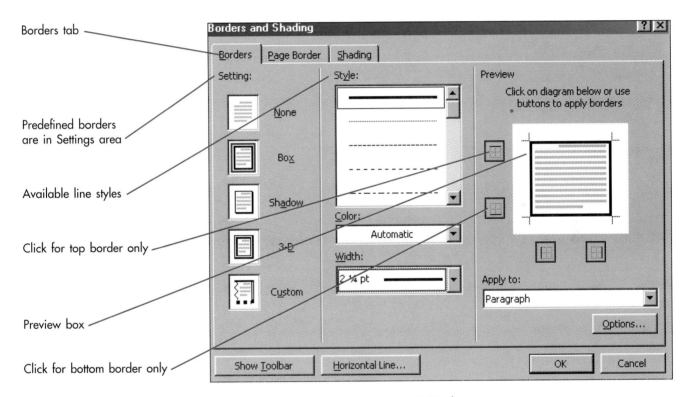

Borders tab

Predefined borders are in Settings area

Available line styles

Click for top border only

Preview box

Click for bottom border only

(a) Borders

FIGURE 2.14   Paragraph Borders and Shading

FORMATTING AND THE PARAGRAPH MARK

The paragraph mark ¶ at the end of a paragraph does more than just indicate the presence of a hard return. It also stores all of the formatting in effect for the paragraph. Hence in order to preserve the formatting when you move or copy a paragraph, you must include the paragraph mark in the selected text. Click the Show/Hide ¶ button on the toolbar to display the paragraph mark and make sure it has been selected.

Columns add interest to a document and are implemented through the **Columns command** in the Format menu as shown in Figure 2.15. You specify the number of columns and, optionally, the space between columns. Microsoft Word does the rest, calculating the width of each column according to the left and right margins on the page and the specified (default) space between columns.

The dialog box in Figure 2.15 implements a design of three equal columns. The 2-inch width of each column is computed automatically based on left and right page margins of 1 inch each and the ¼-inch spacing between columns. The width of each column is determined by subtracting the sum of the margins and the space between the columns (a total of 2½ inches in this example) from the page width of 8½ inches. The result of the subtraction is 6 inches, which is divided by 3, resulting in a column width of 2 inches.

There is, however, one subtlety associated with column formatting, and that is the introduction of the **section,** which controls elements such as the orientation of a page (landscape or portrait), margins, page numbers, and/or the number of columns. All of the documents in the text thus far have consisted of a single section, and therefore section formatting was not an issue. It becomes important only when you want to vary an element that is formatted at the section level. You could, for example, use section formatting to create a document that has one column on its title page and two columns on the remaining pages. This requires you to divide the document two sections through insertion of a **section break.** You then format each section independently and specify the number of columns in each section.

Preset design ————

Column width is calculated automatically ————

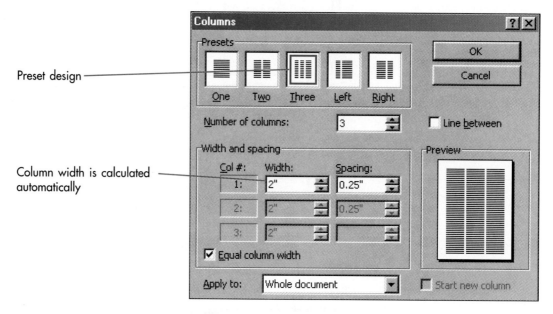

FIGURE 2.15 The Format Columns Command

THE SECTION VERSUS THE PARAGRAPH

Line spacing, alignment, tabs, and indents are implemented at the paragraph level. Change any of these parameters anywhere within the current (or selected) paragraph(s) and you change *only* those paragraph(s). Margins, page numbering, orientation, and columns are implemented at the section level. Change these parameters anywhere within a section and you change the characteristics of every page within that section.

Paragraph Formatting

Objective: To implement line spacing, alignment, and indents; to implement widow and orphan protection; to box and shade a selected paragraph.

STEP 1: Select-Then-Do

➤ Open the **Modified Tips** document from the previous exercise. If necessary, change to the Print Layout view. Click the **Zoom drop-down arrow** and click **Two Pages** to match the view in Figure 2.16a.

➤ Select the entire second page as shown in the figure. Point to the selected text and click the **right mouse button** to produce the shortcut menu. Click **Paragraph.**

Zoom box

Select text on page two

Point to selected text and click right mouse button to display shortcut menu

Print Layout View button

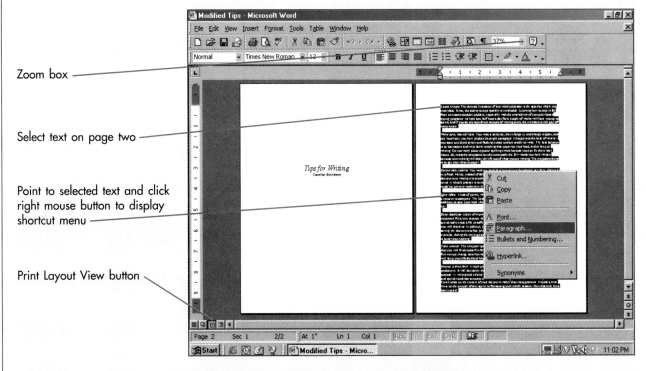

(a) Select-Then-Do (step 1)

FIGURE 2.16   Hands-on Exercise 3

SELECT TEXT WITH THE F8 EXTEND KEY

Move to the beginning of the text you want to select, then press the F8 (extend) key. The letters EXT will appear in the status bar. Use the arrow keys to extend the selection in the indicated direction; for example, press the down arrow key to select the line. You can also press any character—for example, a letter, space, or period—to extend the selection to the first occurrence of that character. Press Esc to cancel the selection mode.

STEP 2: Line Spacing, Justification, and Pagination

➤ If necessary, click the **Indents and Spacing tab** to view the options in Figure 2.16b.

- Click the **down arrow** on the list box for Line Spacing and select **1.5 Lines.**

- Click the **down arrow** on the Alignment list box and select **Justified** as shown in Figure 2.16b.

- The Preview area shows the effect of these settings.

➤ Click the tab for **Line and Page Breaks.**

- Check the box for **Keep Lines Together.** If necessary, check the box for **Widow/Orphan Control.**

➤ Click **OK** to accept all of the settings in the dialog box.

➤ Click anywhere in the document to deselect the text and see the effects of the formatting changes:

- The document is fully justified and the line spacing has increased.

- The document now extends to three pages, with the fifth, sixth, and seventh paragraphs appearing on the last page.

- There is a large bottom margin on the second page as a consequence of keeping the lines together in paragraph five.

➤ Save the document.

Click Indents and Spacing tab

Click to select alignment

Click to select line spacing

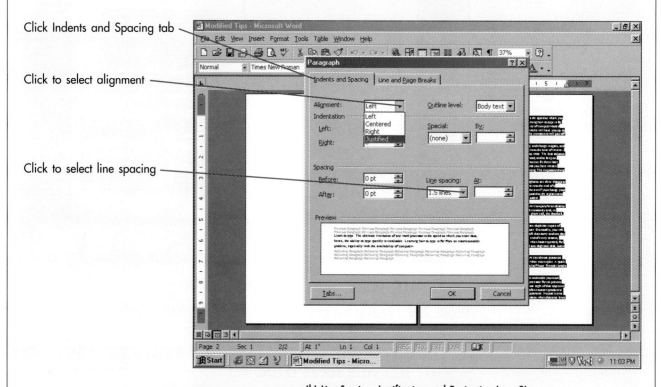

(b) Line Spacing, Justification, and Pagination (step 2)

FIGURE 2.16   Hands-on Exercise 3 (continued)

STEP 3: Indents

➤ Select the second paragraph as shown in Figure 2.16c. (The second paragraph will not yet be indented.)

➤ Pull down the **Format menu** and click **Paragraph** (or press the **right mouse button** to produce the shortcut menu and click **Paragraph**).

➤ If necessary, click the **Indents and Spacing tab** in the Paragraph dialog box. Click the **up arrow** on the Left Indentation text box to set the **Left Indent** to **.5** inch. Set the **Right indent** to **.5** inch. Click **OK.** Your document should match Figure 2.16c.

➤ Save the document.

Click and drag to set right indent

Click and drag to set left indent and first line indent at same time

Select paragraph two

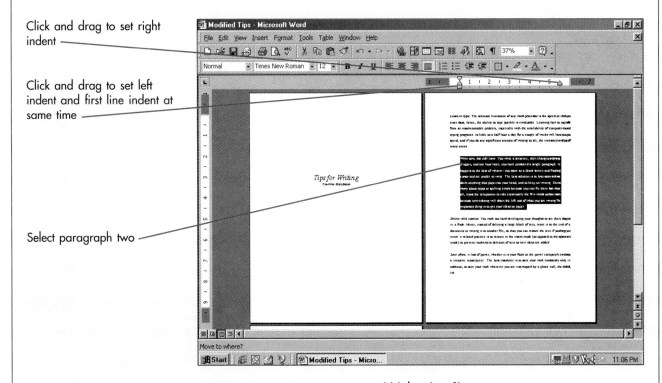

(c) Indents (step 3)

FIGURE 2.16   Hands-on Exercise 3 (continued)

INDENTS AND THE RULER

Use the ruler to change the special, left, and/or right indents. Select the paragraph (or paragraphs) in which you want to change indents, then drag the appropriate indent markers to the new location(s). If you get a hanging indent when you wanted to change the left indent, it means you dragged the bottom triangle instead of the box. Click the Undo button and try again. (You can always use the Format Paragraph command rather than the ruler if you continue to have difficulty.)

STEP 4: Borders and Shading

➤ Pull down the **Format menu.** Click **Borders and Shading** to produce the dialog box in Figure 2.16d.

➤ If necessary, click the **Borders tab.** Select a style and width for the line around the box. Click the rectangle labeled **Box** under Setting.

➤ Click the **Shading Tab.** Click the **down arrow** on the Style list box. Click **10%.**

➤ Click **OK** to accept the settings for both Borders and Shading. Click outside the paragraph.

➤ Save the document.

Click Borders tab

Select a line style

Click Box style

Select a line width

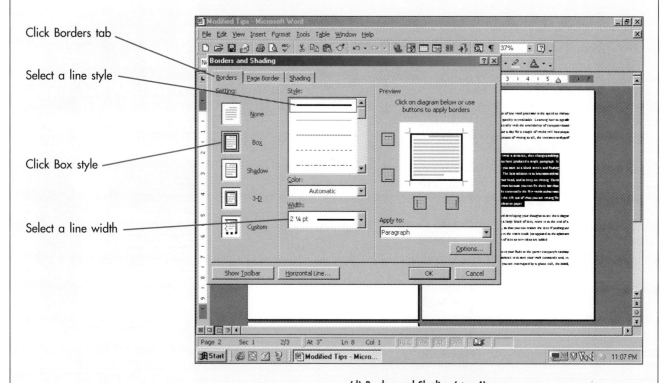

(d) Borders and Shading (step 4)

FIGURE 2.16   Hands-on Exercise 3 (continued)

THE PAGE BORDER COMMAND

You can apply a border to the title page of your document, to every page except the title page, or to every page including the title page. Pull down the Format menu, click Borders and Shading, and click the Page Borders tab. First design the border by selecting a style, color, width, and art (if any). Then choose the page(s) to which you want to apply the border by clicking the drop-down arrow in the Apply to list box. Close the Borders and Shading dialog box. See practice exercise 5 at the end of the chapter.

STEP 5: Help with Formatting

➤ Pull down the **Help menu** and click the **What's This command** (or press **Shift+F1**). The mouse pointer changes to an arrow with a question mark.

➤ Click anywhere inside the boxed paragraph to display the formatting information shown in Figure 2.16e.

➤ Click in a different paragraph to see its formatting. Press the **Esc key** to return the pointer to normal.

DISPLAY THE HARD RETURNS

Many formattting commands are implemented at the paragraph level, and thus it helps to know where a paragraph ends. Click the Show/Hide ¶ button on the Standard toolbar to display the hard returns (paragraph marks) and other nonprinting characters (such as tab characters or blank spaces) contained within a document. The Show/Hide ¶ functions as a toggle switch; the first time you click it the hard returns are displayed, the second time you press it the returns are hidden, and so on.

STEP 6: The Zoom Command

➤ Pull down the **View menu.** Click **Zoom** to produce the dialog box in Figure 2.16f. Click the **Many Pages** option button.

➤ Click the **monitor icon** to display a sample selection box, then click and drag to display three pages across. Release the mouse. Click **OK.**

STEP 7: Help for Word 2000

➤ Display the Office Assistant if it is not already visible on your screen. Pull down the **Help menu** and click the command to **Show the Office Assistant.**

➤ Ask the Assistant a question, then press the **Search button** in the Assistant's balloon to look for the answer. Select (click) the appropriate topic from the list of suggested topics provided by the Assistant.

➤ Click the **Show button** in the Help window that is displayed by the Assistant, then use either the **Contents** or **Index tab** to search for additional information. Close the Help window.

➤ If you have an Internet connection, pull down the **Help menu** and click **Microsoft on the Web** to connect to the Microsoft Web site for additional information. Explore the site, then close the browser and return to your document.

ADVICE FROM THE OFFICE ASSISTANT

The Office Assistant indicates it has a suggestion by displaying a lightbulb. Click the lightbulb to display the tip, then click the OK button to close the balloon and continue working. The Assistant will not, however, repeat a tip from an earlier session unless you reset it at the start of a new session. This is especially important in a laboratory situation where you are sharing a computer with many students. To reset the tips, click the Assistant to display a balloon asking what you want to do, click the Options button in the balloon, click the Options tab, then click the button to Reset my Tips.

Paragraph formatting in effect

Click to display formatting specifications

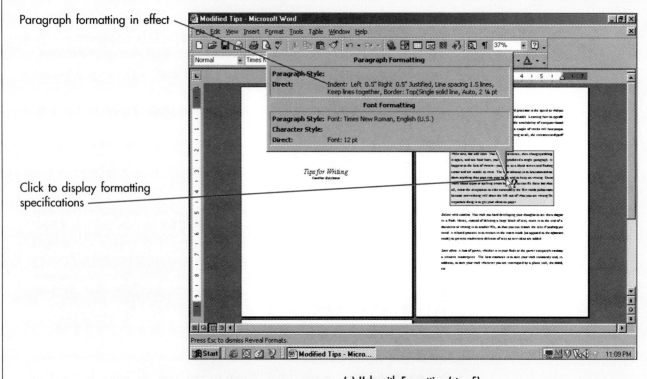

(e) Help with Formatting (step 5)

Many Pages option button

Monitor icon

Click and drag over three pages in same row of grid

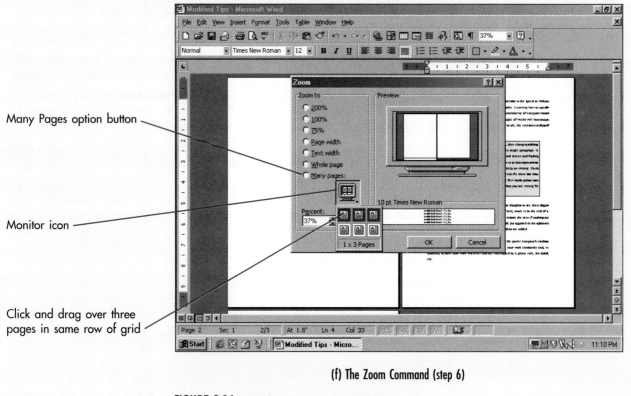

(f) The Zoom Command (step 6)

FIGURE 2.16   Hands-on Exercise 3 (continued)

STEP 8: The Completed Document

➤ Your screen should match the one in Figure 2.16g, which displays all three pages of the document.

➤ The Print Layout view displays both a vertical and a horizontal ruler. The boxed and indented paragraph is clearly shown in the second page.

➤ The soft page break between pages two and three occurs between tips rather than within a tip; that is, the text of each tip is kept together on the same page.

➤ Save the document a final time. Print the completed document and submit it to your instructor.

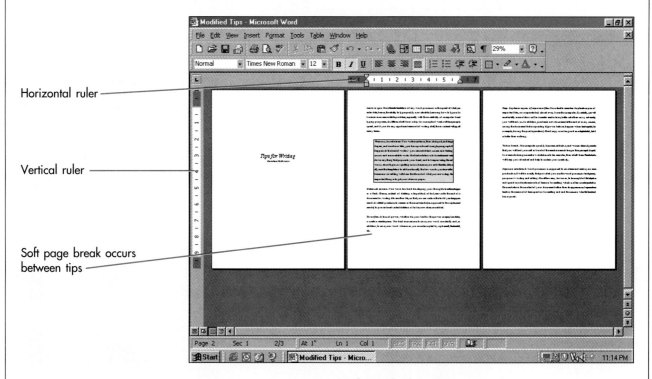

Horizontal ruler

Vertical ruler

Soft page break occurs between tips

(g) The Completed Docment (step 8)

FIGURE 2.16   Hands-on Exercise 3 (continued)

PRINT SELECTED PAGES

Why print an entire document if you want only a few pages? Pull down the File menu and click Print as you usually do to initiate the printing process. Click the Pages option button, then enter the page numbers and/or page ranges you want; for example, 3, 6–8 will print page three and pages six through eight. You can also print multiple copies by entering the appropriate number in the Number of copies list box.

STEP 9: Change the Column Structure

➤ Click the **down arrow** on the Zoom list box and return to **Page Width.** Press the **PgDn key** to scroll until the second page comes into view.

➤ Pull down the **File menu** and click the **Page Setup command** to display the Page Setup dialog box. Click the **Margins tab,** then change the Left and Right margins to 1″ each. Click **OK** to accept the settings and close the dialog box.

➤ Click anywhere in the paragraph, "Write Now but Edit Later". Pull down the **Format menu,** click the **Paragraph command,** click the Indents and Spacing tab if necessary, then change the left and right indents to 0.

➤ All paragraphs in the document should have the same indentation as shown in Figure 2.16h. Pull down the **Format menu** and click the **Columns command** to display the Columns dialog box.

➤ Click the icon for **three columns.** The default spacing between columns is .5″, which leads to a column width of 1.83″. Click in the Spacing list box and change the spacing to **.25″,** which automatically changes the column width to 2″.

➤ Check the box for the **Line Between** columns. Click **OK.**

Select three columns

Change the default spacing to automatically change the column width

Set the indentation for this paragraph to match the other paragraphs

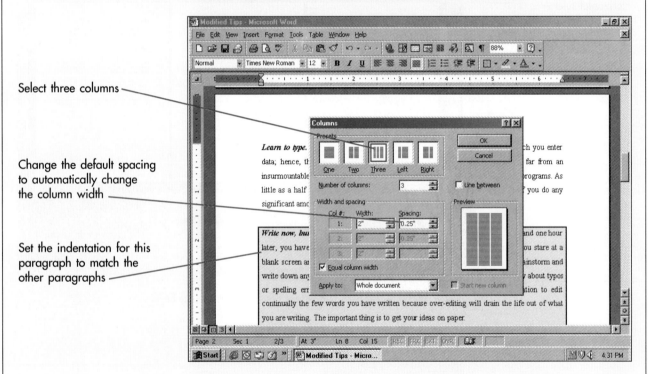

(h) Change the Column Structure (step 9)

FIGURE 2.16   Hands-on Exercise 3 (continued)

USE THE RULER TO CHANGE COLUMN WIDTH

Click anywhere within the column whose width you want to change, then point to the ruler and click and drag the right margin (the mouse pointer changes to a double arrow) to change the column width. Changing the width of one column in a document with equal-sized columns changes the width of all other columns so that they remain equal. Changing the width in a document with unequal columns changes only that column.

STEP 10: Insert a Section Break

➤ Pull down the **View menu,** click the **Zoom command,** then click the **Many Pages** option button. The document has switched to column formatting.

➤ Click at the beginning of the second page, immediately to the left of the first paragraph. Pull down the **Insert menu** and click **Break** to display the dialog box in Figure 2.16i.

➤ Click the **Continuous option button,** then click **OK** to accept the settings and close the dialog box.

➤ Click anywhere on the title page (before the section break you just inserted). Click the **Columns button,** then click the first column.

➤ The formatting for the first section of the document (the title page) should change to one column; the title of the document and your name are centered across the entire page.

➤ Print the document in this format for your instructor. Decide in which format you want to save the document—i.e., as it exists now, or as it existed at the end of step 8. Exit Word.

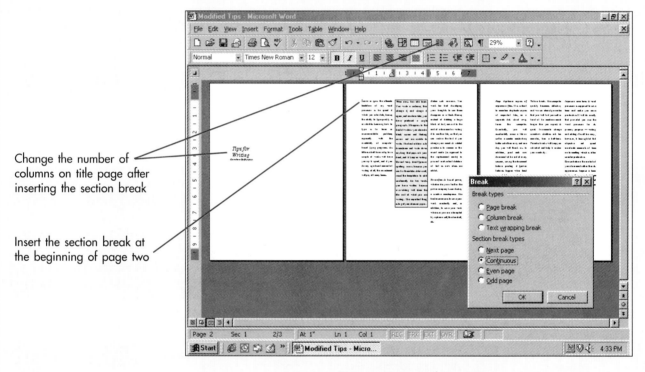

Change the number of columns on title page after inserting the section break

Insert the section break at the beginning of page two

(i) Insert a Section Break (step 10)

FIGURE 2.16   Hands-on Exercise 3 (continued)

THE COLUMNS BUTTON

The Columns button on the Standard toolbar is the fastest way to create columns in a document. Click the button, drag the mouse to choose the number of columns, then release the mouse to create the columns. The toolbar lets you change the number of columns, but not the spacing between columns. The toolbar is also limited, in that you cannot create columns of different widths or select a line between the columns.

Many operations in Word are done within the context of select-then-do; that is, select the text, then execute the necessary command. Text may be selected by dragging the mouse, by using the selection bar to the left of the document, or by using the keyboard. Text is deselected by clicking anywhere within the document.

The Find and Replace commands locate a designated character string and optionally replace one or more occurrences of that string with a different character string. The search may be case-sensitive and/or restricted to whole words as necessary.

Text is moved or copied through a combination of the Cut, Copy, and Paste commands and/or the drag-and-drop facility. The contents of the Windows clipboard are modified by any subsequent Cut or Copy command, but are unaffected by the Paste command; that is, the same text can be pasted into multiple locations.

The Undo command reverses the effect of previous commands. The Undo and Redo commands work in conjunction with one another; that is, every command that is undone can be redone at a later time.

Scrolling occurs when a document is too large to be seen in its entirety. Scrolling with the mouse changes what is displayed on the screen, but does not move the insertion point; that is, you must click the mouse to move the insertion point. Scrolling via the keyboard (for example, PgUp and PgDn) changes what is seen on the screen as well as the location of the insertion point.

The Print Layout view displays top and bottom margins, headers and footers, and other elements not seen in the Normal view. The Normal view is faster because Word spends less time formatting the display. Both views can be seen at different magnifications.

TrueType fonts are scaleable and accessible from any Windows application. The Format Font command enables you to choose the typeface (e.g., Times New Roman or Arial), style (e.g., bold or italic), point size, and color of text.

The Format Paragraph command determines the line spacing, alignment, indents, and text flow, all of which are set at the paragraph level. Borders and shading are also set at the paragraph level. Margins, page size, and orientation, are set in the Page Setup command and affect the entire document (or section).

Alignment
Arial
Automatic replacement
Borders and Shading
  command
Case-insensitive
  replacement
Case-sensitive
  replacement
Clipboard toolbar
Columns command
Copy command
Courier New
Cut command
Drag and drop

Find command
First line indent
Font
Format Font command
Format Painter
Format Paragraph
  command
Go To command
Hanging indent
Hard page break
Hyphenation
Indents
Landscape orientation
Leader character
Left indent

Line spacing
Margins
Monospaced typeface
Nonbreaking hyphen
Normal view
Office clipboard
Page break
Page Setup command
Paste command
Point size
Portrait orientation
Print Layout view
Proportional typeface
Redo command
Repeat command

Replace command	Serif typeface	Typography
Right indent	Shortcut menu	Underlining
Sans serif typeface	Soft page break	Undo command
Scrolling	Special indent	View menu
Section	Tab stop	Whole word replacement
Section break	Times New Roman	Widows and orphans
Select-Then-Do	Typeface	Wild card
Selection bar	Type size	Windows clipboard
Selective replacement	Type style	Zoom command

MULTIPLE CHOICE

1. Which of the following commands does *not* place data onto the clipboard?
   (a) Cut
   (b) Copy
   (c) Paste
   (d) All of the above

2. What happens if you select a block of text, copy it, move to the beginning of the document, paste it, move to the end of the document, and paste the text again?
   (a) The selected text will appear in three places: at the original location, and at the beginning and end of the document
   (b) The selected text will appear in two places: at the beginning and end of the document
   (c) The selected text will appear in just the original location
   (d) The situation is not possible; that is, you cannot paste twice in a row without an intervening cut or copy operation

3. What happens if you select a block of text, cut it, move to the beginning of the document, paste it, move to the end of the document, and paste the text again?
   (a) The selected text will appear in three places: at the original location and at the beginning and end of the document
   (b) The selected text will appear in two places: at the beginning and end of the document
   (c) The selected text will appear in just the original location
   (d) The situation is not possible; that is, you cannot paste twice in a row without an intervening cut or copy operation

4. Which of the following are set at the paragraph level?
   (a) Alignment
   (b) Tabs and indents
   (c) Line spacing
   (d) All of the above

5. How do you change the font for *existing* text within a document?
   (a) Select the text, then choose the new font
   (b) Choose the new font, then select the text
   (c) Either (a) or (b)
   (d) Neither (a) nor (b)

6. The Page Setup command can be used to change:
   (a) The margins in a document
   (b) The orientation of a document
   (c) Both (a) and (b)
   (d) Neither (a) nor (b)

7. Which of the following is a true statement regarding indents?
   (a) Indents are measured from the edge of the page rather than from the margin
   (b) The left, right, and first line indents must be set to the same value
   (c) The insertion point can be anywhere in the paragraph when indents are set
   (d) Indents must be set with the Format Paragraph command

8. The spacing in an existing multipage document is changed from single spacing to double spacing throughout the document. What can you say about the number of hard and soft page breaks before and after the formatting change?
   (a) The number of soft page breaks is the same, but the number and/or position of the hard page breaks is different
   (b) The number of hard page breaks is the same, but the number and/or position of the soft page breaks is different
   (c) The number and position of both hard and soft page breaks is the same
   (d) The number and position of both hard and soft page breaks is different

9. The default tab stops are set to:
   (a) Left indents every ½ inch
   (b) Left indents every ¼ inch
   (c) Right indents every ½ inch
   (d) Right indents every ¼ inch

10. Which of the following describes the Arial and Times New Roman fonts?
    (a) Arial is a sans serif font, Times New Roman is a serif font
    (b) Arial is a serif font, Times New Roman is a sans serif font
    (c) Both are serif fonts
    (d) Both are sans serif fonts

11. The find and replacement strings must be
    (a) The same length
    (b) The same case, either upper or lower
    (c) The same length and the same case
    (d) None of the above

12. Assume that you are in the middle of a multipage document. How do you scroll to the beginning of the document and simultaneously change the insertion point?
    (a) Press Ctrl+Home
    (b) Drag the scroll bar to the top of the scroll box
    (c) Both (a) and (b)
    (d) Neither (a) nor (b)

13. Which of the following substitutions can be accomplished by the Find and Replace command?
- (a) All occurrences of the words "Times New Roman" can be replaced with the word "Arial"
- (b) All text set in the Times New Roman font can be replaced by the Arial font
- (c) Both (a) and (b)
- (d) Neither (a) nor (b)

14. Which of the following deselects a selected block of text?
- (a) Clicking anywhere outside the selected text
- (b) Clicking any alignment button on the toolbar
- (c) Clicking the Bold, Italic, or Underline button
- (d) All of the above

15. Which view, and which magnification, lets you see the whole page, including top and bottom margins?
- (a) Print Layout view at 100% magnification
- (b) Print Layout view at Whole Page magnification
- (c) Normal view at 100% magnification
- (d) Normal view at Whole Page magnification

Answers

1. c	**6.** c	**11.** d
2. a	**7.** c	**12.** a
3. b	**8.** b	**13.** c
4. d	**9.** a	**14.** a
5. a	**10.** a	**15.** b

PRACTICE WITH MICROSOFT WORD

1. Formatting a Document: Open the *Chapter 2 Practice 1* document that is displayed in Figure 2.17 and make the following changes.
- a. Copy the sentence *Discretion is the better part of valor* to the beginning of the first paragraph.
- b. Move the second paragraph to the end of the document.
- c. Change the typeface of the entire document to 12 point Arial.
- d. Change all whole word occurrences of *feel* to *think*.
- e. Change the spacing of the entire document from single spacing to 1.5. Change the alignment of the entire document to justified.
- f. Set the phrases *Format Font command* and *Format Paragraph command* in italics.
- g. Indent the second paragraph .25 inch on both the left and right.
- h. Box and shade the last paragraph.
- i. Create a title page that precedes the document. Set the title, *Discretion in Design,* in 24 point Arial bold and center it approximately two inches from the top of the page. Right align your name toward the bottom of the title page in 12 point Arial regular.
- j. Print the revised document and submit it to your instructor.

It is not difficult, especially with practice, to learn to format a document. It is not long before the mouse goes automatically to the Format Font command to change the selected text to a sans-serif font, to increase the font size, or to apply a boldface or italic style. Nor is it long before you go directly to the Format Paragraph command to change the alignment or line spacing for selected paragraphs.

What is not easy, however, is to teach discretion in applying formats. Too many different formats on one page can be distracting, and in almost all cases, less is better. Be conservative and never feel that you have to demonstrate everything you know how to do in each and every document that you create. Discretion is the better part of valor. No more than two different typefaces should be used in a single document, although each can be used in a variety of different styles and sizes.

It is always a good idea to stay on the lookout for what you feel are good designs and then determine exactly what you like and don't like about each. In that way, you are constantly building ideas for your own future designs.

FIGURE 2.17   Formatting a Document (Exercise 1)

2. Typography: Figure 2.18 displays a completed version of the *Chapter 2 Practice 2* document that exists on the data disk. We want you to retrieve the original document from the data disk, then change the document so that it matches Figure 2.18. No editing is required as the text in the original document is identical to the finished document.

   The only changes are in formatting, but you will have to compare the documents in order to determine the nature of the changes. Color is a nice touch (which depends on the availability of a color printer) and is not required. Add your name somewhere in the document, then print the revised document and submit it to your instructor.

3. The Preamble: Create a simple document containing the text of the Preamble to the Constitution as shown in Figure 2.19.
   a. Set the Preamble in 12 point Times New Roman.
   b. Use single spacing and left alignment.
   c. Copy the Preamble to a new page, then change to a larger point size and more interesting typeface.
   d. Create a title page for your assignment, containing your name, course name, and appropriate title.
   e. Use a different typeface for the title page than in the rest of the document, and set the title in at least 24 points.
   f. Submit all three pages (the title page and both versions of the Preamble) to your instructor.

TYPOGRAPHY

The art of formatting a document is more than just knowing definitions, but knowing the definitions is definitely a starting point. A *typeface* is a complete set of characters with the same general appearance, and can be *serif* (cross lines at the end of the main strokes of each letter) or *sans serif* (without the cross lines). A *type size* is a vertical measurement, made from the top of the tallest letter in the character set to the bottom of the lowest letter in the character set. *Type style* refers to variations in the typeface, such as boldface and italics.

Several typefaces are shipped with Windows, including ***Times New Roman,*** a serif typeface, and ***Arial***, a sans serif typeface. Times New Roman should be used for large amounts of text, whereas Arial is best used for titles and subtitles. It is best not to use too many different typefaces in the same document, but rather to use only one or two and then make the document interesting by varying their size and style.

FIGURE 2.18 Typography (Exercise 2)

We, the people of the United States, in order to form a more perfect Union, establish justice, insure domestic tranquillity, provide for the common defense, promote the general welfare, and secure the blessings of liberty to ourselves and our posterity, do ordain and establish this Constitution for the United States of America.

FIGURE 2.19 The Preamble (Exercise 3)

4. Tab Stops: Anyone who has used a typewriter is familiar with the function of the Tab key; that is, press Tab and the insertion point moves to the next tab stop (a measured position to align text at a specific place). The Tab key is more powerful in Word because you can choose from four different types of tab stops (left, center, right, and decimal). You can also specify a leader character, typically dots or hyphens, to draw the reader's eye across the page.

Create the document in Figure 2.20 and add your name in the indicated position. (Use the Help facility to discover how to work with tab stops.) Submit the completed document to your instructor as proof that you have mastered the Tab key.

EXAMPLES OF TAB STOPS

Example 1 - Right tab at 6":

CIS 120   **Maryann Barber**
Fall 1999   **September 21, 1999**

Example 2 - Right tab with a dot leader at 6":

Chapter 1..1
Chapter 2..31
Chapter 3..56

Example 3 - Right tab at 1" and left tab at 1.25":

To:	Maryann Barber
From:	Joel Stutz
Department:	Computer Information Systems
Subject:	Exams

Example 4 - Left tab at 2" and a decimal tab at 3.5":

Rent	$375.38
Utilities	$125.59
Phone	$56.92
Cable	$42.45

FIGURE 2.20   Tab Stops (Exercise 4)

5. The Page Borders Command: Figure 2.21 illustrates a hypothetical title page for a paper describing the capabilities of borders and shading. The Borders and Shading command is applied at the paragraph level as indicated in the chapter. You can, however, select the Page Border tab within the Borders and Shading dialog box to create an unusual and attractive document. Experiment with the command to create a title page similar to Figure 2.21. Submit the document to your instructor as proof you did the exercise.

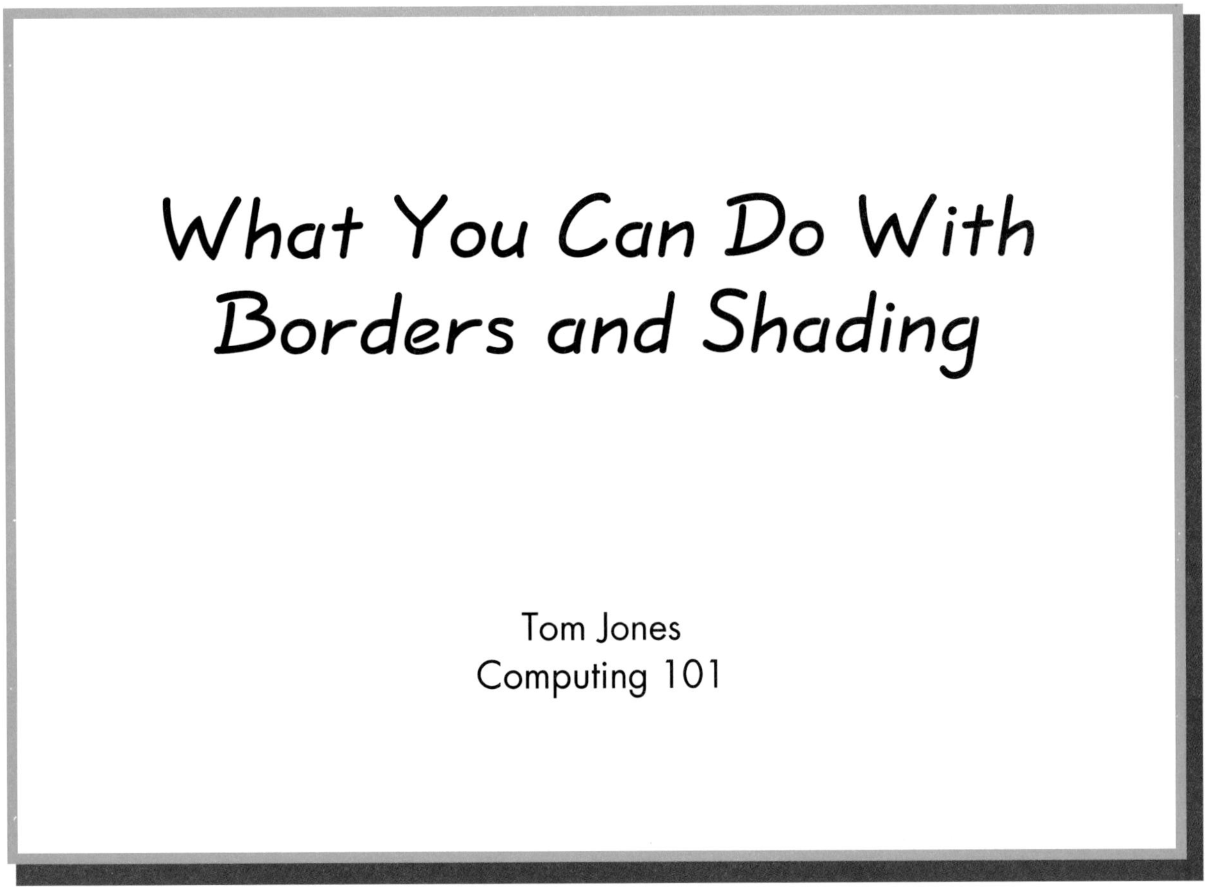

What You Can Do With Borders and Shading

Tom Jones
Computing 101

FIGURE 2.21   The Page Borders Command (Exercise 5)

6. Exploring Fonts: The Font Folder within the Control Panel displays the names of the fonts available on a system and enables you to obtain a printed sample of any specific font. Click the Start button, click (or point to) the Settings command, click (or point to) Control Panel, then double click the Fonts icon to open the font folder and display the fonts on your system.

   a. Double click a font you want to view, then click the Print button to print a sample of the selected font.

   b. Click the Fonts button on the Taskbar to return to the Fonts window and open a different font. Print a sample page of this font as well.

   c. Start Word. Create a title page containing your name, class, date, and the title of this assignment (My Favorite Fonts). Center the title. Use boldface or italics as you see fit. Be sure to use appropriate type sizes.

   d. Staple the three pages together (the title page and two font samples), then submit them to your instructor.

7. Inserting the Date and Time: Create a document similar to Figure 2.22 that describes the Insert Date and Time command. You need not duplicate our document exactly, but you are asked to print the dates in several formats. Use the columns feature to separate the two sets of dates. Note the keyboard shortcut that is described in the document to go to the next column. You will also have to insert a section break before and after the dates to change the number of columns in the document. Create your document on one day, then open it a day later, to be sure that the dates that were entered as fields were updated appropriately.

Inserting the Date and Time

The *Insert Date and Time command* puts the date (and/or time) into a document. The date can be inserted as a specific value (the date and time on which the command is executed) or as a *field*. The latter is updated automatically from the computer's internal clock whenever the document is opened or when the document is printed. You can also update a field manually, by selecting the appropriate command from a shortcut menu. Either way, the date may be printed in a variety of formats as shown below.

Update field box is clear	Update field box is checked
January 21, 1999	February 15, 1999
Thursday, January 21, 1999	Monday, February 15, 1999
1/21/99	2/15/99
21 January 1999	15 February 1999
1/21/99 10:08 AM	2/15/1999

Any date that is entered as a field is shaded by default. You can change that, however, by using the Options command in the Tools menu. (Select the View tab and click the drop-down arrow in the Field Shading list box to choose the option you want.) Note, too, that I created this document using the columns feature. My document has three sections, with the section in the middle containing two columns. (I pressed **Ctrl+Shift+Enter** to go from the bottom of one column to the top of the next.)

Maryann Coulter
January 21, 1999

FIGURE 2.22   Inserting the Date and Time (Exercise 7)

CASE STUDIES

Computers Past and Present

The ENIAC was the scientific marvel of its day and the world's first operational electronic computer. It could perform 5,000 additions per second, weighed 30 tons, and took 1,500 square feet of floor space. The price was a modest $486,000 in 1946 dollars. The story of the ENIAC and other influential computers of the author's choosing is found in the file *History of Computers,* which we forgot to format, so we are asking you to do it for us.

Be sure to use appropriate emphasis for the names of the various computers. Create a title page in front of the document, then submit the completed assignment to your instructor. If you are ambitious, you can enhance this assignment by using your favorite search engine to look for computer museums on the Web. Visit one or two sites, and include this information on a separate page at the end of the document. One last task, and that is to update the description of Today's PC (the last computer in the document).

Your First Consultant's Job

Go to a real installation, such as a doctor's or an attorney's office, the company where you work, or the computer lab at school. Determine the backup procedures that are in effect, then write a one-page report indicating whether the policy is adequate and, if necessary, offering suggestions for improvement. Your report should be addressed to the individual in charge of the business, and it should cover all aspects of the backup strategy—that is, which files are backed up and how often, and what software is used for the backup operation. Use appropriate emphasis (for example, bold italics) to identify any potential problems. This is a professional document (it is your first consultant's job), and its appearance must be perfect in every way.

To Hyphenate or Not to Hyphenate

The best way to learn about hyphenation is to experiment with an existing document. Open the *To Hyphenate or Not to Hyphenate* document that is on the data disk. The document is currently set in 12-point type with hyphenation in effect. Experiment with various formatting changes that will change the soft line breaks to see the effect on the hyphenation within the document. You can change the point size, the number of columns, and/or the right indent. You can also suppress hyphenation altogether, as described within the document. Summarize your findings in a short note to your instructor.

Paper Makes a Difference

Most of us take paper for granted, but the right paper can make a significant difference in the effectiveness of the document. Reports and formal correspondence are usually printed on white paper, but you would be surprised how many different shades of white there are. Other types of documents lend themselves to colored paper for additional impact. In short, which paper you use is far from an automatic decision. Walk into a local copy store and see if they have any specialty papers available. Our favorite source for paper is a company called *Paper Direct* (1-800-APAPERS). Ask for a catalog, then consider the use of a specialty paper the next time you have an important project.

The Invitation

Choose an event and produce the perfect invitation. The possibilities are endless and limited only by your imagination. You can invite people to your wedding or to a fraternity party. Your laser printer and abundance of fancy fonts enable you to do anything a professional printer can do. Special paper (see previous case study) will add the finishing touch. Go to it—this assignment is a lot of fun.

One Space After a Period

Touch typing classes typically teach the student to place two spaces after a period. The technique worked well in the days of the typewriter and monospaced fonts, but it creates an artificially large space when used with proportional fonts and a word processor. Select any document that is at least several paragraphs in length and print the document with the current spacing. Use the Find and Replace commands to change to the alternate spacing, then print the document a second time. Which spacing looks better to you? Submit both versions of the document to your instructor with a brief note summarizing your findings.

The Contest

Almost everyone enjoys some form of competition. Ask your instructor to choose a specific type of document, such as a flyer or résumé, and declare a contest in the class to produce the "best" document. Submit your entry, but write your name on the back of the document so that it can be judged anonymously. Your instructor may want to select a set of semifinalists and then distribute copies of those documents so that the class can vote on the winner.

chapter 3

ENHANCING A DOCUMENT: THE WEB AND OTHER RESOURCES

OBJECTIVES

After reading this chapter you will be able to:

1. Describe object linking and embedding; explain how it is used to create a compound document.
2. Describe the resources in the Microsoft Clip Gallery; insert clip art and/or a photograph into a document.
3. Use the Format Picture command to wrap text around a clip art image.
4. Use WordArt to insert decorative text into a document.
5. Describe the Internet and World Wide Web; download resources from the Web for inclusion in a Word document.
6. Insert a hyperlink into a Word document; save a Word document as a Web page.
7. Use the Drawing toolbar to create and modify lines and objects.
8. Insert a footnote or endnote into a document to cite a reference.
9. Use wizards and templates to create a document.

OVERVIEW

This chapter describes how to enhance a document using applications within Microsoft Office Professional as well as resources on the Internet and World Wide Web. We begin with a discussion of the Microsoft Clip Gallery, a collection of clip art, sound files, and motion clips that can be inserted into any office document. We describe how Microsoft WordArt can be used to create special effects with text and how to create lines and objects through the Drawing toolbar.

These resources pale, however, in comparison to what is available via the Internet. Thus, we also show you how to download an object from the Web and include it in an Office document. We describe how to add footnotes to give appropriate credit to your sources and how to further enhance a document through inclusion of hyperlinks. We also explain how to save a Word document as a Web page so that you can post the documents you create to a Web server or local area network.

The chapter also describes the various wizards and templates that are built into Microsoft Word to help you create professionally formatted documents. We believe this to be a very enjoyable chapter that will add significantly to your capability in Microsoft Word. As always, learning is best accomplished by doing, and the hands-on exercises are essential to master the material.

A COMPOUND DOCUMENT

The applications in Microsoft Office are thoroughly integrated with one another. Equally important, they share information through a technology known as *Object Linking and Embedding (OLE),* which enables you to create a *compound document* containing data (objects) from multiple applications.

Consider, for example, the compound document in Figure 3.1, which was created in Microsoft Word but contains objects (data) from other applications. The *clip art* (a graphic as opposed to a photograph) was taken from the Microsoft Clip Gallery. The title of the document was created using Microsoft WordArt. The document also illustrates the Insert Symbol command to insert special characters such as the Windows logo.

WordArt ———————

Clip art ———————

Enhancing a Document

Clip art is available from a variety of sources, including the Microsoft Clip Gallery, which is part of Microsoft Office. The Clip Gallery contains clip art as well as sound bites and motion clips, although the latter are more common in PowerPoint presentations. Once the object has been inserted into a document, it can be moved and sized using various options in the Format Picture command. You can wrap text around a picture, place a border around the picture or even crop (cut out part of) the picture if necessary.

In addition to clip art, you can use WordArt to create artistic effects to enhance any document. WordArt enables you to create special effects with text. It lets you rotate and/or flip text, display it vertically on the page, shade it, slant it, arch it, or even print it upside down. Best of all, WordArt is intuitive and easy to use. In essence, you enter text into a dialog box, and then you choose a shape for the text from a dialog box. You can create special effects by choosing one of several different shadows. You can vary the image even further by using any TrueType font on your system. It's fun, it's easy, and you can create some truly dynamite documents.

The Insert Symbol command enables you to insert special symbols into a document to give it a professional look. You can, for example, use ™ rather than TM, © rather than (C), or ½ and ¼ rather than 1/2 and 1/4. It also enables you to insert accented characters as appropriate in English, as in the word *résumé,* or in a foreign language to create properly accented words and phrases—for example, *¿Cómo está usted?*

You can insert clip art or WordArt into any Office document using the same commands that you will learn in this chapter. Indeed, that is one of the benefits of the Office suite because the same commands are executed from the same menus as you go from one application to another. In addition, each application also contains a Standard toolbar and a Formatting toolbar.

Windows logo added through
Insert Symbol command ———————

Eric Simon created this document using Microsoft Windows ⊞®

FIGURE 3.1   A Compound Document

Microsoft Clip Gallery

The **Microsoft Clip Gallery** contains clip art, sound files, and motion clips and it is accessible from any application in Microsoft Office. Clip art is inserted into a document in one of two ways—through the **Insert Object command** or more directly through the **Insert Picture command** as shown in Figure 3.2. Choose the type of object and the category (such as a picture in the Animals category in Figure 3.2a), then select the image (the lion in Figure 3.2b) and insert it into the document. After a picture has been placed into a document, it can be moved and sized just like any Windows object.

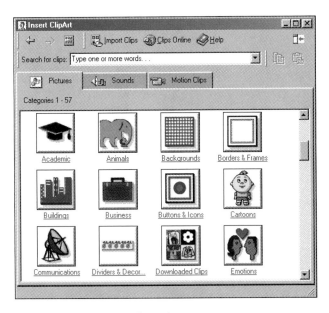

(a) Choose the Category

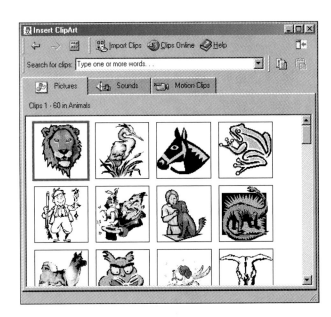

(b) Choose the Image

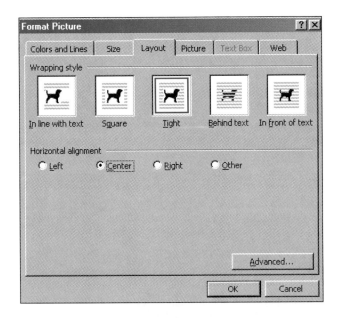

(c) Format the Picture

(d) The Completed Document

FIGURE 3.2   Microsoft Clip Gallery

The **Format Picture command** enables you to further customize the picture. The Layout tab in Figure 3.2c determines the position of the picture with respect to the text. We chose the tight wrapping style, which means that the text comes to the border of the picture. You can also use the **Picture Toolbar** (not shown in Figure 3.2) to **crop** (cut out part of) the picture if necessary. Figure 3.2d shows how the selected object appears in the completed document. Note, too, the **sizing handles** on the graphic that enable you to move and size the picture within the document.

The Insert Symbol Command

One characteristic of a professional document is the use of typographic symbols in place of ordinary typing—for example, ® rather than (R), © rather than (C), or ½ and ¼ rather than 1/2 and 1/4. Much of this formatting is implemented automatically by Word through substitutions built into the **AutoCorrect** feature. Other characters, especially accented characters such as the "é" in résumé, or those in a foreign language (e.g., ¿Cómo está usted?), have to be inserted manually into a document.

Look carefully at the last line of Figure 3.1, and notice the Windows logo at the end of the sentence. The latter was created through the **Insert Symbol command,** as shown in Figure 3.3. You select the font containing the desired character (e.g., Wingdings in Figure 3.3), then you select the character, and finally you click the Insert command button to place the character in the document.

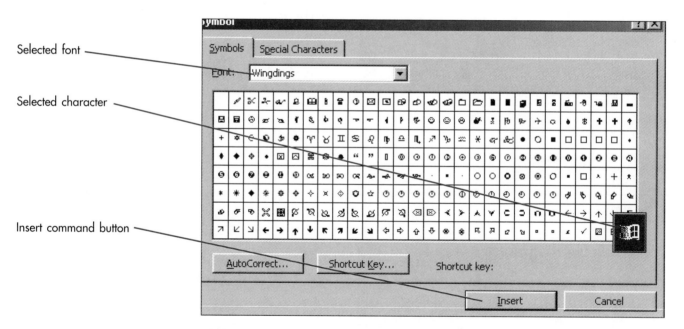

Selected font

Selected character

Insert command button

FIGURE 3.3   The Insert Symbol Command

THE WINGDINGS AND SYMBOLS FONTS

The Wingdings and Symbols fonts are two of the best-kept secrets in Windows 95. Both fonts contain a variety of special characters that can be inserted into a document through the Insert Symbol command. These fonts are scaleable to any point size, enabling you to create some truly unusual documents. (See practice exercise 3 at the end of the chapter.)

Microsoft WordArt

Microsoft WordArt is an application within Microsoft Office that creates decorative text to add interest to a document. You can use WordArt in addition to clip art, as was done in Figure 3.1, or in place of clip art if the right image is not available. You're limited only by your imagination, as you can rotate text in any direction, add three-dimensional effects, display the text vertically down the page, shade it, slant it, arch it, or even print it upside down.

WordArt is intuitive and easy to use. In essence, you choose a style for the text from among the selections in the dialog box of Figure 3.4a, then you enter your specific text as shown in Figure 3.4b. You can modify the style through various special effects, you can use any TrueType font on your system, and you can change the color or shading. Figure 3.4c shows the completed WordArt object. It's fun, it's easy, and you can create some truly dynamite documents.

Selected WordArt style   Selected font   Enter text

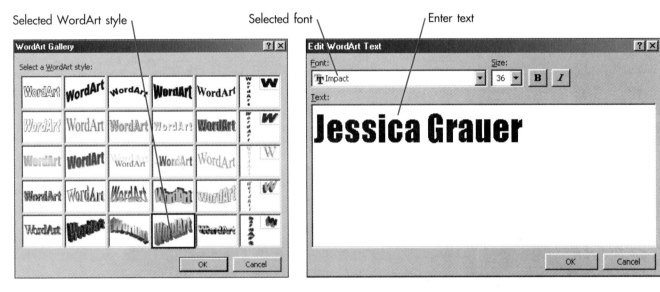

(a) Choose the Style   (b) Enter the Text

(c) Completed WordArt

FIGURE 3.4   Microsoft WordArt

Did you ever stop to think how the images in the Clip Gallery were developed? Undoubtedly they were drawn by someone with artistic ability who used basic shapes, such as lines and curves in various combinations, to create the images. The *Drawing toolbar* in Figure 3.5 contains all of the tools necessary to create original clip art. As with any toolbar, you can point to a button to display a Screen-Tip containing the name of the button that is indicative of its function.

To draw an object, select the appropriate tool, then click and drag in the document to create the object. Select the Line tool, for example, then draw the line. After the line has been created, you can select it and change its properties (such as thickness, style, or color) by using other tools on the Drawing toolbar. To create a drawing, you add other objects such as lines and curves, and soon you have a piece of original clip art.

Once you learn the basics, there are other techniques to master. The Shift key, for example, has special significance when used in conjunction with the Line, Rectangle, and Oval tools. Press and hold the Shift key as you drag the line tool horizontally or vertically to create a perfectly straight line in either direction. Press and hold the Shift key as you drag the Rectangle and Oval tool to create a square or circle, respectively. We don't expect you to create clip art comparable to the images within the Clip Gallery, but you can use the tools on the Drawing toolbar to modify an existing image and/or create simple shapes of your own that can enhance any document.

One tool that is especially useful is the *AutoShapes button* that displays a series of selected shapes such as the callout or banner. And, as with any object, you can change the thickness, color, or fill by selecting the object and choosing the appropriate tool. It's fun, it's easy—just be flexible and willing to experiment. We think you will be pleased at what you will be able to do.

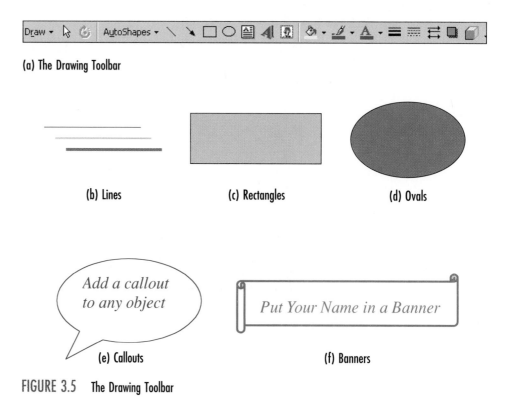

(a) The Drawing Toolbar

(b) Lines (c) Rectangles (d) Ovals

Add a callout to any object *Put Your Name in a Banner*

(e) Callouts (f) Banners

FIGURE 3.5   The Drawing Toolbar

Creating a Compound Document

Objective: To create a compound document containing clip art and WordArt; to illustrate the Insert Symbol command to place typographical symbols into a document. Use Figure 3.6 as a guide in the exercise.

STEP 1: Insert the Clip Art

➤ Start Word. Open the **Clip Art and WordArt** document in the Exploring Word folder. Save the document as **Modified Clip Art and WordArt.**

➤ Check that the insertion point is at the beginning of the document. Pull down the **Insert menu,** click **Picture,** then click **Clip Art** to display the Insert Clip Art dialog box as shown in Figure 3.6a.

➤ If necessary, click the **Pictures tab** and select (click) the **Science and Technology category.** Select the **Computers graphic** (or a different image if you prefer), then click the **Insert Clip button** on the shortcut menu.

➤ The picture should appear in the document where it can be moved and sized as described in the next several steps.

➤ Click the **Close button** on the Insert Clip Art dialog box.

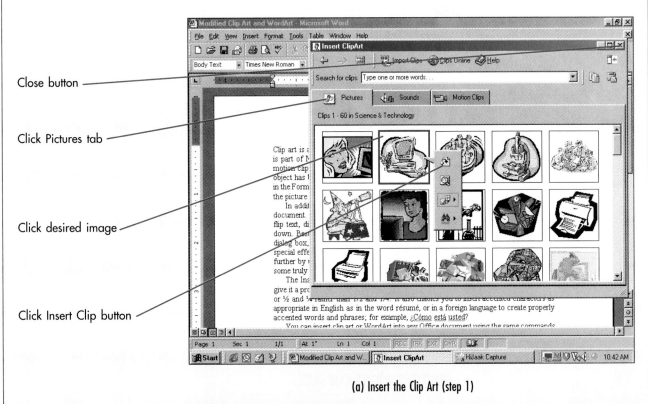

Close button

Click Pictures tab

Click desired image

Click Insert Clip button

(a) Insert the Clip Art (step 1)

FIGURE 3.6   Hands-on Exercise 1

STEP 2: Move and Size the Picture

➤ Change to the Print Layout view in Figure 3.6b. Move and size the image.

➤ To size an object:

* Click the object to display the sizing handles.

* Drag a corner handle (the mouse pointer changes to a double arrow) to change the length and width of the picture simultaneously; this keeps the graphic in proportion as it sizes it.

* Drag a handle on the horizontal or vertical border to change one dimension only; this distorts the picture.

➤ To move an object:

* Click the object to display the sizing handles.

* Point to any part of the image except a sizing handle (the mouse pointer changes to a four-sided arrow), then click and drag to move the image elsewhere in the document. You cannot wrap text around the image until you execute the Format Picture command in step 3.

➤ Save the document.

Picture toolbar is displayed when image is selected

Click and drag sizing handle to size object

Click and drag to move object

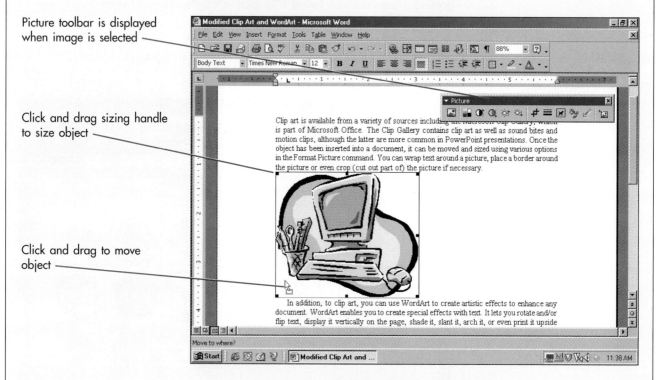

(b) Move and Size the Picture (step 2)

FIGURE 3.6   Hands-on Exercise 1 (continued)

FIND THE RIGHT CLIP ART

Use the search capability within the Clip Gallery to find the right image. Pull down the Insert menu, click Picture, then click Clip Art to display the Insert Clip Art dialog box. Click in the Search for text box, enter a key word such as "women," then press the enter key to display all of the images, regardless of category, that list "women" as a key word.

STEP 3: Format the Picture

➤ Be sure the clip art is still selected, then pull down the **Format menu** and select the **Picture command** to display the Format Picture dialog box in Figure 3.6c.

➤ Click the **Layout tab,** select **Square** as the wrapping style, and choose the **left option button** under horizontal alignment.

➤ The text should be wrapped to the right of the image. Move and size the image until you are satisfied with its position. Note, however, that the image will always be positioned (wrapped) according to the settings in the Format Picture command.

➤ Save the document.

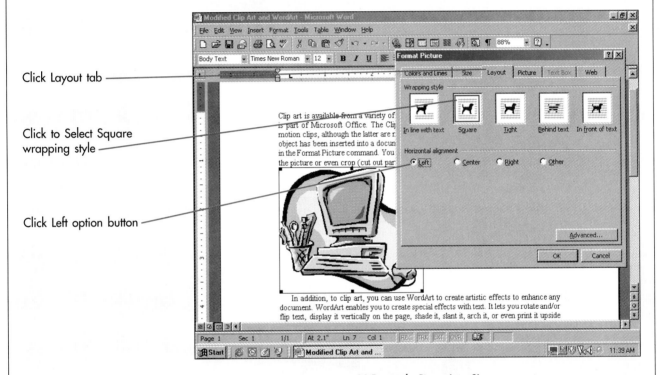

(c) Format the Picture (step 3)

FIGURE 3.6   Hands-on Exercise 1 (continued)

CLIP PROPERTIES

Every clip art image has multiple properties that determine the category (or categories) in which it is listed as well as key words that are reflected in a search of the Clip Gallery. Right click any image within the Insert Clip Art dialog box and click the Click Properties command to display the Clip Properties dialog box. Click the Categories tab, then check any additional categories under which the image should appear. Click the Keywords tab to add (delete) the entries for this item. Click OK to accept the changes and close the Properties dialog box. Check the additional categories or search on a new key word within the Insert Clip Art dialog box to verify the effect of your changes.

STEP 4: WordArt

➤ Press **Ctrl+End** to move to the end of the document. Pull down the **Insert menu,** click **Picture,** then click **WordArt** to display the WordArt Gallery dialog box.

➤ Select the WordArt style you like (you can change it later). Click **OK.** You will see a second dialog box in which you enter the text. Enter **Enhancing a Document.** Click **OK.**

➤ The WordArt object appears in your document in the style you selected. Point to the WordArt object and click the **right mouse button** to display the shortcut menu in Figure 3.6d. Click **Format WordArt** to display the Format WordArt dialog box.

➤ Click the **Layout tab,** then select **Square** as the Wrapping style. Click **OK.** It is important to select this wrapping option to facilitate placing the WordArt at the top of the document. Save the document.

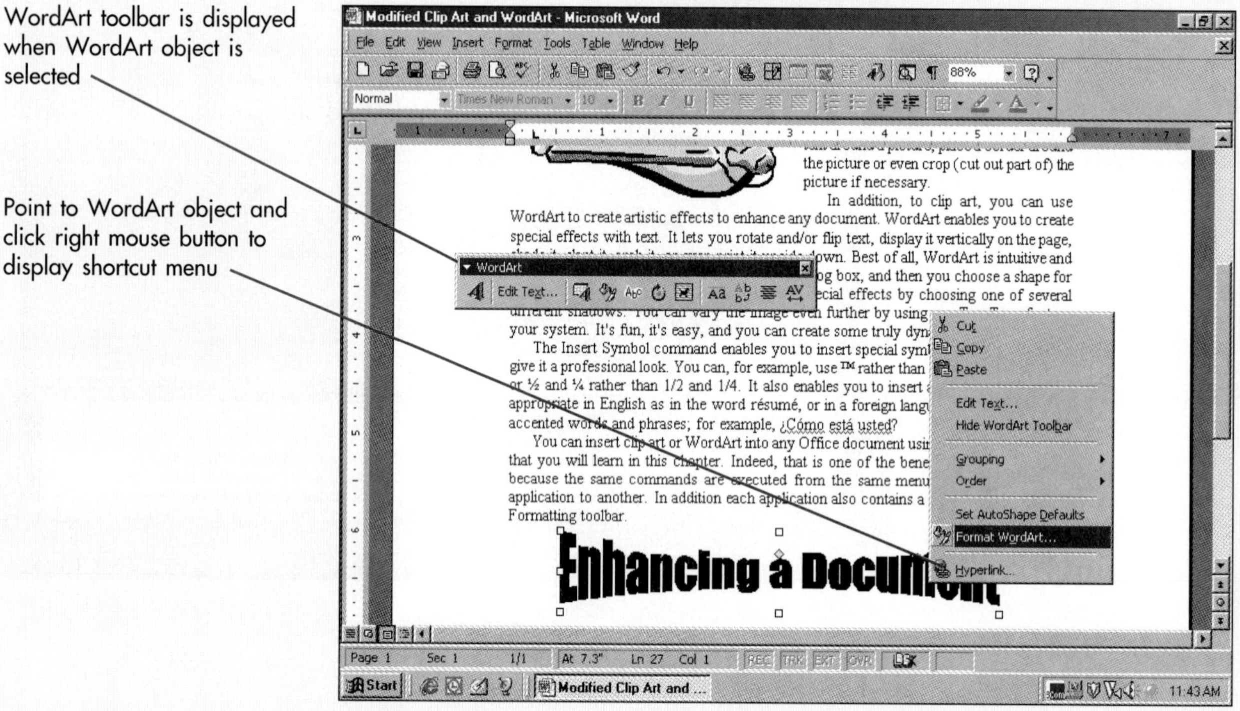

WordArt toolbar is displayed when WordArt object is selected

Point to WordArt object and click right mouse button to display shortcut menu

(d) WordArt (step 4)

FIGURE 3.6   Hands-on Exercise 1 (continued)

FORMATTING WORDART

The WordArt toolbar offers the easiest way to execute various commands associated with a WordArt object. It is displayed automatically when a WordArt object is selected, and suppressed otherwise. As with any toolbar, you can point to a button to display a ScreenTip containing the name of the button, which is indicative of its function. You will find buttons to display the text vertically, change the style or shape, and/or edit the text.

STEP 5: WordArt (continued)

➤ Click and drag the WordArt object to move it the top of the document as shown in Figure 3.6e. (The Format WordArt dialog box is not yet visible.)

➤ Point to the WordArt object, click the **right mouse button** to display a short-cut menu, then click **Format WordArt** to display the Format WordArt dialog box.

➤ Click the **Colors and Lines tab,** then click the **Fill Color drop-down arrow** to display the available colors. Select a different color (e.g., blue). Click **OK.**

➤ Move and/or size the WordArt object as necessary.

➤ Save the document.

Click Colors and Lines tab

Move WordArt object to top of document

Click Fill color drop-down arrow

Select a color

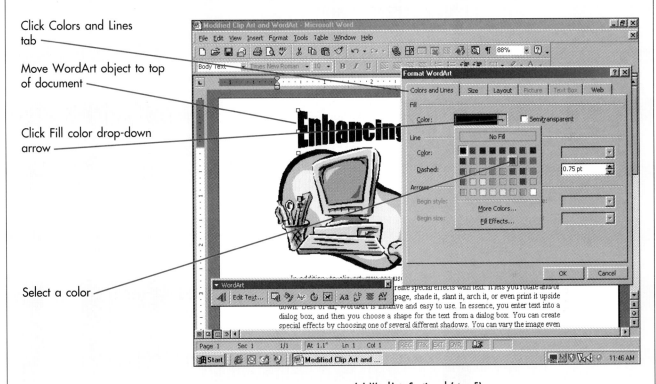

(e) WordArt, Continued (step 5)

FIGURE 3.6   Hands-on Exercise 1 (continued)

THE THIRD DIMENSION

You can make your WordArt images even more dramatic by adding 3-D effects. You can tilt the text up or down, right or left, increase or decrease the depth, and change the shading. Pull down the View menu, click Toolbars, click Customize to display the complete list of available toolbars, click the Toolbars tab, check the box to display the 3-D Settings toolbar, and click the Close button. Select the WordArt object, then experiment with various tools and special effects. The results are even better if you have a color printer.

STEP 6: The Insert Symbol Command

➤ Press **Ctrl+End** to move to the end of the document as shown in Figure 3.6f. Press the **enter key** to insert a blank line at the end of the document.

➤ Type the sentence, **Eric Simon created this document using Microsoft Windows,** substituting your name for Eric Simon. Click the **Center button** on the Formatting toolbar to center the sentence.

➤ Pull down the **Insert menu,** click **Symbol,** then choose **Wingdings** from the Font list box. Click the **Windows logo** (the last character in the last line), click **Insert,** then close the Symbol dialog box.

➤ Click and drag to select the newly inserted symbol, click the **drop-down arrow** on the **Font Size box,** then change the font to **24** points. Press the **right arrow key** to deselect the symbol.

➤ Click the **drop-down arrow** on the **Font Size box** and change to **10 point type** so that subsequent text is entered in this size. Type **(r)** after the Windows logo and try to watch the monitor as you enter the text. The (r) will be converted automatically to ® because of the AutoFormat command.

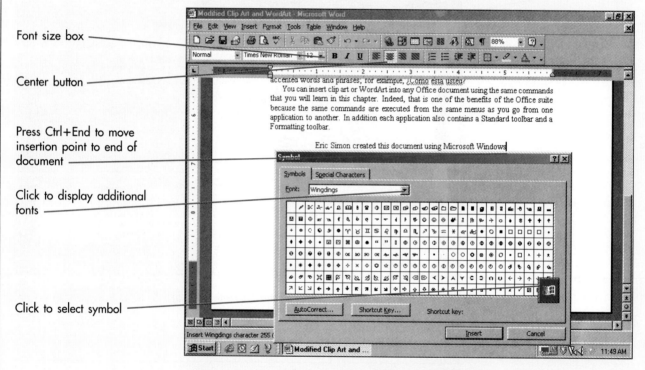

Font size box

Center button

Press Ctrl+End to move insertion point to end of document

Click to display additional fonts

Click to select symbol

(f) Insert Symbol Command (step 6)

FIGURE 3.6 Hands-on Exercise 1 (continued)

AUTOCORRECT AND AUTOFORMAT

The AutoCorrect feature not only corrects mistakes as you type by substituting one character string for another (e.g., *the* for *teh*), but it will also substitute symbols for typewritten equivalents such as © for (c), provided the entries are included in the table of substitutions. The AutoFormat feature is similar in concept and replaces common fractions such as 1/2 or 1/4 with ½ or ¼. It also converts ordinal numbers such as 1st to 1st.

STEP 7: Create the AutoShape

➤ Pull down the **View menu,** click (or point to) the **Toolbars command** to display the list of available toolbars, then click the **Drawing toolbar.**

➤ Press **Ctrl+End** to move to the end of the document. Move up one line and press **enter** to create a blank line. Click the **down arrow** on the AutoShapes button to display the AutoShapes menu. Click the **Stars and Banners submenu** and select (click) the **Horizontal scroll.**

➤ The mouse pointer changes to a tiny crosshair. Click and drag the mouse over the last sentence (that has Eric Simon's name) to create the scroll as shown in Figure 3.6g (the shortcut menus are not yet visible). Release the mouse.

➤ The scroll is still selected but the underlying text has disappeared. Click the **right mouse button** to display a context-sensitive menu, click the **Order command,** then click **Send Behind Text.** The text is now visible.

➤ Click the **Line Style** and/or **Line Color** tools to change the thickness and color of the line, respectively.

➤ Click elsewhere in the document to deselect the scroll. Save the document.

Banner is selected

Send banner behind text

Click the AutoShapes button to display the Stars and Banners submenu

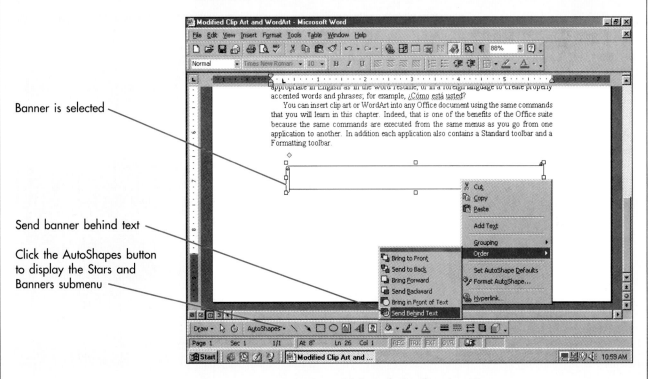

(g) Create the AutoShape (step 7)

FIGURE 3.5   Hands-on Exercise 1 (continued)

DISPLAY THE AUTOSHAPE TOOLBAR

Click the down arrow on the AutoShapes button on the Drawing toolbar to display a cascaded menu listing the various types of AutoShapes, then click and drag the menu's title bar to display the menu as a floating toolbar. Click any tool on the AutoShapes toolbar (such as Stars and Banners), then click and drag its title bar to display the various stars and banners in their own floating toolbar.

STEP 8: The Completed Document

➤ Pull down the **File menu** and click the **Page Setup command** to display the Page Setup dialog box. Click the **Margins tab** and change the top margin to **1.5 inches** (to accommodate the WordArt at the top of the document). Click **OK.**

➤ Click the **drop-down arrow** on the Zoom box and select **Whole Page** to preview the completed document as shown in Figure 3.6h. You can change the size and position of the objects from within this view. For example:

• Click the WordArt to select the object and display the sizing handles and WordArt toolbar.

• Click the banner to deselect the WordArt and display the sizing handles for the banner.

➤ Move and size either object as necessary; then save the document a final time.

➤ Print the document and submit it to your instructor as proof that you did the exercise. Close the document. Exit Word if you do not want to continue with the next exercise at this time.

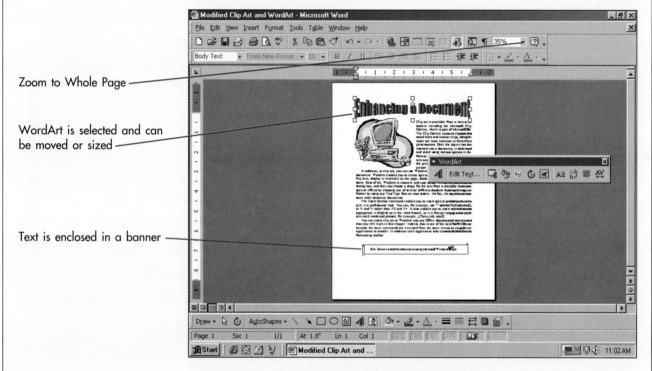

Zoom to Whole Page

WordArt is selected and can be moved or sized

Text is enclosed in a banner

(h) The Completed Document (step 8)

FIGURE 3.6   Hands-on Exercise 1 (continued)

HIGHLIGHT IMPORTANT TEXT

You will love the Highlight text tool, especially if you are in the habit of highlighting text in with a pen. Click the tool to turn the feature on (the button is depressed and the mouse pointer changes to a pen), then paint as many sections as you like. Click the tool a second time to turn the feature off. Click the drop-down arrow on the tool to change the highlighting color.

The emergence of the Internet and World Wide Web has totally changed our society. Perhaps you are already familiar with the basic concepts that underlie the Internet, but if not, a brief review is in order. The **Internet** is a network of networks that connects computers anywhere in the world. The **World Wide Web** (WWW or simply, the Web) is a very large subset of the Internet, consisting of those computers that store a special type of document known as a **Web page** or **HTML document.**

The interesting thing about a Web page is that it contains references called **hyperlinks** to other Web pages, which may in turn be stored on a different computer that may be located anywhere in the world. And therein lies the fascination of the Web, in that you simply click on link after link to go effortlessly from one document to the next. You can start your journey on your professor's home page, then browse through any set of links you wish to follow.

The Internet and World Wide Web are thoroughly integrated into Office 2000 in three important ways. First, you can download resources from any Web page for inclusion in an Office document. Second, you can insert hyperlinks into an Office document, then click those links within Office to display the associated Web page. And finally, you can convert any Office document into a Web page as we will do in Figure 3.7.

All Web pages are developed in a special language called **HTML (Hyper-Text Markup Language).** Initially, the only way to create a Web page was to learn HTML. As indicated, Office 2000 simplifies the process because you can create the document in Word, then simply save it as a Web page. In other words, you start Word in the usual fashion and enter the text of the document with basic formatting. However, instead of saving the document in the default format (as a Word document), you use the **Save As Web Page command** to convert the document to HTML. Microsoft Word does the rest and generates the HTML statements for you.

Footnote

Point to hyperlink to see address associated with hyperlink

Hyperlink

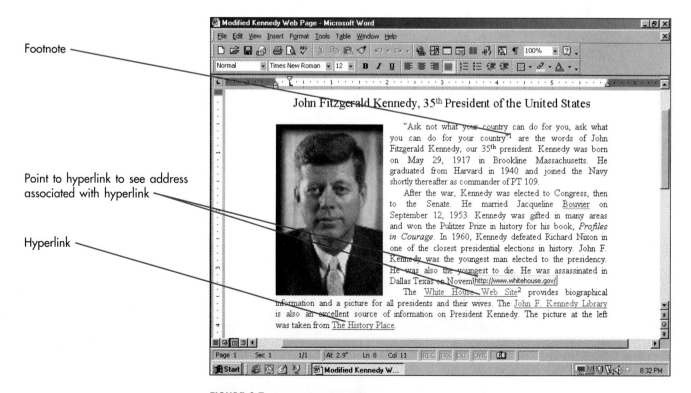

FIGURE 3.7 Creating a Web Page

Figure 3.7 contains the Web page you will create in the next hands-on exercise. The exercise begins by having you search the Web to locate a suitable photograph of President Kennedy for inclusion into the document. You then download the picture to your PC and use the Insert Picture command to insert the photograph into your document. You add formatting, hyperlinks, and footnotes as appropriate, then you save the document as a Web page. The exercise is easy to do and it will give you an appreciation for the various Web capabilities that are built into Office 2000.

Realize, however, that even if you do not place your page on the Web, you can still view it locally on your PC. This is the approach we follow in the next hands-on exercise, which shows you how to save a Word document as a Web page, then see the results of your effort in a Web browser. The Web page is stored on a local drive (e.g., on drive A or drive C) rather than on an Internet server, but it can still be viewed through Internet Explorer (or any other browser).

The ability to create links to local documents and to view those pages through a Web browser has created an entirely new way to disseminate information. Organizations of every size are taking advantage of this capability to develop an *intranet,* in which Web pages are placed on a local area network for use within the organizations. The documents on an intranet are available only to individuals with access to the local area network on which the documents are stored. This is in contrast to loading pages onto a Web server, where they can be viewed by anyone with access to the Web.

THE WEB PAGE WIZARD

The Save As Web Page command converts a Word document to the equivalent HTML document for posting on a Web server. The Web Page Wizard extends the process to create a multipage Web site, complete with navigation and a professionally designed theme. The navigation options let you choose between horizontal and vertical frames so that the user can see the links and content at the same time. The design themes are quite varied and include every element on a Web page. The Wizard is an incredibly powerful tool that rivals any Web-authoring tool we have seen. Try it if a Web project is in your future!

Copyright Protection

A *copyright* provides legal protection for a written or artistic work, giving the author exclusive rights to its use and reproduction, except as governed under the fair use exclusion as explained below. Anything on the Internet or World Wide Web should be considered copyrighted unless the document specifically says it is in the *public domain,* in which case the author is giving everyone the right to freely reproduce and distribute the material.

Does copyright protection mean you cannot quote in your term papers statistics and other facts you find while browsing the Web? Does it mean you cannot download an image to include in your report? The answer to both questions depends on the amount of the material and on your intended use of the information. It is considered *fair use,* and thus not an infringement of copyright, to use a portion of the work for educational, nonprofit purposes, or for the purpose of critical review or commentary. In other words, you can use a quote, downloaded image, or other information from the Web *if* you cite the original work in your footnotes and/or bibliography. Facts themselves are not covered by copyright, so you can use statistical and other data without fear of infringement. You should, however, cite the original source in your document.

Footnotes and Endnotes

A *footnote* provides additional information about an item, such as its source, and appears at the bottom of the page where the reference occurs. An **endnote** is similar in concept but appears at the end of a document. A horizontal line separates the notes from the rest of the document.

The **Insert Footnote command** inserts a note into a document, and automatically assigns the next sequential number to that note. To create a note, position the insertion point where you want the reference, pull down the Insert menu, click Footnote to display the dialog box in Figure 3.8a, then choose either the Footnote or Endnote option button. A superscript reference is inserted into the document, and you will be positioned at the bottom of the page (a footnote) or at the end of the document (an endnote) where you enter the text of the note.

The Options command button in the Footnote and Endnote dialog box enables you to modify the formatting of either type of note as shown in Figure 3.8b. You can change the numbering format (e.g., to Roman numerals) and/or start numbering from a number other than 1. You can also convert footnotes to endnotes or vice versa.

The Insert Footnote command adjusts for last-minute changes, either in your writing or in your professor's requirements. It will, for example, renumber all existing notes to accommodate the addition or deletion of a footnote or endnote. Existing notes are moved (or deleted) within a document by moving (deleting) the reference mark rather than the text of the footnote.

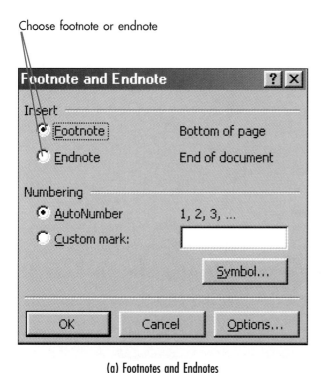

(a) Footnotes and Endnotes

(b) Options

FIGURE 3.8   Footnotes and Endnotes

Word 2000 and the Web

Objective: To download a picture from the Internet for use in a Word document; to insert a hyperlink into a Word document; to save a Word document as a Web page. The exercise requires an Internet connection.

STEP 1: Search the Web

➤ Start **Internet Explorer.** Click the **Maximize button** so that Internet Explorer takes the entire screen.

➤ Click the **Search button** on the Internet Explorer toolbar to open the Explorer bar. The option button to find a Web page is selected by default. Enter **John Kennedy** in the text box, then click the **Search button.**

➤ The results of the search are displayed in the left pane. You can follow any of the links returned by your search engine, or you can attempt to duplicate our results using **Yahoo.** Click the **down arrow** on the **Next button,** then select **Yahoo** as the search engine.

➤ The list of hits is displayed at the bottom of the left pane as shown in Figure 3.9a. (Your list may be different from ours.) Click any link and the associated page is displayed in the right pane. We chose the first category. The links for that category are displayed in the right pane, where we chose the link to **Photo History of JFK.**

➤ Close the left pane to give yourself more room to browse through the site containing the Kennedy photographs. (You can click the **Search button** at any time to reopen the Explorer bar to choose a different site.)

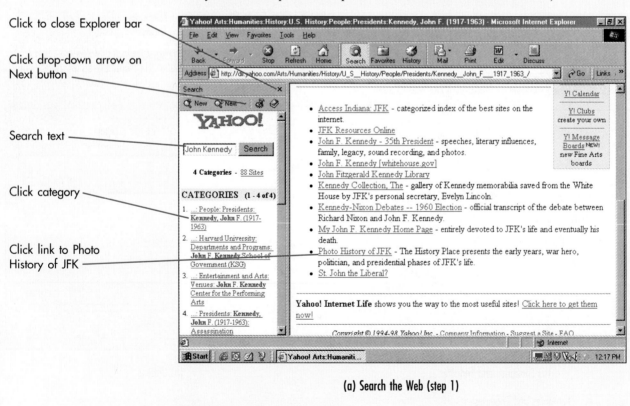

Click to close Explorer bar

Click drop-down arrow on Next button

Search text

Click category

Click link to Photo History of JFK

(a) Search the Web (step 1)

FIGURE 3.9   Hands-on Exercise 2

STEP 2: Save the Picture

➤ Point to the picture of President Kennedy you want to use in your document. Click the **right mouse button** to display a shortcut menu, then click the **Save Picture As command** to display the Save As dialog box in Figure 3.9b.

- Click the **drop-down arrow** in the Save in list box to specify the drive and folder in which you want to save the graphic.
- Internet Explorer supplies the file name and file type for you. You may change the name, but you cannot change the file type.
- Click the **Save button** to download the image. Remember the file name and location, as you will need to access the file in the next step.

➤ The Save As dialog box will close automatically after the picture has been downloaded. Click the **Minimize button** in the Internet Explorer window, since you are temporarily finished using the browser.

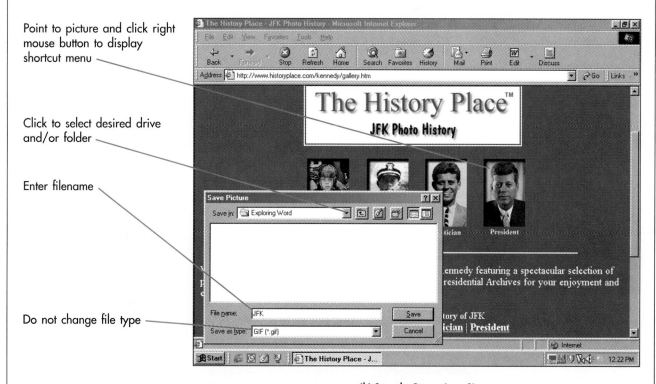

Point to picture and click right mouse button to display shortcut menu

Click to select desired drive and/or folder

Enter filename

Do not change file type

(b) Save the Picture (step 2)

FIGURE 3.9   Hands-on Exercise 2 (continued)

MINIMIZING VERSUS CLOSING AN APPLICATION

Minimizing an application is different from closing it, and you should understand the difference. Minimizing an application leaves the application open in memory, but shrinks its window to a button on the Windows taskbar so that you can return to it later in the session. Closing an application removes the application from memory, so that you have to restart the application if you need it. The advantage to closing an application, however, is that you free system resources, so that your remaining applications will run more efficiently.

STEP 3: Insert the Picture

➤ Start Word and open the **Kennedy document** in the **Exploring Word folder.** Save the document as **Modified Kennedy.**

➤ Pull down the **View menu** to be sure that you are in the **Print Layout view** (or else you will not see the picture after it is inserted into the document). Pull down the **Insert menu,** point to (or click) **Picture command,** then click **From File** to display the Insert Picture dialog box shown in Figure 3.9c.

➤ Click the **drop-down arrow** on the Look in text box to select the drive and folder where you previously saved the picture.

➤ Select (click) **JFK,** which is the file containing the picture of President Kennedy. Click the **drop-down arrow** on the **Views button** to switch to the **Preview button** and display the picture prior to inserting it into the document. Click **Insert.**

➤ Save the document.

Views button

Click to select drive and/or folder

Click file

Print Layout button

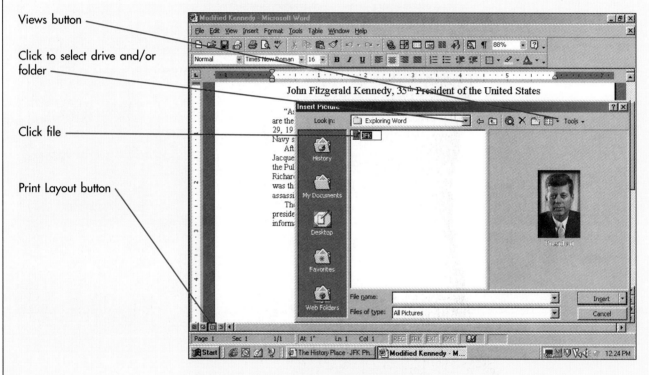

(c) Insert the Picture (step 3)

FIGURE 3.9   Hands-on Exercise 2 (continued)

THE VIEWS BUTTON

Click the Views button to cycle through the four available views, each with a flavor of its own. The Details view shows the file size as well as the date and time the file was last modified. The Preview view displays the beginning of the file without having to open it. The Properties view shows additional characteristics about the file, such as the author's name. The List view displays only icons and file names, but enables you to see the largest number of files without having to scroll. Choose the view that is appropriate for your current task.

STEP 4: Move and Size the Picture

➤ Point to the picture after it is inserted into the document, click the **right mouse button** to display a shortcut menu, then click the **Format Picture command** to display the Format Picture dialog box.

➤ Click the **Layout tab,** choose **Square** as the Wrapping Style, then click the **Left option button** under Horizontal Alignment. Click **OK** to accept the settings and close the Format Picture dialog box. Move and/or size the picture so that it approximates the position in Figure 3.9d.

➤ Check that the picture is still selected, then click the **Crop tool** on the Picture toolbar. The mouse pointer changes to interlocking lines. Click and drag the sizing handle on the bottom of the picture upward to delete the label in the picture. Resize the picture as necessary.

➤ Save the document.

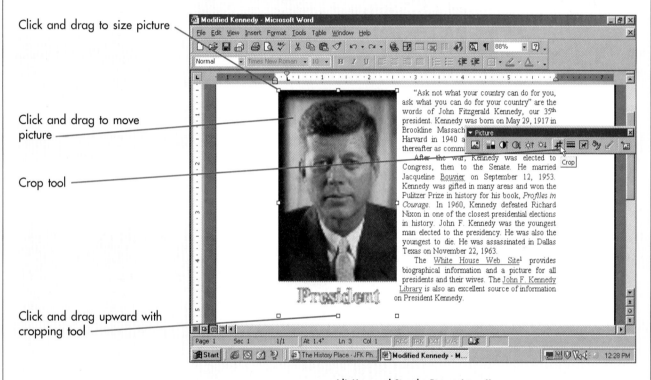

Click and drag to size picture

Click and drag to move picture

Crop tool

Click and drag upward with cropping tool

(d) Move and Size the Picture (step 4)

FIGURE 3.9   Hands-on Exercise 2 (continued)

THE PICTURE TOOLBAR

The Picture Toolbar is displayed automatically when a picture is selected, and suppressed otherwise. As with any toolbar, it may be docked along the edge of the application window or floating within the window. You can move a floating toolbar by dragging its title bar. You can move a docked toolbar by dragging the move handle (the line at the left of the toolbar). If by chance you do not see the Picture toolbar when a picture is selected, pull down the View menu, click the Toolbars command, and check the Picture toolbar. Point to any toolbar button to display a Screen-Tip that is indicative of its function.

STEP 5: Insert a Hyperlink

➤ Press **Ctrl+End** to move to the end of the document, where you will add a sentence to identify the photograph. Enter the text, **The picture at the left was taken from** (the sentence will end with a hyperlink).

➤ Pull down the **Insert menu** and click the **Hyperlink command** (or click the **Insert Hyperlink button** on the Standard toolbar) to display the Insert Hyperlink dialog box as shown in Figure 3.9e.

➤ Click in the **Text to display** text box and enter **The History Place.** Press **Tab.** Enter **www.historyplace.com/kennedy/gallery.htm.** Click **OK.** The hyperlink should appear as an underlined entry in the document. Type a period after the hyperlink. Save the document.

Insert Hyperlink button ——

Enter text of hyperlink ——

Enter Web address ——

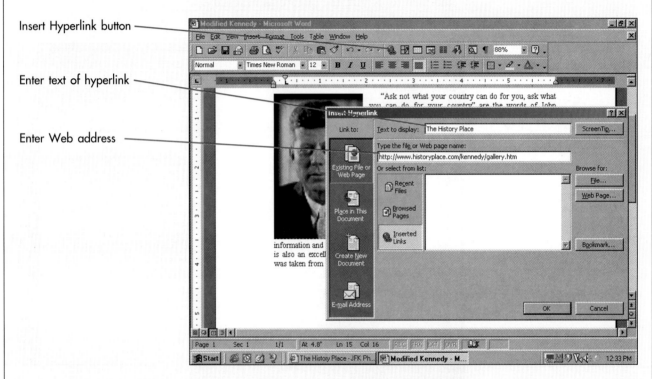

(e) Insert a Hyperlink (step 5)

FIGURE 3.9   Hands-on Exercise 2 (continued)

COPY THE WEB ADDRESS

Use the Copy command to enter a Web address from Internet Explorer into a Word document or dialog box. Not only do you save time by not having to type the address yourself, but you also ensure that it is entered correctly. Click in the Address bar of Internet Explorer to select the URL, then pull down the Edit menu and click the Copy command (or use the Ctrl+C keyboard shortcut). Switch to the Word document, click at the place in the document where you want to insert the URL, pull down the Edit menu and click the Paste command (or use the Ctrl+V keyboard shortcut). You must, however, use the keyboard shortcut if you are pasting the address into a dialog box.

STEP 6: Insert a Footnote

➤ Press **Ctrl+Home** to move to the beginning of the document. Click at the end of the quotation in the first paragraph, where you will insert a new footnote.

➤ Pull down the **Insert menu.** Click **Footnote** to display the Footnote and Endnote dialog as shown in Figure 3.9f. Check that the option buttons for **Footnote** and **AutoNumber** are selected, then click **OK.**

➤ The insertion point moves to the bottom of the page, where you type the text of the footnote. Enter **Inaugural Address, John F. Kennedy, January 20, 1961.** You can expand the footnote to include a Web site that contains the text at **www.cc.columbia.edu/acis/bartleby/inaugural/pres56.html.**

➤ Press **Ctrl+Home** to move to the beginning of the page, where you will see a reference for the footnote you just created. If necessary, you can move (or delete) a footnote by moving (deleting) the reference mark. Save the document.

Click at end of quotation

Click Footnote

Click AutoNunmber

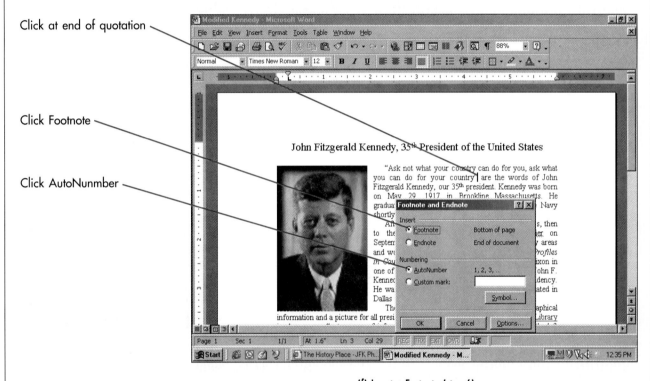

(f) Insert a Footnote (step 6)

FIGURE 3.9   Hands-on Exercise 2 (continued)

CREATE A HYPERLINK AUTOMATICALLY

Type any Internet path (i.e., any text that begins with http:// or www) or e-mail address, and Word will automatically convert the entry to a hyperlink. (If this does not work on your system, pull down the Tools menu, click AutoCorrect, then click the AutoFormat as you Type tab. Check the box in the Replace as you type area for Internet and Network paths, and click OK.) To modify the hyperlink after it is created, right click the link to display a shortcut menu, click the Hyperlink command, then select the Edit Hyperlink command to display the associated dialog box.

STEP 7: Create the Web Page

➤ Pull down the **File menu** and click the **Save as Web Page** command to display the Save as dialog box as shown in Figure 3.9g. Click the drop-down arrow in the Save In list box to select the appropriate drive, then open the **Exploring Word folder** that contains the documents you are using.

➤ Change the name of the Web page to **Modified Kennedy Web Page** (to differentiate it from the Word document). Click the **Save button.**

➤ The title bar changes to reflect the name of the Web page. There are now two versions of this document in the Exploring Word folder—Modified Kennedy, and Modified Kennedy Web Page. The latter has been saved as a Web page (in HTML format).

➤ Print this page for your instructor.

Print button —

Click to select drive and/or folder —

Enter filename —

Internet Explorer button —

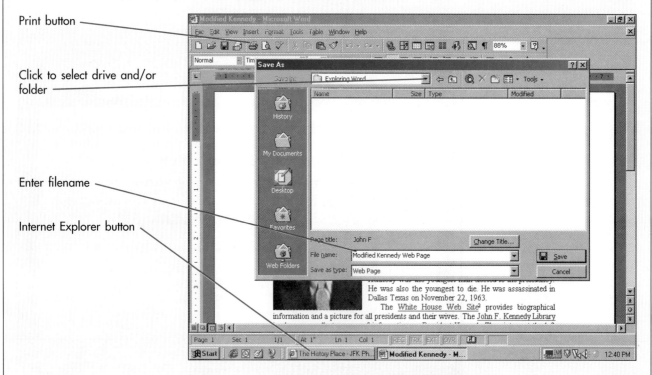

(g) Create the Web Page (step 7)

FIGURE 3.9   Hands-on Exercise 2 (continued)

CHANGE THE DEFAULT FILE LOCATION

The default file location is the folder Word uses to open and save a document unless it is otherwise instructed. To change the default location, pull down the Tools menu, click Options, click the File Locations tab, click the desired File type (documents), then click the Modify command button to display the Modify Location dialog box. Click the drop-down arrow in the Look In box to select the new folder (e.g., C:\Exploring Word). Click OK to accept this selection. Click OK to close the Options dialog box. The next time you access the Open or Save command from the File menu, the Look In text box will reflect the change.

STEP 8: Preview the Web Page

➤ The easiest way to start Internet Explorer is to pull down the **File menu** and click the **Web Page Preview command.** However, we want you to see the extra folder that was created with your Web page. Thus, click the button for Internet Explorer on the Windows taskbar.

➤ Pull down the **File menu** and click the **Open command** to display the Open dialog box. Click the **Browse button,** then select the folder (e.g., Exploring Word) where you saved the Web page. Select (click) the **Modified Kennedy as Web Page** document, click **Open,** then click **OK** to open the document.

➤ You should see the Web page that was created earlier as shown in Figure 3.9h, except that you are viewing the page in Internet Explorer.

➤ Click the **Print button** on the Internet Explorer toolbar to print this page for your instructor. Does this printed document differ from the version that was printed at the end of step 7? Close Internet Explorer.

➤ Exit Word if you do not want to continue with the next exercise at this time.

Print button —

Address bar reflects local address —

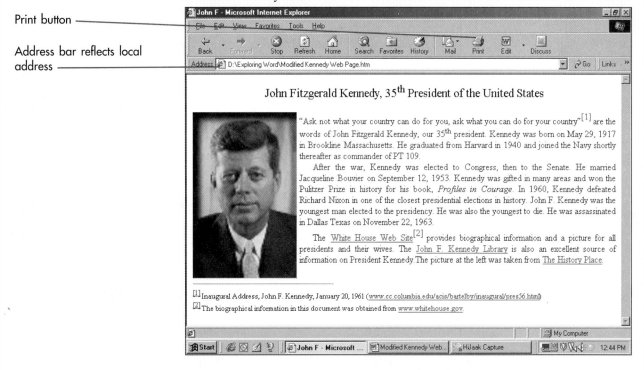

(h) Preview the Web Page (step 8)

FIGURE 3.9 Hands-on Exercise 2 (continued)

AN EXTRA FOLDER

Look carefully at the contents of the Exploring Word folder within the Open dialog box. You see the HTML document you just created, as well as a folder that was created automatically by the Save as Web page command. The latter folder contains the objects that are referenced by the page such as the Kennedy picture and a horizontal line above the footnotes. Be sure to copy the contents of this folder to the Web server in addition to your Web page if you decide to post the page.

We have created some very interesting documents throughout the text, but in every instance we have formatted the document entirely on our own. It is time now to see what is available to "jump start" the process by borrowing professional designs from others. Accordingly, we discuss the wizards and templates that are built into Microsoft Word.

A *template* is a partially completed document that contains formatting, text, and/or graphics. It may be as simple as a memo or as complex as a résumé or newsletter. Microsoft Word provides a variety of templates for common documents including a résumé, agenda, and fax cover sheet. You simply open the template, then modify the existing text as necessary, while retaining the formatting in the template. A *wizard* makes the process even easier by asking a series of questions, then creating a customized document based on your answers. A template or wizard creates the initial document for you. It's then up to you to complete the document by entering the appropriate information.

Figure 3.10 illustrates the use of wizards and templates in conjunction with a résumé. You can choose from one of three existing templates (contemporary, elegant, and professional) to which you add personal information. Alternatively, you can select the ***Résumé Wizard*** to create a customized résumé, as was done in Figure 3.10a.

After the Résumé Wizard is selected, it prompts you for the information it needs to create a basic résumé. You specify the style in Figure 3.10b, enter the requested information in Figure 3.10c, and choose the headings in Figure 3.10d. The wizard continues to ask additional questions (not shown in Figure 3.10), after which it displays the (partially) completed résumé based on your responses. You then complete the résumé by entering the specifics of your employment and/or additional information. As you edit the document, you can copy and paste information within the résumé, just as you would with a regular document. It takes a little practice, but the end result is a professionally formatted résumé in a minimum of time.

Microsoft Word contains templates and wizards for a variety of other documents. (Look carefully at the tabs within the dialog box of Figure 3.10a and you can infer that Word will help you to create letters, faxes, memos, reports, legal pleadings, publications, and even Web pages.) Consider, too, Figure 3.11, which displays four attractive documents that were created using the respective wizards. Realize, however, that while wizards and templates will help you to create professionally designed documents, they are only a beginning. *The content is still up to you.*

THIRTY SECONDS IS ALL YOU HAVE

Thirty seconds is the average amount of time a personnel manager spends skimming your résumé and deciding whether or not to call you for an interview. It doesn't matter how much training you have had or how good you are if your résumé and cover letter fail to project a professional image. Know your audience and use the vocabulary of your targeted field. Be positive and describe your experience from an accomplishment point of view. Maintain a separate list of references and have it available on request. Be sure that all information is accurate. Be conscientious about the design of your résumé, and proofread the final documents very carefully.

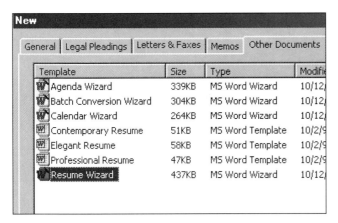

(a) Résumé Wizard

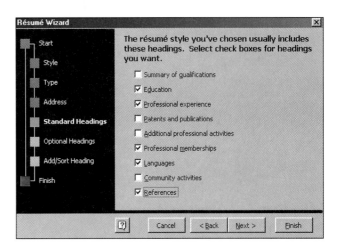

(d) Choose the Headings

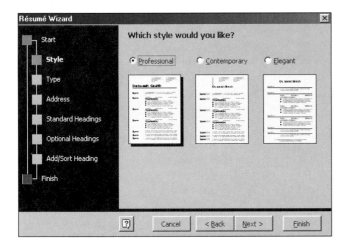

(b) Choose the Style

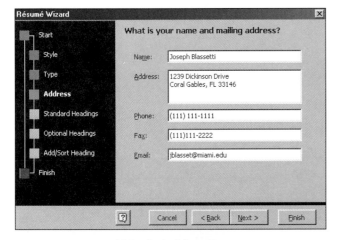

(c) Supply the Information

(e) The Completed Résumé

FIGURE 3.10   Creating a Résumé

(a) Calendar

	Sun	Mon	Tue	Wed	Thu	Fri	Sat
							1
	2	3	4	5	6	7	8
	9	10	11	12	13	14	15
	16	17	18	19	20	21	22
	23	24	25	26	27	28	29
	30	31					

May

1999

(a) Calendar

(b) Agenda

Agenda

Initial Study Group Session

2/20/99
7:30 PM to 8:15 PM
Joe's Place

Note taker:	Jennifer
Attendees:	Jennifer, Susan, Joe, and Paul
Please bring:	Text book, class notes, calendar

Agenda topics

10	Introduction	Susan
20	Semester Plan	Joe
15	Review current assignment	Paul

Special notes: As you can see, the meeting should not take any longer than 45-50 minutes, if everyone is prepared. We can order pizza afterwards, if anyone is interested.

(b) Agenda

277 Riviera Drive
Coral Gables, FL 33146
Phone: (111) 222-4545
Fax: (111) 222-4546

Fax

To:	Jennifer	From:	Susan Peterson
Fax:	(111) 222-3333	Date:	March 13, 1999
Phone:	(111) 222-3344	Pages:	2
Re:	Initial Study Group Session	CC:	

☐ Urgent ☐ For Review ☐ Please Comment ☐ Please Reply ☐ Please Recycle

•**Comments:** Attached you should find the agenda for our initial study group session. Please let me know if you have any questions. I look forward to seeing you on the 20th.

(c) Fax Cover Sheet

Interoffice Memo

Date: 2/15/99
To: Dr. Robert Plant, Dr. John Stewart
From: Jenn Sheridan
RE: CIS 120 Final Exam

The meeting to prepare the final exam for CIS 120 will be on Friday, February 19, 1999 at 3:00PM in my office. I have attached a copy of last semester's final, which I would like for you to review prior to the meeting. In addition, if you could take a few minutes and create approximately 20 new questions for this semester's test, it would make our job at the meeting a lot easier. The meeting should last no longer than an hour, provided that we all do our homework before the meeting. If you have any questions before that time, please let me know.

Attachments

2/15/99   Confidential   1

(d) Memo

FIGURE 3.11   What You Can Do With Wizards

Wizards and Templates

Objective: To use the Agenda Wizard to create an agenda for a study group, then use the Fax Wizard to fax the agenda to your group. Use Figure 3.12 as a guide in the exercise.

STEP 1: The File New Command

➤ Start Word. Pull down the **File menu.** Click **New** to display the New dialog box shown in Figure 3.12a. Click the **Other Documents tab.**

➤ Click the **Details button** to switch to the Details view to see the file name, type, size, and date of last modification. Click and drag the vertical line between the Template and Size columns, to increase the size of the Template column, so that you can see the complete document name.

➤ Select (click) **Agenda Wizard.** If necessary, click the option button to **Create New Document** (as opposed to a template). Click **OK.**

Details button

Click Other Documents tab

Click and drag to change size of column

Click to select Agenda Wizard

Click Document option button

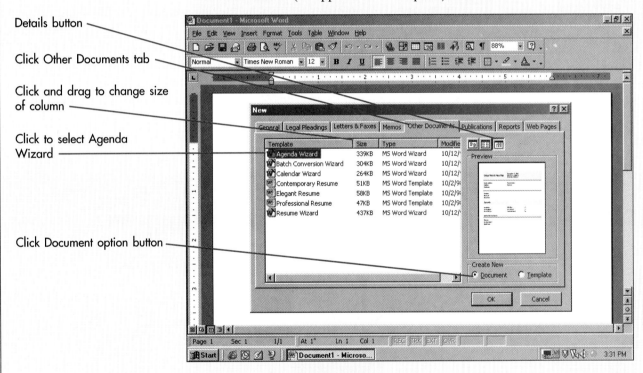

(a) The File New Command (step 1)

FIGURE 3.12 Hands-on Exercise 3

SORT BY NAME, DATE, OR FILE SIZE

The files in the Save As, Open, and New dialog boxes can be displayed in ascending or descending sequence by name, date modified, or size. Change to the Details view, then click the heading of the desired column; e.g., click the Type column to list the files according to file type (to separate the documents from the templates).

STEP 2: The Agenda Wizard

➤ You should see the main screen of the Agenda Wizard as shown in Figure 3.12b. Click **Next** to begin. The Wizard will take you through a series of questions, from start to finish. To create the desired agenda:

• Click **Modern** as the style of the agenda. Click **Next.**

• Enter the date and time of your meeting. Enter **Initial Study Group Session** as the title. Enter **Joe's Place** as the location. Click **Next.**

• The Wizard asks which headings you want and supplies a check box next to each heading. The check boxes function as toggle switches to select (deselect) each heading. We suggest you clear all entries except **Please bring.** Click **Next.**

• The Wizard asks which names you want in the agenda. Clear all headings except **Note Taker** and **Attendees.** Click **Next.**

• Enter at least three topics for the agenda. Press the **Tab key** to move from one text box to the next (e.g., from Agenda topic, to Person, to Minutes). Click the **Add** button when you have completed the information for one topic.

• If necessary, reorder the topics by clicking the desired topic, then clicking the **Move Up** or **Move Down** command button. Click **Next** when you are satisfied with the agenda.

• Click **No** when asked whether you want a form to record the minutes of the meeting. Click **Next.**

➤ The final screen of the Agenda Wizard indicates that the Wizard has all the information it needs. Click the **Finish button.**

Click Next

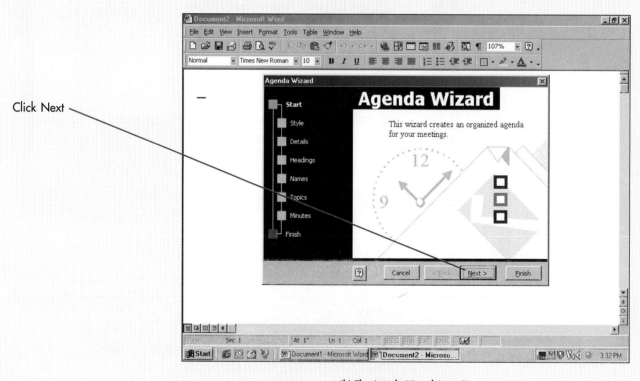

(b) The Agenda Wizard (step 2)

FIGURE 3.12   Hands-on Exercise 3 (continued)

STEP 3: Complete the Agenda

➤ You should see an initial agenda similar to the document in Figure 3.12c. Cancel the Office Assistant if it appears (or you can leave it open and request help as necessary).

➤ Save the agenda as **Initial Study Group Session** in the **Exploring Word** folder. If necessary, change to the **Print Layout view** and zoom to **Page Width** so that your document more closely matches ours.

➤ Complete the Agenda by entering the additional information, such as the names of the note taker and attendees as well as the specifics of what to read or bring, as shown in the figure. Click at the indicated position on the figure prior to entering the text, so that your entries align properly.

➤ Click the **Spelling and Grammar button** to check the agenda for spelling.

➤ Save the document but do not close it.

➤ Click the **Print button** on the Standard toolbar to print the completed document and submit it to your instructor.

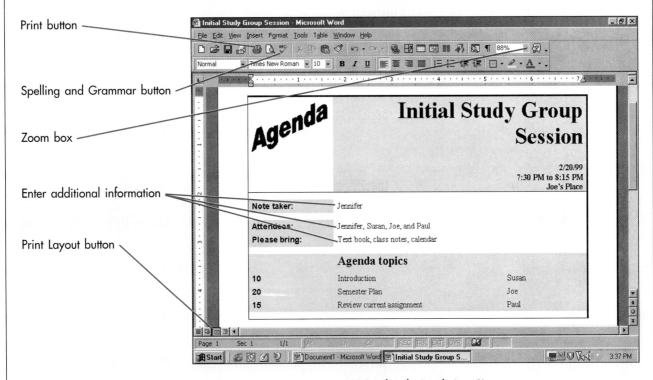

(c) Complete the Agenda (step 3)

FIGURE 3.12   Hands-on Exercise 3 (continued)

RETRACE YOUR STEPS

The Agenda Wizard guides you every step of the way, but what if you make a mistake or change your mind? Click the Back command button at any time to return to a previous screen in order to enter different information, then continue working with the Wizard.

STEP 4: The Fax Wizard

➤ Pull down the **File menu** and click **New** to display the New dialog box. Click the **Letters & Faxes tab** to display the indicated wizards and templates. Check that the **Document option button** is selected. Double click the **Fax Wizard** to start it.

➤ You should see the main screen of the Fax Wizard as shown in Figure 3.12d. Click **Next** to begin.

- The Fax Wizard suggests Initial Study Group as the name of the document you want to fax (because the document is still open). The option button **With a Cover Sheet** is selected. Click **Next**.

- Do not be concerned about the fax software that is installed on your computer, because you're not going to send the fax. Thus, click the option button to print the document (as though you were going to send it from a fax machine). Click **Next**.

- Enter the name and fax number of one person in your group. Complete this entry even if you do not intend to send an actual fax. Click **Next**.

- Choose the style of the cover sheet. We selected **Professional**. Click **Next**.

- If necessary, complete and/or modify the information about the sender so that it reflects your name and telephone number. Click **Next**.

- Read the last screen reminding you about how to list phone numbers correctly. Click **Finish**.

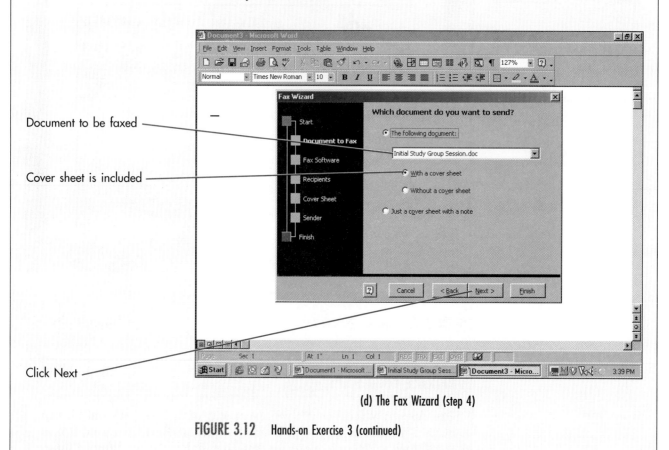

(d) The Fax Wizard (step 4)

FIGURE 3.12   Hands-on Exercise 3 (continued)

STEP 5: Complete the Fax

➤ You should see a fax cover sheet similar to the document in Figure 3.12e.

➤ Save the cover sheet as **Fax Cover Sheet** in the **Exploring Word** folder. If necessary, change to the **Normal view** and zoom to **Page Width** so that your document more closely matches ours.

➤ Complete the cover sheet by entering the additional information as appropriate. Click at the indicated position in Figure 3.12e prior to entering the text, so that your entries align properly.

➤ Click the **Spelling and Grammar button** to check the agenda for spelling.

➤ Save the document a final time. Click the **Print button** on the Standard toolbar to print the completed document, and submit it to your instructor.

➤ Exit Word. Congratulations on a job well done.

Print button —

Spelling and Grammar button —

Zoom box —

Print Layout button —

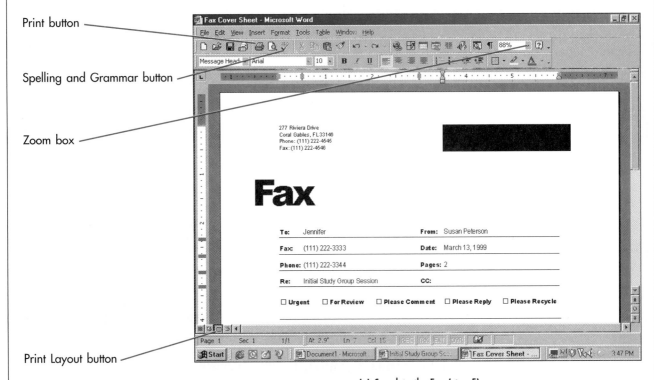

(e) Complete the Fax (step 5)

FIGURE 3.12 Hands-on Exercise 3 (continued)

CHANGING THE VIEW

Word provides different views of a document and different magnifications of each view. The Normal view suppresses the margins, giving you more room in which to work. The Print Layout view, on the other hand, displays the margins, so that what you see on the monitor more closely resembles the printed page. The easiest way to change from one view to the other is by clicking the appropriate icon above the status bar. The easiest way to change the magnification is to click the drop-down arrow in the Zoom box on the Standard toolbar.

SUMMARY

The applications in Microsoft Office are thoroughly integrated with one another. They look alike and work alike. Equally important, they share information through a technology known as Object Linking and Embedding (OLE), which enables you to create a compound document containing data (objects) from multiple applications.

The Microsoft Clip Gallery contains clip art, sound files, and motion clips and it is accessible from any application in Microsoft Office. Clip art is inserted into a document in one of two ways—through the Insert Object command or more directly through the Insert Picture command. Either way, you choose the type of object and the category, then select the image and insert it into the document. Microsoft WordArt is an application within Microsoft Office that creates decorative text, which can be used to add interest to a document.

The Insert Symbol command provides access to special characters, making it easy to place typographic characters into a document. The symbols can be taken from any TrueType font and can be displayed in any point size.

The Internet is a network of networks. The World Wide Web (WWW, or simply the Web) is a very large subset of the Internet, consisting of those computers containing hypertext and/or hypermedia documents. Resources (e.g., clip art or photographs) can be downloaded from the Web for inclusion in a Word document. All Web pages are written in a language called HTML (HyperText Markup Language). The Save As Web Page command saves a Word document as a Web page.

A copyright provides legal protection to a written or artistic work, giving the author exclusive rights to its use and reproduction except as governed under the fair use exclusion. Anything on the Internet or World Wide Web should be considered copyrighted unless the document specifically says it is in the public domain. The fair use exclusion enables you to use a portion of the work for educational, nonprofit purposes, or for the purpose of critical review or commentary.

A footnote provides additional information about an item, such as its source, and appears at the bottom of the page where the reference occurs. The Insert Footnote command inserts a footnote into a document and automatically assigns the next sequential number to that note.

Wizards and templates help create professionally designed documents with a minimum of time and effort. A template is a partially completed document that contains formatting and other information. A wizard is an interactive program that creates a customized template based on the answers you supply.

OBJECT LINKING AND EMBEDDING

Object Linking and Embedding (OLE) enables you to create a compound document containing objects (data) from multiple Windows applications. Each of the techniques, linking and embedding, can be implemented in various ways. Althogh OLE is one of the major benefits of working in the Windows environment, it would be impossible to illustrate all of the techniques in a single exercise. Accordingly, we have created the icon at the left to help you identify the many OLE examples that appear throughout the *Exploring Windows* series.

Agenda Wizard
AutoCorrect
AutoFormat
Clip art
Clipboard
Compound document
Copyright
Crop
Drawing toolbar
Endnote
Fair use exclusion
Fax Wizard
Footnote
Format Picture
   command

HTML document
Hyperlink
Insert Footnote
   command
Insert Hyperlink
   command
Insert Picture command
Insert Symbol
   command
Internet
Intranet
Microsoft Clip Gallery
Microsoft WordArt
Object Linking and
   Embedding (OLE)

Picture toolbar
Public domain
Résumé Wizard
Save as Web Page
   command
Sizing handle
Template
Web page
Wizard
WordArt
WordArt toolbar
World Wide Web

MULTIPLE CHOICE

1. How do you change the size of a selected object so that the height and width change in proportion to one another?
   (a) Click and drag any of the four corner handles in the direction you want to go
   (b) Click and drag the sizing handle on the top border, then click and drag the sizing handle on the left side
   (c) Click and drag the sizing handle on the bottom border, then click and drag the sizing handle on the right side
   (d) All of the above

2. The Microsoft Clip Galley:
   (a) Is accessed through the Insert Picture command
   (b) Is available to every application in the Microsoft Office
   (c) Enables you to search for a specific piece of clip art by specifying a key word in the description of the clip art
   (d) All of the above

3. Which view, and which magnification, offers the most convenient way to position a graphic within a document?
   (a) Page Width in the Print Layout view
   (b) Full Page in the Print Layout view
   (c) Page Width in the Normal view
   (d) Full Page in the Normal view

4. Which of the following can be inserted from the Microsoft Clip Gallery?
   (a) Clip art
   (b) Sound
   (c) Motion clips
   (d) All of the above

5. How do you insert special characters such as the accented letters or typographical symbols into a Word document?
   (a) Use the Insert WordArt command to draw the character
   (b) Use the Insert Picture command to draw the character
   (c) Use the Insert Symbol command
   (d) All of the above

6. How do you format a document so that text in the document wraps around a clip art image?
   (a) Select the text, then use the Format Text command or the Format Text toolbar to specify the desired layout
   (b) Select the picture, then use the Format Picture command or the Format Picture toolbar to specify the desired layout
   (c) Select the text, then click and drag a sizing handle to obtain the desired layout
   (d) You cannot wrap the text around the picture

7. Which of the following is true about footnotes or endnotes?
   (a) The addition of a footnote or endnote automatically renumbers the notes that follow
   (b) The deletion of a footnote or endnote automatically renumbers the notes that follow
   (c) Both (a) and (b)
   (d) Neither (a) nor (b)

8. Which of the following is true about the Insert Symbol command?
   (a) It can insert a symbol in different type sizes
   (b) It can access any TrueType font installed on the system
   (c) Both (a) and (b)
   (d) Neither (a) nor (b)

9. Which of the following is a true statement regarding objects and the toolbars associated with those objects?
   (a) Clicking on a WordArt object displays the WordArt toolbar
   (b) Clicking on a Picture displays the Picture Toolbar
   (c) Both (a) and (b)
   (d) Neither (a) nor (b)

10. How do you insert a hyperlink into a Word document?
    (a) Pull down the Insert menu and click the Hyperlink command
    (b) Click the Insert Hyperlink button on the Standard toolbar
    (c) Both (a) and (b)
    (d) Neither (a) nor (b)

11. A Web browser such as Internet Explorer can display a page from:
    (a) A local drive such as drive A or drive C
    (b) A drive on a local area network
    (c) The World Wide Web
    (d) All of the above

12. What happens if you enter the text *www.intel.com* into a document?
    (a) The entry is converted to a hyperlink, and the text will be underlined and displayed in a different color
    (b) The associated page will be opened, provided your computer has access to the Internet
    (c) Both (a) and (b)
    (d) Neither (a) nor (b)

13. Which of the following is a true statement about wizards?
    (a) They are accessed through the New command in the File menu
    (b) They always produce a finished document
    (c) Both (a) and (b)
    (d) Neither (a) nor (b)

14. How do you access the wizards built into Microsoft Word?
    (a) Pull down the Wizards and Templates menu
    (b) Pull down the Insert menu and choose the Wizards and Templates command
    (c) Pull down the File menu and choose the New command
    (d) None of the above

15. Which of the following is true regarding wizards and templates?
    (a) A wizard may create a template
    (b) A template may create a wizard
    (c) Both (a) and (b)
    (d) Neither (a) nor (b)

Answers

1. a	**6.** b	**11.** d
2. d	**7.** c	**12.** a
3. b	**8.** c	**13.** a
4. d	**9.** c	**14.** c
5. c	**10.** c	**15.** a

PRACTICE WITH MICROSOFT WORD

1. Inserting Objects: Figure 3.13 illustrates a flyer that we created for a hypothetical computer sale. We embedded clip art and WordArt and created what we believe is an attractive flyer. Try to duplicate our advertisement, or better yet, create your own. Include your name somewhere in the document as a sales associate. Be sure to spell check your ad, then print the completed flyer and submit it to your instructor.

2. Exploring TrueType: The installation of Microsoft Windows and/or Office 2000 also installs several TrueType fonts, which in turn are accessible from any application. Two of the fonts, Symbols and Wingdings, contain a variety of special characters that can be used to create some unusual documents. Use the Insert Symbol command, your imagination, and the fact that TrueType fonts are scaleable to any point size to re-create the documents in Figure 3.14. Better yet, use your imagination to create your own documents.

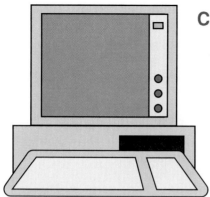

Computer World's Annual Pre-Inventory Sale

When: June 21, 1999
          8:00AM - 10:00PM

Where: 13640 South Dixie Highway

Computer World

Computers
Printers
Fax/Modems
CD-ROM drives
Sound Systems
Software
Etc.

Pre-Inventory Sale

Sales Associate: Bianca Costo

FIGURE 3.13   Inserting Objects (Exercise 1)

Valentine's Day
We'll serenade your sweetheart
Call 284-LOVE

STUDENT COMPUTER LAB
Fall Semester Hours

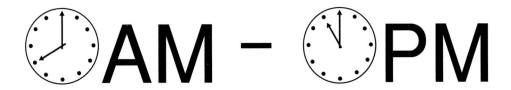

FIGURE 3.14   Exploring TrueType (Exercise 2)

3. Automatic Formatting: The document in Figure 3.15 was created to illustrate the automatic formatting and correction facilities that are built into Microsoft Word. We want you to create the document, include your name at the bottom, then submit the completed document to your instructor as proof that you did the exercise. All you have to do is follow the instructions within the document and let Word do the formatting and correcting for you.

The only potential difficulty is that the options on your system may be set to negate some of the features to which we refer. Accordingly, you need to pull down the Tools menu, click the AutoCorrect command, and click the AutoFormat As You Type tab. Verify that the options referenced in the document are in effect. You also need to review the table of predefined substitutions on the AutoCorrect tab to learn the typewritten characters that will trigger the smiley faces, copyright, and registered trademark substitutions.

It's Easier Than It Looks

This document was created to demonstrate the AutoCorrect and AutoFormat features that are built into Microsoft Word. In essence, you type as you always did and enter traditional characters, then let Word perform its "magic" by substituting symbols and other formatting for you. Among the many features included in these powerful commands are the:

1. Automatic creation of numbered lists by typing a number followed by a period, tab, or right parenthesis. Just remember to press the return key twice to turn off this feature.
2. Symbols for common fractions such as $\frac{1}{2}$ or $\frac{1}{4}$.
3. Ordinal numbers with superscripts created automatically such as 1st, 2nd, or 3rd.
4. Copyright © and Registered trademark ® symbols.

AutoFormat will even add a border to a paragraph any time you type three or more hyphens, equal signs, or underscores on a line by itself.

And finally, the AutoCorrect feature has built-in substitution for smiley faces that look best when set in a larger point size such as 72 points.

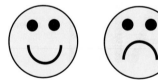

FIGURE 3.15   Automatic Formatting (Exercise 3)

4. Create an Envelope: The Résumé Wizard will take you through the process of creating a résumé, but you need an envelope in which to mail it. Pull down the Tools menu, click the Envelopes and Labels command, click the Envelopes command, then enter the indicated information. Look closely at the dialog box and note that Word will even append a bar code to the envelope if you request it.

You can print the envelope and/or include it permanently in the document as shown in Figure 3.16. *Do not, however, do this exercise in a Computer Lab at school unless envelopes are available for the printer.*

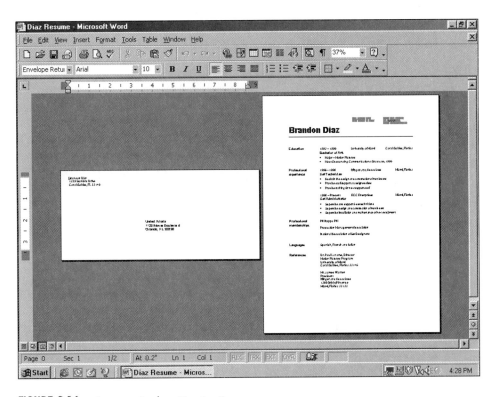

FIGURE 3.16 Create an Envelope (Exercise 4)

5. Presidential Anecdotes: Figure 3.17 displays the finished version of a document containing 10 presidential anecdotes. The anecdotes were taken from the book *Presidential Anecdotes,* by Paul F. Boller, Jr., published by Penguin Books (New York, NY, 1981). Open the *Chapter 3 Practice 5* document that is found on the data disk, then make the following changes:

a. Add a footnote after Mr. Boller's name, which appears at the end of the second sentence, citing the information about the book. This, in turn, renumbers all existing footnotes in the document.

b. Switch the order of the anecdotes for Lincoln and Jefferson so that the presidents appear in order. The footnotes for these references are changed automatically.

c. Convert all of the footnotes to endnotes, as shown in the figure.

d. Go to the White House Web site and download a picture of any of the 10 presidents, then incorporate that picture into a cover page. Remember to cite the reference with an appropriate footnote.

e. Submit the completed document to your instructor.

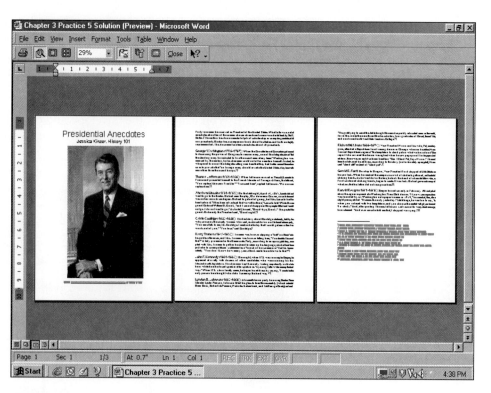

FIGURE 3.17   Presidential Anecdotes (Exercise 5)

6. Photographs Online: The Smithsonian Institution is a priceless resource. Go to the home page of the Smithsonian (www.si.edu), select photography from the subject area, then go to Smithsonian Photographs online to display the page in Figure 3.18. (You can also go to this page directly at photo2.si.edu). Click the link to search the image database, then choose one or two photographs on any subject that you find interesting.

Use the technique described in the chapter to download those photographs to your PC, then use the Insert Picture command to incorporate those pictures into a Word document. Write a short paper (250 to 500 words) describing those photographs and submit the paper to your professor as proof you did this exercise. Be sure to include an appropriate footnote to cite the source of the photographs.

7. Music on the Web: The World Wide Web is a source of infinite variety, including music from your favorite rock group. You can find biographical information and/or photographs such as the one in Figure 3.19. You can even find music, which you can download and play, provided you have the necessary hardware. It's fun, it's easy, so go to it. Use any search engine to find documents about your favorite rock group. Try to find biographical information as well as a picture, then incorporate the results of your research into a short paper to submit to your instructor.

8. The iCOMP Index: The iCOMP index was developed by Intel to compare the speeds of various microprocessors. We want you to search the Web and find a chart showing values in the current iCOMP index. (The chart you find need not be the same as the one in Figure 3.20.) Once you find the chart, download the graphic and incorporate it into a memo to your instructor. Add a paragraph or two describing the purpose of the index as shown in Figure 3.20.

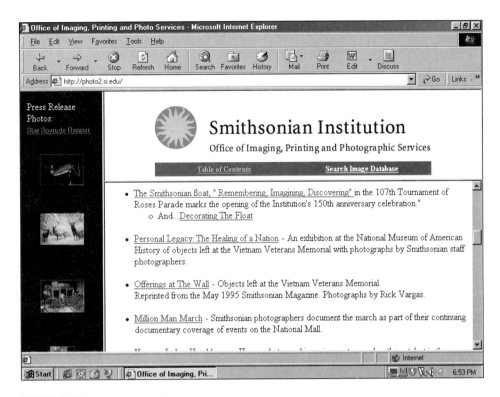

FIGURE 3.18 Photographs Online (Exercise 6)

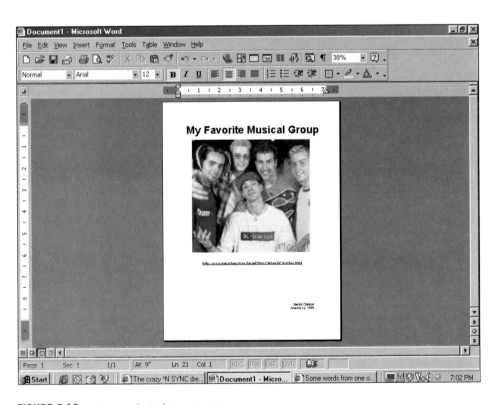

FIGURE 3.19 Music on the Web (Exercise 7)

A Comparison of Microcomputers

James Warren, CIS 120

(http://pentium.intel.com/procs/perf/icomp/index.htm)

The capability of a PC depends on the microprocessor on which it is based. Intel microprocessors are currently in their sixth generation, with each generation giving rise to increasingly powerful personal computers. All generations are upward compatible; that is, software written for one generation will automatically run on the next. This upward compatibility is crucial because it protects your investment in software when you upgrade to a faster computer.

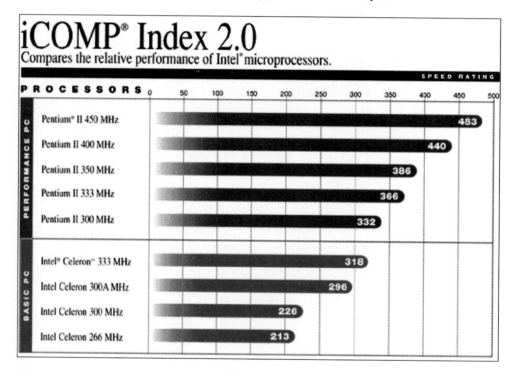

Each generation has multiple microprocessors which are differentiated by *clock speed*, an indication of how fast instructions are executed. Clock speed is measured in *megahertz* (MHz). The higher the clock speed the faster the machine. Thus, all Pentiums are not created equal, because they operate at different clock speeds. The *Intel CPU Performance Index* (see chart) was created to compare the performance of one microprocessor to another. The index consists of a single number to indicate the relative performance of the microprocessor; the higher the number, the faster the processor.

FIGURE 3.20   The iCOMP Index (Exercise 8)

9. Create a Home Page: Creating a home page has never been easier. Start Word, click the File menu, then click the New command to display the New Page dialog box. Select the Web Pages tab, then open the Personal Web page template in Figure 3.21. Add your personal information to the appropriate sections in the template and you have your home page. Pull down the Format menu, click the Themes command, then select a professionally chosen design for your Web page. You can view the completed page locally, or better yet, ask your instructor whether the page can be posted to a Web server.

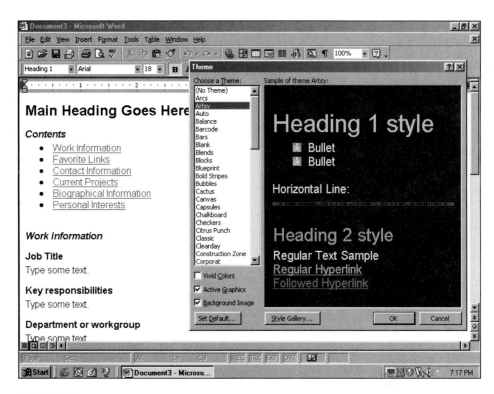

FIGURE 3.21   Create a Home Page (Exercise 9)

CASE STUDIES

The Letterhead

Collect samples of professional stationery, then design your own letterhead, which includes your name, address, phone, and any other information you deem relevant. Try different fonts and/or the Format Border command to add horizontal line(s) under the text. Consider a graphic logo, but keep it simple. You might also want to decrease the top margin so that the letterhead prints closer to the top of the page.

The Cover Page

Use WordArt and/or the Clip Gallery to create a truly original cover page that you can use with all of your assignments. The cover page should include the title of the assignment, your name, course information, and date. (Use the Insert Date and Time command to insert the date as a field so that it will be updated automatically every time you retrieve the document.) The formatting is up to you.

The Résumé

Use your imagination to create a résumé for Benjamin Franklin or Leonardo da Vinci, two acknowledged geniuses. The résumé is limited to one page and will be judged for content (yes, you have to do a little research on the Web) as well as appearance. You can intersperse fact and fiction as appropriate; for example, you may want to leave space for a telephone and/or a fax number, but could indicate that these devices have not yet been invented. You can choose a format for the résumé using the Résumé Wizard, or better yet, design your own.

File Compression

Photographs add significantly to the appearance of a document, but they also add to its size. Accordingly, you might want to consider acquiring a file compression program to facilitate copying large documents to a floppy disk in order to transport your documents to and from school, home, or work. You can download an evaluation copy of the popular WinZip program at *www.winzip.com.* Investigate the subject of file compression, then submit a summary of your findings to your instructor.

Copyright Infringement

It's fun to download images from the Web for inclusion in a document, but is it legal? Copyright protection (infringement) is one of the most pressing legal issues on the Web. Search the Web for sites that provide information on current copyright law. One excellent site is the copyright page at the Institute for Learning Technologies at *www.ilt.columbia.edu/projects/copyright.* Another excellent reference is the page at *www.benedict.com.* Research these and other sites, then summarize your findings in a short note to your instructor.

Macros

The Insert Symbol command can be used to insert foreign characters into a document, but this technique is too slow if you use these characters with any frequency. It is much more efficient to develop a series of macros (keyboard shortcuts) that will insert the characters for you. You could, for example, create a macro to insert an accented *e,* then invoke that macro through the Ctrl+e keyboard shortcut. Parallel macros could be developed for the other vowels or special characters that you use frequently. Use the Help menu to learn about macros, then summarize your findings in a short note to your instructor.

chapter 4

ADVANCED FEATURES: OUTLINES, TABLES, STYLES, AND SECTIONS

OBJECTIVES

After reading this chapter you will be able to:

1. Create a bulleted or numbered list; create an outline using a multi-level list.
2. Describe the Outline view; explain how this view facilitates moving text within a document.
3. Describe the tables feature; create a table and insert it into a document.
4. Explain how styles automate the formatting process and provide a consistent appearance to common elements in a document.
5. Use the AutoFormat command to apply styles to an existing document; create, modify, and apply a style to selected elements of a document.
6. Define a section; explain how section formatting differs from character and paragraph formatting.
7. Create a header and/or a footer; establish different headers or footers for the first, odd, or even pages in the same document.
8. Insert page numbers into a document; use the Edit menu's Go To command to move directly to a specific page in a document.
9. Create an index and a table of contents.

OVERVIEW

This chapter presents a series of advanced features that will be especially useful the next time you have to write a term paper with specific formatting requirements. We show you how to create a bulleted or numbered list to emphasize important items within a term paper, and how to create an outline for that paper. We also introduce the tables feature, which is one of the most powerful features in Microsoft Word as it provides an easy way to arrange text, numbers, and/or graphics.

The second half of the chapter develops the use of styles, or sets of formatting instructions that provide a consistent appearance to similar elements in a document. We describe the AutoFormat command that assigns styles to an existing document and greatly simplifies the formatting process. We show you how to create a new style, how to modify an existing style, and how to apply those styles to text within a document. We introduce the Outline view, which is used in conjunction with styles to provide a condensed view of a document. We also discuss several items associated with longer documents, such as page numbers, headers and footers, a table of contents, and an index.

The chapter contains four hands-on exercises to apply the material at the computer. This is one more exercise than in our earlier chapters, but we think you will appreciate the practical application of these very important capabilities within Microsoft Word.

BULLETS AND LISTS

A list helps you organize information by highlighting important topics. A *bulleted list* emphasizes (and separates) the items. A *numbered list* sequences (and prioritizes) the items and is automatically updated to accommodate additions or deletions. An *outline* (or outline numbered list) extends a numbered list to several levels, and it too is updated automatically when topics are added or deleted. Each of these lists is created through the *Bullets and Numbering command* in the Format menu, which displays the Bullets and Numbering dialog box in Figure 4.1.

The tabs within the Bullets and Numbering dialog box are used to choose the type of list and customize its appearance. The Bulleted tab selected in Figure 4.1a enables you to specify one of several predefined symbols for the bullet. Typically, that is all you do, although you can use the Customize button to change the default spacing (of ¼ inch) of the text from the bullet and/or to choose a different symbol for the bullet.

The Numbered tab in Figure 4.1b lets you choose Arabic or Roman numerals, or upper- or lowercase letters, for a Numbered list. As with a bulleted list, the Customize button lets you change the default spacing, the numbering style, and/or the punctuation before or after the number or letter. Note, too, the option buttons to restart or continue numbering, which become important if a list appears in multiple places within a document. In other words, each occurrence of a list can start numbering anew, or it can continue from where the previous list left off.

The Outline Numbered tab in Figure 4.1c enables you to create an outline to organize your thoughts. As with the other types of lists, you can choose one of several default styles, and/or modify a style through the Customize command button. You can also specify whether each outline within a document is to restart its numbering, or whether it is to continue numbering from the previous outline.

CREATING AN OUTLINE

The following exercise explores the Bullets and Numbering command in conjunction with creating an outline for a hypothetical paper on the United States Constitution. The exercise begins by having you create a bulleted list, then asking you to convert it to a numbered list, and finally to an outline. The end result is the type of outline your professor may ask you to create prior to writing a term paper.

As you do the exercise, remember that a conventional outline is created as an outline numbered list within the Bullets and Numbering command. Text for the outline is entered in the Print Layout or Normal view, *not* the Outline view. The latter provides a completely different capability—a condensed view of a document that is used in conjunction with styles and is discussed later in the chapter. We mention this to avoid confusion should you stumble into the Outline view.

Select Bullet symbol

Click to choose a different bullet symbol or change the default spacing

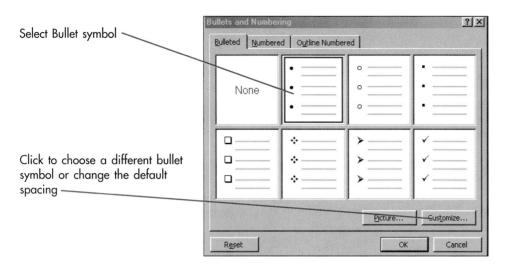

(a) Bulleted List

Select Number style

Restarts numbering for each new list within document

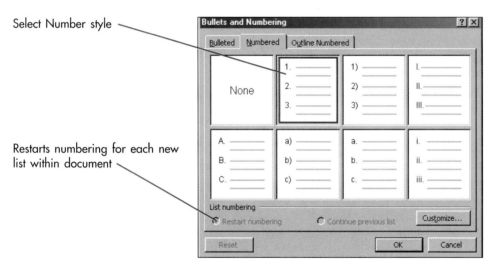

(b) Numbered List

Select Outline style

Click Customize to modify the Outline style

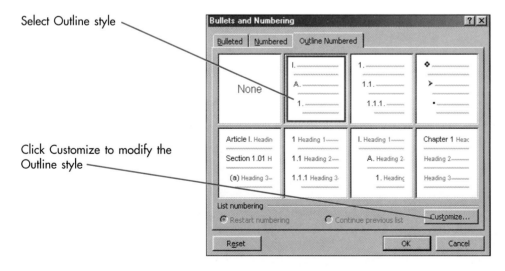

(c) Outline Numbered List

FIGURE 4.1   Bullets and Numbering

Objective: To use the Bullets and Numbering command to create a bulleted list, a numbered list, and an outline. Use Figure 4.2 as a guide in doing the exercise.

STEP 1: Create a Bulleted List

➤ Start Word and begin a new document. Type **Preamble,** the first topic in our list, and press **enter.**

➤ Type the three remaining topics, **Article I—Legislative Branch, Article II—Executive Branch,** and **Article III—Judicial Branch.** Do not press enter after the last item.

➤ Click and drag to select all four topics as shown in Figure 4.2a. Pull down the **Format menu** and click the **Bullets and Numbering command** to display the Bullets and Numbering dialog box.

➤ If necessary, click the **Bulleted tab,** select the type of bullet you want, then click **OK** to accept this setting and close the dialog box. Bullets have been added to the list.

➤ Click after the words **Judicial Branch** to deselect the list and also to position the insertion point at the end of the list. Press **enter** to begin a new line. A bullet appears automatically since Word copies the formatting from one paragraph to the next.

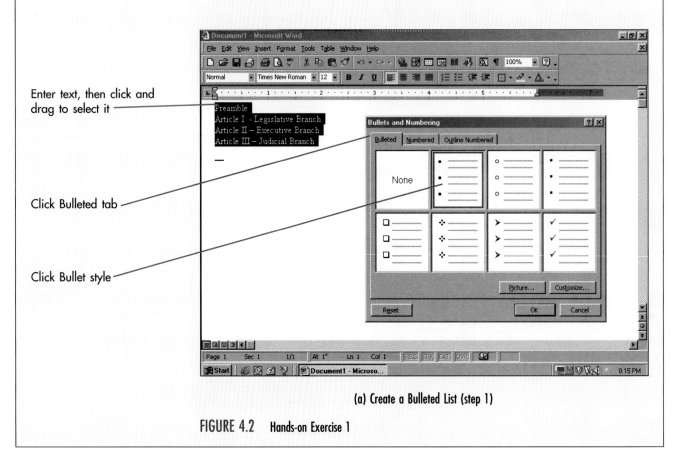

Enter text, then click and drag to select it

Click Bulleted tab

Click Bullet style

(a) Create a Bulleted List (step 1)

FIGURE 4.2   Hands-on Exercise 1

➤ Type **Amendments.** Press **enter** to end this line and begin the next, which already has a bullet. Press **enter** a second time to terminate the bulleted list.

➤ Save the document as **US Constitution** in the **Exploring Word folder.**

THE BULLETS AND NUMBERING BUTTONS

Select the items for which you want to create a list, then click the Numbering or Bullets button on the Formatting toolbar to create a numbered or bulleted list, respectively. The buttons function as toggle switches; that is, click the button once (when the items are selected) and the list formatting is in effect. Click the button a second time and the bullets or numbers disappear. The buttons also enable you to switch from one type of list to another; that is, selecting a bulleted list and clicking the Numbering button changes the list to a numbered list, and vice versa.

STEP 2: Modify a Numbered List

➤ Click and drag to select the five items in the bulleted list, then click the **Numbering button** on the Standard toolbar.

➤ The bulleted list has been converted to a numbered list as shown in Figure 4.2b. (The last two items have not yet been added to the list.)

Numbering button

Click and drag selected text to left of "Preamble"

Click in selection bar to select line

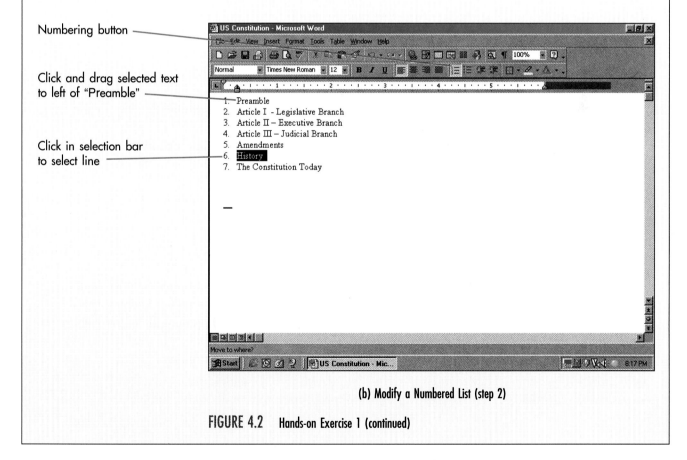

(b) Modify a Numbered List (step 2)

FIGURE 4.2   Hands-on Exercise 1 (continued)

➤ Click immediately after the last item in the list and press **enter** to begin a new line. Word automatically adds the next sequential number to the list.

➤ Type **History** and press **enter.** Type **The Constitution Today** as the seventh (and last) item.

➤ Click in the selection area to the left of the sixth item, **History** (only the text is selected). Now drag the selected text to the beginning of the list, in front of *Preamble.* Release the mouse.

➤ The list is automatically renumbered. *History* is now the first item, *Preamble* is the second item, and so on.

➤ Save the document.

AUTOMATIC CREATION OF A NUMBERED LIST

Word automatically creates a numbered list whenever you begin a paragraph with a number or letter, followed by a period, tab, or right parenthesis. Once the list is started, press the enter key at the end of a line, and Word generates the next sequential number or letter in the list. To end the list, press the backspace key once, or press the enter key twice. To turn the autonumbering feature on or off, pull down the Tools menu, click AutoCorrect to display the AutoCorrect dialog box, click the AutoFormat as you Type tab, then check (clear) the box for Automatic Numbered lists.

STEP 3: Convert to an Outline

➤ Click and drag to select the entire list, then click the **right mouse button** to display a context-sensitive menu.

➤ Click the **Bullets and Numbering command** to display the Bullets and Numbering dialog box in Figure 4.2c.

➤ Click the **Outline Numbered tab,** then select the type of outline you want. (Do not be concerned if the selected formatting does not display Roman numerals as we customize the outline later in the exercise.)

➤ Click **OK** to accept the formatting and close the dialog box. The numbered list has been converted to an outline, although that is difficult to see at this point.

➤ Click at the end of the third item, **Article I—Legislative Branch.** Press **enter.** The number 4 is generated automatically for the next item in the list.

➤ Press the **Tab key** to indent this item and automatically move to the next level of numbering (a lowercase *a*). Type **House of Representatives.**

➤ Press **enter.** The next sequential number (a lowercase *b*) is generated automatically. Type **Senate.**

➤ Save the document.

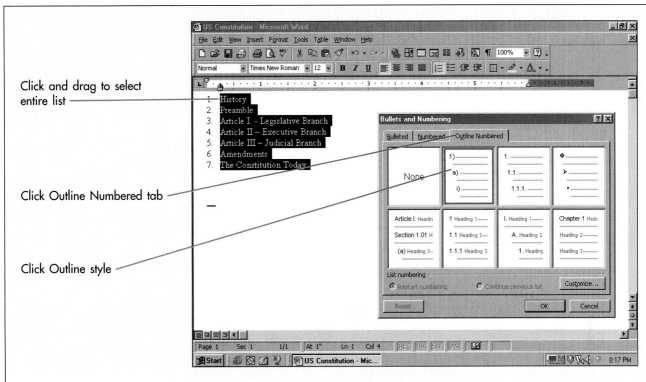

Click and drag to select entire list

Click Outline Numbered tab

Click Outline style

(c) Convert to an Outline (step 3)

FIGURE 4.2   Hands-on Exercise 1 (continued)

THE TAB AND SHIFT+TAB KEYS

The easiest way to enter text into an outline is to type continually from one line to the next, using the Tab and Shift+Tab keys as necessary. Press the enter key after completing an item to move to the next item, which is automatically created at the same level, then continue typing if the item is to remain at this level. To change the level, press the Tab key to demote the item (move it to the next lower level), or the Shift+Tab combination to promote the item (move it to the next higher level).

STEP 4: Enter Text into the Outline

➤ Your outline should be similar in appearance to Figure 4.2d, except that you have not yet entered most of the text. Click at the end of the line containing *House of Representatives.*

➤ Press **enter** to start a new item (which begins with a lowercase *b*). Press **Tab** to indent one level, changing the number to a lowercase *i.* Type **Length of term.** Press **enter.** Type **Requirements for office.** Enter these two items for the Senate as well.

➤ Enter the remaining text as shown in Figure 4.2.d, using the **Tab** and **Shift+Tab** keys to demote and promote the items. Save the document.

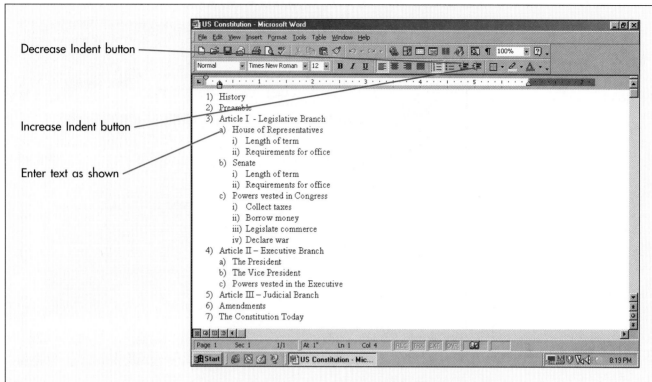

Decrease Indent button

Increase Indent button

Enter text as shown

(d) Enter Text into the Outline (step 4)

FIGURE 4.2 Hands-on Exercise 1 (continued)

THE INCREASE AND DECREASE INDENT BUTTONS

The Increase and Decrease Indent buttons on the Standard toolbar are another way to change the level within an outline. Click anywhere within an item, then click the appropriate button to change the level within the outline. Indentation is implemented at the paragraph level, and hence you can click the button without selecting the entire item. You can also click and drag to select multiple item(s), then click the desired button.

STEP 5: Customize the Outline

➤ Select the entire outline, pull down the **Format menu,** then click **Bullets and Numbering** to display the Bullets and Numbering dialog box.

➤ If necessary, click the Outline Numbered tab and click **Customize** to display the Customize dialog box as shown in Figure 4.2e. Level **1** should be selected in the Level list box.

- Click the **drop-down arrow** in the Number style list box and select **I, II, III** as the style.

- Click in the Number format text box, which now contains the Roman numeral I followed by a right parenthesis. Click and drag to select the parenthesis and replace it with a period.

- Click the **drop-down arrow** in the Number position list box. Click **right** to right-align the Roman numerals that will appear in your outline.

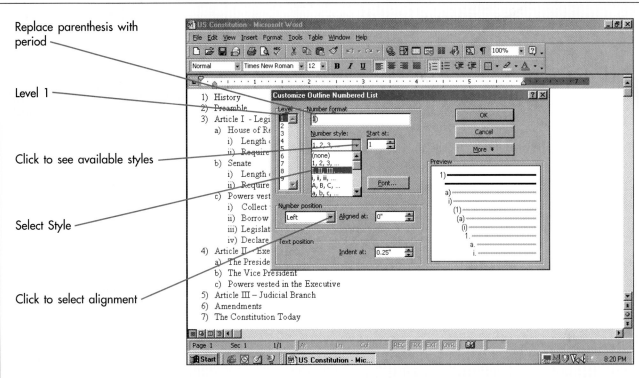

Replace parenthesis with period

Level 1

Click to see available styles

Select Style

Click to select alignment

(e) Customize the Outline (step 5)

FIGURE 4.2   Hands-on Exercise 1 (continued)

➤ Click the number **2** in the Level list box and select **A, B, C** as the Number style. Click in the Number format text box and replace the right parenthesis with a period.

➤ Click the number **3** in the Level list box and select **1, 2, 3** as the Number style. Click in the Number format text box and replace the right parenthesis with a period.

➤ Click **OK** to accept these settings and close the dialog box. The formatting of your outline has changed to match the customization in this step.

CHANGE THE FORMATTING

Word provides several types of default formatting for an outline. Surprisingly, however, Roman numerals are not provided as the default and hence you may want to change the formatting to meet your exact requirements. The formats are changed one level at a time by selecting the style for a level, then changing the punctuation (e.g., by substituting a period for a right parenthesis). If you make a mistake, you can return to the default format by closing the Custom Outline Numbered List dialog box, then clicking the Reset button from within the Bullets and Numbering dialog box.

STEP 6: The Completed Outline

➤ Your outline should reflect the style in Figure 4.2f. The major headings begin with Roman numerals, the second level headings with uppercase letters, and so on.

➤ Press **Ctrl+Home** to move to the beginning of the outline. The insertion point is after Roman numeral I, in front of the word *History.* Type **The United States Constitution.** Press **enter.**

➤ The new text appears as Roman numeral I and all existing entries have been renumbered appropriately.

➤ The insertion point is immediately before the word *History.* Press **enter** to create a blank line (for your name).

➤ The blank line is now Roman numeral II and *History* has been moved to Roman numeral III. Move the insertion point to the blank line.

➤ Press the **Tab** key so that the blank line (which will contain your name) is item A. This also renumbers *History* as Roman numeral II.

➤ Enter your name as shown in Figure 4.2f. Save the document, then print the outline and submit it to your instructor as proof you did this exercise.

➤ Close the document. Exit Word if you do not want to continue with the next exercise at this time.

Enter new text

Press tab key to renumber as item A

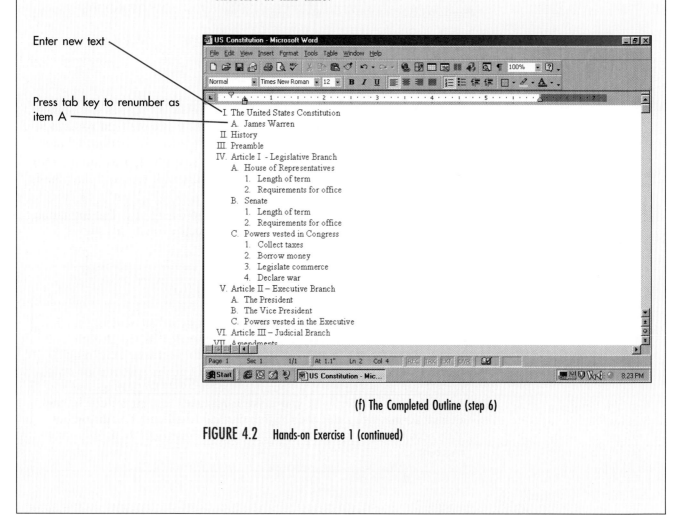

(f) The Completed Outline (step 6)

FIGURE 4.2   Hands-on Exercise 1 (continued)

The **tables feature** is one of the most powerful in Word and is the basis for an almost limitless variety of documents. The study schedule in Figure 4.3a, for example, is actually a 12×8 (12 rows and 8 columns) table as can be seen from the underlying structure in Figure 4.3b. The completed table looks quite impressive, but it is very easy to create once you understand how a table works. (See the practice exercises at the end of the chapter for other examples.)

The rows and columns in a table intersect to form **cells.** Each cell is formatted independently of every other cell and may contain text, numbers and/or graphics. Commands operate on one or more cells. Individual cells can be joined together to form a larger cell as was done in the first and last rows of Figure 4.3a. Conversely, a single cell can be split into multiple cells. The rows within a table can be different heights, just as each column can be a different width. You can specify the height or width explicitly, or you can let Word determine it for you.

A cell can contain anything, even clip art as in the bottom right corner of Figure 4.3a. Just click in the cell where you want the clip art to go, then use the Insert Picture command as you have throughout the text. Use the sizing handles once the clip art has been inserted to move and/or position it within the cell.

A table is created through the **Insert Table command** in the **Table menu.** The command produces a dialog box in which you enter the number of rows and columns. Once the table has been defined, you enter text in individual cells. Text wraps as it is entered within a cell, so that you can add or delete text in a cell without affecting the entries in other cells. You can format the contents of an individual cell the same way you format an ordinary paragraph; that is, you can change the font, use boldface or italics, change the alignment, or apply any other formatting command. You can select multiple cells and apply the formatting to all selected cells at once.

You can also modify the structure of a table after it has been created. The Insert and Delete commands in the Table menu enable you to add new rows or columns, or delete existing rows or columns. You can invoke other commands to shade and/or border selected cells or the entire table.

You can work with a table using commands in the Table menu, or you can use the various tools on the Tables and Borders toolbar. (Just point to a button to display a ScreenTip indicative of its function.) Some of the buttons are simply shortcuts for commands within the Table menu. Other buttons offer new and intriguing possibilities, such as the button to Change Text Direction.

It's easy, and as you might have guessed, it's time for another hands-on exercise in which you create the table in Figure 4.3.

LEFT	CENTER	RIGHT
Many documents call for left, centered, and/or right aligned text on the same line, an effect that is achieved through setting tabs, or more easily through a table. To achieve the effect shown in the heading of this box, create a 1×3 table (one row and three columns), type the text in the three cells as needed, then use the buttons on the Formatting toolbar to left-align, center, and right-align the respective cells. Select the table, pull down the Format menu, click Borders and Shading, then specify None as the Border setting.		

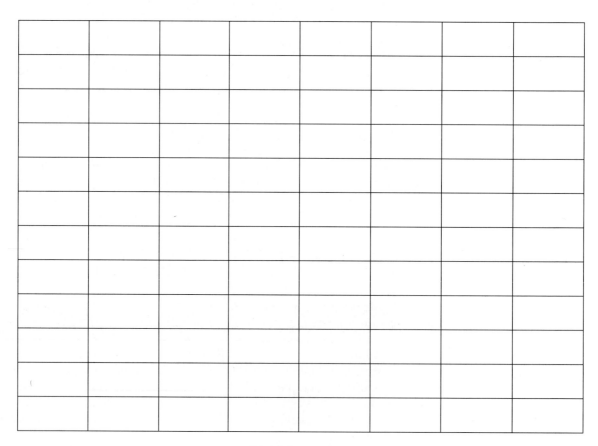

Weekly Class and Study Schedule

	Monday	Tuesday	Wednesday	Thursday	Friday	Saturday	Sunday
8:00AM							
9:00AM							
10:00AM							
11:00AM							
12:00PM							
1:00PM							
2:00PM							
3:00PM							
4:00PM							

Notes:

James Warren

(a) Completed Table

(b) Underlying Structure

FIGURE 4.3 The Tables Feature

Objective: To create a table; to change row heights and column widths; to join cells together; to apply borders and shading to selected cells. Use Figure 4.4 as a guide in the exercise.

STEP 1: The Page Setup Command

➤ Start Word. Click the **Tables and Borders button** on the Standard toolbar to display the Tables and Borders toolbar as shown in Figure 4.4a.

➤ The button functions as a toggle switch—click it once and the toolbar is displayed. Click the button a second time and the toolbar is suppressed.

➤ Pull down the **File menu.** Click **Page Setup.** Click the **Paper Size tab** to display the dialog box in Figure 4.4a. Click the **Landscape option button.**

➤ Click the **Margins tab.** Change the top and bottom margins to **.75** inch. Change the left and right margins to **.5** inch each. Click **OK** to accept the settings and close the dialog box.

➤ Change to the **Print Layout** view. Zoom to **Page Width.**

➤ Save the document as **My Study Schedule** in the Exploring Word folder.

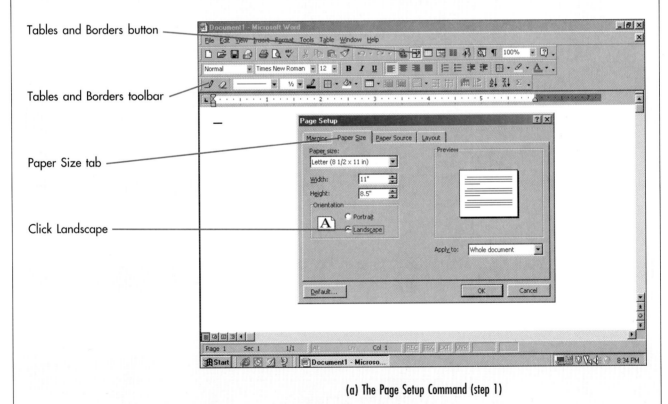

(a) The Page Setup Command (step 1)

FIGURE 4.4   Hands-on Exercise 2

STEP 2: Create the Table

➤ Pull down the **Table menu.** Click **Insert,** then click **Table** to display the dialog box in Figure 4.4b.

➤ Enter **8** as the number of columns. Enter **12** as the number of rows. Click **OK** and the table will be inserted into the document.

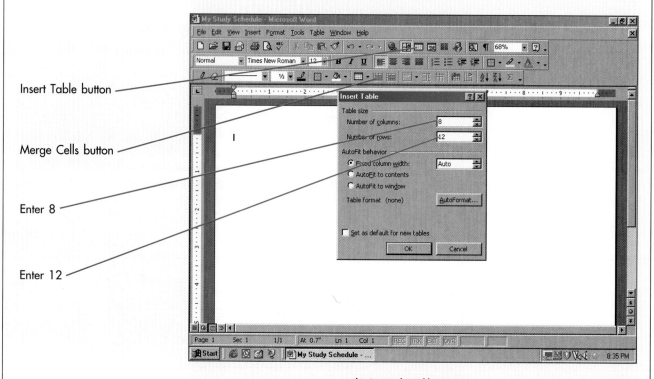

Insert Table button

Merge Cells button

Enter 8

Enter 12

(b) Create the Table (step 2)

FIGURE 4.4   Hands-on Exercise 2 (continued)

STEP 3: Table Basics

➤ Practice moving within the table:

- If the cells in the table are empty (as they are now), press the **left** and **right arrow keys** to move from cell to cell.
- If the cells contain text (as they will later in the exercise), you must press **Tab** and **Shift+Tab** to move from cell to cell.
- Press the **up** and **down arrow keys** to move from row to row. This works for both empty cells and cells with text.

➤ Select a cell row, column, or block of contiguous cells:

- To select a single cell, click immediately to the right of the left cell border (the pointer changes to an arrow when you are in the proper position).
- To select an entire row, click outside the table to the left of the first cell in that row.
- To select a column, click just above the top of the column (the pointer changes to a small black arrow).
- To select adjacent cells, drag the mouse over the cells.
- To select the entire table, drag the mouse over the table.

➤ You can also pull down the **Table menu,** click the **Select command,** then choose table, column, row, or cell as appropriate.

TABS AND TABLES

The Tab key functions differently in a table than in a regular document. Press the Tab key to move to the next cell in the current row (or to the first cell in the next row if you are at the end of a row). Press Tab when you are in the last cell of a table to add a new blank row to the bottom of the table. Press Shift+Tab to move to the previous cell in the current row (or to the last cell in the previous row). You must press Ctrl+Tab to insert a regular tab character within a cell.

STEP 4: Merge the Cells

➤ Click outside the table to the left of the first cell in the first row to select the entire first row as shown in Figure 4.4c.

➤ Pull down the **Table menu** and click **Merge Cells** (or click the **Merge Cells button** on the Tables and Borders toolbar).

➤ Type **Weekly Class and Study Schedule** and format the text in 24 point Arial bold. Center the text within the cell.

➤ Click outside the table to the left of the first cell in the last row to select the entire row. Click the **Merge Cells button** to join the cells into a single cell.

➤ Type **Notes:** and format the entry in 12 point Arial bold.

➤ Save the table.

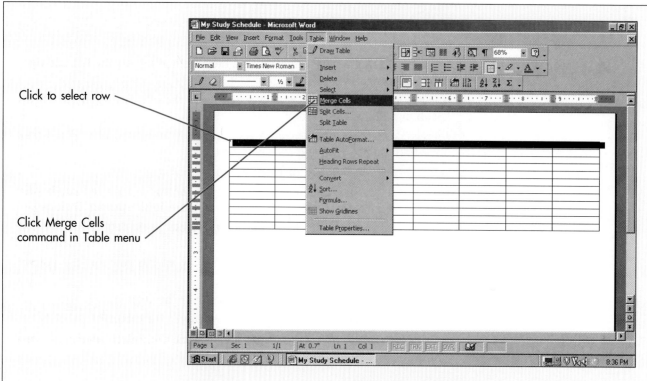

Click to select row

Click Merge Cells
command in Table menu

(c) Merge the Cells (step 4)

FIGURE 4.4   Hands-on Exercise 2 (continued)

STEP 5: Enter the Days and Hours

➤ Click the second cell in the second row. Type **Monday.**

➤ Press the **Tab** (or **right arrow**) **key** to move to the next cell. Type **Tuesday.** Continue until the days of the week have been entered.

➤ Use the Formatting Toolbar to change the font and alignment for the days of the week:

• Select the entire row. Click the **Bold button.**

• Click the **Font List box** to choose an appropriate font such as **Arial.**

• Click the **Font Size List box** to choose an appropriate size such as **10** point.

• Click the **Center button** on the Formatting toolbar.

➤ Click anywhere in the table to deselect the text and see the effect of the formatting change.

➤ Click the first cell in the third row. Type **8:00AM.** Press the **down arrow key** to move to the first cell in the fourth row. Type **9:00AM.**

➤ Continue in this fashion until you have entered the hourly periods up to **3:00PM.** Select the row containing the entry for 3:00PM. Pull down the **Table menu,** click the **Insert command,** then click **Rows Below** to insert a new row. Enter 4:00PM.

➤ Format as appropriate. (We right aligned the time periods and changed the font to 10-point Arial bold.) Your table should match Figure 4.4d. Save the table.

Merge Cells button

Enter table title

Enter days of week

Enter hours

Merge cells in last row

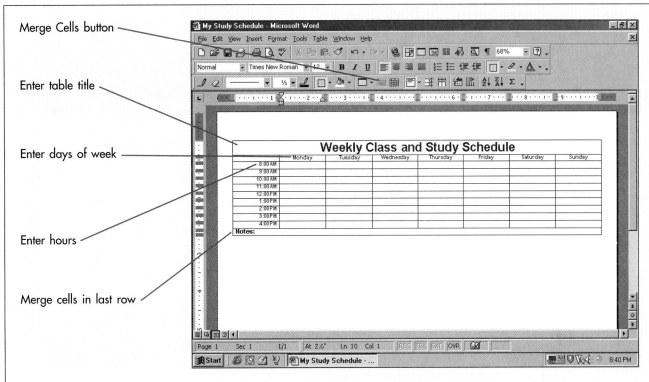

(d) Enter the Days and Hours (step 5)

FIGURE 4.4   Hands-on Exercise 2 (continued)

INSERTING OR DELETING ROWS AND COLUMNS

You can insert or delete rows and columns after a table has been created. To insert a row, select the entire row, pull down the Table menu, click the Insert command, then choose Rows Above or Below as appropriate. Follow a similar procedure to insert columns, then choose whether the column is to go to the left or right of the selected column. You can also right click a row or column, then select the Insert or Delete command from the context-sensitive menu.

STEP 6: Change the Row Heights

> Click immediately after the word *notes.* Press the **enter key** five times. The height of the cell increases automatically to accommodate the blank lines.

> Select the cells containing the hours of the day. Pull down the **Table menu.** Click **Table Properties,** then click the **Row tab** to display the Table Properties dialog box in Figure 4.4e.

> Click the **Specify height** check box. Click the **up arrow** until the height is **.5″,** then click the **drop-down arrow** on the Row Heights list box and select **Exactly.**

> Click the **Cell tab** in the Tables Properties dialog box, then click the **Center button.** Click **OK** to accept the settings and close the dialog box.

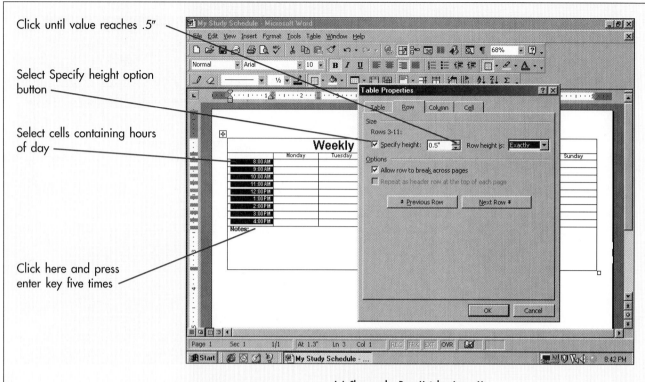

Click until value reaches .5″

Select Specify height option button

Select cells containing hours of day

Click here and press enter key five times

(e) Change the Row Heights (step 6)

FIGURE 4.4   Hands-on Exercise 2 (continued)

STEP 7: Borders and Shading

➤ Click outside the first row (the cell containing the title of the table) to select the cell. Pull down the **Format menu,** click the **Borders and Shading** command to display the Borders and Shading dialog box as shown in Figure 4.4f.

➤ Click the **Shading tab.** Click the **drop-down arrow** on the Style list box, then select **solid (100%)** as the Style pattern. Click **OK.**

➤ Click outside the cell to see the effect of this command. You should see white letters on a solid black background. Save the document.

USE COLOR REVERSES FOR EMPHASIS

White letters on a solid background (technically called a reverse) is a favorite technique of desktop publishers. It looks even better in color. Select the text, click the Shading button on the Tables and Borders toolbar, then click the desired background color (e.g., red) to create the solid background. Next, click the drop-down arrow on the Font Color list box, click white for the text color, and click the Bold button to emphasize the white text. Click elsewhere in the document to see the result.

Shading tab

Click to select first row

Click to see available styles

Click Solid

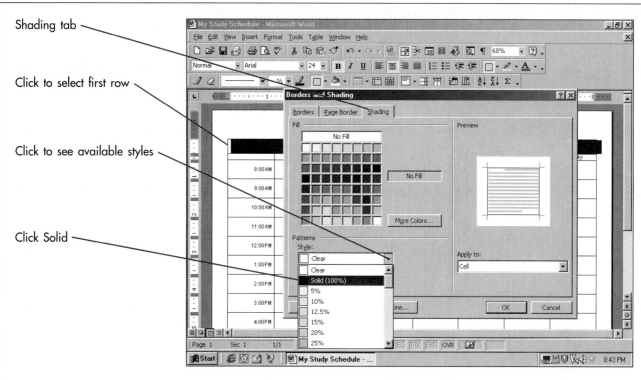

(f) Borders and Shading (step 7)

FIGURE 4.4 Hands-on Exercise 2 (continued)

STEP 8: Insert the Clip Art

➤ Click the **drop-down arrow** on the Zoom list box and zoom to **Whole Page.** Click in the last cell in the table, the cell for your notes.

➤ Pull down the **Insert menu,** click **Picture,** then click **ClipArt** to display the Insert ClipArt dialog box as shown in Figure 4.4g. Click **OK** if you see a dialog box reminding you that additional clip art is available on the Office CD.

➤ If necessary, click the **Pictures tab** and select (click) the **Academic category.** Select the Books (or a different image if you prefer). Click the **Insert Clip** icon.

➤ Close the Insert ClipArt dialog box and the picture will be inserted into the table, where it can be moved and sized as described in step 9. Do not be concerned if the clip art is too large for your table or if it spills to a second page.

FIND THE RIGHT CLIP ART

You can manually search the individual categories within the Clip Gallery to find the image you are looking for. It's faster, however, to use the automated search capability. Pull down the Insert menu, click Picture, then click Clip Art to display the Insert ClipArt dialog box. Click in the Search for text box, enter a key word such as "women," then press the enter key to display all of the images, regardless of category, that list "women" as a key word.

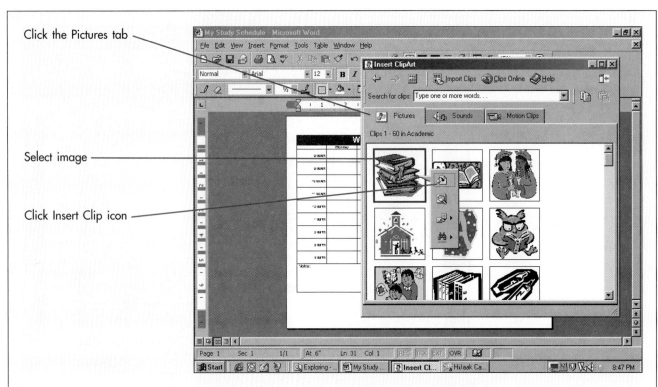

Click the Pictures tab

Select image

Click Insert Clip icon

(g) Insert the Clip Art (step 8)

FIGURE 4.4 Hands-on Exercise 2 (continued)

STEP 9: Complete the Table

➤ Click the picture to select it and display the Picture toolbar. Click the **Format Picture** tool to display the Format Picture dialog box.

➤ Click the **Layout tab,** then click the **Advanced button** to display the Advanced Layout dialog box. Select **In Front of Text** and click **OK.** Click **OK** a second time to close the Format Picture dialog box.

➤ The clip art should still be selected as indicated by the sizing handles in Figure 4.4h. Move and size the clip art until you are satisfied with its position within the table.

➤ Add your name somewhere in the table. Add other finishing touches (especially color if you have a color printer) to further personalize your table. Save the document.

➤ Print the completed table and submit it to your instructor as proof you did this exercise. Close the document. Exit Word if you do not want to continue with the next exercise at this time.

ROTATE TEXT IN A TABLE

Take advantage of the Text Direction command to display text vertically within a cell. Select the cell, pull down the Format menu, and click the Text Direction command to display the Text Direction dialog box. Choose the desired orientation and click OK to accept the settings. The effect is interesting but only in moderation.

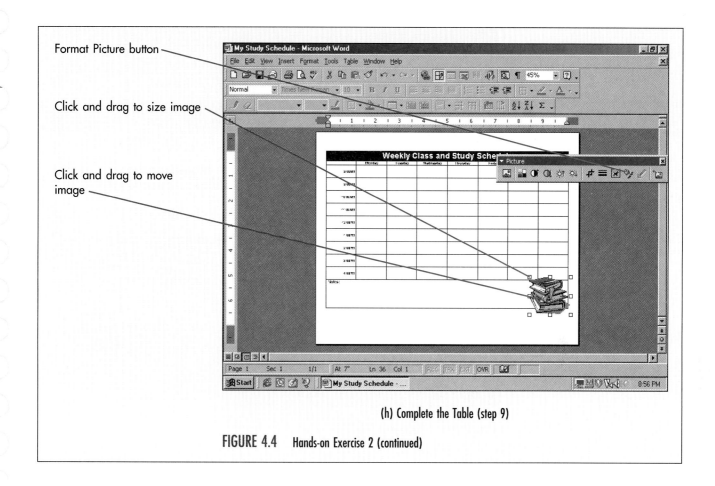

Format Picture button

Click and drag to size image

Click and drag to move image

(h) Complete the Table (step 9)

FIGURE 4.4   Hands-on Exercise 2 (continued)

STYLES

A characteristic of professional documents is the use of uniform formatting for each element. Different elements can have different formatting; for example, headings may be set in one font and the text under those headings in a different font. You may want the headings centered and the text fully justified.

If you are like most people, you will change your mind several times before arriving at a satisfactory design, after which you will want consistent formatting for each element in the document. You can use the Format Painter on the Standard toolbar to copy the formatting from one occurrence of an element to another, but it still requires you to select the individual elements and paint each one whenever formatting changes.

A much easier way to achieve uniformity is to store the formatting information as a *style,* then apply that style to multiple occurrences of the same element within the document. Change the style and you automatically change all text defined by that style.

Styles are created on the character or paragraph level. A *character style* stores character formatting (font, size, and style) and affects only the selected text. A *paragraph style* stores paragraph formatting (alignment, line spacing, indents, tabs, text flow, and borders and shading, as well as the font, size, and style of the text in the paragraph). A paragraph style affects the current paragraph or multiple paragraphs if several paragraphs are selected. The *Style command* in the Format menu is used to create and/or modify either type of style, then enables you to apply that style within a document.

Execution of the Style command displays the dialog box shown in Figure 4.5, which lists the styles in use within a document. The *Normal style* contains the

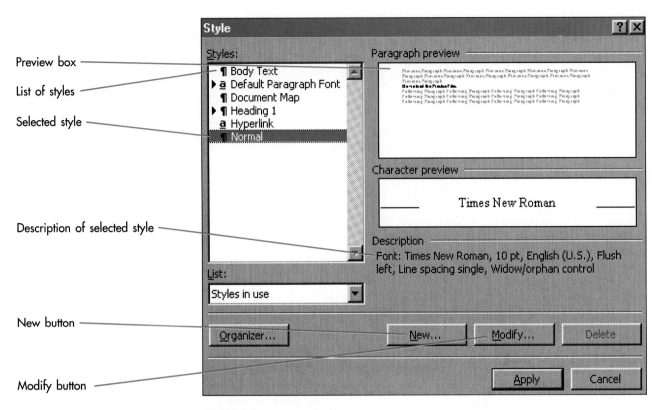

Preview box
List of styles
Selected style
Description of selected style
New button
Modify button

FIGURE 4.5 The Normal Style

default paragraph settings (left aligned, single spacing, and the default font) and is automatically assigned to every paragraph unless a different style is specified. The *Heading 1* and *Body Text* styles are used in conjunction with the AutoFormat command, which applies these styles throughout a document. (The AutoFormat command is illustrated in the next hands-on exercise.) The *Default Paragraph Font* is a character style that specifies the (default) font for new text.

The Description box displays the style definition; for example, Times New Roman, 10 point, flush left, single spacing, and widow/orphan control. The Paragraph Preview box shows how paragraphs formatted in that style will appear. The Modify command button provides access to the Format Paragraph and Format Font commands to change the characteristics of the selected style. The Apply command button applies the style to all selected paragraphs or to the current paragraph. The New command button enables you to define a new style.

Styles automate the formatting process and provide a consistent appearance to a document. Any type of character or paragraph formatting can be stored within a style, and once a style has been defined, it can be applied to multiple occurrences of the same element within a document to produce identical formatting.

STYLES AND PARAGRAPHS

A paragraph style affects the entire paragraph; that is, you cannot apply a paragraph style to only part of a paragraph. To apply a style to an existing paragraph, place the insertion point anywhere within the paragraph, pull down the Style list box on the Formatting toolbar, then click the name of the style you want.

One additional advantage of styles is that they enable you to view a document in the ***Outline view.*** The Outline view does not display a conventional outline (such as the multilevel list created earlier in the chapter), but rather a structural view of a document that can be collapsed or expanded as necessary. Consider, for example, Figure 4.6, which displays the Outline view of a document that will be the basis of the next hands-on exercise. The document consists of a series of tips for Word 2000. The heading for each tip is formatted according to the Heading 1 style. The text of each tip is formatted according to the Body Text style.

The advantage of the Outline view is that you can collapse or expand portions of a document to provide varying amounts of detail. We have, for example, collapsed almost the entire document in Figure 4.6, displaying the headings while suppressing the body text. We also expanded the text for two tips (Download the Practice Files and Moving Within a Document) for purposes of illustration.

Now assume that you want to move the latter tip from its present position to immediately below the first tip. Without the Outline view, the text would stretch over two pages, making it difficult to see the text of both tips at the same time. Using the Outline view, however, you can collapse what you don't need to see, then simply click and drag the headings to rearrange the text within the document.

Outline toolbar

Tip has been expanded (body text is displayed)

Tips are collapsed (body text is not displayed)

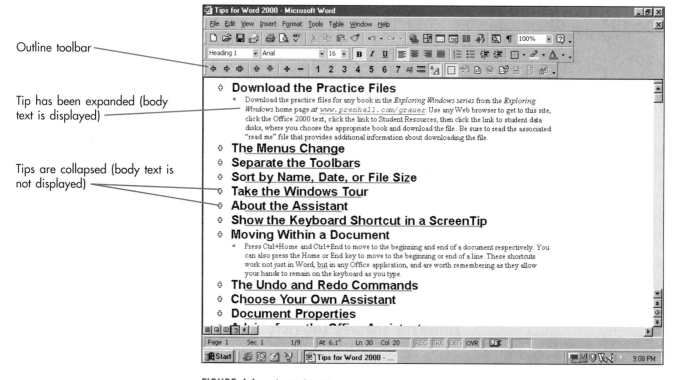

FIGURE 4.6 The Outline View

THE OUTLINE VERSUS THE OUTLINE VIEW

A conventional outline is created as a multilevel list within the Bullets and Numbering command. Text for the outline is entered in the Print Layout or Normal view, *not* the Outline view. The latter provides a condensed view of a document that is used in conjunction with styles.

The AutoFormat Command

Styles are extremely powerful. They enable you to impose uniform formatting within a document and they let you take advantage of the Outline view. What if, however, you have an existing and/or lengthy document that does not contain any styles (other than the default Normal style, which is applied to every paragraph)? Do you have to manually go through every paragraph in order to apply the appropriate style? The AutoFormat command provides a quick solution.

The *AutoFormat command* enables you to format lengthy documents quickly, easily, and in a consistent fashion. In essence, the command analyzes a document and formats it for you. Its most important capability is the application of styles to individual paragraphs; that is, the command goes through an entire document, determines how each paragraph is used, then applies an appropriate style to each paragraph. The formatting process assumes that one-line paragraphs are headings and applies the predefined Heading 1 style to those paragraphs. It applies the Body Text style to ordinary paragraphs and can also detect lists and apply a numbered or bullet style to those lists.

The AutoFormat command will also add special touches to a document if you request those options. It can replace "ordinary quotation marks" with "smart quotation marks" that curl and face each other. It will replace ordinal numbers (1st, 2nd, or 3rd) with the corresponding superscripts (1st, 2nd, or 3rd), or common fractions (1/2 or 1/4) with typographical symbols (½ or ¼).

The AutoFormat command will also replace Internet references (Web addresses and e-mail addresses) with hyperlinks. It will recognize, for example, any entry beginning with http: or www. as a hyperlink and display the entry as underlined blue text (www.microsoft.com). This is not merely a change in formatting, but an actual hyperlink to a document on the Web or corporate Intranet. It also converts entries containing an @ sign, such as rgrauer@umiami.miami.edu to a hyperlink as well. All Office 2000 documents are Web-enabled. Thus, clicking on a hyperlink or e-mail address within a Word document displays the Web page or starts your e-mail program, respectively.

The options for the AutoFormat command are controlled through the Auto-Correct command in the Tools menu as shown in Figure 4.7. Once the options have been set, all formatting is done automatically by selecting the AutoFormat command from the Format menu. The changes are not final, however, as the command gives you the opportunity to review each formatting change individually, then accept the change or reject it as appropriate. (You can also format text automatically as it is entered according to the options specified under the AutoFormat As You Type tab.)

AUTOMATIC BORDERS AND LISTS

The AutoFormat As You Type option applies sophisticated formatting as text is entered. It automatically creates a numbered list any time a number is followed by a period, tab, or right parenthesis (press enter twice in a row to turn off the feature). It will also add a border to a paragraph any time you type three or more hyphens, equal signs, or underscores followed by the enter key. Pull down the Tools menu, click the AutoCorrect command, then click the AutoFormat As You Type tab and select the desired features.

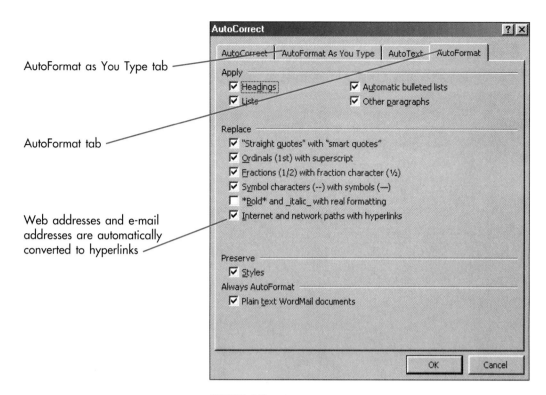

AutoFormat as You Type tab

AutoFormat tab

Web addresses and e-mail addresses are automatically converted to hyperlinks

FIGURE 4.7   The AutoFormat Command

HANDS-ON EXERCISE 3

Styles

Objective: To use the AutoFormat command on an existing document; to modify existing styles; to create a new style. Use Figure 4.8 as a guide.

STEP 1: Load the Practice Document

➤ Start Word. Pull down the **File menu.** Open the document **Tips for Word 2000** from the Exploring Word folder.

➤ Pull down the **File menu** a second time. Save the document as **Modified Tips for Word 2000** so that you can return to the original if necessary.

➤ If necessary, pull down the **View menu** and click **Normal** (or click the **Normal View button** above the status bar). Pull down the **View menu** a second time, click **Zoom,** click **Page Width,** and click **OK** (or click the **arrow** on the **Zoom Control box** on the Standard toolbar and select **Page Width**).

CREATE A NEW FOLDER

Do you work with a large number of documents? If so, it may be useful for you to store those documents in different folders. Pull down the File menu, click the Save As command to display the Save As dialog box, then click the Create New Folder button to display the New Folder dialog box. Enter the name of the folder, then click OK to create the folder.

STEP 2: The AutoFormat Command

➤ Press **Ctrl+Home** to move to the beginning of the document. Pull down the **Format menu.** Click **AutoFormat** to display the AutoFormat dialog box in Figure 4.8a.

➤ Click the **Options command button** to display the AutoCorrect dialog box. Be sure that every check box is selected to implement the maximum amount of automatic formatting. Click **OK.**

➤ Click the **OK command button** in the AutoFormat dialog box to format the document. You will see a message at the left side of the status bar as the formatting is taking place, then you will see the newly formatted document.

➤ Click the title of any tip and you will see the Heading 1 style in the Style box. Click the text of any tip. You will see the Body Text style in the Style box.

➤ Save the document.

Style box

Press Ctrl+Home to move to top of document

Select all of the options

Click Options button

Normal View button

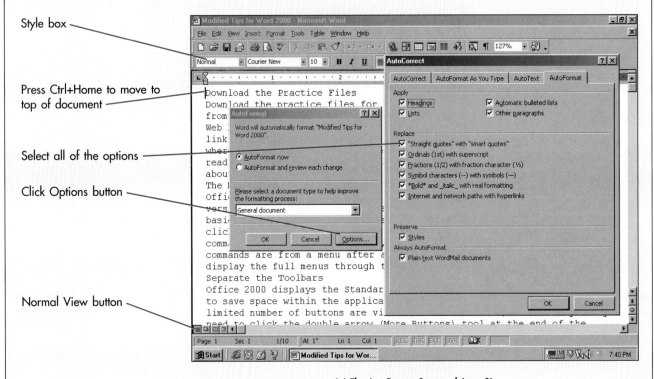

(a) The AutoFormat Command (step 2)

FIGURE 4.8   Hands-on Exercise 3

STEP 3: Modify the Body Text Style

➤ Press **Ctrl+Home** to move to the beginning of the document. Click anywhere in the text of the first tip (except within the hyperlink).

➤ Pull down the **Format menu.** Click **Style.** The Body Text style is automatically selected, and its characteristics are displayed within the description box.

➤ Click the **Modify command button** to display the Modify Style dialog box in Figure 4.8b.

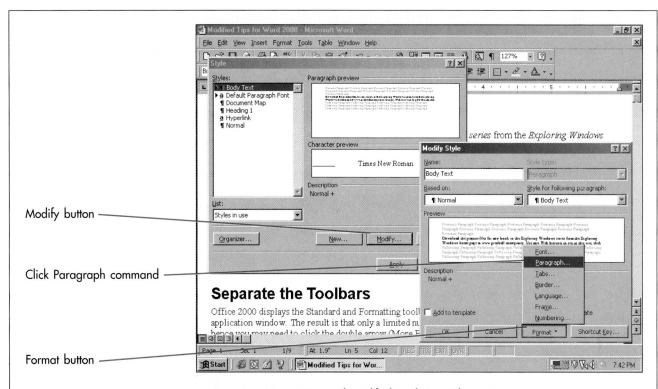

Modify button

Click Paragraph command

Format button

(b) Modify the Body Text Style (step 3)

FIGURE 4.8   Hands-on Exercise 3 (continued)

➤ Click the **Format command button.**
  • Click **Paragraph** to produce the Paragraph dialog box.
  • Click the **Indents and Spacing** tab.
  • Click the **arrow** on the **Alignment list box. Click Justified.**
  • Change the **Spacing After** to **12.**
  • Click the **Line and Page Breaks tab** on the Paragraph dialog box.
  • Click the **Keep Lines Together** check box so an individual tip will not be broken over two pages. Click **OK** to close the Paragraph dialog box.
➤ Click **OK** to close the Modify Style dialog box. Click the **Close command button** to return to the document.
➤ All paragraphs in the document change automatically to reflect the new definition of the Body Text style.

SPACE BEFORE AND AFTER

It's common practice to press the enter key twice at the end of a paragraph (once to end the paragraph, and a second time to insert a blank line before the next paragraph). The same effect can be achieved by setting the spacing before or after the paragraph using the Spacing Before or After list boxes in the Format Paragraph command. The latter technique gives you greater flexibility in that you can specify any amount of spacing (e.g., 6 points to leave only half a line) before or after a paragraph. It also enables you to change the spacing between paragraphs more easily because the information is stored within the paragraph style.

STEP 4: Review the Formatting

➤ Pull down the **Help menu** and click the **What's This command** (or press **Shift+F1**). The mouse pointer changes to a large question mark.

➤ Click in any paragraph to display the formatting in effect for that paragraph as shown in Figure 4.8c.

➤ You will see formatting specifications for the Body Text style—Indent: Left 0″, Right 0″, Justified, Space After 12 pt, Keep Lines Together, Font Times New Roman, 10 pt, and English (US).

➤ Click in any other paragraph to see the formatting in effect for that paragraph. Press **Esc** to return to normal editing.

Style in effect

Paragraph formatting
specifications for Body
Text style

Click in paragraph

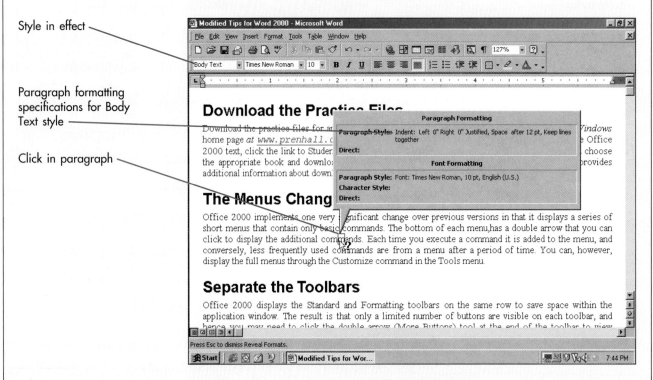

(c) Review the Formatting (step 4)

FIGURE 4.8   Hands-on Exercise 3 (continued)

USE THE DOCUMENT ORGANIZER

Use the Document Organizer to copy styles from one document to another. Start with the document that contains the style you want to copy, pull down the Format menu, and click the Style command to display the Style dialog box. Click the Organizer command button to display the Organizer dialog box. Select (click) the styles you want to copy from your document, then click the Copy button to copy those styles to the Normal template in the right side of the Organizer dialog box. Close the dialog box. The copied styles will now be available to any document that is based on the Normal template.

STEP 5: Modify the Heading 1 Style

➤ Click anywhere in the title of the first tip. The Style box on the Formatting toolbar contains Heading 1 to indicate that this style has been applied to the current paragraph.

➤ Pull down the **Format menu.** Click **Style.** The Heading 1 style is automatically selected, and its characteristics are displayed within the description box.

➤ Click the **Modify command button** to display the Modify Style dialog box.

➤ Click the **Format command button.**

  • Click **Paragraph** to display the Paragraph dialog box. Click the **Indents and Spacing tab.**

  • Change the **Spacing After** to **0** (there should be no space separating the heading and the paragraph).

  • Change the **Spacing Before** to **0** (since there are already 12 points after the Body Text style as per the settings in step 4). Click **OK.**

  • Click the **Format command button** a second time.

  • Click **Font** to display the Font dialog box.

  • Click **10** in the Font size box. Click **OK.**

➤ Click **OK** to close the Modify Style dialog box. Click the **Close command button** to return to the document and view the changes.

➤ Save the document.

MODIFY STYLES BY EXAMPLE

The Modify command button in the Format Style command is one way to change a style, but it prevents the use of the toolbar buttons. Thus it's easier to modify an existing style by example. Select any text that is defined by the style you want to modify, then reformat that text using the Formatting toolbar, shortcut keys, or pull-down menus. Click the Style box on the Formatting toolbar, make sure the selected style is the correct one, press enter, then click OK when asked if you want to update the style to reflect recent changes.

STEP 6: The Outline View

➤ Pull down the **View menu** and click **Outline** (or click the **Outline view button** above the status bar) to display the document in the Outline view.

➤ Pull down the **Edit menu** and click **Select All** (or press **Ctrl+A**) to select the entire document. Click the **Collapse button** on the Outlining toolbar to collapse the entire document so that only the headings are visible.

➤ Click in the heading of the first tip (Download the Practice Files) as shown in Figure 4.7d. Click the **Expand button** on the Outlining toolbar to see the subordinate items under this heading.

➤ Experiment with the Collapse and Expand buttons to display different levels of information in the outline.

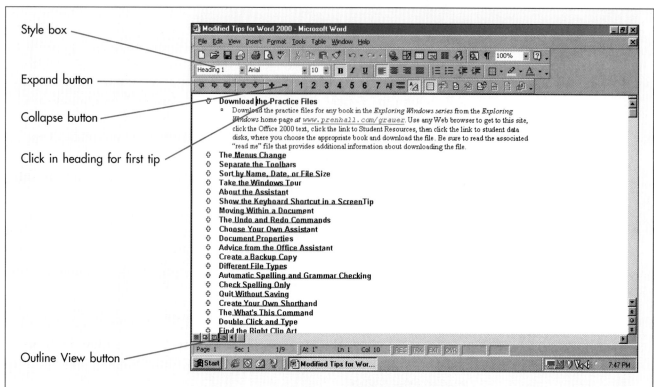

Style box

Expand button

Collapse button

Click in heading for first tip

Outline View button

(d) The Outline View (step 6)

FIGURE 4.8   Hands-on Exercise 3 (continued)

STEP 7: Moving Text

➤ The advantage of the Outline view is that it facilitates moving text in a large document. You can move either an expanded or collapsed item, but the latter is generally easier, as you see the overall structure of the document.

➤ Click the **down arrow** on the vertical scroll bar until you see the tip, **Create Your Own Shorthand.** Click and drag to select the tip as shown in Figure 4.7e.

➤ Point to the **plus sign** next to the selected tip (the mouse pointer changes to a double arrow), then click and drag to move the tip below the **Different File Types** as shown in Figure 4.7e. Release the mouse.

➤ Change to the Print Layout view. Change the magnification to **Page Width.** Save the document.

THE DOCUMENT MAP

The Document Map helps you to navigate within a large document. Click the Document Map button on the Standard toolbar to divide the screen into two panes. The headings in a document are displayed in the left pane and the text of the document is visible in the right pane. To go to a specific point in a document, click its heading in the left pane, and the insertion point is moved automatically to that point in the document, which is visible in the right pane. Click the Map button a second time to turn the feature off.

Document Map button ———

Click and drag tip to below
Different File Types

Click and drag to select text

Print Layout View button ———

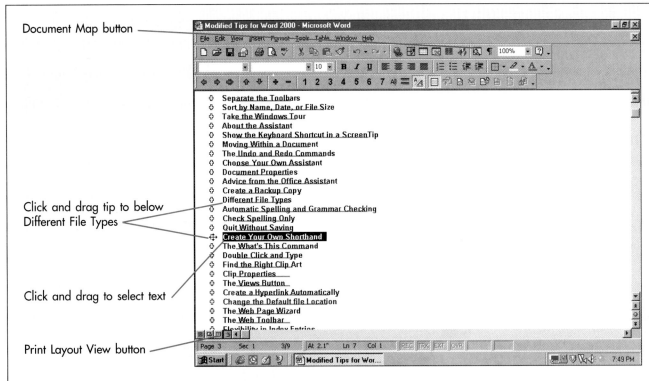

(e) Moving Text (step 7)

FIGURE 4.8   Hands-on Exercise 3 (continued)

STEP 8: Create a New Style

➤ Press **Ctrl+Home** to move to the beginning of the document. Press **Ctrl+enter** to create a page break for a title page.

➤ Move the insertion point on to the new page. Press the **enter key** five to ten times to move to an appropriate position for the title.

➤ Click the **Show/Hide ¶ button** on the Standard toolbar to display the non-printing characters. Select the paragraph marks, pull down the **Style list** on the Formatting toolbar, and click **Normal.**

➤ Deselect the paragraph marks to continue editing.

➤ Place the insertion point immediately to the left of the last hard return above the page break.

➤ Enter the title, **Tips for Microsoft Word 2000,** and format it in 28 Point Arial Bold as shown in Figure 4.8f.

➤ Click the **Center button** on the Formatting toolbar.

➤ Check that the title is still selected, then click in the **Styles List box** on the Formatting toolbar. The style name, Normal, is selected.

➤ Type **My Style** (the name of the new style). Press **enter.** You have just created a new style that we will use in the next exercise.

➤ Save the document.

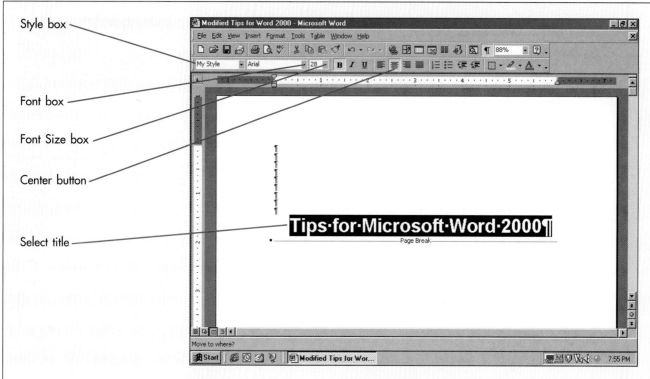

Style box

Font box

Font Size box

Center button

Select title

Tips·for·Microsoft·Word·2000¶

(f) Create a New Style (step 8)

FIGURE 4.8 Hands-on Exercise 3 (continued)

STEP 9: Complete the Title Page

➤ Click the **arrow** on the **Zoom box** on the Standard toolbar. Click **Two Pages.**

➤ Scroll through the document to see the effects of your formatting.

➤ Press **Ctrl+Home** to return to the beginning of the document, then change the magnification to **Page Width** so that you can read what you are typing. Complete the title page as shown in Figure 4.8g.

➤ Click immediately to the left of the ¶ after the title. Press **enter** once or twice.

➤ Click the **arrow** on the **Font Size box** on the Formatting toolbar. Click **12.** Type **by Robert Grauer and Maryann Barber.** Press **enter.**

➤ Save the document. Exit Word if you do not want to continue with the next exercise at this time.

THE PAGE BORDER COMMAND

Add interest to a title page with a border. Click anywhere on the page, pull down the Format menu, click the Borders and Shading command, then click the Page Border tab in the Borders and Shading dialog box. You can choose a box, shadow, or 3-D style in similar fashion to placing a border around a paragraph. You can also click the drop-down arrow on the Art text box to create a border consisting of a repeating clip art image.

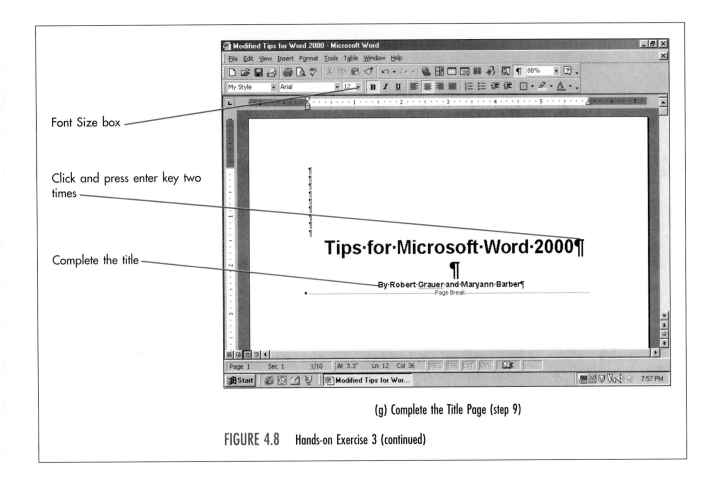

Font Size box

Click and press enter key two times

Complete the title

(g) Complete the Title Page (step 9)

FIGURE 4.8   Hands-on Exercise 3 (continued)

WORKING IN LONG DOCUMENTS

Long documents, such as term papers or reports, require additional formatting for better organization. These documents typically contain page numbers, headers and/or footers, a table of contents, and an index. Each of these elements is discussed in turn and will be illustrated in a hands-on exercise.

Page Numbers

The ***Insert Page Numbers command*** is the easiest way to place ***page numbers*** into a document and is illustrated in Figure 4.9. The page numbers can appear at the top or bottom of a page, and can be left, centered, or right-aligned. Word provides additional flexibility in that you can use Roman rather than Arabic numerals, and you need not start at page number one.

The Insert Page Number command is limited, however, in that it does not provide for additional text next to the page number. You can overcome this restriction by creating a header or footer which contains the page number.

Headers and Footers

Headers and footers give a professional appearance to a document. A ***header*** consists of one or more lines that are printed at the top of every page. A ***footer*** is printed at the bottom of the page. A document may contain headers but not footers, footers but not headers, or both headers and footers.

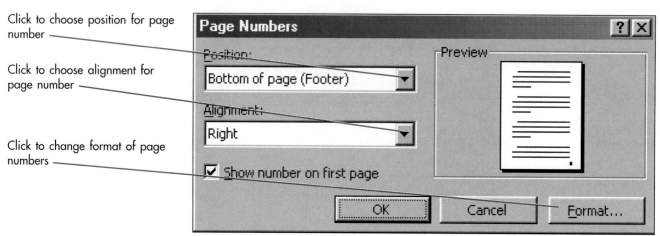

Click to choose position for page number

Click to choose alignment for page number

Click to change format of page numbers

FIGURE 4.9   Page Numbers

Headers and footers are created from the View menu. (A simple header or footer is also created automatically by the Insert Page Number command, depending on whether the page number is at the top or bottom of a page.) Headers and footers are formatted like any other paragraph and can be centered, left- or right-aligned. They can be formatted in any typeface or point size and can include special codes to automatically insert the page number, date, and/or time a document is printed.

The advantage of using a header or footer (over typing the text yourself at the top or bottom of every page) is that you type the text only once, after which it appears automatically according to your specifications. In addition, the placement of the headers and footers is adjusted for changes in page breaks caused by the insertion or deletion of text in the body of the document.

Headers and footers can change continually throughout a document. The Page Setup dialog box (in the File menu) enables you to specify a different header or footer for the first page, and/or different headers and footers for the odd and even pages. If, however, you wanted to change the header (or footer) midway through a document, you would need to insert a section break at the point where the new header (or footer) is to begin.

Sections

Formatting in Word occurs on three levels. You are already familiar with formatting at the character and paragraph levels that have been used throughout the text. Formatting at the section level controls headers and footers, page numbering, page size and orientation, margins, and columns. All of the documents in the text so far have consisted of a single *section,* and thus any section formatting applied to the entire document. You can, however, divide a document into sections and format each section independently.

Formatting at the section level gives you the ability to create more sophisticated documents. You can use section formatting to:

➤ Change the margins within a multipage letter, where the first page (the letterhead) requires a larger top margin than the other pages in the letter.

➤ Change the orientation from portrait to landscape to accommodate a wide table at the end of the document.

➤ Change the page numbering to use Roman numerals at the beginning of the document for a table of contents and Arabic numerals thereafter.

➤ Change the number of columns in a newsletter, which may contain a single column at the top of a page for the masthead, then two or three columns in the body of the newsletter.

In all instances, you determine where one section ends and another begins by using the ***Insert menu*** to create a ***section break.*** You also have the option of deciding how the section break will be implemented on the printed page; that is, you can specify that the new section continue on the same page, that it begin on a new page, or that it begin on the next odd or even page even if a blank page has to be inserted.

Word stores the formatting characteristics of each section in the section break at the end of a section. Thus, deleting a section break also deletes the section formatting, causing the text above the break to assume the formatting characteristics of the next section.

Figure 4.10 displays a multipage view of a ten-page document. The document has been divided into two sections, and the insertion point is currently on the fourth page of the document (page four of ten), which is also the first page of the second section. Note the corresponding indications on the status bar and the position of the headers and footers throughout the document.

Figure 4.10 also displays the Headers and Footers toolbar, which contains various icons associated with these elements. As indicated, a header or footer may contain text and/or special codes—for example, the word "page" followed by a code for the page number. The latter is inserted into the header by clicking the appropriate button on the Headers and Footers toolbar. Remember, headers and footers are implemented at the section level. Thus, changing a header or footer within a document requires the insertion of a section break.

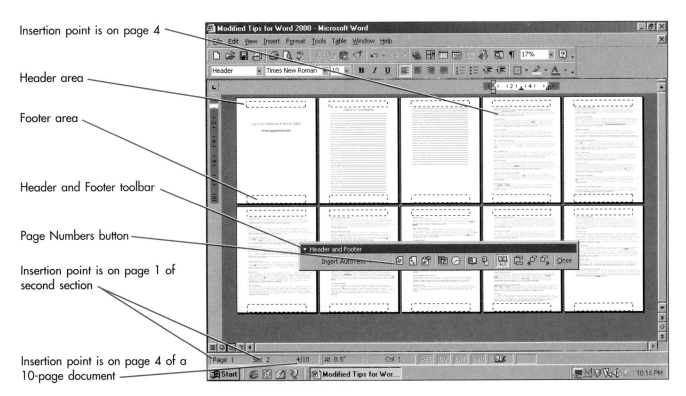

Insertion point is on page 4

Header area

Footer area

Header and Footer toolbar

Page Numbers button

Insertion point is on page 1 of second section

Insertion point is on page 4 of a 10-page document

FIGURE 4.10   Headers and Footers

Table of Contents

A **table of contents** lists headings in the order they appear in a document and the page numbers where the entries begin. Word will create the table of contents automatically, provided you have identified each heading in the document with a built-in heading style (Heading 1 through Heading 9). Word will also update the table automatically to accommodate the addition or deletion of headings and/or changes in page numbers brought about through changes in the document.

The table of contents is created through the **Index and Tables command** from the Insert menu as shown in Figure 4.11a. You have your choice of several

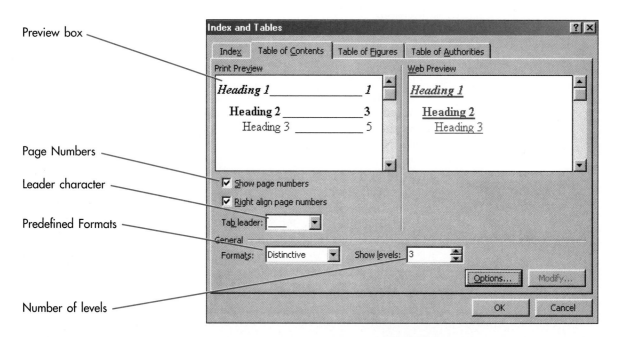

(a) Table of Contents

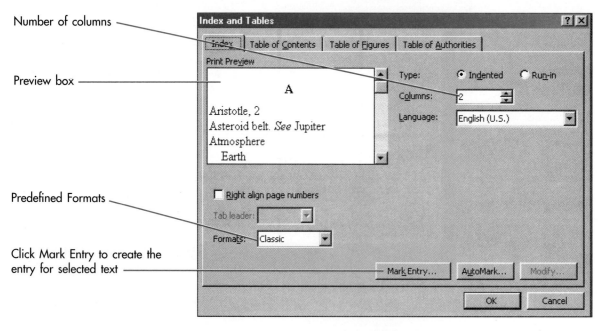

(b) Index

FIGURE 4.11   Index and Tables Command

predefined formats and the number of levels within each format; the latter correspond to the heading styles used within the document. You can also choose the *leader character* and whether or not to right align the page numbers.

Creating an Index

An *index* is the finishing touch in a long document. Word will create an index automatically provided that the entries for the index have been previously marked. This, in turn, requires you to go through a document, and one by one, select the terms to be included in the index and mark them accordingly. It's not as tedious as it sounds. You can, for example, select a single occurrence of an entry and tell Word to mark all occurrences of that entry for the index. You can also create cross-references, such as "see also Internet."

After the entries have been specified, you create the index by choosing the appropriate settings in the Index and Tables command as shown in Figure 4.11b. You can choose a variety of styles for the index just as you can for the table of contents. Word will put the index entries in alphabetical order and will enter the appropriate page references. You can also create additional index entries and/or move text within a document, then update the index with the click of a mouse.

The Go To Command

The *Go To command* moves the insertion point to the top of a designated page. The command is accessed from the Edit menu by pressing the F5 function key, or by double clicking the Page number on the status bar. After the command has been executed, you are presented with a dialog box in which you enter the desired page number. You can also specify a relative page number—for example, P +2 to move forward two pages, or P −1 to move back one page.

HANDS-ON EXERCISE 4

Working in Long Documents

Objective: To create a header (footer) that includes page numbers; to insert and update a table of contents; to add an index entry; to insert a section break and demonstrate the Go To command; to view multiple pages of a document. Use Figure 4.12 as a guide for the exercise.

STEP 1: Applying a Style

➤ Open the **Modified Tips for Word 2000 document** from the previous exercise. Scroll to the top of the second page. Click to the left of the first tip title. (If necessary, click the **Show/Hide ¶ button** on the Standard toolbar to hide the paragraph marks.)

➤ Type **Table of Contents.** Press the **enter key** two times.

➤ Click anywhere within the phrase "Table of Contents". Click the **down arrow** on the **Styles list box** to pull down the styles for this document as shown in Figure 4.12a.

➤ Click **My Style** (the style you created at the end of the previous exercise). "Table of Contents" is centered in 28 point Arial bold according to the definition of My Style.

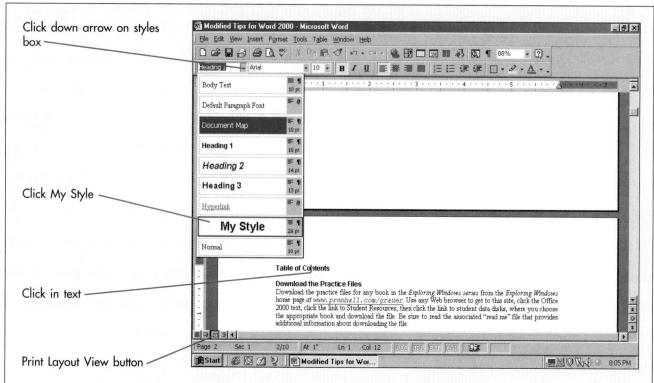

Click down arrow on styles box

Click My Style

Click in text

Print Layout View button

(a) Applying a Style (step 1)

FIGURE 4.12 Hands-on Exercise 4

STEP 2: View Many Pages

➤ If necessary, change to the Print Layout view. Click the line immediately under the title for the table of contents. Pull down the **View menu.** Click **Zoom** to display the dialog box in Figure 4.12b.

➤ Click the **monitor icon.** Click and drag the **page icons** to display two pages down by five pages across as shown in the figure. Release the mouse.

➤ Click **OK.** The display changes to show all ten pages in the document.

STEP 3: Create the Table of Contents

➤ Pull down the **Insert menu.** Click **Index and Tables.** If necessary, click the **Table of Contents tab** to display the dialog box in Figure 4.12c.

➤ Check the boxes to **Show Page Numbers** and to **Right Align Page Numbers.**

➤ Click the **down arrow** on the Formats list box, then click **Distinctive.** Click the **arrow** in the **Tab Leader list box.** Choose a dot leader. Click **OK.** Word takes a moment to create the table of contents, which extends to two pages.

AUTOFORMAT AND THE TABLE OF CONTENTS

Word will create a table of contents automatically, provided you use the built-in heading styles to define the items for inclusion. If you have not applied the styles to the document, the AutoFormat command will do it for you. Once the heading styles are in the document, pull down the Insert command, click Index and Tables, then click the Table of Contents command.

Click Monitor icon

Click and drag 5 pages across by 2 pages down

Text is in My Style style

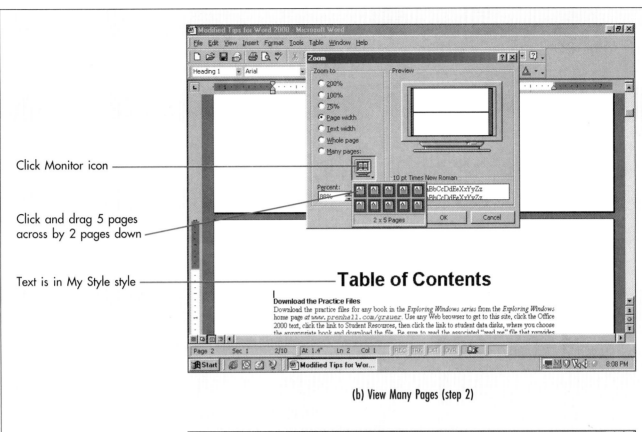

(b) View Many Pages (step 2)

Click Table of Contents tab

Select both options

Click to select dot leader

Click to select Distinctive style

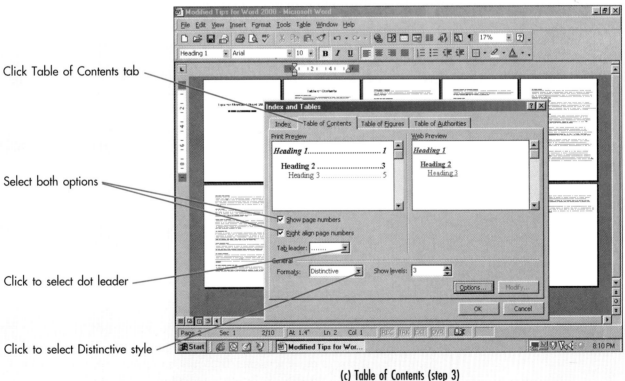

(c) Table of Contents (step 3)

FIGURE 4.12   Hands-on Exercise 4 (continued)

STEP 4: Field Codes versus Field Text

➤ Click the **arrow** on the **Zoom Control box** on the Standard toolbar. Click **Page Width** in order to read the table of contents as in Figure 4.12d.

➤ Use the **up arrow key** to scroll to the beginning of the table of contents. Press **Alt+F9.** The table of contents is replaced by an entry similar to {TOC \o "1-3"} to indicate a field code. The exact code depends on the selections you made in step 4.

➤ Press **Alt+F9** a second time. The field code for the table of contents is replaced by text.

➤ Pull down the **Edit menu.** Click **Go To** to display the dialog box in Figure 4.12d.

➤ Type **3** and press the **enter key** to go to page 3, which contains the bottom portion of the table of contents. Click **Close.**

Click Go To tab ———

Enter 3 ———

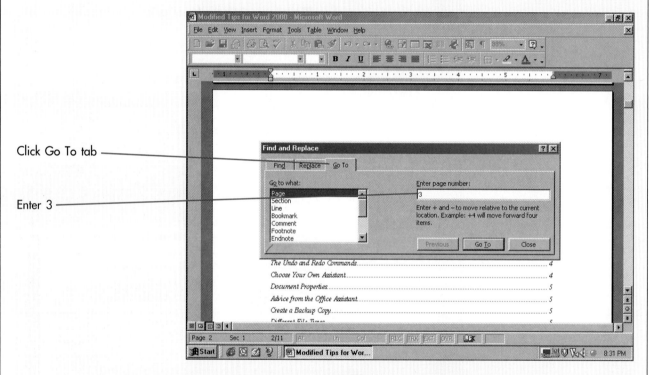

(d) Field Codes versus Field Text (step 4)

FIGURE 4.12   Hands-on Exercise 4 (continued)

THE GO TO AND GO BACK COMMANDS

The F5 key is the shortcut equivalent of the Go To command and displays a dialog box to move to a specific location (a page or section) within a document. The Shift+F5 combination executes the Go Back command and returns to a previous location of the insertion point; press Shift+F5 repeatedly to cycle through the last three locations of the insertion point.

STEP 5: Insert a Section Break

➤ Scroll down page three until you are at the end of the table of contents. Click to the left of the first tip heading as shown in Figure 4.12e.

➤ Pull down the **Insert menu.** Click **Break** to display the Break dialog box. Click the **Next Page button** under Section Breaks. Click **OK** to create a section break, simultaneously forcing the first tip to begin on a new page.

➤ The first tip, Download the Practice Files, moves to the top of the next page (page 4 in the document). If the status bar already displays Page 1 Section 2, a previous user has changed the default numbering to begin each section on its own page and you can go to step 6. If not you need to change the page numbering.

➤ Pull down the **Insert menu** and click **Page Numbers** to display the Page Numbers dialog box. Click the **drop-down arrow** in the Position list box to position the page number at the top of page (in the header).

➤ Click the **Format command button** to display the Page Number Format dialog box. Click the option button to **Start at** page 1 (i.e., you want the first page in the second section to be numbered as page 1), and click **OK** to close the Page Number Format box.

➤ Close the Page Numbers dialog box. The status bar now displays page 1 Sec 2 to indicate that you are on page 1 in the second section. The entry 4/12 indicates that you are physically on the fourth page of a 12-page document.

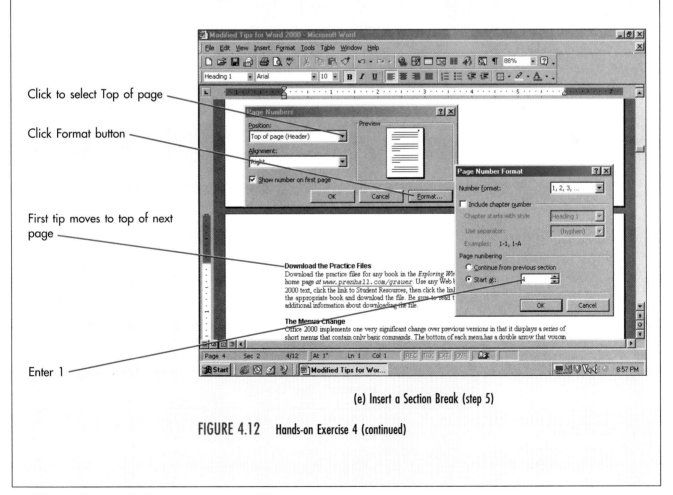

Click to select Top of page

Click Format button

First tip moves to top of next page

Enter 1

(e) Insert a Section Break (step 5)

FIGURE 4.12   Hands-on Exercise 4 (continued)

STEP 6: The Page Setup Command

➤ Pull down the **File menu** and click the **Page Setup** command (or double click the ruler) to display the Page Setup dialog box.

➤ Click the **Layout tab** to display the dialog box in Figure 4.12f.

➤ If necessary, clear the box for Different Odd and Even Pages and for Different First Page, as all pages in this section (section two) are to have the same header. Click **OK.**

➤ Save the document.

Click Layout tab

Check boxes should not be selected

Insertion point is on page 1 of section 2

Insertion point is on page 4 of 12-page document

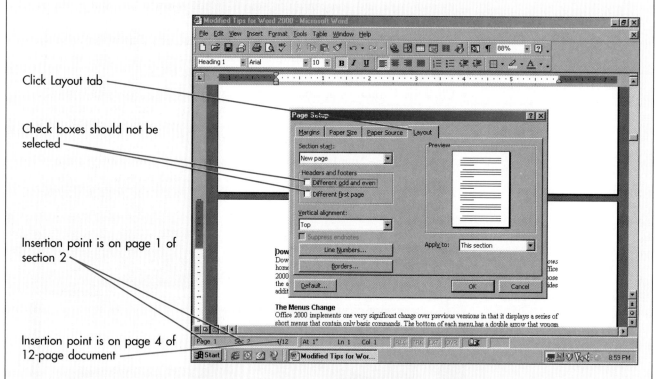

(f) The Page Setup Command (step 6)

FIGURE 4.12   Hands-on Exercise 4 (continued)

MOVING WITHIN LONG DOCUMENTS

Double click the page indicator on the status bar to display the dialog box for the Go To command from where you can go directly to any page within the document. You can also click an entry in the table of contents to go directly to the text of that entry. And finally, you can use the Ctrl+Home and Ctrl+End keyboard shortcuts to move to the beginning or end of the document, respectively.

STEP 7: Create the Header

➤ Pull down the **View menu.** Click **Header and Footer** to produce the screen in Figure 4.12g. The text in the document is faded to indicate that you are editing the header, as opposed to the document.

➤ The "Same as Previous" indicator is on since Word automatically uses the header from the previous section.

➤ Click the **Same as Previous button** on the Header and Footer toolbar to toggle the indicator off and to create a different header for this section.

➤ If necessary, click in the header. Click the **arrow** on the **Font list box** on the Formatting toolbar. Click **Arial.** Click the **arrow** on the Font size box. Click **8.** Type **Tips for Microsoft Word 2000.**

➤ Press the **Tab key** twice. Type **PAGE.** Press the **space bar.** Click the **Insert Page Number button** on the Header and Footer toolbar.

➤ Click the **Close button** on the Header and Footer toolbar. The header is faded, and the document text is available for editing.

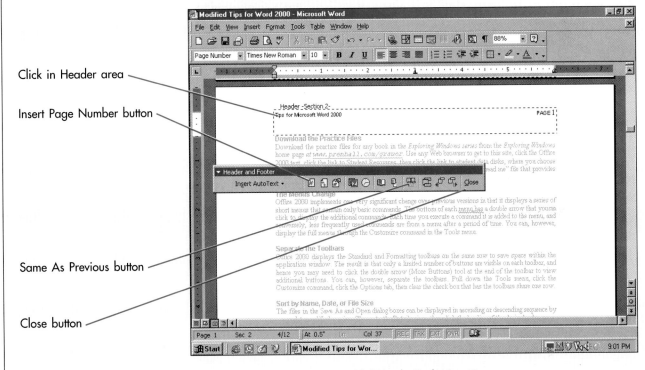

(g) Create the Header (step 7)

FIGURE 4.12   Hands-on Exercise 4 (continued)

HEADERS AND FOOTERS

If you do not see a header or footer, it is most likely because you are in the wrong view. Headers and footers are displayed in the Print Layout view but not in the Normal view. (Click the Print Layout button on the status bar to change the view.)

STEP 8: Update the Table of Contents

➤ Press **Ctrl+Home** to move to the beginning of the document. The status bar indicates Page 1, Sec 1.

➤ Click the **Select Browse Object button** on the Vertical scroll bar, then click the **Browse by Page** icon.

➤ If necessary, click the **Next Page button** or **Previous Page button** on the vertical scroll bar (or press **Ctrl+PgDn**) to move to the page containing the table of contents.

➤ Click to the left of the first entry in the Table of Contents. Press the **F9 key** to update the table of contents. If necessary, click the **Update Entire Table button** as shown in Figure 4.12h, then click **OK.**

➤ The pages are renumbered to reflect the actual page numbers in the second section.

Click to left of first entry

Click Update Entire table

Previous Page button

Select Browse Object button

Next Page button

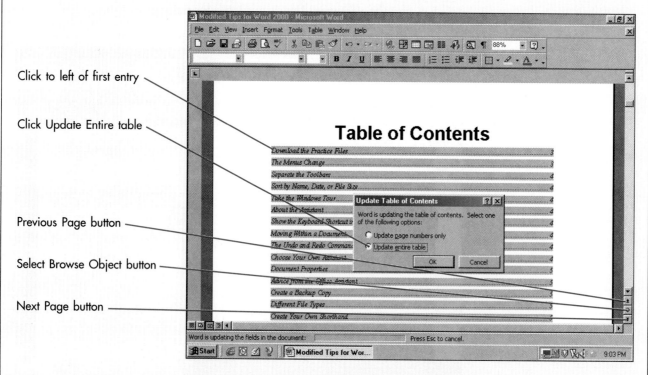

(h) Update the Table of Contents (step 8)

FIGURE 4.12 Hands-on Exercise 4 (continued)

SELECT BROWSE OBJECT

Click the Select Browse Object button toward the bottom of the vertical scroll bar to display a menu in which you specify how to browse through a document. Typically you browse from one page to the next, but you can browse by footnote, section, graphic, table, or any of the other objects listed. Once you select the object, click the Next or Previous buttons on the vertical scroll bar (or press Ctrl+PgDn or Ctrl+PgUp) to move to the next or previous occurrence of the selected object.

STEP 9: Create an Index Entry

➤ Press **Ctrl+Home** to move to the beginning of the document. Pull down the **Edit menu** and click the **Find command.** Search for the first occurrence of the text "Ctrl+Home" within the document, as shown in Figure 4.12i. Close the Find and Replace dialog box.

➤ Click the **Show/Hide ¶ button** so you can see the nonprinting characters in the document, which include the index entries that have been previously created by the authors. (The index entries appear in curly brackets and begin with the letters XE.)

➤ Check that the text "Ctrl+Home" is selected within the document, then press **Alt+Shift+X** to display the Mark Index Entry dialog box. (Should you forget the shortcut, pull down the Insert menu, click the **Index and Tables command,** then click the Mark Entry command button.)

➤ Click the **Mark command button** to create the index entry, after which you see the field code, {XE "Ctrl+Home"} to indicate that the index entry has been created.

➤ The Mark Index Entry dialog box stays open so that you can create additional entries by selecting additional text.

➤ Click the option button to create a **cross-reference.** Type **keyboard shortcut** in the associated text box. Click **Mark.**

➤ Click in the document, click and drag to select the text "Ctrl+End," then click in the dialog box, and the Main entry changes to Ctrl+End automatically. Click the **Mark command button** to create the index entry. Close the Mark Index Entry dialog box. Save the document.

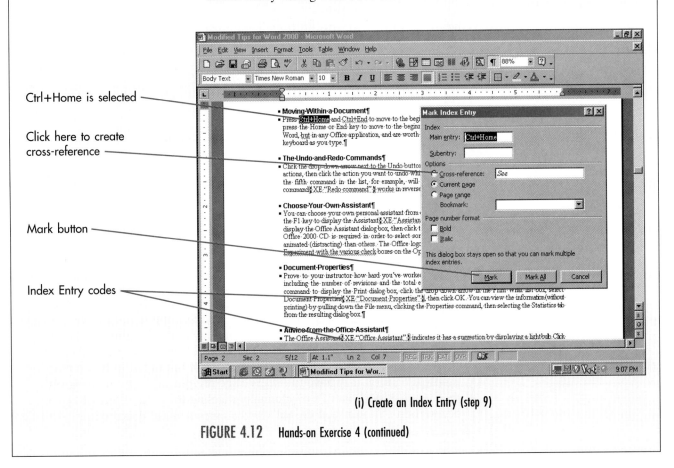

Ctrl+Home is selected

Click here to create cross-reference

Mark button

Index Entry codes

(i) Create an Index Entry (step 9)

FIGURE 4.12 Hands-on Exercise 4 (continued)

STEP 10: Create the Index

➤ Press **Ctrl+End** to move to the end of the document where you will insert the index. Pull down the **Insert menu** and click the **Index and Tables command** to display the Index and Tables dialog box in Figure 4.12j. Click the **Index tab** if necessary.

➤ Choose the type of index you want. We selected a **classic format** over **two columns.** Click **OK** to create the index. Click the **Undo command** if you are not satisfied with the appearance of the index, then repeat the process to create an index with a different style.

➤ Save the document.

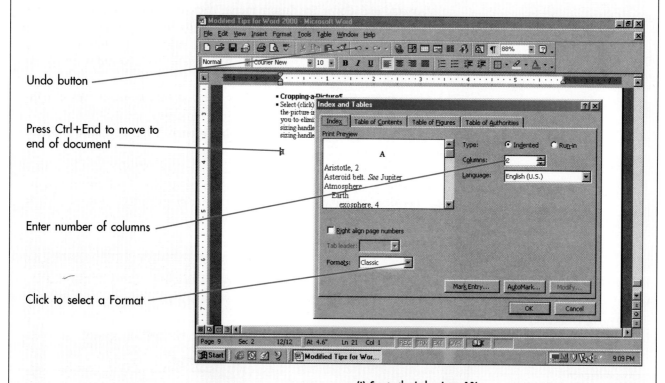

Undo button

Press Ctrl+End to move to end of document

Enter number of columns

Click to select a Format

(j) Create the Index (step 10)

FIGURE 4.12   Hands-on Exercise 4 (continued)

AUTOMARK INDEX ENTRIES

The AutoMark command will, as the name implies, automatically mark all occurrences of all entries for inclusion in an index. To use the feature, you have to create a separate document that lists the terms you want to reference, then you execute the AutoMark command from the Index and Tables dialog box. The advantage is that it is fast. The disadvantage is that every occurrence of an entry is marked in the index so that a commonly used term may have too many page references. You can, however, delete superfluous entries by manually deleting the field codes. Click the Show/Hide button if you do not see the entries in the document.

STEP 11: Complete the Index

➤ Scroll to the beginning of the index and click to the left of the letter "A." Pull down the **File menu** and click the **Page Setup command** to display the Page Setup dialog box and click the **Layout tab.**

➤ Click the **down arrow** in the Section start list box and specify **New page.** Click the **down arrow** in the Apply to list box and specify **This section.** Click **OK.** The index moves to the top of a new page.

➤ Click anywhere in the index, which is contained in its own section since it is displayed over two columns. The status bar displays Page 1, Section 3, 13/13 as shown in Figure 4.12k.

➤ Save the document.

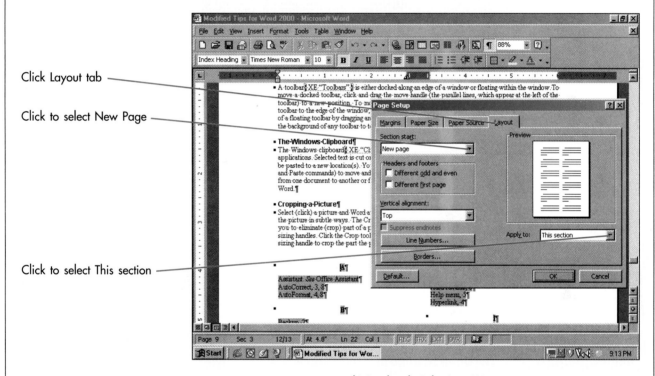

Click Layout tab

Click to select New Page

Click to select This section

(k) Complete the Index (step 11)

FIGURE 4.12   Hands-on Exercise 4 (continued)

SECTION FORMATTING

Page numbering and orientation, headers, footers, and columns are implemented at the section level. Thus the index is automatically placed in its own section because it contains a different number of columns from the rest of the document. The notation on the status bar, Page 1, Section 3, 13/13 indicates that the insertion point is on the first page of section three, corresponding to the 13th page of a 13-page document.

STEP 12: The Completed Document

➤ Pull down the **View menu.** Click **Zoom.** Click **Many Pages.** Click the **monitor icon.** Click and drag the page icon within the monitor to display two pages down by five pages. Release the mouse. Click **OK.**

➤ The completed document is shown in Figure 4.12l. The index appears by itself on the last (13th) page of the document.

➤ Save the document, then print the completed document to prove to your instructor that you have completed the exercise.

➤ Congratulations on a job well done. Exit Word.

Index is on last page

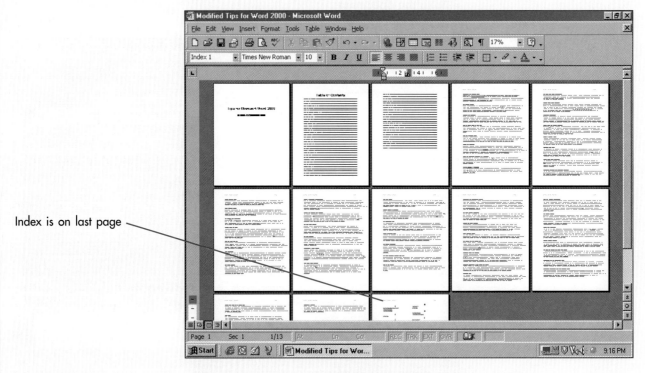

(l) The Completed Document (step 12)

FIGURE 4.12   Hands-on Exercise 4 (continued)

UPDATING THE TABLE OF CONTENTS

Use a Shortcut menu to update the table of contents. Point to any entry in the table of contents, then press the right mouse button to display a shortcut menu. Click Update Field, click the Update Entire Table command button, and click OK. The table of contents will be adjusted automatically to reflect page number changes as well as the addition or deletion of any items defined by any built-in heading style.

A list helps to organize information by emphasizing important topics. A bulleted or numbered list can be created by clicking the appropriate button on the Formatting toolbar or by executing the Bullets and Numbering command in the Format menu. An outline extends a numbered list to several levels.

Tables represent a very powerful capability within Word and are created through the Insert Table command in the Table menu or by using the Insert Table button on the Standard toolbar. Each cell in a table is formatted independently and may contain text, numbers, and/or graphics.

A style is a set of formatting instructions that has been saved under a distinct name. Styles are created at the character or paragraph level and provide a consistent appearance to similar elements throughout a document. Existing styles can be modified to change the formatting of all text defined by that style.

The Outline view displays a condensed view of a document based on styles within the document. Text may be collapsed or expanded as necessary to facilitate moving text within long documents.

The AutoFormat command analyzes a document and formats it for you. The command goes through an entire document, determines how each paragraph is used, then applies an appropriate style to each paragraph.

Formatting occurs at the character, paragraph, or section level. Section formatting controls margins, columns, page orientation and size, page numbering, and headers and footers. A header consists of one or more lines that are printed at the top of every (designated) page in a document. A footer is text that is printed at the bottom of designated pages. Page numbers may be added to either a header or footer.

A table of contents lists headings in the order they appear in a document with their respective page numbers. It can be created automatically, provided the built-in heading styles were previously applied to the items for inclusion. Word will create an index automatically, provided that the entries for the index have been previously marked. This, in turn, requires you to go through a document, select the appropriate text, and mark the entries accordingly. The Edit Go To command enables you to move directly to a specific page, section, or bookmark within a document.

KEY WORDS AND CONCEPTS

AutoFormat command	Go To command	Normal style
AutoMark	Header	Numbered list
Body Text style	Heading 1 style	Outline
Bookmark	Index	Outline view
Bulleted list	Index and Tables command	Page numbers
Bullets and Numbering command	Insert menu	Paragraph style
Cell	Insert Page Numbers command	Section
Character style	Insert Table command	Section break
Default Paragraph Font style	Leader character	Style
Footer	Mark Index entry	Style command
Format Style command	Outline numbered list	Table menu
		Table of contents
		Tables feature

1. Which of the following can be stored within a paragraph style?
   (a) Tabs and indents
   (b) Line spacing and alignment
   (c) Shading and borders
   (d) All of the above

2. What is the easiest way to change the alignment of five paragraphs scattered throughout a document, each of which has been formatted with the same style?
   (a) Select the paragraphs individually, then click the appropriate alignment button on the Formatting toolbar
   (b) Select the paragraphs at the same time, then click the appropriate alignment button on the Formatting toolbar
   (c) Change the format of the existing style, which changes the paragraphs
   (d) Retype the paragraphs according to the new specifications

3. The AutoFormat command will do all of the following except:
   (a) Apply styles to individual paragraphs
   (b) Apply boldface italics to terms that require additional emphasis
   (c) Replace ordinary quotes with smart quotes
   (d) Substitute typographic symbols for ordinary letters—such as © for (C)

4. Which of the following is used to create a conventional outline?
   (a) The Bullets and Numbering command
   (b) The Outline view
   (c) Both (a) and (b)
   (d) Neither (a) nor (b)

5. In which view do you see headers and/or footers?
   (a) Print Layout view
   (b) Normal view
   (c) Both (a) and (b)
   (d) Neither (a) nor (b)

6. Which of the following numbering schemes can be used with page numbers?
   (a) Roman numerals (I, II, III . . . or i, ii, iii)
   (b) Regular numbers (1, 2, 3, . . .)
   (c) Letters (A, B, C . . . or a, b, c)
   (d) All of the above

7. Which of the following is true regarding headers and footers?
   (a) Every document must have at least one header
   (b) Every document must have at least one footer
   (c) Both (a) and (b)
   (d) Neither (a) nor (b)

8. Which of the following is a *false* statement regarding lists?
   (a) A bulleted list can be changed to a numbered list and vice versa
   (b) The symbol for the bulleted list can be changed to a different character
   (c) The numbers in a numbered list can be changed to letters or roman numerals
   (d) The bullets or numbers cannot be removed

9. Page numbers can be specified in:
   (a) A header but not a footer
   (b) A footer but not a header
   (c) A header or a footer
   (d) Neither a header nor a footer

10. Which of the following is true regarding the formatting within a document?
    (a) Line spacing and alignment are implemented at the section level
    (b) Margins, headers, and footers are implemented at the paragraph level
    (c) Both (a) and (b)
    (d) Neither (a) nor (b)

11. What happens when you press the Tab key from within a table?
    (a) A Tab character is inserted just as it would be for ordinary text
    (b) The insertion point moves to the next column in the same row or the first column in the next row if you are at the end of the row
    (c) Both (a) and (b)
    (d) Neither (a) nor (b)

12. Which of the following is true, given that the status bar displays Page 1, Section 3, followed by 7/9?
    (a) The document has a maximum of three sections
    (b) The third section begins on page 7
    (c) The insertion point is on the very first page of the document
    (d) All of the above

13. The Edit Go To command enables you to move the insertion point to:
    (a) A specific page
    (b) A relative page forward or backward from the current page
    (c) A specific section
    (d) Any of the above

14. Once a table of contents has been created and inserted into a document:
    (a) Any subsequent page changes arising from the insertion or deletion of text to existing paragraphs must be entered manually
    (b) Any additions to the entries in the table arising due to the insertion of new paragraphs defined by a heading style must be entered manually
    (c) Both (a) and (b)
    (d) Neither (a) nor (b)

15. Which of the following is *false* about the Outline view?
    (a) It can be collapsed to display only headings
    (b) It can be expanded to show the entire document
    (c) It requires the application of styles
    (d) It is used to create a conventional outline

Answers

1. d	**6.** d	**11.** b
2. c	**7.** d	**12.** b
3. b	**8.** d	**13.** d
4. a	**9.** c	**14.** d
5. a	**10.** d	**15.** d

PRACTICE WITH MICROSOFT WORD

1. Use your favorite search engine to locate the text of the United States Constitution. There are many available sites and associated documents. Once you locate the text of the Constitution, expand the outline created in the first hands-on exercise to include information about the other provisions of the Constitution (Articles IV through VII, the Bill of Rights, and the other amendments). Submit the completed outline to your professor.

2. Sections and Page Orientation: Formatting in Word takes place at the character, paragraph, or section level. The latter controls the margins and page orientation within a document and is illustrated in Figure 4.13. Create the study schedule as described in the second hands-on exercise, then insert a title page in front of the table. Note, however, that the title page and table must appear in different sections so that you can use the portrait and landscape orientations, respectively. Print the two-page document, consisting of the title page and table, and submit it to your instructor.

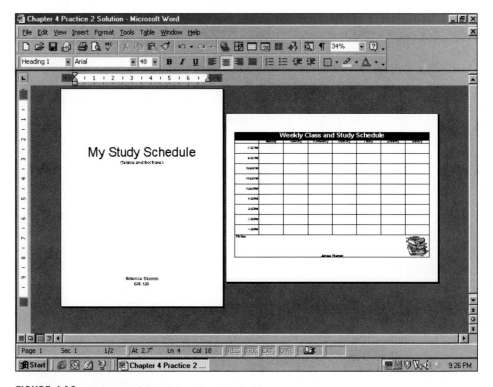

FIGURE 4.13   Sections and Page Orientation (Exercise 2)

3. For the health conscious: Open the *Chapter 4 Practice 3 document* in the *Exploring Word folder,* which consists of a series of tips for healthy living. Modify the document as follows:
   a. Use the AutoFormat command to apply the Heading 1 and Body Text styles throughout the document.
   b. Change the specifications for the Body Text and Heading 1 styles as follows. The Heading 1 style calls for 12 point Arial bold with a blue top border (which requires a color printer). The Body Text style is 12 point Times New Roman, justified, with a ¼ inch left indent.
   c. Create a title page for the document consisting of the title, *Tips for Healthy Living,* the author, *Marion B. Grauer,* and an additional line, indicating that the document was prepared for you.
   d. Create a header for the document consisting of the title, *Tips for Healthy Living,* and a page number. The header is not to appear on the title page, nor should the title page be included in the page numbering.
   e. Print the entire document for your instructor.

4. Graphics: A table may contain anything—text, graphics, or numbers as shown by the document in Figure 4.14. It's not complicated; in fact, it was really very easy; just follow the steps below:
   a. Create a 7 × 4 table.
   b. Merge all of the cells in row one and enter the heading. Merge all of the cells in row two and type the text describing the sale.
   c. Use the Clip Gallery to insert a picture into the table.
   d. Enter the sales data in rows three through seven of the table; all entries are centered within the respective cells.
   e. Change the font, colors, and formatting, then print the completed document. Use any format you think is appropriate.

Of course, it isn't quite as simple as it sounds, but we think you get the idea. Good luck and feel free to improve on our design. Color is a nice touch, but it is definitely not required.

Computers To Go

Our tremendous sales volume enables us to offer the fastest, most powerful Pentium II computers at prices almost too good to be true. Each microprocessor is offered in a variety of configurations so that you get exactly what you need. All configurations include a 17-inch monitor, mouse, and Windows 98.

Capacity	Configuration 1 128 Mb RAM 12 Gb Hard Drive	Configuration 2 96 Mb RAM 10 Gb Hard Drive	Configuration 3 64 Mb RAM 8 Gb Hard Drive
Pentium II – 450 MHz	$2,655	$2,437	$2,341
Pentium II – 400 MHz	$2,367	$2,249	$2,053
Pentium II – 350 MHz	$1,970	$1,769	$1,554
Pentium II – 333 MHz	$1,693	$1,492	$1,277

FIGURE 4.14   Graphics (Exercise 6)

Tips for Windows 98

Open the *Tips for Windows 98* document that can be found in the Exploring Windows folder. The tips are not formatted so we would like you to use the Auto-Format command to create an attractive document. There are lots of tips so a table of contents is also appropriate. Add a cover page with your name and date, then submit the completed document to your instructor.

Milestones in Communications

We take for granted immediate news of everything that is going on in the world, but it was not always that way. Did you know, for example, that it took five months for Queen Isabella to hear of Columbus' discovery, or that it took two weeks for Europe to learn of Lincoln's assassination? We've done some research on milestones in communications and left the file for you (Milestones in Communications). It runs for two, three, or four pages, depending on the formatting, which we leave to you. We would like you to include a header, and we think you should box the quotations that appear at the end of the document (it's your call as to whether to separate the quotations or group them together). Please be sure to number the completed document and don't forget a title page.

The Term Paper

Go to your most demanding professor and obtain the formatting requirements for the submission of a term paper. Be as precise as possible; for example, ask about margins, type size, and so on. What are the requirements for a title page? Is there a table of contents? Are there footnotes or endnotes, headers or footers? What is the format for the bibliography? Summarize the requirements, then indicate the precise means of implementation within Microsoft Word.

Word Outlines and PowerPoint Presentations

A Word document can be the basis of a PowerPoint presentation, provided the document has been formatted to include styles. Each paragraph formatted according to the Heading 1 style becomes the title of a slide, each paragraph formatted with the Heading 2 style becomes the first level of text, and so on.

Use the *Milestones in Communications* document in the Exploring Word folder as the basis of a PowerPoint presentation (see the first case study). Use the AutoFormat command to apply the necessary styles, pull down the File menu, select the Send To command, then choose Microsoft PowerPoint. Your system will start PowerPoint, then convert the styles in the Word document to a PowerPoint outline. Complete the presentation based on facts in the Word document, then submit the completed presentation to your instructor.

chapter 1

INTRODUCTION TO MICROSOFT EXCEL: WHAT IS A SPREADSHEET?

OBJECTIVES

After reading this chapter you will be able to:

1. Describe a spreadsheet and suggest several potential applications; explain how the rows and columns of a spreadsheet are identified, and how its cells are labeled.

2. Distinguish between a formula and a constant; explain the use of a predefined function within a formula.

3. Open an Excel workbook; insert and delete rows and columns of a worksheet; save and print the modified worksheet.

4. Distinguish between a pull-down menu, a shortcut menu, and a toolbar.

5. Describe the three-dimensional nature of an Excel workbook; distinguish between a workbook and a worksheet.

6. Print a worksheet two ways: to show the computed values or the cell formulas.

7. Use the Page Setup command to print a worksheet with or without gridlines and/or row and column headings; preview a worksheet before printing.

OVERVIEW

This chapter provides a broad-based introduction to spreadsheets in general, and to Microsoft Excel in particular. The spreadsheet is the microcomputer application that is most widely used by managers and executives. Our intent is to show the wide diversity of business and other uses to which the spreadsheet model can be applied. For one example, we draw an analogy between the spreadsheet and the accountant's ledger. For a second example, we create an instructor's grade book.

The chapter covers the fundamentals of spreadsheets as implemented in Excel, which uses the term worksheet rather than spreadsheet. It discusses how the rows and columns of an Excel worksheet are labeled, the difference between a formula and a constant, and the ability of a worksheet to recalculate itself after a change is made. We also distinguish between a worksheet and a workbook.

The hands-on exercises in the chapter enable you to apply all of the material at the computer, and are indispensable to the learn-by-doing philosophy we follow throughout the text. As you do the exercises, you may recognize many commands from other Windows applications, all of which share a common user interface and consistent command structure. Excel will be even easier to learn if you already know another application in Microsoft Office.

INTRODUCTION TO SPREADSHEETS

A *spreadsheet* is the computerized equivalent of an accountant's ledger. As with the ledger, it consists of a grid of rows and columns that enables you to organize data in a readily understandable format. Figures 1.1a and 1.1b show the same information displayed in ledger and spreadsheet format, respectively.

"What is the big deal?" you might ask. The big deal is that after you change an entry (or entries), the spreadsheet will, automatically and almost instantly, recompute all of the formulas. Consider, for example, the profit projection spreadsheet shown in Figure 1.1b. As the spreadsheet is presently constructed, the unit price is $20 and the projected sales are 1,200 units, producing gross sales of $24,000 ($20/unit × 1,200 units). The projected expenses are $19,200, which yields a profit of $4,800 ($24,000 − $19,200). If the unit price is increased to $22 per unit, the spreadsheet recomputes the formulas, adjusting the values of gross sales and net profit. The modified spreadsheet of Figure 1.1c appears automatically.

With a calculator and bottle of correction fluid or a good eraser, the same changes could also be made to the ledger. But imagine a ledger with hundreds of entries and the time that would be required to make the necessary changes to the ledger by hand. The same spreadsheet will be recomputed automatically by the computer. And the computer will not make mistakes. Herein lies the advantage of a spreadsheet—the ability to make changes, and to have the computer carry out the recalculation faster and more accurately than could be accomplished manually.

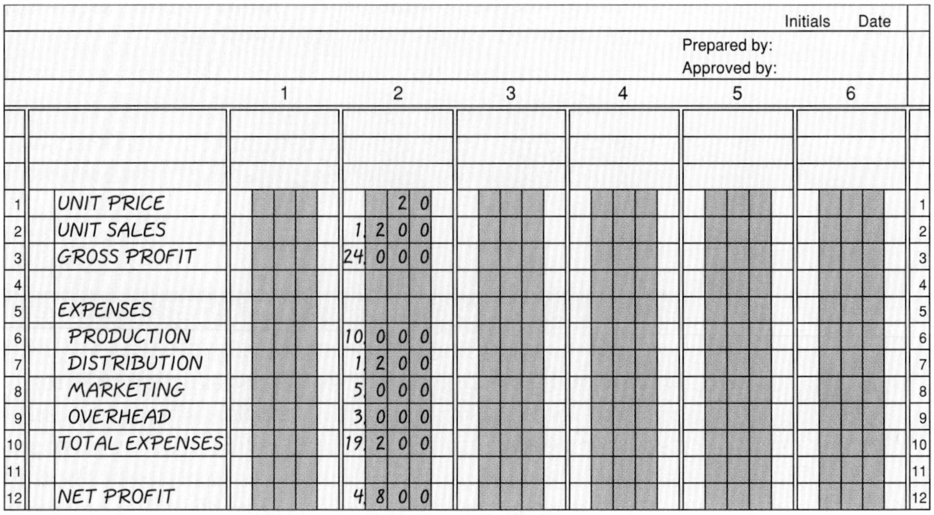

(a) The Accountant's Ledger

FIGURE 1.1   The Accountant's Ledger

Unit price is increased to $22

Formulas recompute automatically

	A	B
1	Profit Projection	
2		
3	Unit Price	$20
4	Unit Sales	1,200
5	Gross Sales	$24,000
6		
7	Expenses	
8	Production	$10,000
9	Distribution	$1,200
10	Marketing	$5,000
11	Overhead	$3,000
12	Total Expenses	$19,200
13		
14	Net Profit	$4,800

(b) Original Spreadsheet

	A	B
1	Profit Projection	
2		
3	Unit Price	$22
4	Unit Sales	1,200
5	Gross Sales	$26,400
6		
7	Expenses	
8	Production	$10,000
9	Distribution	$1,200
10	Marketing	$5,000
11	Overhead	$3,000
12	Total Expenses	$19,200
13		
14	Net Profit	$7,200

(c) Modified Spreadsheet

FIGURE 1.1   The Accountant's Ledger (continued)

The Professor's Grade Book

A second example of a spreadsheet, one with which you can easily identify, is that of a professor's grade book. The grades are recorded by hand in a notebook, which is nothing more than a different kind of accountant's ledger. Figure 1.2 contains both manual and spreadsheet versions of a grade book.

Figure 1.2a shows a handwritten grade book as it has been done since the days of the little red schoolhouse. For the sake of simplicity, only five students are shown, each with three grades. The professor has computed class averages for each exam, as well as a semester average for every student, in which the final counts *twice* as much as either test; for example, Adams's average is equal to $(100+90+81+81)/4 = 88$.

Figure 1.2b shows the grade book as it might appear in a spreadsheet, and is essentially unchanged from Figure 1.2a. Walker's grade on the final exam in Figure 1.2b is 90, giving him a semester average of 85 and producing a class average on the final of 75.2 as well. Now consider Figure 1.2c, in which the grade on Walker's final has been changed to 100, causing Walker's semester average to change from 85 to 90, and the class average on the final to go from 75.2 to 77.2. As with the profit projection, a change to any entry within the grade book automatically recalculates all other dependent formulas as well. Hence, when Walker's final exam was regraded, all dependent formulas (the class average for the final as well as Walker's semester average) were recomputed.

As simple as the idea of a spreadsheet may seem, it provided the first major reason for managers to have a personal computer on their desks. Essentially, anything that can be done with a pencil, a pad of paper, and a calculator can be done faster and far more accurately with a spreadsheet. The spreadsheet, like the personal computer, has become an integral part of every type of business. Indeed, it is hard to imagine that these calculations were ever done by hand.

Final counts twice so average is
computed as (100 + 90 + 81 + 81)/4

	TEST 1	TEST 2	FINAL	AVERAGE
ADAMS	100	90	81	88
BAKER	90	76	87	85
GLASSMAN	90	78	78	81
MOLDOF	60	60	40	50
WALKER	80	80	90	85
CLASS AVERAGE	84.0	76.8	75.2	
NOTE: FINAL COUNTS DOUBLE				

(a) The Professor's Grade Book

	A	B	C	D	E
1	Student	Test 1	Test 2	Final	Average
2					
3	Adams	100	90	81	88.0
4	Baker	90	76	87	85.0
5	Glassman	90	78	78	81.0
6	Moldof	60	60	40	50.0
7	Walker	80	80	90	85.0
8					
9	Class Average	84.0	76.8	75.2	

Walker's original grade is 90

(b) Original Grades

	A	B	C	D	E
1	Student	Test 1	Test 2	Final	Average
2					
3	Adams	100	90	81	88.0
4	Baker	90	76	87	85.0
5	Glassman	90	78	78	81.0
6	Moldof	60	60	40	50.0
7	Walker	80	80	100	90.0
8					
9	Class Average	84.0	76.8	77.2	

Grade on Walker's
final is changed to 100

Formulas recompute automatically

(c) Modified Spreadsheet

FIGURE 1.2   The Professor's Grade Book

Row and Column Headings

A spreadsheet is divided into rows and columns, with each row and column assigned a heading. Rows are given numeric headings ranging from 1 to 65,536 (the maximum number of rows allowed). Columns are assigned alphabetic headings from column A to Z, then continue from AA to AZ and then from BA to BZ and so on, until the last of 256 columns (column IV) is reached.

The intersection of a row and column forms a *cell,* with the number of cells in a spreadsheet equal to the number of rows times the number of columns. The professor's grade book in Figure 1.2, for example, has 5 columns labeled A through E, 9 rows numbered from 1 to 9, and a total of 45 cells. Each cell has a unique *cell reference;* for example, the cell at the intersection of column A and row 9 is known as cell A9. The column heading always precedes the row heading in the cell reference.

Formulas and Constants

Figure 1.3 is an alternate view of the professor's grade book that shows the cell contents rather than the computed values. Cell E3, for example, does not contain the number 88 (Adams' average for the semester), but rather the formula to compute the average from the exam grades. Indeed, it is the existence of the formula that lets you change the value of any cell containing a grade for Adams (cells B3, C3, or D3), and have the computed average in cell E3 change automatically.

To create a spreadsheet, one goes from cell to cell and enters either a *constant* or a *formula.* A *constant* is an entry that does not change. It may be a number, such as a student's grade on an exam, or it may be descriptive text (a label), such as a student's name. A *formula* is a combination of numeric constants, cell references, arithmetic operators, and/or functions (described below) that displays the result of a calculation. You can *edit* (change) the contents of a cell, by returning to the cell and reentering the constant or formula.

A formula always begins with an equal sign. Consider, for example, the formula in cell E3, $=(B3+C3+2*D3)/4$, which computes Adams's semester average. The formula is built in accordance with the professor's rules for computing a student's semester average, which counts the final twice as much as the other tests. Excel uses symbols $+$, $-$, $*$, $/$, and $\wedge$ to indicate addition, subtraction, multiplication, division, and exponentiation, respectively, and follows the normal rules of arithmetic precedence. Any expression in parentheses is evaluated first, then within an expression exponentiation is performed first, followed by multiplication or division in left to right order, then finally addition or subtraction.

The formula in cell E3 takes the grade on the first exam (in cell B3), plus the grade on the second exam (in cell C3), plus two times the grade on the final (in cell D3), and divides the result by four. Thus, should any of the exam grades change, the semester average (a formula whose results depend on the individual exam grades) will also change. This, in essence, is the basic principle behind the spreadsheet and explains why, when one number changes, various other numbers throughout the spreadsheet change as well.

A formula may also include a *function,* or predefined computational task, such as the *AVERAGE function* in cells B9, C9, and D9. The function in cell B9, for example, $=AVERAGE(B3:B7)$, is interpreted to mean the average of all cells starting at cell B3 and ending at cell B7 and is equivalent to the formula $=(B3+B4+B5+B6+B7)/5$. You can appreciate that functions are often easier to use than the corresponding formulas, especially with larger spreadsheets (and classes with many students). Excel contains a wide variety of functions that help you to create very powerful spreadsheets. Financial functions, for example, enable you to calculate the interest payments on a car loan or home mortgage.

Constant (entry that does not change) Function (predefined computational task) Formula (displays the result of a calculation)

	A	B	C	D	E
1	Student	Test 1	Test 2	Final	Average
2					
3	Adams	100	90	81	=(B3+C3+2*D3)/4
4	Baker	90	76	87	=(B4+C4+2*D4)/4
5	Glassman	90	78	78	=(B5+C5+2*D5)/4
6	Moldof	60	60	40	=(B6+C6+2*D6)/4
7	Walker	80	80	90	=(B7+C7+2*D7)/4
8					
9	Class Average	=AVERAGE(B3:B7)	=AVERAGE(C3:C7)	=AVERAGE(D3:D7)	

FIGURE 1.3   The Professor's Grade Book (cell formulas)

Figure 1.4 displays the professor's grade book as it is implemented in Microsoft Excel. Microsoft Excel is a Windows application, and thus shares the common user interface with which you are familiar. (It's even easier to learn Excel if you already know another Office application such as Microsoft Word.) You should recognize, therefore, that the desktop in Figure 1.4 has two open windows—an application window for Microsoft Excel and a document window for the workbook, which is currently open.

Each window has its own Minimize, Maximize (or Restore), and Close buttons. Both windows have been maximized and thus the title bars have been merged into a single title bar that appears at the top of the application window. The title bar reflects the application (Microsoft Excel) as well as the name of the workbook (Grade Book) on which you are working. A menu bar appears immediately below the title bar. Two toolbars, which are discussed in depth on page 8, appear below the menu bar. Vertical and horizontal scroll bars appear at the right and bottom of the document window. The Windows taskbar appears at the bottom of the screen and shows the open applications.

The terminology is important, and we distinguish between spreadsheet, worksheet, and workbook. Excel refers to a spreadsheet as a ***worksheet.*** Spreadsheet is a generic term; *workbook* and *worksheet* are unique to Excel. An Excel ***workbook*** contains one or more worksheets. The professor's grades for this class are contained in the CIS120 worksheet within the Grade Book workbook. This workbook also contains additional worksheets (CIS223 and CIS316) as indicated by the worksheet tabs at the bottom of the window. These worksheets contain the professor's grades for other courses that he or she is teaching this semester. (See practice exercise 1 at the end of the chapter.)

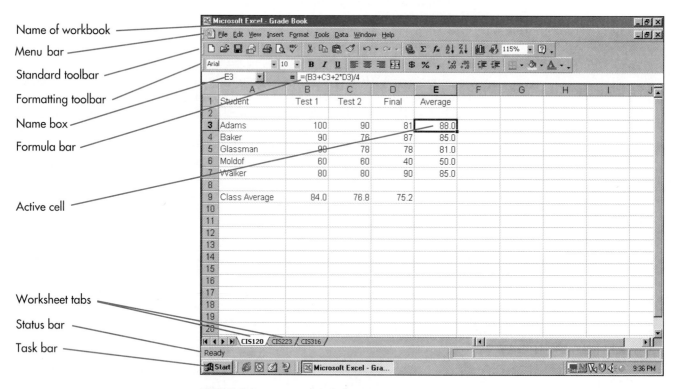

FIGURE 1.4   Professor's Grade Book

Figure 1.4 resembles the grade book shown earlier, but it includes several other elements that enable you to create and/or edit the worksheet. The heavy border around cell E3 indicates that it (cell E3) is the *active cell.* Any entry made at this time is made into the active cell, and any commands that are executed affect the contents of the active cell. The active cell can be changed by clicking a different cell, or by using the arrow keys to move to a different cell.

The displayed value in cell E3 is 88.0, but as indicated earlier, the cell contains a formula to compute the semester average rather than the number itself. The contents of the active cell, =(B3+C3+2*D3)/4, are displayed in the *formula bar* near the top of the worksheet. The cell reference for the active cell, cell E3 in Figure 1.4, appears in the *Name box* at the left of the formula bar.

The *status bar* at the bottom of the worksheet keeps you informed of what is happening as you work within Excel. It displays information about a selected command or an operation in progress.

THE EXCEL WORKBOOK

An Excel workbook is the electronic equivalent of the three-ring binder. A workbook contains one or more worksheets (or chart sheets), each of which is identified by a tab at the bottom of the workbook. The worksheets in a workbook are normally related to one another; for example, each worksheet may contain the sales for a specific division within a company. The advantage of a workbook is that all of its worksheets are stored in a single file, which is accessed as a unit.

Toolbars

Excel provides several different ways to accomplish the same task. Commands may be accessed from a pull-down menu, from a shortcut menu (which is displayed by pointing to an object and clicking the right mouse button), and/or through keyboard equivalents. Commands can also be executed from one of many *toolbars* that appear immediately below the menu bar. The Standard and Formatting toolbars are displayed by default. The toolbars appear initially on the same line, but can be separated as described in the hands-on exercise that follows.

The *Standard toolbar* contains buttons corresponding to the most basic commands in Excel—for example, opening and closing a workbook, printing a workbook, and so on. The icon on the button is intended to be indicative of its function (e.g., a printer to indicate the Print command). You can also point to the button to display a *ScreenTip* showing the name of the button.

The *Formatting toolbar* appears under the Standard toolbar, and provides access to common formatting operations such as boldface, italics, or underlining. It also enables you to change the alignment of entries within a cell and/or change the font or color. The easiest way to master the toolbars is to view the buttons in groups according to their general function, as shown in Figure 1.5.

The toolbars may appear overwhelming at first, but there is absolutely no need to memorize what the individual buttons do. That will come with time. Indeed, if you use another office application such as Microsoft Word, you may already recognize many of the buttons on the Standard and Formatting toolbars. Note, too, that many of the commands in the pull-down menus are displayed with an image that corresponds to a button on a toolbar.

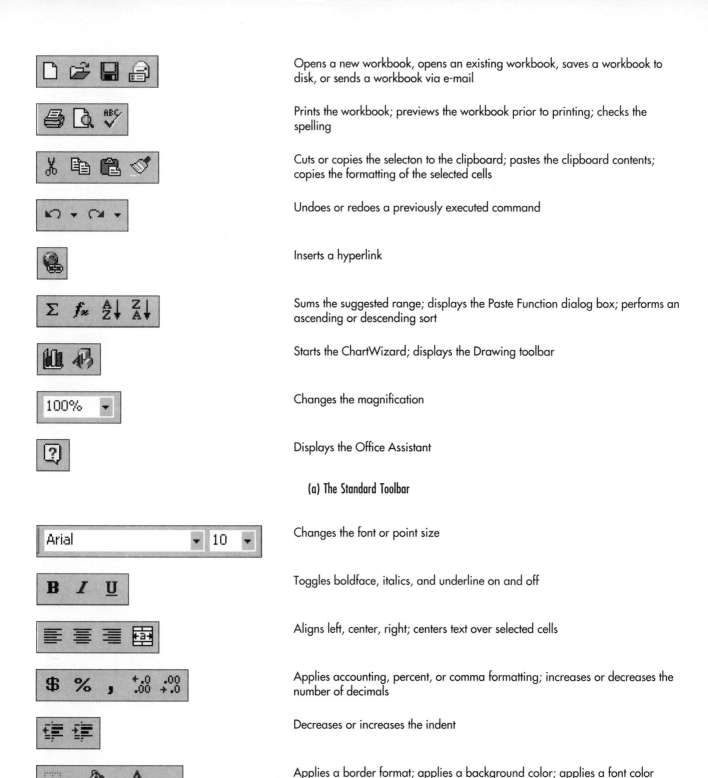

Opens a new workbook, opens an existing workbook, saves a workbook to disk, or sends a workbook via e-mail

Prints the workbook; previews the workbook prior to printing; checks the spelling

Cuts or copies the selecton to the clipboard; pastes the clipboard contents; copies the formatting of the selected cells

Undoes or redoes a previously executed command

Inserts a hyperlink

Sums the suggested range; displays the Paste Function dialog box; performs an ascending or descending sort

Starts the ChartWizard; displays the Drawing toolbar

Changes the magnification

Displays the Office Assistant

(a) The Standard Toolbar

Changes the font or point size

Toggles boldface, italics, and underline on and off

Aligns left, center, right; centers text over selected cells

Applies accounting, percent, or comma formatting; increases or decreases the number of decimals

Decreases or increases the indent

Applies a border format; applies a background color; applies a font color

(b) The Formatting Toolbar

FIGURE 1.5   Toolbars

The *File Menu* is a critically important menu in virtually every Windows application. It contains the Save and Open commands to save a workbook on disk, then subsequently retrieve (open) that workbook at a later time. The File Menu also contains the *Print command* to print a workbook, the *Close command* to close the current workbook but continue working in the application, and the *Exit command* to quit the application altogether.

The *Save command* copies the workbook that you are working on (i.e., the workbook that is currently in memory) to disk. The command functions differently the first time it is executed for a new workbook, in that it displays the Save As dialog box as shown in Figure 1.6a. The dialog box requires you to specify the name of the workbook, the drive (and an optional folder) in which the workbook is to be stored, and its file type. All subsequent executions of the command save the workbook under the assigned name, replacing the previously saved version with the new version.

The *file name* (e.g., My First Spreadsheet) can contain up to 255 characters including spaces, commas, and/or periods. (Periods are discouraged, however, since they are too easily confused with DOS extensions.) The Save In list box is used to select the drive (which is not visible in Figure 1.6a) and the optional folder (e.g., Exploring Excel). The *Places Bar* provides shortcuts to any of its folders without having to search through the Save In list box. Click the Desktop icon, for example, and the file is saved on the Windows desktop. You can also use the Favorites folder, which is accessible from every application in Office 2000.

The *file type* defaults to an Excel 2000 workbook. You can, however, choose a different format such as Excel 95 to maintain compatibility with earlier versions of Microsoft Excel. You can also save any Excel workbook as a Web page or HTML document. (Long-time DOS users will remember the three-character extension at the end of a filename such as XLS to indicate an Excel workbook. The extension is generally hidden in Windows 95/98, according to options that are set through the View menu in My Computer or Windows Explorer.)

The *Open command* is the opposite of the Save command as it brings a copy of an existing workbook into memory, enabling you to work with that workbook. The Open command displays the Open dialog box in which you specify the file name, the drive (and optionally the folder) that contains the file, and the file type. Microsoft Excel will then list all files of that type on the designated drive (and folder), enabling you to open the file you want.

The Save and Open commands work in conjunction with one another. The Save As dialog box in Figure 1.6a, for example, saves the file My First Spreadsheet in the Exploring Excel folder. The Open dialog box in Figure 1.6b loads that file into memory so that you can work with the file, after which you can save the revised file for use at a later time.

The toolbars in the Save As and Open dialog boxes have several buttons in common that facilitate the execution of either command. The Views button lets you display the files in one of four different views. The Details view shows the file size as well as the date and time a file was last modified. The Preview view shows the beginning of a workbook, without having to open the workbook. The List view displays only the file names, and thus lets you see more files at one time. The Properties view shows information about the workbook including the date of creation and number of revisions.

Other buttons provide limited file management without having to go to My Computer or Windows Explorer. You can for example, delete a file, create a new folder, or start your Web browser from either dialog box. The Tools button provides access to additional commands that are well worth exploring as you gain proficiency in Microsoft Office.

Drive/Folder in which file is to be stored

Views button

Places bar

File name

File type

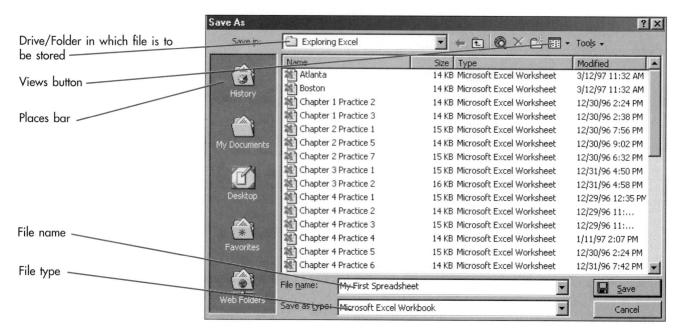

(a) Save As Dialog Box (Details View)

Drive/Folder in which file is stored

Views button

File to be opened

File type

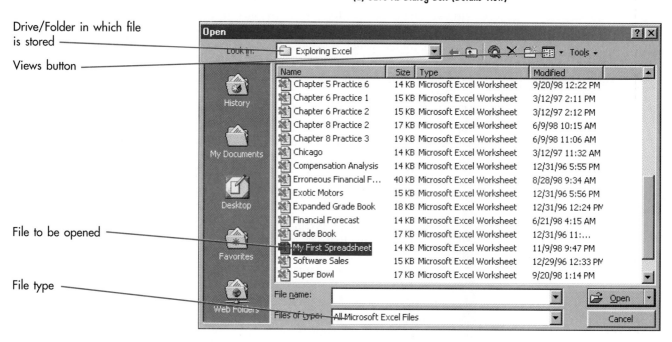

(b) Open Dialog Box (Details Views)

FIGURE 1.6   The Save and Open Commands

SORT BY NAME, DATE, OR FILE SIZE

The files in the Save As and Open dialog boxes can be displayed in ascending or descending sequence by name, date modified, or size. Change to the Details view, then click the heading of the desired column; e.g., click the Modified column to list the files according to the date they were last changed. Click the column heading a second time to reverse the sequence; that is, to switch from ascending to descending, and vice versa.

Introduction to Microsoft Excel

Objective: To start Microsoft Excel; to open, modify, and print an existing workbook. Use Figure 1.7 as a guide in the exercise.

STEP 1: Welcome to Windows

➤ Turn on the computer and all of its peripherals. The floppy drive should be empty prior to starting your machine. This ensures that the system starts by reading from the hard disk, which contains the Windows files, as opposed to a floppy disk, which does not.

➤ Your system will take a minute or so to get started, after which you should see the desktop in Figure 1.7a. Do not be concerned if the appearance of your desktop is different from ours.

➤ You may see additional objects on the desktop in Windows 95 and/or the active desktop in Windows 98. It doesn't matter which operating system you are using because Office 2000 runs equally well under both Windows 95 and Windows 98, as well as Windows NT.

➤ You may also see a Welcome to Windows dialog box with commands to take a tour of the operating system. If so, click the appropriate button(s) or close the dialog box.

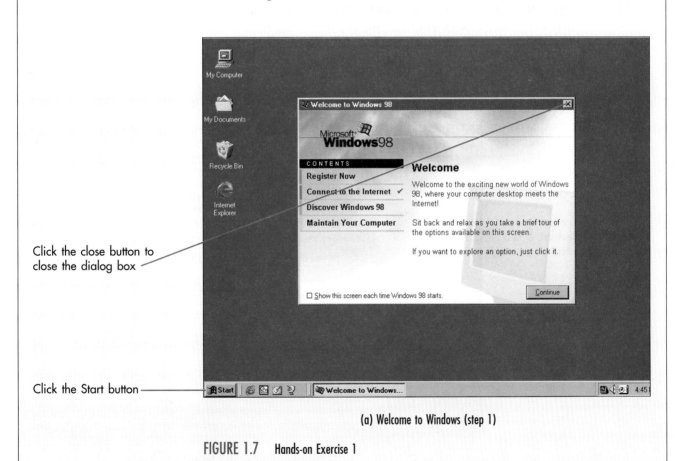

Click the close button to close the dialog box

Click the Start button

(a) Welcome to Windows (step 1)

FIGURE 1.7   Hands-on Exercise 1

STEP 2: Obtain the Practice Files

➤ We have created a series of practice files (also called a "data disk") for you to use throughout the text. Your instructor will make these files available to you in a variety of ways:

- The files may be on a network drive, in which case you use Windows Explorer to copy the files from the network to a floppy disk.

- There may be an actual "data disk" that you are to check out from the lab in order to use the Copy Disk command to duplicate the disk.

➤ You can also download the files from our Web site provided you have an Internet connection. Start Internet Explorer, then go to the Exploring Windows home page at **www.prenhall.com/grauer.**

- Click the book for **Office 2000,** which takes you to the Office 2000 home page. Click the **Student Resources tab** (at the top of the window) to go to the Student Resources page as shown in Figure 1.7b.

- Click the link to **Student Data Disk** (in the left frame), then scroll down the page until you can select Excel 2000. Click the link to download the student data disk.

- You will see the File Download dialog box asking what you want to do. The option button to save this program to disk is selected. Click **OK.** The Save As dialog box appears.

- Click the down arrow in the Save In list box to enter the drive and folder where you want to save the file. It's best to save the file to the Windows desktop or to a temporary folder on drive C

- Double click the file after it has been downloaded to your PC, then follow the onscreen instructions.

➤ Check with your instructor for additional information.

Click here for student data disk

Click here for Companion Web site (see problem 8 at the end of the chapter)

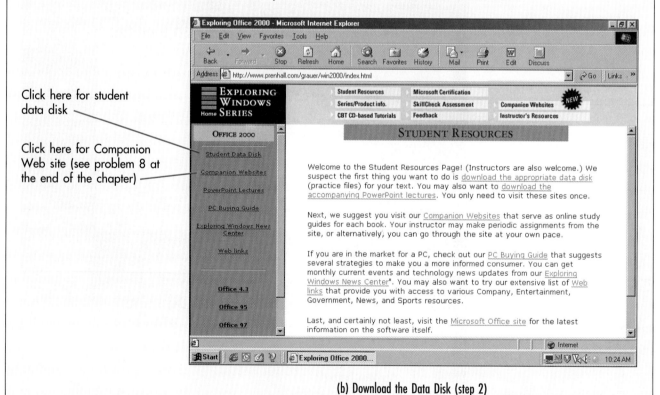

(b) Download the Data Disk (step 2)

FIGURE 1.7 Hands-on Exercise 1 (continued)

STEP 3: Start Excel

➤ Click the **Start button** to display the Start menu. Click (or point to) the **Programs menu,** then click **Microsoft Excel** to start the program.

➤ Click and drag the Office Assistant out of the way. (The Office Assistant is illustrated in step 7 of this exercise.)

➤ If necessary, click the **Maximize button** in the application window so that Excel takes the entire desktop as shown in Figure 1.7c. Click the **Maximize button** in the document window (if necessary) so that the document window is as large as possible.

Click and drag the Office Assistant out of the way

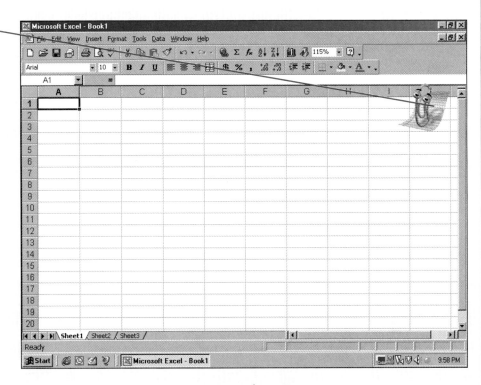

(c) Start Excel (step 3)

FIGURE 1.7   Hands-on Exercise 1 (continued)

ABOUT THE ASSISTANT

The Assistant is very powerful and hence you want to experiment with various ways to use it. To ask a question, click the Assistant's icon to toggle its balloon on or off. To change the way in which the Assistant works, click the Options button within the balloon and experiment with the various check boxes to see their effects. If you find the Assistant distracting, click and drag the character out of the way or hide it altogether by pulling down the Help menu and clicking the Hide the Office Assistant command. Pull down the Help menu and click the Show the Office Assistant command to return the Assistant to the desktop.

STEP 4: Open the Workbook

> ➤ Pull down the **File menu** and click **Open** (or click the **Open button** on the Standard toolbar). You should see a dialog box similar to the one in Figure 1.7d.

> ➤ Click the down-drop arrow on the Views button, then click **Details** to change to the Details view. Click and drag the vertical border between two columns to increase (or decrease) the size of a column.

> ➤ Click the **drop-down arrow** on the Look In list box. Click the appropriate drive, drive C or drive A, depending on the location of your data. Double click the **Exploring Excel folder** to make it the active folder (the folder from which you will retrieve and into which you will save the workbook).

> ➤ Click the **down scroll arrow** if necessary in order to click **Grade Book** to select the professor's grade book. Click the **Open command button** to open the workbook and begin the exercise.

Open button

Views button

Click the drop-down arrow to select the drive and folder

Click and drag to change the column width

Click to select the Grade Book

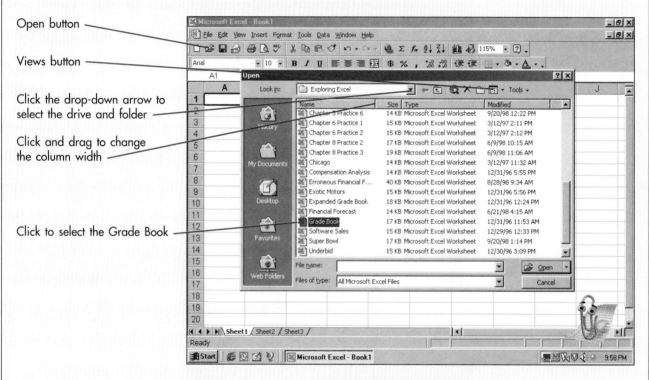

(d) Open the Workbook (step 4)

FIGURE 1.7 Hands-on Exercise 1 (continued)

SEPARATE THE TOOLBARS

Office 2000 displays the Standard and Formatting toolbars on the same row to save space within the application window. The result is that only a limited number of buttons are visible on each toolbar, and hence you may need to click the double arrow (More Buttons) tool at the end of the toolbar to view additional buttons. You can, however, separate the toolbars. Pull down the Tools menu, click the Customize command, click the Options tab, then clear the check box that has the toolbars share one row.

STEP 5: The Active Cell, Formula Bar, and Worksheet Tabs

➤ You should see the workbook in Figure 1.7e. Click in **cell B3,** the cell containing Adams's grade on the first test. Cell B3 is now the active cell and is surrounded by a heavy border. The Name box indicates that cell B3 is the active cell, and its contents are displayed in the formula bar.

➤ Click in **cell B4** (or press the **down arrow key**) to make it the active cell. The Name box indicates cell B4 while the formula bar indicates a grade of 90.

➤ Click in **cell E3,** the cell containing the formula to compute Adams's semester average; the worksheet displays the computed average of 88.0, but the formula bar displays the formula, $=(B3+C3+2*D3)/4$, to compute that average based on the test grades.

➤ Click the **CIS223 tab** to view a different worksheet within the same workbook. This worksheet contains the grades for a different class.

➤ Click the **CIS316 tab** to view this worksheet. Click the **CIS120 tab** to return to this worksheet and continue with the exercise.

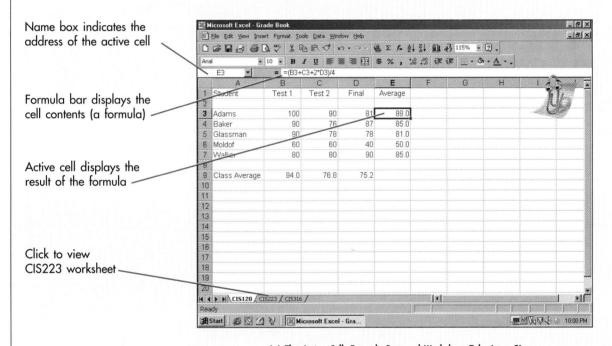

Name box indicates the address of the active cell

Formula bar displays the cell contents (a formula)

Active cell displays the result of the formula

Click to view CIS223 worksheet

(e) The Active Cell, Formula Bar, and Worksheet Tabs (step 5)

FIGURE 1.7   Hands-on Exercise 1 (continued)

THE MENUS CHANGE

All applications in Office 2000 display a series of short menus that contain only basic commands to simplify the application for the new user. There is, however, a double arrow at the bottom of each menu that you can click to display the additional commands. In addition, each time you execute a command it is added to the menu, and conversely, commands are removed from a menu if they are not used after a period of time. You can, however, display the full menus through the Customize command in the Tools menu by clearing the check boxes in the Personalized Menus and Toolbars section.

STEP 6: Experiment (What If?)

➤ Click in **cell C4,** the cell containing Baker's grade on the second test. Enter a corrected value of **86** (instead of the previous entry of 76). Press **enter** (or click in another cell).

➤ The effects of this change ripple through the worksheet, automatically changing the computed value for Baker's average in cell E4 to 87.5. The class average on the second test in cell C9 changes to 78.8.

➤ Change Walker's grade on the final from 90 to **100.** Press **enter** (or click in another cell). Walker's average in cell E7 changes to 90.0, while the class average in cell D9 changes to 77.2.

➤ Your worksheet should match Figure 1.7f.

Change test score to 86

Change grade on final to 100

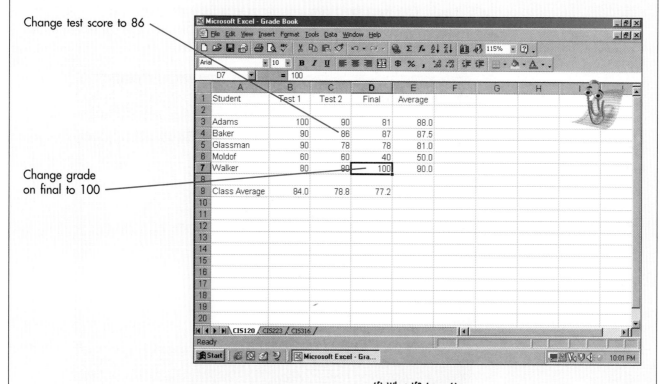

(f) What If? (step 6)

FIGURE 1.7   Hands-on Exercise 1 (continued)

THE UNDO AND REDO COMMANDS

The Undo Command lets you undo the last several changes to a workbook. Click the down arrow next to the Undo button on the Standard toolbar to display a reverse-order list of your previous commands, then click the command you want to undo, which also cancels all of the preceding commands. Undoing the fifth command in the list, for example, will also undo the preceding four commands. The Redo commands redoes (reverses) the last command that was undone. It, too, displays a reverse-order list of commands, so that redoing the fifth command in the list will also redo the preceding four commands.

STEP 7: The Office Assistant

➤ If necessary, pull down the **Help menu** and click the comand to **Show the Office Assistant.** You may see a different character than the one we have selected. Click the Assistant, then enter the question, **How do I use the Office Assistant?** as shown in Figure 1.7g.

➤ Click the **Search button** in the Assistant's balloon to look for the answer. The size of the Assistant's balloon expands as the Assistant suggests several topics that may be appropriate.

➤ Select (click) any topic, which in turn diplays a Help window with multiple links associated with the topic you selected.

➤ Click the Office Assistant to hide the balloon, then click any of the links in the Help window to read the information. You can print the contents of any topic by clicking the **Print button** in the Help window.

➤ Close the Help window when you are finished. If necessary, click the Excel button on the taskbar to return to the workbook.

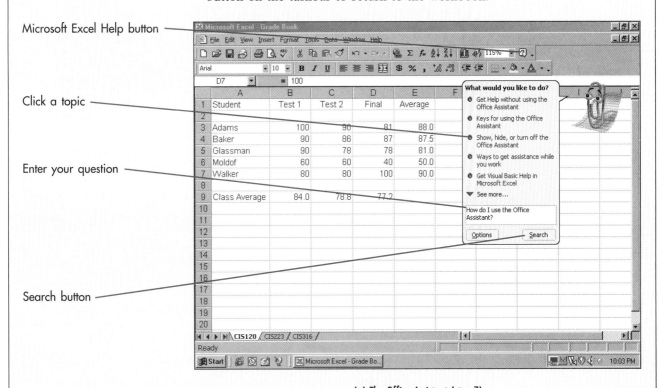

Microsoft Excel Help button

Click a topic

Enter your question

Search button

(g) The Office Assistant (step 7)

FIGURE 1.7   Hands-on Exercise 1 (continued)

ABOUT MICROSOFT EXCEL

Pull down the Help menu and click About Microsoft Excel to display the specific release number as well as other licensing information, including the Product ID. This help screen also contains two very useful command buttons, System Info and Technical Support. The first button displays information about the hardware installed on your system, including the amount of memory and available space on the hard drive. The Technical Support button provides information on obtaining technical assistance.

STEP 8: Print the Workbook

➤ Pull down the **File menu** and click **Save** (or click the **Save button** on the Standard toolbar).

➤ Pull down the **File menu.** Click **Print** to display a dialog box requesting information for the Print command as shown in Figure 1.7h. Click **OK** to accept the default options (you want to print only the selected worksheet).

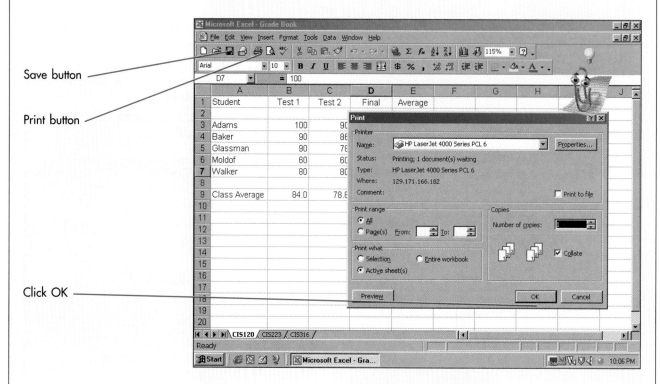

Save button

Print button

Click OK

(h) Print the Workbook (step 8)

FIGURE 1.7   Hands-on Exercise 1 (continued)

THE PRINT PREVIEW COMMAND

The Print Preview command displays the worksheet as it will appear when printed. The command is invaluable and will save you considerable time as you don't have to rely on trial and error to obtain the perfect printout. The Print Preview command can be executed from the File menu, via the Print Preview button on the Standard toolbar, or from the Print Preview command button within the Page Setup command.

STEP 9: Close the Workbook

➤ Pull down the **File menu.** Click **Close** to close the workbook but leave Excel open.

➤ Pull down the **File menu** a second time. Click **Exit** if you do not want to continue with the next exercise at this time.

We trust that you completed the hands-on exercise without difficulty and that you are more confident in your ability than when you first began. The exercise was not complicated, but it did accomplish several objectives and set the stage for a second exercise, which follows shortly.

Consider now Figure 1.8, which contains a modified version of the professor's grade book. Figure 1.8a shows the grade book at the end of the first hands-on exercise and reflects the changes made to the grades for Baker and Walker. Figure 1.8b shows the worksheet as it will appear at the end of the second exercise. Several changes bear mention:

1. One student has dropped the class and two other students have been added. Moldof appeared in the original worksheet in Figure 1.8a, but has somehow managed to withdraw; Coulter and Courier did not appear in the original grade book but have been added to the worksheet in Figure 1.8b.
2. A new column containing the students' majors has been added.

The implementation of these changes is accomplished through a combination of the **Insert Command** (to add individual cells, rows, or columns) and/or the **Delete command** (to remove individual cells, rows, or columns). Execution of either command automatically adjusts the cell references in existing formulas to reflect the insertion or deletion of the various cells. The Insert and Delete commands can also be used to insert or delete a worksheet. The professor could, for example, add a new sheet to a workbook to include grades for another class and/or delete a worksheet for a class that was no longer taught. We focus initially, however, on the insertion and deletion of rows and columns within a worksheet.

Moldof will be dropped from class →

	A	B	C	D	E
1	Student	Test 1	Test 2	Final	Average
2					
3	Adams	100	90	81	88.0
4	Baker	90	86	87	87.5
5	Glassman	90	78	78	81.0
6	Moldof	60	60	40	50.0
7	Walker	80	80	100	90.0
8					
9	Class Average	84.0	78.8	77.2	

(a) After Hands-on Exercise 1

A new column has been added (Major) →

Two new students have been added →

Moldof has been deleted →

	A	B	C	D	E	F
1	Student	Major	Test 1	Test 2	Final	Average
2						
3	Adams	CIS	100	90	81	88.0
4	Baker	MKT	90	86	87	87.5
5	Coulter	ACC	85	95	100	95.0
6	Courier	FIN	75	75	85	80.0
7	Glassman	CIS	90	78	78	81.0
8	Walker	CIS	80	80	100	90.0
9						

(b) After Hands-on Exercise 2

FIGURE 1.8   The Modified Grade Book

Figure 1.9 displays the cell formulas in the professor's grade book and corresponds to the worksheets in Figure 1.8. The "before" and "after" worksheets reflect the insertion of a new column containing the students' majors, the addition of two new students, Coulter and Courier, and the deletion of an existing student, Moldof.

Let us consider the formula to compute Adams's semester average, which is contained in cell E3 of the original grade book, but in cell F3 in the modified grade book. The formula in Figure 1.9a referenced cells B3, C3, and D3 (the grades on test 1, test 2, and the final). The corresponding formula in Figure 1.9b reflects the fact that a new column has been inserted, and references cells C3, D3, and E3. The change in the formula is made automatically by Excel, without any action on the part of the user other than to insert the new column. The formulas for all other students have been adjusted in similar fashion.

Some students (all students below Baker) have had a further adjustment to reflect the addition of the new students through insertion of new rows in the worksheet. Glassman, for example, appeared in row 5 of the original worksheet, but appears in row 7 of the revised worksheet. Hence the formula to compute Glassman's semester average now references the grades in row 7, rather than in row 5 as in the original worksheet.

Finally, the formulas to compute the class averages have also been adjusted. These formulas appeared in row 9 of Figure 1.9a and averaged the grades in rows 3 through 7. The revised worksheet has a net increase of one student, which automatically moves these formulas to row 10, where the formulas are adjusted to average the grades in rows 3 through 8.

Formula references grades in B3, C3, and D3 ⟶

Function references grades in rows 3–7 ⟶

	A	B	C	D	E
1	Student	Test1	Test2	Final	Average
2					
3	Adams	100	90	81	=(B3+C3+2*D3)/4
4	Baker	90	86	87	=(B4+C4+2*D4)/4
5	Glassman	90	78	78	=(B5+C5+2*D5)/4
6	Moldof	60	60	40	=(B6+C6+2*D6)/4
7	Walker	80	80	100	=(B7+C7+2*D7)/4
8					
9	Class Average	=AVERAGE(B3:B7)	=AVERAGE(C3:C7)	=AVERAGE(D3:D7)	

(a) Before

	A	B	C	D	E	F
1	Student	Major	Test1	Test2	Final	Average
2						
3	Adams	CIS	100	90	81	=(C3+D3+2*E3)/4
4	Baker	MKT	90	86	87	=(C4+D4+2*E4)/4
5	Coulter	ACC	85	95	100	=(C5+D5+2*E5)/4
6	Courier	FIN	75	75	85	=(C6+D6+2*E6)/4
7	Glassman	CIS	90	78	78	=(C7+D7+2*E7)/4
8	Walker	CIS	80	80	100	=(C8+D8+2*E8)/4
9						
10	Class Average		=AVERAGE(C3:C8)	=AVERAGE(D3:D8)	=AVERAGE(E3:E8)	

Function changes to reference grades in rows 3–8 (due to addition of 2 new students and deletion of 1)

Formula changes to reference grades in C3, D3, and E3 due to addition of new column

(b) After

FIGURE 1.9   The Insert and Delete Commands

THE PAGE SETUP COMMAND

The Print command was used at the end of the first hands-on exercise to print the completed workbook. The *Page Setup command* gives you complete control of the printed worksheet as illustrated in Figure 1.10. Many of the options may not appear important now, but you will appreciate them as you develop larger and more complicated worksheets later in the text.

The Page tab in Figure 1.10a determines the orientation and scaling of the printed page. *Portrait orientation* ($8\frac{1}{2} \times 11$) prints vertically down the page. *Landscape orientation* ($11 \times 8\frac{1}{2}$) prints horizontally across the page and is used

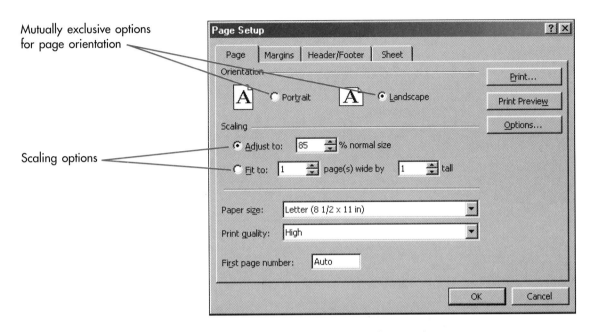

Mutually exclusive options for page orientation

Scaling options

(a) The Page Tab

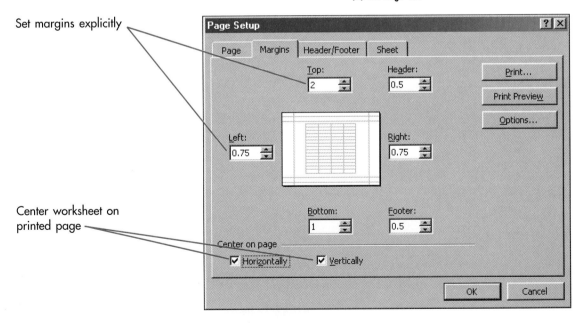

Set margins explicitly

Center worksheet on printed page

(b) The Margins Tab

FIGURE 1.10   The Page Setup Command

when the worksheet is too wide to fit on a portrait page. The option buttons indicate mutually exclusive items, one of which *must* be selected; that is, a worksheet must be printed in either portrait or landscape orientation. Option buttons are also used to choose the scaling factor. You can reduce (enlarge) the output by a designated scaling factor, or you can force the output to fit on a specified number of pages. The latter option is typically used to force a worksheet to fit on a single page.

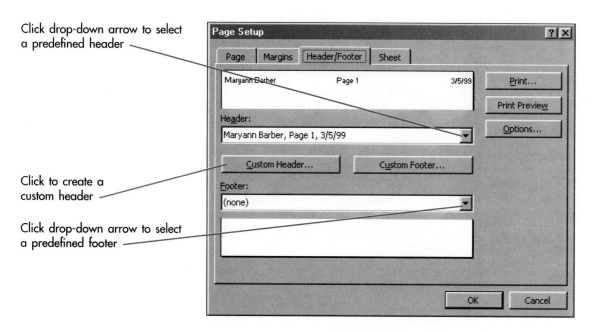

(c) The Header/Footer Tab

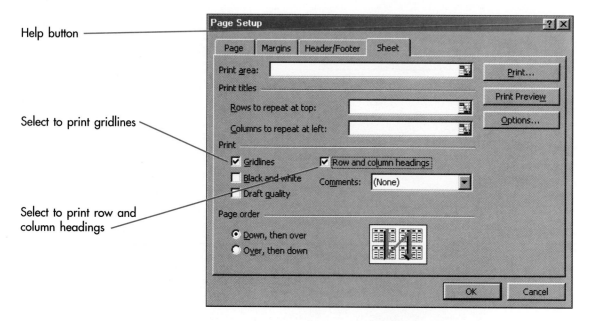

(d) The Sheet Tab

FIGURE 1.10   The Page Setup Command (continued)

The Margins tab in Figure 1.10b not only controls the margins, but will also center the worksheet horizontally and/or vertically. Check boxes are associated with the centering options and indicate that multiple options can be chosen; for example, horizontally and vertically are both selected. The Margins tab also determines the distance of the header and footer from the edge of the page.

The Header/Footer tab in Figure 1.10c lets you create a header (and/or footer) that appears at the top (and/or bottom) of every page. The pull-down list boxes let you choose from several preformatted entries, or alternatively, you can click the appropriate command button to customize either entry.

The Sheet tab in Figure 1.10d offers several additional options. The Gridlines option prints lines to separate the cells within the worksheet. The Row and Column Headings option displays the column letters and row numbers. Both options should be selected for most worksheets. Information about the additional entries can be obtained by clicking the Help button.

The Print Preview command button is available from all four tabs within the Page Setup dialog box. The command shows you how the worksheet will appear when printed and saves you from having to rely on trial and error.

HANDS-ON EXERCISE 2

Modifying a Worksheet

Objective: To open an existing workbook; to insert and delete rows and columns in a worksheet; to print cell formulas and displayed values; to use the Page Setup command to modify the appearance of a printed workbook. Use Figure 1.11 as a guide in doing the exercise.

STEP 1: Open the Workbook

➤ Open the grade book as you did in the previous exercise. Pull down the **File menu** and click **Open** (or click the **Open button** on the Standard toolbar) to display the Open dialog box.

➤ Click the **drop-down arrow** on the Look In list box. Click the appropriate drive, drive C or drive A, depending on the location of your data. Double click the **Exploring Excel folder** to make it the active folder (the folder from which you will open the workbook).

➤ Click the **down scroll arrow** until you can select (click) the **Grade Book** workbook. Click the **Open button** to open the workbook and begin the exercise.

THE MOST RECENTLY OPENED FILE LIST

The easiest way to open a recently used workbook is to select the workbook directly from the File menu. Pull down the File menu, but instead of clicking the Open command, check to see if the workbook appears on the list of the most recently opened workbooks located at the bottom of the menu. If it does, you can click the workbook name rather than having to make the appropriate selections through the Open dialog box.

STEP 2: The Save As Command

➤ Pull down the **File menu.** Click **Save As** to display the dialog box shown in Figure 1.11a.

➤ Enter **Finished Grade Book** as the name of the new workbook. (A filename may contain up to 255 characters. Spaces and commas are allowed in the file-name.)

➤ Click the **Save button.** Press the **Esc key** or click the **Close button** if you see a Properties dialog box.

➤ There are now two identical copies of the file on disk: "Grade Book," which is the completed workbook from the previous exercise, and "Finished Grade Book," which you just created. The title bar shows the latter name, which is the workbook currently in memory.

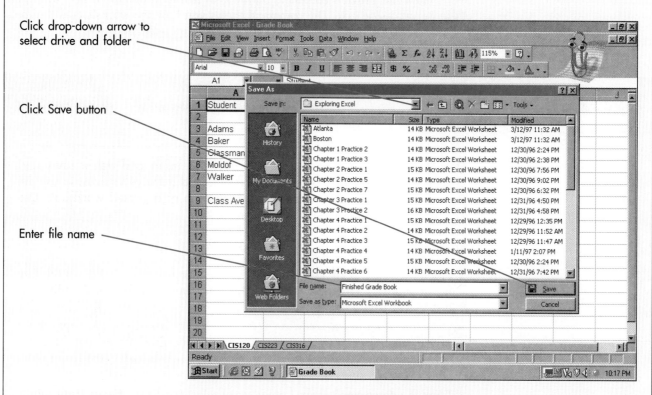

Click drop-down arrow to select drive and folder

Click Save button

Enter file name

(a) Save As Command (step 2)

FIGURE 1.11   Hands-on Exercise 2

INCOMPATIBLE FILE TYPES

The file format for Excel 2000 is compatible with Excel 97, but incompatible with earlier versions such as Excel 95. The newer releases can open a workbook that was created using the older program (Excel 95), but the reverse is not true; that is, you cannot open a workbook that was created in Excel 2000 in Excel 95 unless you change the file type. Pull down the File menu, click the Save As command, then specify the earlier (Microsoft Excel 5.0/ 95 workbook) file type. You will be able to read the file in Excel 95, but will lose any formatting that is unique to the newer release.

STEP 3: Delete a Row

➤ Click any cell in **row 6** (the row you will delete). Pull down the **Edit menu.** Click **Delete** to display the dialog box in Figure 1.11b. Click **Entire Row.** Click **OK** to delete row 6.

➤ Moldof has disappeared from the grade book, and the class averages (now in row 8) have been updated automatically.

➤ Pull down the **Edit menu** and click **Undo Delete** (or click the **Undo button** on the Standard toolbar) to reverse the last command.

➤ The row for Moldof has been put back in the worksheet.

➤ Click any cell in **row 6,** and this time delete the entire row for good.

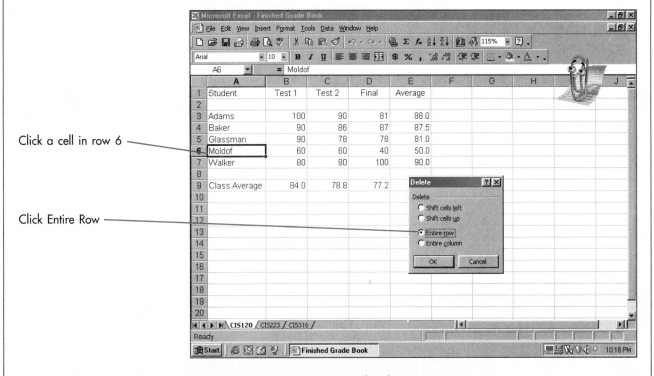

Click a cell in row 6

Click Entire Row

(b) Delete a Row (step 3)

FIGURE 1.11   Hands-on Exercise 2 (continued)

EDIT CLEAR VERSUS EDIT DELETE

The Edit Delete command deletes the selected cell, row, or column from the worksheet, and thus its execution will adjust cell references throughout the worksheet. It is very different from the Edit Clear command, which erases the contents (and/or formatting) of the selected cells, but does not delete the cells from the worksheet and hence has no effect on the cell references in other cells. Pressing the Del key erases the contents of a cell and thus corresponds to the Edit Clear command.

STEP 4: Insert a Row

➤ Click any cell in **row 5** (the row containing Glassman's grades).

➤ Pull down the **Insert menu.** Click **Rows** to add a new row above the current row. Row 5 is now blank (it is the newly inserted row), and Glassman (who was in row 5) is now in row 6.

➤ Enter the data for the new student in row 5 as shown in Figure 1.11c. Click in **cell A5.** Type **Coulter.** Press the **right arrow key** or click in **cell B5.** Enter the test grades of 85, 95, 100 in cells B5, C5, and D5.

➤ Enter the formula to compute the semester average, **=(B5+C5+2*D5)/4.** Be sure to begin the formula with an equal sign. Press **enter.**

➤ Click the **Save button** on the Standard toolbar, or pull down the **File menu** and click **Save** to save the changes made to this point.

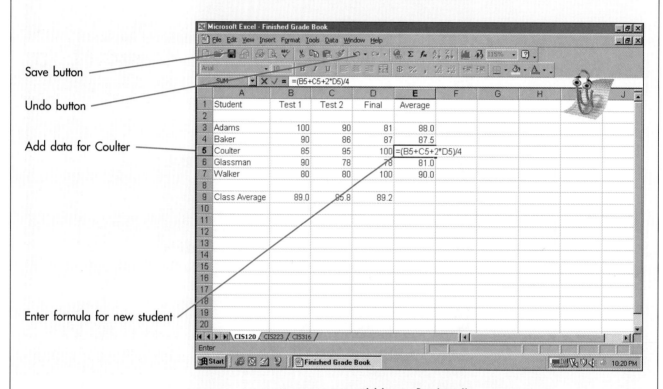

(c) Insert a Row (step 4)

FIGURE 1.11   Hands-on Exercise 2 (continued)

INSERTING (DELETING) ROWS AND COLUMNS

The fastest way to insert or delete a row is to point to the row number, then click the right mouse button to simultaneously select the row and display a shortcut menu. Click Insert to add a row above the selected row, or click Delete to delete the selected row. Use a similar technique to insert or delete a column, by pointing to the column heading, then clicking the right mouse button to display a shortcut menu from which you can select the appropriate command.

STEP 5: The AutoComplete Feature

➤ Point to the row heading for **row 6** (which now contains Glassman's grades), then click the **right mouse button** to select the row and display a shortcut menu. Click **Insert** to insert a new row 6, which moves Glassman to row 7 as shown in Figure 1.11d.

➤ Click in **cell A6.** Type **C,** the first letter in "Courier," which also happens to be the first letter in "Coulter," a previous entry in column A. If the Auto-Complete feature is on (see boxed tip), Coulter's name will be automatically inserted in cell A6 with "oulter" selected.

➤ Type **ourier** (the remaining letters in "Courier," which replace "oulter."

➤ Enter Courier's grades in the appropriate cells (75, 75, and 85 in cells B6, C6, and D6, respectively). Click in **cell E6.** Enter the formula to compute the semester average, **=(B6+C6+2*D6)/4.** Press **enter.**

Coulter is selected and will be replaced if you continue to type

Click in A6 and type a C

Glassman moves to row 7

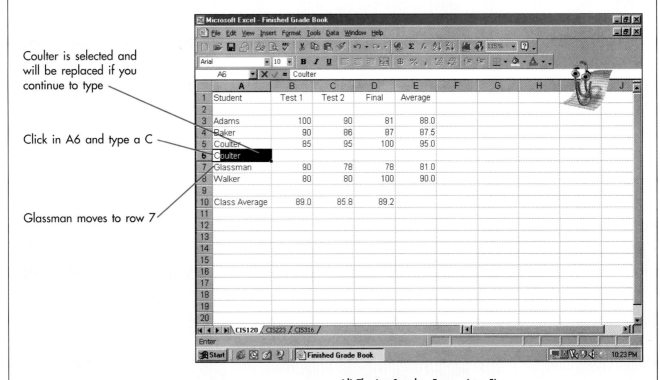

(d) The AutoComplete Feature (step 5)

FIGURE 1.11   Hands-on Exercise 2 (continued)

AUTOCOMPLETE

As soon as you begin typing a label into a cell, Excel searches for and (automatically) displays any other label in that column that matches the letters you typed. It's handy if you want to repeat a label, but it can be distracting if you want to enter a different label that just happens to begin with the same letter. To turn the feature on (off), pull down the Tools menu, click Options, then click the Edit tab. Check (clear) the box to enable the AutoComplete feature.

STEP 6: Insert a Column

➤ Point to the column heading for column B, then click the **right mouse button** to display a shortcut menu as shown in Figure 1.11e.

➤ Click **Insert** to insert a new column, which becomes the new column B. All existing columns have been moved to the right.

➤ Click in **cell B1.** Type **Major.**

➤ Click in **cell B3.** Enter **CIS** as Adams's major. Press the **down arrow** to move automatically to the major for the next student.

➤ Type **MKT** in cell B4. Press the **down arrow.** Type **ACC** in cell B5. Press the **down arrow.** Type **FIN** in cell B6.

➤ Press the **down arrow** to move to cell B7. Type **C** (AutoComplete will automatically enter "IS" to complete the entry). Press the **down arrow** to move to cell B8. Type **C** (the AutoComplete feature again enters "IS"), then press **enter** to complete the entry.

Point to column heading and click right mouse button to display shortcut menu

Click Insert

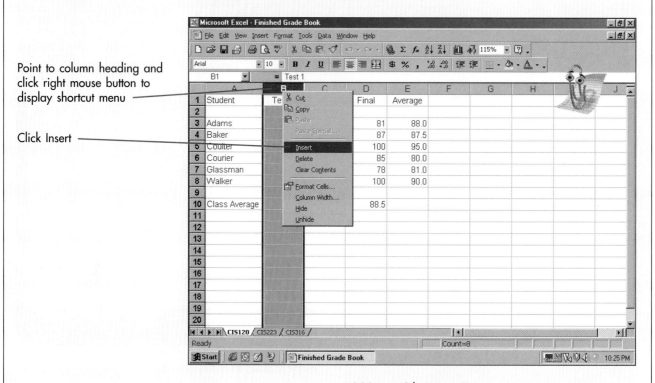

(e) Insert a Column (step 6)

FIGURE 1.11   Hands-on Exercise 2 (continued)

INSERTING AND DELETING INDIVIDUAL CELLS

You can insert and/or delete individual cells as opposed to an entire row or column. To insert a cell, click in the cell to the left or above of where you want the new cell to go, pull down the Insert menu, then click Cells to display the Insert dialog box. Click the appropriate option button to shift cells right or down and click OK. To delete a cell or cells, select the cell(s), pull down the Edit menu, click the Delete command, then click the option button to shift cells left or up.

STEP 7: Display the Cell Formulas

➤ Pull down the **Tools menu.** Click **Options** to display the Options dialog box. Click the **View tab.** Check the box for **Formulas.** Click **OK.**

➤ The worksheet should display the cell formulas as shown in Figure 1.11f. If necessary, click the **right scroll arrow** on the horizontal scroll bar until column F, the column containing the formulas to compute the semester averages, comes into view.

➤ If necessary (i.e., if the formulas are not completely visible), double click the border between the column headings for columns F and G. This increases the width of column F to accommodate the widest entry in that column.

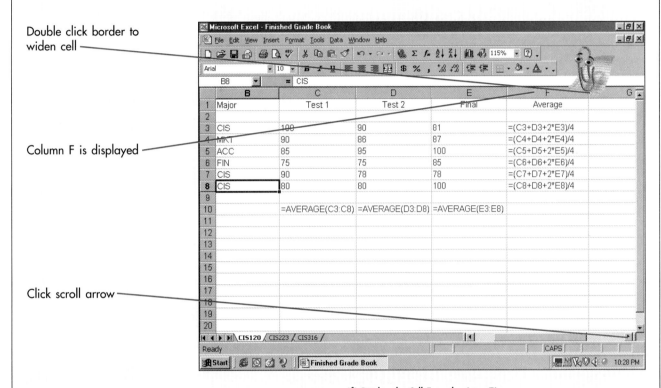

(f) Display the Cell Formulas (step 7)

FIGURE 1.11   Hands-on Exercise 2 (continued)

DISPLAY CELL FORMULAS

A worksheet should always be printed twice, once to show the computed results, and once to show the cell formulas. The fastest way to toggle (switch) between cell formulas and displayed values is to use the Ctrl+` keyboard shortcut. (The ` is on the same key as the ~ at the upper left of the keyboard.) Press Ctrl+` to switch from displayed values to cell formulas. Press Ctrl+` a second time and you are back to the displayed values.

STEP 8: The Page Setup Command

➤ Pull down the **File menu.** Click the **Page Setup command** to display the Page Setup dialog box as shown in Figure 1.11g.

- Click the **Page tab.** Click the **Landscape option button.** Click the option button to **Fit to 1 page.**
- Click the **Margins tab.** Check the box to center the worksheet horizontally.
- Click the **Header/Footer tab.** Click the **drop-down arrow** on the Footer list box. Scroll to the top of the list and click **(none)** to remove the footer.
- Click the **Sheet tab.** Check the boxes to print Row and Column Headings and Gridlines.

➤ Click **OK** to exit the Page Setup dialog box. Save the workbook.

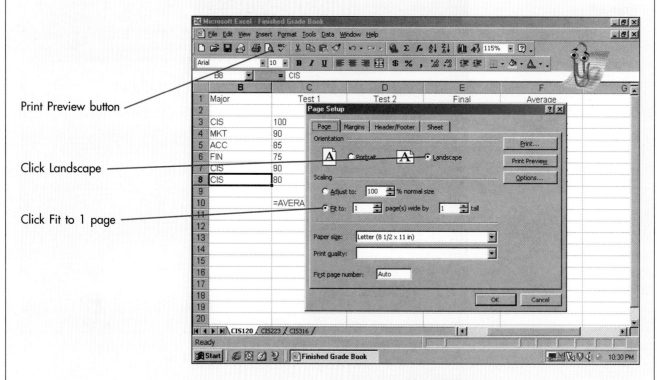

Print Preview button

Click Landscape

Click Fit to 1 page

(g) The Page Setup Command (step 8)

FIGURE 1.11   Hands-on Exercise 2 (continued)

KEYBOARD SHORTCUTS—THE DIALOG BOX

Press Tab or Shift+Tab to move forward (backward) between fields in a dialog box, or press the Alt key plus the underlined letter to move directly to an option. Use the space bar to toggle check boxes on or off and the up (down) arrow keys to move between options in a list box. Press enter to activate the highlighted command button and Esc to exit the dialog box without accepting the changes.

STEP 9: The Print Preview Command

➤ Pull down the **File menu** and click **Print Preview** (or click the **Print Preview button** on the Standard toolbar). Your monitor should match the display in Figure 1.11h.

➤ Click the **Print command button** to display the Print dialog box, then click **OK** to print the worksheet.

➤ Press **Ctrl+`** to switch to displayed values rather than cell formulas. Click the **Print button** on the Standard toolbar to print the worksheet without displaying the Print dialog box.

Click Print command button

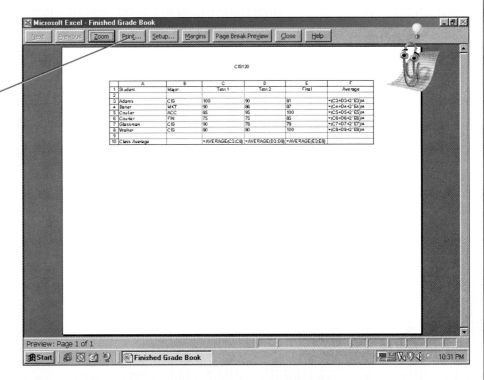

(h) The Print Preview Command (step 9)

FIGURE 1.11   Hands-on Exercise 2 (continued)

CREATE A CUSTOM VIEW

Use the Custom View command to store the different column widths associated with printing cell formulas versus displayed values. Start with either view, pull down the View menu, and click Custom Views to display the Custom Views dialog box. Click the Add button, enter the name of the view (e.g., Cell formulas), and click OK to close the Custom View dialog box. Press Ctrl+` to switch to the other view, change the column widths as appropriate, then pull down the View menu a second time to create the second custom view (e.g., Displayed Values). You can then switch from one view to the other at any time by pulling down the View menu, clicking the Custom Views command, and double clicking the desired view.

STEP 10: Insert and Delete a Worksheet

➤ Pull down the **Insert menu** and click the **Worksheet command** to insert a new worksheet. The worksheet is inserted as Sheet1.

➤ Click in cell **A1,** type **Student,** and press **enter.** Enter the labels and student data as shown in Figure 1.11i. Enter the formulas to calculate the students' semester averages. (The midterm and final count equally.)

➤ Enter the formulas in row 7 to compute the class averages on each exam. If necessary, click and drag the column border between columns A and B to widen column A.

➤ Double click the name of the worksheet (Sheet1) to select the name. Type a new name, **CIS101,** to replace the selected text and press enter.

➤ Click the worksheet tab for **CIS223.** Pull down the **Edit menu** and click the **Delete Sheet command.** Click **OK** when you are warned that the worksheet will be permanently deleted.

➤ Save the workbook. Print the new worksheet. Exit Excel.

Pull down Insert menu to insert new worksheet

Click tab, then pull down the Edit menu to delete

Double click worksheet tab to rename the sheet

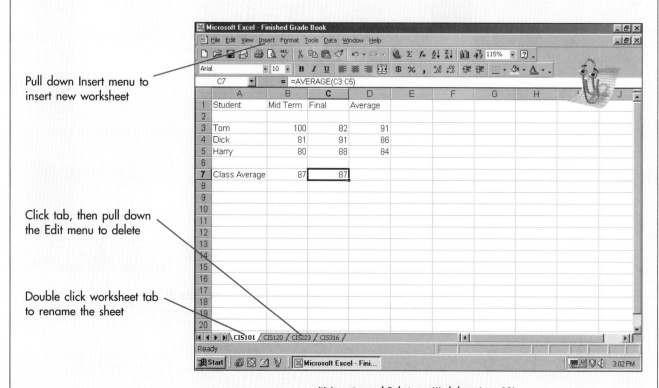

(i) Inserting and Deleting a Worksheet (step 10)

FIGURE 1.11   Hands-on Exercise 2 (continued)

MOVING, COPYING, AND RENAMING WORKSHEETS

The fastest way to move a worksheet is to click and drag the worksheet tab. You can copy a worksheet in similar fashion by pressing and holding the Ctrl key as you drag the worksheet tab. To rename a worksheet, double click its tab to select the current name, type the new name, and press the enter key.

SUMMARY

A spreadsheet is the computerized equivalent of an accountant's ledger. It is divided into rows and columns, with each row and column assigned a heading. The intersection of a row and column forms a cell. Spreadsheet is a generic term. Workbook and worksheet are Excel specific. An Excel workbook contains one or more worksheets.

Every cell in a worksheet (spreadsheet) contains either a formula or a constant. A formula begins with an equal sign; a constant does not. A constant is an entry that does not change and may be numeric or descriptive text. A formula is a combination of numeric constants, cell references, arithmetic operators, and/or functions that produces a new value from existing values.

The Insert and Delete commands add or remove individual cells, rows, or columns from a worksheet. The commands are also used to insert or delete worksheets within a workbook. The Open command brings a workbook from disk into memory. The Save command copies the workbook in memory to disk.

The Page Setup command provides complete control over the printed page, enabling you to print a worksheet with or without gridlines or row and column headings. The Page Setup command also controls margins, headers and footers, centering, and orientation. The Print Preview command shows the worksheet as it will print and should be used prior to printing.

A worksheet should always be printed twice, once with displayed values and once with cell formulas. The latter is an important tool in checking the accuracy of a worksheet, which is far more important than its appearance.

KEY WORDS AND CONCEPTS

Active cell	Formula	Save command
AutoComplete	Formula bar	ScreenTip
AVERAGE function	Function	Spreadsheet
Cell	Insert command	Standard toolbar
Cell contents	Landscape orientation	Status bar
Cell reference	Name box	Text box
Close command	Office Assistant	Toolbar
Constant	Open command	Undo command
Delete command	Page Setup command	Value
Exit command	Portrait orientation	Workbook
File menu	Print command	Worksheet
Formatting toolbar	Print Preview command	

MULTIPLE CHOICE

1. Which of the following is true?
 (a) A worksheet contains one or more workbooks
 (b) A workbook contains one or more worksheets
 (c) A spreadsheet contains one or more worksheets
 (d) A worksheet contains one or more spreadsheets

2. A worksheet is superior to manual calculation because:
   (a) The worksheet computes its entries faster
   (b) The worksheet computes its results more accurately
   (c) The worksheet recalculates its results whenever cell contents are changed
   (d) All of the above

3. The cell at the intersection of the second column and third row has the cell reference:
   (a) B3
   (b) 3B
   (c) C2
   (d) 2C

4. A right-handed person will normally:
   (a) Click the right and left mouse button to access a pull-down menu and shortcut menu, respectively
   (b) Click the left and right mouse button to access a pull-down menu and shortcut menu, respectively
   (c) Click the left mouse button to access both a pull-down menu and a shortcut menu
   (d) Click the right mouse button to access both a pull-down menu and a shortcut menu

5. What is the effect of typing F5+F6 into a cell without a beginning equal sign?
   (a) The entry is equivalent to the formula =F5+F6
   (b) The cell will display the contents of cell F5 plus cell F6
   (c) The entry will be treated as a text entry and display F5+F6 in the cell
   (d) The entry will be rejected by Excel, which will signal an error message

6. The Open command:
   (a) Brings a workbook from disk into memory
   (b) Brings a workbook from disk into memory, then erases the workbook on disk
   (c) Stores the workbook in memory on disk
   (d) Stores the workbook in memory on disk, then erases the workbook from memory

7. The Save command:
   (a) Brings a workbook from disk into memory
   (b) Brings a workbook from disk into memory, then erases the workbook on disk
   (c) Stores the workbook in memory on disk
   (d) Stores the workbook in memory on disk, then erases the workbook from memory

8. How do you open an Excel workbook?
   (a) Pull down the File menu and click the Open command
   (b) Click the Open button on the Standard toolbar
   (c) Either (a) or (b)
   (d) Neither (a) nor (b)

9. In the absence of parentheses, the order of operation is:
   (a) Exponentiation, addition or subtraction, multiplication or division
   (b) Addition or subtraction, multiplication or division, exponentiation
   (c) Multiplication or division, exponentiation, addition or subtraction
   (d) Exponentiation, multiplication or division, addition or subtraction

10. Given that cells A1, A2, and A3 contain the values 10, 20, and 40, respectively, what value will be displayed in a cell containing the cell formula =A1/A2*A3+1?
    (a) 1.125
    (b) 21
    (c) 20.125
    (d) Impossible to determine

11. The entry =AVERAGE(A4:A6):
    (a) Is invalid because the cells are not contiguous
    (b) Computes the average of cells A4 and A6
    (c) Computes the average of cells A4, A5, and A6
    (d) None of the above

12. Which of the following was suggested with respect to printing a workbook?
    (a) Print the displayed values only
    (b) Print the cell formulas only
    (c) Print both the displayed values and cell formulas
    (d) Print neither the displayed values nor the cell formulas

13. Which of the following is true regarding a printed worksheet?
    (a) It may be printed with or without the row and column headings
    (b) It may be printed with or without the gridlines
    (c) Both (a) and (b) above
    (d) Neither (a) nor (b)

14. Which options are mutually exclusive in the Page Setup menu?
    (a) Portrait and landscape orientation
    (b) Cell gridlines and row and column headings
    (c) Headers and footers
    (d) Left and right margins

15. Which of the following is controlled by the Page Setup command?
    (a) Headers and footers
    (b) Margins
    (c) Orientation
    (d) All of the above

ANSWERS

1. b	**6.** a	**11.** c
2. d	**7.** c	**12.** c
3. a	**8.** c	**13.** c
4. b	**9.** d	**14.** a
5. c	**10.** b	**15.** d

1. The Grading Assistant: Your professor is very impressed with the way you did the hands-on exercises in the chapter and has hired you as his grading assistant to handle all of his classes this semester. He would like you to take the Finished Grade Book that you used in the chapter, and save it as *Chapter 1 Practice 1 Solution.* Make the following changes in the new workbook:

   a. Click the worksheet tab for CIS120. Add Milgrom as a new student majoring in Finance with grades of 88, 80, and 84, respectively. Delete Baker. Be sure that the class averages adjust automatically for the insertion and deletion of these students.

   b. Click the worksheet tab for CIS316 to move to this worksheet. Insert a new column for the Final, then enter the following grades for the students in this class (Bippen, 90; Freeman, 75; Manni, 84; Peck, 93; Tanney, 87).

   c. Enter the formulas to compute the semester average for each student in the class. (Tests 1, 2, and 3 each count 20%. The final counts 40%.)

   d. Enter the formulas to compute the class average on each test and the final.

   e. Enter the label *Grading Assistant* followed by your name on each worksheet. Print the entire workbook and submit all three pages of the printout to your instructor as proof that you did this exercise.

2. Exotic Gardens: The worksheet in Figure 1.12 displays last week's sales from the Exotic Gardens Nurseries. There are four locations, each of which divides its sales into three general areas.

   a. Open the partially completed *Chapter 1 Practice 2* workbook on the data disk. Save the workbook as *Chapter 1 Practice 2 Solution.*

   b. Enter the appropriate formulas in row 5 of the worksheet to compute the total sales for each location. Use the SUM function to compute the total for each location; for example, type =SUM(B2:B4) in cell B5 (as opposed to =B2+B3+B4) to compute the total sales for the Las Olas location.

   c. Insert a new row 4 for a new category of product. Type *Insecticides* in cell A4, and enter $1,000 for each store in this category. The total sales for each store should adjust automatically to include the additional business.

   d. Enter the appropriate formulas in column F of the worksheet to compute the total sales for each category.

   e. Delete column D, the column containing sales for the Galleria location.

   f. Add your name somewhere in the worksheet as the bookkeeper.

   g. Print the completed worksheet two times, to show both displayed values and cell formulas. Submit both pages to your instructor.

	A	B	C	D	E	F
1		Las Olas	Coral Gables	Galleria	Miracle Mile	Total
2	Indoor Plants	$1,500	$3,000	$4,500	$800	$9,800
3	Accessories	$350	$725	$1,200	$128	$2,403
4	Landscaping	$3,750	$7,300	$12,000	$1,500	$24,550
5	Total	$5,600	$11,025	$17,700	$2,428	$36,753
6						
7						
8						

FIGURE 1.12   Exotic Gardens (Exercise 2)

3. Residential Colleges: Formatting is not covered until Chapter 2, but we think you are ready to try your hand at basic formatting now. Most formatting operations are done in the context of select-then-do. You select the cell or cells you want to format, then you execute the appropriate formatting command, most easily by clicking the appropriate button on the Formatting toolbar. The function of each button should be apparent from its icon, but you can simply point to a button to display a ScreenTip that is indicative of the button's function.

Open the unformatted version of the *Chapter 1 Practice 3* workbook on the data disk, and save it as *Chapter 1 Practice 3 Solution.* Add a new row 6 and enter data for Hume Hall as shown in Figure 1.13. Enter formulas for totals. Format the remainder of the worksheet so that it matches the completed worksheet in Figure 1.13. Add your name in bold italics somewhere in the worksheet as the Residence Hall Coordinator, then print the completed worksheet and submit it to your instructor.

	A	B	C	D	E	F	G
1	Residential Colleges						
2							
3		Freshmen	Sophomores	Juniors	Seniors	Graduates	Totals
4	Broward Hall	176	143	77	29	13	438
5	Graham Hall	375	112	37	23	7	554
6	Hume Hall	212	108	45	43	12	420
7	Jennnings Hall	89	54	23	46	23	235
8	Rawlings Hall	75	167	93	145	43	523
9	Tolbert Hall	172	102	26	17	22	339
10	Totals	1099	686	301	303	120	2509

FIGURE 1.13   Residential Colleges (Exercise 3)

4. Companion Web Sites: A Companion Web site (or online study guide) accompanies each book in the *Exploring Microsoft Office 2000* series. Go to the Exploring Windows home page at www.prenhall.com/grauer, click the book to Office 2000, and click the Companion Web site tab at the top of the screen. Choose the appropriate text (Exploring Excel 2000) and the chapter within the text (e.g., Chapter 1).

Each chapter contains a series of short-answer exercises (multiple-choice, true/false, and matching) to review the material in the chapter. You can take practice quizzes by yourself and/or e-mail the results to your instructor. You can try the essay questions for additional practice and engage in online chat sessions. We hope you will find the online guide to be a valuable resource.

5. Student Budget: Create a worksheet that shows your income and expenses for a typical semester according to the format in Figure 1.14. Enter your budget rather than ours by entering your name in cell A1.

   a. Enter at least five different expenses in consecutive rows, beginning in A6, and enter the corresponding amounts in column B.

   b. Enter the text *Total Expenses* in the row immediately below your last expense item and then enter the formula to compute the total in the corresponding cells in columns B through E.

   c. Skip one blank row and then enter the text *What's Left for Fun* in column A and the formula to compute how much money you have left at the end of the month in columns B through E.

d. Insert a new row 8. Add an additional expense that you left out, entering the text in A8 and the amount in cells B8 through E8. Do the formulas for total expenses reflect the additional expense? If not, change the formulas so they adjust automatically.

e. Save the workbook as *Chapter 1 Practice 5 Solution*. Center the worksheet horizontally, then print the worksheet two ways, to show cell formulas and displayed values. Submit both printed pages to your instructor.

	A	B	C	D	E
1	Maryann Barber's Budget				
2		Sept	Oct	Nov	Dec
3	Monthly Income	$1,000	$1,000	$1,000	$1,400
4					
5	Monthly Expenses				
6	Food	$250	$250	$250	$250
7	Rent	$350	$350	$350	$350
8	Cable	$40	$40	$40	$40
9	Utilities	$100	$100	$125	$140
10	Phone	$30	$30	$30	$20
11	Gas	$40	$40	$40	$75
12	Total Expenses	$810	$810	$835	$875
13					
14	What's Left for Fun	$190	$190	$165	$525

FIGURE 1.14   Student Budget (Exercise 5)

6. Vacation to Europe: Figure 1.15 displays a spreadsheet that plans for a summer vacation in Europe. The spreadsheet includes fixed costs such as airfare and a Euro Rail pass. It also has variable costs for each day of the vacation. Develop a spreadsheet similar to the one in Figure 1.15. You need not follow our format exactly, but you should include all expenses for your vacation. Add your name somewhere in the worksheet, then print it two ways, once with displayed values and once with the cell formulas. Create a title page, then submit all three pages to your instructor as proof you did this exercise.

	A	B	C	D
1	My Vacation to Europe			
2				
3	Daily Expenses	Cost	Number of Days	Amount
4	Hotel	$95	5	$475
5	Youth Hostel	$45	16	$720
6	Food	$30	21	$630
7	Touring/Shopping	$45	21	$945
8	One time expenses			
9	Round Trip Airfare			$750
10	EuroRail Pass			$200
11				
12	Subtotal			$3,720
13	Contingency (10% of total)			$372
14	Estimated cost			$4,092

FIGURE 1.15   Vacation to Europe (Exercise 6)

chapter 2

GAINING PROFICIENCY: COPYING, FORMATTING, AND ISOLATING ASSUMPTIONS

OBJECTIVES

After reading this chapter you will be able to:

1. Explain the importance of isolating assumptions within a worksheet.
2. Define a cell range; select and deselect ranges within a worksheet.
3. Copy and/or move cells within a worksheet; differentiate between relative, absolute, and mixed addresses.
4. Format a worksheet to include boldface, italics, shading, and borders; change the font and/or alignment of a selected entry.
5. Change the width of a column; explain what happens if a column is too narrow to display the computed result.
6. Insert a hyperlink into an Excel workbook; save a workbook as a Web page.

OVERVIEW

This chapter continues the grade book example of Chapter 1. It is perhaps the most important chapter in the entire text as it describes the basic commands to create a worksheet. We begin with the definition of a cell range and the commands to build a worksheet without regard to its appearance. We focus on the Copy command and the difference between relative and absolute addresses. We stress the importance of isolating the assumptions within a worksheet so that alternative strategies may be easily evaluated.

The second half of the chapter presents formatting commands to improve the appearance of a worksheet after it has been created. You will be pleased with the dramatic impact you can achieve with a few simple commands, but we emphasize that accuracy in a worksheet is much more important than appearance. The chapter also describes the relationship between Office 2000, the Internet, and the World Wide Web.

The hands-on exercises are absolutely critical if you are to master the material. As you do the exercises, you will realize that there are many different ways to accomplish the same task. Our approach is to present the most basic way first and the shortcuts later. You will like the shortcuts better, but you may not remember them all. Do not be concerned because it is much more important to understand the underlying concepts. You can always find the necessary command from the appropriate menu, and if you don't know which menu, you can always look to online help.

A BETTER GRADE BOOK

Figure 2.1 contains a much improved version of the professor's grade book over the one from the previous chapter. The most obvious difference is in the appearance of the worksheet, as a variety of formatting commands have been used to make it more attractive. The exam scores and semester averages are centered under the appropriate headings. The exam weights are formatted with percentages, and all averages are displayed with exactly one decimal point. Boldface and italics are used for emphasis. Shading and borders are used to highlight various areas of the worksheet. The title has been centered over the worksheet and is set in a larger typeface.

The most *significant* differences, however, are that the weight of each exam is indicated within the worksheet, and that the formulas to compute the students' semester averages reference these cells in their calculations. The professor can change the contents of the cells containing the exam weights and see immediately the effect on the student averages.

The isolation of cells whose values are subject to change is one of the most important concepts in the development of a spreadsheet. This technique lets the professor explore alternative grading strategies. He or she may notice, for example, that the class did significantly better on the final than on either of the first two exams. The professor may then decide to give the class a break and increase the weight of the final relative to the other tests. But before the professor says anything to the class, he or she wants to know the effect of increasing the weight of the final to 60%. What if the final should count 70%? The effect of these and other changes can be seen immediately by entering the new exam weights in the appropriate cells at the bottom of the worksheet.

Title is centered and in larger font size ——

Exam scores are centered ——

Boldface, italics, shading, and borders are used

Exam weights are used to calculate the Semester Average ——

	A	B	C	D	E
1		CIS120 - Spring 2000			
2					
3	Student	Test 1	Test 2	Final	Average
4	Costa, Frank	70	80	90	82.5
5	Ford, Judd	70	85	80	78.8
6	Grauer, Jessica	90	80	98	91.5
7	Howard, Lauren	80	78	98	88.5
8	Krein, Darren	85	70	95	86.3
9	Moldof, Adam	75	75	80	77.5
10					
11	Class Averages	78.3	78.0	90.2	
12					
13	Exam Weights	25%	25%	50%	

FIGURE 2.1   A Better Grade Book

CELL RANGES

Every command in Excel operates on a rectangular group of cells known as a *range*. A range may be as small as a single cell or as large as the entire worksheet. It may consist of a row or part of a row, a column or part of a column, or multiple rows and/or columns. The cells within a range are specified by indicating the diagonally opposite corners, typically the upper-left and lower-right corners of the rectangle. Many different ranges could be selected in conjunction with the worksheet of Figure 2.1. The exam weights, for example, are found in the range B13:D13. The students' semester averages are found in the range E4:E9. The student data is contained in the range A4:E9.

The easiest way to select a range is to click and drag—click at the beginning of the range, then press and hold the left mouse button as you drag the mouse to the end of the range where you release the mouse. Once selected, the range is highlighted and its cells will be affected by any subsequent command. The range remains selected until another range is defined or until you click another cell anywhere on the worksheet.

COPY COMMAND

The *Copy command* duplicates the contents of a cell, or range of cells, and saves you from having to enter the contents of every cell individually. It is much easier, for example, to enter the formula to compute the class average once (for test 1), then copy it to obtain the average for the remaining tests, rather than explicitly entering the formula for every test.

Figure 2.2 illustrates how the Copy command can be used to duplicate the formula to compute the class average. The cell(s) that you are copying from, cell B11, is called the *source range.* The cells that you are copying to, cells C11 and D11, are the *destination* (or target) *range*. The formula is not copied exactly, but is adjusted as it is copied, to compute the average for the pertinent test.

The formula to compute the average on the first test was entered in cell B11 as =AVERAGE(B4:B9). The range in the formula references the cell seven rows above the cell containing the formula (i.e., cell B4 is seven rows above cell B11) as well as the cell two rows above the formula (i.e., cell B9). When the formula in cell B11 is copied to C11, it is adjusted so that the cells referenced in the new formula are in the same relative position as those in the original formula; that is, seven and two rows above the formula itself. Thus, the formula in cell C11 becomes =AVERAGE(C4:C9). In similar fashion, the formula in cell D11 becomes =AVERAGE(D4:D9).

	A	B	C	D	E
1			CIS120 - Spring 2000		
2					
3	Student	Test 1	Test 2	Final	Average
4	Costa, Frank	70	80	90	=$B$13*B4+$C$13*C4+$D$13*D4
5	Ford, Judd	70	85	80	=$B$13*B5+$C$13*C5+$D$13*D5
6	Grauer, Jessica	90	80	98	=$B$13*B6+$C$13*C6+$D$13*D6
7	Howard, Lauren	80	78	98	=$B$13*B7+$C$13*C7+$D$13*D7
8	Krein, Darren	85	70	95	=$B$13*B8+$C$13*C8+$D$13*D8
9	Moldof, Adam	75	75	80	=$B$13*B9+$C$13*C9+$D$13*D9
10					
11	Class Averages	=AVERAGE(B4:B9)	=AVERAGE(C4:C9)	=AVERAGE(D4:D9)	
12					
13	Exam Weights	25%	25%	50%	

FIGURE 2.2   The Copy Command

Figure 2.2 also illustrates how the Copy command is used to copy the formula for a student's semester average, from cell E4 (the source range) to cells E5 through E9 (the destination range). This is slightly more complicated than the previous example because the formula is based on a student's grades, which vary from one student to the next, and on the exam weights, which do not. The cells referring to the student's grades should adjust as the formula is copied, but the addresses referencing the exam weights should not.

The distinction between cell references that remain constant versus cell addresses that change is made by means of a dollar sign. An **absolute reference** remains constant throughout the copy operation and is specified with a dollar sign in front of the column and row designation, for example, $B$13. A **relative reference**, on the other hand, adjusts during a copy operation and is specified without dollar signs; for example, B4. (A **mixed reference** uses a single dollar sign to make the column absolute and the row relative; for example, $A5. Alternatively, you can make the column relative and the row absolute as in A$5.)

Consider, for example, the formula to compute a student's semester average as it appears in cell E4 of Figure 2.2:

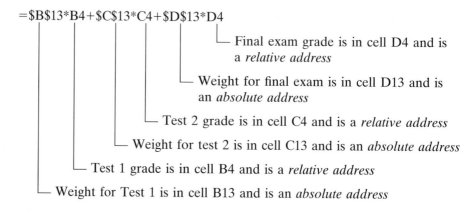

=$B$13*B4+$C$13*C4+$D$13*D4

       Final exam grade is in cell D4 and is a *relative address*

       Weight for final exam is in cell D13 and is an *absolute address*

       Test 2 grade is in cell C4 and is a *relative address*

       Weight for test 2 is in cell C13 and is an *absolute address*

       Test 1 grade is in cell B4 and is a *relative address*

       Weight for Test 1 is in cell B13 and is an *absolute address*

The formula in cell E4 uses a combination of relative and absolute addresses to compute the student's semester average. Relative addresses are used for the exam grades (found in cells B4, C4, and D4) and change automatically when the formula is copied to the other rows. Absolute addresses are used for the exam weights (found in cells B13, C13, and D13) and remain constant.

The copy operation is implemented by using the **clipboard** common to all Windows applications and a combination of the **Copy** and **Paste commands** from the Edit menu. (Office 2000 also supports the Office Clipboard that can hold 12 separate items. All references to the "clipboard" in this chapter, however, are to the Windows clipboard.) The contents of the source range are copied to the clipboard, from where they are pasted to the destination range. The contents of the clipboard are replaced with each subsequent Copy command but are unaffected by the Paste command. Thus, you can execute the Paste command several times in succession to paste the contents of the clipboard to multiple locations.

MIXED REFERENCES

Most spreadsheets can be developed using only absolute or relative references such as $A1$1 or A, respectively. Mixed references, where only the row ($A1) or column (A$1) changes, are more subtle, and thus are typically not used by beginners. Mixed references are necessary in more sophisticated worksheets and add significantly to the power of Excel. See practice exercise 4 at the end of the chapter.

The ***move operation*** is not used in the grade book, but its presentation is essential for the sake of completeness. The move operation transfers the contents of a cell (or range of cells) from one location to another. After the move is completed, the cells where the move originated (that is, the source range) are empty. This is in contrast to the Copy command, where the entries remain in the source range and are duplicated in the destination range.

A simple move operation is depicted in Figure 2.3a, in which the contents of cell A3 are moved to cell C3, with the formula in cell C3 unchanged after the move. In other words, the move operation simply picks up the contents of cell A3 (a formula that adds the values in cells A1 and A2) and puts it down in cell C3. The source range, cell A3, is empty after the move operation has been executed.

Figure 2.3b depicts a situation where the formula itself remains in the same cell, but one of the values it references is moved to a new location; that is, the

Source range
is empty after move

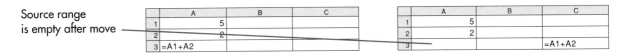

(a) Example 1 (only cell A3 is moved)

Cell reference is adjusted
to follow moved entry

(b) Example 2 (only cell A1 is moved)

Both cell references adjust
to follow moved entries

(c) Example 3 (all three cells in column A are moved)

Cell reference adjusts to
follow moved entry

Moved formula
is unchanged

(d) Example 4 (dependent cells)

FIGURE 2.3   The Move Command

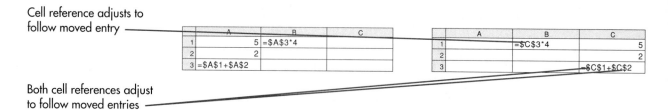

(e) Example 5 (absolute cell addresses)

FIGURE 2.3 The Move Command (continued)

entry in A1 is moved to C1. The formula in cell A3 is adjusted to follow the moved entry to its new location; that is, the formula is now =C1+A2.

The situation is different in Figure 2.3c as the contents of all three cells— A1, A2, and A3—are moved. After the move has taken place, cells C1 and C2 contain the 5 and the 2, respectively, with the formula in cell C3 adjusted to reflect the movement of the contents of cells A1 and A2. Once again the source range (A1:A3) is empty after the move is completed.

Figure 2.3d contains an additional formula in cell B1, which is *dependent* on cell A3, which in turn is moved to cell C3. The formula in cell C3 is unchanged after the move because *only* the formula was moved, *not* the values it referenced. The formula in cell B1 changes because cell B1 refers to an entry (cell A3) that was moved to a new location (cell C3).

Figure 2.3e shows that the specification of an absolute reference has no meaning in a move operation, because the cell addresses are adjusted as necessary to reflect the cells that have been moved. Moving a formula that contains an absolute reference does not adjust the formula. Moving a value that is specified as an absolute reference, however, adjusts the formula to follow the cell to its new location. Thus all of the absolute references in Figure 2.3e are changed to reflect the entries that were moved.

The move operation is a convenient way to improve the appearance of a worksheet after it has been developed. It is subtle in its operation, and we suggest you think twice before moving cell entries because of the complexities involved.

The move operation is implemented by using the Windows clipboard and a combination of the **Cut** and **Paste commands** from the Edit menu. The contents of the source range are transferred to the clipboard, from which they are pasted to the destination range. (Executing a Paste command after a Cut command empties the clipboard. This is different from pasting after a Copy command, which does not affect the contents of the clipboard.)

LEARNING BY DOING

As we have already indicated, there are many different ways to accomplish the same task. You can execute commands using a pull-down menu, a shortcut menu, a toolbar, or the keyboard. In the exercise that follows we emphasize pull-down menus (the most basic technique) but suggest various shortcuts as appropriate.

Realize, however, that while the shortcuts are interesting, it is far more important to focus on the underlying concepts in the exercise, rather than specific key strokes or mouse clicks. The professor's grade book was developed to emphasize the difference between relative and absolute cell references. The grade book also illustrates the importance of isolating assumptions so that alternative strategies (e.g., different exam weights) can be considered.

Creating a Workbook

Objective: To create a new workbook; to develop a formula containing relative and absolute references; to use the Copy command within a worksheet. Use Figure 2.4 as a guide.

STEP 1: Create a New Workbook

➤ Click the **Start button,** click (or point to) the **Programs command,** then click **Microsoft Excel** to start the program. If Excel is already open, click the **New button** on the Standard toolbar to begin a new workbook.

➤ Click and drag the Office Assistant out of the way or hide it altogether. (Pull down the **Help menu** and click the **Hide the Office Assistant.**)

➤ If necessary, separate the Standard and Formatting toolbars. Pull down the **View menu,** click **Toolbars,** click **Customize,** and click the **Options tab.** Clear the check box that indicates the Standard and Formatting toolbars should share the same row.

➤ Click in **cell A1.** Enter the title of the worksheet, **CIS120 - Spring 2000** as in Figure 2.4a. (The Save As dialog box is not yet visible.)

➤ Press the **down arrow key** twice to move to cell A3. Type **Student.**

➤ Press the **right arrow key** to move to cell B3. Type **Test 1.**

➤ Press the **right arrow key** to move to cell C3. Type **Test 2.**

➤ Press the **right arrow key** to move to cell D3. Type **Final.**

➤ Press the **right arrow key** to move to cell E3. Type **Average.** Press **enter.**

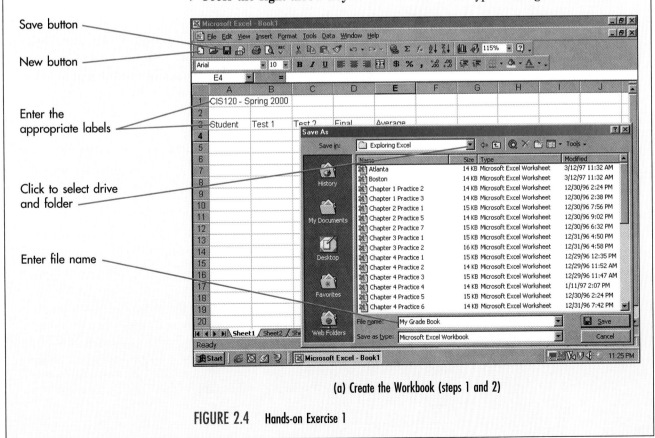

(a) Create the Workbook (steps 1 and 2)

FIGURE 2.4   Hands-on Exercise 1

STEP 2: Save the Workbook

➤ Pull down the **File menu** and click **Save** (or click the **Save button** on the Standard toolbar) to display the Save As dialog box as shown in Figure 2.4d.

➤ Click the **drop-down arrow** on the Save In list box. Click the appropriate drive, drive C or drive A, depending on where you are saving your Excel workbook.

➤ Double click the **Exploring Excel folder** to make it the active folder (the folder in which you will save the document).

➤ Click and drag to select **Book1** (the default entry) in the File name text box. Type **My Grade Book** as the name of the workbook. Press the **enter key.**

➤ The title bar changes to reflect the name of the workbook.

CREATE A NEW FOLDER

Do you work with a large number of workbooks? If so, it may be useful for you to store those workbooks in different folders. You could, for example, create one folder for school and one for work. Pull down the File menu, click the Save As command to display the Save As dialog box, then click the Create New Folder button to display the New Folder dialog box. Enter the name of the folder, then click OK to close the New Folder dialog box and create the folder. Once the folder has been created, use the Look In box to change to that folder the next time you open or save a workbook.

STEP 3: Enter Student Data

➤ Click in **cell A4** and type **Costa, Frank.** Move across row 4 and enter Frank's grades on the two tests and the final. Use Figure 2.4b as a guide.

• Do *not* enter Frank's average in cell E4 as that will be entered as a formula in step 5.

• Do *not* be concerned that you cannot see Frank's entire name because the default width of column A is not wide enough to display the entire name.

➤ Enter the names and grades for the other students in rows 5 through 9. Do *not* enter their averages.

➤ Complete the entries in column A by typing **Class Averages** and **Exam Weights** in cells **A11** and **A13,** respectively.

CHANGE THE ZOOM SETTING

You can increase or decrease the size of a worksheet as it appears on the monitor. If you find yourself squinting because the numbers are too small, click the down arrow on the Zoom box and choose a larger magnification. Conversely, if you are working with a large spreadsheet and cannot see it at one time, choose a number less than 100 percent. Changing the magnification on the screen does not affect printing; that is, worksheets are printed at 100% unless you change the scaling within the Page Setup command.

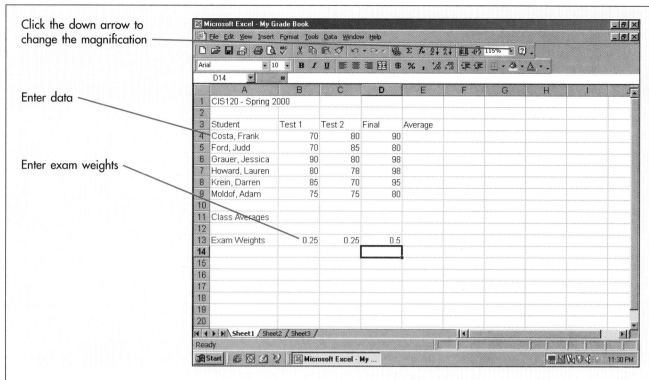

Click the down arrow to change the magnification

Enter data

Enter exam weights

(b) Enter Student Data (steps 3 and 4)

FIGURE 2.4   Hands-on Exercise 1 (continued)

STEP 4: Enter Exam Weights

➤ Click in **cell B13** and enter **.25** (the weight for the first exam).

➤ Press the **right arrow key** to move to cell C13 and enter **.25** (the weight for the second exam).

➤ Press the **right arrow key** to move to cell D13 and enter **.5** (the weight for the final). Press **enter.** Do *not* be concerned that the exam weights do not appear as percentages; they will be formatted in the next exercise.

➤ The worksheet should match Figure 2.4b except that column A is too narrow to display the entire name of each student.

STEP 5: Compute the Semester Average

➤ Click in **cell E4** and type the formula **=$B$13*B4+$C$13*C4+$D$13*D4** as shown in Figure 2.4c. Press **enter** when you have completed the formula.

➤ Check that the displayed value in cell E4 is 82.5, which indicates you entered the formula correctly. Correct the formula if necessary. Save the workbook.

CORRECTING MISTAKES

The most basic way to correct an erroneous entry is to click in the cell, then re-enter the cell contents in their entirety. It's often faster, however, to edit the cell contents rather than retyping them. Click in the cell whose contents you want to change, then make the necessary changes in the formula bar near the top of the Excel window. Use the mouse or arrow keys to position the insertion point. Make the necessary correction(s), then press the enter key.

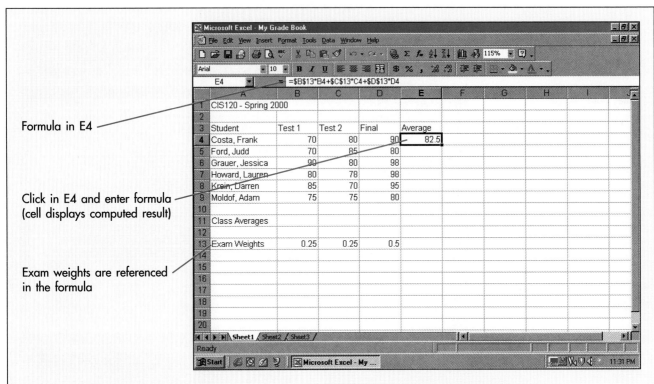

Formula in E4

Click in E4 and enter formula
(cell displays computed result)

Exam weights are referenced
in the formula

E4 = =$B$13*B4+$C$13*C4+$D$13*D4

	A	B	C	D	E	F	G	H	I
1	CIS120 - Spring 2000								
2									
3	Student	Test 1	Test 2	Final	Average				
4	Costa, Frank	70	80	90	82.5				
5	Ford, Judd	70	85	80					
6	Grauer, Jessica	90	80	98					
7	Howard, Lauren	80	78	98					
8	Krein, Darren	85	70	95					
9	Moldof, Adam	75	75	80					
10									
11	Class Averages								
12									
13	Exam Weights	0.25	0.25	0.5					
14									
15									
16									
17									
18									
19									
20									

(c) Compute the Semester Average (step 5)

FIGURE 2.4   Hands-on Exercise 1 (continued)

STEP 6: Copy the Semester Average

➤ Click in **cell E4.** Pull down the **Edit menu** and click **Copy** (or click the **copy button** on the standard toolbar). A moving border will surround cell E4.

➤ Click **cell E5.** Drag the mouse over cells **E5** through **E9** to select the destination range as in Figure 2.4d.

➤ Pull down the **Edit menu** and click **Paste** to copy the contents of the clipboard to the destination range.

➤ Press **Esc** to remove the moving border around cell E4. Click anywhere in the worksheet to deselect cells E5 through E9.

➤ Click in **cell E5** and look at the formula. The cells that reference the grades have changed to B5, C5, and D5. The cells that reference the exam weights—$B$13, $C$13, and $D$13—are the same as in the formula in cell E4.

CUT, COPY, AND PASTE

Ctrl+X (the X is supposed to remind you of a pair of scissors), Ctrl+C, and Ctrl+V are keyboard equivalents to cut, copy, and paste, respectively, and apply to Excel, Word, PowerPoint and Access, as well as Windows applications in general. (The keystrokes are easier to remember when you realize that the operative letters, X, C, and V, are next to each other at the bottom-left side of the keyboard.) Alternatively, you can use the Cut, Copy, and Paste buttons on the Standard toolbar, which are also found on the Standard toolbar in the other Office applications.

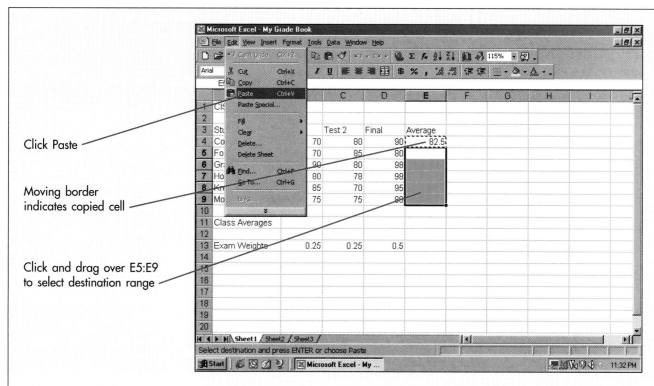

Click Paste

Moving border
indicates copied cell

Click and drag over E5:E9
to select destination range

(d) Copy the Semester Average (step 6)

FIGURE 2.4   Hands-on Exercise 1 (continued)

STEP 7: Compute Class Averages

➤ Click in **cell B11** and type the formula **=AVERAGE(B4:B9)** to compute the class average on the first test. Press the **enter key** when you have completed the formula.

➤ Point to **cell B11,** then click the **right mouse button** to display the shortcut menu in Figure 2.4e. Click **Copy,** which produces the moving border around cell B11.

➤ Click **cell C11.** Drag the mouse over cells **C11** and **D11,** the destination range for the Copy command.

➤ Click the **Paste button** on the Standard toolbar (or press Ctrl+V) to paste the contents of the clipboard to the destination range.

➤ Press **Esc** to remove the moving border. Click anywhere in the worksheet to deselect cells C11 through D11.

THE RIGHT MOUSE BUTTON

Point to a cell (or cell range), a worksheet tab, or a toolbar, then click the right mouse button to display a context-sensitive menu with commands appropriate to the item you are pointing to. Right clicking a cell, for example, displays a menu with selected commands from the Edit, Insert, and Format menus. Right clicking a toolbar displays a menu that lets you display (hide) additional toolbars. Right clicking a worksheet tab enables you to rename, move, copy, or delete the worksheet.

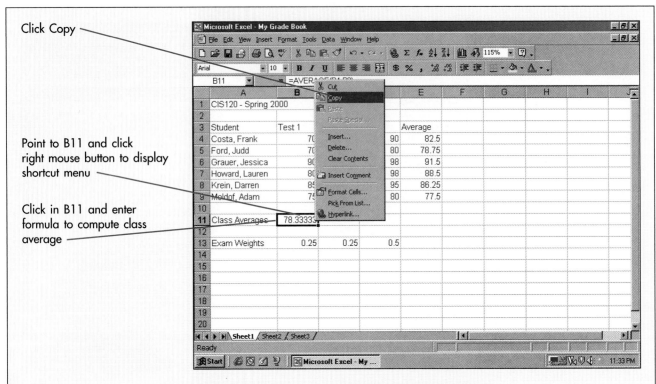

Click Copy

Point to B11 and click right mouse button to display shortcut menu

Click in B11 and enter formula to compute class average

(e) Compute Class Averages (step 7)

FIGURE 2.4   Hands-on Exercise 1 (continued)

STEP 8: What If? Change Exam Weights

➤ Change the entries in cells B13 and C13 to **.20** and the entry in cell D13 to **.60.** The semester average for every student changes automatically; for example, Costa and Moldof change to 84 and 78, respectively.

➤ The professor decides this does not make a significant difference and wants to go back to the original weights. Click the **Undo button** three times to reverse the last three actions. You should see .25, .25, and .50 in cells B13, C13, and D13, respectively.

➤ Click the **Save button.**

STEP 9: Exit Excel

➤ Exit Excel if you are not ready to begin the next exercise at this time.

ISOLATE ASSUMPTIONS

The formulas in a worksheet should always be based on cell references rather than on specific values—for example, B13 or $B13 rather than .25. The cells containing these values should be clearly labeled and set apart from the rest of the worksheet. You can then vary the inputs (or assumptions on which the worksheet is based) to see the effect within the worksheet. The chance for error is also minimized because you are changing the contents of a single cell rather than changing the multiple formulas that reference those values.

FORMATTING

Figure 2.5a shows the grade book as it exists at the end of the first hands-on exercise, without concern for its appearance. Figure 2.5b shows the grade book as it will appear at the end of the next exercise after it has been formatted. The differences between the two are due entirely to formatting. Consider:

- The exam weights are formatted as percentages in Figure 2.5b, as opposed to decimals in Figure 2.5a. The class and semester averages are displayed with a single decimal place in Figure 2.5b.
- Boldface and italics are used for emphasis, as are shading and borders.
- Exam grades and computed averages are centered under their respective headings, as are the exam weights.
- The worksheet title is centered across all five columns.
- The width of column A has been increased so that the students' names are completely visible. The other columns have been widened as well.

Column A is too narrow

	A	B	C	D	E
1	CIS120 - Spring 2000				
2					
3	Student	Test 1	Test 2	Final	Average
4	Costa, Fra	70	80	90	82.5
5	Ford, Judd	70	85	80	78.75
6	Grauer, Je	90	80	98	91.5
7	Howard, La	80	78	98	88.5
8	Krein, Darr	85	70	95	86.25
9	Moldof, Ad	75	75	80	77.5
10					
11	Class Aver	78.33333	78	90.16667	
12					
13	Exam Weig	0.25	0.25	0.5	

Class averages are not uniformly formatted

(a) At the End of Hands-on Exercise 1

Title is centered across columns and set in a larger font size

Boldface, italics, shading and borders are used for emphasis

Test scores are centered in cells

Results are displayed with 1 decimal place

Exam weights are formatted as a percentage

	A	B	C	D	E
1	CIS120 - Spring 2000				
2					
3	Student	Test 1	Test 2	Final	Average
4	Costa, Frank	70	80	90	82.5
5	Ford, Judd	70	85	80	78.8
6	Grauer, Jessica	90	80	98	91.5
7	Howard, Lauren	80	78	98	88.5
8	Krein, Darren	85	70	95	86.3
9	Moldof, Adam	75	75	80	77.5
10					
11	Class Averages	78.3	78.0	90.2	
12					
13	Exam Weights	25%	25%	50%	

(b) At the End of Hands-on Exercise 2

FIGURE 2.5   Developing the Grade Book

Column Widths

A column is often too narrow to display the contents of one or more cells in that column. When this happens, the display depends on whether the cell contains a text or numeric entry, and if it is a text entry, on whether or not the adjacent cell is empty.

The student names in Figure 2.5a, for example, are partially hidden because column A is too narrow to display the entire name. Cells A4 through A9 contain the complete names of each student, but because the adjacent cells in column B contain data, the displayed entries in column A are truncated (cut off) at the cell width. The situation is different for the worksheet title in cell A1. This time the adjacent cell (cell B1) is empty, so that the contents of cell A1 overflow into that cell and are completely visible.

Numbers are treated differently from text and do not depend on the contents of the adjacent cell. Excel will automatically increase the column width to accommodate a formatted number unless the column width has been previously adjusted. In that event, Excel displays a series of number signs (######) when a cell containing a numeric entry is too narrow to display the entry in its current format. You may be able to correct the problem by changing the format of the number (e.g., display the number with fewer decimal places). Alternatively, you can increase the column width by using the **Column command** in the Format menu.

Row Heights

The **row height** changes automatically as the font size is increased. Row 1 in Figure 2.5b, for example, has a greater height than the other rows to accommodate the larger font size in the title of the worksheet. The row height can also be changed manually through the **Row command** in the Format menu.

FORMAT CELLS COMMAND

The **Format Cells command** controls the formatting for numbers, alignment, fonts, borders, and patterns (color). Execution of the command produces a tabbed dialog box in which you choose the particular formatting category, then enter the desired options. All formatting is done within the context of **select-then-do.** You select the cells to which the formatting is to apply, then you execute the Format Cells command (or click the appropriate button on the Formatting toolbar).

Once a format has been assigned to a cell, the formatting remains in the cell and is applied to all subsequent values that are entered into that cell. You can, however, change the formatting by executing a new formatting command. You can also remove the formatting by using the Clear command in the Edit menu. Note, too, that changing the format of a number changes the way the number is displayed, but does not change its value. If, for example, you entered 1.2345 into a cell, but displayed the number as 1.23, the actual value (1.2345) would be used in all calculations involving that cell.

Numeric Formats

General format is the default format for numeric entries and displays a number according to the way it was originally entered. Numbers are shown as integers (e.g., 123), decimal fractions (e.g., 1.23), or in scientific notation (e.g., 1.23E+10) if the number exceeds 11 digits. You can also display a number in one of several built-in formats as shown in Figure 2.6a:

■ *Number format,* which displays a number with or without the 1000 separator (e.g., a comma) and with any number of decimal places. Negative numbers can be displayed with parentheses and/or can be shown in red.

■ *Currency format,* which displays a number with the 1000 separator and an optional dollar sign (which is placed immediately to the left of the number). Negative values can be preceded by a minus sign or displayed with parentheses and/or can be shown in red.

■ *Accounting format,* which displays a number with the 1000 separator, an optional dollar sign (at the left border of the cell, which vertically aligns the dollar signs within a column), negative values in parentheses, and zero values as hyphens.

■ *Date format,* which displays the date in different ways, such as March 4, 1998, 3/4/98, or 4-Mar-98.

■ *Time format,* which displays the time in different formats, such as 10:50 PM or the equivalent 22:50 (24-hour time).

■ *Percentage format,* whereby the number is multiplied by 100 for display purposes only, a percent sign is included, and any number of decimal places can be specified.

■ *Fraction format,* which displays a number as a fraction, and is appropriate when there is no exact decimal equivalent, for example, ⅓.

■ *Scientific format,* which displays a number as a decimal fraction followed by a whole number exponent of 10; for example, the number 12345 would

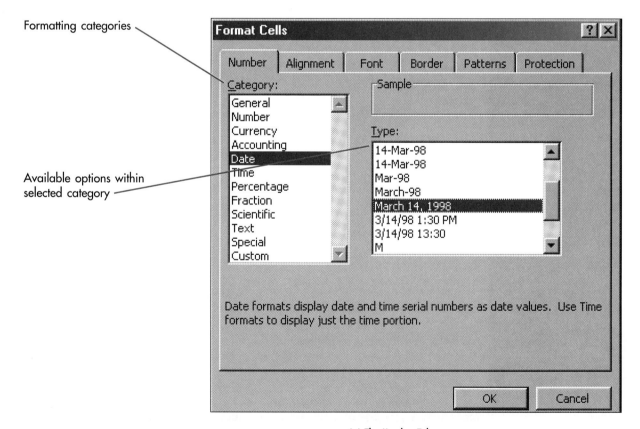

(a) The Number Tab

FIGURE 2.6 The Format Cells Command

appear as 1.2345E+04. The exponent, +04 in the example, is the number of places the decimal point is moved to the left (or right if the exponent is negative). Very small numbers have negative exponents; for example, the entry .0000012 would be displayed as 1.2E−06. Scientific notation is used only with very large or very small numbers.

- **Text format,** which left aligns the entry and is useful for numerical values that have leading zeros and should be treated as text, such as ZIP codes.
- **Special format,** which displays a number with editing characters, such as hyphens in a social security number or parentheses around the area code of a telephone number.
- **Custom format,** which allows you to develop your own formats.

DATES VERSUS FRACTIONS

A fraction may be entered into a cell by preceding the fraction with an equal sign, for example, =1/3. The fraction is converted to its decimal equivalent and displayed in that format in the worksheet. Omission of the equal sign causes Excel to treat the entry as a date; that is, 1/3 will be stored as January 3 (of the current year).

Alignment

The contents of a cell (whether text or numeric) may be aligned horizontally and/or vertically as indicated by the dialog box of Figure 2.6b. The default horizontal alignment is general, which left-aligns text and right-aligns date and numbers. You can also center an entry across a range of selected cells (or merge the selected cells), as in the professor's grade book, which centered the title in cell A1 across columns A through E. The Fill option duplicates the characters in the cell across the entire width of that cell.

Vertical alignment is important only if the row height is changed and the characters are smaller than the height of the row. Entries may be vertically aligned at the top, center, or bottom (the default) of a cell.

It is also possible to wrap the text within a cell to emulate the word wrap of a word processor. You select multiple cells and merge them together. And finally, you can achieve some very interesting effects by rotating text up to 90° in either direction.

Fonts

You can use the same fonts (typefaces) in Excel as you can in any other Windows application. Windows itself includes a limited number of fonts (Arial, Times New Roman, Courier New, Symbol, and Wingdings) to provide variety in creating documents. (Additional fonts are also installed with Microsoft Office.) All fonts are WYSIWYG (What You See Is What You Get), meaning that the worksheet you see on the monitor will match the worksheet produced by the printer.

Any entry in a worksheet may be displayed in any font, style, or point size as indicated by the dialog box of Figure 2.6c. The example shows Arial, Bold Italic, and 14 points, and corresponds to the selection for the worksheet title in the improved grade book. Special effects, such as subscripts or superscripts, are also possible. You can even select a different color, but you will need a color printer to see the effect on the printed page. The Preview box shows the text as it will appear in the worksheet.

Horizontal alignment options

Vertical alignment options

Click to wrap text in cell

Click and drag to rotate text in cell

Click to merge cells

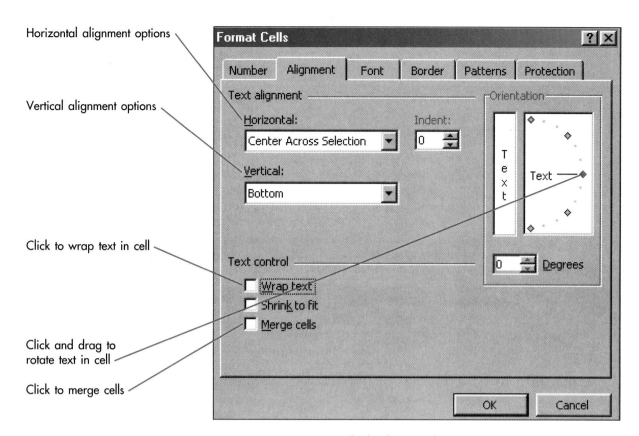

(b) The Alignment Tab

List of available sizes

List of available fonts

Preview of font

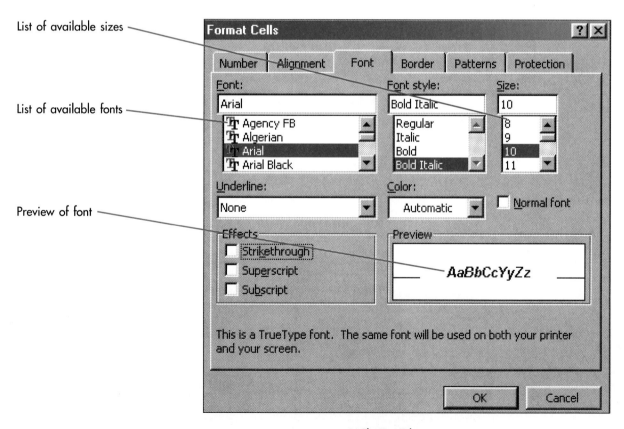

(c) The Font Tab

FIGURE 2.6   The Format Cells Command (continued)

Borders, Patterns, and Shading

The *Border tab* in Figure 2.6d enables you to create a border around a cell (or cells) for additional emphasis. You can outline the entire selection, or you can choose the specific side or sides; for example, thicker lines on the bottom and right sides produce a drop shadow, which is very effective. You can also specify a different line style and/or a different color for the border, but you will need a color printer to see the effect on the printed output.

The *Patterns tab* in Figure 2.6e lets you choose a different color in which to shade the cell and further emphasize its contents. The Pattern drop-down list box lets you select an alternate pattern, such as dots or slanted lines.

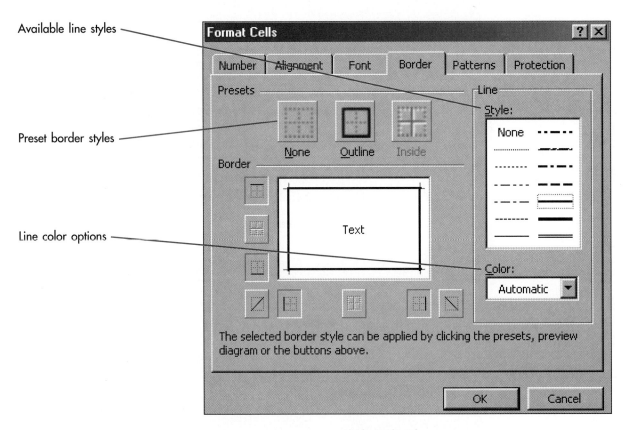

Available line styles

Preset border styles

Line color options

(d) The Border Tab

FIGURE 2.6   The Format Cells Command (continued)

USE RESTRAINT

More is not better, especially in the case of too many typefaces and styles, which produce cluttered worksheets that impress no one. Limit yourself to a maximum of two typefaces per worksheet, but choose multiple sizes and/or styles within those typefaces. Use boldface or italics for emphasis, but do so in moderation, because if you emphasize too many elements, the effect is lost.

Color options —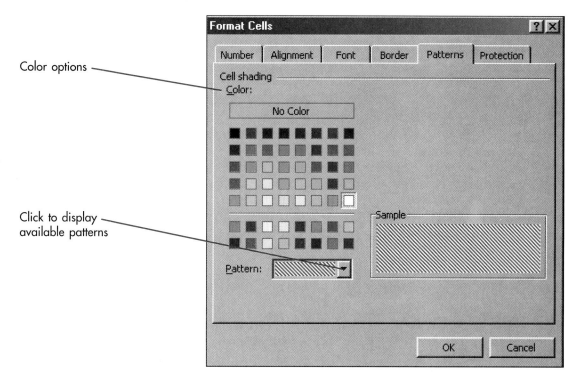

Click to display available patterns —

(e) The Patterns Tab

FIGURE 2.6   The Format Cells Command (continued)

HANDS-ON EXERCISE 2

Formatting a Worksheet

Objective: To format a worksheet using both pull-down menus and the Formatting toolbar; to use boldface, italics, shading, and borders; to change the font and/or alignment of a selected entry; to change the width of a column. Use Figure 2.7 as a guide in the exercise.

STEP 1: Center Across Selection

➤ Click the **Open button** on the Standard toolbar to display the Open dialog box, then click the **drop-down arrow** on the Look In list box and choose the appropriate drive. Double click the **Exploring Excel folder,** then double click the **My Grade Book** workbook that was created in the previous exercise.

➤ Click in **cell A1** to select the cell containing the title of the worksheet.

➤ Pull down the **Format menu.** Click **Cells.** If necessary, click the **Font tab.** Click **Arial** in the Font list box, **Bold Italic** in the Font Style box, and then scroll to select **14** from the Size box. Click **OK.**

➤ Click and drag to select cells **A1** through **E1,** which represents the width of the entire worksheet.

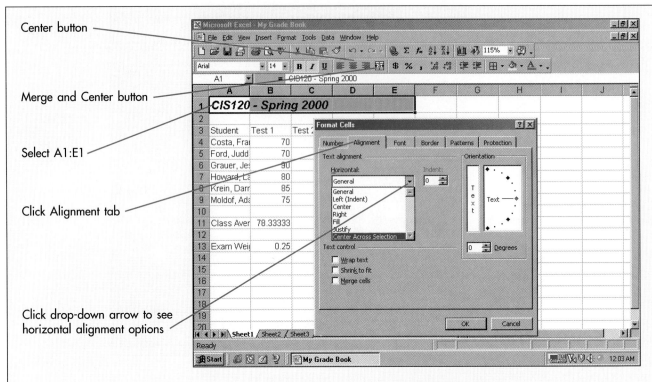

Center button

Merge and Center button

Select A1:E1

Click Alignment tab

Click drop-down arrow to see
horizontal alignment options

(a) Center Across Selection (step 1)

FIGURE 2.7   Hands-on Exercise 2

➤ Pull down the **Format menu** a second time. Click **Cells.** Click the **Alignment tab.** Click the **down arrow** in the Horizontal list box, then click **Center Across Selection** as in Figure 2.7a. Click **OK.**

➤ Click and drag over cells **B3** through **E13.** Click the **Center button** on the Formatting toolbar.

STEP 2: Increase the Width of Column A

➤ Click in **cell A4.** Drag the mouse over cells **A4** through **A13.**

➤ Pull down the **Format menu,** click **Column,** then click **AutoFit Selection** as shown in Figure 2.7b.

➤ The width of the selected cells increases to accommodate the longest entry in the selected range.

➤ Save the workbook.

COLUMN WIDTHS AND ROW HEIGHTS

Drag the border between column headings to change the column width; for example, to increase (decrease) the width of column A, drag the border between column headings A and B to the right (left). Double click the right boundary of a column heading to change the column width to accommodate the widest entry in that column. Use the same techniques to change the row heights.

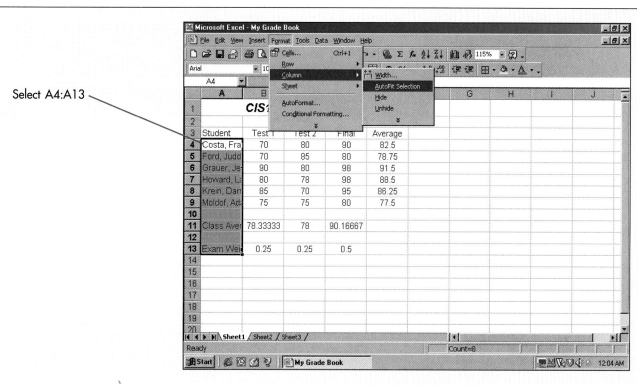

Select A4:A13

(b) Increase the Width of Column A (step 2)

FIGURE 2.7　Hands-on Exercise 2 (continued)

STEP 3: Format the Exam Weights

➤ Click and drag to select cells **B13** through **D13.** Point to the selected cells and click the **right mouse button** to display the shortcut menu in Figure 2.7c. Click **Format Cells** to produce the Format Cells dialog box.

➤ If necessary, click the **Number tab.** Click **Percentage** in the Category list box. Click the **down arrow** in the Decimal Places box to reduce the number of decimals to zero, then click **OK.** The exam weights are displayed with percent signs and no decimal places.

➤ Click the **Undo button** on the Standard toolbar to cancel the formatting command.

➤ Click the **% button** on the Formatting toolbar to reformat the exam weights as percentages. (This is an alternate and faster way to change to the percent format.)

AUTOMATIC FORMATTING

Excel converts any number entered with a beginning dollar sign to currency format, and any number entered with an ending percent sign to percentage format. The automatic formatting enables you to save a step by typing $100,000 or 7.5% directly into a cell, rather than entering 100000 or .075 and having to format the number. The formatting is applied to the cell and affects any subsequent numbers entered in that cell.

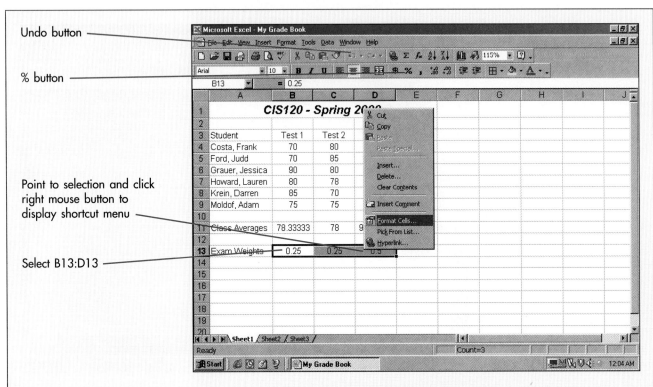

Undo button

% button

Point to selection and click right mouse button to display shortcut menu

Select B13:D13

(c) Format the Exam Weights (step 3)

FIGURE 2.7   Hands-on Exercise 2 (continued)

STEP 4: Noncontiguous Ranges

➤ Select cells **B11** through **D11.** Press *and* hold the **Ctrl key** as you click and drag to select cells **E4** through **E9.** Release the **Ctrl key.**

➤ You will see two noncontiguous (nonadjacent) ranges highlighted, cells B11:D11 and cells E4:E9 as in Figure 2.7d. Format the selected cells using either the Formatting toolbar or the Format menu:

• To use the Formatting toolbar, click the appropriate button to increase or decrease the number of decimal places to one.

• To use the Format menu, pull down the **Format menu,** click **Cells,** click the **Number tab,** then click **Number** in the Category list box. Click the **down arrow** in the Decimal Places text box to reduce the decimal places to one. Click **OK.**

THE FORMAT PAINTER

The Format Painter copies the formatting of the selected cell to other cells in the worksheet. Click the cell whose formatting you want to copy, then double click the Format Painter button on the Standard toolbar. The mouse pointer changes to a paintbrush to indicate that you can copy the current formatting; just click and drag the paintbrush over the additional cells to which you want to apply the formatting. Repeat the painting process as often as necessary, then click the Format Painter button a second time to return to normal editing.

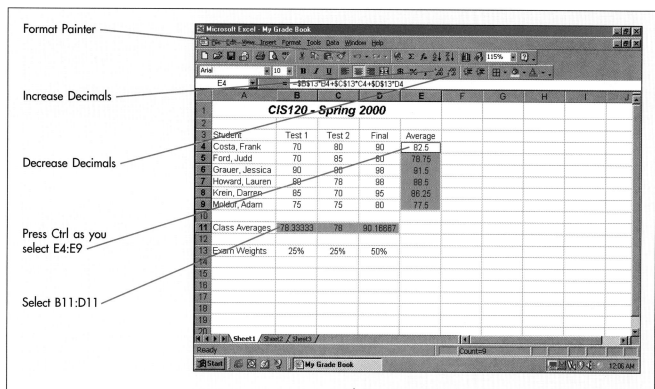

Format Painter

Increase Decimals

Decrease Decimals

Press Ctrl as you
select E4:E9

Select B11:D11

(d) Noncontiguous Ranges (step 4)

FIGURE 2.7   Hands-on Exercise 2 (continued)

STEP 5: The Border Command

➤ Click and drag to select cells **A3** through **E3.** Press *and* hold the **Ctrl key** as
you click and drag to select the range **A11:E11.**

➤ Continue to press and hold the **Ctrl key** as you click and drag to select cells
A13:E13.

➤ Pull down the **Format menu** and click **Cells** (or click the **right mouse button**
to produce a shortcut menu, then click **Format Cells**). Click the **Border tab**
to access the dialog box in Figure 2.7e.

➤ Choose a line width from the Style section. Click the **Top** and **Bottom** boxes
in the Border section. Click **OK** to exit the dialog box and return to the worksheet.

SELECTING NONCONTIGUOUS RANGES

Dragging the mouse to select a range always produces some type of rectangle; that is, a single cell, a row or column, or a group of rows and
columns. You can, however, select noncontiguous (nonadjacent) ranges
by selecting the first range in the normal fashion, then pressing and holding the Ctrl key as you select the additional range(s). This is especially
useful when the same command is to be applied to multiple ranges within
a worksheet.

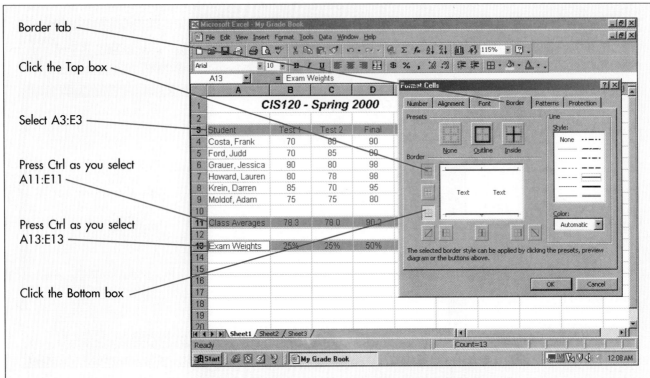

Border tab

Click the Top box

Select A3:E3

Press Ctrl as you select A11:E11

Press Ctrl as you select A13:E13

Click the Bottom box

(e) The Border Command (step 5)

FIGURE 2.7 Hands-on Exercise 2 (continued)

STEP 6: Add Color

➤ Check that all three ranges are still selected (A3:E3, A11:E11, *and* A13:E13).

➤ Click the **down arrow** on the **Fill Color button** on the Formatting toolbar. Click yellow (or whatever color appeals to you) as shown in Figure 2.7f.

➤ Click the **boldface** and **italics buttons** on the Formatting toolbar. Click outside the selected cells to see the effects of the formatting change.

➤ Save the workbook.

THE FORMATTING TOOLBAR

The Formatting toolbar is the fastest way to implement most formatting operations. There are buttons for boldface, italics, and underlining, alignment (including merge and center), currency, percent, and comma formats, as well as buttons to increase or decrease the number of decimal places. There are also several list boxes to choose the font, point size, and font color as well as the type of border and shading. Be sure to separate the Formatting and Standard toolbars to see all of the available buttons, as described at the beginning of the first hands-on exercise.

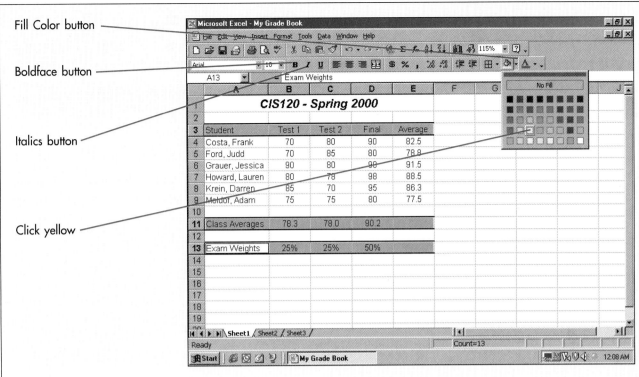

Fill Color button

Boldface button

Italics button

Click yellow

(f) Add Color (step 6)

FIGURE 2.7   Hands-on Exercise 2 (continued)

STEP 7: Enter Your Name and Social Security Number

➤ Click in **cell A15.** Type **Grading Assistant.** Press the **down arrow key.** Type your name, press the **down arrow key,** and enter your social security number *without* the hyphens. Press **enter.**

➤ Point to **cell A17,** then click the **right mouse button** to display a shortcut menu. Click **Format Cells** to display the dialog box in Figure 2.7g.

➤ Click the **Number tab,** click **Special** in the Category list box, then click **Social Security Number** in the Type list box. Click **OK.** Hyphens have been inserted into your social security number.

TIME STAMP YOUR SPREADSHEETS

The Now( ) function displays the current date and time and is continually updated throughout a session. The Today( ) function is similar in concept except it displays only the date. To change the format of either function, pull down the Format menu and click the Cells command to display the Format Cells dialog box. Click the Number tab, choose the Date category, select the desired format, then click OK to accept the setting and close the Format Cells dialog box.

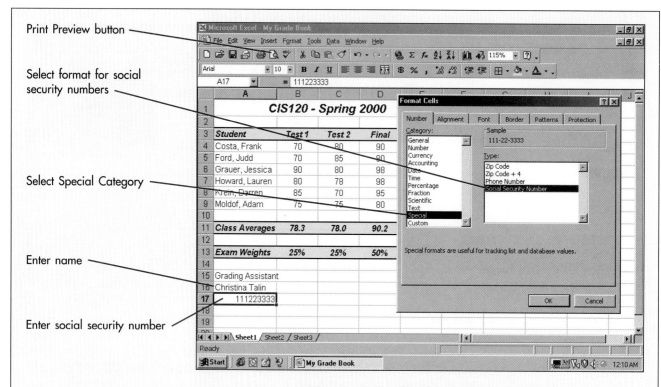

Print Preview button

Select format for social security numbers

Select Special Category

Enter name

Enter social security number

(g) Enter Your Name and Social Security Number (step 7)

FIGURE 2.7 Hands-on Exercise 2 (continued)

STEP 8: The Page Setup Command

➤ Pull down the **File menu.** Click **Page Setup** to display the Page Setup dialog box.

- Click the **Margins tab.** Check the box to center the worksheet Horizontally.
- Click the **Sheet tab.** Check the boxes to print Row and Column Headings and Gridlines.
- Click **OK** to exit the Page Setup dialog box.

➤ Click the **Print Preview button** to preview the worksheet before printing:

- If you are satisfied with the appearance of the worksheet, click the **Print button** within the Preview window, then click **OK** to print the worksheet.
- If you are not satisfied with the appearance of the worksheet, click the **Setup button** within the Preview window to make the necessary changes, after which you can print the worksheet.

➤ Save the workbook.

THE INSERT COMMENT COMMAND

You can add a comment, which displays a ScreenTip, to any cell in a worksheet. Click in the cell, pull down the Insert menu, and click Comment to display a box in which you enter the comment. Click outside the box when you have completed the entry. Point to the cell (which should have a tiny red triangle) and you will see the ScreenTip you just created. (If you do not see the triangle or the tip, pull down the Tools menu, click Options, click the View tab, then click the options button for Comment Indicator Only in the Comments area.)

STEP 9: Print the Cell Formulas

➤ Pull down the **Tools menu,** click **Options,** click the **View tab,** check the box for **Formulas,** then click **OK** (or use the keyboard shortcut **Ctrl+`**). The worksheet should display the cell formulas.

➤ If necessary, click the right arrow on the horizontal scroll bar so that column E, the column containing the cell formulas, comes into view.

➤ Double click the border between the column headings for columns E and F to increase the width of column E to accommodate the widest entry in the column.

➤ Pull down the **File menu.** Click the **Page Setup** command to display the Page Setup dialog box.

  • Click the **Page tab.** Click the **Landscape orientation button.**

  • Click the option button to **Fit to 1 page.** Click **OK** to exit the Page Setup dialog box.

➤ Click the **Print Preview button** to preview the worksheet before printing. It should match the display in Figure 2.7h:

  • If you are satisfied with the appearance of the worksheet, click the **Print button** within the Preview window, then click **OK** to print the worksheet.

  • If you are not satisfied with the appearance of the worksheet, click the **Setup button** within the Preview window to make the necessary changes, after which you can print the worksheet.

➤ Pull down the **File menu.** Click **Close.** Click **No** if prompted to save changes.

➤ Exit Excel if you do not want to continue with the next exercise at this time.

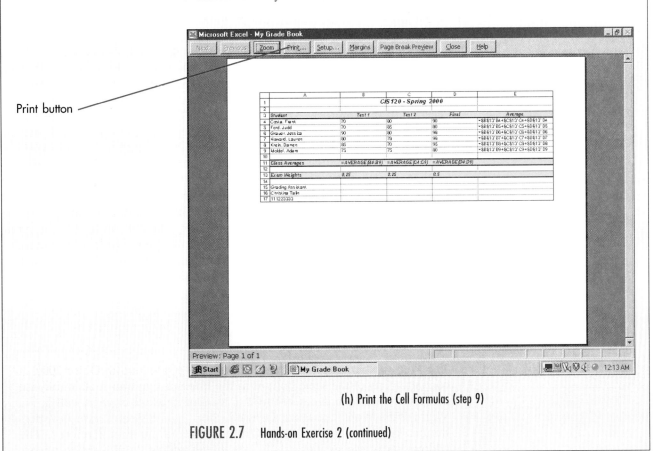

Print button

(h) Print the Cell Formulas (step 9)

FIGURE 2.7   Hands-on Exercise 2 (continued)

The growth of the Internet and World Wide Web has been astounding and has totally changed our society. You may be familiar with the basic concepts that underlie the Internet, but we think a brief review is in order. The **Internet** is a network of networks that connects computers anywhere in the world. The **World Wide Web** (WWW, or simply, the Web) is a very large subset of the Internet, consisting of those computers that store a special type of document known as a **Web page** or **HTML document.**

The interesting thing about a Web page or HTML document is that it contains references (called **hyperlinks**) to other Web pages, which may be stored on the same computer, or even on a different computer, with the latter located anywhere in the world. And therein lies the fascination of the Web, in that you simply click on link after link to go effortlessly from one document to the next. You can start your journey on your professor's home page, then browse through any set of links you wish to follow.

The Internet and World Wide Web are thoroughly integrated into Office 2000 through two basic capabilities. You can insert a hyperlink into any Office document, then view the associated Web page by clicking the link without having to start your Web browser manually. You can also save any Office document as a Web page, which in turn can be stored on a Web server and displayed through a browser such as Internet Explorer or Netscape Navigator.

Consider, for example, Figure 2.8a, which displays a slightly modified version of the grade book that we have been using throughout the chapter. The grade book contains an additional column that identifies students by number (e.g., the last four digits of the Social Security number) rather than by name. In addition, a hyperlink to the professor's home page has been inserted into cell B15. You can click the link from within Excel, and provided you have an Internet connection, your Web browser will display the associated page.

Figure 2.8b displays the grade book using Internet Explorer rather than Excel. This was accomplished by saving the grade book in Excel as a Web page (or HTML document), then opening the document in Internet Explorer. The page can be posted to the professor's Web site, where it can be accessed by students connecting to the Internet. Alternatively, the HTML version of the grade book could be stored on a local area network to prevent access by individuals outside the organization. (Look carefully at the address bar in Figure 2.8b and you will see that we are viewing the document locally rather than from the Internet.)

Note, too, that the student names do not appear in Figure 2.8b because the professor elected to hide the column of student names prior to creating the Web page. (This is accomplished through the **Hide Column command** in the Format menu.) Hiding a column is different from deleting the column in that the information remains in the workbook but is hidden from view. The professor can display (unhide) the column at any time; for example, he can view the student names during data entry.

THE WEB TOOLBAR

The Web toolbar may be displayed from any application in Office 2000. It contains many of the same buttons as the Internet Explorer toolbar and can be used to display a document from a local or network drive as well as the World Wide Web. The Back, Forward, Stop, Home, Search, and Favorites buttons function identically in Office 2000 and Internet Explorer. The address bar is also similar and displays the address of the current document.

Additional column for
Student Numbers

Professor's Home Page is
accessed by clicking hyperlink

Hyperlink to professor's
home page

Hyperlink to professor's
home page

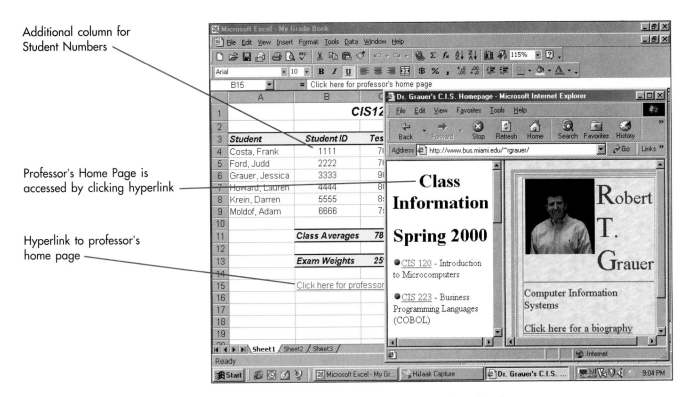

(a) Hyperlinks and the Web Toolbar

Internet Explorer is used to
display the Grade Book

Document is viewed from
a local drive

Student names do not appear

Hyperlink to professor's
home page

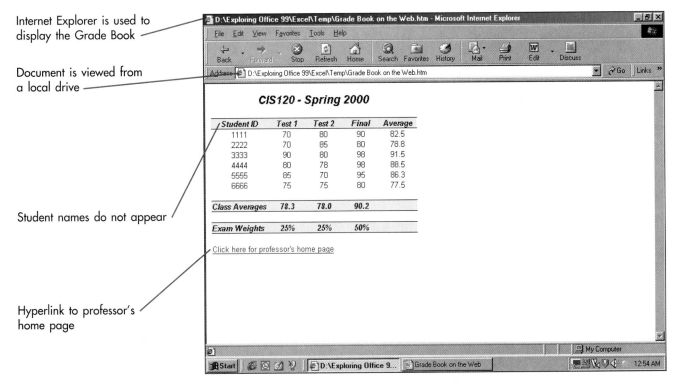

(b) Viewing the Web Page

FIGURE 2.8   Excel 2000 and the Internet

Objective: To insert a hyperlink into an Excel workbook; to save a workbook as an HTML document. Use Figure 2.9 as a guide in the exercise. The exercise requires that you have an Internet connection to test the hyperlink.

STEP 1: Insert the Student IDs

➤ Open the **My Grade Book workbook** from the previous exercise. Move the contents of cell A1 to cell B1. Click the column header for column B.

➤ Pull down the **Insert menu** and click the **Columns command** to insert a new column to the left of column B; i.e., the grades for Test 1 are now in column C as shown in Figure 2.9a.

➤ Enter the label **Student ID** in cell B3, then enter the Student ID for each student as shown in the figure. Click and drag to select cells B3 through B9, then click the **Center button** on the Formatting toolbar.

➤ Click in cell **A11** to select this cell. Click and drag the top border (the mouse pointer changes from a cross to an arrow), to cell B11 to move the contents of cell A11 to B11. Move the contents of cell A13 to cell B13.

➤ Click the column header for column A to select the entire column as shown in Figure 2.9a. Pull down the **Format menu,** click (or point to) the **Column command** to display a cascaded menu, then click the **Hide command.** Column A (the student names) is no longer visible.

➤ Save the workbook.

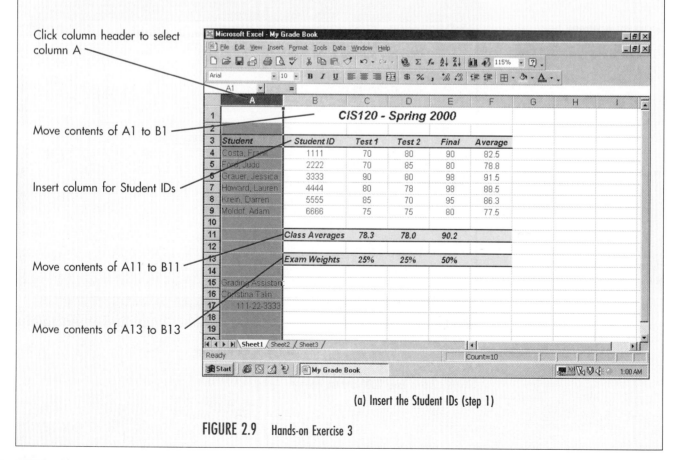

(a) Insert the Student IDs (step 1)

FIGURE 2.9 Hands-on Exercise 3

STEP 2: Insert a Hyperlink

➤ Click in cell **B15.** Pull down the **Insert menu** and click the **Hyperlink command** (or click the **Insert Hyperlink button** on the Standard toolbar) to display the Insert Hyperlink dialog box in Figure 2.9b.

➤ Click in the **Text to display** text box and enter **Click here for professor's home page.** Click in the second text box and enter the desired Web address; e.g., **www.bus.miami.edu/~rgrauer** (the http:// is assumed).

➤ Click **OK** to accept the settings and close the dialog box. The hyperlink should appear as an underlined entry in the worksheet.

➤ Save the workbook.

Insert Hyperlink button

Enter text to be displayed

Enter address

Click in B15

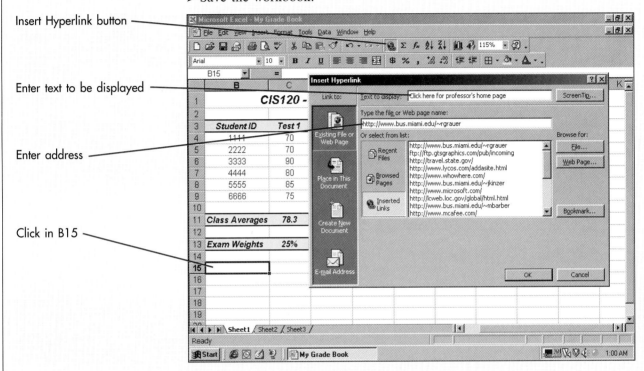

(b) Insert a Hyperlink (step 2)

FIGURE 2.9 Hands-on Exercise 3 (continued)

SELECTING (EDITING) A HYPERLINK

In an ideal world, you will enter all the information for a hyperlink correctly on the first attempt. But what if you make a mistake and need to edit the information? You cannot select a hyperlink by clicking it, because that displays the associated Web page. You can, however, right click the cell containing the hyperlink to display a context-sensitive menu. Click the Hyperlink command from that menu, then select the Edit Hyperlink command to display the associated dialog box in which to make the necessary changes.

STEP 3: Test the Hyperlink

➤ Point to the hyperlink (the Web address should appear as a ScreenTip), then click the link to start your browser and view the Web page. (You need an Internet connection to see the actual page.)

➤ If necessary, click the **maximize button** in your Web browser so that it takes the entire desktop as shown in Figure 2.9c. You are now running two applications, Excel and the Web browser, each of which has its own button on the Windows taskbar.

➤ Click the **Excel button** to continue working on the workbook.

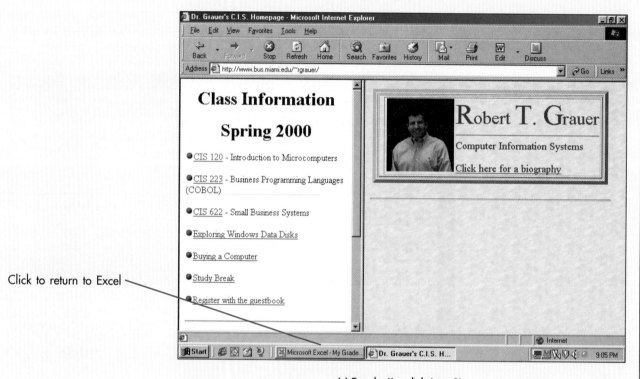

(c) Test the Hyperlink (step 3)

FIGURE 2.9   Hands-on Exercise 3 (continued)

MULTITASKING

Multitasking, the ability to run multiple applications at the same time, is one of the primary advantages of the Windows environment. Minimizing an application is different from closing it, and you want to minimize, rather than close, an application to take advantage of multitasking. Closing an application removes it from memory so that you have to restart the application if you want to return to it later in the session. Minimizing, however, leaves the application open in memory, but shrinks its window to a button on the Windows taskbar.

STEP 4: Save as a Web Page

➤ Pull down the **File menu** and click the **Save as Web Page** command to display the Save as dialog box in Figure 2.9d. (The Web page can be saved and viewed on a local drive prior to posting it on the Web.)

➤ Click the drop-down arrow in the Save In list box to select the appropriate drive, drive C or drive A, then open the **Exploring Excel folder**.

➤ Change the name of the Web page to **My Grade Book as Web Page** (to differentiate it from the Excel workbook of the same name). Click the **Save button** to save the page.

➤ The title bar changes to reflect the name of the Web page. There are now two versions of this workbook in the Exploring Excel folder, My Grade Book, and My Grade Book as Web Page. The latter has been saved as a Web page (in HTML format) and can be viewed by any Web browser.

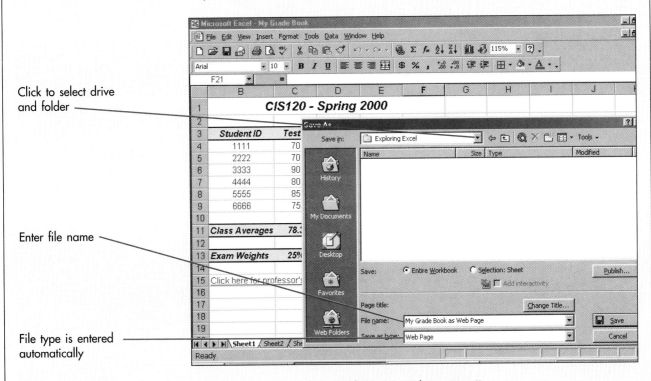

Click to select drive and folder

Enter file name

File type is entered automatically

(d) Save as a Web Page (step 4)

FIGURE 2.9 Hands-on Exercise 3 (continued)

HIDING AND UNHIDING ROWS AND COLUMNS

Excel enables you to hide a column from view while retaining the data in the workbook. Select the column(s) you wish to hide, click the right mouse button, then select the Hide command from the shortcut menu. Reverse the process to unhide the column; i.e., right click the column header to the left of the hidden column, then click the Unhide command. To unhide column A, however, click in the Name box and enter A1. Pull down the Format menu, click Column, then click the Unhide command. Follow a similar process to hide and unhide a row.

STEP 5: View the Web Page

➤ You can preview the Web page by pulling down the **File menu** and clicking the **Web Page Preview command.** We prefer, however that you start Internet Explorer by clicking its button on the Windows taskbar to open the Web page explicitly.

➤ Pull down the **File menu** and click the **Open command** to display the Open dialog box in Figure 2.9e. Click the **Browse button,** then select the drive and folder where you saved the Web page in the previous step.

➤ Click the **Details button** on the Open toolbar to display the date and time the Web page was created.

➤ Select (click) **My Grade Book as Web Page,** then click **Open** to close the dialog box. Click **OK** to open the document. You should see the professor's grade book with the students listed by Student ID, rather than name.

➤ Close Excel and Internet Explorer.

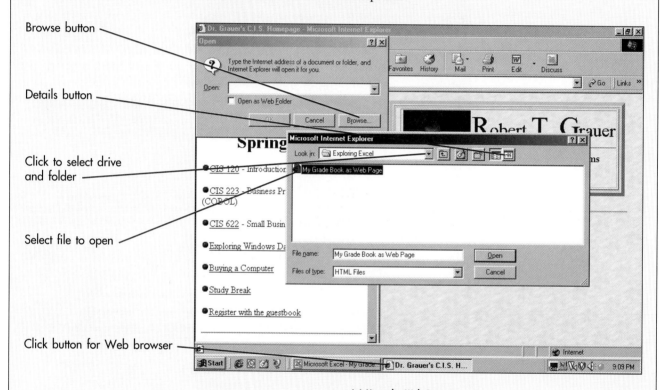

Browse button

Details button

Click to select drive and folder

Select file to open

Click button for Web browser

(e) View the Web Page (step 5)

FIGURE 2.9   Hands-on Exercise 3 (continued)

THE CORPORATE INTRANET

The ability to create links to local documents and to view those pages through a Web browser has created an entirely new way to disseminate information. Organizations of every size are taking advantage of this capability to develop a corporate intranet in which Web pages are placed on a local area network for use within the organizations. The documents on an intranet are available only to individuals with access to the local area network on which the documents are stored.

All worksheet commands operate on a cell or group of cells known as a range. A range is selected by dragging the mouse to highlight the range. The range remains selected until another range is defined or you click another cell in the worksheet. Noncontiguous (nonadjacent) ranges may be selected in conjunction with the Ctrl key.

The formulas in a cell or range of cells may be copied or moved anywhere within a worksheet. An absolute reference remains constant throughout a copy operation, whereas a relative address is adjusted for the new location. Absolute and relative references have no meaning in a move operation. The copy and move operations are implemented through the Copy and Paste commands, and the Cut and Paste commands, respectively.

Formatting is done within the context of select-then-do; that is, select the cell or range of cells, then execute the appropriate command. The Format Cells command controls the formatting for Numbers, Alignment, Fonts, Borders, and Patterns (colors). The Formatting toolbar simplifies the formatting process.

A spreadsheet is first and foremost a tool for decision making, and as such, the subject of continual what-if speculation. It is critical, therefore, that the initial conditions and assumptions be isolated and clearly visible, and further that all formulas in the body of the spreadsheet be developed using these cells.

The Internet and World Wide Web are thoroughly integrated into Office 2000 through two basic capabilities. You can insert a hyperlink into any Office document, then view the associated Web page from within the document. You can also save any Office document as a Web page, which in turn can be displayed through a Web browser.

KEY WORDS AND CONCEPTS

Absolute reference
Accounting format
Alignment
Assumptions
Automatic formatting
Border tab
Cell formulas
Clipboard
Column command
Column width
Copy command
Currency format
Custom format
Cut command
Date format
Destination range
Format cells command
Format menu

Format Painter
Formatting toolbar
Fraction format
General format
Horizontal alignment
Hyperlink
Initial conditions
Insert Hyperlink
    command
Internet
Mixed reference
Move operation
Noncontiguous range
Now( ) function
Number format
Paste command
Patterns tab
Percentage format

Range
Relative reference
Row command
Row height
Save as Web Page
    command
Scientific format
Select-then-do
Source range
Special format
Text format
Time format
Today( ) function
Vertical alignment
Web toolbar
World Wide Web

1. Cell F6 contains the formula =AVERAGE(B6:D6). What will be the contents of cell F7 if the entry in cell F6 is *copied* to cell F7?
   (a) =AVERAGE(B6:D6)
   (b) =AVERAGE(B7:D7)
   (c) =AVERAGE($B$6:$D$6)
   (d) =AVERAGE($B$7:$D$7)

2. Cell F6 contains the formula =AVERAGE(B6:D6). What will be the contents of cell F7 if the entry in cell F6 is *moved* to cell F7?
   (a) =AVERAGE(B6:D6)
   (b) =AVERAGE(B7:D7)
   (c) =AVERAGE($B$6:$D$6)
   (d) =AVERAGE($B$7:$D$7)

3. A formula containing the entry =$A$4 is copied to a cell one column over and two rows down. How will the entry appear in its new location?
   (a) Both the row and column will change
   (b) Neither the row nor column will change
   (c) The row will change but the column will remain the same
   (d) The column will change but the row will remain the same

4. Which commands are necessary to implement a move?
   (a) Cut and Paste commands
   (b) Move command from the Edit menu
   (c) Either (a) or (b)
   (d) Neither (a) nor (b)

5. A cell range may consist of:
   (a) A single cell
   (b) A row or set of rows
   (c) A column or set of columns
   (d) All of the above

6. Which command will take a cell, or group of cells, and duplicate them elsewhere in the worksheet, without changing the original cell references?
   (a) Copy command, provided relative addresses were specified
   (b) Copy command, provided absolute addresses were specified
   (c) Move command, provided relative addresses were specified
   (d) Move command, provided absolute addresses were specified

7. The contents of cell B4 consist of the formula =B2*B3, yet the displayed value in cell B4 is a series of pound signs. What is the most likely explanation for this?
   (a) Cells B2 and B3 contain text entries rather than numeric entries and so the formula in cell B4 cannot be evaluated
   (b) Cell B4 is too narrow to display the computed result
   (c) Both (a) and (b)
   (d) Neither (a) nor (b)

8. The Formatting toolbar contains buttons to
   (a) Change to percent format
   (b) Increase or decrease the number of decimal places
   (c) Center an entry across columns
   (d) All of the above

9. Given that the percentage format is in effect, and that the number .056 has been entered into the active cell, how will the contents of the cell appear?
   (a) .056
   (b) 5.6%
   (c) .056%
   (d) 56%

10. Which of the following entries is equivalent to the decimal number .2?
    (a) ⅕
    (b) =1/5
    (c) Both (a) and (b)
    (d) Neither (a) nor (b)

11. What is the effect of two successive Undo commands, one right after the other?
    (a) The situation is not possible because the Undo command is not available in Microsoft Excel
    (b) The situation is not possible because the Undo command cannot be executed twice in a row
    (c) The Undo commands cancel each other out; that is, the worksheet is as it was prior to the first Undo command
    (d) The last two commands prior to the first Undo command are reversed

12. A formula containing the entry =$B3 is copied to a cell one column over and two rows down. How will the entry appear in its new location?
    (a) =$B3
    (b) =B3
    (c) =$C5
    (d) =$B5

13. What will be stored in a cell if 2/5 is entered in it?
    (a) 2/5
    (b) .4
    (c) The date value February 5 of the current year
    (d) 2/5 or .4 depending on the format in effect

14. Which of the following is true regarding numeric formatting changes versus the numeric values?
    (a) When you change the numeric formatting the value will change
    (b) When you change the numeric formatting the value will not be changed
    (c) When you change the numeric formatting the value will be truncated
    (d) None of the above is true

15. Which of the following may be copied using the Copy command?
    (a) A cell
    (b) A range of cells
    (c) A function
    (d) All of the above

16. A numerical entry may be
    (a) Displayed in boldface and/or italics
    (b) Left, centered, or right aligned in a cell
    (c) Displayed in any TrueType font in any available point size
    (d) All of the above

17. How do you insert a hyperlink into an Excel workbook?
    (a) Pull down the Insert menu and click the Hyperlink command
    (b) Click the Insert Hyperlink button on the Standard toolbar
    (c) Right click a cell and click the Hyperlink command
    (d) All of the above

18. A Web browser such as Internet Explorer can display a page from
    (a) A local drive such as drive A or drive C
    (b) A drive on a local area network
    (c) The World Wide Web
    (d) All of the above

ANSWERS

1. b	**6.** b	**11.** d	**16.** d
2. a	**7.** b	**12.** d	**17.** d
3. b	**8.** d	**13.** c	**18.** d
4. a	**9.** b	**14.** b	
5. d	**10.** b	**15.** d	

PRACTICE WITH EXCEL 2000

1. Coaches Realty: Figure 2.10 contains a worksheet that was used to calculate the difference between the Asking Price and Selling Price on various real estate listings that were sold during June, as well as the commission paid to the real estate agency as a result of selling those listings. Complete the worksheet, following the steps on the next page.

	A	B	C	D	E	F
1	Coaches Realty - Sales for June					
2						
3						
4	Customer	Address	Asking Price	Selling Price	Difference	Commission
5	Landry	122 West 75 Terr.	450000	350000		
6	Spurrier	4567 S.W. 95 Street	750000	648500		
7	Shula	123 Alamo Road	350000	275000		
8	Lombardi	9000 Brickell Place	275000	250000		
9	Johnson	5596 Powerline Road	189000	189000		
10	Erickson	8900 N.W. 89 Street	456000	390000		
11	Bowden	75 Maynada Blvd.	300000	265000		
12						
13		Totals:				
14						
15	Commission %:		0.035			

FIGURE 2.10   Coaches Realty (Exercise 1)

a. Open the partially completed *Chapter 2 Practice 1* workbook on the data disk, then save the workbook as *Chapter 2 Practice 1 Solution.*

b. Click cell E5 and enter the formula to calculate the difference between the asking price and the selling price.

c. Click cell F5 and enter the formula to calculate the commission paid to the agency as a result of selling the property. (Pay close attention to the difference between relative and absolute cell references.)

d. Select cells E5:F5 and copy the formulas to E6:F11 to calculate the difference and commission for the rest of the properties.

e. Click cell C13 and enter the formula to calculate the total asking price, which is the sum of the asking prices for the individual listings.

f. Copy the formula in C13 to the range D13:F13.

g. Select the range C5:F13 and format the numbers so that they display with dollar signs and commas, and no decimal places (e.g., $450,000).

h. Click cell B15 and format the number as a percentage.

i. Click cell A1 and center the title across the width of the worksheet. With the cell still selected, select cells A2:F4 as well and change the font to 12 point Arial bold italic.

j. Select cells A4:F4 and create a bottom border to separate the headings from the data. Select cells F5:F11 and shade the commissions.

k. Add your name in cell A20. Print the worksheet.

2. **The Sales Invoice:** Use Figure 2.11 as the basis for a sales invoice that you will create and submit to your instructor. Your spreadsheet should follow the general format shown in the figure with respect to including a uniform discount for each item. Your spreadsheet should also include the sales tax. The discount percentage and sales tax percentage should be entered in a separate area so that they can be easily modified.

Use your imagination and sell any product at any price. You must, however, include at least four items in your invoice. Formatting is important, but you need not follow our format exactly. See how creative you can be, then submit your completed invoice to your instructor for inclusion in a class contest for the best invoice. Be sure your name appears somewhere on the worksheet as a sales associate. If you are really ambitious, you might include an object from the Microsoft Clip Gallery.

	A	B	C	D	E	F
1			Bargain Basement Shopping			
2	**Item**		**Quantity**	**List Price**	**Discount**	**Your Price**	**Total**
3	U.S. Robotics 56K Internal Faxmodem		2	$129.95	$25.99	$103.96	$207.92
4	Seagate 9.1Gb Hard Drive		6	$289.00	$57.80	$231.20	$1,387.20
5	Yamaha CD-R Drive		4	$249.95	$49.99	$199.96	$799.84
6	Iomega Zip Drive		10	$119.95	$23.99	$95.96	$959.60
7							
8	Subtotal						$3,354.56
9	Tax						$218.05
10	Amount Due						$3,572.61
11							
12	Discount Percentage		20.0%				
13	Sales Tax Percentage		6.5%				
14	Sales Associate		Conner Smith				

FIGURE 2.11 The Sales Invoice (Exercise 2)

3. The Checkbook: Figure 2.12 displays a worksheet that can be used to balance your checkbook. You can create the worksheet, and apply basic formatting by following these directions.

a. Start Excel. If necessary, click the New button on the Standard toolbar to display a blank workbook. Click in cell A1 and enter the title with your name as shown. Enter the labels for cells A3 through F3. Do not worry about formatting at this time.

b. Enter the initial balance in cell F4. Enter the data for your first check in row 5 and for your first deposit in row 6. (To enter a date, just type the date without an equal sign; e.g., enter 6/2/99 to enter June 2, 1999.) Use real or hypothetical data as you see fit.

c. Click in cell F5 and enter the formula to compute your balance. Develop the formula in such a way that it can be copied to the remaining cells in column F; that is, the formula should compute the balance after the current transaction, regardless of whether the transaction is a check or deposit.

d. Enter the data for at least four additional transactions in cells A through E of the appropriate row. Copy the formula to compute the balance for these transactions from cell F5.

e. Skip one row after the last transaction, then enter the formulas to verify that the balance is correct. The formula for cell F12 (in our worksheet) is the initial balance, minus the sum of all check amounts, plus the sum of all deposits. The displayed value should equal the balance after the last transaction.

f. Format the completed worksheet as appropriate. Print the worksheet twice, once to show the displayed values and once to show the cell contents. Submit both printouts to your instructor as proof that you did this exercise.

	A	B	C	D	E	F
1			Jessica Benjamin's Checkbook			
2	Check #	Date	Description	Amount	Deposit	Balance
3						$1,000.00
4	1	2-Jun	Rent	$345.00		$655.00
5		2-Jun	DEPOSIT		$125.00	$780.00
6	2	3-Jun	Utilities	$45.43		$734.57
7			ATM Withdrawal	$50.00		$684.57
8	3	6-Jun	Computer Repair	$84.25		$600.32
9	4	6-Jun	AOL	$19.99		$580.33
10						
11	Verification			$544.67	$125.00	$580.33

FIGURE 2.12   The Checkbook (Exercise 3)

4. Mixed References: Develop the multiplication table for a younger sibling shown in Figure 2.13. Creating the row and column headings is easy in that you can enter the numbers manually, or you can use online help to learn about the AutoFill feature. The hard part is creating the formulas in the body of the worksheet (we don't want you to enter the numbers manually).

The trick is to use mixed references for the formula in cell B4, then copy that single cell to the remainder of the table. The formula in cell B4 will be the product of two numbers. To develop the proper mixed reference, you need to think about what will vary and what will remain constant (e.g., you will always be using one value from column A and another value from row 3).

Add your name to the worksheet and submit it to your instructor. Remember, this worksheet is for a younger sibling, and so formatting is important. Print the cell formulas as well so that you can see how the mixed reference changes throughout the worksheet. Submit the complete assignment (title page, displayed values, and cell formulas) to your instructor. Using mixed references correctly is challenging, but once you arrive at the correct solution, you will have learned a lot about this very powerful spreadsheet feature.

	A	B	C	D	E	F	G	H	I	J	K	L	M
1	A Multiplication Table for My Younger Sister												
2													
3		1	2	3	4	5	6	7	8	9	10	11	12
4	1	1	2	3	4	5	6	7	8	9	10	11	12
5	2	2	4	6	8	10	12	14	16	18	20	22	24
6	3	3	6	9	12	15	18	21	24	27	30	33	36
7	4	4	8	12	16	20	24	28	32	36	40	44	48
8	5	5	10	15	20	25	30	35	40	45	50	55	60
9	6	6	12	18	24	30	36	42	48	54	60	66	72
10	7	7	14	21	28	35	42	49	56	63	70	77	84
11	8	8	16	24	32	40	48	56	64	72	80	88	96
12	9	9	18	27	36	45	54	63	72	81	90	99	108
13	10	10	20	30	40	50	60	70	80	90	100	110	120
14	11	11	22	33	44	55	66	77	88	99	110	121	132
15	12	12	24	36	48	60	72	84	96	108	120	132	144

FIGURE 2.13   Mixed References (Exercise 4)

5. Payroll: Figure 2.14 illustrates how a spreadsheet can be used to compute a payroll for hourly employees. A partially completed version of the worksheet can be found in the file *Chapter 2 Practice 5*. Your job is to complete the worksheet by developing the entries for the first employee, then copying those entries to the remaining rows. (An employee receives time and a half for overtime.)

To receive full credit for this assignment, the formulas for the withholding and Social Security taxes must reference the percentages in cells C12 and C13, respectively. Format the worksheet after it has been completed. Add your name anywhere in the worksheet, then print it two ways, once with displayed values and once with cell contents; then submit both pages to your instructor.

	A	B	C	D	E	F	G	H
1	Employee Name	Hourly Wage	Regular Hours	Overtime Hours	Gross Pay	Withholding Tax	Soc Sec Tax	Net Pay
2								
3	Jones	$8.00	40	10	$440.00	$123.20	$28.60	$288.20
4	Smith	$9.00	35	0	$315.00	$88.20	$20.48	$206.33
5	Baker	$7.20	40	0	$288.00	$80.64	$18.72	$188.64
6	Barnard	$7.20	40	8	$374.40	$104.83	$24.34	$245.23
7	Adams	$10.00	40	4	$460.00	$128.80	$29.90	$301.30
8								
9	Totals				$1,877.40	$525.67	$122.03	$1,229.70
10								
11	Assumptions							
12	Withholding tax		28.0%					
13	FICA		6.5%					

FIGURE 2.14   Payroll (Exercise 5)

6. Exchange Rates: The attractive worksheet in Figure 2.15 is based on a simple monetary conversion formula whereby specified dollar amounts are converted to British pounds and vice versa. Your assignment is to create the equivalent worksheet, based on today's rate of exchange for any foreign currency. The most important part of the assignment is to create an accurate spreadsheet. The inclusion of the flags is optional.

a. Choose any foreign currency you like, then use your favorite search engine to locate today's rate of exchange. Enter the conversion factors in the appropriate cells in the worksheet.

b. Enter the fixed amounts of the foreign currency in cells B4 through B7, then enter the appropriate formulas in cells C4 through C7.

c. Enter the fixed amounts of the U.S. currency in cells B10 through B13, then enter the appropriate formulas in cells C10 through C13.

d. Use the Currency category in the Format Cells command to display the symbol for your selected currency in the appropriate cells.

e. Click in cell C15 and enter the label, "Click here to obtain today's rate of Exchange." Click the Insert Hyperlink button on the Standard toolbar to display the Insert Hyperlink dialog box in which you enter the Web address of the site you used to obtain the exchange rate.

f. This step requires the installation of additional clip art from the Office 2000 CD. Pull down the Insert menu, click (or point to) the Picture command, then choose Clip Art to display the Microsoft Clip Gallery dialog box. Select the Flags category, then insert the appropriate flags into your worksheet.

g. Click in cell B19 and enter =today( ) to display the current date. Add your name elsewhere in the worksheet. Save the workbook. Print the workbook with today's conversion rates.

h. Open the workbook on a different day and note that the displayed value in cell B19 changes automatically. Click the hyperlink to go to the Web site containing the rates of exchange and enter the new values, which in turn should change the other values in the body of the spreadsheet. Print the workbook a second time to reflect these rates.

	A	B	C
1	Currency Conversion		
2			
3	Pounds to Dollars	Cost in Pounds	Cost in Dollars
4		£1.00	$1.63
5		£5.00	$8.15
6		£10.00	$16.30
7		£25.00	$40.75
8			
9	Dollars to Pounds	Cost in Dollars	Cost in Pounds
10		$1.00	£0.61
11		$5.00	£3.07
12		$10.00	£6.13
13		$25.00	£15.34
14			
15	Click here to obtain today's rate of exchange		
16	Convert dollars to pounds		1.63
17	Convert pounds to dollars		0.61
18			
19	Today's Date	2/4/99	
20	Your friendly banker	Andrea Carrion	

FIGURE 2.15   Exchange Rates (Exercise 6)

7. Get Rich Quick: Financial planning and budgeting is one of the most common business applications of spreadsheets. Figure 2.16 depicts one such illustration, in which the income and expenses of Get Rich Quick Enterprises are projected over a five-year period. Your assignment is to create the spreadsheet from the partially completed version, *Chapter 2 Practice 7* that is found on the data disk. You don't have to be an accountant to do the assignment, which computes an estimated profit by subtracting expenses from income.

The projected income in 1999, for example, is $300,000 based on sales of 100,000 units at a price of $3.00 per unit. The variable costs for the same year are estimated at $150,000 (100,000 units times $1.50 per unit). The production facility costs an additional $50,000 and administrative expenses add another $25,000. Subtracting the total expenses from the estimated income yields a net income before taxes of $75,000. The estimated income and expenses for each succeeding year are based on an assumed percentage increase over the previous year. The projected rates of increase as well as the initial conditions are shown at the bottom of the worksheet.

Open the partially completed spreadsheet in *Chapter 2 Practice 7,* then complete the spreadsheet so that it matches Figure 2.16. The assignment is not difficult, provided you follow these basic steps.

a. Develop the formulas for the first year of the forecast based on the initial conditions at the bottom of the spreadsheet; e.g., the entry in cell B4 should be =B18 (or =$B$18).

b. Develop the formulas for the second year based on the values in year one and the assumed rates of change. Use the appropriate combination of relative and absolute addresses; e.g., the entry in cell C4 should be =B4+B4*$D$18.

c. Copy the formulas for year two to the remaining years of the forecast.

d. Format the spreadsheet, then print the completed forecast. Add your name somewhere in the worksheet, then submit the completed spreadsheet to your instructor.

	A	B	C	D	E	F
1	Get Rich Quick Enterprises					
2		1999	2000	2001	2002	2003
3	Income					
4	Units Sold	100,000	110,000	121,000	133,100	146,410
5	Unit Price	$3.00	$3.15	$3.31	$3.47	$3.65
6	Gross Revenue	$300,000	$346,500	$400,208	$462,240	$533,887
7						
8	Fixed costs					
9	Production facility	$50,000	$54,000	$58,320	$62,986	$68,024
10	Administration	$25,000	$26,250	$27,563	$28,941	$30,388
11	Variable cost					
12	Unit mfg cost	$1.50	$1.65	$1.82	$2.00	$2.20
13	Variable mfg cost	$150,000	$181,500	$219,615	$265,734	$321,538
14						
15	Earnings before taxes	$75,000	$84,750	$94,710	$104,579	$113,936
16						
17	Initial conditions			Annual increase		
18	First year sales	100,000		10.0%		
19	Selling price	$3.00		5.0%		
20	Unit mfg cost	$1.50		10.0%		
21	Production facility	$50,000		8.0%		
22	Administration	$25,000		5.0%		
23	First year of forecast	1999				

FIGURE 2.16   Get Rich Quick (Exercise 7)

Establishing a Budget

Create a detailed budget for your four years at school. Your worksheet should include all sources of income (scholarships, loans, summer jobs, work-study, etc.) as well as all expenses (tuition, books, room and board, and entertainment). Make the budget as realistic as possible by building in projected increases over the four-year period. Be sure to isolate the assumptions and initial conditions so that your spreadsheet is amenable to change. Print the spreadsheet twice, once to show displayed values, and once to show the cell formulas. Submit both pages to your instructor together with a cover page.

Two Different Clipboards

The Office clipboard is different from the Windows clipboard, but both clipboards share some functionality. Thus, whenever you copy an object to the Office clipboard, it is also copied to the Windows clipboard. However, each successive copy operation adds an object to the Office clipboard (up to a maximum of 12 objects), whereas it replaces the contents of the Windows clipboard. The Office clipboard also has its own toolbar. Experiment with the Office clipboard from different applications, then summarize your findings in a brief note to your instructor.

Break-even Analysis

Widgets of America has developed the perfect product and is ready to go into production, pending a review of a five-year break-even analysis. The manufacturing cost in the first year is $1.00 per unit and is estimated to increase at 5% annually. The projected selling price is $2.00 per unit and can increase at 10% annually. Overhead expenses are fixed at $100,000 per year over the life of the project. The advertising budget is $50,000 in the first year but will decrease 15% a year as the product gains acceptance. How many units have to be sold each year for the company to break even?

As in the previous case, your worksheet should be completely flexible and capable of accommodating a change in any of the initial conditions or projected rates of increase or decrease. Be sure to isolate all of the assumptions (i.e., the initial conditions and rates of increase) in one area of the worksheet, and then reference these cells as absolute references when building the formulas.

chapter 3

SPREADSHEETS IN DECISION MAKING: WHAT IF?

OBJECTIVES

After reading this chapter you will be able to:

1. Describe the use of spreadsheets in decision making; explain how the Goal Seek command and Scenario Manager facilitate the decision making process.
2. List the arguments of the PMT function and describe its use in financial decisions.
3. Use the Paste Function dialog box to select a function, identify the function arguments, then enter the function into a worksheet.
4. Use the fill handle to copy a cell range to a range of adjacent cells; use the AutoFill capability to enter a series into a worksheet.
5. Use pointing to create a formula; explain the advantage of pointing over explicitly typing cell references.
6. Use the AVERAGE, MAX, MIN, and COUNT functions in a worksheet.
7. Use the IF function to implement a decision; explain the VLOOKUP function and how it is used in a worksheet.
8. Describe the additional measures needed to print large worksheets; explain how freezing panes may help in the development of a large worksheet.

OVERVIEW

Excel is a fascinating program, but it is only a means to an end. A spreadsheet is first and foremost a tool for decision making, and the objective of this chapter is to show you just how valuable that tool can be. We begin by presenting two worksheets that we think will be truly useful to you. The first evaluates the purchase of a car and helps you determine just how much car you can afford. The second will be of interest when you are looking for a mortgage to buy a home.

The chapter continues to develop your knowledge of Excel with emphasis on the predefined functions that are built into the program. We consider financial functions such as the PMT function to determine the monthly payment on a loan. We introduce the MAX, MIN, COUNT, and COUNTA statistical functions. We also present the IF and VLOOKUP functions that provide decision making within a worksheet.

The chapter also discusses two important commands that facilitate the decision-making process. The Goal Seek command lets you enter the desired end result (such as the monthly payment on a car loan) and from that, determines the input (e.g., the price of the car) to produce that result. The Scenario Manager enables you to specify multiple sets of assumptions and input conditions (scenarios), then see at a glance the results of any given scenario.

The examples in this chapter review the important concepts of relative and absolute cell references, as well as the need to isolate the assumptions and initial conditions in a worksheet. The hands-on exercises introduce new techniques in the form of powerful shortcuts that will make you more proficient in Excel. We show you how to use the fill handle to copy cells within a worksheet and how to use the AutoFill capability to enter a data series. We also explain how to enter formulas by pointing to cells within a worksheet, as opposed to having to explicitly type the cell references.

ANALYSIS OF A CAR LOAN

Figure 3.1 shows how a worksheet might be applied to the purchase of a car. In essence, you need to know the monthly payment, which depends on the price of the car, the down payment, and the terms of the loan. In other words:

- Can you afford the monthly payment on the car of your choice?
- What if you settle for a less expensive car and receive a manufacturer's rebate?
- What if you work next summer to earn money for a down payment?
- What if you extend the life of the loan and receive a more favorable interest rate?

The answers to these and other questions determine whether you can afford a car, and if so, which car, and how you will pay for it. The decision is made easier by developing the worksheet in Figure 3.1, and then by changing the various parameters as indicated.

Figure 3.1a contains the *template*, or "empty" worksheet, in which the text entries and formulas have already been entered, the formatting has already been applied, but no specific data has been input. The template requires that you enter the price of the car, the manufacturer's rebate, the down payment, the interest rate, and the length of the loan. The worksheet uses these parameters to compute the monthly payment. (Implicit in this discussion is the existence of a PMT function within the worksheet program, which is explained in the next section.)

The availability of the worksheet lets you consider several alternatives, and therein lies its true value. You quickly realize that the purchase of a $14,999 car as shown in Figure 3.1b is prohibitive because the monthly payment is almost $500. Settling for a less expensive car, coming up with a substantial down payment, and obtaining a manufacturer's rebate in Figure 3.1c help considerably, but the $317 monthly payment is still too steep. Extending the loan to a fourth year at a lower interest rate in Figure 3.1d reduces the monthly payment to (a more affordable) $244.

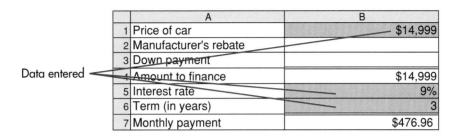

	A	B
1	Price of car	
2	Manufacturer's rebate	
3	Down payment	
4	Amount to finance	=B1-(B2+B3)
5	Interest rate	
6	Term (in years)	
7	Monthly payment	=PMT(B5/12,B6*12,-B4)

No specific data has been input

(a) The Template

	A	B
1	Price of car	$14,999
2	Manufacturer's rebate	
3	Down payment	
4	Amount to finance	$14,999
5	Interest rate	9%
6	Term (in years)	3
7	Monthly payment	$476.96

Data entered

(b) Initial Parameters

	A	B
1	Price of car	$13,999
2	Manufacturer's rebate	$1,000
3	Down payment	$3,000
4	Amount to finance	$9,999
5	Interest rate	9%
6	Term (in years)	3
7	Monthly payment	$317.97

Less expensive car
Rebate
Down payment made

(c) Less Expensive Car with Down Payment and Rebate

	A	B
1	Price of car	$13,999
2	Manufacturer's rebate	$1,000
3	Down payment	$3,000
4	Amount to finance	$9,999
5	Interest rate	8%
6	Term (in years)	4
7	Monthly payment	$244.10

Lower interest rate
Longer term

(d) Longer Term and Better Interest Rate

FIGURE 3.1   Spreadsheets in Decision Making

CAR SHOPPING ON THE WEB

Why guess about the price of a car or its features if you can obtain exact information from the Web? You can go to the site of a specific manufacturer, usually by entering an address of the form www.company.com (e.g., www.ford.com). You can also go to a site that provides information about multiple vendors. Our favorite is carpoint.msn.com, which provides detailed information about specifications and current prices. See practice exercise 6 at the end of the chapter.

PMT Function

A *function* is a predefined formula that accepts one or more *arguments* as input, performs the indicated calculation, then returns another value as output. Excel has more than 100 different functions in various categories. Financial functions, such as the PMT function we are about to study, are especially important in business.

The **PMT function** requires three arguments (the interest rate per period, the number of periods, and the amount of the loan) from which it computes the associated payment on a loan. The arguments are placed in parentheses and are separated by commas. Consider, for example, the PMT function as it might apply to Figure 3.1b:

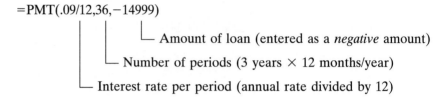

=PMT(.09/12,36,−14999)

Amount of loan (entered as a *negative* amount)

Number of periods (3 years × 12 months/year)

Interest rate per period (annual rate divided by 12)

Instead of using specific values, however, the arguments in the PMT function are supplied as cell references, so that the computed payment can be based on values supplied by the user elsewhere in the worksheet. Thus, the PMT function is entered as =PMT(B5/12,B6*12,−B4) to reflect the terms of a specific loan whose arguments are in cells B4, B5, and B6. (The principal is entered as a negative amount because the money is lent to you and represents an outflow of cash from the bank.)

The Goal Seek Command

The analysis in Figure 3.1 enabled us to reduce the projected monthly payment from $476 to a more affordable $244. What if, however, you can afford a payment of only $200, and you want to know the maximum you can borrow in order to keep the payment to the specified amount. The **Goal Seek command** is designed to solve this type of problem, as it enables you to set an end result (e.g., the monthly payment) in order to determine the input (the price of the car) to produce that result. Only one input (e.g., the price of the car *or* the interest rate) can be varied at a time.

Figure 3.2 extends our earlier analysis to illustrate the Goal Seek command. You create the spreadsheet as usual, then you pull down the Tools menu, and select the Goal Seek command to display the dialog box in Figure 3.2a. Enter the address of the cell containing the dependent formula (the monthly payment in cell B7) and the desired value of this cell ($200). Indicate the cell whose contents should be varied (the price of the car in cell B1), then click OK to execute the command. The Goal Seek command then varies the price of the car until the monthly payment returns the desired value of $200. (Not every problem has a solution, in which case Excel returns a message indicating that a solution cannot be found.)

In this example, the Goal Seek command is able to find a solution and returns a purchase price of $12,192 as shown in Figure 3.2b. You now have all the information you need. Find a car that sells for $12,192 (or less), hold the other parameters to the values shown in the figure, and your monthly payment will be (at most) $200. The analyses in Figures 3.1 and 3.2 illustrate how a worksheet is used in the decision-making process. An individual defines a problem, then develops a worksheet that includes all of the associated parameters. He or she can then plug in specific numbers, changing one or more of the variables until a decision can be reached.

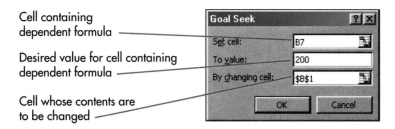

Cell containing
dependent formula

Desired value for cell containing
dependent formula

Cell whose contents are
to be changed

(a) Set the Maximum Payment

Required purchase price for
a $200 monthly payment

	A	B
1	Price of car	$12,192
2	Manufacturer's rebate	$1,000
3	Down payment	$3,000
4	Amount to finance	$8,192
5	Interest rate	8%
6	Term (in years)	4
7	Monthly payment	$200.00

(b) Solution

FIGURE 3.2   The Goal Seek Command

HANDS-ON EXERCISE 1

Analysis of a Car Loan

Objective: To create a spreadsheet that will analyze a car loan; to illustrate the PMT function and the Goal Seek command. Use Figure 3.3 as a guide.

STEP 1: Enter the Descriptive Labels

➤ Start Excel. If necessary, click the **New button** on the Standard toolbar to open a new workbook.

➤ Click in **cell A1,** type **Price of car,** then press the **enter key** or **down arrow** to complete the entry and move to cell A2.

➤ Enter the remaining labels for column A as shown in Figure 3.3a.

➤ Click and drag the column border between columns A and B to increase the width of column A to accommodate its widest entry.

➤ Save the workbook as **Analysis of a Car Loan** in the **Exploring Excel folder** as shown in Figure 3.3a.

THE INCREASE INDENT BUTTON

Take advantage of the familiar buttons on the Formatting toolbar to improve the look of the descriptive information in a worksheet. Enter the descriptive labels as indicated, press and hold the Ctrl key to select cells A2 and A3, then click the Increase Indent button on the Formatting toolbar to indent these labels under the price of the car. Indent the loan parameters in cells A5 and A6 in similar fashion.

New button

Click and drag column border to widen column A

Click to select drive and folder

Enter file name

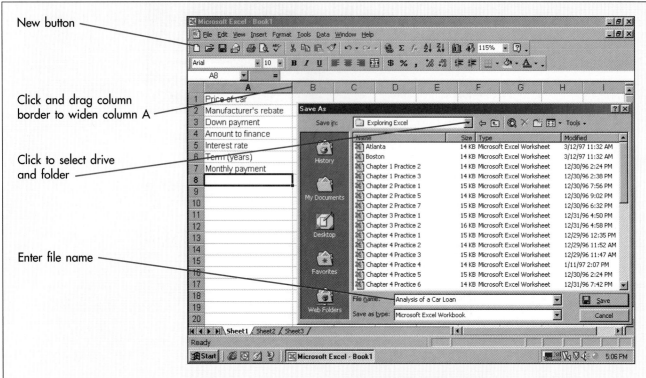

(a) Enter the Descriptive Labels (step 1)

FIGURE 3.3 Hands-on Exercise 1

STEP 2: Enter the PMT Function and Its Parameters

➤ Enter **$14,999** in cell B1 as shown in Figure 3.3b.

➤ Click in **cell B4.** Enter **=B1−(B2+B3),** which calculates the amount to finance (i.e., the principal of the loan).

➤ Enter **9%** and **3** in cells B5 and B6 as shown in Figure 3.3b.

➤ Click in **cell B7.** Enter **=PMT(B5/12,B6*12,−B4)** as the payment function. The arguments in the PMT function are the interest rate per period, the number of periods, and the principal, and correspond to the parameters of the loan. Save the workbook.

STEP 3: What If?

➤ Click in **cell B1** and change the price of the car to **$13,999.** The monthly payment drops to $445.16.

➤ Click in **cell B2** and enter a manufacturer's rebate of **$1,000.** The monthly payment drops to $413.36.

➤ Click in **cell B3** and enter a down payment of **$3,000.** The monthly payment drops to $317.97.

➤ Change the interest rate to **8%** and the term of the loan to **4** years. The payment drops to $244.10.

Formula in active cell (B7)

Enter PMT function in B7

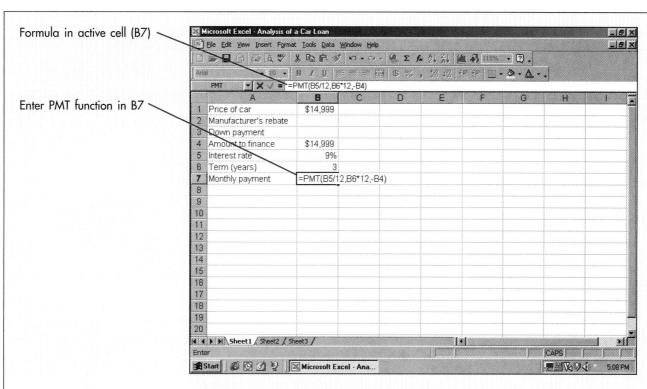

(b) Enter the PMT Function and Its Parameters (step 2)

FIGURE 3.3   Hands-on Exercise 1 (continued)

STEP 4: The Goal Seek Command

➤ Click in **cell B7,** the cell containing the formula for the monthly payment. This is the cell whose value we want to set to a fixed amount.

➤ Pull down the **Tools menu.** Click **Goal Seek** to display the dialog box in Figure 3.3c. (You may have to click the double arrow at the bottom of the Tools menu to display the Goal Seek command.) If necessary, click and drag the title bar of the Goal Seek dialog box so that you can see the cells containing the data for your loan.

➤ The Set Cell parameter is already set to B7, as that is the selected cell. Click in the **To value** text box. Type **200** (the desired value of the monthly payment).

➤ Click in the **By changing cell** text box. Type **B1,** the cell containing the price of the car. This is the cell whose value will be determined. Click **OK.**

STEP 5: The Completed Worksheet

➤ The Goal Seek command returns a successful solution as indicated by the dialog box in Figure 3.3d. The worksheet changes to display $12,192 and $200 in cells B1 and B7, respectively, corresponding to the parameters in the Goal Seek command:

  • Click **OK** to accept the solution and close the Goal Seek dialog box, *or*

  • Click **Cancel** if you don't like the solution and want to return to the original values.

➤ Save the workbook. Close the workbook. Exit Excel if you do not want to continue with the next exercise at this time.

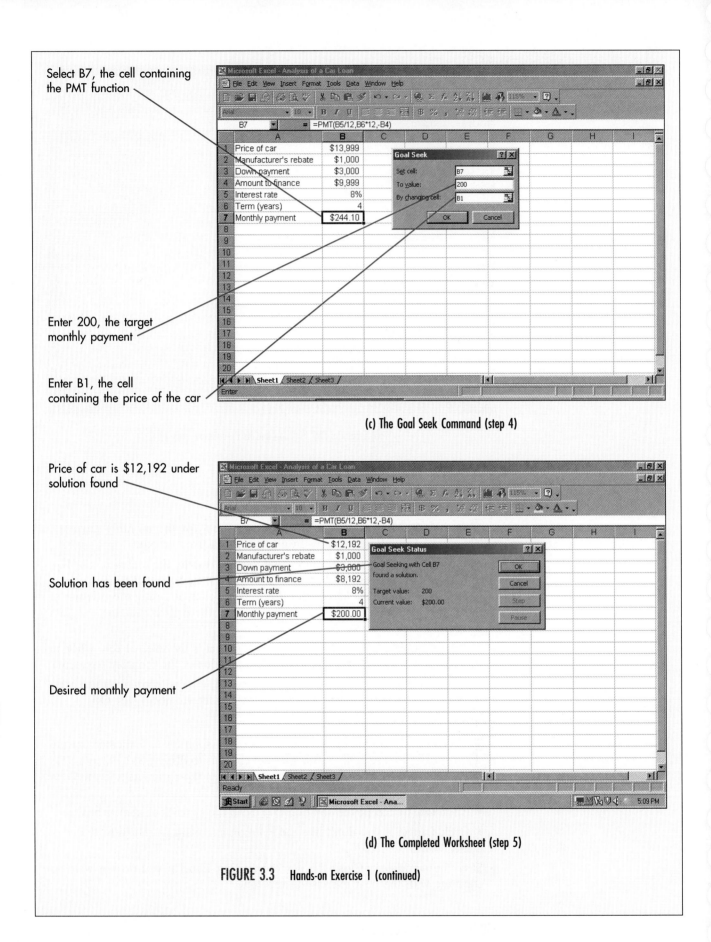

Select B7, the cell containing the PMT function

Enter 200, the target monthly payment

Enter B1, the cell containing the price of the car

(c) The Goal Seek Command (step 4)

Price of car is $12,192 under solution found

Solution has been found

Desired monthly payment

(d) The Completed Worksheet (step 5)

FIGURE 3.3   Hands-on Exercise 1 (continued)

The PMT function is used in our next example in conjunction with the purchase of a home. The example also reviews the concept of relative and absolute addresses from Chapter 2. In addition, it introduces several other techniques to make you more proficient in Excel.

The spreadsheets in Figure 3.4 illustrate a variable rate mortgage, which will be developed over the next several pages. The user enters the amount he or she wishes to borrow and a starting interest rate, and the spreadsheet displays the associated monthly payment. The spreadsheet in Figure 3.4a enables the user to see the monthly payment at varying interest rates, and to contrast the amount of the payment for a 15- and a 30-year mortgage.

Most first-time buyers opt for the longer term, but they would do well to consider a 15-year mortgage. Note, for example, that the difference in monthly payments for a $100,000 mortgage at 7.5% is only $227.80 (the difference between $927.01 for a 15-year mortgage versus $699.21 for the 30-year mortgage). This is a significant amount of money, but when viewed as a percentage of the total cost of a home (property taxes and maintenance), it becomes less important, especially when you consider the substantial saving in interest over the life of the mortgage.

Figure 3.4b expands the spreadsheet to show the total interest over the life of the loan for both the 15- and the 30-year mortgage. The total interest on a $100,000 loan at 7.5% is $151,717 for a 30-year mortgage, but only $66,862 for a 15-year mortgage. In other words, you will pay back the $100,000 in principal plus another $151,717 in interest if you select the longer term.

Difference in monthly payment between a 30-year and a 15-year mortgage at 7.5%

	A	B	C	D
1	Amount Borrowed		$100,000	
2	Starting Interest		7.50%	
3				
4		Monthly Payment		
5	Interest	30 Years	15 Years	Difference
6	7.50%	$699.21	$927.01	$227.80
7	8.50%	$768.91	$984.74	$215.83
8	9.50%	$840.85	$1,044.22	$203.37
9	10.50%	$914.74	$1,105.40	$190.66
10	11.50%	$990.29	$1,168.19	$177.90
11	12.50%	$1,067.26	$1,232.52	$165.26

(a) Difference in Monthly Payment

Less interest is paid on a 15-year loan ($66,862 vs $151,717 on a 30-year loan)

	A	B	C	D	E
1	Amount Borrowed			$100,000	
2	Starting Interest			7.50%	
3					
4		30 Years		15 Years	
5	Interest	Monthly Payment	Total Interest	Monthly Payment	Total Interest
6	7.50%	$699.21	$151,717	$927.01	$66,862
7	8.50%	$768.91	$176,809	$984.74	$77,253
8	9.50%	$840.85	$202,708	$1,044.22	$87,960
9	10.50%	$914.74	$229,306	$1,105.40	$98,972
10	11.50%	$990.29	$256,505	$1,168.19	$110,274
11	12.50%	$1,067.26	$284,213	$1,232.52	$121,854

(b) Total Interest

FIGURE 3.4   15- Versus 30-Year Mortgage

Figure 3.5 presents another variation of the spreadsheet in which we show the amortization (payoff) schedule of the loan. The monthly payment is divided into two components, for interest and principal, respectively, with the latter reducing the balance of the loan. The amount allocated for interest decreases each period, and, conversely, the amount that goes toward the principle increases. These values can be computed through the **IPMT** and **PPMT functions,** respectively. The sum of the two components remains constant and is equal to the monthly payment.

You can see from the spreadsheet that most of the early payments go toward interest rather than principal. If, for example, you were to move at the end of five years (60 months), less than $6,000 (of the $44,952 you paid during those five years) goes toward the principal. (A 15-year mortgage, however, would pay off almost $22,000 during the same five-year period. The latter number is not shown, but can be displayed by changing the term of the mortgage in cell C5.)

Our objective is not to convince you of the merits of one loan over another, but to show you how useful a worksheet can be in the decision-making process. If you do eventually buy a home, and you select a 15-year mortgage, think of us.

	A	B	C	D
1	Amortization Schedule			
2				
3	Principal		$100,000	
4	Annual Interest		7.50%	
5	Term (in years)		30	
6	Monthly Payment		$699.21	
7				
8	Month	Toward Interest	Toward Principal	Balance
9				$100,000.00
10	1	$625.00	$74.21	$99,925.79
11	2	$624.54	$74.68	$99,851.11
12	3	$624.07	$75.15	$99,775.96
13	4	$623.60	$75.61	$99,700.35
14	5	$623.13	$76.09	$99,624.26
15	6	$622.65	$76.56	$99,547.70
65	56	$594.67	$104.55	$95,042.20
66	57	$594.01	$105.20	$94,937.00
67	58	$593.36	$105.86	$94,831.14
68	59	$592.69	$106.52	$94,724.62
69	60	$592.03	$107.19	$94,617.44

Less than $6,000 of the principal has been paid off

5 years (60 months)

FIGURE 3.5 Amortization Schedule

THE FV (FUTURE VALUE) FUNCTION

The FV function returns the value of a periodic investment after a specified number of periods at a fixed rate of interest. It can be used to compute the amount you will have at retirement if you save a constant amount each year. It can also compute the amount of money that would be available for college, given that a child's parents save a constant amount for each year until their child is ready to enroll.

Relative versus Absolute Addresses

Figure 3.6 displays the cell formulas for the mortgage analysis. All of the formulas are based on the amount borrowed and the starting interest, in cells C1 and C2, respectively. You can vary either or both of these parameters, and the worksheet will automatically recalculate the monthly payments.

The similarity in the formulas from one row to the next implies that the copy operation will be essential to the development of the worksheet. You must, however, remember the distinction between a *relative* and an *absolute reference*—that is, a cell reference that changes during a copy operation (relative) versus one that does not (absolute). Consider the PMT function as it appears in cell B6:

=PMT(A6/12,30*12,−$C$1)

                    The amount of the loan, −$C$1, is an absolute reference that remains constant

           Number of periods (30 years*12 months/year)

      The interest rate, A6/12, is a relative reference that changes

The entry A6/12 (which is the first argument in the formula in cell B6) is interpreted to mean "divide the contents of the cell one column to the left by 12." Thus, when the PMT function in cell B6 is copied to cell B7, it (the copied formula) is adjusted to maintain this relationship and will contain the entry A7/12. The Copy command does not duplicate a relative address exactly, but adjusts it from row to row (or column to column) to maintain the relative relationship. The cell reference for the amount of the loan should not change when the formula is copied, and hence it is specified as an absolute address.

Relative reference (adjusts during copy operation)

Absolute reference (doesn't adjust during copy operation)

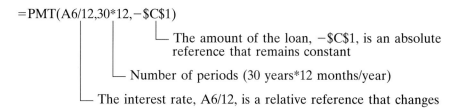

	A	B	C	D
1	Amount Borrowed		$100,000	
2	Starting Interest		7.50%	
3				
4		Monthly Payment		
5	Interest	30 Years	15 Years	Difference
6	=C2	=PMT(A6/12,30*12,-$C$1)	=PMT(A6/12,15*12,-$C$1)	=C6-B6
7	=A6+0.01	=PMT(A7/12,30*12,-$C$1)	=PMT(A7/12,15*12,-$C$1)	=C7-B7
8	=A7+0.01	=PMT(A8/12,30*12,-$C$1)	=PMT(A8/12,15*12,-$C$1)	=C8-B8
9	=A8+0.01	=PMT(A9/12,30*12,-$C$1)	=PMT(A9/12,15*12,-$C$1)	=C9-B9
10	=A9+0.01	=PMT(A10/12,30*12,-$C$1)	=PMT(A10/12,15*12,-$C$1)	=C10-B10
11	=A10+0.01	=PMT(A11/12,30*12,-$C$1)	=PMT(A11/12,15*12,-$C$1)	=C11-B11

FIGURE 3.6   Cell Formulas

ISOLATE ASSUMPTIONS

The formulas in a worksheet should be based on cell references rather than specific values—for example, C1 or $C$1 rather than $100,000. The cells containing these values should be clearly labeled and set apart from the rest of the worksheet. You can then vary the inputs (assumptions) to the worksheet and immediately see the effect. The chance for error is also minimized because you are changing the contents of a single cell, rather than changing multiple formulas.

You already know enough about Excel to develop the worksheet for the mortgage analysis. Excel is so powerful, however, and offers so many shortcuts, that we would be remiss not to show you alternative techniques. This section introduces the fill handle as a shortcut for copying cells, and pointing as a more accurate way to enter cell formulas.

The Fill Handle

The *fill handle* is a tiny black square that appears in the lower-right corner of the selected cells—it is the fastest way to copy a cell (or range of cells) to an *adjacent* cell (or range of cells). The process is quite easy, and you get to practice in the exercise (see Figure 3.8b) that follows shortly. In essence, you:

- Select the cell or cells to be copied.
- Point to the fill handle for the selected cell(s), which changes the mouse pointer to a thin crosshair.
- Click and drag the fill handle over the destination range. A border appears to outline the destination range.
- Release the mouse to complete the copy operation.

Pointing

A cell address is entered into a formula by typing the reference explicitly (as we have done throughout the text) or by pointing. If you type the address, it is all too easy to make a mistake, such as typing A40 when you really mean A41. *Pointing* is more accurate, since you use the mouse or arrow keys to select the cell directly as you build the formula. The process is much easier than it sounds, and you get to practice in the hands-on exercise (see Figure 3.8d). In essence, you:

- Select (click) the cell to contain the formula.
- Type an equal sign to begin entering the formula. The status bar indicates that you are in the *Enter mode,* which means that the formula bar is active and the formula can be entered.
- Click the cell you want to reference in the formula (or use the arrow keys to move to the cell). A moving border appears around the cell, and the cell reference is displayed in both the cell and formula bar. The status bar indicates the *Point mode.*
- Type any arithmetic operator to place the cell reference in the formula and return to the Enter mode.
- Continue pointing to additional cells and entering arithmetic operators until you complete the formula. Press the enter key to complete the formula.

As with everything else, the more you practice, the easier it is. The hands-on exercises will give you ample opportunity to practice everything you have learned.

Functions

The functions in Excel are grouped into categories, as shown in the Paste Function dialog box in Figure 3.7a. Select the category you want, then choose the desired function from within that category. Click OK to display the dialog box in Figure 3.7b, in which you specify the arguments for the function.

Select category

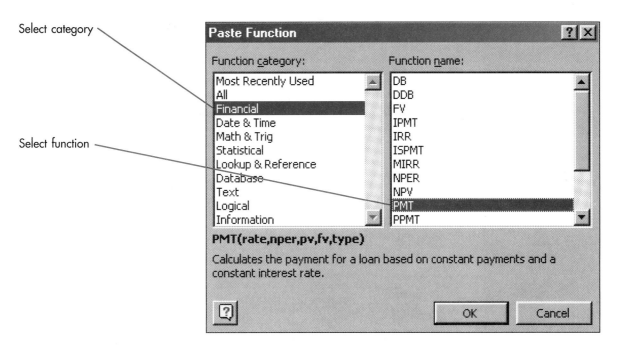

Select function

(a) Select the Function

Text boxes for function arguments

Calculated value of the individual arguments

Computed value of function

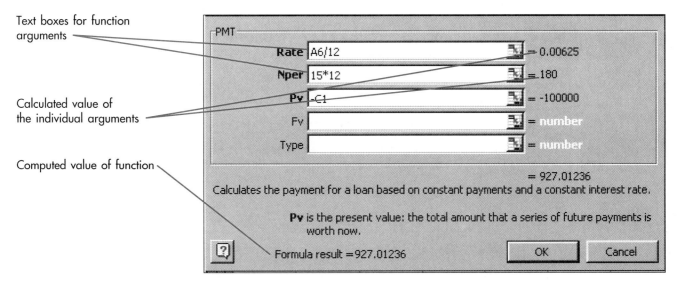

(b) Enter the Arguments

FIGURE 3.7 The Paste Function

The dialog box contains a text box for each argument, a description of each argument (as the text box is selected), and an indication of whether or not the argument is required. (Only the first three arguments are required in the PMT function.) Enter the value, cell reference, or formula for each argument by clicking in the text box and typing the entry, or by clicking the appropriate cell(s) in the worksheet.

Excel displays the calculated value for each argument immediately to the right of the argument. It also shows the computed value for the function as a whole at the bottom of the dialog box. All you need to do is click the OK button to insert the function into the worksheet.

Mortgage Analysis

Objective: To develop the worksheet for the mortgage analysis; to use pointing to enter a formula and drag-and-drop to copy a formula. Use Figure 3.8 as a guide in the exercise.

STEP 1: Enter the Descriptive Labels and Initial Conditions

➤ Start Excel. Click in **cell A1.** Type **Amount Borrowed.** Do not be concerned that the text is longer than the cell width, as cell B1 is empty and thus the text will be displayed in its entirety. Press the **enter key** or **down arrow** to complete the entry and move to cell A2.

➤ Type **Starting Interest** in cell A2. Click in **cell A4.** Type **Monthly Payment.** Enter the remaining labels in cells A5 through D5 as shown in Figure 3.8a. Do not worry about formatting at this time as all formatting will be done at the end of the exercise.

➤ Click in **cell C1.** Type **$100,000** (include the dollar sign and comma). Press the **enter key** or **down arrow** to complete the entry and move to cell C2. Type **7.5%** (include the percent sign). Press **enter.**

➤ Save the workbook as **Variable Rate Mortgage** in the **Exploring Excel folder.**

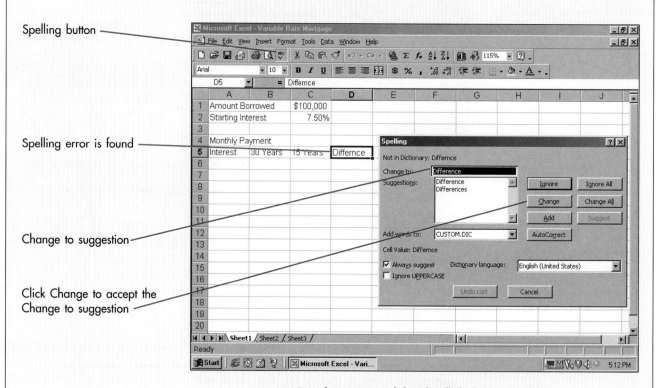

(a) Enter the Descriptive Labels and Spell Check (steps 1 and 2)

FIGURE 3.8   Hands-on Exercise 2

DISPLAY THE FULL MENUS

The default menus in Office 2000 show only basic commands so as not to overwhelm the user, and thus it may be necessary to click the double arrow at the bottom of the menu to view the complete set of commands. Once you use a command, however, it is added to the menu. Alternatively, you can customize Office to always display the full menus by default. Pull down the Tools menu, click Customize, click the Options tab, then clear the Menus show recently used commands first check box.

STEP 2: The Spell Check

➤ Click in **cell A1** to begin the spell check at the beginning of the worksheet.

➤ Click the **Spelling button** on the Standard toolbar to initiate the spell check as shown in Figure 3.8a. If you don't see the Spelling button, click the More Buttons (») to see more tools.

➤ Make corrections, as necessary, just as you would in Microsoft Word. Click Ok when the Spell Check is complete.

➤ Save the workbook.

FIND AND REPLACE

Anyone familiar with a word processor takes the Find and Replace commands for granted, but did you know the same capabilities exist in Excel? Pull down the Edit menu and choose either command. You have the same options as in the parallel command in Word, such as a case-sensitive (or insensitive) search or a limitation to the contents of an entire cell (similar to a whole word search). Use the command in the current workbook to change "Interest" to "Interest Rate".

STEP 3: The Fill Handle

➤ Click in **cell A6.** Type **=C2** to reference the starting interest rate in cell C2.

➤ Click in **cell A7.** Type the formula **=A6+.01** to compute the interest rate in this cell, which is one percent more than the interest rate in row 6. Press **enter.**

➤ Click in **cell A7.** Point to the **fill handle** in the lower corner of cell A7. The mouse pointer changes to a thin crosshair.

➤ Drag the **fill handle** over cells **A8** through **A11.** A border appears, indicating the destination range as in Figure 3.8b. Release the mouse to complete the copy operation. The formula and associated percentage format in cell A7 have been copied to cells A8 through A11.

➤ Click in **cell C2.** Type **5%.** The entries in cells A6 through A11 change automatically. Click the **Undo button** on the Standard toolbar to return to the 7.5% interest rate.

➤ Save the workbook.

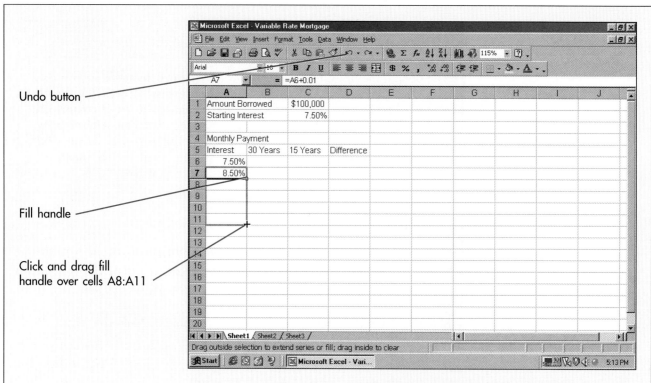

Undo button

Fill handle

Click and drag fill
handle over cells A8:A11

(b) The Fill Handle (step 3)

FIGURE 3.8   Hands-on Exercise 2 (continued)

STEP 4: Determine the 30-Year Payments

➤ Click in **cell B6.** Type the formula **=PMT(A6/12,30*12,−$C$1).** Press the **enter key.** Click in cell B6, which should display $699.21 as shown in Figure 3.8c.

➤ Click in **cell B6.** Point to the **fill handle** in the bottom-right corner of cell B6. The mouse pointer changes to a thin crosshair. Drag the **fill handle** over cells **B7** through **B11.** A border appears to indicate the destination range. Release the mouse to complete the copy operation.

➤ The PMT function in cell B6 has been copied to cells B7 through B11. (You may see a series of pound signs in cell B11, meaning that the column is too narrow to display the computed results in the selected format. Increase the column width.)

➤ Save the workbook.

THE OPTIMAL (AUTOFIT) COLUMN WIDTH

The appearance of pound signs within a cell indicates that the cell width (column width) is insufficient to display the computed results in the selected format. Double click the right border of the column heading to change the column width to accommodate the widest entry in that column. For example, to increase the width of column B, double click the border between the column headings for columns B and C.

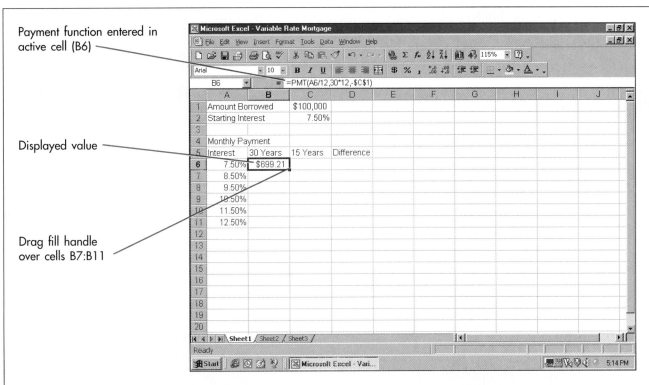

Payment function entered in active cell (B6)

Displayed value

Drag fill handle over cells B7:B11

	A	B	C	D	E
1	Amount Borrowed		$100,000		
2	Starting Interest		7.50%		
3					
4	Monthly Payment				
5	Interest	30 Years	15 Years	Difference	
6	7.50%	$699.21			
7	8.50%				
8	9.50%				
9	10.50%				
10	11.50%				
11	12.50%				

B6 = =PMT(A6/12,30*12,-$C$1)

(c) Determine the 30-Year Payments (step 4)

FIGURE 3.8   Hands-on Exercise 2 (continued)

STEP 5: Paste the PMT Function

➤ Click in **cell C6.** Pull down the **Insert menu** and click **Function** (or click the **Paste Function button** on the Standard toolbar) to display the Paste Function dialog box. If the Office Assistant offers help, click **No.**

➤ Click **Financial** in the Function Category list box. Click **PMT** in the Function Name list box. Click **OK.** Click and drag the Formula Palette so that you can see the underlying cells as shown in Figure 3.8d.

➤ Click the text box for **rate.** Type **A6/12.** The Formula Palette displays the computed value of .00625.

➤ Click the text box for the number of periods **(Nper).** Type **15*12,** corresponding to 15 years and 12 months per year.

➤ Click the text box for the present value **(Pv).** Type **−$C$1.**

➤ Check that the computed values on your monitor match those in Figure 3.8d. Make corrections as necessary. Click **OK.**

USE THE FORMULA PALETTE

Use the Formula Palette as a convenient shortcut to enter a function in a worksheet. Click in the cell that is to contain the function, click the = sign in the formula bar, then click the down arrow to display a list of recently used functions. Select the function and enter its arguments in the resulting Paste Function dialog box. You can save a step if you already know the name of the function by clicking the equal sign, and typing the function name followed by the left parenthesis to display the Paste Function dialog box.

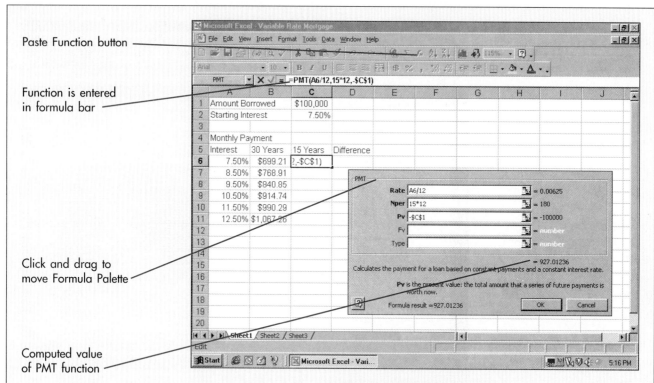

Paste Function button

Function is entered in formula bar

Click and drag to move Formula Palette

Computed value of PMT function

(d) The Paste the PMT Function (step 5)

FIGURE 3.8   Hands-on Exercise 2 (continued)

STEP 6: Copy the 15-Year Payments

➤ Cell C6 should display $927.01. If not, return to step 5 and correct the error.

➤ Check that cell C6 is still selected. Point to the **fill handle** in the lower-right corner of cell C6. The mouse pointer changes to a thin crosshair.

➤ Drag the **fill handle** to copy the PMT function to cells **C7** through **C11.** Adjust the width of these cells so that you can see the displayed values.

➤ Cell C11 should display $1,232.52 if you have done this step correctly. Save the workbook.

PASTE SPECIAL COMMAND

The fill handle is the easiest way to copy the entire contents of a cell or range of cells. But what if you want to copy the formulas without the formatting, or vice versa? You might even want to convert a formula to its computed numeric value. Any of these tasks can be accomplished through the Paste Special command. Select the cell or cells you want to copy, click the Copy button, select the destination range, then pull down the Edit menu and click the Paste Special command to display the Paste Special dialog box. Click the appropriate option button, then click OK to copy the selected item.

STEP 7: Compute the Monthly Difference (Pointing)

➤ Click in **cell D6.** Type **=** to begin the formula. Press the **left arrow key** (or click in **cell C6**), which produces the moving border around the entry in cell C6. The status bar indicates the point mode as shown in Figure 3.8e.

➤ Press the **minus sign,** then press the **left arrow key** twice (or click in **cell B6**).

➤ Press **enter** to complete the formula. Cell D6 should display $227.80.

➤ Use the **fill handle** to copy the contents of cell D6 to cells **D7** through **D11.** If you have done the step correctly, cell D11 will display $165.26.

➤ Save the workbook.

Cell address is entered in formula bar when you point to cell

Moving border is displayed as you point to cell

Point mode

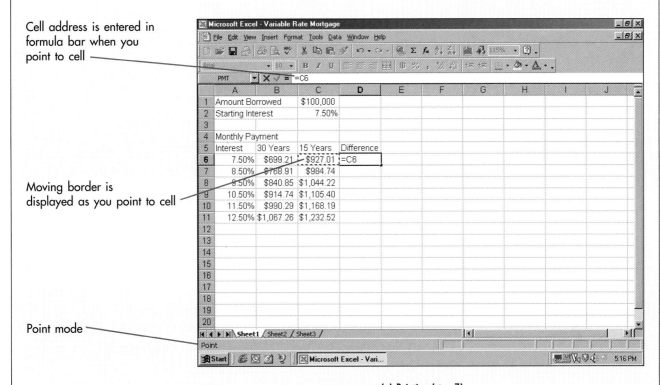

(e) Pointing (step 7)

FIGURE 3.8   Hands-on Exercise 2 (continued)

STEP 8: The Finishing Touches

➤ Type **Financial consultant:** in cell A13. Enter **your name** in cell C13 as shown in Figure 3.8f.

➤ Add formatting as necessary, using Figure 3.8f as a guide:

• Click **cell A4.** Drag the mouse over cells **A4** through **D4.** Click the **Merge and Center button** on the Formatting toolbar to center the entry over four columns.

• Center the column headings in row 5. Add boldface and/or italics to the text and/or numbers as you see fit.

➤ Save the workbook.

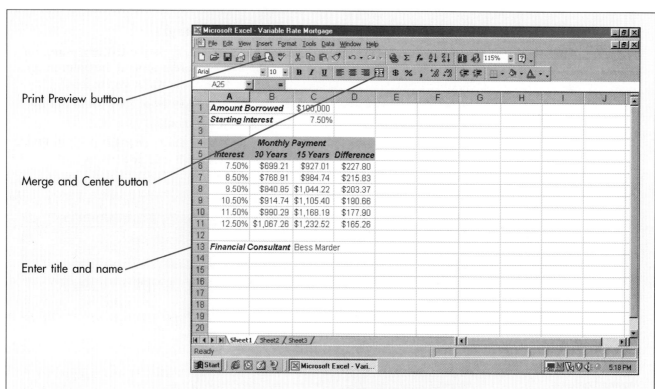

Print Preview buttton

Merge and Center button

Enter title and name

(f) The Finishing Touches (step 8)

FIGURE 3.8   Hands-on Exercise 2 (continued)

STEP 9: Print the Worksheet

➤ Pull down the **File menu** and click **Print Preview** (or click the **Print Preview button** on the Standard toolbar).

➤ Click the **Setup command button** to display the Page Setup dialog box.

  • Click the **Margins tab.** Check the box to center the worksheet Horizontally.

  • Click the **Sheet tab.** Check the boxes to include Row and Column Headings and Gridlines.

  • Click **OK** to exit the Page Setup dialog box.

➤ Click the **Print command button** to display the Print dialog box, then click **OK** to print the worksheet.

➤ Press **Ctrl+`** to display the cell formulas. (The left quotation mark is on the same key as the ~.) Widen the cells as necessary to see the complete cell formulas.

➤ Click the **Print button** on the Standard toolbar to print the cell formulas.

➤ Close the workbook. Click **No** when asked whether you want to save the changes, or else you will save the workbook with the settings to print the cell formulas rather than the displayed values.

➤ Exit Excel if you do not want to continue with the next exercise at this time.

THE GRADE BOOK REVISITED

Financial functions are only one of several categories of functions that are included in Excel. Our next example presents an expanded version of the professor's grade book. It introduces several new functions and shows how those functions can aid in the professor's determination of a student's grade. The worksheet shown in Figure 3.9 also illustrates several additional features. Consider:

Statistical functions: The AVERAGE, MAX, and MIN functions are used to compute the statistics on each test for the class as a whole. The range on each test is computed by subtracting the minimum value from the maximum value.

IF function: The IF function conditionally adds a homework bonus of three points to the semester average, prior to determining the letter grade. The bonus is awarded to those students whose homework is "OK." Students whose homework is not "OK" do not receive the bonus.

VLOOKUP function: The expanded grade book converts a student's semester average to a letter grade, in accordance with the table shown in the lower-right portion of the worksheet. A student with an average of 60 to 69 will receive a D, 70 to 79 a C, and so on. Any student with an average less than 60 receives an F.

The Sort Command: The rows within a spreadsheet can be displayed in any sequence by clicking on the appropriate column within the list of students, then clicking the Ascending or Descending sort button on the Standard toolbar. The students in Figure 3.9 are listed alphabetically, but could just as easily have been listed by social security number.

	A	B	C	D	E	F	G	H	I	J
1					Professor's Grade Book					
2										
3	Name	Student ID	Test 1	Test 2	Test 3	Test 4	Test Average	Homework	Semester Average	Grade
4	Adams, John	011-12-2333	80	71	70	84	77.8	Poor	77.8	C
5	Barber, Maryann	444-55-6666	96	98	97	90	94.2	OK	97.2	A
6	Boone, Dan	777-88-9999	78	81	70	78	77.0	OK	80.0	B
7	Borow, Jeff	123-45-6789	65	65	65	60	63.0	OK	66.0	D
8	Brown, James	999-99-9999	92	95	79	80	85.2	OK	88.2	B
9	Carson, Kit	888-88-8888	90	90	90	70	82.0	OK	85.0	B
10	Coulter, Sara	100-00-0000	60	50	40	79	61.6	OK	64.6	D
11	Fegin, Richard	222-22-2222	75	70	65	95	80.0	OK	83.0	B
12	Ford, Judd	200-00-0000	90	90	80	90	88.0	Poor	88.0	B
13	Glassman, Kris	444-44-4444	82	78	62	77	75.2	OK	78.2	C
14	Goodman, Neil	555-55-5555	92	88	65	78	80.2	OK	83.2	B
15	Milgrom, Marion	666-66-6666	94	92	86	84	88.0	OK	91.0	A
16	Moldof, Adam	300-00-0000	92	78	65	84	80.6	OK	83.6	B
17	Smith, Adam	777-77-7777	60	50	65	80	67.0	Poor	67.0	D
18										
19	Average		81.9	78.3	71.4	80.6	HW Bonus:	3	Grading Criteria	
20	Highest Grade		96	98	97	95			(No Curve)	
21	Lowest Grade		60	50	40	60			0	F
22	Range		36	48	57	35			60	D
23									70	C
24	Exam Weights		20%	20%	20%	40%			80	B
25									90	A

Statistical functions   IF function   Table Lookup function

FIGURE 3.9   The Expanded Grade Book

Statistical Functions

The **MAX, MIN,** and **AVERAGE** functions return the highest, lowest, and average values, respectively, from an argument list. The list may include individual cell references, ranges, numeric values, functions, or mathematical expressions (formulas). The **statistical functions** are illustrated in the worksheet of Figure 3.10.

The first example, =AVERAGE(A1:A3), computes the average for cells A1 through A3 by adding the values in the indicated range (70, 80, and 90), then dividing the result by three, to obtain an average of 80. Additional arguments in the form of values and/or cell addresses can be specified within the parentheses; for example, the function =AVERAGE(A1:A3,200), computes the average of cells A1, A2, and A3, and the number 200.

Cells that are empty or cells that contain text values are *not* included in the computation. Thus, since cell A4 is empty, the function =AVERAGE(A1:A4) also returns an average of 80 (240/3). In similar fashion, the function =AVERAGE(A1:A3,A5) includes only three values in its computation (cells A1, A2, and A3), because the text entry in cell A5 is excluded. The results of the MIN and MAX functions are obtained in a comparable way, as indicated in Figure 3.10. Empty cells and text entries are not included in the computation.

The COUNT and COUNTA functions each tally the number of entries in the argument list and are subtly different. The **COUNT function** returns the number of cells containing a numeric entry, including formulas that evaluate to numeric results. The **COUNTA function** includes cells with text as well as numeric values. The functions =COUNT(A1:A3) and =COUNTA(A1:A3) both return a value of 3 as do the two functions =COUNT(A1:A4) and =COUNTA(A1:A4). (Cell A4 is empty and is excluded from the latter computations.) The function =COUNT(A1:A3,A5) also returns a value of 3 because it does not include the text entry in cell A5. However, the function =COUNTA(A1:A3,A5) returns a value of 4 because it includes the text entry in cell A5.

Function	Value
=AVERAGE(A1:A3)	80
=AVERAGE(A1:A3,200)	110
=AVERAGE(A1:A4)	80
=AVERAGE(A1:A3,A5)	80
=MAX(A1:A3)	90
=MAX(A1:A3,200)	200
=MAX(A1:A4)	90
=MAX(A1:A3,A5)	90
=MIN(A1:A3)	70
=MIN(A1:A3,200)	70
=MIN(A1:A4)	70
=MIN(A1:A3,A5)	70
=COUNT(A1:A3)	3
=COUNT(A1:A3,200)	4
=COUNT(A1:A4)	3
=COUNT(A1:A3,A5)	3
=COUNTA(A1:A3)	3
=COUNTA(A1:A3,200)	4
=COUNTA(A1:A4)	3
=COUNTA(A1:A3,A5)	4

Empty and/or text values are not included in the computation

Empty and/or text values are not included in the computation (COUNT)

Empty cells are not included in the computation (COUNTA)

Text values are included in the computation (COUNTA)

Illustrative functions

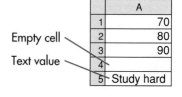

	A
1	70
2	80
3	90
4	
5	Study hard

Empty cell

Text value

The spreadsheet

FIGURE 3.10 Statistical Functions with a Text Entry

Arithmetic Expressions versus Functions

Many worksheet calculations, such as an average or a sum, can be performed in two ways. You can enter a formula such as =(A1+A2+A3)/3, or you can use the equivalent function =AVERAGE(A1:A3). *The use of functions is generally preferable* as shown in Figure 3.11.

The two worksheets in Figure 3.11a may appear equivalent, but the SUM function is superior to the arithmetic expression. This is true despite the fact that the entries in cell A5 of both worksheets return a value of 100.

Consider what happens if a new row is inserted between existing rows 2 and 3, with the entry in the new cell equal to 25 as shown in Figure 3.11b. The **SUM function** adjusts automatically to include the new value (returning a sum of 125) because the SUM function was defined originally for the cell range *A1 through A4*. The new row is inserted within these cells, moving the entry in cell A4 to cell A5, and changing the range to include cell A5.

No such accommodation is made in the arithmetic expression, which was defined to include four *specific* cells rather than a range of cells. The addition of the new row modifies the cell references (since the values in cells A3 and A4 have been moved to cells A4 and A5), and does not include the new row in the adjusted expression.

Similar reasoning holds for deleting a row. Figure 3.11c deletes row two from the *original* worksheets, which moves the entry in cell A4 to cell A3. The SUM function adjusts automatically to =SUM(A1:A3) and returns the value 80. The formula, however, returns an error (to indicate an illegal cell reference) because it is still attempting to add the entries in four cells, one of which no longer exists. In summary, a function expands and contracts to adjust for insertions or deletions, and should be used wherever possible.

#REF!—ILLEGAL CELL REFERENCE

The #REF! error occurs when you refer to a cell that is not valid. The error is displayed whenever Excel is unable to evaluate a formula because of an illegal cell reference. The most common cause of the error is deleting the row, column, or cell that contained the original cell reference.

AutoFill

The **AutoFill capability** is a wonderful shortcut and the fastest way to enter certain series into adjacent cells. In essence, you enter the first value(s) of a series, then drag the fill handle to the adjacent cells that are to contain the remaining values in that series. Excel creates the series for you based on the initial value(s) you supply. If, for example, you wanted the months of the year to appear in 12 successive cells, you would enter January (or Jan) in the first cell, then drag the fill handle over the next 11 cells in the direction you want to fill. Excel will enter the remaining months of the year in those cells.

Excel "guesses" at the type of series you want and fills the cells accordingly. You can type Monday (rather than January), and Excel will return the days of the week. You can enter a text and numeric combination, such as Quarter 1 or 1st Quarter, and Excel will extend the series appropriately. You can also create a numeric series by entering the first two numbers in that series; for example, to enter the years 1990 through 1999, type 1990 and 1991 in the first two cells, select both of these cells, and drag the fill handle in the appropriate direction over the destination range.

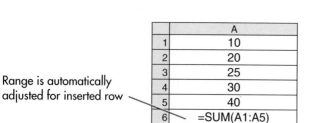

(a) Spreadsheets as Initially Entered

Function → | | A |
|---|---|
| 1 | 10 |
| 2 | 20 |
| 3 | 30 |
| 4 | 40 |
| 5 | =SUM(A1:A4) |

Formula → | | A |
|---|---|
| 1 | 10 |
| 2 | 20 |
| 3 | 30 |
| 4 | 40 |
| 5 | =A1+A2+A3+A4 |

Cell references adjust to follow moved entries

Range is automatically adjusted for inserted row →

	A
1	10
2	20
3	25
4	30
5	40
6	=SUM(A1:A5)

	A
1	10
2	20
3	25
4	30
5	40
6	=A1+A2+A4+A5

(b) Spreadsheets after the Addition of a New Row

#REF! indicates that a referenced cell has been deleted

Range is automatically adjusted for deleted row →

	A
1	10
2	30
3	40
4	=SUM(A1:A3)

	A
1	10
2	30
3	40
4	=A1+#REF!+A2+A3

(c) Spreadsheets after the Deletion of a Row

FIGURE 3.11 Arithmetic Expressions vs. Functions

IF Function

The *IF function* enables decision making to be implemented within a worksheet—for example, a conditional bonus for students whose homework is satisfactory. Students with inferior homework do not get this bonus.

The IF function has three arguments: a condition that is evaluated as true or false, the value to be returned if the condition is true, and the value to be returned if the condition is false. Consider:

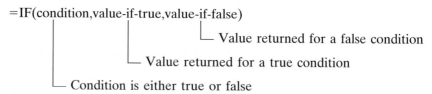

=IF(condition,value-if-true,value-if-false)

— Value returned for a false condition

— Value returned for a true condition

— Condition is either true or false

The IF function returns either the second or third argument, depending on the result of the condition; that is, if the condition is true, the function returns the second argument, whereas if the condition is false, the function returns the third argument.

The condition is based on one of the six *relational operators* in Figure 3.12a. The IF function is illustrated in the worksheet in Figure 3.12b, which is used to create the examples in Figure 3.12c. In every instance the condition is evaluated, then the second or third argument is returned, depending on whether the condition is true or false. The arguments may be numeric (1000 or 2000), a cell reference to display the contents of the specific cell (B1 or B2), a formula (=B1+10 or =B1−10), a function (MAX(B1:B2) or MIN(B1:B2)), or a text entry enclosed in quotation marks ("Go" or "Hold").

Operator	Description
=	Equal to
<>	Not equal to
<	Less than
>	Greater than
<=	Less than or equal to
>=	Greater than or equal to

(a) Relational Operators

	A	B	C
1	10	15	April
2	10	30	May

(b) The Spreadsheet

IF Function	Evaluation	Result
=IF(A1=A2,1000,2000)	10 is equal to 10: TRUE	1000
=IF(A1<>A2,1000,2000)	10 is not equal to 10: FALSE	2000
=IF(A1<>A2,B1,B2)	10 is not equal to 10:FALSE	30
=IF(A1<B2,MAX(B1:B2),MIN(B1:B2))	10 is less than 30: TRUE	30
=IF(A1<A2,B1+10,B1-10)	10 is less than 10:FALSE	5
=IF(A1=A2,C1,C2)	10 is equal to 10: TRUE	April
=IF(SUM(A1:A2)>20,"Go","Hold")	10+10 is greater than 20:FALSE	Hold

(c) Examples

FIGURE 3.12   The IF Function

The IF function is used in the grade book of Figure 3.9 to award a bonus for homework. Students whose homework is "OK" receive the bonus, whereas other students do not. The IF function to implement this logic for the first student is entered in cell H4 as follows:

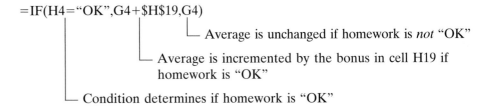

=IF(H4="OK",G4+$H$19,G4)

└─ Average is unchanged if homework is *not* "OK"

└─ Average is incremented by the bonus in cell H19 if homework is "OK"

└─ Condition determines if homework is "OK"

The IF function compares the value in cell H4 (the homework grade) to the literal "OK." If the condition is true (the homework is "OK"), the bonus in cell H19 is added to the student's test average in cell G4. If, however, the condition is false (the homework is not "OK"), the average is unchanged.

The bonus is specified as a cell address rather than a specific value so that the number of bonus points can be easily changed; that is, the professor can make a single change to the worksheet by increasing (decreasing) the bonus in cell H19 and see immediately the effect on every student without having to edit or retype any other formula. An absolute (rather than a relative) reference is used to reference the homework bonus so that when the IF function is copied to the other rows in the column, the address will remain constant. A relative reference, however, was used for the student's homework and semester averages, in cells H4 and G4, because these addresses change from one student to the next.

VLOOKUP Function

Consider, for a moment, how the professor assigns letter grades to students at the end of the semester. He or she computes a test average for each student and conditionally awards the bonus for homework. The professor then determines a letter grade according to a predetermined scale; for example, 90 or above is an A, 80 to 89 is a B, and so on.

The ***VLOOKUP*** (vertical lookup) ***function*** duplicates this process within a worksheet, by assigning an entry to a cell based on a numeric value contained in another cell. The ***HLOOKUP*** (horizontal lookup) ***function*** is similar in concept except that the table is arranged horizontally. In other words, just as the professor knows where on the grading scale a student's numerical average will fall, the VLOOKUP function determines where within a specified table (the grading criteria) a numeric value (a student's average) is found, and retrieves the corresponding entry (the letter grade).

The VLOOKUP function requires three arguments: the numeric value to look up, the range of cells containing the table in which the value is to be looked up, and the column-number within the table that contains the result. These concepts are illustrated in Figure 3.13, which was taken from the expanded grade book in Figure 3.9. The table in Figure 3.13 extends over two columns (I and J), and five rows (21 through 25); that is, the table is located in the range I21:J25. The ***breakpoints*** or matching values (the lowest numeric value for each grade) are contained in column I (the first column in the table) and are in ascending order. The corresponding letter grades are found in column J.

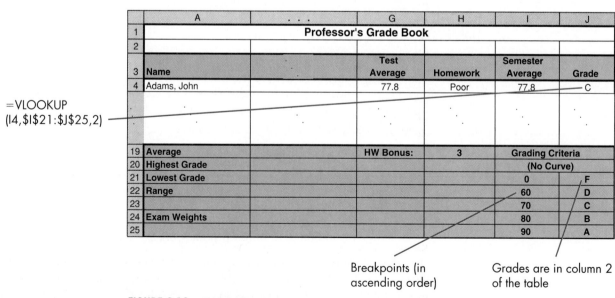

=VLOOKUP
(I4,$I$21:$J$25,2)

	A	. . .	G	H	I	J
1			Professor's Grade Book			
2						
3	Name		Test Average	Homework	Semester Average	Grade
4	Adams, John		77.8	Poor	77.8	C
.		.				
.			.	.	.	.
.		.	.		.	.
19	Average		HW Bonus:	3	Grading Criteria	
20	Highest Grade				(No Curve)	
21	Lowest Grade				0	F
22	Range				60	D
23					70	C
24	Exam Weights				80	B
25					90	A

Breakpoints (in ascending order)

Grades are in column 2 of the table

FIGURE 3.13   Table Lookup Function

The VLOOKUP function in cell J4 determines the letter grade (for John Adams) based on the computed average in cell I4. Consider:

=VLOOKUP(I4,$I$21:$J$25,2)

— The column number containing the letter grade

— The range of the table

— Numeric value to look up (the student's average)

The first argument is the value to look up, which in this example is Adams's computed average, found in cell I4. A relative reference is used so that the address will adjust when the formula is copied to the other rows in the worksheet.

The second argument is the range of the table, found in cells I21 through J25, as explained earlier. Absolute references are specified so that the addresses will not change when the function is copied to determine the letter grades for the other students. The first column in the table (column I in this example) contains the breakpoints, which must be in ascending order.

The third argument indicates the column containing the value to be returned (the letter grades). To determine the letter grade for Adams (whose computed average is 77.8), the VLOOKUP function searches cells I21 through I25 for the largest value less than or equal to 77.8 (the computed average in cell I4). The lookup function finds the number 70 in cell I23. It then retrieves the corresponding letter grade from the second column in that row (cell J23). Adams, with an average of 77.8, is assigned a grade of C.

WORKING WITH LARGE SPREADSHEETS

A large worksheet, such as the extended grade book, can seldom be seen on the monitor in its entirety. It becomes necessary, therefore, to learn how to view the distant parts of a worksheet and/or to keep certain parts of the worksheet in constant view. Figure 3.14 illustrates these concepts.

The specific rows and columns that are displayed are determined by an operation called *scrolling,* which shows different parts of a worksheet at different times. Scrolling enables you to see any portion of the worksheet at the expense of not seeing another portion. The worksheet in Figure 3.14a, for example, displays column J containing the students' grades, but not columns A and B, which contain the students' names and social security numbers. In similar fashion, you can see rows 21 through 25 that display the grading criteria, but you cannot see the column headings, which identify the data in those columns.

Scrolling comes about automatically as the active cell changes and may take place in both horizontal and vertical directions. Clicking the right arrow on the horizontal scroll bar (or pressing the right arrow key when the active cell is already in the rightmost column of the screen) causes the entire screen to move one column to the right. In similar fashion, clicking the down arrow in the vertical scroll bar (or pressing the down arrow key when the active cell is in the bottom row of the screen) causes the entire screen to move down one row.

Freezing Panes

Scrolling brings distant portions of a large worksheet into view, but it also moves the descriptive headings for existing rows and/or columns off the screen. You can, however, retain these headings by freezing panes as shown in Figure 3.14b. The grades and grading criteria are visible as in the previous figure, but so too are the student names at the left of the worksheet and the column headings at the top.

Can't see columns A and B

Can't see rows 1–9

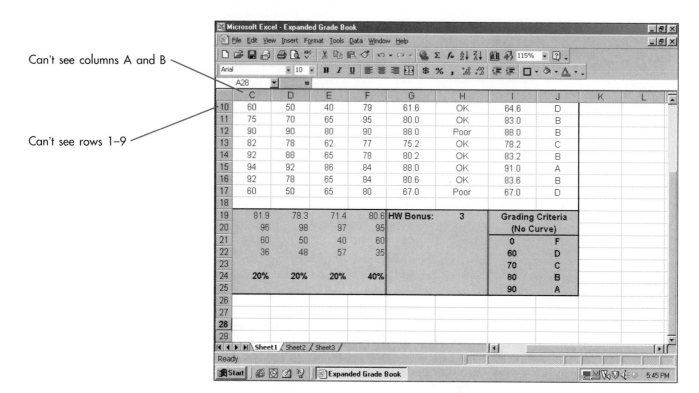

(a) Scrolling

Column A remains on the screen as you scroll (columns B–D have scrolled off the screen)

Rows 1,2, and 3 remain on the screen as you scroll (rows 4–9 have scrolled off the screen)

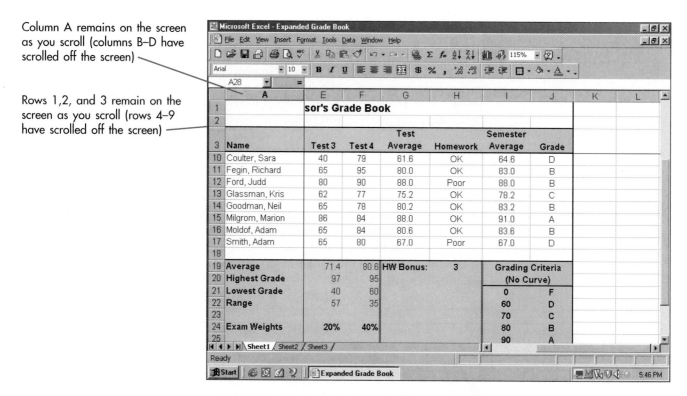

(b) Freezing Panes

FIGURE 3.14   Large Spreadsheets

Look closely at Figure 3.12b and you will see that columns B through D (social security number, test 1, and test 2) are missing, as are rows 4 through 9 (the first six students). You will also notice a horizontal line under row 3, and a vertical line after column A, to indicate that these rows and columns have been frozen. Scrolling still takes place as you move beyond the rightmost column or below the bottom row, but you will always see column A and rows 1, 2, and 3.

The **Freeze Panes command,** in the Window menu, displays the desired rows or columns regardless of the scrolling in effect. It is especially helpful when viewing or entering data in a large worksheet. The rows and/or columns that are frozen are the ones above and to the left of the active cell when the command is issued. You may still access (and edit) cells in the frozen area by clicking the desired cell. The **Unfreeze Panes command** returns to normal scrolling.

Grouping and Outlines

Figure 3.14c illustrates how the records within a worksheet may be grouped within an outline to show different levels of detail with a single click. Look carefully at the worksheet and note the outlining symbols to the left of the student names.

The students have been placed into a group through the **Group and Outline command** in the Data menu. The group is defined by the vertical line; the minus sign at the end of the line indicates all the records within the group are visible. A plus sign (not shown in the figure) is just the opposite and indicates that the group has been collapsed and that the detail information is suppressed. Click the minus sign in the figure, and rows 4 through 17 will disappear from view and a plus sign will appear in place of the minus sign. Click the plus sign and the rows will reappear. There can be up to eight levels of detail (groups within groups).

The Grouping and Outline feature is useful for any type of list in which aggregation or summarization is required. It is illustrated further in a practice problem at the end of the chapter.

Students have been placed into a group

Click the minus sign to collapse the student records

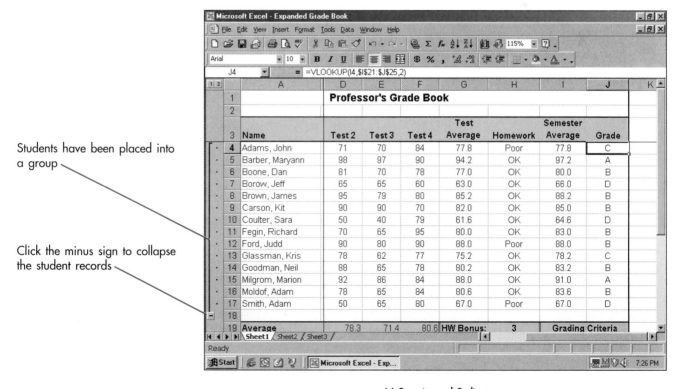

(c) Grouping and Outlines

FIGURE 3.14   Large Spreadsheets (continued)

Scenario Manager

The *Scenario Manager* enables you to evaluate and compare multiple sets of initial conditions and assumptions (scenarios). Each *scenario* represents a different set of what-if conditions that you want to consider in assessing the outcome of a spreadsheet model. The professor, for example, will use the Scenario Manager to evaluate his semester grades with and without a curve.

Figure 3.15 illustrates the use of the Scenario Manager in conjunction with the expanded grade book. Each scenario is stored under its own name, such as "Curve" and "No Curve" as shown in Figure 3.15a. Each scenario is comprised of a set of cells whose values vary from scenario to scenario, as well as the values for those cells. Figure 3.15b shows the scenario when no curve is in effect and contains the values for the homework bonus and the breakpoints for the grade distribution table. Figure 3.15c displays a different scenario in which the professor increases the homework bonus and introduces a curve in computing the grades for the class.

Once the individual scenarios have been defined, you can display the worksheet under any scenario by clicking the Show button in the Scenario Manager dialog box. The professor can consider the outcome (the grades assigned to individual students) under the different scenarios and arrive at the best possible decision (the grading criteria to use).

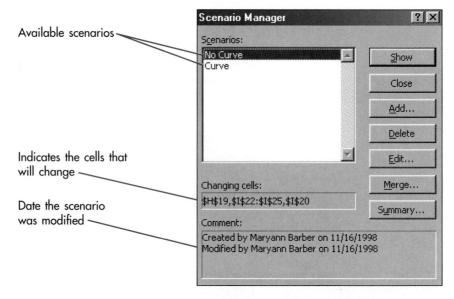

(a) Existing Scenarios

(b) Scenario Values (No Curve)

(c) Scenario Values (Curve)

FIGURE 3.15   Scenario Manager

Objective: To develop the expanded grade book; to use statistical (AVERAGE, MAX, and MIN) and logical (IF and VLOOKUP) functions; to demonstrate scrolling and the Freeze Panes command; to illustrate the AutoFill capability and the Scenario Manager. Use Figure 3.16 as a guide in the exercise.

STEP 1: Open the Extended Grade Book

➤ Pull down the **File menu** and click **Open** (or click the **Open button** on the Standard toolbar) to display the Open dialog box.

➤ Click the **drop-down arrow** on the Look In list box. Click the appropriate drive, drive C or drive A, depending on the location of your data. Double click the **Exploring Excel folder** to make it the active folder.

➤ Double click **Expanded Grade Book** to open the workbook.

➤ Pull down the **File menu** and save the workbook as **Finished Expanded Grade Book** so that you can always return to the original workbook if necessary.

SORTING THE STUDENT LIST

The students are listed in the gradebook in alphabetical order, but you can rearrange the list according to any other field, such as the test average. Click in the row containing the data for any student, click in the column on which you want to sort, then click the Ascending or Descending Sort button on the Standard toolbar. Click the Undo command if the result is different from what you intended.

STEP 2: The Fill Handle

➤ Click in **cell C3,** the cell containing the label Test 1. Point to the **fill handle** in the lower-right corner, as shown in Figure 3.16a. The mouse pointer changes to a thin crosshair.

➤ Click and drag the **fill handle** over cells **D3, E3,** and **F3** (a ScreenTip shows the projected result in cell F3), then release the mouse. Cells D3, E3, and F3 now contain the labels Test 2, Test 3, and Test 4, respectively.

THE AUTOFILL CAPABILITY

The AutoFill capability is a wonderful shortcut and the fastest way to enter certain series into contiguous cells. In essence, you enter the starting value(s) in a series, then drag the fill handle to the adjacent cells. Excel completes the series based on the initial value; e.g., type January (or Jan) into a cell, then drag the fill handle over the desired number of cells in the direction you want to fill. Excel will enter the appropriate months in sequence. You can type Monday (or Mon) for the days of the week or Quarter 1 to get to Quarter 2, etc.

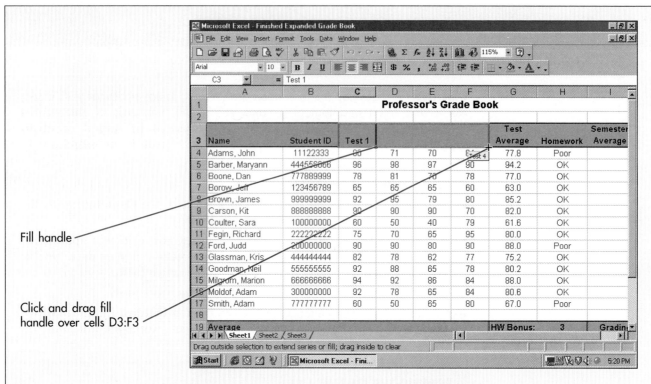

Fill handle

Click and drag fill handle over cells D3:F3

(a) The Fill Handle (step 2)

FIGURE 3.16 Hands-on Exercise 3

STEP 3: Format the Social Security Numbers

➤ Click and drag to select cells **B4** through **B17,** the cells containing the unformatted social security numbers.

➤ Point to the selected cells and click the **right mouse button** to display a shortcut menu. Click the **Format Cells command,** click the **Number tab,** then click **Special** in the Category list box.

➤ Click **Social Security Number** in the Type box, then click **OK** to accept the formatting and close the Format Cells dialog box. The social security numbers are displayed with hyphens.

➤ Save the workbook.

CREATE YOUR OWN STYLE

You can save the complete set of formatting specifications that have been applied to a specific cell as a style, then apply that formatting elsewhere in the worksheet with a simple click. Click in the cell that contains the desired formatting, pull down the Format menu and click the Style command to display the Style dialog box. Enter a name for your style (e.g., Blue Borders), then click OK to accept the style and close the dialog box. To apply the style, click in another cell, pull down the Format menu, click the Style command, then choose the newly created style from the Style Name list box.

STEP 4: The Freeze Panes Command

➤ Press **Ctrl+Home** to move to cell A1. Click the **right arrow** on the horizontal scroll bar until column A scrolls off the screen. Cell A1 is still the active cell, because scrolling with the mouse does not change the active cell.

➤ Press **Ctrl+Home.** Press the **right arrow key** until column A scrolls off the screen. The active cell changes as you scroll with the keyboard.

➤ Press **Ctrl+Home** again, then click in **cell B4.** Pull down the **Window menu.** Click **Freeze Panes** as shown in Figure 3.16b. You will see a line to the right of column A and below row 3.

➤ Click the **right arrow** on the horizontal scroll bar (or press the **right arrow key**) repeatedly until column J is visible. Note that column A is visible (frozen), but that one or more columns are not shown.

➤ Click the **down arrow** on the vertical scroll bar (or press the **down arrow key**) repeatedly until row 25 is visible. Note that rows one through three are visible (frozen), but that one or more rows are not shown.

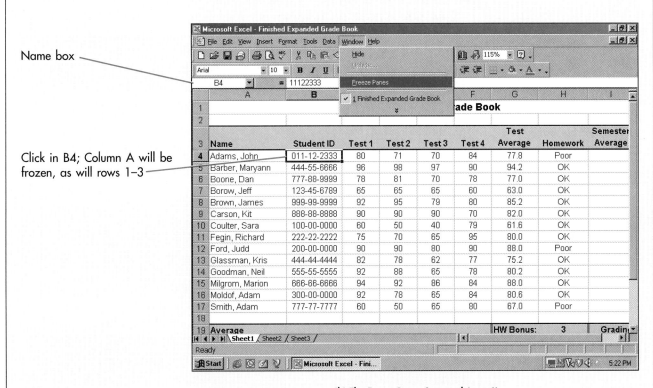

Name box

Click in B4; Column A will be frozen, as will rows 1–3

(b) The Freeze Panes Command (step 4)

FIGURE 3.16   Hands-on Exercise 3 (continued)

GO TO A SPECIFIC CELL

Ctrl+Home and Ctrl+End will take you to the upper-left and bottom-right cells within a worksheet, but how do you get to a specific cell? One way is to click in the Name box (to the left of the formula bar), enter the cell reference (e.g., K250), and press the enter key. You can also press the F5 key to display the Go To dialog box, enter the name of the cell in the Reference text box, then press enter to go directly to the cell.

STEP 5: The IF Function

➤ Scroll until Column I is visible on the screen. Click in **cell I4.**

➤ Click the **Paste Function button** on the Standard toolbar. Click **Logical** in the Function category list box. Click **IF** in the Function name list box, then click **OK** to display the Formula Palette in Figure 3.16c.

➤ You can enter the arguments directly, or you can use pointing as follows:

- Click the **Logical_test** text box. Click **cell H4** in the worksheet. (You may need to click and drag the top border of the Formula Palette of the dialog box to move it out of the way.) Type **="OK"** to complete the logical test.

- Click the **Value_if_true** text box. Click **cell G4** in the worksheet, type a **plus sign,** click **cell H19** in the worksheet (scrolling if necessary), and finally press the **F4 key** (see boxed tip) to convert the reference to cell H19 to an absolute reference ($H$19).

- Click the **Value_if_false** text box. Click **cell G4** in the worksheet.

➤ Check that the dialog box on your worksheet matches the one in Figure 3.16c. Click **OK** to insert the function into your worksheet. Save the workbook.

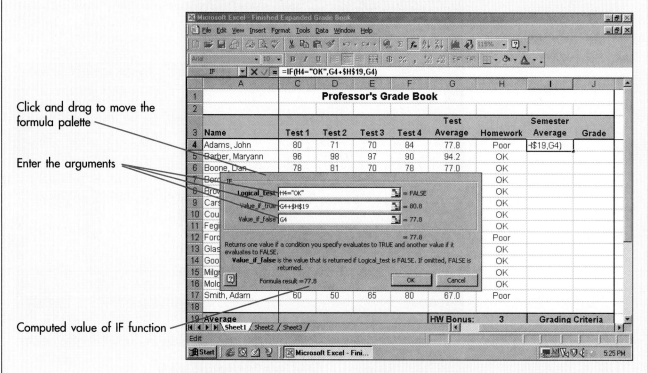

Click and drag to move the formula palette

Enter the arguments

Computed value of IF function

(c) The IF Function (step 5)

FIGURE 3.16   Hands-on Exercise 3 (continued)

THE F4 KEY

The F4 key cycles through relative, absolute, and mixed addresses. Click on any reference within the formula bar; for example, click on A1 in the formula =A1+A2. Press the F4 key once, and it changes to an absolute reference. Press the F4 key a second time, and it becomes a mixed reference, A$1; press it again, and it is a different mixed reference, $A1. Press the F4 key a fourth time, and return to the original relative address, A1.

STEP 6: The VLOOKUP Function

➤ Click in **cell J4.** Click the **Paste Function button** on the Standard toolbar. Click **Lookup & Reference** in the Function category list box. Scroll in the Function name list box until you can select **VLOOKUP.** Click **OK** to display the Formula Palette in Figure 3.16d.

➤ Enter the arguments for the VLOOKUP function as shown in the figure. You can enter the arguments directly, or you can use pointing as follows:

- Click the **Lookup_value** text box. Click **cell I4** in the worksheet.
- Click the **Table_array** text box. Click **cell I21** and drag to cell **J25** (scrolling if necessary). Press the **F4 key** to convert to an absolute reference.
- Click the **Col_index_num** text box. Type **2.**

➤ Check that the dialog box on your worksheet matches the one in Figure 3.16d. Make corrections as necessary. Click **OK** to insert the function into your worksheet. Save the workbook.

Paste Function button ————

Enter the arguments ————

Computed value of VLOOKUP function ————

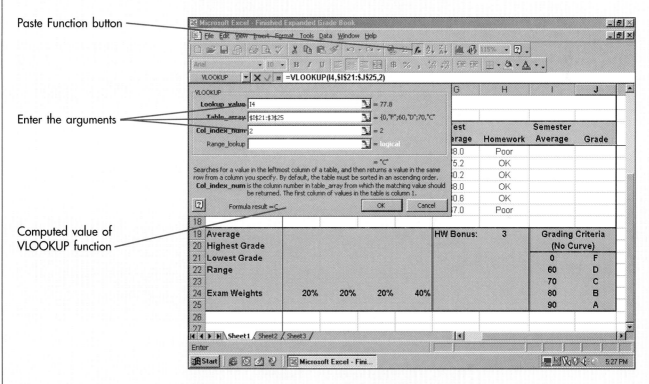

(d) The VLOOKUP Function (step 6)

FIGURE 3.16   Hands-on Exercise 3 (continued)

THE COLLAPSE DIALOG BUTTON

You can enter a cell reference in one of two ways: you can type it directly in the Formula Palette, or click the cell in the worksheet. The Formula Palette typically hides the necessary cell, however, in which case you can click the Collapse Dialog button (which appears to the right of any parameter within the dialog box). This collapses (hides) the Formula Palette so that you can click the underlying cell, which is now visible. Click the Collapse Dialog button a second time to display the entire dialog box.

STEP 7: Copy the IF and VLOOKUP Functions

➤ If necessary, scroll to the top of the worksheet. Select cells **I4** and **J4** as in Figure 3.16e.

➤ Point to the **fill handle** in the lower-right corner of the selected range. The mouse pointer changes to a thin crosshair.

➤ Drag the **fill handle** over cells **I5** through **J17.** A border appears, indicating the destination range as shown in Figure 3.16e. Release the mouse to complete the copy operation. If you have done everything correctly, Adam Smith should have a grade of D based on a semester average of 67. Format the semester averages in column I to one decimal place.

➤ Save the workbook.

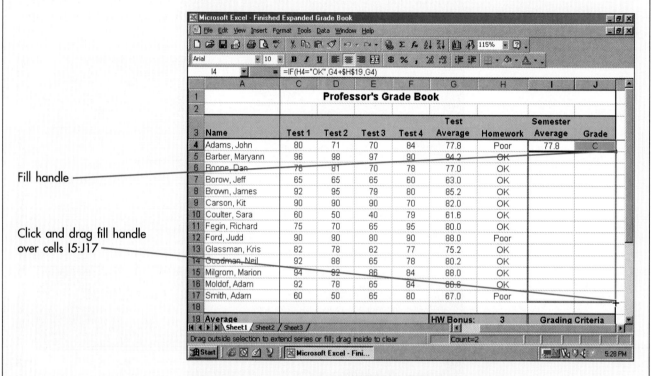

(e) Copy the IF and VLOOKUP Functions (step 7)

FIGURE 3.16   Hands-on Exercise 3 (continued)

STEP 8: Statistical Functions

➤ Scroll until you can click in **cell C19.** Type **=AVERAGE(C4:C17).** Press **enter.** Cell C19 should display 81.857. Format the average to one decimal place.

➤ Click in **cell C20.** Type **=MAX(C4:C17).** Press **enter.** Cell C20 should display a value of 96.

➤ Click in **cell C21.** Type **=MIN(C4:C17).** Press **enter.** Cell C21 should display a value of 60.

➤ Click in **cell C22.** Type **=C20-C21.** Press **enter.** Cell C22 should display 36.

STEP 9: Copy the Statistical Functions

➤ Select cells **C19** through **C22** as shown in Figure 3.16f. Click the **right mouse button** to display the shortcut menu shown in the figure. Click **Copy.** A moving border appears around the selected cells.

➤ Drag the mouse over cells **D19** through **F19.** Click the **Paste button** on the Standard toolbar to complete the copy operation, then press **Esc** to remove the moving border.

➤ If you have done everything correctly, cells F19, F20, F21, and F22 will display 80.6, 95, 60, and 35, respectively.

➤ Save the workbook.

Point to selection and click right mouse button to display shortcut menu

Select cells C19:C22

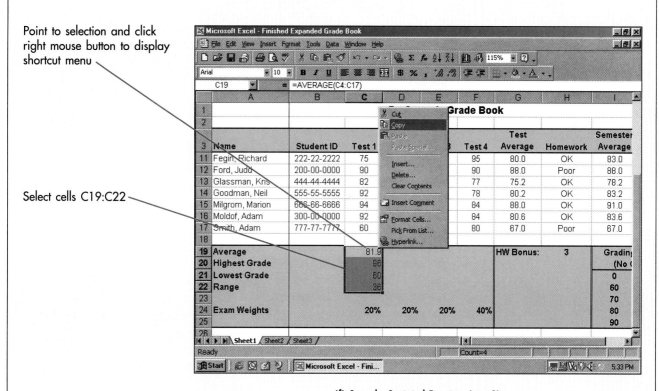

(f) Copy the Statistical Functions (step 9)

FIGURE 3.16   Hands-on Exercise 3 (continued)

STEP 10: Create the No Curve Scenario

➤ Click in **cell H19.** Pull down the **Tools menu.** Click **Scenarios** to display the Scenario Manager dialog box. Click the **Add command button** to display the Add Scenario dialog box in Figure 3.16g.

➤ Type **No Curve** in the Scenario Name text box.

➤ Click in the **Changing Cells text box** to the right of H19. Cell H19 (the active cell) is already entered as the first cell in the scenario.

➤ Type a **comma,** then click and drag to select cells **I22** through **I25** (the cells containing the breakpoints for the grade distribution table). Scroll to these cells if necessary.

➤ Type another **comma,** then click in **cell I20.** The Add Scenarios dialog box should match the display in Figure 3.16g. Click **OK.**

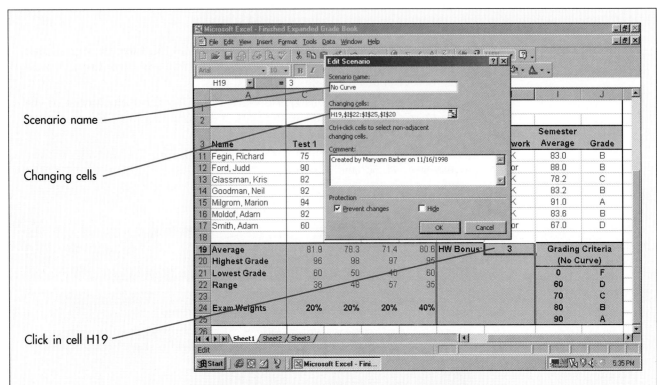

Scenario name

Changing cells

Click in cell H19

(g) Create the No Curve Scenario (step 10)

FIGURE 3.16   Hands-on Exercise 3 (continued)

➤ You should see the Scenario Values dialog box with the values of this scenario (No Curve) already entered. Only the first five cells are displayed, and you must scroll to see the others.

➤ Click **OK** to complete the No Curve scenario and close the Scenario Values dialog box.

STEP 11: Add the Curve Scenario

➤ The Scenario Manager dialog box should still be open. Click the **Add button** to add a second scenario and display the Add Scenario dialog box.

➤ Type **Curve** in the Scenario name text box. The changing cells are already entered and match the changing cells in the No Curve scenario. Click **OK.**

➤ Enter **5** as the new value for cell H19 (the bonus for homework). Press the **Tab key** to move to the text box for the next cell. Enter 55, 65, 76, and 88 as the values for cells I22 through I25, respectively.

➤ Enter **(Curve)** as the value for cell I20. Click **OK** to complete the scenario and close the Scenario Values dialog box.

INCLUDE THE SCENARIO NAME

A scenario is composed of one or more changing cells whose values you want to consider in evaluating the outcome of a spreadsheet model. We find it useful to include an additional cell within the scenario that contains the name of the scenario itself, so that the scenario name appears within the worksheet when the worksheet is printed.

STEP 12: View the Scenarios

➤ The Scenario Manager dialog box should still be open as shown in Figure 3.16h. (If necessary, pull down the **Tools menu** and click the **Scenarios command** to reopen the Scenario Manager.) There should be two scenarios listed, No Curve and Curve, corresponding to the scenarios that were just created.

➤ Select the **Curve** scenario, then click the **Show button** to display the grade book under this scenario. Some, but not all, of the grades will change under the easier criteria. Ford, for example, goes from a B to an A.

➤ Select the **No Curve** scenario. Click the **Show button** to display the grades under the initial set of assumptions. Click the **Close button** and review the changes. Ford goes from an A back to a B.

➤ Show the grades under the **Curve** scenario a second time, then click the **Close button** to exit the Scenario Manager. Save the workbook.

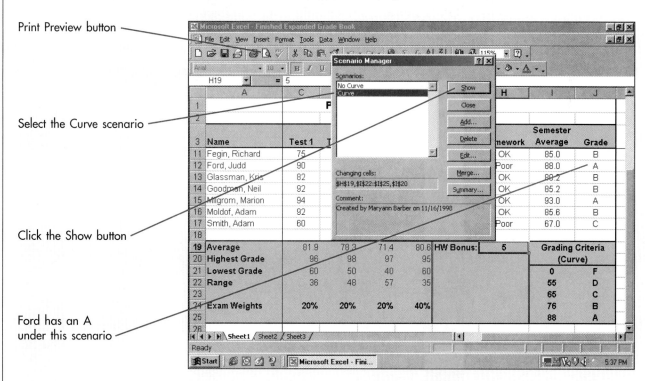

Print Preview button

Select the Curve scenario

Click the Show button

Ford has an A under this scenario

(h) View the Scenarios (step 12)

FIGURE 3.16   Hands-on Exercise 3 (continued)

THE SCENARIO MANAGER LIST BOX

The Scenario Manager List Box enables you to select a scenario directly from a toolbar. Point to any toolbar, click the right mouse button to display a shortcut menu, then click Customize to display the Customize dialog box. Click the Commands tab, click Tools in the Categories list box, then scroll until you can click and drag the Scenario list box to an empty space within a toolbar. Close the dialog box. Click the down arrow on the Scenario list box, which now appears on the toolbar, to choose from the scenarios that have been defined within the current workbook.

STEP 13: The Print Preview Command

➤ Add your name and title (**Grading Assistant**) in cells G26 and G27. Save the workbook.

➤ Pull down the **File menu.** Click **Page Setup** to display the Page Setup dialog box. Click the **Page tab.** Click the **Landscape option button.** Click the option button to **Fit to 1 page.**

➤ Click the **Margins tab.** Check the box to center the worksheet horizontally on the page. Click the **Sheet tab.** Check the boxes for **Row and Column Headings** and for **Gridlines.**

➤ Click the **Print Preview button** to display the completed spreadsheet in Figure 3.16i. Click the **Print button** and click **OK** to print the workbook.

➤ Press **Ctrl+´** to show the cell formulas rather than the displayed values. Click the **Print Preview button** as previously, click the **Setup button** (within the Print Preview window), then make the necessary changes to show the cell formulas on a single page.

➤ Print the worksheet with the cell formulas. Exit Excel.

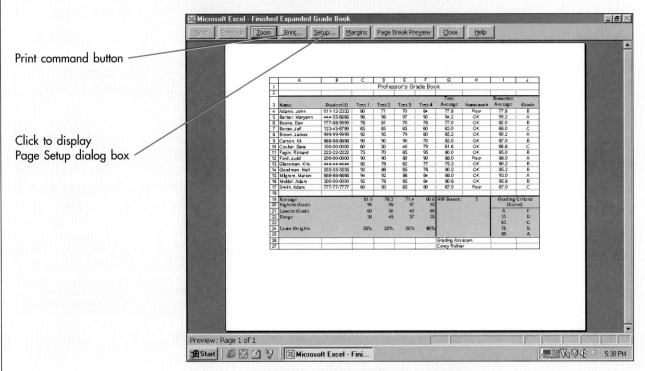

Print command button

Click to display
Page Setup dialog box

(i) The Print Preview Command (step 13)

FIGURE 3.16   Hands-on Exercise 3 (continued)

PRINT ONLY WHAT YOU NEED

Why print an entire spreadsheet if you need to see only a portion of it? Click and drag to select the desired area, pull down the File menu, click the Print command, then choose the option to print the selection, as opposed to the entire worksheet or workbook. You can also set a print area that will print the selected cells automatically, without having to specify the selection. See exercise 5 at the end of the chapter.

Excel contains several categories of built-in functions. The PMT function computes the periodic payment for a loan based on three arguments (the interest rate per period, the number of periods, and the amount of the loan). The IPMT and PPMT functions determine the amount of each payment that goes toward interest and principal, respectively.

Statistical functions were also discussed. The AVERAGE, MAX, and MIN functions return the average, highest, and lowest values in the argument list. The COUNT function returns the number of cells with numeric entries. The COUNTA function displays the number of cells with numeric and/or text entries.

The IF, VLOOKUP, and HLOOKUP functions implement decision making within a worksheet. The IF function has three arguments: a condition, which is evaluated as true or false; a value if the test is true; and a value if the test is false. The VLOOKUP and HLOOKUP functions also have three arguments: the numeric value to look up, the range of cells containing the table, and the column or row number within the table that contains the result.

The hands-on exercises introduced several techniques to make you more proficient. The fill handle is used to copy a cell or group of cells to a range of adjacent cells. Pointing is a more accurate way to enter a cell reference into a formula as it uses the mouse or arrow keys to select the cell as you build the formula. The AutoFill capability creates a series based on the initial value(s) you supply.

Scrolling enables you to view any portion of a large worksheet but moves the labels for existing rows and/or columns off the screen. The Freeze Panes command keeps the row and/or column headings on the screen while scrolling in a large worksheet. The Group and Outline command groups the records in a worksheet to show different levels of detail.

A spreadsheet is first and foremost a tool for decision making, and thus Excel includes several commands to aid in that process. The Goal Seek command lets you enter the desired end result of a spreadsheet model (such as the monthly payment on a car loan) and determines the input (the price of the car) necessary to produce that result. The Scenario Manager enables you to specify multiple sets of assumptions (scenarios), and see at a glance the results of any scenario.

The assumptions and initial conditions in a spreadsheet should be clearly labeled and set apart from the rest of the worksheet. This facilitates change and reduces the chance for error.

KEY WORDS AND CONCEPTS

=AVERAGE	Absolute reference	Pointing
=COUNT	Arguments	Point mode
=COUNTA	Assumptions	Relational operator
=HLOOKUP	AutoFill capability	Relative reference
=IF	Breakpoint	Scenario
=IPMT	Custom series	Scenario Manager
=MAX	Enter mode	Scrolling
=MIN	Fill handle	Spell check
=PMT	Freeze Panes command	Statistical functions
=PPMT	Function	Template
=SUM	Goal Seek command	Unfreeze Panes command
=VLOOKUP	Group and Outline command	

1. Which of the following options may be used to print a large worksheet?
   (a) Landscape orientation
   (b) Scaling
   (c) Reduced margins
   (d) All of the above

2. If the results of a formula contain more characters than can be displayed according to the present format and cell width,
   (a) The extra characters will be truncated under all circumstances
   (b) All of the characters will be displayed if the cell to the right is empty
   (c) A series of asterisks will be displayed
   (d) A series of pound signs will be displayed

3. Which cell—A1, A2, or A3—will contain the amount of the loan, given the function =PMT(A1,A2,A3)?
   (a) A1
   (b) A2
   (c) A3
   (d) Impossible to determine

4. Which of the following will compute the average of the values in cells D2, D3, and D4?
   (a) The function =AVERAGE(D2:D4)
   (b) The function =AVERAGE(D2,D4)
   (c) Both (a) and (b)
   (d) Neither (a) nor (b)

5. The function =IF(A1>A2,A1+A2,A1*A2) returns
   (a) The product of cells A1 and A2 if cell A1 is greater than A2
   (b) The sum of cells A1 and A2 if cell A1 is less than A2
   (c) Both (a) and (b)
   (d) Neither (a) nor (b)

6. Which of the following is the preferred way to sum the values contained in cells A1 to A4?
   (a) =SUM(A1:A4)
   (b) =A1+A2+A3+A4
   (c) Either (a) or (b) is equally good
   (d) Neither (a) nor (b) is correct

7. Which of the following will return the highest and lowest arguments from a list of arguments?
   (a) HIGH/LOW
   (b) LARGEST/SMALLEST
   (c) MAX/MIN
   (d) All of the above

8. Which of the following is a *required* technique to develop the worksheet for the mortgage analysis?
   (a) Pointing
   (b) Copying with the fill handle
   (c) Both (a) and (b)
   (d) Neither (a) nor (b)

9. Given that cells B6, C6, and D6 contain the numbers 10, 20, and 30, respectively, what value will be returned by the function =IF(B6>10,C6*2,D6*3)?
   (a) 10
   (b) 40
   (c) 60
   (d) 90

10. Which of the following is not an input to the Goal Seek command?
    (a) The cell containing the end result
    (b) The desired value of the end result
    (c) The cell whose value will change to reach the end result
    (d) The value of the input cell that is required to reach the end result

11. Each scenario in the Scenario Manager:
    (a) Is stored in a separate worksheet
    (b) Contains the value of a single assumption or input condition
    (c) Both (a) and (b)
    (d) Neither (a) nor (b)

12. Which function will return the number of nonempty cells in the range A2 through A6, including in the result cells that contain text as well as numeric entries?
    (a) =COUNT(A2:A6)
    (b) =COUNTA(A2:A6)
    (c) =COUNT(A2,A6)
    (d) =COUNTA(A2,A6)

13. What happens if you select a range, then press the right (alternate) mouse button?
    (a) The range will be deselected
    (b) Nothing; that is, the button has no effect
    (c) The Edit and Format menus will be displayed in their entirety
    (d) A shortcut menu with commands from both the Edit and Format menus will be displayed

14. The worksheet displayed in the monitor shows columns A and B, skips columns D, E, and F, then displays columns G, H, I, J, and K. What is the most likely explanation for the missing columns?
    (a) The columns were previously deleted
    (b) The columns are empty and thus are automatically hidden from view
    (c) Either (a) or (b) is a satisfactory explanation
    (d) Neither (a) nor (b) is a likely reason

15. Given the function =VLOOKUP(C6,D12:F18,3)
    (a) The entries in cells D12 through D18 are in ascending order
    (b) The entries in cells D12 through D18 are in descending order
    (c) The entries in cells F12 through F18 are in ascending order
    (d) The entries in cells F12 through F18 are in descending order

ANSWERS

1. d	**6.** a	**11.** d
2. d	**7.** c	**12.** b
3. c	**8.** d	**13.** d
4. a	**9.** d	**14.** d
5. d	**10.** d	**15.** a

PRACTICE WITH EXCEL 2000

1. Startup Airlines: The spreadsheet in Figure 3.17 is used by a new airline to calculate the fuel requirements and associated cost for its available flights. The airline has only two types of planes, B27s and DC-9s. The fuel needed for any given flight depends on the aircraft and number of flying hours; for example, a five-hour flight in a DC-9 can be expected to use 40,000 gallons. In addition, the plane must carry an additional 10% of the required fuel to maintain a holding pattern (4,000 gallons in this example) and an additional 20% as reserve (8,000 gallons in this example).

   Retrieve the partially completed *Chapter 3 Practice 1* from the data disk and save it as *Chapter 3 Practice 1 Solution*. Compute the fuel necessary for the listed flights based on a fuel price of $1.00 per gallon. Your worksheet should be completely flexible and amenable to change; that is, the hourly fuel requirements, price per gallon, holding and reserve percentages are all subject to change at a moment's notice. Thus, all formulas in the body of the worksheet should be based on the "fuel facts" in rows 11 through 14.

   After completing the cell formulas, format the spreadsheet as you see fit or follow the formatting in our figure. Add your name somewhere in the worksheet, then print the completed worksheet and cell formulas, and submit the assignment to your instructor.

	A	B	C	D	E	F	G	H
1				**Fuel Estimates**				
2								
3	**Plane**	**Flight**	**Flying Hours**	**Flying Fuel**	**Reserve Fuel**	**Holding Fuel**	**Total Fuel Needed**	**Estimated Fuel Cost**
4	Boeing-727	MIA-JFK	2.75	27,500	5,500	2,750	35,750	$35,750
5	DC-9	MIA-ATL	1.25	10,000	2,000	1,000	13,000	$13,000
6	Boeing-727	MIA-IAH	2.25	22,500	4,500	2,250	29,250	$29,250
7	Boeing-727	MIA-LAX	5.5	55,000	11,000	5,500	71,500	$71,500
8	DC-9	MIA-MSY	1.5	12,000	2,400	1,200	15,600	$15,600
9		Totals	13.25	127,000	25,400	12,700	165,100	$165,100
10								
11	**Fuel Facts:**							
12	Gallons per hour: Boeing-727		10,000			% of Flying Fuel required for:		
13	Gallons per hour: DC-9		8,000			Reserve Fuel		20%
14	Fuel cost per gallon		$1.00			Holding Fuel		10%

FIGURE 3.17   Startup Airlines (Exercise 1)

2. A partially completed version of the worksheet in Figure 3.18 can be found on the data disk as *Chapter 3 Practice 2*. To complete the spreadsheet, you need to understand the discount policy, which states that a discount is given if the total sale is equal to or greater than the discount threshold. (The amount of the discount is the total sale multiplied by the discount percentage.)

Complete the worksheet in Figure 3.18, then create two additional scenarios for different selling strategies. In one scenario lower the discount threshold and discount percentage to $3000 and 12%, respectively. Increase these values in a second scenario to $10,000 and 20%. Print all three scenarios and submit the completed assignment.

	A	B	C	D	E	F	G	H	I
1					Hot Spot Software Distributors				
2					Miami, Florida				
3									
4	Customer Name	Program	Current Price	Units Sold	Total Sale	Amount of Discount	Discounted Total	Sales Tax	Amount Due
5	AAA Software Sales	Norton Utilities	$116.99	35	$4,094.65	$0.00	$4,094.65	$266.15	$4,360.80
6	CompuSoft, Inc.	Microsoft Office 2000	$317.95	45	$14,307.75	$2,146.16	$12,161.59	$790.50	$12,952.09
7	Kings Bay Software	Adobe Photoshop	$159.55	15	$2,393.25	$0.00	$2,393.25	$155.56	$2,548.81
8	MicroSales, Inc	Quicken Deluxe	$59.99	30	$1,799.70	$0.00	$1,799.70	$116.98	$1,916.68
9	PC and Me Software	Microsoft Office 2000	$317.95	17	$5,405.15	$810.77	$4,594.38	$298.63	$4,893.01
10	Personal Software Sales	Quicken Deluxe	$59.99	30	$1,799.70	$0.00	$1,799.70	$116.98	$1,916.68
11	Service Software	Adobe Photoshop	$159.99	35	$5,599.65	$839.95	$4,759.70	$309.38	$5,069.08
12	Software and More	Norton Utilities	$116.99	50	$5,849.50	$877.43	$4,972.08	$323.18	$5,295.26
13	Software To Go	Norton Utilities	$116.99	35	$4,094.65	$0.00	$4,094.65	$266.15	$4,360.80
14	Unique Software Sales	Microsoft Office 2000	$317.95	50	$15,897.50	$2,384.63	$13,512.88	$878.34	$14,391.21
15									
16	Discount threshold	$5,000.00					Number of customers		10
17	Discount percentage	15.0%					Highest current price		$317.95
18	Sales tax	6.5%					Fewest units sold		15
19							Average discount		$705.89
20							Total amount due		$57,704.43

FIGURE 3.18 Spreadsheet (Exercise 2)

3. Object Linking and Embedding: Figure 3.19 extends the analysis of a car loan to include monthly expenditures for gas, insurance, and maintenance. It also includes an IF function in cell B13 that compares the total monthly cost to $500 (the maximum you can afford), and prints "Yes" or "No" depending on the answer. You can also use the Insert Picture command to insert a picture of the car. (The Microsoft Clip Gallery has a picture of a car, but we chose our picture from outside the gallery.) Add your name somewhere in the worksheet, then print the completed worksheet and submit it to your instructor.

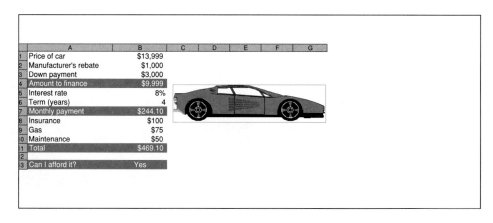

FIGURE 3.19 Object Linking and Embedding (Exercise 3)

4. Grouping and Outlines: The Grouping and Outline feature is ideal with any type of list in which aggregation or summarization is required. The capability is illustrated in Figure 3.20, which displays a list of transactions for salespersons at the Coral Park Auto Mall.
   a. Open the partially completed workbook, *Chapter 3 Practice 4,* which contains the individual transactions. Save the workbook as *Chapter 3 Practice 4 Solution.*
   b. Move to the bottom of the list and add two transactions for yourself in the amounts of $20,000 and $25,000. Use today's date for both transactions. Enter the date by typing just the month and day; for example 2/27 to enter February 27 of the current year. Excel changes the formatting automatically.
   c. Click in either cell that contains your name and click the Sort Ascending button on the Standard toolbar. The transactions are now arranged in alphabetical order by salesperson.
   d. Pull down the Data menu and click the Subtotals command to display the Subtotals dialog box. Check that the subtotals will be computed at each change in salesperson, using the Sum function, and the subtotal will be added to the Amount field. Click OK. If the subtotals are not correct, it is most likely because you forgot to sort the list. Click the Undo button and repeat the earlier step to place the transactions in alphabetical order by salesperson.
   e. Complete the worksheet by formatting the entries in rows 1 and 3 to match our figure. Click in any cell that contains a total in column A, click the Format Painter button on the Formatting toolbar, then copy that format to the column headings in row 3. Click in cell A1, click and drag to select cells A1 through A3, then click the Merge and Center button. Change the font to 14 point Arial bold.
   f. Print the worksheet as it appears in Figure 3.20. Click the Level 2 button to outline the data (i.e., to omit the detail transactions and show only the salesperson total). Print the worksheet a second time in this format.
   g. Submit both worksheets to your instructor.

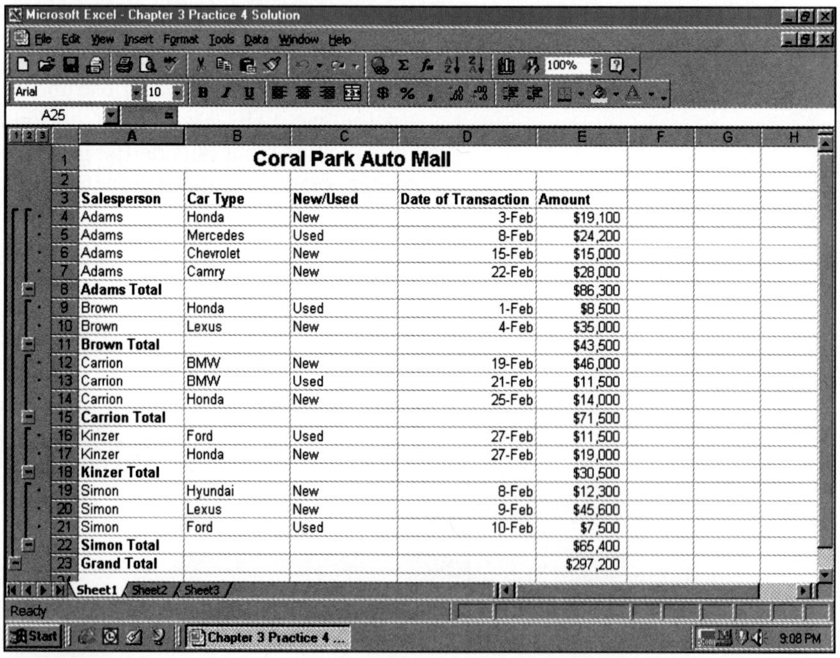

Coral Park Auto Mall

Salesperson	Car Type	New/Used	Date of Transaction	Amount
Adams	Honda	New	3-Feb	$19,100
Adams	Mercedes	Used	8-Feb	$24,200
Adams	Chevrolet	New	15-Feb	$15,000
Adams	Camry	New	22-Feb	$28,000
Adams Total				$86,300
Brown	Honda	Used	1-Feb	$8,500
Brown	Lexus	New	4-Feb	$35,000
Brown Total				$43,500
Carrion	BMW	New	19-Feb	$46,000
Carrion	BMW	Used	21-Feb	$11,500
Carrion	Honda	New	25-Feb	$14,000
Carrion Total				$71,500
Kinzer	Ford	Used	27-Feb	$11,500
Kinzer	Honda	New	27-Feb	$19,000
Kinzer Total				$30,500
Simon	Hyundai	New	8-Feb	$12,300
Simon	Lexus	New	9-Feb	$45,600
Simon	Ford	Used	10-Feb	$7,500
Simon Total				$65,400
Grand Total				$297,200

FIGURE 3.20 **Grouping and Outlines (Exercise 4)**

5. The Amortization Table: The worksheet in Figure 3.21 illustrates the use of three different financial functions to compute the amortization (payoff) schedule for a loan. The top portion contains the input values on which the worksheet is based, as well as some fancy formatting. Follow these instructions:

a. Enter the labels in cells B3:B6, the associated parameters in cells D3:D5, and the PMT function (based on the entries in cells D3:D5) in cell D6.

b. Enter the labels in row 8. Click in cell D9 and enter the formula =D3.

c. Type the numbers 1 and 2 in cells A10 and A11, respectively. Select both cells, then click and drag the fill handle to cell until you reach the number 360 (cell A369).

d. Enter the appropriate IPMT and PPMT functions in cells B10 and C10, respectively. Use the Paste Function button to create these entries so that you will see the nature of each argument.

e. Compute the balance of the loan after the first payment in cell D10. The balance is equal to the value in cell D9 minus the amount of the payment that went toward principal (cell C10).

f. Copy the entries in row 10 to the remaining rows in the worksheet (through row 369).

g. Click in cell A3 and enter the label shown in the figure. Click and drag to select cells A3 through A6. Pull down the Format menu and click the Cells command to display the Format Cells dialog box, click the Alignment tab, check the box to merge cells, then drag the red diamond within the orientation area until you get the proper angle (−45 degrees). Click OK. Change the font size to 14 or 16 point.

h. Click in cell A1, type Amortization Schedule, click and drag to select cells A1 through D1, then click the merge and center button. Change the point size to 14 or 16 point.

i. Select cells A1:D1, then press and hold the Ctrl key as you select A3 and A8:D8. Change the fill color for the selected cells to blue, the text to white, and the style to boldface. Change column widths as needed.

	A	B	C	D
1	Amortization Schedule			
2				
3	*Terms*	Principal		$100,000
4		Annual Interest		7.50%
5		Length of loan (years)		30
6		Monthly payment		$699.21
7				
8	Payment Number	Toward Interest	Toward Principal	Balance
9				$100,000
10	1	$625.00	$74.21	$99,925.79
11	2	$624.54	$74.68	$99,851.11
12	3	$624.07	$75.15	$99,775.96
13	4	$623.60	$75.61	$99,700.35
14	5	$623.13	$76.09	$99,624.26
15	6	$622.65	$76.56	$99,547.70
16	7	$622.17	$77.04	$99,470.66
17	8	$621.69	$77.52	$99,393.13
18	9	$621.21	$78.01	$99,315.13

FIGURE 3.21 The Amortization Table (Exercise 5)

j. Select cells A8:D8, pull down in the Format menu, click the Cells command, click the Alignment tab, and check the box to Wrap Text.

k. You don't have to print the entire spreadsheet, but only a selected area. Click and drag the first 45 rows (through the 36th payment), pull down the File menu, click the Print Area command, then click Set Print Area. A dashed line will appear to indicate the part of the spreadsheet that will be printed. Click the Print button. Now pull down the File menu a second time, click Print Area, then click Clear Print Area so that you will be able to print the entire spreadsheet.

l. If you elect to print the entire spreadsheet, you can insert the page breaks to override the breaks that are inserted by Excel. Click the heading below the row where you want the break to occur, pull down the Insert menu, and click the Page break command.

6. Information from the Web: The compound document in Figure 3.22 contains a spreadsheet to compute a car payment together with a description and picture of the associated car. The latter two were taken from the Web site carpoint.msn.com. Choose any car you like, then go to the indicated Web site to obtain the retail price of that car so you can create the spreadsheet. In addition, download a picture and description of the car so that you can create a compound document similar to Figure 3.22. *Be sure to credit the source in your document.* Add your name to the completed document and submit it to your instructor.

The Camaro Coupe

The description and picture of the Camaro was taken from the Microsoft site, carpoint.msn.com. The spreadsheet calculations are mine. The calculations are based on the retail price of the 1999 fully loaded Z28 convertible. The monthly payment is well beyond my budget, but it never hurts to dream.

Price of car	$27,850
Manufacturer's rebate	$0
Down payment	$0
Amount to finance	$27,850
Interest rate	8%
Term (years)	4
Monthly payment	$679.90

"Chevrolet introduced the Camaro in 1967 as its entry into what came to be called the 'pony car' segment created by the Ford Mustang. Although it has always been available with options to suit a wide range of sports-coupe buyers, performance has been what the name Camaro brings to mind for most people. Since its early days the Camaro has been a successful race car. Even today, there's bound to be a Camaro racing somewhere in America on any given race weekend. The current car, a fourth-generation model introduced in 1993, offers a high level of performance at a competitive price."

FIGURE 3.22   Information from the Web (Exercise 6)

7. Mixed References: Figure 3.23 contains another variation on the mortgage example in which we vary the principal and interest rate. The user inputs an initial principal (e.g., $200,000) and interest rate (e.g., 8%) and the amounts by which to vary those values ($10,000 and 1%, respectively). The spreadsheet then computes the monthly payment for different combinations of the interest and principal. Your assignment is to duplicate the spreadsheet in Figure 3.23.

The trick to the assignment is to develop a formula with mixed references in cell B11 that can be copied to the remaining rows and columns. Your spreadsheet is to be completely flexible in that the user can input any assumption or initial condition in cells B4 through B8, then see the results in the body of the spreadsheet. Print the cell formulas and displayed values and submit both to your instructor as proof that you did this exercise.

	A	B	C	D	E	F	G
1	\multicolumn{7}{c}{**Mortgage Calculator**}
2	\multicolumn{7}{c}{*Change any parameter in cells B4 through B8 and the table is recalculated automatically*}
3							
4	**Initial principal**	$200,000					
5	*Increment*	$10,000					
6	**Starting Interest**	6.00%					
7	*Increment*	1.00%					
8	**Term (years)**	15					
9							
10		$200,000	$210,000	$220,000	$230,000	$240,000	$250,000
11	6.00%	$1,687.71	$1,772.10	$1,856.49	$1,940.87	$2,025.26	$2,109.64
12	7.00%	$1,797.66	$1,887.54	$1,977.42	$2,067.31	$2,157.19	$2,247.07
13	8.00%	$1,911.30	$2,006.87	$2,102.43	$2,198.00	$2,293.57	$2,389.13
14	9.00%	$2,028.53	$2,129.96	$2,231.39	$2,332.81	$2,434.24	$2,535.67
15	10.00%	$2,149.21	$2,256.67	$2,364.13	$2,471.59	$2,579.05	$2,686.51
16	11.00%	$2,273.19	$2,386.85	$2,500.51	$2,614.17	$2,727.83	$2,841.49
17	12.00%	$2,400.34	$2,520.35	$2,640.37	$2,760.39	$2,880.40	$3,000.42
18	13.00%	$2,530.48	$2,657.01	$2,783.53	$2,910.06	$3,036.58	$3,163.11

FIGURE 3.23   Mixed References (Exercise 7)

8. The Birthday Problem: How much would you bet *against* two people in your class having the same birthday? Don't be too hasty, for the odds of two classmates sharing the same birthday (month and day) are much higher than you would expect; e.g., there is a fifty percent chance (.5063) in a class of 23 students that two people will have been born on the same day. The probability jumps to seventy percent (.7053) in a class of thirty, and to ninety percent (.9025) in a class of forty-one. We encourage you to conduct an experiment in your class to see if the probabilities hold.

Your assignment is to create the worksheet in Figure 3.24 that displays the set of probabilities. Enter your name and birth date in cells B3 and B4, respectively, then use the Now() function to compute your age in cell B5. Change the default alignment and number of decimal places in cell B5 so that your worksheet matches ours.

You need a basic knowledge of probability to create the remainder of the spreadsheet. In essence you calculate the probability of individuals not having the same birthday, then subtract this number from one, to obtain the probability of the event coming true. In a group of two people, for example, the probability of not being born on the same day is 365/366; i.e., the second person can be born on any of 365 days and still have a different birthday. The probability of two people having the same birthday becomes 1 − 365/366.

The probability for different birthdays in a group of three is (365/366)*(364/366); the probability of not having different birthdays; i.e., of two people having the same birthday, is one minus this number. Each row in the spreadsheet calculated from the previous row. It's not as hard as it looks and the results are quite interesting!

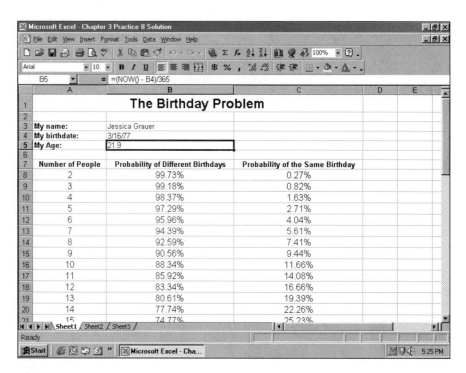

FIGURE 3.24   The Birthday Problem (Exercise 8)

CASE STUDIES

The Financial Consultant

A friend of yours is in the process of buying a home and has asked you to compare the payments and total interest on a 15- and a 30-year loan. You want to do as professional a job as possible and have decided to analyze the loans in Excel, then incorporate the results into a memo written in Microsoft Word. As of now, the principal is $150,000, but it is very likely that your friend will change his mind several times, and so you want to use the OLE capability within Windows to dynamically link the worksheet to the word processing document. Your memo should include a letterhead that takes advantage of the formatting capabilities within Word; a graphic logo would be a nice touch.

Compensation Analysis

A corporation typically uses several different measures of compensation in an effort to pay its employees fairly. Most organizations closely monitor an employee's salary history, keeping both the present and previous salary in order to compute various statistics, including:

- The percent salary increase, which is computed by taking the difference between the present and previous salary, and dividing by the previous salary.
- The months between increase, which is the elapsed time between the date the present salary took effect and the date of the previous salary. (Assume 30 days per month for ease of calculation.)
- The annualized rate of increase, which is the percent salary increase divided by the months between increase; for example, a 5% raise after 6 months is equivalent to an annualized increase of 10%; a 5% raise after two years is equivalent to an annual increase of 2.5%.

Use the data in the *Compensation Analysis* workbook on the data disk to compute salary statistics for the employees who have had a salary increase; employees who have not received an increase should have a suitable indication in the cell. Compute the average, minimum, and maximum value for each measure of compensation for those employees who have received an increase.

The Automobile Dealership

The purchase of a car usually entails extensive bargaining between the dealer and the consumer. The dealer has an asking price but typically settles for less. The commission paid to a salesperson depends on how close the selling price is to the asking price. Exotic Motors has the following compensation policy for its sales staff:

- A 3% commission on the actual selling price for cars sold at 95% or more of the asking price.
- A 2% commission on the actual selling price for cars sold at 90% or more (but less than 95%) of the asking price
- A 1% commission on the actual selling price for cars sold at less than 90% of the asking price. The dealer will not go below 85% of his asking price.

The dealer's asking price is based on the dealer's cost plus a 20% markup; for example, the asking price on a car that cost the dealer $20,000 would be $24,000. Develop a worksheet to be used by the dealer that shows his profit (the selling price minus the cost of the car minus the salesperson's commission) on every sale. The worksheet should be completely flexible and allow the dealer to vary the markup or commission percentages without having to edit or recopy any of the formulas. Use the data in the *Exotic Motors* workbook to test your worksheet.

The Lottery

Many states raise money through lotteries that advertise prizes of several million dollars. In reality, however, the actual value of the prize is considerably less than the advertised value, although the winners almost certainly do not care. One state, for example, recently offered a twenty million dollar prize that was to be distributed in twenty annual payments of one million dollars each. How much was the prize actually worth, assuming a long-term interest rate of seven percent?

A Penny a Day

What if you had a rich uncle who offered to pay you "a penny a day," then double your salary each day for the next month? It does not sound very generous, but you will be surprised at how quickly the amount grows. Create a simple worksheet that enables you to use the Goal Seek command to answer the following questions. On what day of the month (if any) will your uncle pay you more than one million dollars? How much money will your uncle pay you on the 31st day?

Data Tables

A data table is a tool that shows the effect of varying one or two variables in a formula. You could, for example, use a data table to show how changes in principal and/or interest affect the monthly payment on a loan. Data tables do not really represent a new capability, as you can achieve the same result by building a worksheet with the appropriate combination of relative, absolute, and/or mixed references. Use the Help command in Excel to learn about data tables, then construct a data table that is equivalent to the spreadsheet in Figure 3.23 in conjunction with practice exercise 7. Which technique do you prefer, mixed references or data tables? Why?

The Power of Compound Interest

A Roth IRA, or Individual Retirement Account, is one of the best tax breaks you will ever receive. The money that you contribute is on an "after tax basis" (it has already been taxed), but the interest it earns is tax-free. Even if you live from paycheck to paycheck, as most of us do, it is well worth it to try to save a constant amount every month. The maximum contribution is $2,000 a year. Let's assume that you contribute that amount for 40 years, from age 25 to age 65. How much will you have at the end of 40 years? Answer for interest rates of 6%, 8%, and 10%. Hint: use the Future Value (FV) function.

chapter 4

GRAPHS AND CHARTS: DELIVERING A MESSAGE

OBJECTIVES

After reading this chapter you will be able to:

1. Distinguish between the different types of charts, stating the advantages and disadvantages of each.
2. Distinguish between a chart embedded in a worksheet and one in a separate chart sheet; explain how many charts can be associated with the same worksheet.
3. Use the Chart Wizard to create and/or modify a chart.
4. Use the Drawing toolbar to enhance a chart by creating lines, objects, and 3-D shapes.
5. Differentiate between data series specified in rows and data series specified in columns.
6. Describe how a chart can be statistically accurate yet totally misleading.
7. Create a compound document consisting of a word processing memo, a worksheet, and a chart.

OVERVIEW

Business has always known that the graphic representation of data is an attractive, easy-to-understand way to convey information. Indeed, business graphics has become one of the most exciting Windows applications, whereby charts (graphs) are easily created from a worksheet, with just a few simple keystrokes or mouse clicks.

The chapter begins by emphasizing the importance of determining the message to be conveyed by a chart. It describes the different types of charts available within Excel and how to choose among them. It explains how to create a chart using the Chart Wizard, how to embed a chart within a worksheet, and how to create a chart in a separate chart sheet. It also describes how to use the Drawing toolbar to enhance a chart by creating lines, objects, and 3-D shapes.

The second half of the chapter explains how one chart can plot multiple sets of data, and how several charts can be based on the same worksheet. It also describes how to create a compound document, in which a chart and its associated worksheet are dynamically linked to a memo created by a word processor. All told, we think you will find this to be one of the most enjoyable chapters in the text.

CHART TYPES

A *chart* is a graphic representation of data in a worksheet. The chart is based on descriptive entries called *category labels,* and on numeric values called *data points.* The data points are grouped into one or more *data series* that appear in row(s) or column(s) on the worksheet. In every chart there is exactly one data point in each data series for each value of the category label.

The worksheet in Figure 4.1 will be used throughout the chapter as the basis for the charts we will create. Your manager believes that the sales data can be understood more easily from charts than from the strict numerical presentation of a worksheet. You have been given the assignment of analyzing the data in the worksheet and are developing a series of charts to convey that information.

	A	B	C	D	E	F
1		Superior Software Sales				
2						
3		Miami	Denver	New York	Boston	Total
4	Word Processing	$50,000	$67,500	$9,500	$141,000	$268,000
5	Spreadsheets	$44,000	$18,000	$11,500	$105,000	$178,500
6	Database	$12,000	$7,500	$6,000	$30,000	$55,500
7	Total	$106,000	$93,000	$27,000	$276,000	$502,000

FIGURE 4.1 Superior Software

The sales data in the worksheet can be presented several ways—for example, by city, by product, or by a combination of the two. Ask yourself which type of chart is best suited to answer the following questions:

- What percentage of total revenue comes from each city? from each product?
- What is the dollar revenue produced by each city? by each product?
- What is the rank of each city with respect to sales?
- How much revenue does each product contribute in each city?

In every instance, realize that a chart exists only to deliver a message, and that you cannot create an effective chart unless you are sure of what that message is. The next several pages discuss various types of business charts, each of which is best suited to a particular type of message.

KEEP IT SIMPLE

Keep it simple. This rule applies to both your message and the means of conveying that message. Excel makes it almost too easy to change fonts, styles, type sizes, and colors, but such changes will often detract from, rather than enhance, a chart. More is not necessarily better, and you do not have to use the features just because they are there. Remember that a chart must ultimately succeed on the basis of content, and content alone.

Pie Charts

A **pie chart** is the most effective way to display proportional relationships. It is the type of chart to select whenever words like *percentage* or *market share* appear in the message to be delivered. The pie, or complete circle, denotes the total amount. Each slice of the pie corresponds to its respective percentage of the total.

The pie chart in Figure 4.2a divides the pie representing total sales into four slices, one for each city. The size of each slice is proportional to the percentage of total sales in that city. The chart depicts a single data series, which appears in cells B7 through E7 on the associated worksheet. The data series has four data points corresponding to the total sales in each city.

To create the pie chart, Excel computes the total sales ($502,000 in our example), calculates the percentage contributed by each city, and draws each slice of the pie in proportion to its computed percentage. Boston's sales of $276,000 account for 55 percent of the total, and so this slice of the pie is allotted 55 percent of the area of the circle.

An **exploded pie chart,** as shown in Figure 4.2b, separates one or more slices of the pie for emphasis. Another way to achieve emphasis in a chart is to choose a title that reflects the message you are trying to deliver. The title in Figure 4.2a, for example, *Revenue by Geographic Area*, is neutral and leaves the reader to develop his or her own conclusion about the relative contribution of each area. By contrast, the title in Figure 4.2b, *New York Accounts for Only 5% of Revenue*, is more suggestive and emphasizes the problems in this office. Alternatively, the title could be changed to *Boston Exceeds 50% of Total Revenue* if the intent were to emphasize the contribution of Boston.

Three-dimensional pie charts may be created in exploded or nonexploded format as shown in Figures 4.2c and 4.2d, respectively. Excel also enables you to add arrows and text for emphasis.

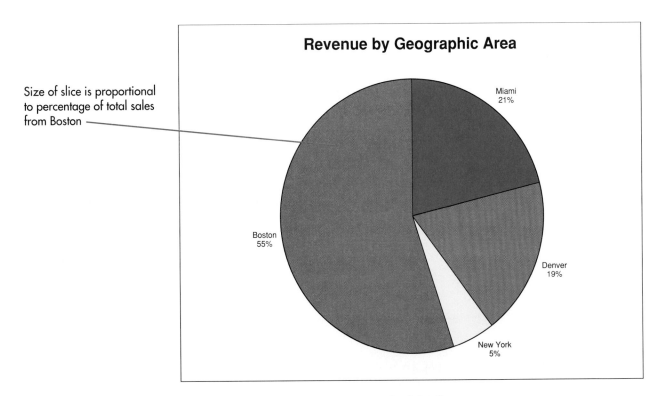

Size of slice is proportional to percentage of total sales from Boston

(a) Simple Pie Chart

FIGURE 4.2   Pie Charts

Title emphasizes
problems in New York

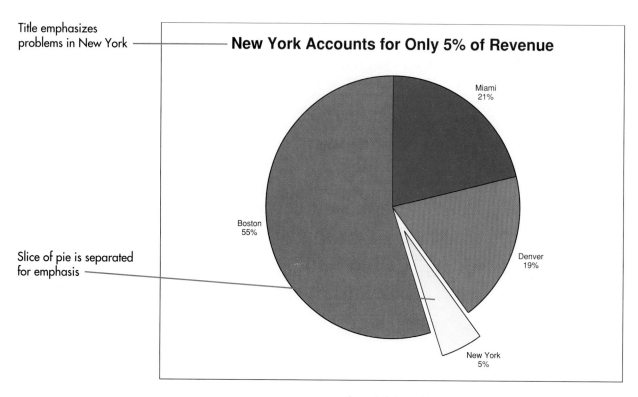

New York Accounts for Only 5% of Revenue

Miami
21%

Denver
19%

New York
5%

Boston
55%

Slice of pie is separated
for emphasis

(b) Exploded Pie Chart

Title emphasizes
Boston's contribution

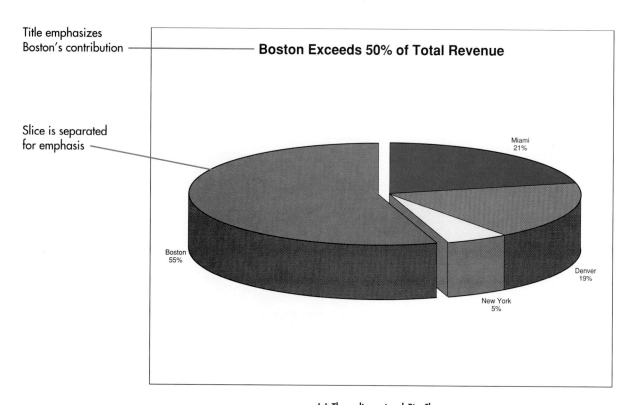

Boston Exceeds 50% of Total Revenue

Miami
21%

Denver
19%

New York
5%

Boston
55%

Slice is separated
for emphasis

(c) Three-dimensional Pie Chart

FIGURE 4.2   Pie Charts (continued)

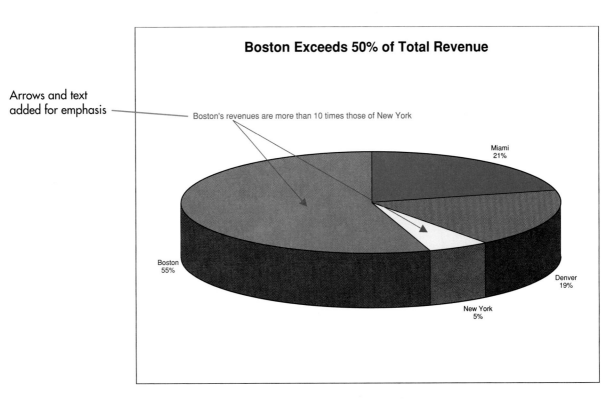

Boston Exceeds 50% of Total Revenue

Arrows and text added for emphasis

Boston's revenues are more than 10 times those of New York

Miami
21%

Boston
55%

New York
5%

Denver
19%

(d) Enhanced Pie Chart

FIGURE 4.2   Pie Charts (continued)

A pie chart is easiest to read when the number of slices is limited (i.e., not more than six or seven), and when small categories (percentages less than five) are grouped into a single category called "Other."

EXPLODED PIE CHARTS

Click and drag wedges out of a pie chart to convert an ordinary pie chart to an exploded pie chart. For best results pull the wedge out only slightly from the main body of the pie.

Column and Bar Charts

A *column chart* is used when there is a need to show actual numbers rather than percentages. The column chart in Figure 4.3a plots the same data series as the earlier pie chart, but displays it differently. The category labels (Miami, Denver, New York, and Boston) are shown along the *X* (horizontal) *axis.* The data points (monthly sales) are plotted along the *Y* (vertical) *axis,* with the height of each column reflecting the value of the data point.

A column chart can be given a horizontal orientation and converted to a *bar chart* as in Figure 4.3b. Some individuals prefer the bar chart over the corresponding column chart because the longer horizontal bars accentuate the difference between the items. Bar charts are also preferable when the descriptive labels are long, to eliminate the crowding that can occur along the horizontal axis of a

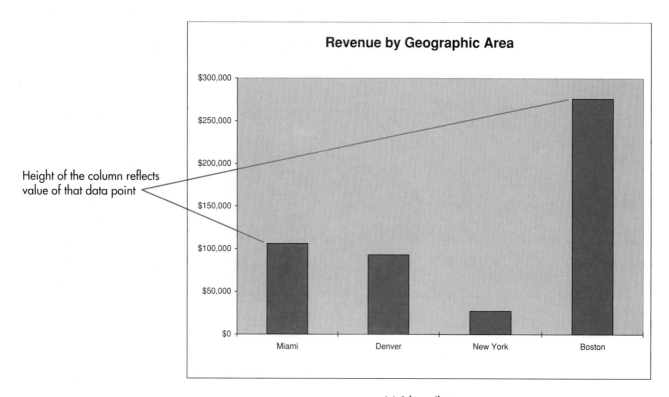

Height of the column reflects value of that data point

(a) Column Chart

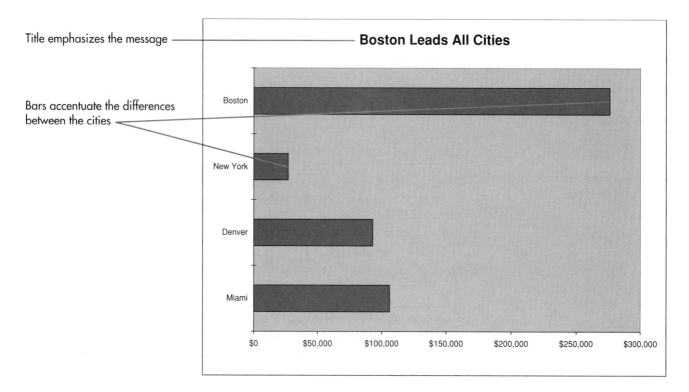

Title emphasizes the message

Bars accentuate the differences between the cities

(b) Horizontal Bar Chart

FIGURE 4.3   Column/Bar Charts

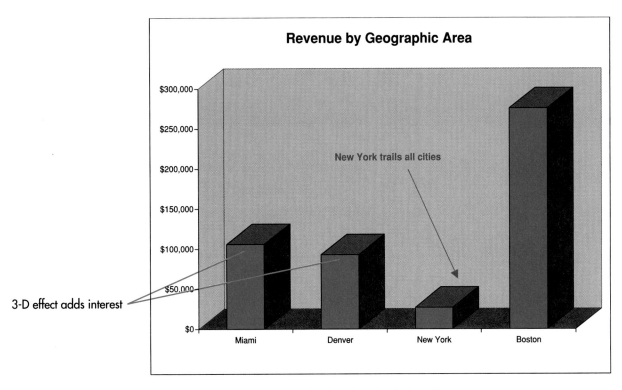

(c) Three-dimensional Column Chart

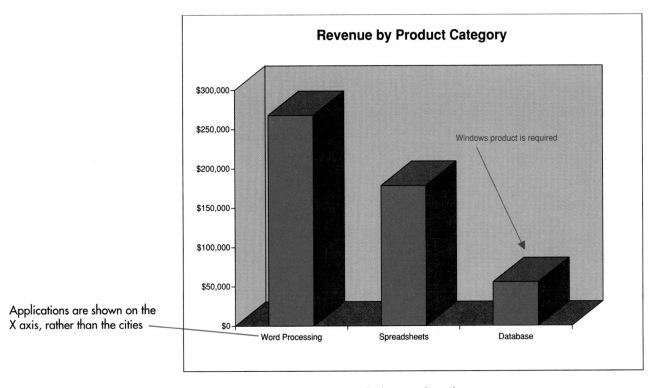

(d) Alternate Column Chart

FIGURE 4.3   Column/Bar Charts (continued)

column chart. As with the pie chart, a title can lead the reader and further emphasize the message, as with *Boston Leads All Cities* in Figure 4.3b.

A three-dimensional effect can produce added interest as shown in Figures 4.3c and 4.3d. Figure 4.3d plots a different set of numbers than we have seen so far (the sales for each product, rather than the sales for each city). The choice between the charts in Figures 4.3c and 4.3d depends on the message you want to convey—whether you want to emphasize the contribution of each city or each product. The title can be used to emphasize the message. Arrows, text, and 3-D shapes can be added to either chart to enhance the message.

As with a pie chart, column and bar charts are easiest to read when the number of categories is relatively small (seven or fewer). Otherwise, the columns (bars) are plotted so close together that labeling becomes impossible.

CREATING A CHART

There are two ways to create a chart in Excel. You can *embed* the chart in a worksheet, or you can create the chart in a separate *chart sheet.* Figure 4.4a displays an embedded column chart. Figure 4.4b shows a pie chart in its own chart sheet. Both techniques are valid. The choice between the two depends on your personal preference.

Regardless of where it is kept (embedded in a worksheet or in its own chart sheet), a chart is linked to the worksheet on which it is based. The charts in Figure 4.4 plot the same data series (the total sales for each city). Change any of these data points on the worksheet, and both charts will be updated automatically to reflect the new data.

Both charts are part of the same workbook (Software Sales) as indicated in the title bar of each figure. The tabs within the workbook have been renamed to indicate the contents of the associated sheet. Additional charts may be created and embedded in the worksheet and/or placed on their own chart sheets. And, as previously stated, if you change the worksheet, the chart (or charts) based upon it will also change.

Study the column chart in Figure 4.4a to see how it corresponds to the worksheet on which it is based. The descriptive names on the X axis are known as *category labels* and match the entries in cells B3 through E3. The quantitative values (data points) are plotted on the Y axis and match the total sales in cells B7 through E7. Even the numeric format matches; that is, the currency format used in the worksheet appears automatically on the scale of the Y axis.

The *sizing handles* on the embedded chart indicate it is currently selected and can be sized, moved, or deleted the same way as any other Windows object:

- To size the selected chart, point to a sizing handle (the mouse pointer changes to a double arrow), then drag the handle in the desired direction.
- To move the selected chart, point to the chart (the mouse pointer is a single arrow), then drag the chart to its new location.
- To copy the selected chart, click the Copy button to copy the chart to the clipboard, click in the workbook where you want the copied chart to go, then click the Paste button to paste the chart at that location.
- To delete the selected chart, press the Del key.

The same operations apply to any of the objects within the chart (e.g., its title), as will be discussed in the section on enhancing a chart. Note, too, that both figures contain a chart toolbar that enables you to modify a chart after it has been created.

Workbook name

Chart toolbar

Sizing handles

Data points (match entries
in B7:E7)

Category labels (match entries
in B3:E3)

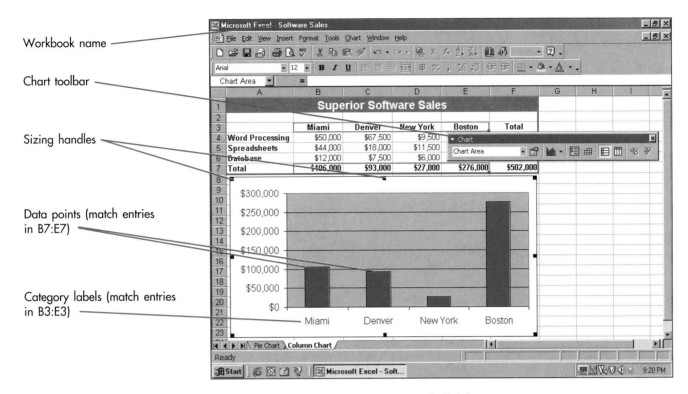

(a) Embedded Chart

Workbook name

Chart toolbar

Chart sheet is selected

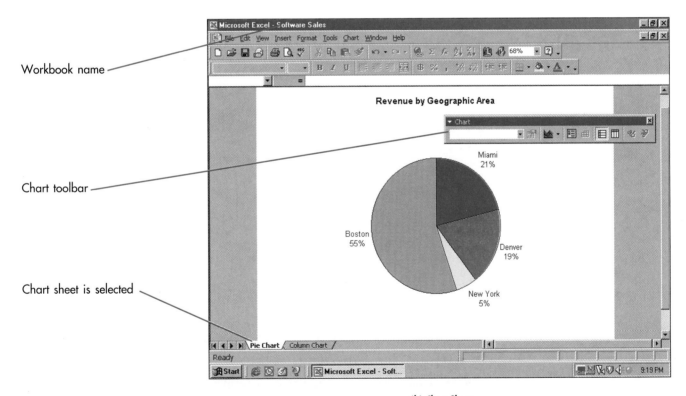

(b) Chart Sheet

FIGURE 4.4   Creating a chart

The Chart Wizard

The **Chart Wizard** is the easiest way to create a chart. Just select the cells that contain the data as shown in Figure 4.5a, click the Chart Wizard button on the Standard toolbar, and let the wizard do the rest. The process is illustrated in Figure 4.5, which shows how the Wizard creates a column chart to plot total sales by geographic area (city).

The steps in Figure 4.5 appear automatically as you click the Next command button to move from one step to the next. You can retrace your steps at any time by pressing the Back command button, access the Office Assistant for help with the Chart Wizard, or abort the process with the Cancel command button.

Step 1 in the Chart Wizard (Figure 4.5b) asks you to choose one of the available chart types. Step 2 (Figure 4.5c) shows you a preview of the chart and enables you to confirm (and, if necessary, change) the category names and data series specified earlier. (Only one data series is plotted in this example. Multiple data series are illustrated later in the chapter.) Step 3 (Figure 4.5d) asks you to complete the chart by entering its title and specifying additional options (such as the position of a legend and gridlines). And finally, step 4 (Figure 4.5e) has you choose whether the chart is to be created as an embedded chart (an object) within a specific worksheet, or whether it is to be created in its own chart sheet. The entire process takes but a few minutes.

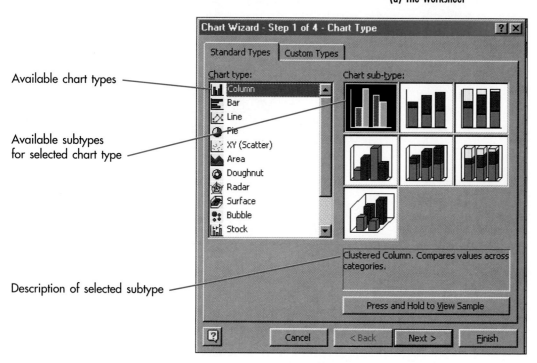

Selected cells (B3:E3 and B7:E7)

	A	B	C	D	E	F
1		Superior Software Sales				
2						
3		Miami	Denver	New York	Boston	Total
4	Word Processing	$50,000	$67,500	$9,500	$141,000	$268,000
5	Spreadsheets	$44,000	$18,000	$11,500	$105,000	$178,500
6	Database	$12,000	$7,500	$6,000	$30,000	$55,500
7	Total	$106,000	$93,000	$27,000	$276,000	$502,000

(a) The Worksheet

Available chart types

Available subtypes for selected chart type

Description of selected subtype

(b) Select the Chart Type (step 1)

FIGURE 4.5   The Chart Wizard

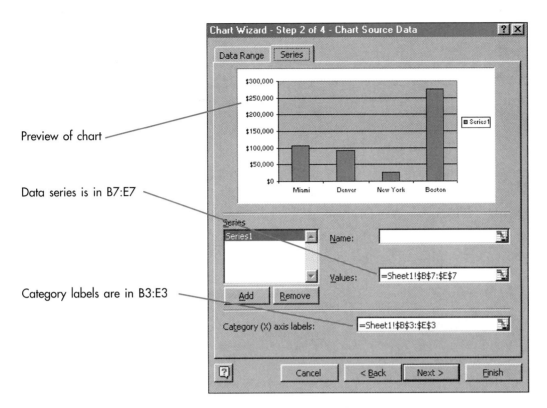

Preview of chart

Data series is in B7:E7

Category labels are in B3:E3

(c) Check the Data Series (step 2)

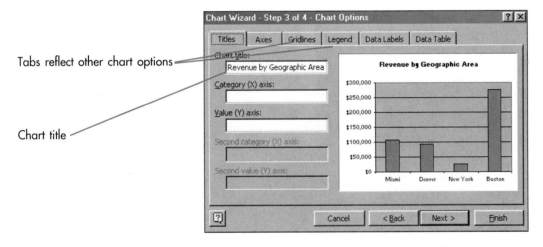

Tabs reflect other chart options

Chart title

(d) Complete the Chart Options (step 3)

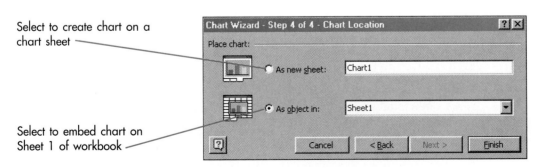

Select to create chart on a chart sheet

Select to embed chart on Sheet 1 of workbook

(e) Choose the Location (step 4)

FIGURE 4.5   The Chart Wizard (continued)

Modifying a Chart

A chart can be modified in several ways after it has been created. You can change the chart type and/or the color, shape, or pattern of the data series. You can add (or remove) gridlines and/or a legend. You can add labels to the data series. You can also change the font, size, color, and style of existing text anywhere in the chart by selecting the text, then changing its format. All of these features are implemented from the Chart menu or by using the appropriate button on the *Chart toolbar.*

You can also use the *Drawing toolbar* to add text boxes, arrows, and other objects for added emphasis. Figure 4.6, for example, contains a three-dimensional arrow with a text box within the arrow to call attention to the word processing sales. It also contains a second text box with a thin arrow in reference to the database product. Each of these objects is created separately using the appropriate tool from the Drawing toolbar. It's easy, as you will see in our next exercise.

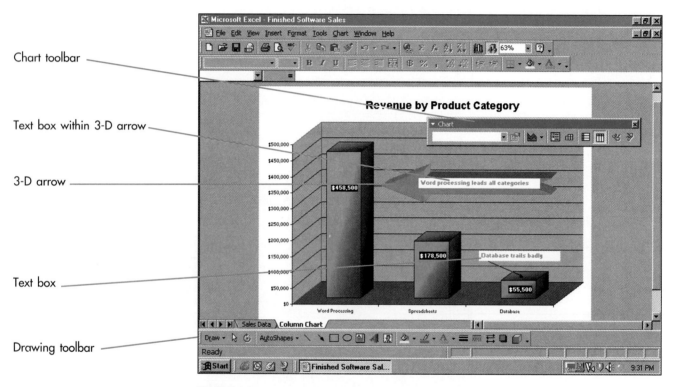

FIGURE 4.6   Enhancing a Chart

SET A TIME LIMIT

Excel enables you to customize virtually every aspect of every object within a chart. That is the good news. It's also the bad news, because you can spend inordinate amounts of time for little or no gain. It's fun to experiment, but set a time limit and stop when you reach the allocated time. The default settings are often adequate to convey your message, and further experimentation might prove counterproductive.

The Chart Wizard

Objective: To create and modify a chart by using the Chart Wizard; to embed a chart within a worksheet; to enhance a chart to include arrows and text. Use Figure 4.7 as a guide in the exercise.

STEP 1: The AutoSum Command

➤ Start Excel. Open the Software Sales workbook in the Exploring Excel folder. Save the workbook as **Finished Software Sales.**

➤ Click and drag to select the entries in cells **B7 through E7** (the cells that will contain the total sales for each location). Click the **AutoSum button** on the Standard toolbar.

➤ The totals are computed automatically as shown in Figure 4.7a. The formula bar shows that Cell B7 contains the Sum function to total all of the numeric entries immediately above the cell.

➤ Click and drag to select cells **F4 through F7,** then click the **AutoSum button.** The Sum function is entered automatically into these cells to total the entries to the left of the selected cells.

➤ Click and drag to select cells **B4 through F7** to format these cells with the currency symbol and no decimal places. Boldface the row and column headings and the totals. Add a red border and center the headings. Save the workbook.

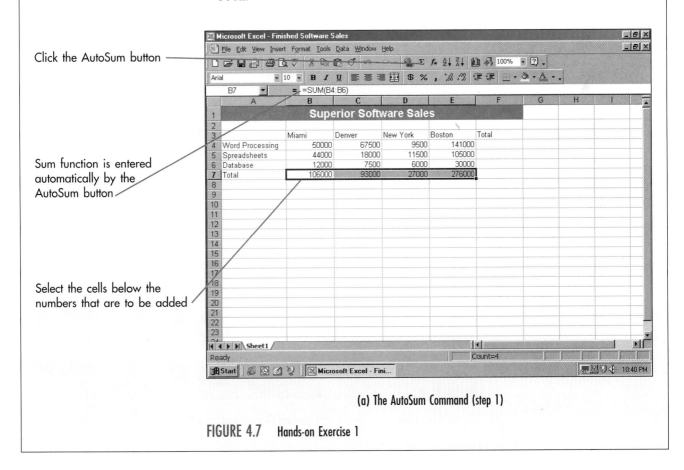

Click the AutoSum button

Sum function is entered automatically by the AutoSum button

Select the cells below the numbers that are to be added

(a) The AutoSum Command (step 1)

FIGURE 4.7 Hands-on Exercise 1

THE AUTOFORMAT COMMAND

The AutoFormat command does not do anything that could not be done through individual formatting commands, but it does provide inspiration by suggesting several attractive designs. Select the cells you want to format, pull down the Format menu, and click the AutoFormat command to display the AutoFormat dialog box. Select (click) a design, then click the Options button to determine the formats to apply (font, column width, patterns, and so on). Click OK to close the dialog box and apply the formatting. Click the Undo button if you do not like the result.

STEP 2: Start the Chart Wizard

➤ Separate the toolbars if they occupy the same row. Pull down the **Tools menu,** click the **Customize command,** click the **Options tab,** then clear the check box that has the toolbars share one row.

➤ Drag the mouse over cells **B3 through E3** to select the category labels (the names of the cities). Press and hold the **Ctrl key** as you drag the mouse over cells **B7 through E7** to select the data series (the cells containing the total sales for the individual cities).

➤ Check that cells B3 through E3 and B7 through E7 are selected. Click the **Chart Wizard button** on the Standard toolbar to start the wizard. If you don't see the button, pull down the **Insert menu** and click the **Chart command.**

➤ You should see the dialog box for step 1 as shown in Figure 4.7b. The **Column** chart type and **Clustered column** subtype are selected. Click **Next.**

Chart Wizard button

Select the category labels (B3:E3)

Select the data series (B7:E7)

Select Clustered column subtype

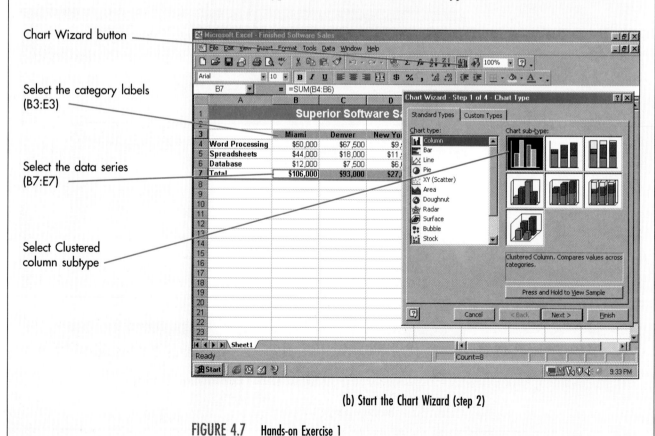

(b) Start the Chart Wizard (step 2)

FIGURE 4.7   Hands-on Exercise 1

STEP 3: The Chart Wizard (continued)

➤ You should see step 2 of the Chart Wizard. Click the **Series tab** in the dialog box so that your screen matches Figure 4.7c. Note that the values (the data being plotted) are in cells B7 through E7, and that the Category labels for the X axis are in cells B3 through E3. Click **Next** to continue.

➤ You should see step 3 of the Chart Wizard. If necessary, click the **Titles tab,** then click in the text box for the Chart title. Type **Revenue by Geographic Area.** Click the **Legend tab** and clear the box to show a legend. Click **Next.**

➤ You should see step 4 of the Chart Wizard. If necessary, click the option button to place the chart **As object** in Sheet1 (the name of the worksheet in which you are working). Click **Finish.**

RETRACE YOUR STEPS

The Chart Wizard guides you every step of the way, but what if you make a mistake or change your mind? Click the Back command button at any time to return to a previous screen in order to enter different information, then continue working with the wizard.

STEP 4: Move and Size the Chart

➤ You should see the completed chart as shown in Figure 4.7d. The sizing handles indicate that the chart is selected and will be affected by subsequent commands. The Chart toolbar is displayed automatically whenever a chart is selected.

➤ Move and/or size the chart just as you would any other Windows object:

• To move the chart, click the chart (background) area to select the chart (a ScreenTip, "Chart Area," is displayed), then click and drag (the mouse pointer changes to a four-sided arrow) to move the chart.

• To size the chart, drag a corner handle (the mouse pointer changes to a double arrow) to change the length and width of the chart simultaneously, keeping the chart in proportion as it is resized.

➤ Click outside the chart to deselect it. The sizing handles disappear and the Chart toolbar is no longer visible.

EMBEDDED CHARTS

An embedded chart is treated as an object that can be moved, sized, copied, or deleted just as any other Windows object. To move an embedded chart, click the background of the chart to select the chart, then drag it to a new location in the worksheet. To size the chart, select it, then drag any of the eight sizing handles in the desired direction. To delete the chart, select it, then press the Del key. To copy the chart, select it, click the Copy button on the Standard toolbar to copy the chart to the clipboard, click elsewhere in the workbook where you want the copied chart to go, then click the Paste button.

Series tab

Data series is in B7:E7

Category labels are in B3:E3

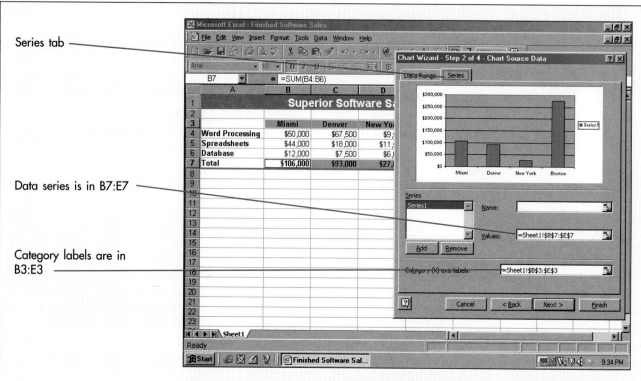

(c) The Chart Wizard (step 3)

Chart toolbar

Sizing handles

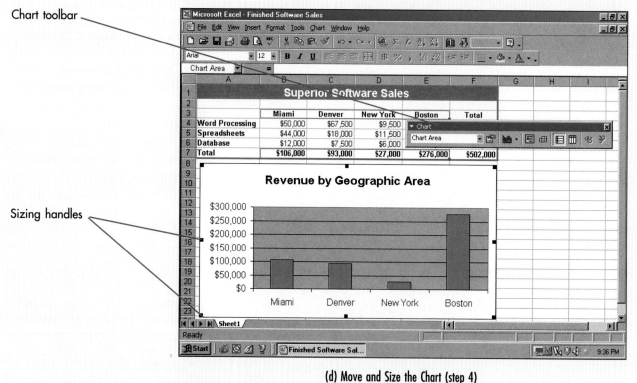

(d) Move and Size the Chart (step 4)

FIGURE 4.7   Hands-on Exercise 1   (continued)

STEP 5: Change the Worksheet

➤ Any changes in a worksheet are automatically reflected in the associated chart. Click in cell **B4,** change the entry to **$400,000,** and press the **enter key.**

➤ The total sales for Miami in cell B7 change automatically to reflect the increased sales for word processing, as shown in Figure 4.7e. The column for Miami also changes in the chart and is now larger than the column for Boston.

➤ Click in cell **B3.** Change the entry to **Chicago.** Press **enter.** The category label on the X axis changes automatically.

➤ Click the **Undo button** to change the city back to Miami. Click the **Undo button** a second time to return to the initial value of $50,000. The worksheet and chart are restored to their earlier values.

CREATE AN ATTRACTIVE CHART BORDER

Dress up an embedded chart by changing its border. Point to the chart area (the white background area near the border), click the right mouse button to display a shortcut menu, then click Format Chart Area to display the Format Chart Area dialog box. If necessary, click the Patterns tab, click the option button for a Custom border, then check the boxes for a Shadow and Round corners. Click the drop-down arrows in the style, color, and weight list boxes to specify a different border style, thickness (weight), or color. Click OK to accept these settings.

STEP 6: Change the Chart Type

➤ Click the chart (background) area to select the chart, click the **drop-down arrow** on the Chart type button on the Chart toolbar, then click the **3-D Pie Chart icon.** The chart changes to a three-dimensional pie chart.

➤ Point to the chart area, click the **right mouse button** to display a shortcut menu, then click the **Chart Options command** to display the Chart Options dialog box shown in Figure 4.7f.

➤ Click the **Data Labels tab,** then click the option button to **Show label and percent.** Click **OK** to accept the settings and close the Chart Options dialog box.

➤ The pie chart changes to reflect the options you just specified, although the chart may not appear exactly as you would like. Accordingly, you can modify each component as necessary:

• Select (click) the (gray) **Plot area.** Click and drag the sizing handles to increase the size of the plot area within the embedded chart.

• Point to any of the labels, click the **right mouse button** to display a shortcut menu, and click **Format Data Labels** to display a dialog box. Click the **Font tab,** and select a smaller point size. It may also be necessary to click and drag each label away from the plot area.

➤ Make other changes as necessary. Save the workbook.

Undo button

Change entry in B4 to $400,000

Total for Miami changes

Column for Miami reflects increased sales

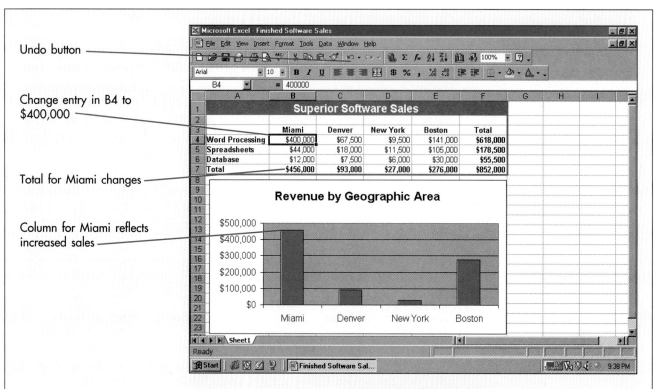

(e) Change the Worksheet (step 5)

Chart Type button

Data Labels tab

Click chart background area

Right Click chart area to display shortcut menu

Click and drag to size plot area

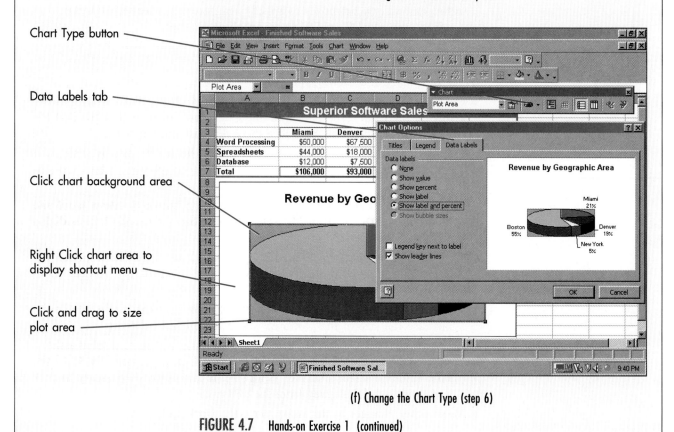

(f) Change the Chart Type (step 6)

FIGURE 4.7 Hands-on Exercise 1 (continued)

STEP 7: Create a Second Chart

➤ Click and drag to select cells **A4 through A6** in the worksheet. Press and hold the **Ctrl key** as you drag the mouse over cells **F4 through F6** to select the data series.

➤ Click the **Chart Wizard button** on the Standard toolbar to start the Chart Wizard and display the dialog box for step 1 as shown in Figure 4.7g. The Column Chart type is already selected. Click the **Clustered column with a 3-D visual effect subtype.** Press and hold the indicated button to preview the chart with your data. Click **Next.**

➤ Click the **Series tab** in the dialog box for step 2 to confirm that you selected the correct data points. The values for series1 should consist of cells F4 through F6. The Category labels for the X axis should be cells A4 through A6. Click **Next.**

➤ You should see step 3 of the Chart Wizard. Click the **Titles tab,** then click in the text box for the Chart title. Type **Revenue by Product Category.** Click the **Legend tab** and clear the box to show a legend. Click **Next.**

➤ You should see step 4 of the Chart Wizard. Select the option button to create the chart **As new sheet** (Chart1). Click **Finish.**

➤ The 3-D column chart has been created in the chart sheet labeled Chart1. Save the workbook.

ANATOMY OF A CHART

A chart is composed of multiple components (objects), each of which can be selected and changed separately. Point to any part of a chart to display a ScreenTip indicating the name of the component, then click the mouse to select that component and display the sizing handles. You can then click and drag the object within the chart and/or click the right mouse button to display a shortcut menu with commands pertaining to the selected object.

STEP 8: Add a Text Box

➤ Point to any visible toolbar, click the **right mouse button** to display a shortcut menu listing the available toolbars, then click **Drawing** to display the Drawing toolbar as shown in Figure 4.7h. Your toolbar may be in a different position from ours.

➤ Click the **TextBox button** on the Drawing toolbar. Click in the chart (the mouse pointer changes to a thin crosshair), then click and drag to create a text box. Release the mouse, then enter the text, **Word Processing leads all categories.**

➤ Point to the thatched border around the text box, then right click the border to display a context-sensitive menu. Click **Format Text Box** to display the Format Text dialog box. Click the **Font tab** and change the font to **12 point bold.** Choose **Red** as the font color.

Chart Wizard button

Select Cells A4:A6
and F4:F6

Select Clustered column with
3-D visual effect subtype

Click and hold this
button to preview the
chart with your data

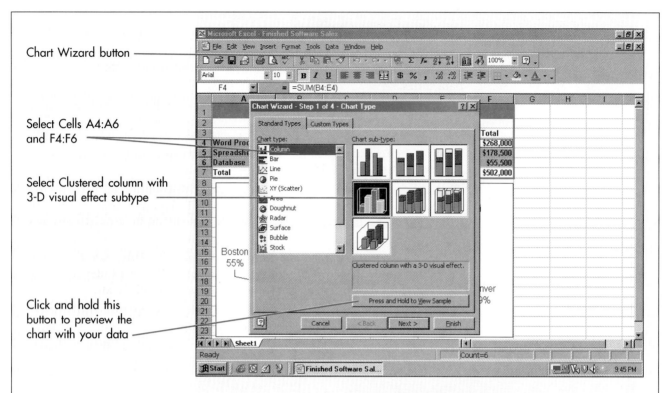

(g) Create a Second Chart (step 7)

Point to thatched border and
right click

Click and drag to create the
text box

Text box button

Drawing toolbar

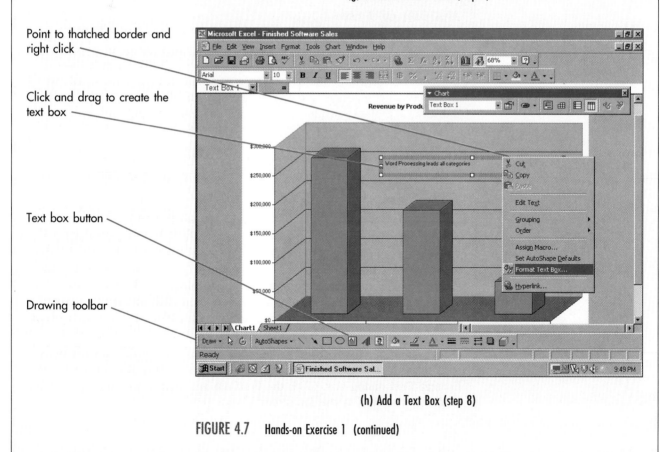

(h) Add a Text Box (step 8)

FIGURE 4.7   Hands-on Exercise 1 (continued)

➤ Click the **Colors and Lines tab** and select **white** as the fill color. Click **OK.** You should see red text on a white background. If necessary, size the text box so that the text fits on one line. Do not worry about the position of the text box at this time.

➤ Click the title of the chart. You will see sizing handles around the title to indicate it has been selected. Click the **drop-down arrow** in the Font Size box on the Formatting toolbar. Click **22** to increase the size of the title. Save the workbook.

FLOATING TOOLBARS

Any toolbar can be docked along the edge of the application window, or it can be displayed as a floating toolbar within the application window. To move a docked toolbar, drag the toolbar background or the move handles. To move a floating toolbar, drag its title bar. To size a floating toolbar, drag any border in the direction you want to go. Double click the background of any toolbar to toggle between a floating toolbar and a docked (fixed) toolbar.

STEP 9: Create a 3-D Shape

➤ Click on the **AutoShapes button** and, if necessary, click the double arrow to display additional commands. Click **Block Arrows** to display the various styles of arrows, then click the left arrow.

➤ Click in the chart (the mouse pointer changes to a thin crosshair), then click and drag to create an arrow. Release the mouse.

➤ Click the **3-D button** on the drawing toolbar and click **3-D Style 1** as shown in figure 4.7i. Right click the arrow and click the **Format AutoShape** command to display the Format AutoShape dialog box. If necessary, click the **Colors and Lines tab.** Choose **Red** as the fill color. Click **OK,** then size the arrow as necessary.

➤ Select (click) the text box you created in the previous step, then click and drag the text box out of the way. Select (click) the 3-D arrow and position it next to the word processing column.

➤ Click and drag the text box into position on top of the arrow. If you do not see the text, right click the arrow, click the **Order command,** and click **Send to Back.** (This moves the arrow behind the text box.)

➤ Save the workbook, but do not print it at this time. Exit Excel if you do not want to continue with the next exercise at this time.

FORMAT THE DATA SERIES

Use the Format Data Series command to change the color, shape, or pattern of the columns within the chart. Right click any column to select the data series (be sure that all three columns are selected), then click Format Data Series to display the Format Data Series dialog box. Experiment with the various options, especially those on the Shapes and Patterns tabs within the dialog box. Click OK when you are satisfied with the changes. We warn you, it's addictive, so set a time limit in advance.

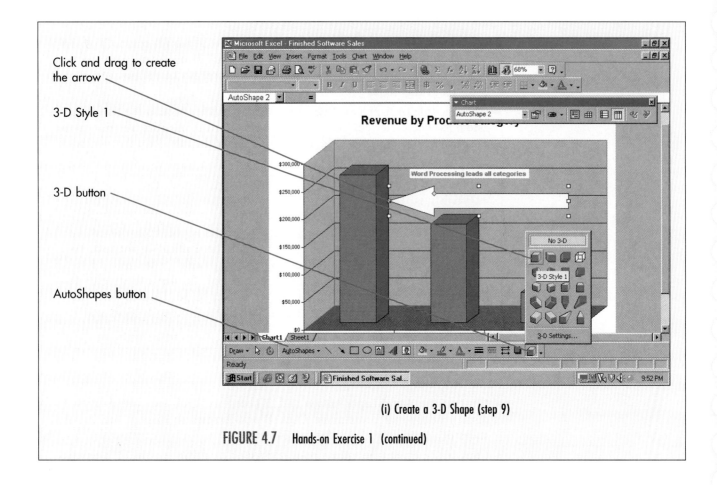

Click and drag to create the arrow

3-D Style 1

3-D button

AutoShapes button

(i) Create a 3-D Shape (step 9)

FIGURE 4.7   Hands-on Exercise 1   (continued)

MULTIPLE DATA SERIES

The charts presented so far displayed only a single data series—for example, the total sales by location or the total sales by product category. Although such charts are useful, it is often necessary to view *multiple data series* on the same chart.

Figure 4.8a displays the sales in each location according to product category. We see how the products compare within each city, and further, that word processing is the leading application in three of the four cities. Figure 4.8b plots the identical data but in *stacked columns* rather than side-by-side.

The choice between the two types of charts depends on your message. If, for example, you want your audience to see the individual sales in each product category, the side-by-side columns are more appropriate. If, on the other hand, you want to emphasize the total sales for each city, the stacked columns are preferable. Note, too, the different scale on the Y axis in the two charts. The side-by-side columns in Figure 4.8a show the sales of each product category and so the Y axis goes only to $160,000. The stacked columns in Figure 4.8b, however, reflect the total sales for each city and thus the scale goes to $300,000.

The biggest difference is that the stacked column explicitly totals the sales for each city while the side-by-side column does not. The advantage of the stacked column is that the city totals are clearly shown and can be easily compared, and further the relative contributions of each product category within each city are apparent. The disadvantage is that the segments within each column do not start at the same point, making it difficult to determine the actual sales for the individual product categories or to compare the product categories among cities.

Realize, too, that for a stacked column chart to make sense, its numbers must be additive. This is true in Figure 4.8b, where the stacked columns consist of three

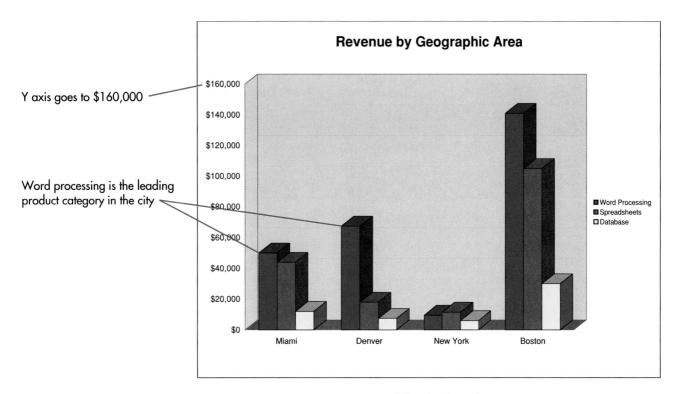

Y axis goes to $160,000

Word processing is the leading product category in the city

(a) Side-by-Side Column Chart

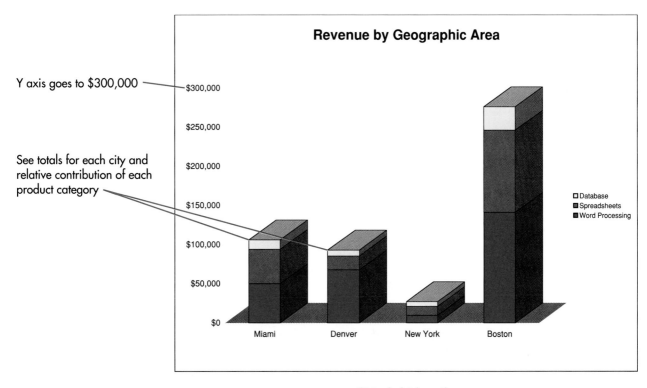

Y axis goes to $300,000

See totals for each city and relative contribution of each product category

(b) Stacked Column Chart

FIGURE 4.8 Column Charts

components, each of which is measured in dollars, and which can be logically added together to produce a total. You shouldn't, however, automatically convert a side-by-side column chart to its stacked column equivalent. It would not make sense, for example, to convert a column chart that plots unit sales and dollar sales side-by-side, into a stacked column chart that adds the two, because units and dollars represent different physical concepts and are not additive.

Rows versus Columns

Figure 4.9 illustrates a critical concept associated with multiple data series—whether the data series are in rows or columns. Figure 4.9a displays the worksheet with multiple data series selected. (Column A and Row 3 are included in the selection to provide the category labels and legend.) Figure 4.9b contains the chart when the data series are in rows (B4:E4, B5:E5, and B6:E6). Figure 4.9c displays the chart based on data series in columns (B4:B6, C4:C6, D4:D6, and E4:E6).

Both charts plot a total of twelve data points (three product categories for each of four locations), but they group the data differently. Figure 4.9b displays the data by city; that is, the sales of three product categories are shown for each of four cities. Figure 4.9c is the reverse and groups the data by product category; this time the sales in the four cities are shown for each of the three product categories. The choice between the two depends on your message and whether you want to emphasize revenue by city or by product category. The *legend,* an explanation of the data series, appears on the chart to distinguish the series from one another.

- If the data series are in rows (Figure 4.9b):
  - Use the first row (cells B3 through E3) in the selected range for the category labels on the X axis
  - Use the first column (cells A4 through A6) for the legend text
- If the data series are in columns (Figure 4.9c):
  - Use the first column (cells A4 through A6) in the selected range for the category labels on the X axis
  - Use the first row (cells B3 through E3) for the legend text

Stated another way, the data series in Figure 4.9b are in rows. Thus, there are three data series (B4:E4, B5:E5, and B6:E6), one for each product category. The first data series plots the word processing sales in Miami, Denver, New York, and Boston; the second series plots the spreadsheet sales for each city, and so on.

The data series in Figure 4.9c are in columns. This time there are four data series (B4:B6, C4:C6, D4:D6, and E4:E6), one for each city. The first series plots the Miami sales for word processing, spreadsheets, and database; the second series plots the Denver sales for each software category, and so on.

A3:E6 is selected

	A	B	C	D	E	F
1	Superior Software Sales					
2						
3		Miami	Denver	New York	Boston	Total
4	Word Processing	$50,000	$67,500	$9,500	$141,000	$268,000
5	Spreadsheets	$44,000	$18,000	$11,500	$105,000	$178,500
6	Database	$12,000	$7,500	$6,000	$30,000	$55,500
7	Total	$106,000	$93,000	$27,000	$276,000	$502,000

(a) The Worksheet

FIGURE 4.9   Multiple Data Series

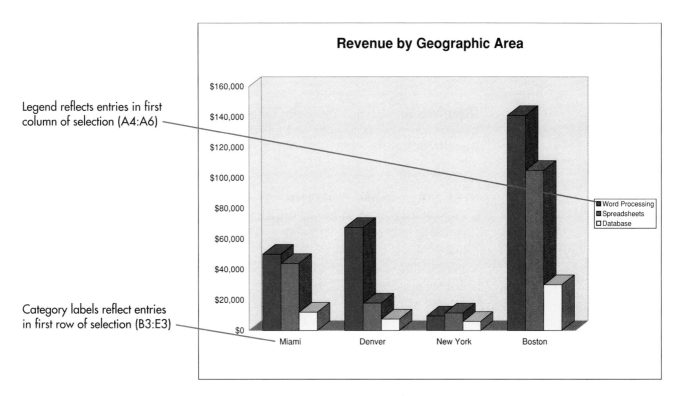

Legend reflects entries in first column of selection (A4:A6)

Category labels reflect entries in first row of selection (B3:E3)

(b) Data in Rows

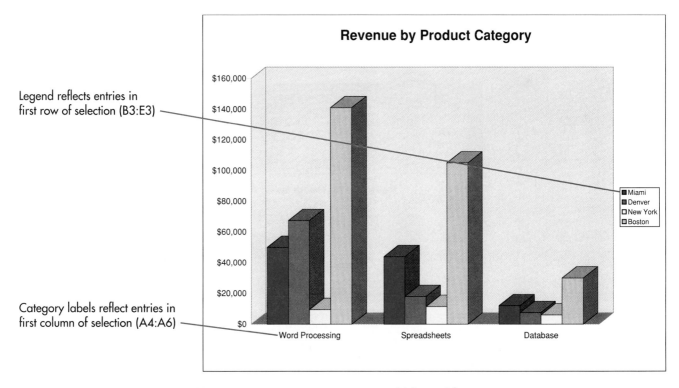

Legend reflects entries in first row of selection (B3:E3)

Category labels reflect entries in first column of selection (A4:A6)

(c) Data in Columns

FIGURE 4.9   Multiple Data Series (continued)

Objective: To plot multiple data series in the same chart; to differentiate between data series in rows and columns; to create and save multiple charts associated with the same worksheet. Use Figure 4.10 as a guide in the exercise.

STEP 1: Rename the Worksheets

➤ Open the **Finished Software Sales** workbook from the previous exercise as shown in Figure 4.10a. The workbook contains an embedded chart and a separate chart sheet.

➤ Point to the workbook tab labeled **Sheet1,** click the **right mouse button** to display a shortcut menu, then click the **Rename** command. The name of the worksheet (Sheet1) is selected. Type **Sales Data** to change the name of the worksheet to the more descriptive name. Press the **enter key.**

➤ Point to the tab labeled **Chart1** (which contains the three-dimensional column chart created in the previous exercise). Click the **right mouse button** to display a shortcut menu, click **Rename,** then enter **Column Chart** as the name of the chart sheet. Press the **enter key.**

➤ Save the workbook.

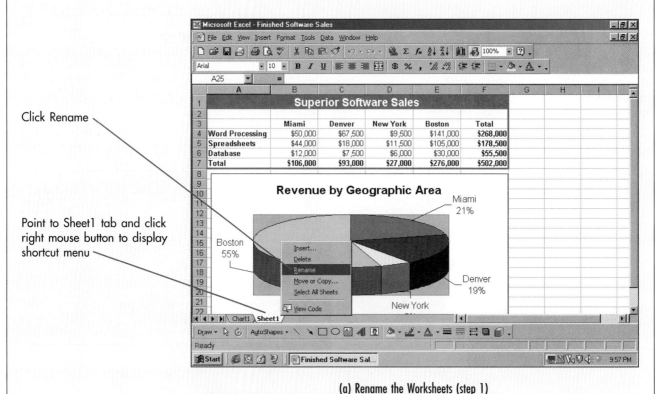

Click Rename

Point to Sheet1 tab and click right mouse button to display shortcut menu

(a) Rename the Worksheets (step 1)

FIGURE 4.10   Hands-on Exercise 2

STEP 2: The Office Assistant

➤ Click the **Sales Data tab,** then click and drag to select cells **A3 through E6.**
Click the **Chart Wizard button** on the Standard toolbar to start the wizard
and display the dialog box shown in Figure 4.10b.

➤ If necessary, click the **Office Assistant button** in the Chart Wizard dialog box
to display the Office Assistant and the initial help screen. Click the option
button for **Help with this feature.**

➤ The display for the Assistant changes to offer help about the various chart
types available. (It's up to you whether you want to explore the advice at this
time. You can close the Assistant, or leave it open and drag the title bar out
of the way.)

➤ Select **Column** as the chart type and **Clustered column** with a 3-D visual
effect as the subtype. Click **Next** to continue with the Chart Wizard.

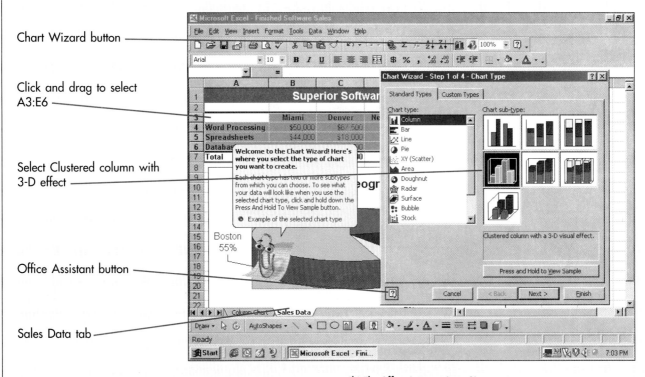

Chart Wizard button

Click and drag to select
A3:E6

Select Clustered column with
3-D effect

Office Assistant button

Sales Data tab

(b) The Office Assistant (step 2)

FIGURE 4.10   Hands-on Exercise 2 (continued)

THE OFFICE ASSISTANT

The Office Assistant button is common to all Office applications and is an
invaluable source of online help. You can activate the Assistant at any
time by clicking its button on the Standard toolbar or from within a specialized dialog box. You can ask the Assistant a specific question and/or
you can have the Assistant monitor your work and suggest tips as appropriate. You can tell that the Assistant has a suggestion when you see a
lightbulb appear adjacent to the character.

STEP 3: View the Data Series

➤ You should see step 2 of the Chart Wizard as shown in Figure 4.10c. The help supplied by the Office Assistant changes automatically with the steps in the Chart Wizard.

➤ The data range should be specified as **Sales Data!$A$3:$E$6** as shown in Figure 4.10c. The option button for **Series in Rows** should be selected. To appreciate the concept of data series in rows (versus columns), click the **Series tab:**

- The series list box shows three data series (Word Processing, Spreadsheets, and Database) corresponding to the legends for the chart.

- The **Word Processing** series is selected by default. The legend in the sample chart shows that the data points in the series are plotted in blue. The values are taken from cells B4 through E4 in the Sales Data Worksheet.

- Click **Spreadsheets** in the series list box. The legend shows that the series is plotted in red. The values are taken from cells B5 through E5 in the Sales Data worksheet.

- Click **Database** in the series list box. The legend shows that the series is plotted in yellow. The values are taken from cells B6 through E6 in the Sales Data worksheet.

DEFAULT SELECTIONS

Excel makes a default determination as to whether the data is in rows or columns by assuming that you want fewer data series than categories. Thus, if the selected cells contain fewer rows than columns (or if the number of rows and columns are equal), it assumes the data series are in rows. If, on the other hand, there are fewer columns than rows, it will assume the data series are in columns.

STEP 4: Complete the Chart

➤ Click **Next** to continue creating the chart. You should see step 3 of the Chart Wizard. Click the **Titles tab.** Click the text box for Chart title. Type **Revenue by City.** Click **Next.**

➤ You should see step 4 of the Chart Wizard. Click the option button for **As new sheet.** Type **Revenue by City** in the associated text box to give the chart sheet a meaningful name. Click **Finish.**

➤ Excel creates the new chart in its own sheet named Revenue by City. Click **No** to tell the Assistant that you don't need further help. Right click the Assistant. Click **Hide.** Save the workbook.

THE F11 KEY

The F11 key is the fastest way to create a chart in its own sheet. Select the data, including the legends and category labels, then press the F11 key to create the chart according to the default format built into the Excel column chart. After the chart has been created, you can use the menu bar, Chart toolbar, or shortcut menus to choose a different chart type and/or customize the formatting.

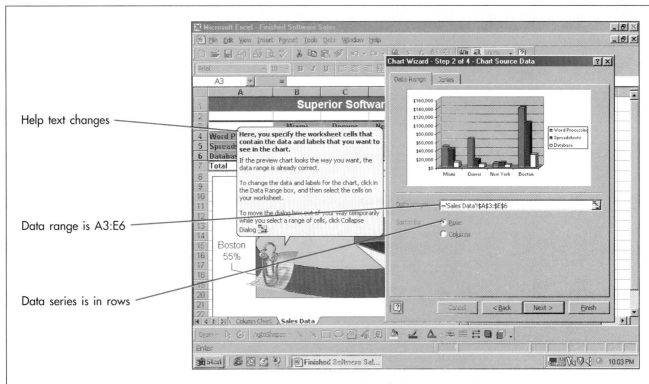

Help text changes

Data range is A3:E6

Data series is in rows

(c) View the Data Series (step 3)

FIGURE 4.10 Hands-on Exercise 2 (continued)

STEP 5: Copy the Chart
➤ Point to the tab named **Revenue by City.** Click the **right mouse button.** Click **Move or Copy** to display the dialog box in Figure 4.10d.
➤ Click **Sales Data** in the Before Sheet list box. Check the box to **Create a Copy.** Click **OK.**
➤ A duplicate worksheet called Revenue by City(2) is created and appears before (to the left of) the Sales Data worksheet.
➤ Rename the copied sheet **Revenue by Product.** Save the workbook.

MOVING AND COPYING A CHART SHEET

The fastest way to move or copy a chart sheet is to drag its tab. To move a sheet, point to its tab, then click and drag the tab to its new position. To copy a sheet, press and hold the Ctrl key as you drag the tab to the desired position for the second sheet. Rename the copied sheet (or any sheet for that matter) by double clicking its tab to select the existing name. Enter a new name for the worksheet, then press the enter key.

Click Sales Data

Check box to create a copy

Point to tab and click right mouse button to display shortcut menu

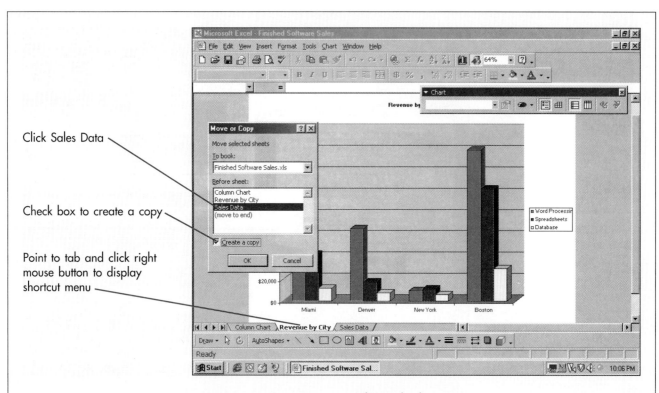

(d) Copy the Chart (step 5)

FIGURE 4.10   Hands-on Exercise 2 (continued)

STEP 6: Change the Source Data

➤ Click the **Revenue by Product tab** to make it the active sheet. Click anywhere in the title of the chart, drag the mouse over the word **City** to select the text, then type **Product Category** to replace the selected text. Click outside the title to deselect it.

➤ Pull down the **Chart menu.** If necessary, click the double arrow to see more commands, click **Source Data** (you will see the Sales Data worksheet), then click the **Columns option button** so that your screen matches Figure 4.10e. Click the **Series tab** and note the following:

• The current chart plots the data in rows. There are three data series (one series for each product).

• The new chart (shown in the dialog box) plots the data in columns. There are four data series (one for each city as indicated in the Series list box).

➤ Click **OK** to close the Source Data dialog box. Save the workbook.

THE HORIZONTAL SCROLL BAR

The horizontal scroll bar contains four scrolling buttons to scroll through the sheet tabs in a workbook. Click ◄ or ► to scroll one tab to the left or right. Click |◄ or ►| to scroll to the first or last tab in the workbook. Once the desired tab is visible, click the tab to select it.

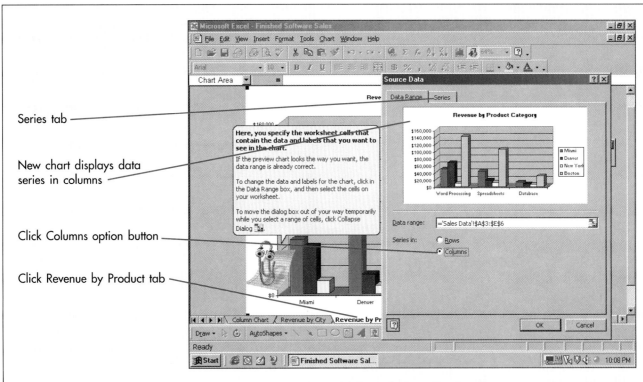

Series tab

New chart displays data series in columns

Click Columns option button

Click Revenue by Product tab

(e) Change the Source Data (step 6)

FIGURE 4.10   Hands-on Exercise 2 (continued)

STEP 7: Change the Chart Type

➤ Point to the chart area, click the **right mouse button** to display a shortcut menu, then click the **Chart Type** command to display the Chart Type dialog box.

➤ Select the **Stacked Column with a 3-D visual effect chart** (the middle entry in the second row). Click **OK.** The chart changes to a stacked column chart as shown in Figure 4.10f. Save the workbook.

➤ Pull down the File menu, click the **Print command,** then click the option button to print the **Entire Workbook.** Click **OK.**

➤ Submit the workbook to your instructor as proof that you completed the exercise. Close the workbook. Exit Excel if you do not want to continue with the next exercise at this time.

THE RIGHT MOUSE BUTTON

Point to a cell (or group of selected cells), a chart or worksheet tab, a toolbar, or chart (or a selected object on the chart), then click the right mouse button to display a shortcut menu. All shortcut menus are context-sensitive and display commands appropriate for the selected item. Right clicking a toolbar, for example, enables you to display (hide) additional toolbars. Right clicking a sheet tab enables you to rename, move, copy, or delete the sheet.

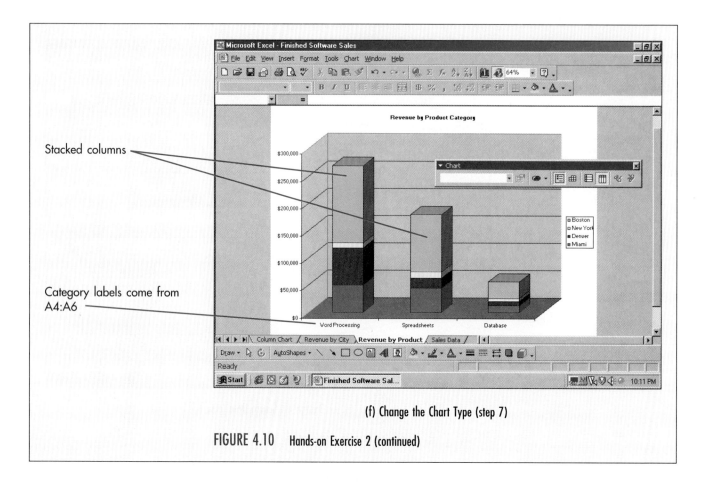

Stacked columns

Category labels come from A4:A6

(f) Change the Chart Type (step 7)

FIGURE 4.10   Hands-on Exercise 2 (continued)

OBJECT LINKING AND EMBEDDING

One of the primary advantages of the Windows environment is the ability to create a *compound document* that contains data *(objects)* from multiple applications. The memo in Figure 4.11 is an example of a compound document. The memo was created in Microsoft Word, and it contains objects (a worksheet and a chart) that were developed in Microsoft Excel. *Object Linking and Embedding* (*OLE,* pronounced "oh-lay") is the means by which you create the compound document.

The essential difference between linking and embedding is whether the object is stored within the compound document *(embedding)* or in its own file *(linking).* An *embedded object* is stored in the compound document, which in turn becomes the only client for that object. A *linked object* is stored in its own file, and the compound document is one of many potential clients for that object. The compound document does not contain the linked object per se, but only a representation of the object as well as a pointer (link) to the file containing the object. The advantage of linking is that any document that is linked to the object is updated automatically if the object is changed.

The choice between linking and embedding depends on how the object will be used. Linking is preferable if the object is likely to change and the compound document requires the latest version. Linking should also be used when the same object is in many documents, so that any change to the object has to be made in only one place. Embedding should be used if you need the actual object—for example, if you intend to edit the compound document on a different computer.

The following exercise uses linking to create a Word document containing an Excel worksheet and chart. As you do the exercise, both applications (Word and Excel) will be open, and it will be necessary to switch back and forth between the two. This in turn demonstrates the *multitasking* capability within Windows and the use of the Windows taskbar to switch between the open applications.

Superior Software

Miami, Florida

To: Mr. White
               Chairman, Superior Software

From: Heather Bond
               Vice President, Marketing

Subject: May Sales Data

The May sales data clearly indicate that Boston is outperforming our other geographic areas. It is my feeling that Ms. Brown, the office supervisor, is directly responsible for its success and that she should be rewarded accordingly. In addition, we may want to think about transferring her to New York, as they are in desperate need of new ideas and direction. I will be awaiting your response after you have time to digest the information presented.

Superior Software Sales

	Miami	Denver	New York	Boston	Total
Word Processing	$50,000	$67,500	$9,500	$141,000	$268,000
Spreadsheets	$44,000	$18,000	$11,500	$105,000	$178,500
Database	$12,000	$7,500	$6,000	$30,000	$55,500
Total	$106,000	$93,000	$27,000	$276,000	$502,000

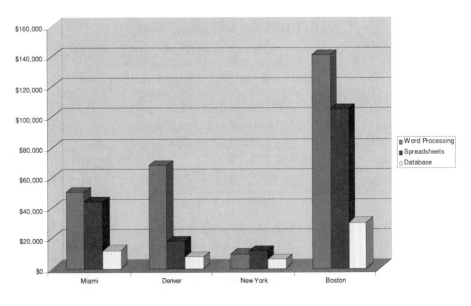

FIGURE 4.11   Object Linking and Embedding

Objective: To create a compound document consisting of a memo, worksheet, and chart. Use Figure 4.12 as a guide in the exercise.

STEP 1: Open the Software Sales Document

➤ Click the **Start button** on the taskbar to display the Start menu. Click (or point to) the **Programs menu,** then click **Microsoft Word 2000** to start the program. Hide the Office Assistant if it appears.

➤ Word is now active, and the taskbar contains a button for Microsoft Word. It may (or may not) contain a button for Microsoft Excel, depending on whether or not you closed Excel at the end of the previous exercise.

➤ If necessary, click the **Maximize button** in the application window so that Word takes the entire desktop as shown in Figure 4.12a. (The Open dialog box is not yet visible.)

➤ Pull down the **File menu** and click **Open** (or click the **Open button** on the Standard toolbar).

- Click the **drop-down arrow** in the Look In list box. Click the appropriate drive, drive C or drive A, depending on the location of your data.

- Double click the **Exploring Excel folder** (we placed the Word memo in the Exploring Excel folder) to open the folder. Double click the **Software Memo** to open the document.

- Save the document as **Finished Software Memo.**

➤ Pull down the **View menu.** Click **Print Layout** to change to the Print Layout view. Pull down the **View menu.** Click **Zoom.** Click **Page Width.**

OBJECT LINKING AND EMBEDDING

Object Linking and Embedding (OLE) enables you to create a compound document containing objects (data) from multiple Windows applications. The two techniques, linking and embedding, can be implemented in different ways. Although OLE is one of the major benefits of working in the Windows environment, it would be impossible to illustrate all of the techniques in a single exercise. Accordingly, we have created the icon at the left to help you identify the many examples of object linking and embedding that appear throughout the *Exploring Windows* series.

STEP 2: Copy the Worksheet

➤ Open (or return to) the **Finished Software Sales workbook** from the previous exercise.

- If you did not close Microsoft Excel at the end of the previous exercise, you will see its button on the taskbar. Click the **Microsoft Excel button** to return to or open the Finished Software Sales workbook.

- If you closed Microsoft Excel, click the **Start button** to start Excel, then open the Finished Software Sales workbook.

➤ The taskbar should now contain a button for both Microsoft Word and Microsoft Excel. Click either button to move back and forth between the open applications. End by clicking the Microsoft Excel button so that you see the Finished Software Sales workbook.

➤ Click the tab for **Sales Data.** Click and drag to select **A1** through **F7** to select the entire worksheet as shown in Figure 4.12b.

➤ Point to the selected area and click the **right mouse button** to display the shortcut menu. Click **Copy.** A moving border appears around the entire worksheet, indicating that it has been copied to the clipboard.

Open button

Click to select drive/folder

Double click to open Software Memo

Start button

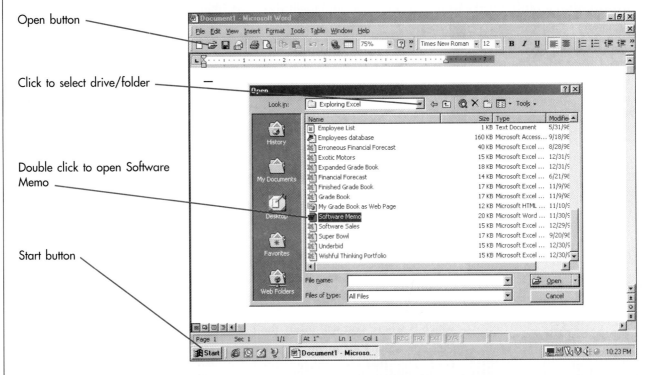

(a) Open the Software Sales Document (step 1)

FIGURE 4.12   Hands-on Exercise 3

THE WINDOWS TASKBAR

Multitasking, the ability to run multiple applications at the same time, is one of the primary advantages of the Windows environment. Each button on the taskbar appears automatically when its application or folder is opened, and disappears upon closing. (The buttons are resized automatically according to the number of open windows.) The taskbar can be moved to the left or right edge of the desktop, or to the top of the desktop, by dragging a blank area of the taskbar to the desired position.

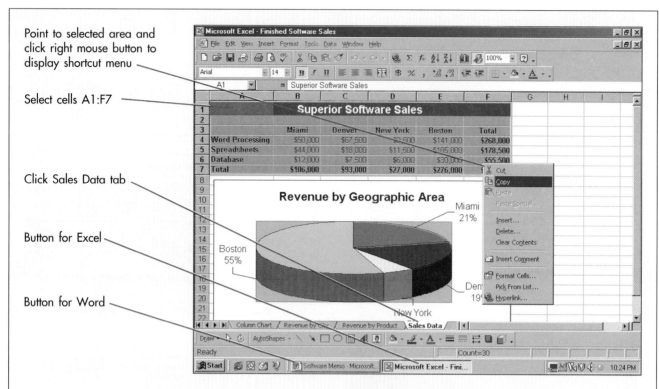

Point to selected area and click right mouse button to display shortcut menu

Select cells A1:F7

Click Sales Data tab

Button for Excel

Button for Word

(b) Copy the Worksheet (step 2)

FIGURE 4.12   Hands-on Exercise 3 (continued)

STEP 3: Create the Link

➤ Click the **Microsoft Word button** on the taskbar to return to the memo as shown in Figure 4.12c. Press **Ctrl+End** to move to the end of the memo, which is where you will insert the Excel worksheet.

➤ Pull down the **Edit menu.** If necessary, click the double arrow to see more commands, then click **Paste Special** to display the dialog box in Figure 4.12c.

➤ Click **Microsoft Excel Worksheet Object** in the As list. Click the **Paste Link option button.** Click **OK** to insert the worksheet into the document.

➤ Click and drag the worksheet to center it between the margins. Save the memo.

THE COMMON USER INTERFACE

The common user interface provides a sense of familiarity from one Windows application to the next. Even if you have never used Microsoft Word, you will recognize many of the elements present in Excel. The applications share a common menu structure with consistent ways to execute commands from those menus. The Standard and Formatting toolbars are present in both applications. Many keyboard shortcuts are also common, such as Ctrl+Home and Ctrl+End to move to the beginning and end of a document.

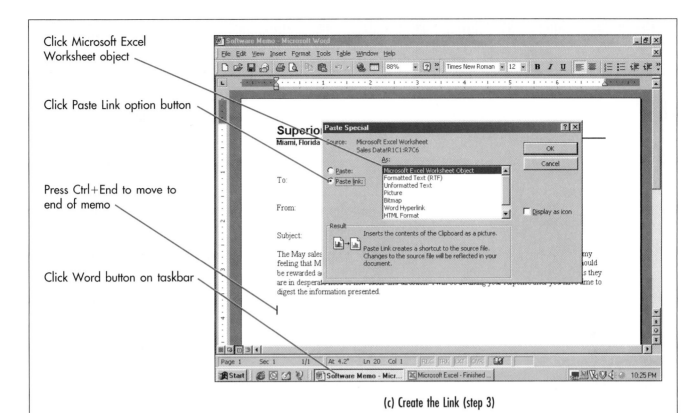

Click Microsoft Excel
Worksheet object

Click Paste Link option button

Press Ctrl+End to move to
end of memo

Click Word button on taskbar

(c) Create the Link (step 3)

FIGURE 4.12   Hands-on Exercise 3 (continued)

STEP 4: Copy the Chart

➤ Click the **Microsoft Excel button** on the taskbar to return to the worksheet.
Click outside the selected area (cells A1 through F7) to deselect the cells.
Press **Esc** to remove the moving border.

➤ Click the **Revenue by City tab** to select the chart sheet. Point to the chart
area, then click the left mouse button to select the chart. Be sure you have
selected the entire chart and that you see the same sizing handles as in Figure 4.12d.

➤ Pull down the **Edit menu** and click **Copy** (or click the **Copy button** on the
Standard toolbar). A moving border appears around the entire chart.

ALT+TAB STILL WORKS

Alt+Tab was a treasured shortcut in Windows 3.1 that enabled users to
switch back and forth between open applications. The shortcut also works
in Windows 95/98. Press and hold the Alt key while you press and release
the Tab key repeatedly to cycle through the open applications, whose
icons are displayed in a small rectangular window in the middle of the
screen. Release the Alt key when you have selected the icon for the application you want.

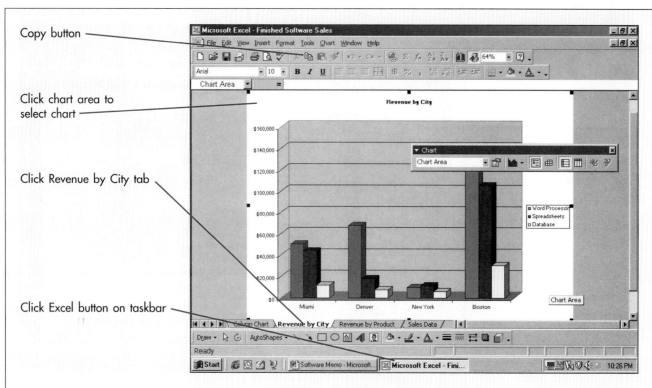

Copy button

Click chart area to select chart

Click Revenue by City tab

Click Excel button on taskbar

(d) Copy the Chart (step 4)

FIGURE 4.12 Hands-on Exercise 3 (continued)

STEP 5: Add the Chart

➤ Click the **Microsoft Word button** on the taskbar to return to the memo. If necessary, press **Ctrl+End** to move to the end of the Word document. Press the **enter key** to add a blank line.

➤ Pull down the **Edit menu.** Click **Paste Special.** Click the **Paste Link** option button. If necessary, click **Microsoft Excel Chart Object.** Click **OK** to insert the chart into the document.

➤ Zoom to **Whole Page** to facilitate moving and sizing the chart. You need to reduce its size so that it fits on the same page as the memo. Thus, scroll to the chart and click it to select it and display the sizing handles as shown in Figure 4.12e.

➤ Click and drag a corner sizing handle inward to make the chart smaller, then move it to the first page and center it on the page.

➤ Zoom to **Page Width.** Look carefully at the worksheet and chart in the document. The sales for Word Processing in New York are currently $9,500, and the chart reflects this amount. Save the memo.

➤ Point to the **Microsoft Excel button** on the taskbar and click the **right mouse button** to display a shortcut menu. Click **Close** to close Excel. Click **Yes** if prompted whether to save the changes to the Finished Software Sales workbook.

➤ Pull down the **File menu** and click the **Exit command.** The Microsoft Excel button disappears from the taskbar, indicating that Excel has been closed. Word is now the only open application.

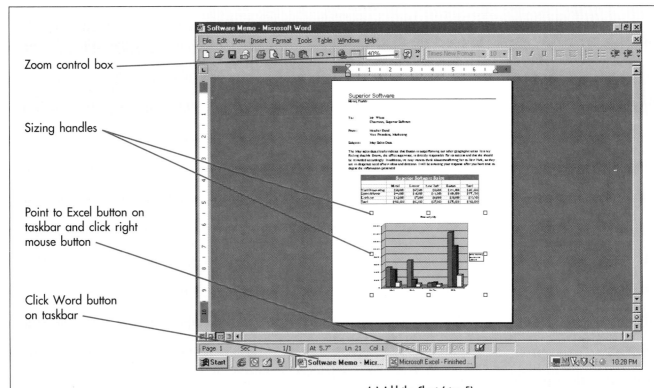

Zoom control box

Sizing handles

Point to Excel button on taskbar and click right mouse button

Click Word button on taskbar

(e) Add the Chart (step 5)

FIGURE 4.12   Hands-on Exercise 3 (continued)

STEP 6: Modify the Worksheet

➤ Click anywhere in the worksheet to select the worksheet and display the sizing handles as shown in Figure 4.12f.

➤ The status bar indicates that you can double click to edit the worksheet. Double click anywhere within the worksheet to reopen Excel in order to change the data.

➤ The system pauses as it loads Excel and reopens the Finished Software Sales workbook. If necessary, click the **Maximize button** to maximize the Excel window. Hide the Office Assistant if it appears.

➤ If necessary, click the **Sales Data tab** within the workbook. Click in **cell D4.** Type **$200,000.** Press **enter.**

➤ Click the **I◄ button** to scroll to the first tab. Click the **Revenue by City tab** to select the chart sheet. The chart has been modified automatically and reflects the increased sales for New York.

LINKING VERSUS EMBEDDING

A linked object maintains its connection to the source file. An embedded object does not. Thus, a linked object can be placed in any number of destination files, each of which maintains a pointer (link) to the same source file. Any change to the object in the source file is reflected automatically in every destination file containing that object.

Double click to edit worksheet

Word is only open application

Status bar

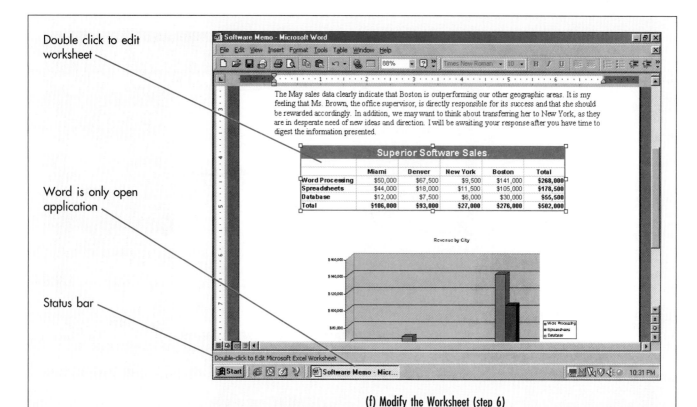

(f) Modify the Worksheet (step 6)

FIGURE 4.12   Hands-on Exercise 3 (continued)

STEP 7: Update the Links

➤ Click the **Microsoft Word button** on the taskbar to return to the Software memo. The links for the worksheet and chart should be updated automatically. If not:

• Pull down the **Edit menu.** Click **Links to** display the Links dialog box in Figure 4.12g.

• Select the link(s) to update. (You can press and hold the **Ctrl key** to select multiple links simultaneously.)

• Click the **Update Now button** to update the selected links.

• Close the Links dialog box.

➤ The worksheet and chart should both reflect $200,000 for word processing sales in New York. Save the Word document.

LINKING WORKSHEETS

A Word document can be linked to an Excel chart and/or worksheet; i.e., change the chart in Excel, and the Word document changes automatically. The chart itself is linked to the underlying worksheet; i.e, change the worksheet, and the chart changes. Worksheets can also be linked to one another; for example, a summary worksheet for the corporation as a whole can reflect data from detail worksheets for individual cities. See problem 4 at the end of the chapter.

Click Update Now

Select link to update

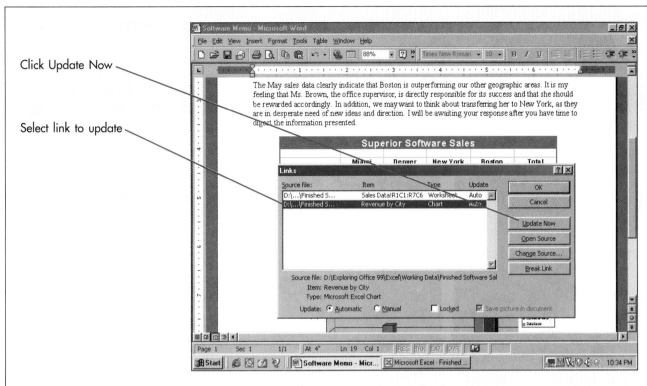

(g) Update the Links (step 7)

FIGURE 4.12   Hands-on Exercise 3 (continued)

STEP 8: The Finishing Touches

➤ Point to the chart, click the **right mouse button** to display a shortcut menu, then click the **Format Object command** to display the Format Object dialog box in Figure 4.12h.

➤ Click the **Colors and Lines Tab,** click the **drop-down arrow** in the Line Color box, then click **black** to display a line (border) around the worksheet. Click **OK.** Deselect the chart to see the border.

➤ Zoom to the **Whole Page** to view the completed document. Click and drag the worksheet and/or the chart within the memo to make any last minute changes. Save the memo a final time.

➤ Print the completed memo and submit it to your instructor. Exit Word. Exit Excel. Save the changes to the Finished Software Sales workbook.

➤ Congratulations on a job well done.

TO CLICK OR DOUBLE CLICK

Clicking an object selects the object after which you can move and/or size the object or change its properties. Double clicking an object starts the application that created the object and enables you to change underlying data. Any changes to the object in the source file (e.g., the worksheet) are automatically reflected in the object in the destination file (e.g., the Word document) provided the two are properly linked to one another.

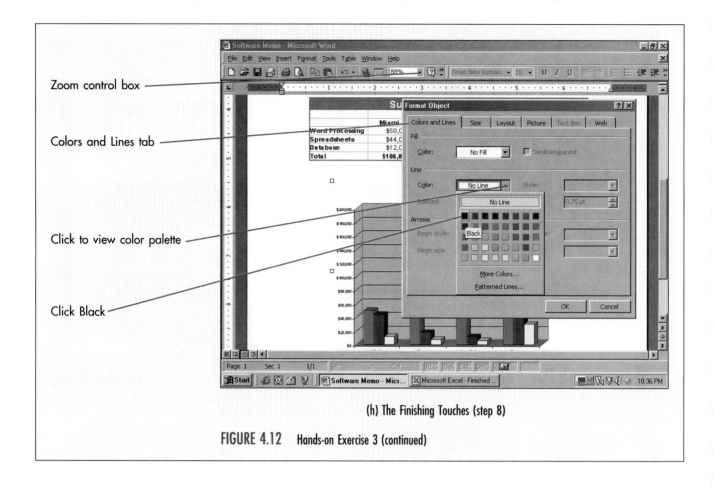

Zoom control box

Colors and Lines tab

Click to view color palette

Click Black

(h) The Finishing Touches (step 8)

FIGURE 4.12   Hands-on Exercise 3 (continued)

ADDITIONAL CHART TYPES

Excel offers a total of 14 standard *chart types,* each with several formats. The chart types are displayed in the Chart Wizard (see Figure 4.5b) and are listed here for convenience. The chart types are: Column, Bar, Line, Pie, XY (scatter), Area, Doughnut, Radar, Surface, Bubble, Stock, Cylinder, Cone, and Pyramid.

It is not possible to cover every type of chart, and so we concentrate on the most common. We have already presented the bar, column, and pie charts and continue with the line and combination charts. We use a different example, the worksheet in Figure 4.13a, which plots financial data for the National Widgets Corporation in Figures 4.13b and 4.13c. Both charts were created through the Chart Wizard, then modified as necessary using the techniques from the previous exercises.

	A	B	C	D	E	F
1		National Widgets Financial Data				
2						
3		*1992*	*1993*	*1994*	*1995*	*1996*
4	*Revenue*	$50,000,000	$60,000,000	$70,000,000	$80,000,000	$90,000,000
5	*Profit*	$10,000,000	$8,000,000	$6,000,000	$4,000,000	$2,000,000
6	*Stock Price*	$40	$35	$36	$31	$24

(a) The Worksheet

FIGURE 4.13   Additional Chart Types

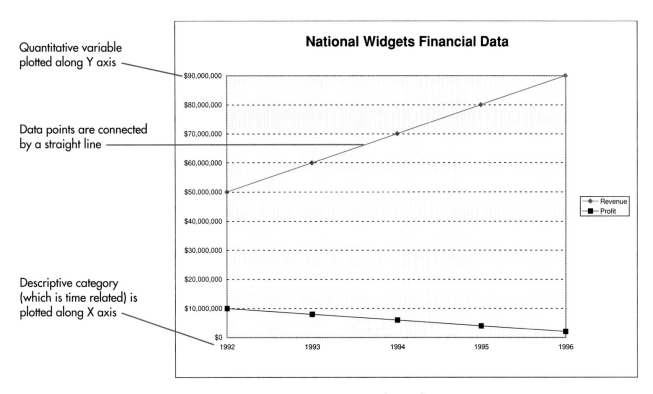

Quantitative variable plotted along Y axis

Data points are connected by a straight line

Descriptive category (which is time related) is plotted along X axis

(b) Line Chart

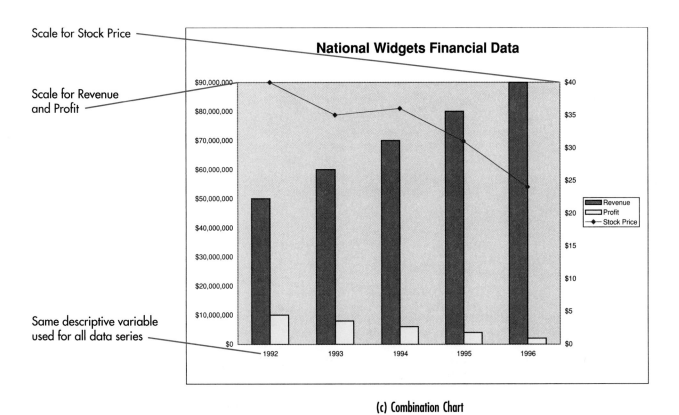

Scale for Stock Price

Scale for Revenue and Profit

Same descriptive variable used for all data series

(c) Combination Chart

FIGURE 4.13   Additional Chart Types (continued)

Line Chart

A **line chart** is best to display time-related information, such as the five-year trend of revenue and profit in Figure 4.13b. A line chart plots one or more data series (e.g., revenue and profit) against a descriptive category (e.g., year). As with a column chart, the quantitative values are plotted along the vertical scale (Y axis) and the descriptive category along the horizontal scale (X axis).

Combination Chart

A **combination chart** uses two or more chart types to display different kinds of information or when different scales are required for multiple data series. The chart in Figure 4.13c plots revenue, profit, and stock price over the five-year period. The same scale can be used for revenue and profit (both are in millions of dollars), but an entirely different scale is needed for the stock price. Investors in National Widgets can see at a glance the true status of their company.

USE AND ABUSE OF CHARTS

The hands-on exercises in the chapter demonstrate how easily numbers in a worksheet can be converted to their graphic equivalent. *The numbers can, however, just as easily be converted into erroneous or misleading charts, a fact that is often overlooked.* Indeed, some individuals are so delighted just to obtain the charts, that they accept the data without question. Accordingly, we present two examples of statistically accurate yet entirely misleading graphical data, drawn from charts submitted by our students in response to homework assignments.

> Lying graphics cheapen the graphical art everywhere ... When a chart on television lies, it lies millions of times over; when a *New York Times* chart lies, it lies 900,000 times over to a great many important and influential readers. The lies are told about the major issues of public policy—the government budget, medical care, prices, and fuel economy standards, for example. The lies are systematic and quite predictable, nearly always exaggerating the rate of recent change.
>
> **Edward Tufte**

Improper (Omitted) Labels

The difference between *unit sales* and *dollar sales* is a concept of great importance, yet one that is often missed. Consider, for example, the two pie charts in Figures 4.14a and 4.14b, both of which are intended to identify the leading salesperson, based on the underlying worksheet in Figure 4.14c. The charts yield two different answers, Jones and Smith, respectively, depending on which chart you use.

As you can see, the two charts reflect different percentages and would appear therefore to contradict each other. Both charts, however, are technically correct, as the percentages depend on whether they express unit sales or dollar sales. *Jones is the leader in terms of units, whereas Smith is the leader in terms of dollars.* The latter is generally more significant, and hence the measure that is probably most important to the reader. Neither chart, however, was properly labeled (there is no indication of whether units or dollars are plotted), which in turn may lead to erroneous conclusions on the part of the reader.

Omitted titles can lead to erroneous conclusions

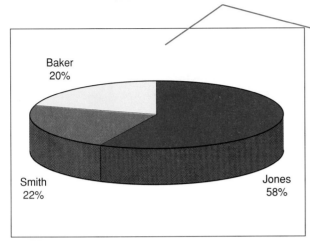

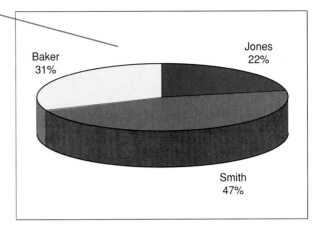

(a) Units

(b) Dollars

Sales Data - First Quarter							
		Jones		Smith		Baker	
	Price	Units	Dollars	Units	Dollars	Units	Dollars
Product 1	$1	200	$200	20	$20	30	$30
Product 2	$5	50	$250	30	$150	30	$150
Product 3	$20	5	$100	50	$1,000	30	$600
	Totals	255	$550	100	$1,170	90	$780

(c) Underlying Spreadsheet

FIGURE 4.14   Omitted Labels

Good practice demands that every chart have a title and that as much information be included on the chart as possible to help the reader interpret the data. Use titles for the X axis and Y axis if necessary. Add text boxes for additional explanation.

Adding Dissimilar Quantities

The conversion of a side-by-side column chart to a stacked column chart is a simple matter, requiring only a few mouse clicks. Because the procedure is so easy, however, it can be done without thought, and in situations where the stacked column chart is inappropriate.

Figures 4.15a and 4.15b display a side-by-side and a stacked column chart, respectively. One chart is appropriate and one chart is not. The side-by-side columns in Figure 4.15a indicate increasing sales in conjunction with decreasing profits. This is a realistic portrayal of the company, which is becoming less efficient because profits are decreasing as sales are increasing.

The stacked column chart in Figure 4.15b plots the identical numbers. It is deceptive, however, as it implies an optimistic trend whose stacked columns reflect a nonsensical addition. The problem is that although sales and profits are both measured in dollars, they should not be added together because the sum does not represent a meaningful concept.

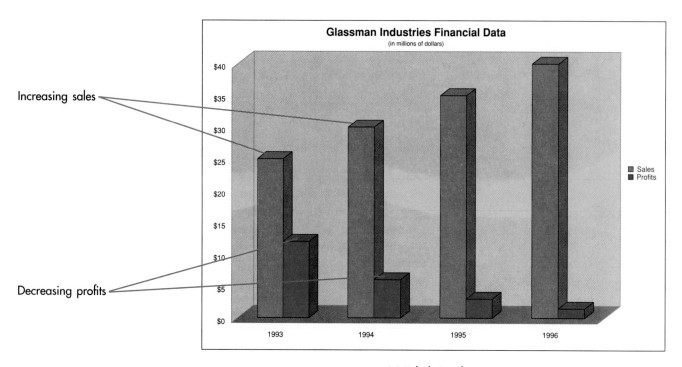

(a) Multiple Bar Chart

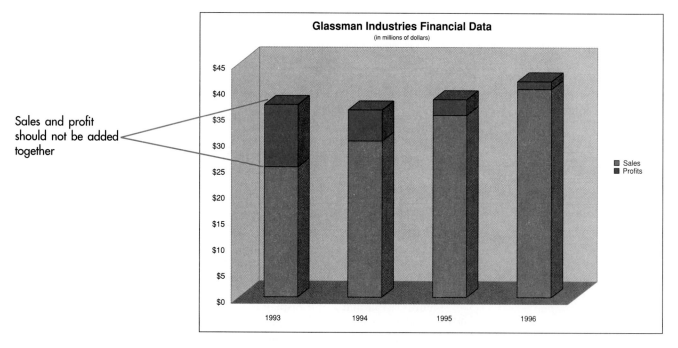

(b) Stacked Bar Chart

FIGURE 4.15   Adding Dissimilar Quantities

SUMMARY

A chart is a graphic representation of data in a worksheet. The type of chart chosen depends on the message to be conveyed. A pie chart is best for proportional relationships. A column or bar chart is used to show actual numbers rather than percentages. A line chart is preferable for time-related data. A combination chart uses two or more chart types when different scales are required for different data series.

The Chart Wizard is an easy way to create a chart. Once created, a chart can be enhanced with arrows and text boxes found on the Drawing toolbar.

A chart may be embedded in a worksheet or created in a separate chart sheet. An embedded chart may be moved within a worksheet by selecting it and dragging it to its new location. An embedded chart may be sized by selecting it and dragging any of the sizing handles in the desired direction.

Multiple data series may be specified in either rows or columns. If the data is in rows, the first row is assumed to contain the category labels, and the first column is assumed to contain the legend. Conversely, if the data is in columns, the first column is assumed to contain the category labels, and the first row the legend. The Chart Wizard makes it easy to switch from rows to columns and vice versa.

Object Linking and Embedding enables the creation of a compound document containing data (objects) from multiple applications. The essential difference between linking and embedding is whether the object is stored within the compound document (embedding) or in its own file (linking). An embedded object is stored in the compound document, which in turn becomes the only user (client) of that object. A linked object is stored in its own file, and the compound document is one of many potential clients of that object.

It is important that charts are created accurately and that they do not mislead the reader. The difference between dollar sales and unit sales is an important concept, which should be clearly indicated. Stacked column charts should not add dissimilar quantities.

KEY WORDS AND CONCEPTS

Bar chart
Category label
Chart
Chart sheet
Chart toolbar
Chart type
Chart Wizard
Column chart
Combination chart
Common user interface
Compound document
Data point
Data series
Default chart

Docked toolbar
Drawing toolbar
Embedded chart
Embedded object
Embedding
Exploded pie chart
Floating toolbar
Legend
Line chart
Linked object
Linking
Multiple data series
Multitasking
Object

Object Linking and
  Embedding (OLE)
Pie chart
Sizing handles
Stacked columns
Taskbar
Three-dimensional
  column chart
Three-dimensional pie
  chart
X axis
Y axis

1. Which type of chart is best to portray proportion or market share?
   (a) Pie chart
   (b) Line
   (c) Column chart
   (d) Combination chart

2. Which of the following is a true statement about the Chart Wizard?
   (a) It is accessed via a button on the Standard toolbar
   (b) It enables you to choose the type of chart you want as well as specify the location for that chart
   (c) It enables you to retrace your steps via the Back command button
   (d) All of the above

3. Which of the following chart types is *not* suitable to display multiple data series?
   (a) Pie chart
   (b) Horizontal bar chart
   (c) Column chart
   (d) All of the above are equally suitable

4. Which of the following is best to display additive information from multiple data series?
   (a) A column chart with the data series stacked one on top of another
   (b) A column chart with the data series side by side
   (c) Both (a) and (b) are equally appropriate
   (d) Neither (a) nor (b) is appropriate

5. A workbook must contain:
   (a) A separate chart sheet for every worksheet
   (b) A separate worksheet for every chart sheet
   (c) Both (a) and (b)
   (d) Neither (a) nor (b)

6. Which of the following is true regarding an embedded chart?
   (a) It can be moved elsewhere within the worksheet
   (b) It can be made larger or smaller
   (c) Both (a) and (b)
   (d) Neither (a) nor (b)

7. Which of the following will produce a shortcut menu?
   (a) Pointing to a workbook tab and clicking the right mouse button
   (b) Pointing to an embedded chart and clicking the right mouse button
   (c) Pointing to a selected cell range and clicking the right mouse button
   (d) All of the above

8. Which of the following is done *prior* to invoking the Chart Wizard?
   (a) The data series are selected
   (b) The location of the embedded chart within the worksheet is specified
   (c) Both (a) and (b)
   (d) Neither (a) nor (b)

9. Which of the following will display sizing handles when selected?
   (a) An embedded chart
   (b) The title of a chart
   (c) A text box or arrow
   (d) All of the above

10. How do you switch between open applications?
    (a) Click the appropriate button on the taskbar
    (b) Use Alt+Tab to cycle through the applications
    (c) Both (a) and (b)
    (d) Neither (a) nor (b)

11. Which of the following is true regarding the compound document (the memo containing the worksheet and chart) that was created in the chapter?
    (a) The compound document contains more than one object
    (b) Excel is the server application and Word for Windows is the client application
    (c) Both (a) and (b)
    (d) Neither (a) nor (b)

12. In order to represent multiple data series on the same chart:
    (a) The data series must be in rows and the rows must be adjacent to one another on the worksheet
    (b) The data series must be in columns and the columns must be adjacent to one another on the worksheet
    (c) The data series may be in rows or columns so long as they are adjacent to one another
    (d) The data series may be in rows or columns with no requirement to be next to one another

13. If multiple data series are selected and rows are specified:
    (a) The first row will be used for the category (X axis) labels
    (b) The first column will be used for the legend
    (c) Both (a) and (b)
    (d) Neither (a) nor (b)

14. If multiple data series are selected and columns are specified:
    (a) The first column will be used for the category (X axis) labels
    (b) The first row will be used for the legend
    (c) Both (a) and (b)
    (d) Neither (a) nor (b)

15. Which of the following is true about the scale on the Y axis in a column chart that plots multiple data series side-by-side versus one that stacks the values one on top of another?
    (a) The scale for the stacked columns will contain larger values than if the columns are plotted side-by-side
    (b) The scale for the side-by-side columns will contain larger values than if the columns are stacked
    (c) The values on the scale will be the same regardless of whether the columns are stacked or side-by-side
    (d) The values on the scale will be different but it is not possible to tell which chart will contain the higher values

ANSWERS

1. a	**6.** c	**11.** c
2. d	**7.** d	**12.** d
3. a	**8.** a	**13.** c
4. a	**9.** d	**14.** c
5. d	**10.** c	**15.** a

PRACTICE WITH EXCEL 2000

1. Michael Moldof Boutique: A partially completed version of the worksheet in Figure 4.16 is available in the Exploring Excel folder as *Chapter 4 Practice 1.* Open the workbook and save it as *Chapter 4 Practice 1 Solution.* Follow the directions in steps (a) and (b) to compute the totals and format the worksheet, then create each of the charts listed below.

a. Use the AutoSum command to enter the formulas to compute the totals for each store and each product.

b. Select the whole worksheet. Use the AutoFormat command as the basis of a design for the worksheet. You do not have to accept the entire design and/or you can modify the design after it has been applied to the worksheet. For example, you may want to add currency formatting and change the column widths.

c. A pie chart showing the percentage of total sales attributed to each store.

d. A column chart showing the total sales for each store.

e. A stacked column chart showing total sales for each store, broken down by clothing category.

f. A stacked column chart showing total dollars for each clothing category, broken down by store.

g. Create each chart in its own chart sheet. Rename the various chart sheets to reflect the charts they contain.

h. Title each chart appropriately and enhance each chart as you see fit.

i. Print the entire workbook (the worksheet and all four chart sheets).

j. Add a title page with your name and date, then submit the completed assignment to your instructor.

	A	B	C	D	E	F
1	Michael Moldof Men's Boutique					
2	January Sales					
3						
4		Store 1	Store 2	Store 3	Store 4	Total
5	Slacks	$ 25,000	$ 28,750	$ 21,500	$ 9,400	$ 84,650
6	Shirts	$ 43,000	$ 49,450	$ 36,900	$ 46,000	$ 175,350
7	Underwear	$ 18,000	$ 20,700	$ 15,500	$ 21,000	$ 75,200
8	Accessories	$ 7,000	$ 8,050	$ 8,000	$ 4,000	$ 27,050
9						
10	Total	$ 93,000	$ 106,950	$ 81,900	$ 80,400	$ 362,250

FIGURE 4.16 Michael Moldof Boutique (Exercise 1)

2. Unique Boutiques: The worksheet in Figure 4.17 is to be used by the corporate marketing manager in a presentation in which she describes sales over the past four years. The worksheet is in the *Chapter 4 Practice 2* workbook. Do the following:

a. Format the worksheet attractively so that it can be used as part of the presentation. Include your name somewhere in the worksheet.

b. Create any chart(s) you think appropriate to emphasize the successful performance enjoyed by the London office.

c. Use the same data and chart type(s) as in part (a) but modify the title to emphasize the disappointing performance of the Paris office.

d. Print the worksheet together with all charts and submit them to your instructor. Be sure to title all charts appropriately and to use the text and arrow tools to add the required emphasis.

	A	B	C	D	E	F
1	Unique Boutiques					
2	Sales for 1995-1998					
3						
4	Store	1995	1996	1997	1998	Totals
5	Miami	1500000	2750000	3000000	3250000	10500000
6	London	4300000	5500000	6700000	13000000	29500000
7	Paris	2200000	1800000	1400000	1000000	6400000
8	Rome	2000000	3000000	4000000	5000000	14000000
9	Totals	10000000	13050000	15100000	22250000	60400000

FIGURE 4.17   Unique Boutiques (Exercise 2)

3. Hotel Capacities: The worksheet in Figure 4.18 is to be used as the basis for several charts depicting information on hotel capacities. Each of the charts is to be created in its own chart sheet within the *Chapter 4 Practice 3* workbook on the data disk. We describe the message we want to convey, but it is up to you to determine the appropriate chart and associated data range(s). Accordingly, you are to create a chart that:

a. Compares the total capacity of the individual hotels to one another.

b. Shows the percent of total capacity for each hotel.

c. Compares the number of standard and deluxe rooms for all hotels, with the number of standard and deluxe rooms side-by-side for each hotel.

d. Compares the standard and deluxe room rates for all hotels, with the two different rates side-by-side for each hotel.

e. Add your name to the worksheet as the Hotel Manager, then print the complete workbook, which will consist of the original worksheet plus the four chart sheets you created.

	A	B	C	D	E	F
1		**Hotel Capacities and Room Rates**				
2						
3	Hotel	No. of Standard Rooms	Standard Rate	No. of Deluxe Rooms	Deluxe Rate	Total Number of Rooms
4	Holiday Inn	300	100	100	150	400
5	Hyatt	225	120	50	175	275
6	Ramada Inn	150	115	35	190	185
7	Sheraton	175	95	25	150	200
8	Marriott	325	100	100	175	425
9	Hilton	250	80	45	120	295
10	Best Western	150	75	25	125	175
11	Days Inn	100	50	15	100	115

FIGURE 4.18   Hotel Capacities (Exercise 3)

4. Linking Worksheets: This chapter described how a chart is linked to the data in an underlying worksheet. It is also possible to link the data from one worksheet to another as can be seen in Figure 4.19. The figure contains a table, which at first glance is very similar to the example that was used throughout the chapter. Look closely, however, and you will see that the workbook contains four worksheets, for the corporation as a whole, as well as for Phoenix, Minneapolis, and Los Angeles.

The numbers in the corporate worksheet are linked to the numbers in the worksheets for the individual cities. The entry in cell B4 of the Corporate worksheet contains the formula =Phoenix!F2 to indicate that the entry comes from cell F2 in the Phoenix worksheet. Other cells in the table reference other cells in the Phoenix worksheet as well as cells in the other worksheets.

a. Open the *Chapter 4 Practice 4* workbook. Check that you are viewing the Corporate worksheet, then click in cell B4 of this worksheet. Type an = sign, click the Phoenix worksheet tab, click in cell F2 of this worksheet, and press the enter key. Click in cell C4, type an = sign, click the Minneapolis worksheet tab, click in cell F2 of that worksheet and press enter. Repeat this process to enter the sales for Los Angeles.

b. Click and drag cells B4 through D4, then drag the fill handle to row 6 to copy the formulas for the other products. The operation works because the worksheet references are absolute, but the cell references are relative.

c. Use the AutoSum button to compute the totals for the corporation as a whole as shown in the figure.

d. Use the completed worksheet in Figure 4.19 as the basis of a side-by-side column chart with the data plotted in rows. Plot a second side-by-side chart with the data in columns. Put each chart in a separate chart sheet.

e. Print the entire workbook for your instructor.

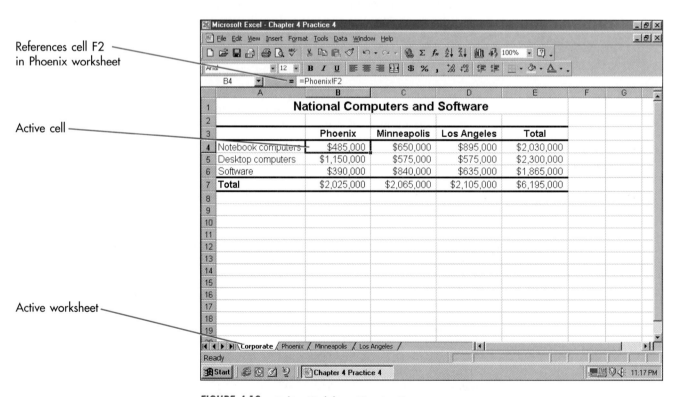

FIGURE 4.19 Linking Worksheets (Exercise 4)

5. Ralph Cordell Sporting Goods: A partially completed version of the worksheet in Figure 4.19 can be found on the data disk in the file *Chapter 4 Practice 5*. Open the workbook and make all necessary entries so that your worksheet matches the one in Figure 4.20. Next, create a memo to your instructor containing the worksheet and a chart that plots the sales data in columns to emphasize the contribution of each salesperson. Use any wording you think is appropriate for the memo. Print the completed memo, add your name, and submit it to your instructor as proof you did this exercise.

	A	B	C	D	E	F
1		**Ralph Cordell Sporting Goods**				
2		Quarterly Sales Report				
3						
4	Salesperson	1st Qtr	2nd Qtr	3rd Qtr	4th Qtr	Total
5	Powell	$50,000	$55,000	$62,500	$85,400	$252,900
6	Blaney	$34,000	$48,500	$62,000	$62,000	$206,500
7	Rego	$49,000	$44,000	$42,500	$41,000	$176,500
8	Total	$133,000	$147,500	$167,000	$188,400	$635,900

FIGURE 4.20   *Ralph Cordell Sporting goods (Exercise 5)*

6. Object Linking and Embedding: The compound document in Figure 4.21 contains a memo and combination chart. (The worksheet is contained in the *Chapter 4 Practice 6* workbook. The text of the memo is in the *Chapter 4 Practice 6 Memo*, which exists as a Word document in the Exploring Excel folder on the data disk.) You are to complete the compound document and submit it to your instructor by completing the following steps:

   a. Create a letterhead for the memo containing your name, address, phone number, and any other information you deem appropriate.

   b. Create the combination chart that appears in the memo. Select the data for the Chart Wizard in the usual fashion. You must specify the custom chart type (Line–Column on 2 Axis) as opposed to a standard line or column chart. (Click the Custom Types tab in step 1 of the Chart Wizard.)

   c. Link the chart to the memo.

   d. Print the compound document and submit it to your instructor.

7. Object Linking and Embedding: Create the document in Figure 4.22 based on the partially completed worksheet in *Chapter 4 Practice 7*. You need to enter the text of the memo yourself, and in addition, create an interesting letterhead using Microsoft WordArt. You need not duplicate our letterhead exactly. This exercise gives you the opportunity to practice a variety of skills.

CASE STUDIES

University Enrollments

Your assistantship has placed you in the Provost's office, where you are to help create a presentation for the Board of Trustees. The Provost is expected to make recommendations to the Board regarding the expansion of some programs and the reduction of others. You are expected to help the Provost by developing a series of charts to illustrate enrollment trends. The Provost has created the *Student Enrollments workbook* on the data disk, which contains summary data.

Steven Stocks

100 Century Tower • New York, NY 10021 • (212) 333-3333

To: Carlos Rosell

From: Steven Stocks

Subject: Status Report on National Widgets

I have uncovered some information that I feel is important to the overall health of your investment portfolio. The graph below clearly shows that while revenues for National Widgets have steadily increased since 1996, profits have steadily decreased. In addition, the stock price is continuing to decline. Although at one time I felt that a turnaround was imminent, I am no longer so optimistic and am advising you to cut your losses and sell your National Widgets stock as soon as possible.

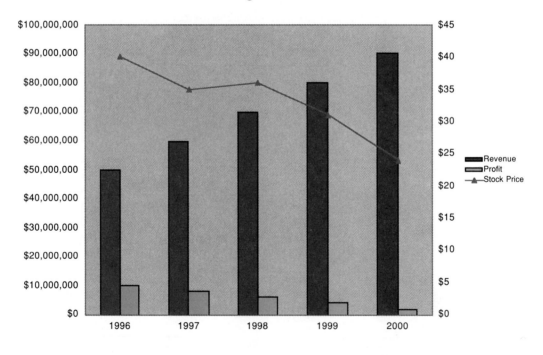

FIGURE 4.21   Compound Document for Practice (Exercise 6)

Office of Residential Living

| University of Miami | ∞ | P.O. Box 248904 | ∞ | Coral Gables, FL 33124 |

January 10, 2000

Mr. Jeffrey Redmond, President
Dynamic Dining Services
4329 Palmetto Lane
Miami, FL 33157

Dear Jeff,

As per our conversation, occupancy is projected to be back up from last year. I have enclosed a spreadsheet and chart that show the total enrollment for the past four school years. Please realize, however, that the 1999-2000 figures are projections, as the Spring 2000 numbers are still incomplete. The final 1999-2000 numbers should be confirmed within the next two weeks. I hope that this helps with your planning. If you need further information, please contact me at the above address.

Dorm Occupancy

	96-97	97-98	98-99	99-00
Beatty	330	285	270	250
Broward	620	580	620	565
Graham	450	397	352	420
Rawlings	435	470	295	372
Tolbert	550	554	524	635
Totals	2385	2286	2061	2242

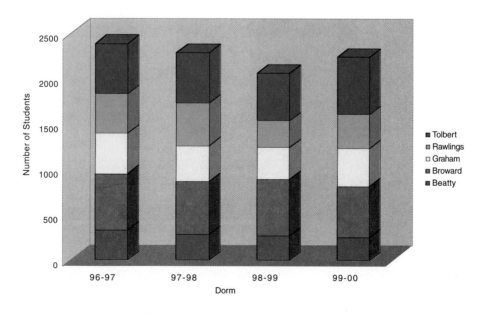

FIGURE 4.22   Compound Document for Practice (Exercise 7)

The Federal Budget

The National debt is staggering—in excess of $5 trillion, more than $1 trillion of which has been added under President Clinton. The per capita share is almost $20,000 for every man, woman, and child in the United States. The annual budget is approximately $1.5 trillion, with the deficit in the neighborhood of $150 billion. Medicare, defense, and interest on the debt itself are the largest expenditures and consume approximately 35%, 24%, and 14%, respectively. Personal income taxes and Social Security (including Medicare) taxes account for approximately 36% and 31% of the government's income.

Use the Internet to obtain exact figures for the current year, then create the appropriate charts to reflect the government's distribution of income and expenditures. Do some additional research and obtain data on the budget, the deficit, and the national debt for the years 1945, 1967, and 1980. The numbers may surprise you. For example, how does the interest expense for the current year compare to the total budget in 1967 (at the height of the Viet Nam War)? To the total budget in 1945 (at the end of World War II)?

The Annual Report

Corporate America spends a small fortune to produce its annual reports, which are readily available to the public at large. Choose any company and obtain a copy of its most recent annual report. Consolidate the information in the company's report to produce a two-page document of your own. Your report should include a description of the company's progress in the last year, a worksheet with any data you deem relevant, and at least two charts in support of the worksheet or written material. Use Microsoft Word in addition to the worksheet to present the information in an attractive manner.

Computer Mapping

Your boss has asked you to look into computer mapping in an effort to better analyze sales data for your organization. She suggested you use the online help facility to explore the Data Map feature within Excel, which enables you to create color-coded maps from columns of numerical data. You mentioned this assignment to a colleague who suggested that you open the *Mapstats workbook* that is installed with Excel to see the sample maps and demographic data included with Excel. You have two days to learn the potential for computer mapping. Your boss expects at least a three-page written report with real examples.

The Census Bureau

Use your favorite search engine to locate the home page of the United States Census Bureau, then download one or more series of population statistics of interest to you. Use the data to plot one or more charts that describe the population growth of the United States. There is an abundance of information available and you are free to choose any statistics you deem relevant.

chapter 1

INTRODUCTION TO MICROSOFT ACCESS: WHAT IS A DATABASE?

OBJECTIVES

After reading this chapter you will be able to:

1. Define the terms field, record, table, and database.
2. Start Microsoft Access; describe the Database window and the objects in an Access database.
3. Add, edit, and delete records within a table; use the Find command to locate a specific record.
4. Describe the record selector; explain when changes are saved to a table.
5. Explain the importance of data validation in table maintenance.
6. Apply a filter (by form or by selection) to a table; sort a table on one or more fields.
7. Describe a relational database; identify the one-to-many relationships that exist within a database.

OVERVIEW

All businesses and organizations maintain data of one kind or another. Companies store data about their employees. Schools and universities store data about their students and faculties. Magazines and newspapers store data about their subscribers. The list goes on and on, and while each of these examples refers to different types of data, they all operate under the same basic principles of database management.

The chapter introduces you to Microsoft Access, the application in the Microsoft Office suite that performs database management. We describe the objects in an Access database and show you how to add, edit, and delete records to a table. We explain how to obtain information from the database by running reports and queries that have been previously created. We discuss how to display selected records through a filter and how to display those records in different sequences. And finally, we provide a look ahead, by showing how the real power of Access is derived from a relational database that contains multiple tables.

The hands-on exercises in the chapter enable you to apply all of the material at the computer, and are indispensable to the learn-by-doing philosophy we follow throughout the text. As you do the exercises, you may recognize many commands from other Windows applications, all of which share a common user interface and consistent command structure.

CASE STUDY: THE COLLEGE BOOKSTORE

Imagine, if you will, that you are the manager of a college bookstore and that you maintain data for every book in the store. Accordingly, you have recorded the specifics of each book (the title, author, publisher, price, and so on) in a manila folder, and have stored the folders in one drawer of a file cabinet.

One of your major responsibilities is to order books at the beginning of each semester, which in turn requires you to contact the various publishers. You have found it convenient, therefore, to create a second set of folders with data about each publisher such as the publisher's phone number, address, discount policy, and so on. You also found it necessary to create a third set of folders with data about each order such as when the order was placed, the status of the order, which books were ordered, how many copies, and so on.

Normal business operations will require you to make repeated trips to the filing cabinet to maintain the accuracy of the data and keep it up to date. You will have to create a new folder whenever a new book is received, whenever you contract with a new publisher, or whenever you place a new order. Each of these folders must be placed in the proper drawer in the filing cabinet. In similar fashion, you will have to modify the data in an existing folder to reflect changes that occur, such as an increase in the price of a book, a change in a publisher's address, or an update in the status of an order. And, lastly, you will need to remove the folder of any book that is no longer carried by the bookstore, or of any publisher with whom you no longer have contact, or of any order that was canceled.

The preceding discussion describes the bookstore of 40 years ago—before the advent of computers and computerized databases. The bookstore manager of today needs the same information as his or her predecessor. Today's manager, however, has the information readily available, at the touch of a key or the click of a mouse, through the miracle of modern technology. The concepts are identical in both the manual and computerized systems.

Information systems have their own vocabulary. A *field* is a basic fact (or data element) such as the name of a book or the telephone number of a publisher. A *record* is a set of fields. A *table* is a set of records. Every record in a table contains the same fields in the same order. A *database* consists of one or more tables. In our example, each record in the Books table will contain the identical six fields—ISBN (a unique identifying number for the book), title, author, year of publication, price, and publisher. In similar fashion, every record in the Publishers table will have the same fields for each publisher just as every record in the Orders table has the same fields for each order. This terminology (field, record, file, and database) is extremely important and will be used throughout the text.

You can think of the file cabinet in the manual system as a database. Each set of folders in the file cabinet corresponds to a table within the database. Thus the bookstore database consists of three separate tables—for books, publishers, and orders. Each table, in turn, consists of multiple *records,* corresponding to the folders in the file cabinet. The Books table, for example, contains a record for every book title in the store. The Publishers table has a record for each publisher, just as the Orders table has a record for each order.

Microsoft Access, the fourth major application in the Microsoft Office, is used to create and manage a database such as the one for the college bookstore. Consider now Figure 1.1, which shows how Microsoft Access appears on the desktop. Our discussion assumes a basic familiarity with the Windows operating system and the user interface that is common to all Windows applications. You should recognize, therefore, that the desktop in Figure 1.1 has two open windows—an application window for Microsoft Access and a document (database) window for the database that is currently open.

Each window has its own title bar and Minimize, Maximize (or Restore), and Close buttons. The title bar in the application window contains the name of the application (Microsoft Access). The title bar in the document (database) window contains the name of the database that is currently open (Bookstore). The application window for Access has been maximized to take up the entire desktop, and hence the Restore button is visible. The database window has not been maximized.

A menu bar appears immediately below the application title bar. A toolbar (similar to those in other Office applications) appears below the menu bar and offers alternative ways to execute common commands. The Windows taskbar appears at the bottom of the screen and shows the open applications.

The Database Window

The *Database window* displays the various objects in an Access database. There are seven types of objects—tables, queries, forms, reports, pages, macros, and modules. Every database must contain at least one table, and it may contain any

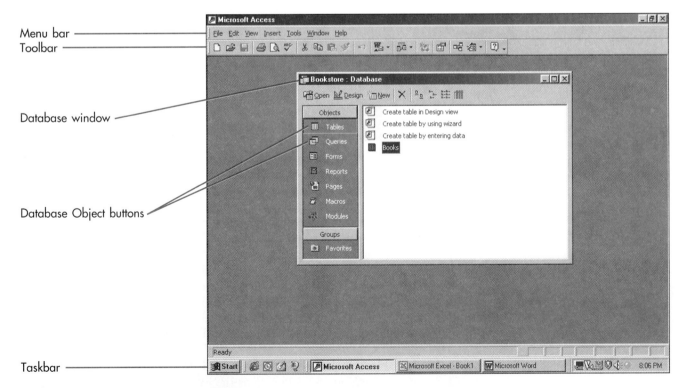

FIGURE 1.1   The Database Window

or all (or none) of the other objects. Each object type is accessed through the appropriate button within the Database window. In this chapter we concentrate on tables, but we briefly describe the other types of objects as a preview of what you will learn as you read our book.

- A *table* stores data about an entity (a person, place, or thing) and is the basic element in any database. A table is made up of records, which in turn are made up of fields. It is columnar in appearance, with each record in a separate row of the table and each field in a separate column.
- A *form* provides a more convenient and attractive way to enter, display, and/or print the data in a table.
- A *query* answers a question about the database. The most common type of query specifies a set of criteria, then searches the database to retrieve the records that satisfy the criteria.
- A *report* presents the data in a table or query in attractive fashion on the printed page.
- A *page* is an HTML document that can be posted to a Web server or Local Area Network, and which can be viewed by a Web browser.
- A *macro* is analogous to a computer program and consists of commands that are executed automatically one after the other. Macros are used to automate the performance of any repetitive task.
- A *module* provides a greater degree of automation through programming in Visual Basic for Applications (VBA).

ONE FILE HOLDS ALL

All of the objects in an Access database (tables, forms, queries, reports, pages, macros, and modules) are stored in a single file on disk. The database itself is opened through the Open command in the File menu or by clicking the Open button on the Database toolbar. The individual objects within a database are opened through the database window.

Tables

A table (or set of tables) is the heart of any database, as it contains the actual data. In Access a table is displayed in one of two views—the Design view or the Datasheet view. The *Design view* is used to define the table initially and to specify the fields it will contain. It is also used to modify the table definition if changes are subsequently necessary. The Design view is discussed in detail in Chapter 2. The *Datasheet view*—the view you use to add, edit, or delete records—is the view on which we focus in this chapter.

Figure 1.2 shows the Datasheet view for the Books table in our bookstore. The first row in the table contains the *field names.* Each additional row contains a record (the data for a specific book). Each column represents a field (one fact about a book). Every record in the table contains the same fields in the same order: ISBN Number, Title, Author, Year, List Price, and Publisher.

The status bar at the bottom of Figure 1.2a indicates that there are five records in the table and that you are positioned on the first record. This is the record you are working on and is known as the *current record.* (You can work on only one record at a time.) There is a *record selector symbol* (a triangle, asterisk, or pencil) next to the current record to indicate its status.

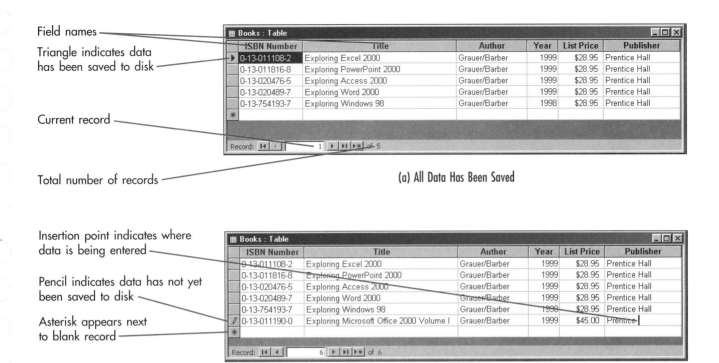

Field names

Triangle indicates data
has been saved to disk

Current record

Total number of records

(a) All Data Has Been Saved

Insertion point indicates where
data is being entered

Pencil indicates data has not yet
been saved to disk

Asterisk appears next
to blank record

(b) During Data Entry

FIGURE 1.2   Tables

A *triangle* indicates that the record has been saved to disk. A *pencil* indicates that you are working on the record and that the changes have not yet been saved. As soon as you move to the next record, however, the pencil changes to a triangle to indicate that the record on which you were working has been saved. (Access, unlike other Office applications, automatically saves changes made to a record without your having to execute the Save command.) An *asterisk* appears next to the blank record at the end of every table.

Figure 1.2a shows the table as it would appear immediately after you opened it. The first field in the first record is selected (highlighted), and anything you type at this point will replace the selected data. (This is the same convention as in any other Windows application.) The triangle next to the current record (record 1) indicates that changes have not yet been made. An asterisk appears as the record selector symbol next to the blank record at the end of the table. The blank record is used to add a record to the table and is not counted in determining the number of records in the table.

Figure 1.2b shows the table as you are in the process of entering data for a new record at the end of the table. The current record is now record 6. The *insertion point* (a flashing vertical bar) appears at the point where text is being entered. The record selector for the current record is a pencil, indicating that the record has not yet been saved. The asterisk has moved to the blank record at the end of the table, which now contains one more record than the table in Figure 1.2a.

Note, too, that each table in a database must have a field (or combination of fields) known as the *primary key,* which is unique for every record in the table. The ISBN (International Standard Book Number) is the primary key in our example, and it ensures that each record in the Books table is different from every other record. (Other fields may also have a unique value for every record, but only one field is designated as the primary key.)

Objective: To open an existing database; to add a record to a table within the database. Use Figure 1.3 as a guide in the exercise.

STEP 1: Welcome to Windows

➤ Turn on the computer and all of its peripherals. The floppy drive should be empty prior to starting your machine. This ensures that the system starts by reading from the hard disk, which contains the Windows files, as opposed to a floppy disk, which does not.

➤ Your system will take a minute or so to get started, after which you should see the desktop in Figure 1.3a. Do not be concerned if the appearance of your desktop is different from ours. If necessary, click the **Close button** to close the Welcome window.

Start button

(a) Welcome to Windows (step 1)

FIGURE 1.3   Hands-on Exercise 1

TAKE THE WINDOWS TOUR

Windows 98 greets you with a Welcome window that describes the highlights in the operating system. Click Discover Windows 98 to take a guided tour or select one of the topics at the left of the window. If you do not see the Welcome window when you start your computer, click the Start button, click Run, type C:\Windows\Welcome in the text box, and press the enter key. Relax and enjoy the show.

STEP 2: Obtain the Practice Files:

➤ We have created a series of practice files for you to use throughout the text. Your instructor will make these files available to you in a variety of ways:

- You can download the files from our Web site if you have access to the Internet and World Wide Web (see boxed tip).
- The files may be on a network drive, in which case you use the Windows Explorer to copy the files from the network to a floppy disk.
- There may be an actual "data disk" that you are to check out from the lab in order to use the Copy Disk command to duplicate the disk.

➤ Check with your instructor for additional information.

DOWNLOAD THE PRACTICE FILES

Download the practice files for any book in the *Exploring Windows* series from the Exploring Windows home page. Go to www.prenhall.com/grauer, click the Office 2000 text, click the link to student resources, then click the link to download the student data disk. Our Web site has many other features such as the Companion Web Sites (online study guides) to enhance your learning experience. See problem 6 at the end of the chapter.

STEP 3: Start Microsoft Access

➤ Click the **Start button** to display the Start menu. Click (or point to) the **Programs menu,** then click **Microsoft Access** to start the program. Click and drag the Office Assistant out of the way if it appears. (The Office Assistant is described in the next hands-on exercise.)

➤ You should see the Microsoft Access dialog box with the option button to **Open an existing file** already selected. Click **More Files,** then click **OK** to display the Open dialog box in Figure 1.3b.

➤ Click the **down arrow** on the Views button, then click **Details** to change to the Details view. Click and drag the vertical border between columns to increase (or decrease) the size of a column.

➤ Click the **drop-down arrow** on the Look In list box. Click the appropriate drive (drive C is recommended rather than drive A), depending on the location of your data. Double click the **Exploring Access folder.**

➤ Click the **down scroll arrow** until you can click the **Bookstore database.** Click the **Open command button** to open the database.

WORK ON DRIVE C

Even in a lab setting it is preferable to work on the local hard drive, as opposed to a floppy disk. The hard drive is much faster, which becomes especially important when working with the large file sizes associated with Access. Use the Windows Explorer to copy the database from the network drive to the local hard drive prior to the exercise, then work on drive C throughout the exercise. Once you have completed the exercise, use the Explorer a second time to copy the modified database to a floppy disk that you can take with you.

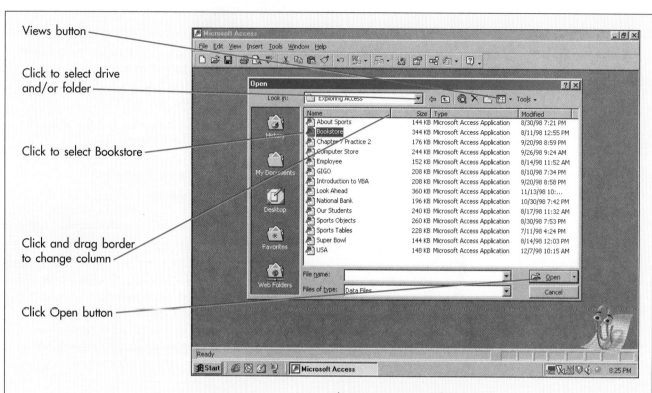

Views button

Click to select drive and/or folder

Click to select Bookstore

Click and drag border to change column

Click Open button

(b) Open an Existing Database (step 3)

FIGURE 1.3   Hands-on Exercise (continued)

STEP 4: Open the Books Table

➤ If necessary, click the **Maximize button** in the application window so that Access takes the entire desktop.

➤ You should see the Database window for the Bookstore database with the **Tables button** already selected. Double click the **Books table** to open the table as shown in Figure 1.3c.

➤ Click the **Maximize button** so that the Books table fills the Access window and reduces the clutter on the screen.

A SIMPLER DATABASE

The real power of Access is derived from a database with multiple tables that are related to one another. For the time being, however, we focus on a database with only one table so that you can learn the basics of Access. After you are comfortable working with a single table, we will show you how to work with multiple tables and how to relate them to one another.

STEP 5: Moving within a Table

➤ Click in any field in the first record. The status bar at the bottom of the Books Table indicates record 1 of 22.

➤ The triangle symbol in the record selector indicates that the record has not changed since it was last saved.

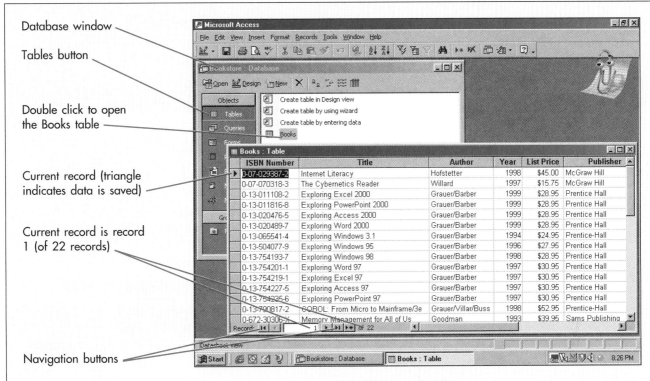

Database window

Tables button

Double click to open
the Books table

Current record (triangle
indicates data is saved)

Current record is record
1 (of 22 records)

Navigation buttons

(c) Open the Books Table (step 4)

FIGURE 1.3 Hands-on Exercise 1 (continued)

➤ You can move from record to record (or field to field) using either the mouse
or the arrow keys:

- Click in any field in the second record. The status bar indicates record 2
  of 22.
- Press the **down arrow key** to move to the third record. The status bar indicates record 3 of 22.
- Press the **left and right arrow keys** to move from field to field within the
  third record.

➤ You can also use the navigation buttons above the status bar to move from
one record to the next:

- Click |◀ to move to the first record in the table.
- Click ▶ to move forward in the table to the next record.
- Click ◀ to move back in the table to the previous record.

MOVING FROM FIELD TO FIELD

Press the Tab key, the right arrow key, or the enter key to move to the
next field in the current record (or the first field in the next record if you
are already in the last field of the current record). Press Shift+Tab or the
left arrow key to return to the previous field in the current record (or the
last field in the previous record if you are already in the first field of the
current record).

- Click ▶| to move to the last record in the table.
- Click ▶* to move beyond the last record in order to insert a new record.

➤ Click |◀ to return to the first record in the table.

STEP 6: Add a New Record

➤ Pull down the **Insert menu** and click **New Record** (or click the **New Record button** on the Table Datasheet toolbar). The record selector moves to the last record (now record 23). The insertion point is positioned in the first field (ISBN Number).

➤ Enter data for the new record as shown in Figure 1.3d. The record selector changes to a pencil as soon as you enter the first character in the new record.

➤ Press the **enter key** when you have entered the last field for the record. The new record is saved, and the record selector changes to a triangle and moves automatically to the next record.

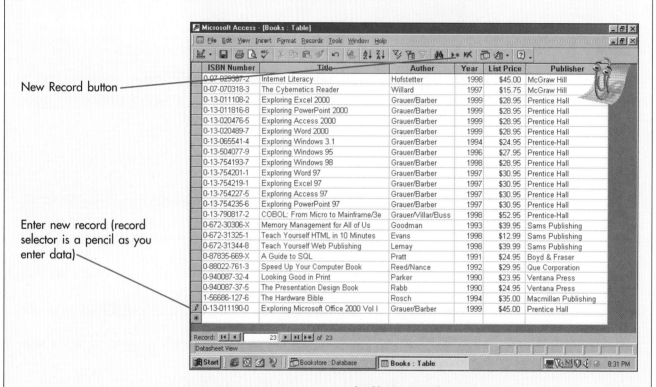

New Record button

Enter new record (record selector is a pencil as you enter data)

(d) Add a New Record (step 6)

FIGURE 1.3   Hands-on Exercise 1 (continued)

WHEN IS DATA SAVED?

There is one critical difference between Access and other Office applications such as Word for Windows or Microsoft Excel. *Access automatically saves any changes in the current record as soon as you move to the next record or when you close the table.* In other words, you do *not* have to execute the Save command explicitly to save the data in the table.

STEP 7: Add a Second Record

➤ The record selector is at the end of the table where you can add another record. Enter **0-07-054048-9** as the ISBN number for this record. Press the **Tab, enter,** or **right arrow key** to move to the Title field.

➤ Enter the title of this book as **Ace teh Technical Interview** (deliberately misspelling the word "the"). Try to look at the monitor as you type to see the AutoCorrect feature (common to all Office applications) in action. Access will correct the misspelling and change *teh* to *the*.

➤ If you did not see the correction being made, press the **backspace key** several times to erase the last several characters in the title, then re-enter the title.

➤ Complete the entry for this book. Enter **Rothstein** for the author. Enter **1998** for the year of publication. Enter **24.95** for the list price. Enter **McGraw Hill** for the publisher, then press **enter.**

CREATE YOUR OWN SHORTHAND

Use the AutoCorrect feature that is common to all Office applications to expand abbreviations such as "PH" for Prentice Hall. Pull down the Tools menu, click AutoCorrect, type the abbreviation in the Replace text box and the expanded entry in the With text box. Click the Add command button, then click OK to exit the dialog box and return to the document. The next time you type PH (in uppercase) as you enter a record, it will automatically be expanded to Prentice Hall.

STEP 8: Print the Table

➤ Pull down the **File menu.** Click **Page Setup** to display the Page Setup dialog box in Figure 1.3e.

➤ Click the **Page tab.** Click the **Landscape option button.** Click **OK** to accept the settings and close the dialog box.

➤ Click the **Print button** on the toolbar to print the table. Alternatively, you can pull down the **File menu,** click **Print** to display the Print dialog box, click the **All option button,** then click **OK.**

ABOUT MICROSOFT ACCESS

Pull down the Help menu and click About Microsoft Access to display the specific release number as well as other licensing information, including the Product ID. This help screen also contains two very useful command buttons, System Info and Tech Support. The first button displays information about the hardware installed on your system, including the amount of memory and available space on the hard drive. The Tech Support button provides telephone numbers for technical assistance.

Print button ——

Page tab ——

Landscape option ——

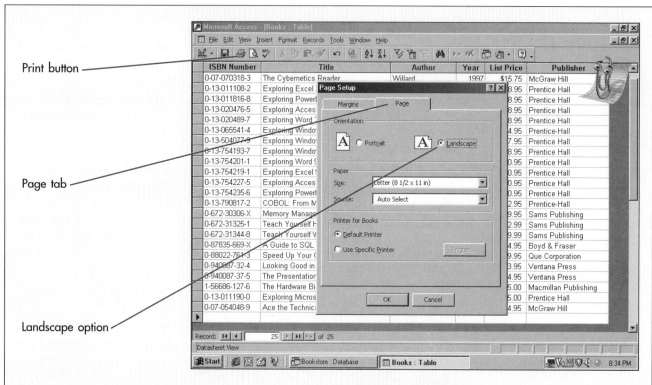

(e) Print the Table (step 8)

FIGURE 1.3   Hands-on Exercise 1 (continued)

STEP 9: Exit Access

➤ You need to close both the Books table and the Bookstore database:

• Pull down the **File menu** and click **Close** (or click the **Close button)** to close the Books table. Answer **Yes** if asked to save changes to the layout of the table.

• Pull down the **File menu** and click **Close** (or click the **Close button)** to close the Bookstore database.

➤ Pull down the **File menu** and click **Exit** to close Access if you do not want to continue with the next exercise at this time.

OUR FAVORITE BOOKSTORE

This exercise has taken you through our hypothetical bookstore database. It's more fun, however, to go to a real bookstore. Amazon Books (www.amazon.com), with a virtual inventory of more than three million titles, is one of our favorite sites on the Web. You can search by author, subject, or title, read reviews written by other Amazon visitors, or contribute your own review. It's not as cozy as your neighborhood bookstore, but you can order any title for mail-order delivery. And you never have to leave home.

The exercise just completed showed you how to open an existing table and add records to that table. You will also need to edit and/or delete existing records in order to maintain the data as changes occur. These operations require you to find the specific record and then make the change. You can search the table manually, or more easily through the Find and Replace commands.

Find and Replace Commands

The Find and Replace commands are similar in function to the corresponding commands in all other Office applications. (The commands are executed from within the same dialog box by selecting the appropriate tab.) The **Find command** enables you to locate a specific record(s) by searching a table for a particular value. You could, for example, search the Books table for the title of a book, then move to the appropriate field to change its price. The **Replace command** incorporates the Find command and allows you to locate and optionally replace (one or more occurrences of) one value with another. The Replace command in Figure 1.4 searches for *PH* in order to substitute *Prentice Hall.*

Searches can be made more efficient by making use of the various options. A case-sensitive search, for example, matches not only the specific characters, but also the use of upper- and lowercase letters. Thus, *PH* is different from *ph,* and a case-sensitive search on one will not identify the other. A case-insensitive search (where Match Case is *not* selected) will find both *PH* and *ph.* Any search may specify a match on whole fields to identify *Davis,* but not *Davison.* And finally, a search can also be made more efficient by restricting it to the current field.

The replacement can be either selective or automatic. Selective replacement lets you examine each successful match in context and decide whether to replace it. Automatic replacement makes the substitution without asking for confirmation (and is generally not recommended). Selective replacement is implemented by clicking the Find Next command button, then clicking (or not clicking) the Replace button to make (or not make) the substitution. Automatic replacement (through the entire table) is implemented by clicking the Replace All button.

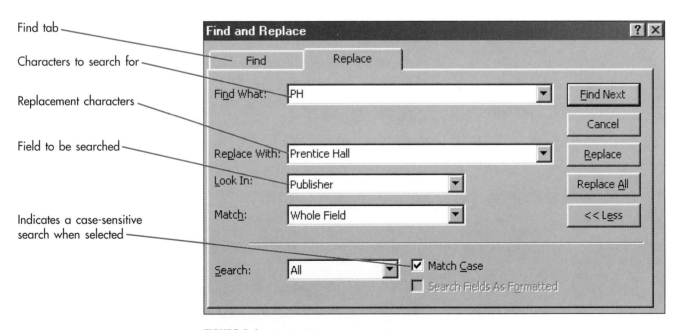

FIGURE 1.4   Find and Replace Commands

Data Validation

It is unwise to simply add (edit or delete) a record without adequate checks on the validity of the data. Ask yourself, for example, whether a search for all books by Prentice Hall (without a hyphen) will also return all books by *Prentice-Hall* (with a hyphen). The answer is *no* because the publisher's name is spelled differently and a search for one will not locate the other. *You* know the publisher is the same in both instances, but the computer does not.

Data validation is a crucial part of any system. Good systems are built to anticipate errors you might make and reject those errors prior to accepting data. Access automatically implements certain types of data validation. It will not, for example, let you enter letters where a numeric value is expected (such as the Year and List Price fields in our example). More sophisticated types of validation are implemented by the user when the table is created. You may decide, for example, to reject any record that omits the title or author. Data validation is described more completely in Chapter 2.

GARBAGE IN, GARBAGE OUT (GIGO)

A computer does exactly what you tell it to do, which is not necessarily what you want it to do. It is absolutely critical, therefore, that you validate the data that goes into a system, or else the associated information may not be correct. No system, no matter how sophisticated, can produce valid output from invalid input. In other words: garbage in, garbage out.

FORMS, QUERIES, AND REPORTS

As previously indicated, an Access database can contain as many as seven different types of objects. Thus far we have concentrated on tables. Now we extend the discussion to include other objects such as forms, queries, and reports as illustrated in Figure 1.5.

Figure 1.5a contains the Books table as it exists after the first hands-on exercise. There are 24 records in the table and six fields for each record. The status bar indicates that you are currently positioned in the first record. You can enter new records in the table as was done in the previous exercise. You can also edit or delete an existing record, as will be illustrated in the next exercise.

Figure 1.5b displays a form that is based on the table of Figure 1.5a. A form provides a friendlier interface than does a table and is easier to understand and use. Note, for example, the command buttons in the form to add a new record, or to find and/or delete an existing record. The status bar at the bottom of the form indicates that you are on the first of 24 records, and is identical to the status bar for the table in Figure 1.5a.

Figure 1.5c displays a query to list the books for a particular publisher (Prentice Hall in this example). A query consists of a question (e.g., enter the publisher name) and an answer (the records that satisfy the query). The results of the query are similar in appearance to that of a table, except that the query results contain selected records and/or selected fields for those records. The query may also list the records in a different sequence from that of the table.

Current record

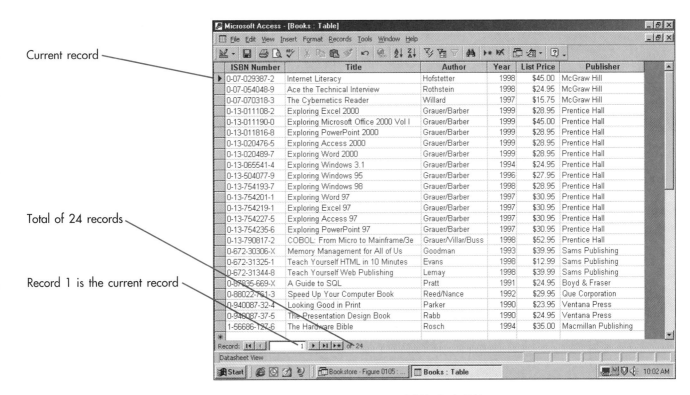

Total of 24 records

Record 1 is the current record

(a) The Books Table

Command buttons

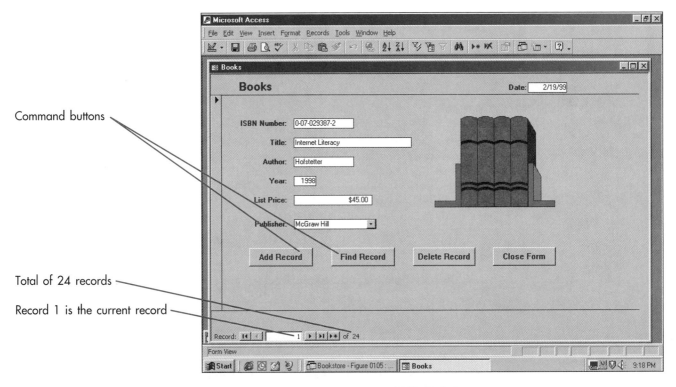

Total of 24 records

Record 1 is the current record

(b) The Books Form

FIGURE 1.5   The Objects in a Database

Records are sequenced by title within author

Query has total of 13 records

Publisher	Author	Title	ISBN Number	Year	List Price
Prentice Hall	Grauer/Barber	Exploring Access 2000	0-13-020476-5	1999	$28.95
Prentice Hall	Grauer/Barber	Exploring Access 97	0-13-754227-5	1997	$30.95
Prentice Hall	Grauer/Barber	Exploring Excel 2000	0-13-011108-2	1999	$28.95
Prentice Hall	Grauer/Barber	Exploring Excel 97	0-13-754219-1	1997	$30.95
Prentice Hall	Grauer/Barber	Exploring Microsoft Office 2000 Vol I	0-13-011190-0	1999	$45.00
Prentice Hall	Grauer/Barber	Exploring PowerPoint 2000	0-13-011816-8	1999	$28.95
Prentice Hall	Grauer/Barber	Exploring PowerPoint 97	0-13-754235-6	1997	$30.95
Prentice Hall	Grauer/Barber	Exploring Windows 3.1	0-13-065541-4	1994	$24.95
Prentice Hall	Grauer/Barber	Exploring Windows 95	0-13-504077-9	1996	$27.95
Prentice Hall	Grauer/Barber	Exploring Windows 98	0-13-754193-7	1998	$28.95
Prentice Hall	Grauer/Barber	Exploring Word 2000	0-13-020489-7	1999	$28.95
Prentice Hall	Grauer/Barber	Exploring Word 97	0-13-754201-1	1997	$30.95
Prentice Hall	Grauer/Villar/Buss	COBOL: From Micro to Mainframe/3e	0-13-790817-2	1998	$52.95

Record: 1 of 13

(c) The Publisher Query

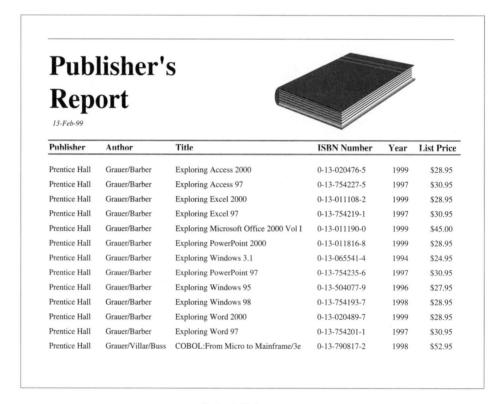

Publisher's Report

13-Feb-99

Publisher	Author	Title	ISBN Number	Year	List Price
Prentice Hall	Grauer/Barber	Exploring Access 2000	0-13-020476-5	1999	$28.95
Prentice Hall	Grauer/Barber	Exploring Access 97	0-13-754227-5	1997	$30.95
Prentice Hall	Grauer/Barber	Exploring Excel 2000	0-13-011108-2	1999	$28.95
Prentice Hall	Grauer/Barber	Exploring Excel 97	0-13-754219-1	1997	$30.95
Prentice Hall	Grauer/Barber	Exploring Microsoft Office 2000 Vol I	0-13-011190-0	1999	$45.00
Prentice Hall	Grauer/Barber	Exploring PowerPoint 2000	0-13-011816-8	1999	$28.95
Prentice Hall	Grauer/Barber	Exploring Windows 3.1	0-13-065541-4	1994	$24.95
Prentice Hall	Grauer/Barber	Exploring PowerPoint 97	0-13-754235-6	1997	$30.95
Prentice Hall	Grauer/Barber	Exploring Windows 95	0-13-504077-9	1996	$27.95
Prentice Hall	Grauer/Barber	Exploring Windows 98	0-13-754193-7	1998	$28.95
Prentice Hall	Grauer/Barber	Exploring Word 2000	0-13-020489-7	1999	$28.95
Prentice Hall	Grauer/Barber	Exploring Word 97	0-13-754201-1	1997	$30.95
Prentice Hall	Grauer/Villar/Buss	COBOL:From Micro to Mainframe/3e	0-13-790817-2	1998	$52.95

(d) The Publisher's Report

FIGURE 1.5   The Objects in a Database (continued)

Figure 1.5d illustrates a report that includes only the books from Prentice Hall. A report provides presentation-quality output and is preferable to printing the datasheet view of a table or query. Note, too, that a report may be based on either a table or a query. You could, for example, base the report in Figure 1.5d on the Books table, in which case it would list every book in the table. Alternatively, the report could be based on a query, as in Figure 1.5d, and list only the books that satisfy the criteria within the query.

Later chapters discuss forms, queries, and reports in depth. The exercise that follows is intended only as a brief introduction to what can be accomplished in Access.

Maintaining the Database

Objective: To add, edit, and delete a record; to demonstrate data validation; to introduce forms, queries, and reports. Use Figure 1.6 as a guide.

STEP 1: Open the Bookstore Database

➤ Start Access. The Bookstore database should appear within the list of recently opened databases as shown in Figure 1.6a.

➤ Select the **Bookstore database** (its drive and folder may be different from that in Figure 1.6a). Click **OK** to open the database.

➤ Right click the Office Assistant if it appears and click the **Hide** command.

Right click the Office
Assistant for shortcut menu —

Click Bookstore to select it —

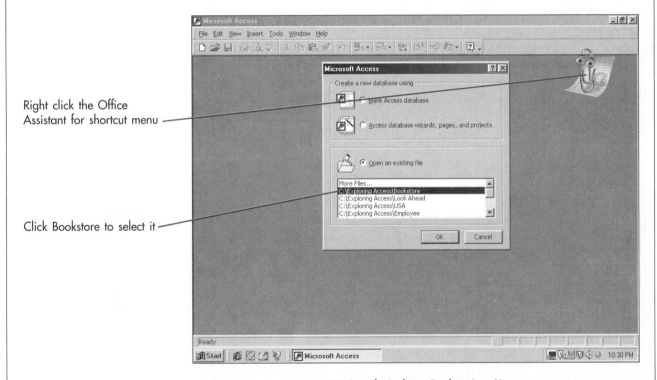

(a) Open the Bookstore Database (step 1)

FIGURE 1.6   Hands-on Exercise 2

ABOUT THE ASSISTANT

The Assistant is very powerful and hence you want to experiment with various ways to use it. To ask a question, click the Assistant's icon to toggle its balloon on or off. If you find the Assistant distracting, click and drag the character out of the way or hide it altogether by pulling down the Help menu and clicking the Hide the Office Assistant command. Pull down the Help menu and click the Show the Office Assistant command to return the Assistant to the desktop.

STEP 2: The Find Command

➤ If necessary, click the **Tables button** in the Database window. Double click the icon for the **Books table** to open the table from the previous exercise.

➤ You should see the Books table in Figure 1.6b. (The Find dialog box is not yet displayed).

➤ If necessary, click the **Maximize button** to maximize the Books table within the Access window.

➤ *Exploring Microsoft Office 2000 Vol 1* and *Ace the Technical Interview,* the books you added in the previous exercise, appear in sequence according to the ISBN number because this field is the primary key for the Books table.

➤ Click in the **Title field** for the first record. Pull down the **Edit menu** and click **Find** (or click the **Find button** on the toolbar) to display the dialog box in Figure 1.6b. (You are still positioned in the first record.)

➤ Enter **Exploring Windows 95** in the Find What text box. Check that the other parameters for the Find command match the dialog box in Figure 1.6b. Be sure that the **Title field** is selected in the Look in list.

➤ Click the **Find Next command button.** Access moves to record 10, the record containing the designated character string, and selects the Title field for that record. Click **Cancel** to close the Find dialog box.

➤ Press the **tab key** three times to move from the Title field to the List Price field. The current price ($27.95) is already selected. Type **28.95,** then press the **enter key** to change the price to $28.95.

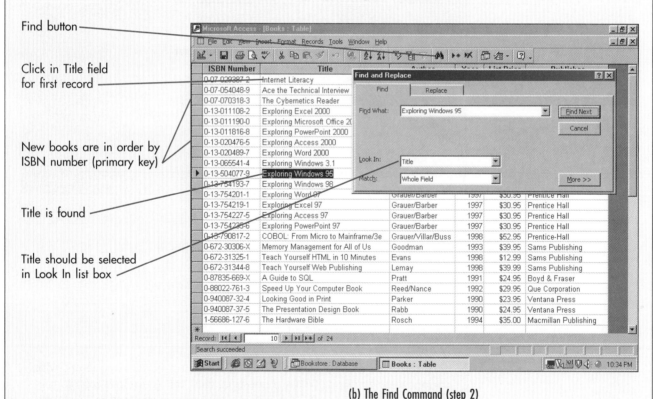

Find button

Click in Title field for first record

New books are in order by ISBN number (primary key)

Title is found

Title should be selected in Look In list box

(b) The Find Command (step 2)

FIGURE 1.6   Hands-on Exercise 2 (continued)

EDITING A RECORD

The fastest way to replace the value in an existing field is to select the field, then type the new value. Access automatically selects the field for you when you use the keyboard (Tab, enter, or arrow keys) to move from one field to the next. Click the mouse within the field (to deselect the field) if you are replacing only one or two characters rather than the entire field.

STEP 3: The Undo Command

➤ Pull down the **Edit menu** and click **Undo Current Field/Record** (or click the **Undo button** on the toolbar). The price for Exploring Windows 95 returns to its previous value.

➤ Pull down the **Edit menu** a second time. The Undo command is dim (as is the Undo button on the toolbar), indicating that you can no longer undo any changes. Press **Esc.**

➤ Correct the List Price field a second time and move to the next record to save your change.

THE UNDO COMMAND

The Undo command is common to all Office applications, but is implemented differently from one application to the next. Microsoft Word, for example, enables you to undo multiple operations. Access, however, because it saves changes automatically as soon as you move to the next record, enables you to undo only the most recent command.

STEP 4: The Delete Command

➤ Click any field in the record for **A Guide to SQL.** (You can also use the **Find command** to search for the title and move directly to its record.)

➤ Pull down the **Edit menu.** Click **Select Record** to highlight the entire record.

➤ Press the **Del key** to delete the record. You will see a dialog box as shown in Figure 1.6c, indicating that you are about to delete a record and asking you to confirm the deletion. Click **Yes.**

➤ Pull down the **Edit menu.** The Undo command is dim, indicating that you cannot undelete a record. Press **Esc** to continue working.

THE RECORD SELECTOR

Click the record selector (the box immediately to the left of the first field in a record) to select the record without having to use a pull-down menu. Click and drag the mouse over the record selector for multiple rows to select several sequential records at the same time.

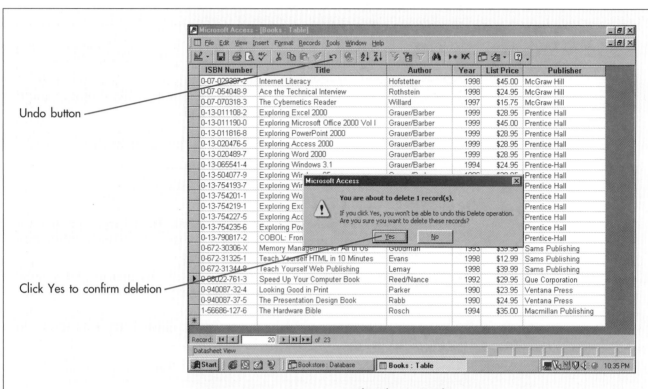

Undo button

Click Yes to confirm deletion

(c) The Delete Command (step 4)

FIGURE 1.6   Hands-on Exercise 2 (continued)

STEP 5: Data Validation

➤ Click the **New Record button** on the toolbar. The record selector moves to the last record (record 24).

➤ Add data as shown in Figure 1.6d, being sure to enter an invalid price **(XXX)** in the List Price field. Press the **Tab key** to move to the next field.

➤ Access displays the dialog box in Figure 1.6d, indicating that the value you entered (XXX) is inappropriate for the List Price field; in other words, you cannot enter letters when Access is expecting a numeric entry.

➤ Click the **OK command button** to close the dialog box and return to the table. Drag the mouse to select XXX, then enter the correct price of **$39.95.**

➤ Press the **Tab key** to move to the Publisher field. Type **McGraw Hill.** Press the **Tab key, right arrow key,** or **enter key** to complete the record.

➤ Click the **Close button** to close the Books table.

STEP 6: Open the Books Form

➤ Click the **Forms button** in the Database window. Double click the **Books form** to open the form as shown in Figure 1.6e, then (if necessary) maximize the form so that it takes the entire window.

➤ Click the **Add Record command button** to move to a new record. The status bar shows record 25 of 25.

➤ Click in the text box for **ISBN number,** then use the **Tab key** to move from field to field as you enter data for the book as shown in Figure 1.6e.

➤ Click the **drop-down arrow** on the Publisher's list box to display the available publishers and to select the appropriate one. The use of a list box ensures that you cannot misspell a publisher's name.

New Record button

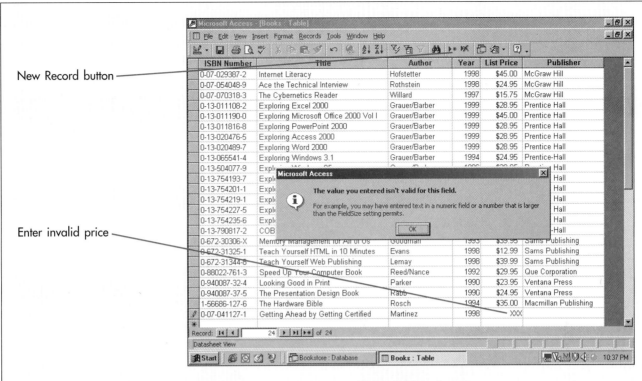

Enter invalid price

(d) Data Validation (step 5)

Click and enter data

Click to display list
of publishers

Add Record button

Current record is record 25

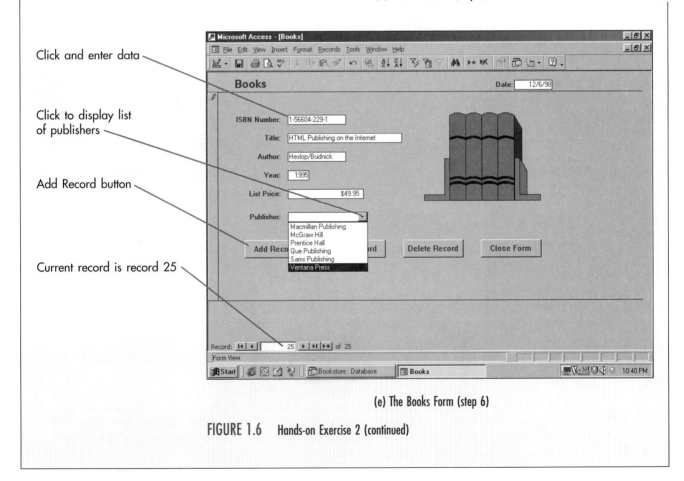

(e) The Books Form (step 6)

FIGURE 1.6   Hands-on Exercise 2 (continued)

STEP 7: The Replace Command

➤ Pull down the **View menu.** Click **Datasheet View** to switch from the Form view to the Datasheet view and display the table on which the form is based.

➤ Press **Ctrl+Home** to move to the first record in the Books table, then click in the **Publisher field** for that record. Pull down the **Edit menu.** Click **Replace.**

➤ Enter the parameters as they appear in Figure 1.6f, then click the **Find Next button** to move to the first occurrence of Prentice-Hall.

➤ Click **Replace** to make the substitution in this record and move to the next occurrence.

➤ Click **Replace** to make the second (and last) substitution, then close the dialog box when Access no longer finds the search string. Close the table.

Click in Publisher field for first record

Enter Prentice-Hall

Enter Prentice Hall (without hyphen)

Search Publisher field

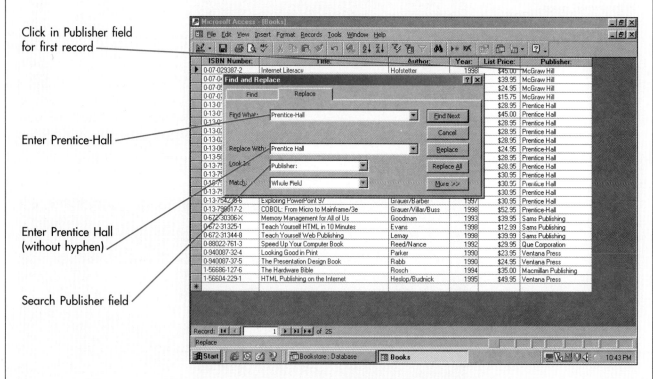

(f) The Replace Command (step 7)

FIGURE 1.6   Hands-on Exercise 2 (continued)

THE MENUS CHANGE

All applications in Office 2000 display a series of short menus that contain only basic commands. There is, however, a double arrow at the bottom of each menu that you can click to display the additional commands. In addition, each time you execute a command it is added to the menu, and conversely, commands are removed from a menu if they are not used after a period of time. You can, however, display the full menus through the Customize command in the Tools menu by clearing the check boxes in the Personalized Menus and Toolbars section.

STEP 8: Print a Report

➤ Click the **Reports button** in the Database window to display the available reports. Double click the icon for the **Publisher report.**

➤ Type **Prentice Hall** (or the name of any other publisher) in the Parameter dialog box. Press **enter** to create the report.

➤ If necessary, click the **Maximize button** in the Report Window so that the report takes the entire screen as shown in Figure 1.6g.

➤ Click the **drop-down arrow** on the Zoom box, then click **Fit** to display the whole page. Note that all of the books in the report are published by Prentice Hall, which is consistent with the parameter you entered earlier.

➤ Click the **Print button** on the Report toolbar to print the report.

➤ Click the **Close button** on the Print Review toolbar to close the Report window.

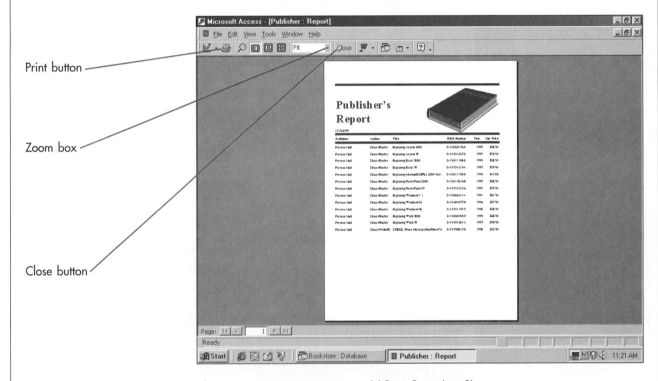

(g) Run a Report (step 8)

FIGURE 1.6 Hands-on Exercise 2 (continued)

TIP OF THE DAY

You can set the Office Assistant to greet you with a "tip of the day" each time you start Access. Click the Microsoft Access Help button (or press the F1 key) to display the Assistant, then click the Options button to display the Office Assistant dialog box. Click the Options tab, then check the Show the Tip of the Day at Startup box and click OK. The next time you start Access, you will be greeted by the Assistant, who will offer you the tip of the day.

STEP 9: The Office Assistant

➤ If necessary, pull down the **Help menu** and click the command to **Show the Office Assistant.** (You may see a different character.) Click the Assistant, then enter the question, **How do I get Help** in the balloon.

➤ Click the **Search button** in the Assistant's balloon to look for the answer. The size of the Assistant's balloon expands as the Assistant suggests several topics that may be appropriate.

➤ Select any topic (we selected **Ways to get assistance while you work**), which in turn displays a Help window with multiple links as shown in Figure 1.6h. Click any of the links in the Help window to read the information.

➤ Click the **Show button** in the Help window to display the Contents, Answer Wizard, and Index tabs. Click the **Contents tab,** then click the **plus sign** that appears next to the various book icons to expand the various help topics. Click the **icon** next to any topic to display the associated information.

➤ Continue to experiment, then close the Help window when you are finished.

➤ Exit Access if you do not want to continue with the next exercise at this time.

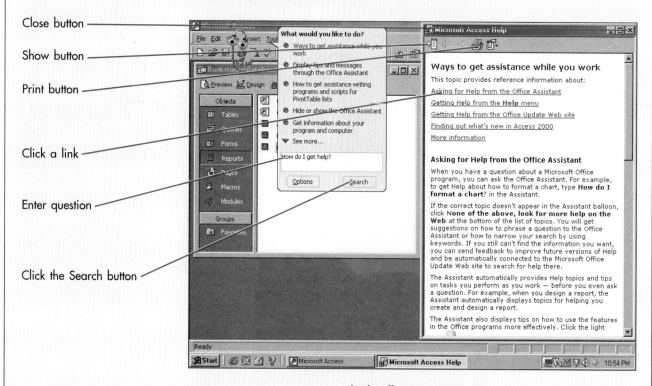

Close button

Show button

Print button

Click a link

Enter question

Click the Search button

(h) The Office Assistant (step 9)

FIGURE 1.6 Hands-on Exercise 2 (continued)

CHOOSE YOUR OWN ASSISTANT

Choose your own personal assistant from one of several available candidates. Press the F1 key to display the Assistant, click the Assistant to display the balloon, click the Options button to display the Office Assistant dialog box, then click the Gallery tab where you choose your character. (The Office 2000 CD is required to select some characters.)

The exercise just completed described how to use an existing report to obtain information from the database. But what if you are in a hurry and don't have the time to create the report? There is a faster way. You can open the table in the Datasheet view, then apply a filter and/or a sort to the table to display selected records in any order. A *filter* displays a subset of records from the table according to specified criteria. A *sort* lists those records in a specific sequence such as alphabetically by last name or by social security number. We illustrate these concepts in conjunction with Figure 1.7.

Figure 1.7a displays an employee table with 14 records. Each record has 8 fields. The records in the table are displayed in sequence according to the social security number, which is also the primary key (the field or combination of fields that uniquely identifies a record). The status bar indicates that there are 14 records in the table.

Figure 1.7b displays a filtered view of the same table in which we see only the Account Reps. The status bar shows that this is a filtered list, and that there are 8 records that satisfy the criteria. (The employee table still contains the original 14 records, but only 8 records are visible with the filter in effect.) Note, too, that the selected employees are displayed in alphabetical order as opposed to social security order.

Two operations are necessary to go from Figure 1.7a to Figure 1.7b—filtering and sorting. The easiest way to implement a filter is to click in any cell that contains the value of the desired criterion (such as any cell that contains "Account Rep" in the Title field) then click the *Filter by Selection button* on the Database toolbar. To sort the table, click in the field on which you want to sequence the records (the LastName field in this example) then click the *Sort Ascending button* on the Database toolbar. The *Sort Descending button* is appropriate for numeric fields such as salary, if you want to display the records with the highest value listed first.

The operations can be done in any order; that is, you can filter a table to show only selected records, then you can sort the filtered table to display the records in a different order. Conversely, you can sort a table and then apply a filter. It does not matter which operation is performed first, and indeed, you can go back and forth between the two. You can also filter the table further, by applying a second (or third) criterion; e.g., click in a cell containing "Good," then click the Filter by Selection button a second time to display the Account Reps with good performance. You can also click the *Remove Filter button* at any time to display the complete table.

Figure 1.7c illustrates an alternate and more powerful way to apply a filter known as *Filter by Form,* in which you can select the criteria from a drop-down list, and/or apply multiple criteria simultaneously. However, the real advantage of the Filter by Form command extends beyond these conveniences to two additional capabilities. First, you can specify relationships within a criterion; for example, you can select employees with a salary greater than (or less than) $40,000. Filter by Selection, on the other hand, requires you to specify criteria equal to an existing value. Figure 1.7d displays the filtered table of Chicago employees earning more than $40,000.

A second advantage of the Filter by Form command is that you can specify alternative criterion (such as employees in Chicago *or* employees who are account reps) by clicking the Or tab. (The latter capability is not implemented in Figure 1.7.) Suffice it to say, however, that the availability of the various filter and sort commands enable you to obtain information from a database quickly and easily. And as you may have guessed, it's time for another hands-on exercise.

Records are in sequence by SSN
(primary key)

Total of 14 records in table

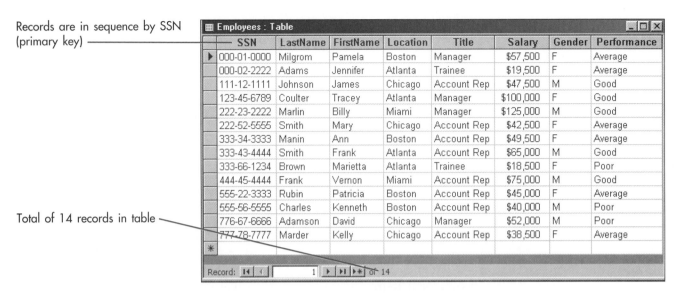

(a) The Employee Table (by Social Security Number)

Records are in alphabetical
order by last name

Total of 8 records in filtered list

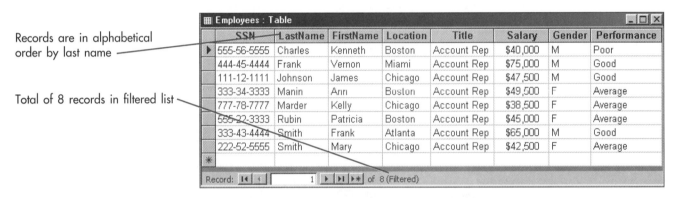

(b) A Filtered List (Account Reps by last name)

Select from a drop-down list
to establish criteria

Or tab

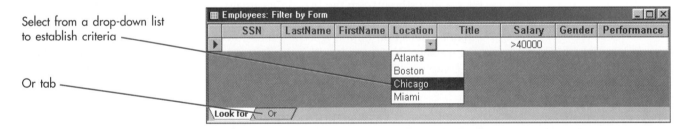

(c) Filter by Form

(d) Filtered List

FIGURE 1.7   Filters and Sorting

Filters and Sorting

Objective: To display selected records within a table by applying the Filter by Selection and Filter by Form criteria; to sort the records in a table. Use Figure 1.8 as a guide in the exercise.

STEP 1: Open the Employees Table

➤ Start Access as you did in the previous exercises, but this time you will open a different database. Click **More Files,** and click **OK** (if you see the Microsoft Access dialog box) or pull down the **File menu** and click the **Open command.** Either way, open the **Employees database** in the **Exploring Access folder.**

➤ If necessary, click the **Tables button** in the database window, then double click the **Employees table,** as shown in Figure 1.8a. Click the **maximize button** so that the Employees table fills the Access window. If necessary, click the **maximize button** in the application window so that Access takes the entire desktop.

➤ Pull down the **Insert menu** and click **New Record** (or click the **New Record button** on either the toolbar or the status bar). The record selector moves to the last record (now record 15).

➤ Add data for yourself, using your own social security number, and your first and last name. Assign yourself to **the Miami office** as an **Account Rep** with a salary of **$32,000** and a **Good performance.**

➤ Press **enter** after you have completed the last field.

New Record button

Add data for yourself

Total of 15 records in table

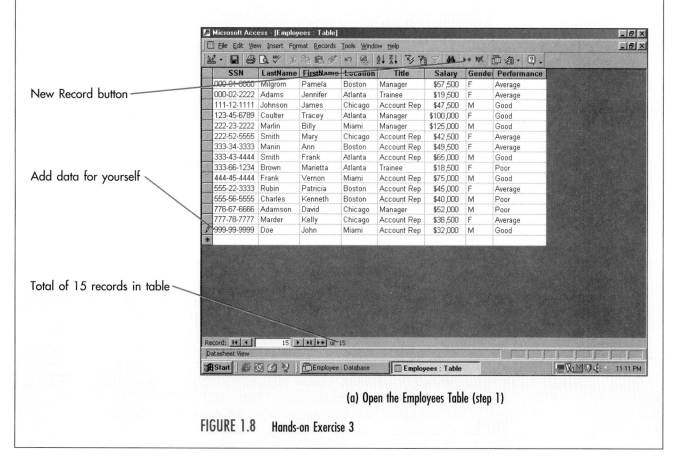

(a) Open the Employees Table (step 1)

FIGURE 1.8   Hands-on Exercise 3

STEP 2: Filter By Selection

➤ The Employees table should contain 15 records, including the record you added for yourself. Click in the Title field of any record that contains the title **Account Rep,** then click the **Filter by Selection button.**

➤ You should see 9 employees, all of whom are Account Reps, as shown in Figure 1.8b. The status bar indicates that there are 9 records (as opposed to 15) and that there is a filter condition in effect.

➤ Click in the performance field of any employee with a good performance (we clicked in the performance field of the first record, which should be yours), then click the **Filter by Selection button** a second time.

➤ This time you see 4 employees, each of whom is an Account Rep with a performance evaluation of good. The status bar indicates that 4 records satisfy this filter condition.

➤ Click the **Print button** to print the filtered table.

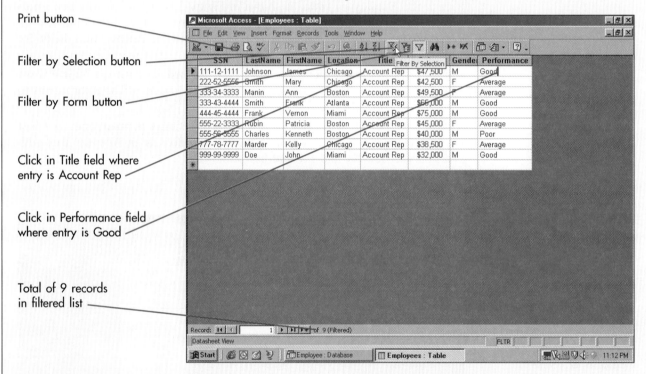

Print button

Filter by Selection button

Filter by Form button

Click in Title field where entry is Account Rep

Click in Performance field where entry is Good

Total of 9 records in filtered list

(b) Filter by Selection (step 2)

FIGURE 1.8   Hands-on Exercise 3 (continued)

FILTER EXCLUDING SELECTION

The Filter by Selection button on the Database toolbar selects all records that meet the designated criterion. The Filter Excluding Selection command does just the opposite and displays all records that do not satisfy the criterion. First, click the Remove Filter button to remove any filters that are in effect, then click in the appropriate field of any record that contains the value you want to exclude. Pull down the Records menu, click (or point to) the Filter command, then click the Filter Excluding Selection command to display the records that do not meet the criterion.

STEP 3: Filter by Form

➤ Click the **Filter by Form button** to display the form in Figure 1.8c where you can enter or remove criteria in any sequence. Each time you click in a field, a drop-down list appears that displays all of the values for the field that occur within the table.

➤ Click in the columns for Title and Performance to remove the criteria that were entered in the previous step. Select the existing entries and press the **Del key.**

➤ Click in the cell underneath the Salary field and type **>30000** (as opposed to selecting a specific value). Click in the cell underneath the Location Field and select **Chicago.**

➤ Click the **Apply Filter button** to display the records that satisfy these criteria. (You should see 4 records.) Click the **Print button.**

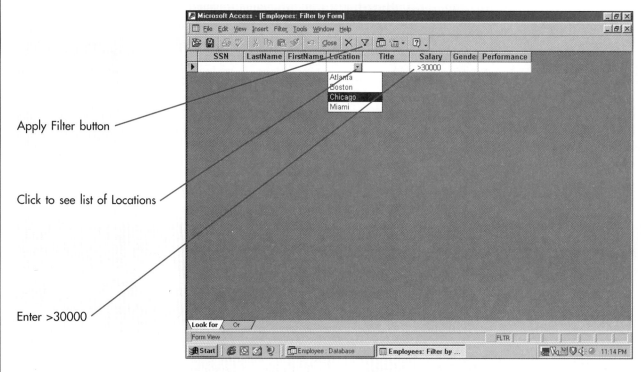

Apply Filter button

Click to see list of Locations

Enter >30000

(c) Filter by Form (step 3)

FIGURE 1.8 Hands-on Exercise 3 (continued)

FILTER BY FORM VERSUS FILTER BY SELECTION

The Filter by Form command has all of the capabilities of the Filter by Selection command, and provides two additional capabilities. First, you can use relational operators such as >, >=, <, or <=, as opposed to searching for an exact value. Second, you can search for records that meet one of several conditions (the equivalent of an "Or" operation). Enter the first criteria as you normally would, then click the Or tab at the bottom of the window to display a second form in which you enter the alternate criteria. (To delete an alternate criterion, click the associated tab, then click the Delete button on the toolbar.)

STEP 4: Sort the Table

➤ Click the **Remove Filter button** to display the complete table of 15 employees. Click in the LastName field of any record, then click the **Sort Ascending button.** The records are displayed in alphabetical (ascending) order by last name.

➤ Click in the Salary field of any record, then click the **Sort Descending button.** The records are in descending order of salary; that is, the employee with the highest salary is listed first.

➤ Click in the Location field of any record, then click the **Sort Ascending button** to display the records by location, although the employees within a location are not in any specific order. You can sort on two fields at the same time provided the fields are next to each other, as described in the next step.

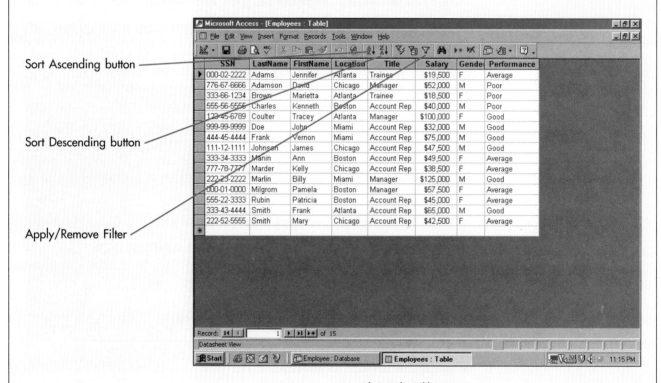

(d) Sort the Table (step 4)

FIGURE 1.8   Hands-on Exercise 3 (continued)

THE SORT OR FILTER—WHICH IS FIRST?

It doesn't matter whether you sort a table and then apply a filter, or filter first and then sort. The operations are cumulative. Thus, once a table has been sorted, any subsequent display of filtered records for that table will be in the specified sequence. Alternatively, you can apply a filter, then sort the filtered table by clicking in the desired field and clicking the appropriate sort button. Remember, too, that all filter commands are cumulative, and hence you must remove the filter to see the original table.

STEP 5: Sort on Two Fields

➤ Click the header for the Location field to select the entire column. Click and drag the Location header so that the Location field is moved to the left of the LastName field as shown in Figure 1.8e.

➤ Click anywhere to deselect the column, then click on the Location header and click and drag to select both the Location header and the LastName Header. Click the **Sort Ascending button.** The records are sorted by location and alphabetically within location.

➤ Click the **Print button** to print the table to prove to your instructor that you completed the exercise. Click the **close button** to close the Employees table.

➤ Click **Yes** when asked whether to save the changes to the Employees table. Saving the table automatically saves the filter and the associated sort.

➤ Exit Access if you do not want to continue with the next exercise at this time.

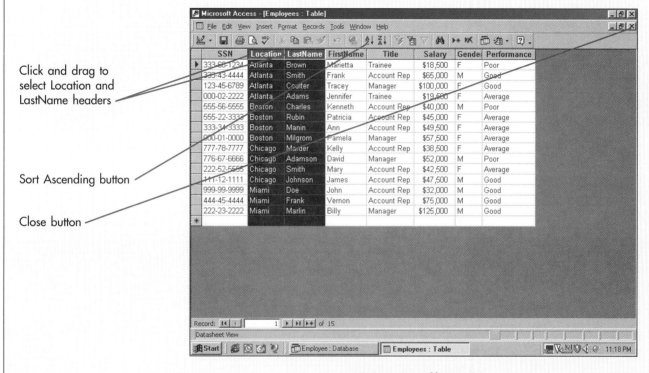

Click and drag to select Location and LastName headers

Sort Ascending button

Close button

(e) Sort on Two Fields (step 5)

FIGURE 1.8   Hands-on Exercise 3 (continued)

REMOVING VERSUS DELETING A FILTER

Removing a filter displays all of the records in a table, but it does not delete the filter because the filter is stored permanently with the table. To delete the filter entirely is more complicated than simply removing it. Pull down the Record menu, click Filter, then click the Advanced Filter/Sort command to display a grid containing the criteria for the filter. Clear the Sort and Criteria rows by clicking in any cell containing an entry and deleting that entry, then click the Apply Filter button when all cells are clear to return to the Datasheet view. The Apply Filter button should be dim, indicating that the table does not contain a filter.

LOOKING AHEAD:
A RELATIONAL DATABASE

The Bookstore and Employee databases are both examples of simple databases in that they each contained only a single table. The real power of Access, however, is derived from multiple tables and the relationships between those tables. This type of database is known as a *relational database* and is illustrated in Figure 1.9. This figure expands the original Employee database by adding two tables, for locations and titles, respectively.

The Employees table in Figure 1.9a is the same table we used at the beginning of the previous exercise, except for the substitution of a LocationID and TitleID for the location and title, respectively. The Locations table in turn has all

SSN	LastName	FirstName	LocationID	TitleID	Salary	Gender	Performance
000-01-0000	Milgrom	Pamela	L02	T02	$57,500	F	Average
000-02-2222	Adams	Jennifer	L01	T03	$19,500	F	Average
111-12-1111	Johnson	James	L03	T01	$47,500	M	Good
123-45-6789	Coulter	Tracey	L01	T02	$100,000	F	Good
222-23-2222	Marlin	Billy	L04	T02	$125,000	M	Good
222-52-5555	Smith	Mary	L03	T01	$42,500	F	Average
333-34-3333	Manin	Ann	L02	T01	$49,500	F	Average
333-43-4444	Smith	Frank	L01	T01	$65,000	M	Good
333-66-1234	Brown	Marietta	L01	T03	$18,500	F	Poor
444-45-4444	Frank	Vernon	L04	T01	$75,000	M	Good
555-22-3333	Rubin	Patricia	L02	T01	$45,000	F	Average
555-56-5555	Charles	Kenneth	L02	T01	$40,000	M	Poor
776-67-6666	Adamson	David	L03	T02	$52,000	M	Poor
777-78-7777	Marder	Kelly	L03	T01	$38,500	F	Average

(a) The Employees Table

LocationID	Location	Address	State	Zipcode	OfficePhone
L01	Atlanta	450 Peachtree Road	GA	30316	(404) 333-5555
L02	Boston	3 Commons Blvd	MA	02190	(617) 123-4444
L03	Chicago	500 Loop Highway	IL	60620	(312) 444-6666
L04	Miami	210 Biscayne Blvd	FL	33103	(305) 787-9999

(b) The Locations Table

TitleID	Title	Description	EducationRequired	MinimumSalary	MaximumSalary
T01	Account Rep	A marketing ...	Four year degree	$25,000	$75,000
T02	Manager	A supervisory ...	Four year degree	$50,000	$150,000
T03	Trainee	An entry-level ...	Two year degree	$18,000	$25,000

(c) The Titles Table

FIGURE 1.9   A Relational Database

of the fields that pertain to each location: LocationID, Location, Address, State, Zipcode, and Office Phone. One field, the LocationID, appears in both Employees and Locations tables and links the two tables to one another. In similar fashion, the Titles table has the information for each title: the TitleID, Title, Description, Education Required, and Minimum and Maximum Salary. The TitleID appears in both the Employees and Titles tables to link those tables to one another.

It sounds complicated, but it is really quite simple and very elegant. More importantly, it enables you to obtain detailed information about any employee, location, or title. To show how it works, we will ask a series of questions that require you to look in one or more tables for the answer. Consider:

Query: At which location does Pamela Milgrom work? What is the phone number of her office?

Answer: Pamela works in the Boston office, at 3 Commons Blvd., Boston, MA, 02190. The phone number is (617) 123-4444.

Did you answer the question correctly? You had to search the Employees table for Pamela Milgrom to obtain the LocationID (L02 in this example) corresponding to her office. You then searched the Locations table for this LocationID to obtain the address and phone number for that location. The process required you to use both the Locations and Employees tables, which are linked to one another through a ***one-to-many relationship.*** One location can have many employees, but a specific employee can work at only one location. Let's try another question:

Query: Which employees are managers?

Answer: There are four managers: Pamela Milgrom, Tracey Coulter, Billy Marlin, and David Adamson

The answer to this question is based on the one-to-many relationship that exists between titles and employees. One title can have many employees, but a given employee has only one title. To answer the query, you search the Titles table for "manager" to determine its TitleID (T02). You then go to the Employees table and select those records that have this value in the TitleID field.

The design of a relational database enables us to extract information from multiple tables in a single query. Equally important, it simplifies the way data is changed in that modifications are made in only one place. Consider:

Query: Which employees work in the Boston office? What is their phone number? How many changes would be necessary if the Boston office were to get a new phone number?

Answer: There are four employees in Boston: Pamela Milgrom, Ann Manin, Patricia Rubin, and Kenneth Charles, each with the same number (617 123-4444). Only one change (in the Locations table) would be necessary if the phone number changed.

Once again, we draw on the one-to-many relationship between locations and employees. Thus, we begin in the Locations table where we search for "Boston" to determine its LocationID (L02) and phone number (617 123-4444). Then we go to the Employees table to select those records with this value in the LocationID field. Realize, however, that the phone number is stored in the Locations table. Thus, the new phone number is entered in the Boston record, where it is reflected automatically for each employee with a LocationID of L02 (corresponding to the Boston office).

Objective: To open a database with multiple tables; to identify the one-to-many relationships within the database and to produce reports based on those relationships. Use Figure 1.10 as a guide in the exercise.

STEP 1: Open the Relationships Window

➤ Start Access, click the **More Files option button,** and click **OK.** If Access is already open, pull down the **File menu** and click the **Open command.** Open the **Look Ahead database** in the **Exploring Access folder.**

➤ The Tables button should be selected as in Figure 1.10a. The database contains the Employees, Locations, and Titles tables.

➤ Pull down the **Tools menu** and click the **Relationships command** to open the Relationships window as shown in Figure 1.10a. (The tables are not yet visible in this window.)

➤ Pull down the **Relationships menu** and click the **Show Table command** to display the Show Table dialog box. Click (select) the **Locations table** (within the Show Table dialog box) then click the **Add button** to add this table to the Relationships window.

➤ Double click the **Titles** and **Employees tables** to add these tables to the Relationships window.

➤ Close the Show Table dialog box.

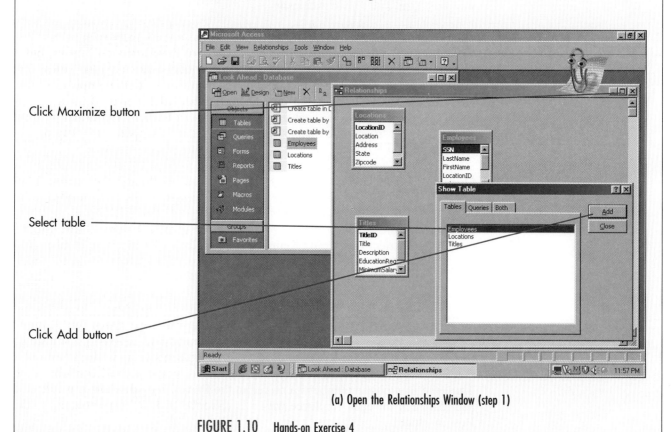

Click Maximize button

Select table

Click Add button

(a) Open the Relationships Window (step 1)

FIGURE 1.10 Hands-on Exercise 4

STEP 2: Create the Relationships

➤ Maximize the Relationships windows so that you have more room in which to work. Click and drag the title bar of each table so that the positions of the tables match those in Figure 1.10b. Click and drag the bottom (and/or right) border of each table so that you see all of the fields in each table.

➤ Click and drag the **LocationID field** in the Locations table field list to the **LocationID field** in the Employees field list. You will see the Edit Relationships dialog box. Check the box to **Enforce Referential Integrity.** Click the **Create button** to create the relationship.

➤ Click and drag the **TitleID field** in the Locations table field list to the **TitleID field** in the Employees field list. You will see the Edit Relationships dialog box. Check the box to **Enforce Referential Integrity** as shown in Figure 1.10b. Click the **Create button** to create the relationship.

➤ Click the **Save button** on the Relationship toolbar to save the Relationships window, then close the Relationships window.

Save button

Click and drag to see all fields

Click and drag TitleID from Titles field list to TitleID in Employees field list

Click Enforce Referential Integrity

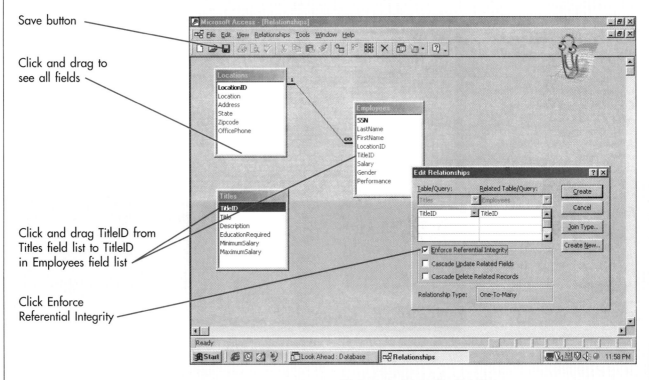

(b) Create the Relationships (step 2)

FIGURE 1.10   Hands-on Exercise 4 (continued)

THE RELATIONSHIPS ARE VISUAL

The tables in an Access database are created independently, then related to one another through the Relationships window. The number 1 and the infinity symbol (∞) appear at the ends of the line to indicate the nature of the relationship; e.g., a one-to-many relationship between the Locations and Employees tables.

STEP 3: Enter Your Own Record

➤ Double click the **Employees table** to open the table. Maximize the window. Pull down the **Insert** menu and click the **New Record** command (or click the **New Record button**) on the Table Datasheet toolbar.

➤ Enter data for yourself, using your own social security number, and your first and last name as shown in Figure 1.10c. Enter an invalid LocationID (e.g., **L44**) then complete the record as shown in the figure.

➤ Press the **enter key** when you have completed the data entry, then click **OK** when you see the error message. Access prevents you from entering a location that does not exist.

➤ Click in the **LocationID field** and enter **L04**, the LocationID for Miami. Press the **down arrow key** to move to the next record, which automatically saves the current record. Close the Employees table.

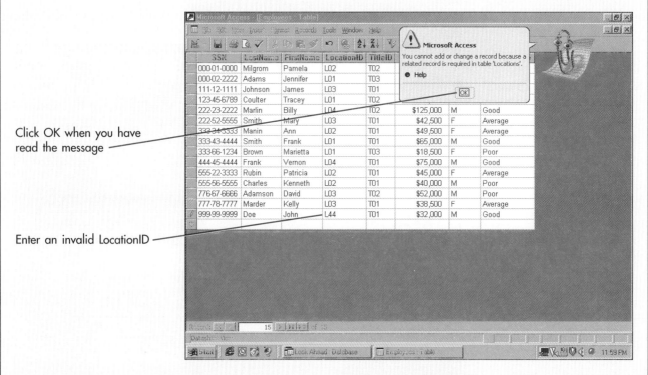

Click OK when you have read the message

Enter an invalid LocationID

(c) Referential Integrity (step 3)

FIGURE 1.10   Hands-on Exercise 4 (continued)

REFERENTIAL INTEGRITY

The tables in a database must be consistent with one another, a concept known as referential integrity. Thus, Access automatically implements certain types of data validation to prevent such errors from occurring. You cannot, for example, enter a record in the Employees table that contains an invalid value for either the LocationID or the TitleID. Nor can you delete a record in the Locations or Titles table if it has related records in the Employees table.

STEP 4: Simplified Data Entry

➤ Click the **Forms button** in the Database window, then double click the **Employees Form** to open this form as shown in Figure 1.10d. Click the **Add Record button** then click in the text box for the Social Security Number.

➤ Enter the data for **Bob Grauer** one field at a time, pressing the **Tab key** to move from one field to the next. Click the **down arrow** when you come to the location field to display the available locations, then select (click) **Miami.**

➤ Press the **Tab key** to move to the Title field and choose **Account Rep.** Complete the data for Bob's record by entering **$150,000, M,** and **Excellent** in the Salary, Gender, and Performance fields, respectively.

➤ Click the **Close Form button** when you have finished entering the data.

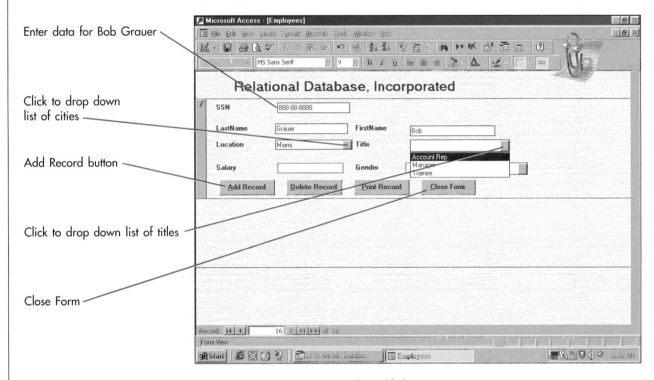

Enter data for Bob Grauer

Click to drop down list of cities

Add Record button

Click to drop down list of titles

Close Form

(d) Simplified Data Entry (step 4)

FIGURE 1.10   Hands-on Exercise 4 (continued)

SIMPLIFIED DATA ENTRY

The success of any system depends on the accuracy of its data as well as its ease of use. Both objectives are met through a well-designed form that guides the user through the process of data entry and simultaneously rejects invalid responses. The drop-down list boxes for the Location, Title, and Performance fields ensure that the user can enter only valid values in these fields. Data entry is also simplified in these fields in that you can enter just the first letter of a field, then press the Tab key to move to the next field.

STEP 5: View the Employee Master List

➤ Click the **Reports button** in the Database window. Double click the **Employee Master List** report to open the report as shown in figure 1.10e.

➤ This report lists selected fields for all employees in the database. Note that the two new employees, you and Bob Grauer, appear in alphabetical order. Both employees are in the Miami Office.

➤ Close the Report window.

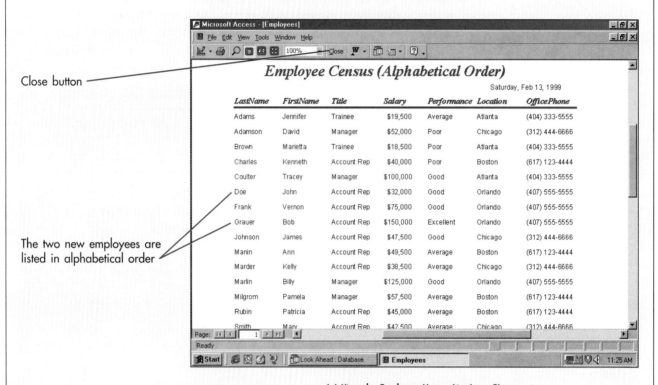

Close button

The two new employees are listed in alphabetical order

(e) View the Employee Master List (step 5)

FIGURE 1.10   Hands-on Exercise 4 (continued)

ADVICE FROM THE ASSISTANT

The Office Assistant monitors your work and displays a lightbulb when it has a suggestion to help you work more efficiently. Click the lightbulb to display the tip, then click OK or press the Esc key after you have read the information. The Assistant will not, however, repeat a tip from an earlier session unless it is reset at the start of a session. This is especially important in a laboratory situation where you are sharing a computer with many students. To reset the tips, click the Assistant to display its balloon, click the Options button in the balloon, then click the Options tab, then click the button to Reset My Tips.

STEP 6: Change the Locations Table

➤ Click the **Tables button** in the Database window, then double click the **Locations table** to open this table as shown in figure 1.10f. Maximize the window.

➤ Click the **plus sign** next to location L04 (Miami) to view the employees in this office. The plus sign changes to a minus sign as the employee records for this location are shown. Your name appears in this list as does Bob Grauer's. Click the **minus sign** and the list of related records disappears.

➤ Click and drag to select **Miami** (the current value in the Location field). Type **Orlando** and press the **Tab key.** Enter the corresponding values for the other field: **1000 Kirkman Road, FL, 32801** and **(407) 555-5555** for the address, state, zip code, and office phone, respectively.

➤ Close the **Locations table.** You have moved the Miami Office to Orlando.

Change address and phone number

Change Miami to Orlando

Click + sign to display employees at Location LO4 (+ changes to a −)

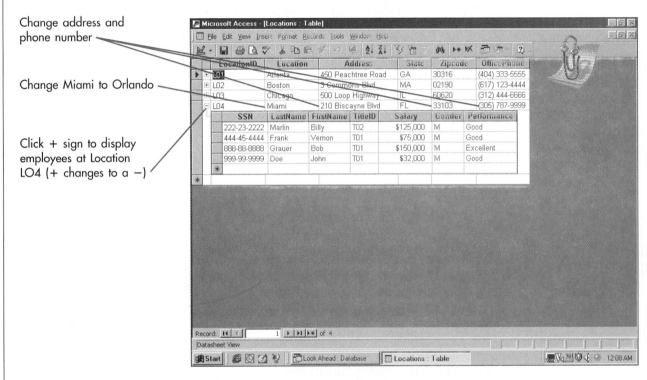

(f) Change the Locations Table (step 6)

FIGURE 1.10   Hands-on Exercise 4 (continued)

ADD AND DELETE RELATED RECORDS

Take advantage of the one-to-many relationship between locations and employees (or titles and employees) to add and/or delete records in the Employees table. Open the Locations table, then click the plus sign next to the location where you want to add or delete an employee record. To add a new employee, click the New Record navigation button within the Employees table for that location, then add the new data. To delete a record, click the record, then click the Delete Record button on the Table Datasheet toolbar. Click the minus sign to close the employee list.

STEP 7: View the Employees by Title Report

➤ Click the **Reports button** in the Database window, then double click the **Employees by Title** report to open the report shown in Figure 1.10g.

➤ This report lists employees by title, rather than alphabetically. Note that you and Bob Grauer are both listed as Account Reps in the Orlando office; i.e., the location of the office was changed in the Locations table and that change is automatically reflected for all employees assigned to that office.

➤ Close the Report window. Close the Database window. Exit Access. Welcome to the world of relational databases.

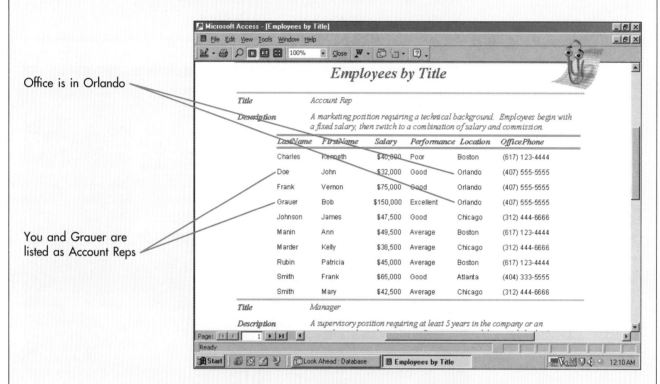

Office is in Orlando

You and Grauer are listed as Account Reps

(g) View the Employees by Title Report (step 7)

FIGURE 1.10   Hands-on Exercise 4 (continued)

THE WHAT'S THIS COMMAND

Use the What's This command to obtain a detailed explanation for any toolbar button. Pull down the Help menu and click the What's This command (or press the Shift+F1 key) to change the mouse pointer to an arrow with a question mark. Now click any toolbar button for an explanation of that button. Press the Esc key to return the mouse pointer to normal and continue working.

An Access database has seven types of objects—tables, forms, queries, reports, pages, macros, and modules. The database window displays these objects and enables you to open an existing object or create a new object.

Each table in the database is composed of records, and each record is in turn composed of fields. Every record in a given table has the same fields in the same order.

A table is displayed in one of two views—the Design view or the Datasheet view. The Design view is used to define the table initially and to specify the fields it will contain. The Datasheet view is the view you use to add, edit, or delete records.

A record selector symbol is displayed next to the current record and signifies the status of that record. A triangle indicates that the record has been saved. A pencil indicates that the record has not been saved and that you are in the process of entering (or changing) the data. An asterisk appears next to the blank record present at the end of every table, where you add a new record to the table.

Access automatically saves any changes in the current record as soon as you move to the next record or when you close the table. The Undo Current Record command cancels (undoes) the changes to the previously saved record.

No system, no matter how sophisticated, can produce valid output from invalid input. Data validation is thus a critical part of any system. Access automatically imposes certain types of data validation during data entry. Additional checks can be implemented by the user.

A filter is a set of criteria that is applied to a table in order to display a subset of the records in that table. Microsoft Access lets you filter by selection or filter by form. The application of a filter does not remove the records from the table, but simply suppresses them from view. The records in a table can be displayed in ascending or descending sequence by clicking the appropriate button on the Database toolbar.

A relational database contains multiple tables and enables you to extract information from those tables in a single query. The tables must be consistent with one another, a concept known as referential integrity. Thus, Access automatically implements certain types of data validation to prevent such errors from occurring.

KEY WORDS AND CONCEPTS

Asterisk (record selector) symbol
AutoCorrect
Current record
Data validation
Database
Database window
Datasheet view
Design view
Field
Field name
Filter
Filter by Form
Filter by Selection
Filter Excluding Selection

Find command
Form
GIGO (garbage in, garbage out)
Insertion point
Macro
Microsoft Access
Module
One-to-many relationship
Page
Pencil (record selector) symbol
Primary key
Query
Record

Record selector symbol
Referential Integrity
Relational database
Remove filter
Replace command
Report
Sort
Sort Ascending
Sort Descending
Table
Triangle (record selector) symbol
Undo command

1. Which sequence represents the hierarchy of terms, from smallest to largest?
   (a) Database, table, record, field
   (b) Field, record, table, database
   (c) Record, field, table, database
   (d) Field, record, database, table

2. Which of the following is true regarding movement within a record (assuming you are not in the first or last field of that record)?
   (a) Press Tab or the right arrow key to move to the next field
   (b) Press Shift+Tab or the left arrow key to return to the previous field
   (c) Both (a) and (b)
   (d) Neither (a) nor (b)

3. You're performing routine maintenance on a table within an Access database. When should you execute the Save command?
   (a) Immediately after you add, edit, or delete a record
   (b) Periodically during a session—for example, after every fifth change
   (c) Once at the end of a session
   (d) None of the above since Access automatically saves the changes as they are made

4. Which of the following objects are contained within an Access database?
   (a) Tables and forms
   (b) Queries and reports
   (c) Macros and modules
   (d) All of the above

5. Which of the following is true about the objects in an Access database?
   (a) Every database must contain at least one object of every type
   (b) A database may contain at most one object of each type
   (c) Both (a) and (b)
   (d) Neither (a) nor (b)

6. Which of the following is true of an Access database?
   (a) Every record in a table has the same fields as every other record in that table
   (b) Every table contains the same number of records as every other table
   (c) Both (a) and (b)
   (d) Neither (a) nor (b)

7. Which of the following is a *false* statement about the Open Database command?
   (a) It can be executed from the File menu
   (b) It can be executed by clicking the Open button on the Database toolbar
   (c) It loads a database from disk into memory
   (d) It opens the selected table from the Database window

8. Which of the following is true regarding the record selector symbol?
    (a) A pencil indicates that the current record has already been saved
    (b) A triangle indicates that the current record has not changed
    (c) An asterisk indicates the first record in the table
    (d) All of the above

9. Which view is used to add, edit, and delete records in a table?
    (a) The Design view
    (b) The Datasheet view
    (c) Either (a) or (b)
    (d) Neither (a) nor (b)

10. Which of the following is true with respect to a table within an Access database?
    (a) Ctrl+End moves to the last field in the last record of a table
    (b) Ctrl+Home moves to the first field in the first record of a table
    (c) Both (a) and (b)
    (d) Neither (a) nor (b)

11. What does GIGO stand for?
    (a) Gee, I Goofed, OK
    (b) Grand Illusions, Go On
    (c) Global Indexing, Global Order
    (d) Garbage In, Garbage Out

12. The find and replace values in a Replace command must be:
    (a) The same length
    (b) The same case
    (c) Both (a) and (b)
    (d) Neither (a) nor (b)

13. An Access table containing 10 records, and 10 fields per record, requires two pages for printing. What, if anything, can be done to print the table on one page?
    (a) Print in Landscape rather than Portrait mode
    (b) Decrease the left and right margins
    (c) Both (a) and (b)
    (d) Neither (a) nor (b)

14. Which of the following capabilities is available through Filter by Selection?
    (a) The imposition of a relational condition
    (b) The imposition of an alternate (OR) condition
    (c) Both (a) and (b)
    (d) Neither (a) nor (b)

15. Which of the following best describes the relationship between locations and employees as implemented in the Look Ahead database within the chapter?
    (a) One to one
    (b) One to many
    (c) Many to many
    (d) Impossible to determine

Answers

PRACTICE WITH ACCESS 2000

1. The Employee Database: Review and/or complete the third hands-on exercise that introduced the Employee database. Be sure to remove any filters that are in effect at the end of the exercise, then implement the following transactions:

   a. Delete the record for Kelly Marder.

   b. Change Pamela Milgrom's salary to $59,500.

   c. Use the Replace command to change all occurrences of "Manager" to "Supervisor."

   d. Print the Employee Census Report as shown in Figure 1.11 after making the changes in parts (a) through (c).

   e. Create a cover page (in Microsoft Word) and submit the assignment to your instructor.

FIGURE 1.11 The Employee Database (Exercise 1)

2. Do the two hands-on exercises in the chapter, then modify the Bookstore database to accommodate the following:

   a. Add the book, *Exploring Microsoft Office 2000 Vol II* (ISBN: 013-011100-7) by Grauer/Barber, published in 1999 by Prentice Hall, selling for $45.00.

   b. Change the price of *Memory Management for All of Us* to $29.95.

   c. Delete *The Presentation Design Book*.

   d. Print the *All Books Report* after these changes have been made.

3. The United States: Figure 1.12 displays a table from the United States (USA) database that is one of our practice files. The database contains statistical data about all 50 states and enables you to produce various reports such as the 10 largest states in terms of population.

   a. Open the USA database, then open the USstates table. Click anywhere in the Population field, then click the Sort Descending button to list the states in descending order. Click and drag to select the first ten records so that you have selected the ten most populous states.

   b. Pull down the File menu, click the Print command, then click the option button to print the selected records. Be sure to print in Landscape mode so that all of the data fits on one page. (Use the Page Setup command in the File menu prior to printing.)

   c. Repeat the procedure in steps a and b, but this time print the ten states with the largest area.

   d. Repeat the procedure once again to print the first thirteen states admitted to the Union. (You have to sort in ascending rather than descending sequence.)

   e. Submit all three pages together with a title page (created in Microsoft Word) to your instructor.

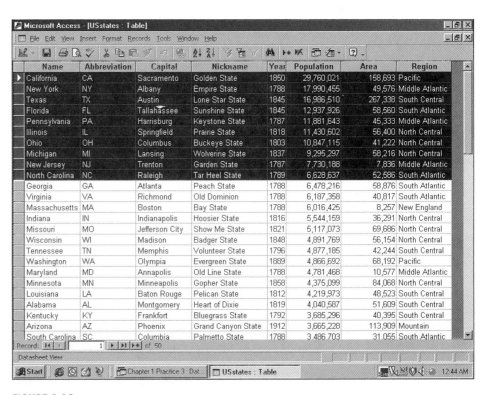

FIGURE 1.12 The United States Database (Exercise 3)

4. The Super Bowl: Open the Super Bowl database on the data disk and display the table in Figure 1.13. Our data stops with the 1999 Super Bowl and it may no longer be current. Thus, the first thing you will need to do is update our table.

a. Pull down the View menu, click Toolbars, then toggle the Web toolbar on. Enter the address of the NFL home page (www.nfl.com) in the Address bar, then click the link to the Super Bowl. Follow the links that will allow you to determine the teams and score of any game(s) not included in our table.

b. Click the New Record button and enter the additional data in the table. The additional data will be entered at the end of the table, and hence you need to sort the data after it is entered. Click anywhere in the Year field, then click the Descending Sort button to display the most recent Super Bowl first as shown in Figure 1.13c.

c. Select the winner in any year that the AFC won. Click the Filter by Selection button to display only those records (i.e., the years in which the AFC won the game). Print these records.

d. Click the Remove Filter button. Select any year in which the NFC won, then click the Filter by Selection button to display the years in which the NFC won. Print these records. Remove the filter.

e. Create one additional filter (e.g., the years in which your team won the big game). Print these records as well.

f. Create a cover sheet, then submit all three reports to your instructor.

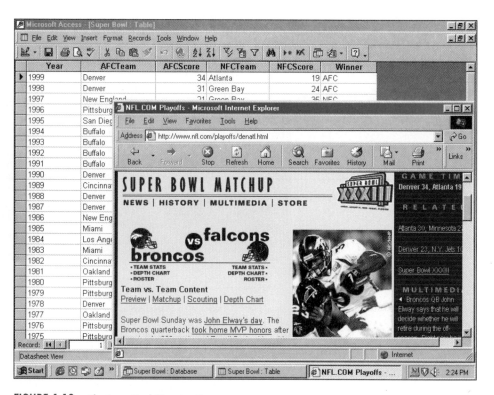

FIGURE 1.13 The Super Bowl (Exercise 4)

5. A Look Ahead: Review and/or complete the fourth hands-on exercise that pertained to the Look Ahead database. Enter the following additional transactions, then print the Employees by Location report shown in Figure 1.14.

   a. Add a new location to the Locations table. Use L05, New York, 1000 Broadway, NY, 10020, and (212) 666-6666 for the LocationID, Location, Address, State, ZipCode, and OfficePhone fields, respectively.

   b. Change the assigned location for Bob Grauer, Frank Smith, and yourself to the New York Office. Bob will be the manager of the New York office.

   c. Delete the record for Kenneth Charles.

   d. Change the title, "Account Rep" to "Account Exec."

   e. Print the Employees by Location report and submit it to your instructor as proof you did this exercise.

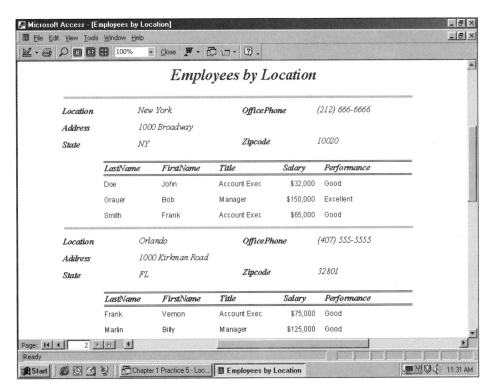

FIGURE 1.14   A Look Ahead (Exercise 5)

6. A Companion Web site (or online study guide) accompanies each book in the *Exploring Microsoft Office 2000* series. Go to the Exploring Windows home page at www.prenhall.com/grauer, click the book to Office 2000, and click the Companion Web site tab at the top of the screen. Choose the appropriate text (Exploring Access 2000) and the chapter within the text (e.g., Chapter 1).

   Each chapter contains a series of short-answer exercises (multiple-choice, true/false, and matching) to review the material in the chapter. You can take practice quizzes by yourself and/or e-mail the results to your instructor. You can try the essay questions for additional practice and engage in online chat sessions. We hope you will find the online guide to be a valuable resource.

Planning for Disaster

This case has nothing to do with databases per se, but it is perhaps the most important case of all, as it deals with the question of backup. Do you have a backup strategy? Do you even know what a backup strategy is? Now is a good time to learn because sooner or later you will wish you had one. There will come a time when you will accidentally erase a file, be unable to read from a floppy disk, or worse yet, suffer a hardware failure in which you are unable to access the hard drive. The problem always seems to occur the night before an assignment is due. The ultimate disaster is the disappearance of your computer, by theft or natural disaster (e.g., Hurricane Andrew, the floods in the Midwest, or the Los Angeles earthquake). Describe in 250 or fewer words the backup strategy you plan to implement in conjunction with your work in this class.

The Common User Interface

One of the most significant benefits of the Windows environment is the common user interface, which provides a sense of familiarity when you go from one application to another—for example, when you go from Excel to Access. How many similarities can you find between these two applications? Which menus are common to both? Which keyboard shortcuts? Which formatting conventions? Which toolbar icons? Which shortcut menus?

Garbage In, Garbage Out

Your excellent work in this class has earned you an internship in the registrar's office. Your predecessor has created a student database that appears to work well, but in reality has several problems in that many of its reports do not produce the expected information. One problem came to light in conjunction with a report listing business majors: the report contained far fewer majors than were expected. Open the GIGO database on the data disk and see if you can find and correct the problem.

Changing Menus and Toolbars

Office 2000 implements one very significant change over previous versions of Office in that it displays a series of short menus that contain only basic commands. The additional commands are made visible by clicking the double arrow that appears at the bottom of the menu. New commands are added to the menu as they are used, and conversely, other commands are removed if they are not used. A similar strategy is followed for the Standard and Formatting toolbars which are displayed on a single row, and thus do not show all of the buttons at one time. The intent is to simplify Office 2000 for the new user by limiting the number of commands that are visible. The consequence, however, is that the individual is not exposed to new commands, and hence may not use Office to its full potential. Which set of menus do you prefer? How do you switch from one set to the other?

chapter 2

TABLES AND FORMS: DESIGN, PROPERTIES, VIEWS, AND WIZARDS

OBJECTIVES

After reading this chapter you will be able to:

1. Describe in general terms how to design a table; discuss three guidelines you can use in the design process.
2. Describe the data types and properties available within Access and the purpose of each; set the primary key for a table.
3. Use the Table Wizard to create a table; add and delete fields in an existing table.
4. Discuss the importance of data validation and how it is implemented in Access.
5. Use the Form Wizard to create one of several predefined forms.
6. Distinguish between a bound control, an unbound control, and a calculated control; explain how each type of control is entered on a form.
7. Modify an existing form to include a combo box, command buttons, and color.
8. Switch between the Form view, Design view, and Datasheet view; use a form to add, edit, and delete records in a table.

OVERVIEW

This chapter introduces a new case study, that of a student database, which we use to present the basic principles of table and form design. Tables and forms are used to input data into a system from which information can be produced. The value of that information depends entirely on the quality of the underlying data, which must be both complete and accurate. We begin, therefore, with a conceptual discussion emphasizing the importance of proper design and develop essential guidelines that are used throughout the book.

After the design has been developed, we turn our attention to implementing that design in Access. We show you how to create a table using the Table Wizard, then show you how to refine its design by changing the properties of various fields within the table. We also stress the importance of data validation during data entry.

The second half of the chapter introduces forms as a more convenient way to enter and display data. We introduce the Form Wizard to create a basic form, then show you how to modify that form to include command buttons, a list box, a check box, and an option group.

As always, the hands-on exercises in the chapter enable you to apply the conceptual material at the computer. This chapter contains three exercises, after which you will be well on your way toward creating a useful database in Access.

CASE STUDY: A STUDENT DATABASE

As a student you are well aware that your school maintains all types of data about you. They have your social security number. They have your name and address and phone number. They know whether or not you are receiving financial aid. They know your major and the number of credits you have completed.

Think for a moment about the information your school requires, then write down all of the data needed to produce that information. This is the key to the design process. You must visualize the output the end user will require to determine the input to produce that output. Think of the specific fields you will need. Try to characterize each field according to the type of data it contains (such as text, numbers, or dates) as well as its size (length).

Our solution is shown in Figure 2.1, which may or may not correspond to what you have written down. The order of the fields within the table is not significant. Neither are the specific field names. What is important is that the table contain all necessary fields so that the system can perform as intended.

Field Name	Type
SSN	Text
FirstName	Text
LastName	Text
Address	Text
City	Text
State	Text
PostalCode	Text
PhoneNumber	Text
Major	Text
BirthDate	Date/Time
FinancialAid	Yes/No
Gender	Text
Credits	Number
QualityPoints	Number

FIGURE 2.1   The Students Table

Figure 2.1 may seem obvious upon presentation, but it does reflect the results of a careful design process based on three essential guidelines:

1. Include all of the necessary data
2. Store data in its smallest parts
3. Do not use calculated fields

Each guideline is discussed in turn. As you proceed through the text, you will be exposed to many applications that help you develop the experience necessary to design your own systems.

Include the Necessary Data

How do you determine the necessary data? The best way is to create a rough draft of the reports you will need, then design the table so that it contains the fields necessary to create those reports. In other words, ask yourself what information will be expected from the system, then determine the data required to produce that information. Consider, for example, the type of information that can and cannot be produced from the table in Figure 2.1:

- You can contact a student by mail or by telephone. You cannot, however, contact the student's parents if the student lives on campus or has an address different from his or her parents.
- You can calculate a student's grade point average (GPA) by dividing the quality points by the number of credits. You cannot produce a transcript listing the courses a student has taken.
- You can calculate a student's age from his or her date of birth. You cannot determine how long the student has been at the university because the date of admission is not in the table.

Whether or not these omissions are important depends on the objectives of the system. Suffice it to say that you must design a table carefully, so that you are not disappointed when it is implemented. *You must be absolutely certain that the data entered into a system is sufficient to provide all necessary information;* otherwise the system is almost guaranteed to fail.

DESIGN FOR THE NEXT 100 YEARS

Your system will not last 100 years, but it is prudent to design as though it will. It is a fundamental law of information technology that systems evolve continually and that information requirements will change. Try to anticipate the future needs of the system, then build in the flexibility to satisfy those demands. Include the necessary data at the outset and be sure that the field sizes are large enough to accommodate future expansion.

Store Data in Its Smallest Parts

Figure 2.1 divides a student's name into two fields (first name and last name) to reference each field individually. You might think it easier to use a single field consisting of both the first and last name, but that approach is inadequate. Consider, for example, the following list in which the student's name is stored as a single field:

Allison Foster
Brit Reback
Carrie Graber
Danielle Ferrarro

The first problem in this approach is one of flexibility, in that you cannot separate a student's first name from her last name. You could not, for example, create a salutation of the form "Dear Allison" or "Dear Ms. Foster" because the first and last name are not accessible individually.

A second difficulty is that the list of students cannot be put into alphabetical order because the last name begins in the middle of the field. Indeed, whether you realize it or not, the names in the list are already in alphabetical order (according to the design criteria of a single field) because sorting always begins with the leftmost position in a field. Thus the "A" in Allison comes before the "B" in Brit, and so on. The proper way to sort the data is on the last name, which can be done only if the last name is stored as a separate field.

CITY, STATE, AND ZIP CODE: ONE FIELD OR THREE?

The city, state, and zip code should always be stored as separate fields. Any type of mass mailing requires you to sort on zip code to take advantage of bulk mail. Other applications may require you to select records from a particular state or zip code, which can be done only if the data is stored as separate fields. The guideline is simple—store data in its smallest parts.

Avoid Calculated Fields

A *calculated field* is a field whose value is derived from a formula or function that references an existing field or combination of fields. Calculated fields should not be stored in a table because they are subject to change, waste space, and are otherwise redundant.

The Grade Point Average (GPA) is an example of a calculated field as it is computed by dividing the number of quality points by the number of credits. It is both unnecessary and undesirable to store GPA in the Students table, because the table contains the fields on which the GPA is based. In other words, Access is able to calculate the GPA from these fields whenever it is needed, which is much more efficient than doing it manually. Imagine, for example, having to manually recalculate the GPA for 10,000 students each semester.

BIRTH DATE VERSUS AGE

A person's age and date of birth provide equivalent information, as one is calculated from the other. It might seem easier, therefore, to store the age rather than the birth date, and thus avoid the calculation. That would be a mistake because age changes continually (and would need to be updated continually), whereas the date of birth remains constant. Similar reasoning applies to an employee's length of service versus date of hire.

There are two ways to create a table. The easier way is to use the **Table Wizard,** an interactive coach that lets you choose from many predefined tables. The Table Wizard asks you questions about the fields you want to include in your table, then creates the table for you. Alternatively, you can create a table yourself by defining every field in the table. Regardless of how a table is created, you can modify it to include a new field or to delete an existing field.

Every field has a **field name** to identify the data that is entered into the field. The field name should be descriptive of the data and can be up to 64 characters in length, including letters, numbers, and spaces. We do not, however, use spaces in our field names, but use uppercase letters to distinguish the first letter of a new word. This is consistent with the default names provided by Access in its predefined tables.

Every field also has a **data type** that determines the type of data that can be entered and the operations that can be performed on that data. Access recognizes nine data types: Number, Text, Memo, Date/Time, Currency, Yes/No, OLE Object, AutoNumber, and Hyperlink.

- A **Number field** contains a value that can be used in a calculation such as the number of quality points or credits a student has earned. The contents of a number field are restricted to numbers, a decimal point, and a plus or minus sign.
- A **Text field** stores alphanumeric data such as a student's name or address. It can contain alphabetic characters, numbers, and/or special characters (e.g., an apostrophe in O'Malley). Fields that contain only numbers but are not used in a calculation (e.g., social security number, telephone number, or zip code) should be designated as text fields for efficiency purposes. A text field can hold up to 255 characters.
- A **Memo field** can be up to 64,000 characters long. Memo fields are used to hold lengthy, descriptive data (several sentences or paragraphs).
- A **Date/Time field** holds formatted dates or times (e.g., mm/dd/yy) and allows the values to be used in date or time arithmetic.
- A **Currency field** can be used in a calculation and is used for fields that contain monetary values.
- A **Yes/No field** (also known as a Boolean or Logical field) assumes one of two values such as Yes or No, or True or False, or On or Off.
- An **OLE Object field** contains an object created by another application. OLE objects include pictures, sounds, or graphics.
- An **AutoNumber field** is a special data type that causes Access to assign the next consecutive number each time you add a record. The value of an AutoNumber field is unique for each record in the file, and thus AutoNumber fields are frequently used as the primary key.
- A **Hyperlink field** stores a Web address (URL). All Office 97 documents are Web-enabled so that you can click a hyperlink within an Access database and display the associated Web page, provided that you have access to the Internet.

Primary Key

The **primary key** is a field (or combination of fields) that uniquely identifies a record. There can be only one primary key per table and, by definition, every record in the table must have a different value for the primary key.

A person's name is not used as the primary key because names are not unique. A social security number, on the other hand, is unique and is a frequent choice for the primary key, as in the Students table in this chapter. The primary key emerges naturally in many applications, such as a part number in an inventory system, or the ISBN in the Books table of Chapter 1. If there is no apparent primary key, a new field can be created with the AutoNumber field type.

Views

A table has two views—the Datasheet view and the Design view. The Datasheet view is the view you used in Chapter 1 to add, edit, and delete records. The Design view is the view you will use in this chapter to create (and modify) a table.

Figure 2.2a shows the Datasheet view corresponding to the table in Figure 2.1. (Not all of the fields are visible.) The **Datasheet view** displays the record selector symbol for the current record (a pencil or a triangle). It also displays an asterisk in the record selector column next to the blank record at the end of the table.

Figure 2.2b shows the Design view of the same table. The **Design view** displays the field names in the table, the data type of each field, and the properties of the selected field. The Design view also displays a key indicator next to the field (or combination of fields) designated as the primary key.

Current Record

Blank Record

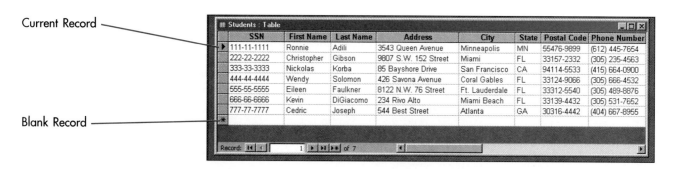

(a) Datasheet View

Primary Key

Properties of selected field

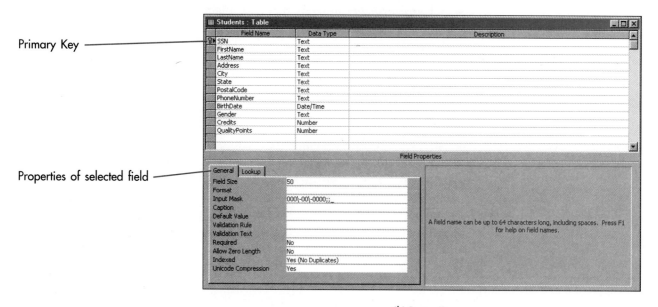

(b) Design View

FIGURE 2.2   The Views of a Table

Properties

A *property* is a characteristic or attribute of an object that determines how the object looks and behaves. Every Access object (tables, forms, queries, and reports) has a set of properties that determine the behavior of that object. The properties for an object are displayed and/or changed in a *property sheet,* which is described in more detail later in the chapter.

Each field has its own set of properties that determine how the data in the field are stored and displayed. The properties are set to default values according to the data type, but can be modified as necessary. The properties are displayed in the Design view and described briefly below:

- The *Field Size property* adjusts the size of a text field or limits the allowable value in a number field. Microsoft Access uses only the amount of space it needs even if the field size allows a greater number.
- The *Format property* changes the way a field is displayed or printed, but does not affect the stored value.
- The *Input Mask property* facilitates data entry by displaying literal characters, such as hyphens in a social security number or slashes in a date. It also imposes data validation by ensuring that the data entered by the user fits within the mask.
- The *Caption property* specifies a label other than the field name for forms and reports.
- The *Default Value property* automatically enters a designated (default) value for the field in each record that is added to the table.
- The *Validation Rule property* rejects any record where the data entered does not conform to the specified rules for data entry.
- The *Validation Text property* specifies the error message that is displayed when the validation rule is violated.
- The *Required property* rejects any record that does not have a value entered for this field.
- The *Allow Zero Length property* allows text or memo strings of zero length.
- The *Indexed property* increases the efficiency of a search on the designated field. (The primary key in a table is always indexed.)

The following exercise has you create a table using the Table Wizard and then modify the table by including additional fields. It also has you change the properties for various fields within the table.

CHANGE THE DEFAULT FOLDER

The default folder is the folder Access uses to retrieve (and save) a database unless it is otherwise instructed. To change the default folder, pull down the Tools menu, click Options, then click the General tab in the Options dialog box. Enter the name of the default database folder (e.g., C:\Exploring Access), then click OK to accept the settings and close the Options dialog box. The next time you access the File menu the default folder will reflect the change.

Creating a Table

Objective: To use the Table Wizard to create a table; to add and delete fields in an existing table; to change the primary key of an existing table; to establish an input mask and validation rule for fields within a table; to switch between the Design and Datasheet views of a table. Use Figure 2.3 as a guide.

STEP 1: Create a New Database

➤ Click the **Start button** to display the Start menu. Click (or point to) the **Programs menu,** then click **Microsoft Access** to start the program.

➤ You should see the Microsoft Access dialog box. Click the option button to create a new database using a **Blank Access Database.** Click **OK.** You should see the File New Database dialog box shown in Figure 2.3a.

➤ Click the **drop-down arrow** on the Save In list box. Click the appropriate drive (e.g., drive C), depending on the location of your data. Double click the **Exploring Access folder** to make it the active folder.

➤ Click in the **File Name text box** and drag to select **db1.** Type **My First Database** as the name of the database you will create. Click the **Create button.**

Click to select drive and/or folder

Create Button

Enter file name

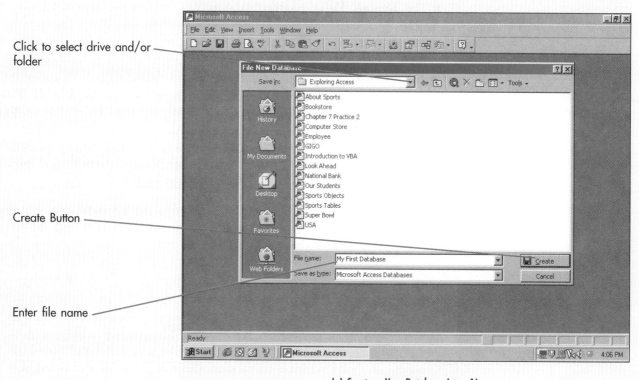

(a) Create a New Database (step 1)

FIGURE 2.3   Hands-on Exercise 1

STEP 2: Create the Table

➤ The Database window for My First Database should appear on your monitor. The **Tables button** is selected by default.

➤ Click and drag an edge or border of the Database window to change its size to match that in Figure 2.3b. Click and drag the title bar of the Database window to change its position on the desktop.

➤ Click the **New button** to display the New Table dialog box shown in Figure 2.3b. Click (select) **Table Wizard** in the New Table dialog box, then click **OK** to start the Table Wizard.

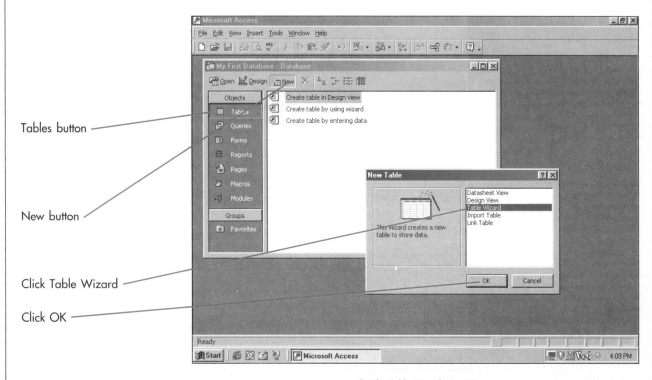

Tables button

New button

Click Table Wizard

Click OK

(b) The Table Wizard (step 2)

FIGURE 2.3   Hands-on Exercise 1 (continued)

STEP 3: The Table Wizard

➤ If necessary, click the **Business option button.** Click the **down arrow** on the **Sample Tables list box** to scroll through the available business tables. Click (select) **Students** within the list of sample tables. The tables are *not* in alphabetical order, and the Students table is found near the very bottom of the list.

➤ The **StudentID field** is already selected in the Sample Fields list box. Click the > **button** to enter this field in the list of fields for the new table as shown in Figure 2.3c.

➤ Enter the additional fields for the new table by selecting the field and clicking the > **button** (or by double clicking the field). The fields to enter are: **FirstName, LastName, Address, City,** and **StateOrProvince** as shown in the figure.

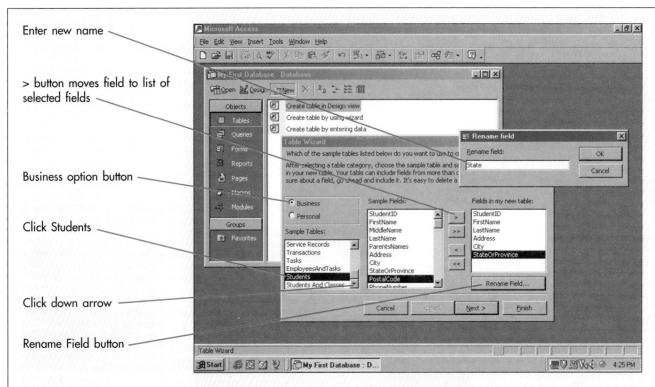

Enter new name

> button moves field to list of selected fields

Business option button

Click Students

Click down arrow

Rename Field button

(c) The Table Wizard (step 3)

FIGURE 2.3   Hands-on Exercise 1 (continued)

➤ Click the **Rename Field command button** after adding the StateOrProvince field to display the Rename Field dialog box. Enter **State** to shorten the name of this field. Click **OK.**

➤ Add **PostalCode** and **PhoneNumber** as the last two fields in the table. Click the **Next command button** when you have entered all the fields.

WIZARDS AND BUTTONS

Many Wizards present you with two open list boxes and expect you to copy some or all fields from the list box on the left to the list box on the right. The > and >> buttons work from left to right. The < and << buttons work in the opposite direction. The > button copies the selected field from the list box on the left to the box on the right. The >> button copies all of the fields. The < button removes the selected field from the list box on the right. The << removes all of the fields.

STEP 4: The Table Wizard (continued)

➤ The next screen in the Table Wizard asks you to name the table and determine the primary key.

• Accept the Wizard's suggestion of **Students** as the name of the table.

• Make sure that the option button **Yes, set a primary key for me** is selected.

• Click the **Next command button** to accept both of these options.

➤ The final screen in the Table Wizard asks what you want to do next.
- Click the option button to **Modify the table design.**
- Click the **Finish command button.** The Students table should appear on your monitor.

➤ Pull down the **File menu** and click **Save** (or click the **Save button** on the Table Design toolbar) to save the table.

STEP 5: Add the Additional Fields

➤ Click the **Maximize button** to give yourself more room to work. Click the cell immediately below the last field in the table (PhoneNumber). Type **Birth-Date** as shown in Figure 2.3d.

➤ Press the **Tab key** to move to the Data Type column. Click the **down arrow** on the drop-down list box. Click **Date/Time.**

➤ Add the remaining fields to the Students table. Add **Gender** as a Text field. Add **Credits** as a Number field. Add **QualityPoints** as a Number field. (There is no space in the field name.)

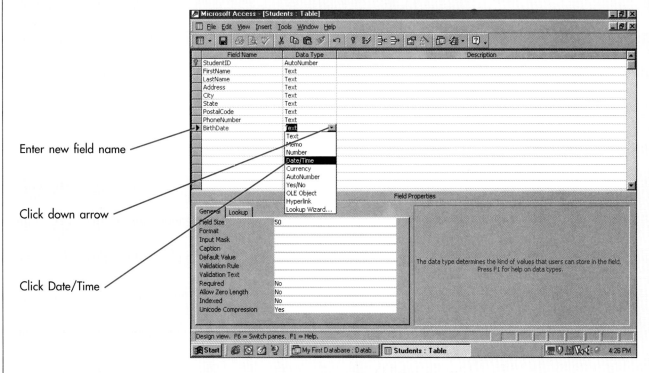

Enter new field name

Click down arrow

Click Date/Time

(d) Add the Additional Fields (step 5)

FIGURE 2.3   Hands-on Exercise 1 (continued)

CHOOSING A DATA TYPE

The fastest way to specify the data type is to type the first letter—T for Text, D for Date/Time, N for Number, and Y for Yes/No. Text is the default data type and is entered automatically.

STEP 6: Change the Primary Key

➤ Point to the first field in the table and click the **right mouse button** to display the shortcut menu in Figure 2.3e. Click **Insert Rows.**

➤ Click the **Field Name column** in the newly inserted row. Type **SSN** (for social security number) as the name of the new field. Press **enter.** The data type will be set to Text by default.

➤ Click the **Required box** in the Properties area. Click the drop-down arrow and select **Yes.**

➤ Click in the Field Name column for **SSN,** then click the **Primary Key button** on the Table Design toolbar to change the primary key to social security number. The primary key symbol has moved to SSN.

➤ Point to the **StudentID field** in the second row. Click the **right mouse button** to display the shortcut menu. Click **Delete Rows** to remove this field from the table definition. Save the table.

Point to first row and click right mouse button to display shortcut menu

Click Insert Rows

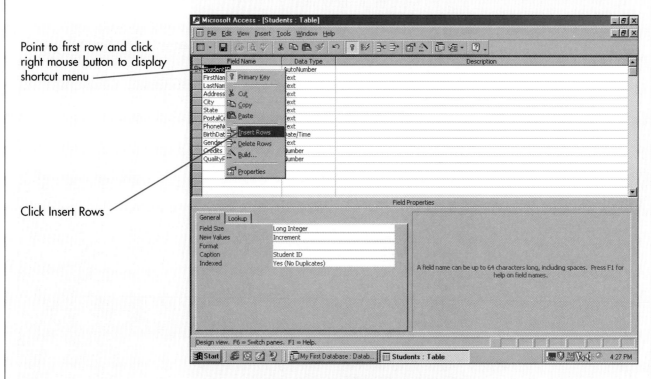

(e) Change the Primary Key (step 6)

FIGURE 2.3   Hands-on Exercise 1 (continued)

INSERTING OR DELETING FIELDS

To insert or delete a field, point to an existing field, then click the right mouse button to display a shortcut menu. Click Insert Rows or Delete Rows to add or remove a field as appropriate. To insert (or delete) multiple fields, point to the field selector to the left of the field name, click and drag the mouse over multiple rows to extend the selection, then click the right mouse button to display a shortcut menu.

STEP 7: Add an Input Mask

➤ Click the field selector column for **SSN.** Click the **Input Mask box** in the Properties area. (The box is currently empty.)

➤ Click the **Build button** to display the Input Mask Wizard. Click **Social Security Number** in the Input Mask Wizard dialog box as shown in Figure 2.3f.

➤ Click the **Try It** text box and enter a social security number to see how the mask works. If necessary, press the **left arrow key** until you are at the beginning of the text box, then enter a social security number (digits only). Click the **Finish command button** to accept the input mask.

➤ Click the field selector column for **BirthDate,** then follow the steps detailed above to add an input mask. (Choose the **Short Date** format.) Click **Yes** if asked whether to save the table.

➤ Save the table.

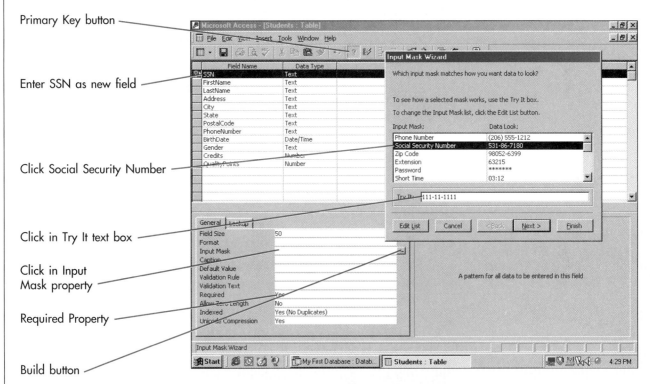

Primary Key button

Enter SSN as new field

Click Social Security Number

Click in Try It text box

Click in Input Mask property

Required Property

Build button

(f) Create an Input Mask (step 7)

FIGURE 2.3   Hands-on Exercise 1 (continued)

SHOW THE KEYBOARD SHORTCUT IN A SCREENTIP

You can expand the ScreenTip associated with any toolbar button to include the equivalent keyboard shortcut. Pull down the View menu, click Toolbars, then click Customize to display the Customize dialog box. Click the Options tab and check the box to show the shortcut keys in the Screen-Tips. Close the dialog box, then point to any toolbar button and you should see the name of the button as well as the equivalent keyboard shortcut.

STEP 8: Change the Field Properties

➤ Click the field selector column for the **FirstName** field:

- Click the **Field Size box** in the Properties area and change the field size to **25.** (You can press the F6 key to toggle between the field name and the Properties area.)

- Click the **Required box** in the Properties area. Click the **drop-down arrow** and select **Yes.**

➤ Click the field selector column for the **LastName** field:

- Click the **Field Size box** in the Properties area. Change the field size to **25.**

- Click the **Required box** in the Properties area. Click the **drop-down arrow** and select **Yes.**

➤ Click the field selector column for the **State** field.

- Click the **Field Size box** in the Properties area and change the field size to **2,** corresponding to the accepted abbreviation for a state.

- Click the **Format box** in the Properties area. Type a **> sign** to display the data in uppercase.

➤ Click the field selector column for the **Credits** field:

- Click the **Field Size box** in the Properties area, click the **drop-down arrow** to display the available field sizes, then click **Integer.**

- Click the **Default Value box** in the Properties area. Delete the **0.**

➤ Click the field selector column for the **QualityPoints** field:

- Click the **Field Size box** in the Properties area, click the **drop-down arrow** to display the available field sizes, then click **Integer.**

- Click the **Default Value box** in the Properties area. Delete the **0.**

➤ Save the table.

THE FIELD SIZE PROPERTY

The field size property for a Text or Number field determines the maximum number of characters that can be stored in that field. The property should be set to the smallest possible setting because smaller data sizes are processed more efficiently. A text field can hold from 0 to 255 characters (50 is the default). Number fields (which do not contain a decimal value) can be set to Byte, Integer, or Long Integer field sizes, which hold values up to 255, or 32,767, or 2,147,483,647, respectively. The Single or Double sizes are required if the field is to contain a decimal value, as they specify the precision with which a value will be stored. (See online Help for details.)

STEP 9: Add a Validation Rule

➤ Click the field selector column for the **Gender** field. Click the **Field Size box** and change the field size to **1** as shown in Figure 2.3g.

➤ Click the **Format box** in the Properties area. Type a **> sign** to display the data entered in uppercase.

➤ Click the **Validation Rule box.** Type **"M" or "F"** to accept only these values on data entry.

➤ Click the **Validation Text box.** Type **You must specify M or F.**

➤ Save the table.

Click field selector column for Gender ⎯

Enter 1 as field size ⎯

Enter > as format ⎯

Enter validation rule ⎯

Enter validation text ⎯

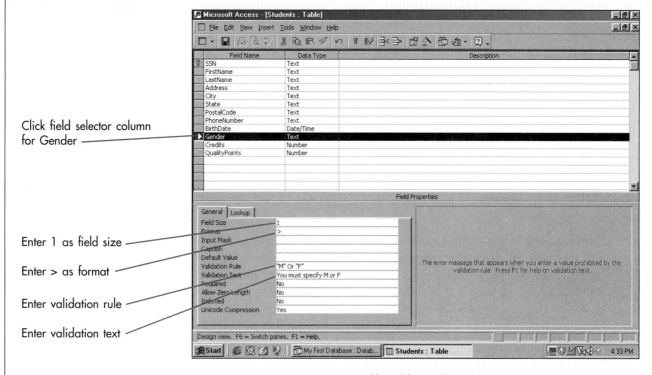

(g) Add a Validation Rule (step 9)

FIGURE 2.3   Hands-on Exercise 1 (continued)

STEP 10: The Datasheet View

➤ Pull down the **View menu** and click **Datasheet View** (or click the **View button** on the toolbar) to change to the Datasheet view as shown in Figure 2.3h.

➤ The insertion point (a flashing vertical line indicating the position where data will be entered) is automatically set to the first field of the first record.

➤ Type **111111111** to enter the social security number for the first record. (The input mask will appear as soon as you enter the first digit.)

➤ Press the **Tab key,** the **right arrow key,** or the **enter key** to move to the First-Name field. Enter the data for Ronnie Adili as shown in Figure 2.3h. Make up data for the fields you cannot see.

➤ Scrolling takes place automatically as you move within the record.

CHANGE THE FIELD WIDTH

Drag the border between field names to change the displayed width of a field. Double click the right boundary of a field name to change the width to accommodate the widest entry in that field.

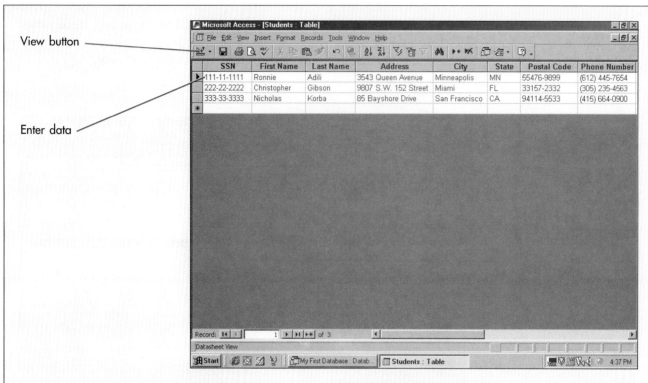

View button

Enter data

(h) Datasheet View (steps 10 & 11)

FIGURE 2.3 Hands-on Exercise 1 (continued)

STEP 11: Enter Additional Data

➤ Enter data for the two additional students shown in the figure, but enter deliberately invalid data to experiment with the validation capabilities built into Access. Here are some of the errors you may encounter:

- The message, *The value you entered isn't valid for this field,* implies that the data type is wrong—for example, alphabetic characters in a numeric field such as Credits.

- The message, *You must specify M or F,* means you entered a letter other than "M" or "F" in the Gender field (or you didn't enter a value at all).

- The message, *The changes you requested to the table were not successful because they would create duplicate values in the index, primary key, or relationship,* indicates that the value of the primary key is not unique.

- The message, *The field 'Students.LastName' can't contain a Null value,* implies that you left a required field blank.

- If you encounter a data validation error, press **Esc** (or click **OK**), then reenter the data.

STEP 12: Print the Students Table

➤ Pull down the **File menu** and click **Print** (or click the **Print button**). Click the **All option button** to print the entire table. Click **OK.** Do not be concerned if the table prints on multiple pages. (You can, however, use the Page Setup command to change the way the data are printed.)

➤ Pull down the **File menu** and click **Close** to close the Students table. Click **Yes** if asked to save the changes to the layout of the table.

➤ Pull down the **File menu** and click the **Close** command to close the database and remain in Access.

➤ Pull down the **File menu** a second time and click **Exit** if you do not want to continue with the next exercise at this time.

THE PAGE SETUP COMMAND

The Page Setup command controls the margins and orientation of the printed page and may enable you to keep all fields for a single record on the same page. Pull down the File menu, click Page Setup, click the Margins tab, then decrease the left and right margins (to .5 inch each) to increase the amount of data that is printed on one line. Be sure to check the box to Print Headings so that the field names appear with the table. Click the Page tab, then click the Landscape option button to change the orientation, which further increases the amount of data printed on one line. Click OK to exit the Page Setup dialog box.

FORMS

A *form* provides an easy way to enter and display the data stored in a table. You type data into a form, such as the one in Figure 2.4, and Access stores the data in the corresponding (underlying) table in the database. One advantage of using a form (as opposed to entering records in the Datasheet view) is that you can see all of the fields in a single record without scrolling. A second advantage is that a form can be designed to resemble a paper form, and thus provide a sense of familiarity for the individuals who actually enter the data.

A form has different views, as does a table. The *Form view* in Figure 2.4a displays the completed form and is used to enter or modify the data in the underlying table. The *Design view* in Figure 2.4b is used to create or modify the form.

Controls

All forms consist of *controls* (objects) that accept and display data, perform a specific action, decorate the form, or add descriptive information. There are three types of controls—bound, unbound, and calculated. A *bound control* (such as the text boxes in Figure 2.4a) has a data source (a field in the underlying table) and is used to enter or modify the data in that table. An *unbound control* has no data source. Unbound controls are used to display titles, labels, lines, graphics, or pictures. Note, too, that every bound control (*text box*) in Figure 2.4a is associated with an unbound control (*label*). The bound control for social security number, for example, is preceded by a label (immediately to the left of the control) that indicates to the user the value that is to be entered.

A *calculated control* has as its data source an expression rather than a field. An *expression* is a combination of operators (e.g., +, −, *, and /), field names, constants, and/or functions. A student's Grade Point Average (GPA in Figure 2.4a) is an example of a calculated control, since it is computed by dividing the number of quality points by the number of credits.

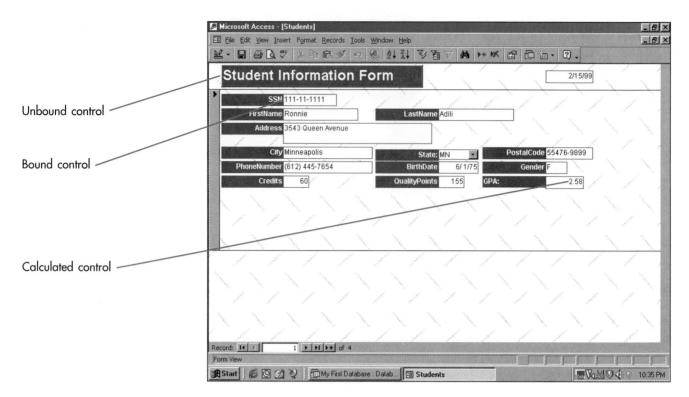

(a) Form View

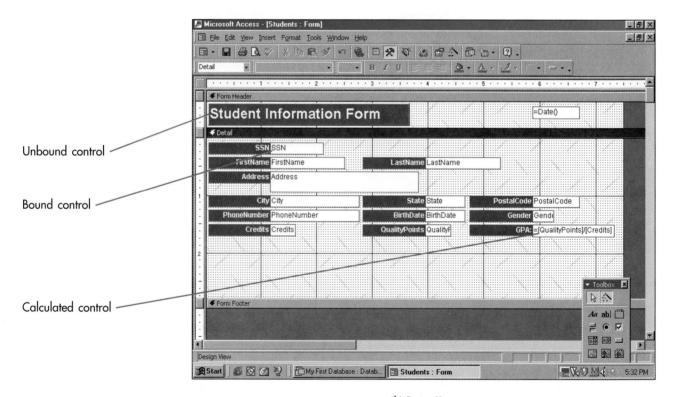

(b) Design View

FIGURE 2.4   Forms

Properties

As previously stated, a ***property*** is a characteristic or attribute of an object that determines how the object looks and behaves. Each control in a form has its own set of properties, just as every field in a table has its own set of properties. The properties for a control are displayed in a ***property sheet,*** as shown in Figure 2.5.

Figure 2.5a displays the property sheet for the Form Header Label. There are many different properties (note the vertical scroll bar) that control every aspect of the label's appearance. The properties are determined automatically as the object is created; that is, as you move and size the label on the form, the properties related to its size and position (Left, Top, Width, and Height in Figure 2.5a) are established for you.

Other actions, such as various formatting commands, set the properties that determine the font name and size (MS Sans Serif and 14 point in Figure 2.5a). You can change the appearance of an object in two ways—by executing a command to change the object on the form, which in turn changes the property sheet, *or* by changing the property within the property sheet, which in turn changes the object's appearance on the form.

Figure 2.5b displays the property sheet for the bound SSN control. The name of the control is SSN. The source for the control is the SSN field in the Students table. Thus, various properties of the SSN control, such as the input mask, are inherited from the SSN field in the underlying table. Note, too, that the list of properties in Figure 2.5b, which reflects a bound control, is different from the list of properties in Figure 2.5a for an unbound control. Some properties, however (such as left, top, width, and height, which determine the size and position of an object), are present for every control and determine its location on the form.

The Form Wizard

The easiest way to create a form is with the ***Form Wizard.*** The Form Wizard asks a series of questions, then builds a form according to your answers. You can use the form as is, or you can customize it to better suit your needs.

Figure 2.6 displays the Database Window from which you call the Form Wizard. The Form Wizard, in turn, requires that you specify the table or query on which the form will be based. (Queries are discussed in Chapter 3.) The form in this example will be based on the Students table created in the previous exercise. Once you specify the underlying table, you select one or more fields from that table as shown in Figure 2.6b. Each field that is selected is entered automatically on the form as a bound control. The Form Wizard asks you to select a layout (e.g., Columnar in Figure 2.6c) and a style (e.g., Blends in Figure 2.6d). The Form Wizard then has all of the information it needs, and creates the form for you. You can enter data immediately, or you can modify the form in the Form Design view.

ANATOMY OF A FORM

A form is divided into one or more sections. Virtually every form has a detail section to display or enter the records in the underlying table. You can, however, increase the effectiveness or visual appeal of a form by adding a header and/or footer. Either section may contain descriptive information about the form such as a title, instructions for using the form, or a graphic or logo.

Properties for Form Header Label —

Properties related to size —

Font name —

Font size —

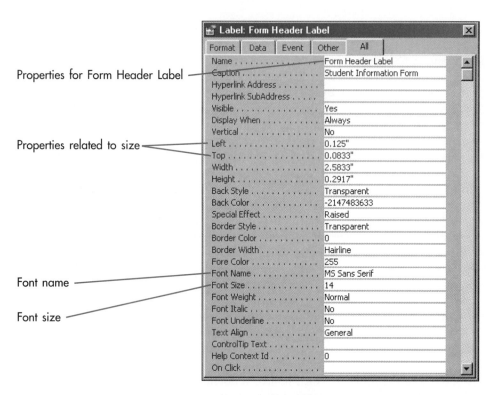

(a) Form Header Label (unbound control)

Properties for SSN —

SSN is data source
for this control —

Input mask was inherited from
table design for underlying table —

Properties related to size —

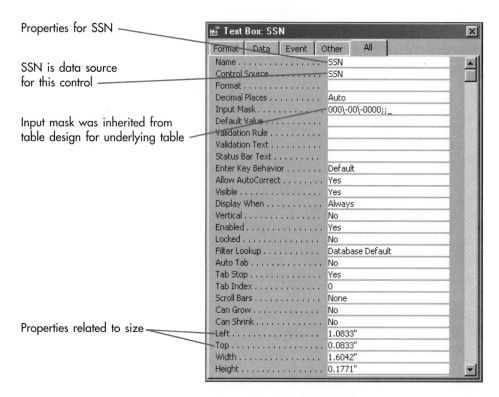

(b) SSN Text Box (bound control)

FIGURE 2.5   Property Sheets

Table on which form will be based

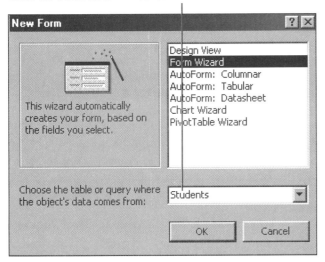

(a) Specify the Underlying Table

Underlying table   Available fields   Selected fields

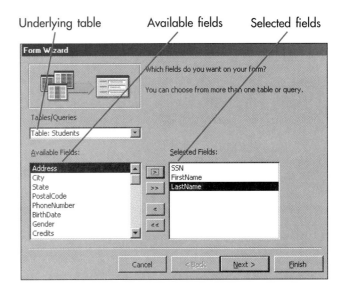

(b) Select the Fields

Selected layout

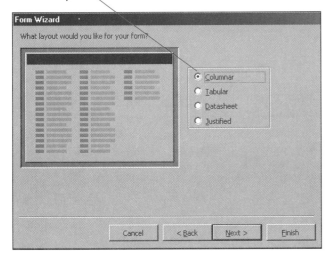

(c) Choose the Layout

Selected style

(d) Choose the Style

FIGURE 2.6   The Form Wizard

Modifying a Form

The Form Wizard provides an excellent starting point, but you typically need to customize the form by adding other controls (e.g., the calculated control for GPA) and/or by modifying the controls that were created by the Wizard. Each control is treated as an object, and moved or sized like any other Windows object. In essence, you select the control, then click and drag to resize the control or position it elsewhere on the form. You can also change the properties of the control through buttons on the various toolbars or by displaying the property sheet for the control and changing the appropriate property. Consider:

- *To select a bound control and its associated label (an unbound control),* click either the control or the label. If you click the control, the control has sizing handles and a move handle, but the label has only a move handle. If you click the label, the opposite occurs; that is, the label will have both sizing handles and a move handle, but the control will have only a move handle.

- *To size a control,* click the control to select the control and display the sizing handles, then drag the sizing handles in the appropriate direction. Drag the handles on the top or bottom to size the box vertically. Drag the handles on the left or right side to size the box horizontally. Drag the handles in the corner to size both horizontally and vertically.

- *To move a control and its label,* click and drag the border of either object. To move either the control or its label, click and drag the move handle (a tiny square in the upper left corner) of the appropriate object.

- *To change the properties of a control,* point to the control, click the right mouse button to display a shortcut menu, then click Properties to display the property sheet. Click the text box for the desired property, make the necessary change, then close the property sheet.

- *To select multiple controls,* press and hold the Shift key as you click each successive control. The advantage of selecting multiple controls is that you can modify the selected controls at the same time rather than working with them individually.

HANDS-ON EXERCISE 2

Creating a Form

Objective: To use the Form Wizard to create a form; to move and size controls within a form; to use the completed form to enter data into the associated table. Use Figure 2.7 as a guide in the exercise.

STEP 1: Open the Existing Database

➤ Start Access as you did in the previous exercise. Select (click) **My First Database** from the list of recently opened databases, then click **OK.** (Click **More Files** if you do not see My First Database.)

➤ Click the **Forms button** in the Database window. Click the **New command button** to display the New Form dialog box as shown in Figure 2.7a.

➤ Click **Form Wizard** in the list box. Click the **drop-down arrow** to display the available tables and queries in the database on which the form can be based.

➤ Click **Students** to select the Students table from the previous exercise. Click **OK** to start the Form Wizard.

THE MOST RECENTLY OPENED FILE LIST

The easiest way to open a recently used database is to select it from the Microsoft Access dialog box that appears when Access is first started. Check to see if your database appears on the list of the four most recently opened databases, and if so, simply double click the database to open it. The list of the most recently opened databases can also be found at the bottom of the File menu.

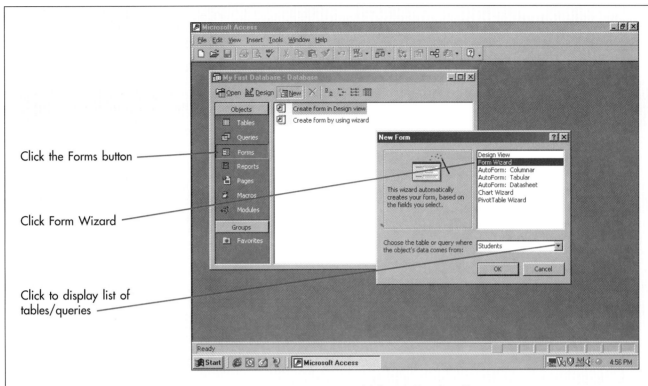

Click the Forms button

Click Form Wizard

Click to display list of tables/queries

(a) Create a Form (step 1)

FIGURE 2.7   Hands-on Exercise 2

STEP 2: The Form Wizard

➤ You should see the dialog box in Figure 2.7b, which displays all of the fields in the Students table. Click the **>> button** to enter all of the fields in the table on the form. Click the **Next command button.**

➤ The **Columnar layout** is already selected. Click the **Next command button.**

➤ Click **Industrial** as the style for your form. Click the **Next command button.**

➤ The Form Wizard asks you for the title of the form and what you want to do next.

 • The Form Wizard suggests **Students** as the title of the form. Keep this entry.

 • Click the option button to **Modify the form's design.**

➤ Click the **Finish command button** to display the form in Design view.

FLOATING TOOLBARS

A toolbar is typically docked (fixed) along the edge of the application window, but it can be displayed as a floating toolbar within the application window. To move a docked toolbar, drag the toolbar background (or the toolbar's move handle). To move a floating toolbar, drag its title bar. To size a floating toolbar, drag any border in the direction you want to go. Double click the background of any toolbar to toggle between a floating toolbar and a docked (fixed) toolbar.

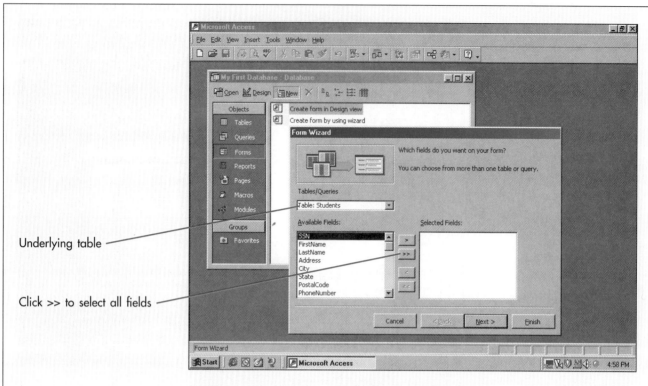

Underlying table

Click >> to select all fields

(b) The Form Wizard (step 2)

FIGURE 2.7   Hands-on Exercise 2 (continued)

STEP 3: Move the Controls

➤ If necessary, click the **Maximize button** so that the form takes the entire screen as shown in Figure 2.7c. The Form Wizard has arranged the controls in columnar format, but you need to rearrange the controls.

➤ Click the **LastName control** to select the control and display the sizing handles. (Be sure to select the text box and *not* the attached label.) Click and drag the **border** of the control (the pointer changes to a hand) so that the LastName control is on the same line as the FirstName control. Use the grid to space and align the controls.

➤ Click and drag the **Address control** under the FirstName control (to take the space previously occupied by the last name).

➤ Click and drag the **border** of the form to **7 inches** so that the City, State, and PostalCode controls will fit on the same line. (Click and drag the title bar of the Toolbox toolbar to move the toolbar out of the way.)

➤ Click and drag the **State control** so that it is next to the City control, then click and drag the **PostalCode control** so that it is on the same line as the other two. Press and hold the **Shift key** as you click the **City, State,** and **PostalCode controls** to select all three, then click and drag the selected controls under the Address control.

➤ Place the controls for **PhoneNumber, BirthDate,** and **Gender** on the same line. Move the controls under City, State, PostalCode.

➤ Place the controls for **Credits** and **QualityPoints** on the same line. Move the controls under PhoneNumber.

➤ Pull down the **File menu** and click **Save** (or click the **Save button**) to save the form.

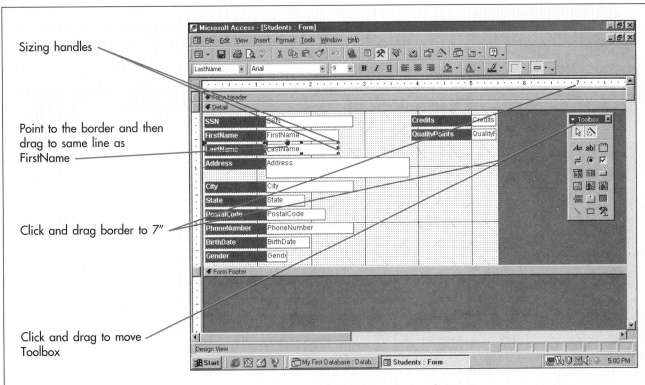

Sizing handles

Point to the border and then drag to same line as FirstName

Click and drag border to 7"

Click and drag to move Toolbox

(c) Move the Controls (step 3)

FIGURE 2.7   Hands-on Exercise 2 (continued)

THE UNDO COMMAND

The Undo command is invaluable at any time, and is especially useful when moving and sizing controls. Pull down the Edit menu and click Undo (or click the Undo button on the toolbar) immediately to reverse the effects of the last command.

STEP 4: Add a Calculated Control (GPA)

➤ Click the **Text Box tool** in the toolbox as shown in Figure 2.7d. The mouse pointer changes to a tiny crosshair with a text box attached.

➤ Click and drag in the form where you want the text box (the GPA control) to go. Release the mouse. You will see an Unbound control and an attached label containing a field number (e.g., Text25) as shown in Figure 2.7d.

➤ Click in the **text box** of the control. The word Unbound will disappear, and you can enter an expression:

- Enter **=[QualityPoints]/[Credits]** to calculate a student's GPA. Do not be concerned if you cannot see the entire entry as scrolling will take place as necessary.

- You must enter the field names *exactly* as they were defined in the table; that is, do *not* include a space between Quality and Points.

➤ Select the attached label (Text25), then click and drag to select the text in the attached label. Type **GPA** as the label for this control and press enter.

Save button

Click and drag to select
Text25, then enter GPA

Click and drag to create text
box (unbound control); click
in text box and enter formula

Text box tool

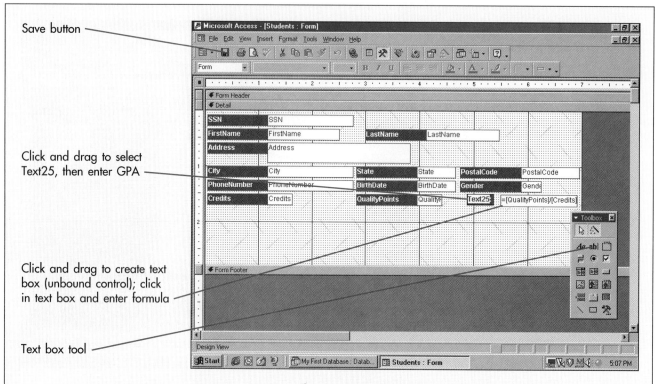

(d) Add a Calculated Control (step 4)

FIGURE 2.7   Hands-on Exercise 2 (continued)

➤ Size the text box appropriately for GPA. Size the bound control as well.
Move either control as necessary.

➤ Click the **Save button.**

SIZING OR MOVING A CONTROL AND ITS LABEL

A bound control is created with an attached label. Select (click) the control, and the control has sizing handles and a move handle, but the label has only a move handle. Select the label (instead of the control), and the opposite occurs; the control has only a move handle, but the label will have both sizing handles and a move handle. To move a control and its label, click and drag the border of either object. To move either the control or its label, click and drag the move handle (a tiny square in the upper left corner) of the appropriate object.

STEP 5: Modify the Property Sheet

➤ Point to the GPA control and click the **right mouse button** to display a shortcut menu. Click **Properties** to display the Properties dialog box.

➤ If necessary, click the **All tab** as shown in Figure 2.7e. The Control Source text box contains the entry =[QualityPoints]/[Credits] from the preceding step.

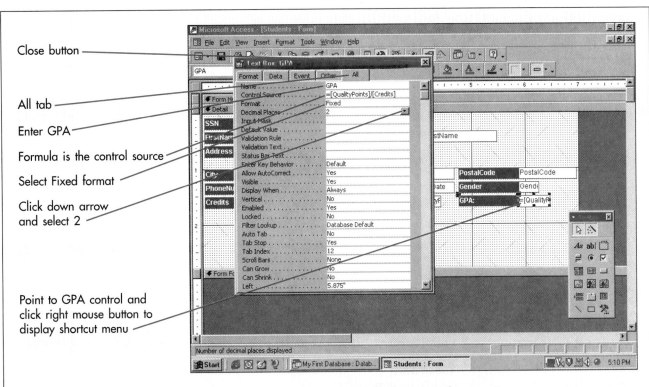

Close button

All tab

Enter GPA

Formula is the control source

Select Fixed format

Click down arrow and select 2

Point to GPA control and click right mouse button to display shortcut menu

(e) Modify the Property Sheet (step 5)

FIGURE 2.7   Hands-on Exercise 2 (continued)

➤ Click the **Name text box.** Replace the original name (e.g., Text24) with **GPA.**
➤ Click the **Format box.** Click the **drop-down arrow,** then scroll until you can select **Fixed.**
➤ Click the box for the **Decimal places.** Click the **drop-down arrow** and select **2** as the number of decimal places.
➤ Close the Properties dialog box to accept these settings and return to the form.

USE THE PROPERTY SHEET

You can change the appearance or behavior of a control in two ways—by changing the actual control on the form itself or by changing the underlying property sheet. Anything you do to the control automatically changes the associated property, and conversely, any change to the property sheet is reflected in the appearance or behavior of the control. In general, you can obtain greater precision through the property sheet, but we find ourselves continually switching back and forth between the two techniques.

STEP 6: Align the Controls

➤ Click the label for SSN, then press and hold the **Shift key** as you click the label for the other controls on the form. This enables you to select multiple controls at the same time in order to apply uniform formatting to the selected controls.

➤ All labels should be selected as shown in Figure 2.7f. Click the **Align Right button** on the Formatting toolbar to move the labels to the right so that each label is closer to its associated control.

➤ Click anywhere on the form to deselect the controls, then fine-tune the form as necessary to make it more attractive. We moved LastName to align it with State. We also made the SSN and PostalCode controls smaller.

➤ Save the form.

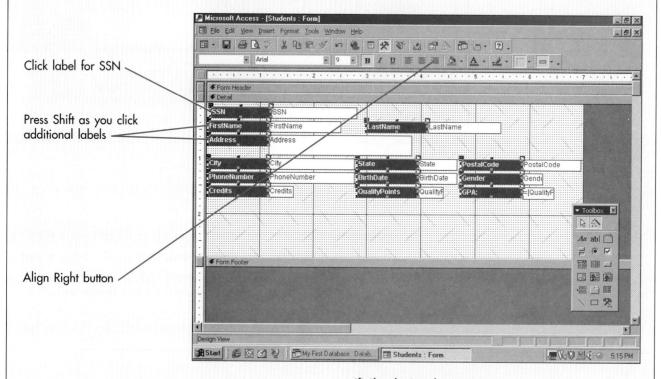

Click label for SSN

Press Shift as you click additional labels

Align Right button

(f) Align the Controls (step 6)

FIGURE 2.7 Hands-on Exercise 2 (continued)

ALIGN THE CONTROLS

To align controls in a straight line (horizontally or vertically), press and hold the Shift key and click the labels of the controls to be aligned. Pull down the Format menu, click Align, then select the edge to align (Left, Right, Top, and Bottom). Click the Undo command if you are not satisfied with the result.

STEP 7: Create the Form Header

➤ Click and drag the line separating the border of the Form Header and Detail to provide space for a header as shown in Figure 2.7g.

➤ Click the **Label tool** on the Toolbox toolbar (the mouse pointer changes to a cross hair combined with the letter A). Click and drag the mouse pointer to create a label within the header. The insertion point (a flashing vertical line) is automatically positioned within the label.

➤ Type **Student Information Form.** Do not be concerned about the size or alignment of the text at this time. Click outside the label when you have completed the entry, then click the control to select it.

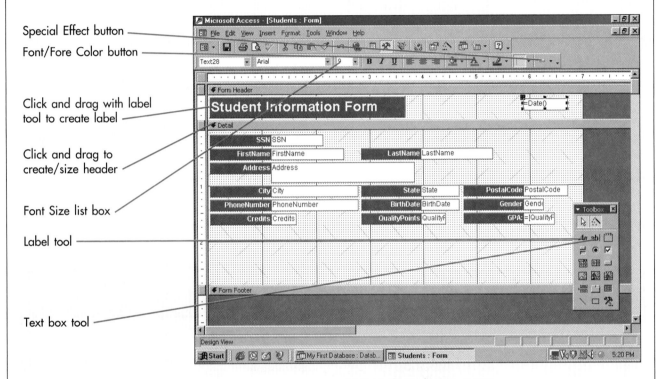

(g) Create the Header (steps 7 & 8)

FIGURE 2.7   Hands-on Exercise 2 (continued)

THE FORMATTING TOOLBAR

The Formatting toolbar contains many of the same buttons that are found on the Formatting toolbars of the other Office applications. These include buttons for boldface, italics, and underlining, as well as left, center, and right alignment. You will find drop-down list boxes to change the font or point size. The Formatting toolbar also contains drop-down palettes to change the foreground or background color, the border color and width, and the special effect.

➤ Click the **drop-down arrow** on the **Font Size list box** on the Formatting toolbar. Click **18.** The size of the text changes to the larger point size.

➤ Click the **drop-down arrow** next to the **Special Effect button** on the Formatting toolbar to display the available effects. Click the **Raised button** to highlight the label.

➤ Click outside the label to deselect it. Click the **Save button** to save the form.

STEP 8: Add the Date

➤ Click the **Textbox tool** on the Toolbox toolbar. The mouse pointer changes to a tiny crosshair with a text box attached.

➤ Click and drag in the form where you want the text box for the date, then release the mouse.

➤ You will see an Unbound control and an attached label containing a number (e.g., Text28). Click in the text box, and the word Unbound will disappear. Type **=Date().** Click the attached label. Press the **Del key** to delete the label.

STEP 9: The Form View

➤ Click the **View button** to switch to the Form view. You will see the first record in the table that was created in the previous exercise.

➤ Click the **New Record button** to move to the end of the table to enter a new record as shown in Figure 2.7h. Enter data for yourself:

• The record selector symbol changes to a pencil as you begin to enter data.

• Press the **Tab key** to move from one field to the next within the form. All properties (masks and data validation) have been inherited from the Students table created in the first exercise.

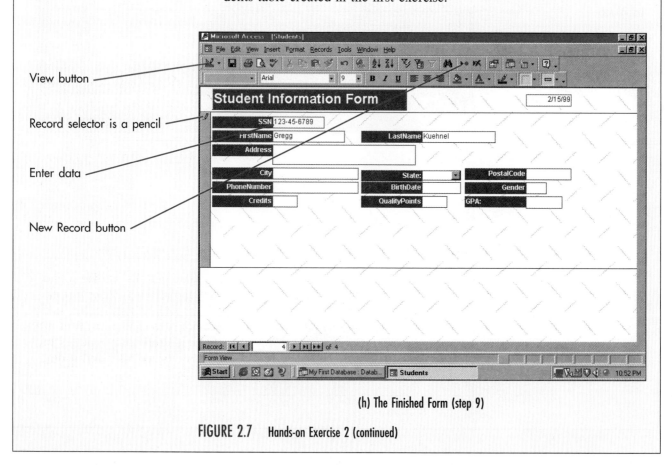

(h) The Finished Form (step 9)

FIGURE 2.7   Hands-on Exercise 2 (continued)

➤ Pull down the **File menu** and click **Close** to close the form. Click **Yes** if asked to save the changes to the form.

➤ Pull down the **File menu** and click **Close** to close the database and remain in Access. Pull down the **File menu** a second time and click **Exit** if you do not want to continue with the next exercise at this time.

ERROR MESSAGES—#NAME? OR #ERROR?

The most common reason for either message is that the control source references a field that no longer exists, or a field whose name is misspelled. Go to the Design view, right click the control, click the Properties command, then click the All tab within the Properties dialog box. Look at the Control Source property and check the spelling of every field. Be sure there are brackets around each field in a calculated control; for example =[QualityPoints]/[Credits].

A MORE SOPHISTICATED FORM

The Form Wizard provides an excellent starting point but stops short of creating the form you really want. The exercise just completed showed you how to add controls to a form that were not in the underlying table, such as the calculated control for the GPA. The exercise also showed how to move and size existing controls to create a more attractive and functional form.

Consider now Figure 2.8, which further improves on the form from the previous exercise. Three additional controls have been added—for major, financial

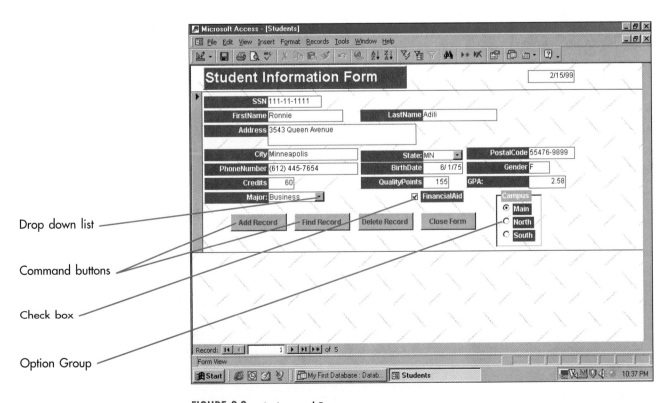

FIGURE 2.8   An Improved Form

aid, and campus—to illustrate other ways to enter data than through a text box. The student's major is selected from a **drop-down list box.** The indication of financial aid (a Yes/No field) is entered through a **check box.** The student's campus is selected from an **option group,** in which you choose one of three mutually exclusive options.

Command buttons have also been added to the bottom of the form to facilitate the way in which the user carries out certain procedures. To add a record, for example, the user simply clicks the Add Record command button, as opposed to having to click the New Record button on the Database toolbar or having to pull down the Insert menu. The next exercise has you retrieve the form you created in Hands-on Exercise 2 in order to add these enhancements.

HANDS-ON EXERCISE 3

A More Sophisticated Form

Objective: To add fields to an existing table; to use the Lookup Wizard to create a combo box; to add controls to an existing form to demonstrate inheritance; to add command buttons to a form. Use Figure 2.9 as a guide in the exercise.

STEP 1: Modify the Table

➤ Open **My First Database** that we have been using throughout the chapter. If necessary, click the **Tables button** in the Database window. The **Students table** is already selected since that is the only table in the database.

➤ Click the **Design command button** to open the table in Design view as shown in Figure 2.9a. (The FinancialAid, Campus, and Major fields have not yet been added.) Maximize the window.

➤ Click the **Field Name box** under QualityPoints. Enter **FinancialAid** as the name of the new field. Press the **enter (Tab,** or **right arrow) key** to move to the Data Type column. Type **Y** (the first letter in a Yes/No field) to specify the data type.

➤ Click the **Field Name box** on the next row. Type **Campus.** (There is no need to specify the Data Type since Text is the default.)

➤ Press the **down arrow key** to move to the Field Name box on the next row. Enter **Major.** Press the **enter (Tab,** or **right arrow) key** to move to the Data Type column. Click the **drop-down arrow** to display the list of data types as shown in Figure 2.9a. Click **Lookup Wizard.**

STEP 2: The Lookup Wizard

➤ The first screen in the Lookup Wizard asks how you want to look up the data. Click the option button that indicates **I will type in the values that I want.** Click **Next.**

➤ You should see the dialog box in Figure 2.9b. The number of columns is already entered as one. Click the **text box** to enter the first major. Type **Business.** Press **Tab** or the **down arrow key** (do *not* press the enter key) to enter the next major.

➤ Complete the entries shown in Figure 2.9b. Click **Next.** The Wizard asks for a label to identify the column. (Major is already entered.) Click **Finish** to exit the Wizard and return to the Design View.

➤ Click the **Save button** to save the table. Close the table.

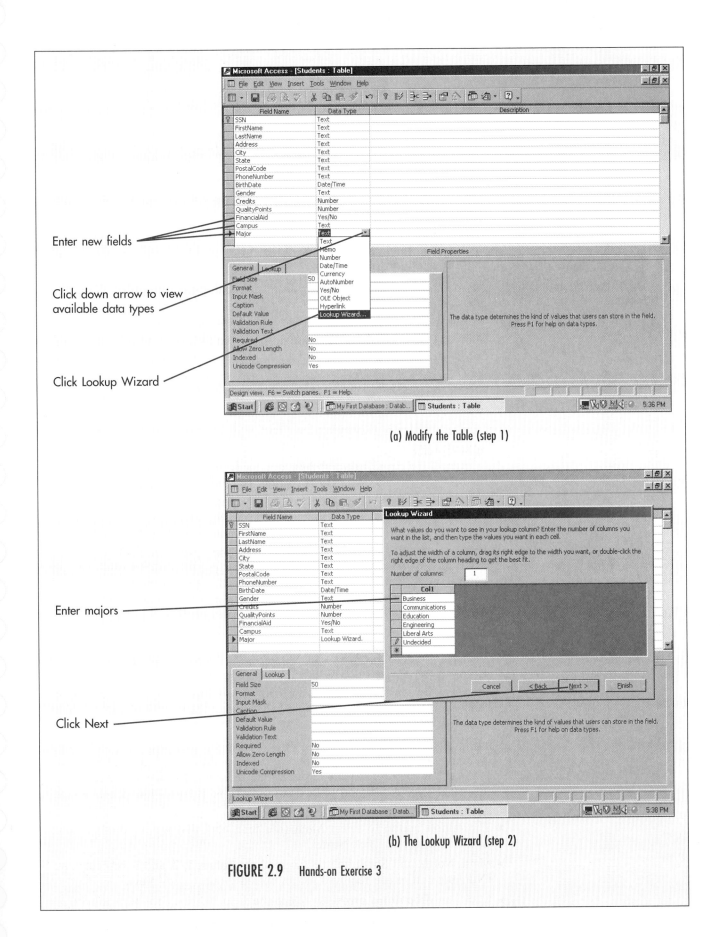

Enter new fields

Click down arrow to view available data types

Click Lookup Wizard

(a) Modify the Table (step 1)

Enter majors

Click Next

(b) The Lookup Wizard (step 2)

FIGURE 2.9   Hands-on Exercise 3

STEP 3: Add the New Controls

➤ Click the **Forms button** in the Database window. If necessary, click the Students form to select it.

➤ Click the **Design command button** to open the form from the previous exercise. If necessary, click the **Maximize button** so that the form takes the entire window.

➤ Pull down the **View menu.** Click **Field List** to display the field list for the table on which the form is based. You can move and size the field list just like any other Windows object.

- Click and drag the **title bar** of the field list to the position in Figure 2.9c.

- Click and drag a **corner** or **border** of the field list so that you can see all of the fields at the same time.

➤ Fields can be added to the form from the field list in any order. Click and drag the **Major field** from the field list to the form. The Major control is created as a combo box because of the lookup list in the underlying table.

➤ Click and drag the **FinancialAid field** from the list to the form. The FinancialAid control is created as a check box because FinancialAid is a Yes/No field in the underlying table.

➤ Save the form.

INHERITANCE

A bound control inherits its properties from the associated field in the underlying table. A check box, for example, appears automatically next to any bound control that was defined as a Yes/No field. In similar fashion, a drop-down list will appear next to any bound control that was defined through the Lookup Wizard. Changing the property setting of a field *after* the form has been created will *not* change the property of the associated control. And finally, changing the property setting of a control does *not* change the property setting of the field because the control inherits the properties of the field rather than the other way around.

STEP 4: Create an Option Group

➤ Click the **Option Group button** on the Toolbox toolbar. The mouse pointer changes to a tiny crosshair attached to an option group icon when you point anywhere in the form. Click and drag in the form where you want the option group to go, then release the mouse.

➤ You should see the Option Group Wizard as shown in Figure 2.9d. Enter **Main** as the label for the first option, then press the **Tab key** to move to the next line. Type **North** and press **Tab** to move to the next line. Enter **South** as the third and last option. Click **Next.**

➤ The option button to select Main (the first label that was entered) as the default is selected. Click **Next.**

➤ Main, North, and South will be assigned the values 1, 2, and 3, respectively. (Numeric entries are required for an option group.) Click **Next.**

➤ Click the **drop-down arrow** to select the field in which to store the value selected through the option group, then scroll until you can select **Campus.** Click **Next.**

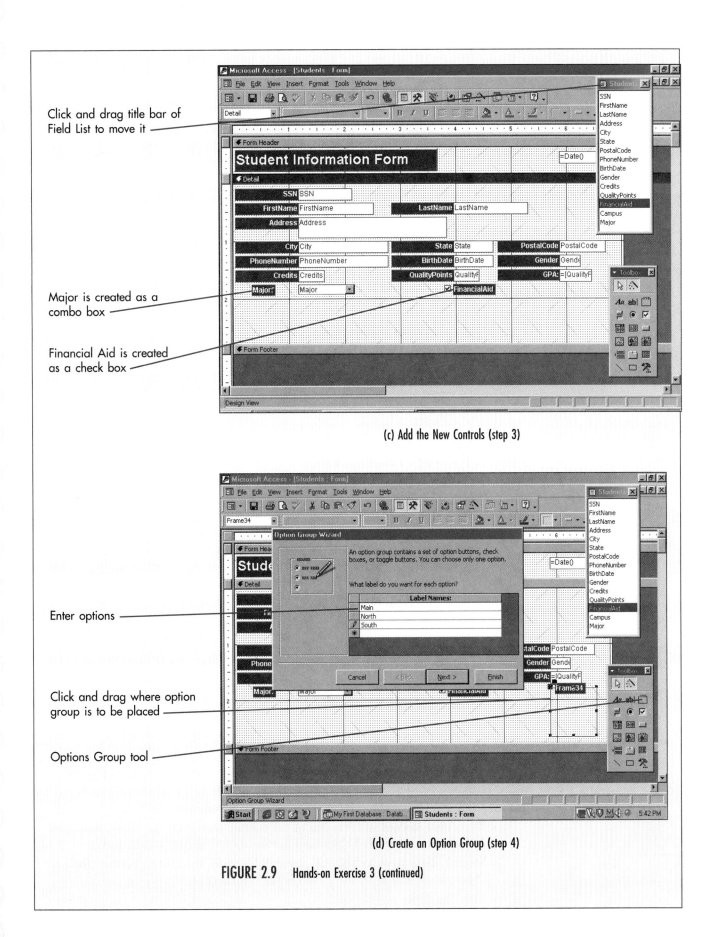

Click and drag title bar of
Field List to move it

Major is created as a
combo box

Financial Aid is created
as a check box

(c) Add the New Controls (step 3)

Enter options

Click and drag where option
group is to be placed

Options Group tool

(d) Create an Option Group (step 4)

FIGURE 2.9   Hands-on Exercise 3 (continued)

➤ Make sure the Option button is selected as the type of control.

➤ Click the option button for the **Sunken style** to match the other controls on the form. Click **Next.**

➤ Enter **Campus** as the caption for the group. Click the **Finish command button** to create the option group on the form. Click and drag the option group to position it on the form under the GPA control.

➤ Point to the border of the option group on the form, click the **right mouse button** to display a shortcut menu, and click **Properties.** Click the **All tab.** Change the name to **Campus.**

➤ Close the dialog box. Close the field list. Save the form.

MISSING TOOLBARS

The Form Design, Formatting, and Toolbox toolbars appear by default in the Form Design view, but any (or all) of these toolbars may be hidden at the discretion of the user. Point to any visible toolbar, click the right mouse button to display a shortcut menu, then check the name of any toolbar you want to display. You can also click the Toolbox button on the Form Design toolbar to display (hide) the Toolbox toolbar.

STEP 5: Add a Command Button

➤ Click the **Command Button tool.** The mouse pointer changes to a tiny crosshair attached to a command button when you point anywhere in the form.

➤ Click and drag in the form where you want the button to go, then release the mouse. This draws a button and simultaneously opens the Command Button Wizard as shown in Figure 2.9e. (The number in your button may be different from ours.)

➤ Click **Record Operations** in the Categories list box. Choose **Add New Record** as the operation. Click **Next.**

➤ Click the **Text option button** in the next screen. Click **Next.**

➤ Type **Add Record** as the name of the button, then click the **Finish command button.** The completed command button should appear on your form. Save the form.

STEP 6: Create the Additional Command Buttons

➤ Click the **Command Button tool.** Click and drag on the form where you want the second button to go.

➤ Click **Record Navigation** in the Categories list box. Choose **Find Record** as the operation. Click the **Next command button.**

➤ Click the **Text option button.** Click the **Next command button.**

➤ Type **Find Record** as the name of the button, then click the **Finish command button.** The completed command button should appear on the form.

➤ Repeat these steps to add the command buttons to delete a record (Record Operations) and close the form (Form Operations).

➤ Save the form.

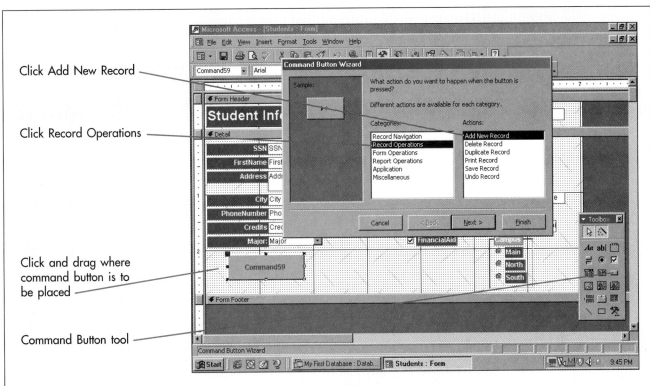

Click Add New Record

Click Record Operations

Click and drag where command button is to be placed

Command Button tool

(e) Add a Command Button (step 5)

FIGURE 2.9   Hands-on Exercise 3 (continued)

STEP 7: Align the Command Buttons

➤ Select the four command buttons by pressing and holding the **Shift key** as you click each button. Release the Shift key when all buttons are selected.

➤ Pull down the **Format menu.** Click **Size** to display the cascade menu shown in Figure 2.9f. (Click the double arrow at the bottom of the menu if you don't see the Size command.) Click **to Widest** to set a uniform width.

➤ Pull down the **Format menu** a second time, click **Size,** then click **to Tallest** to set a uniform height.

➤ Pull down the **Format menu** again, click **Horizontal Spacing,** then click **Make Equal** so that each button is equidistant from the other buttons.

➤ Pull down the **Format menu** a final time, click **Align,** then click **Bottom** to complete the alignment. Drag the buttons to the center of the form.

MULTIPLE CONTROLS AND PROPERTIES

Press and hold the Shift key as you click one control after another to select multiple controls. To view or change the properties for the selected controls, click the right mouse button to display a shortcut menu, then click Properties to display a property sheet. If the value of a property is the same for all selected controls, that value will appear in the property sheet; otherwise the box for that property will be blank. Changing a property when multiple controls are selected changes the property for all selected controls.

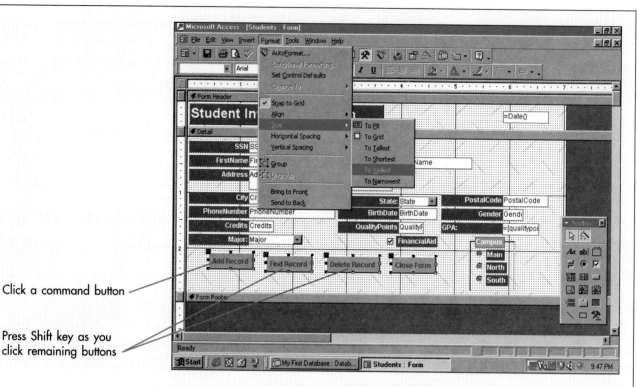

Click a command button

Press Shift key as you click remaining buttons

(f) Align the Buttons (step 7)

FIGURE 2.9   Hands-on Exercise 3 (continued)

STEP 8: Reset the Tab Order

➤ Click anywhere in the Detail section. Pull down the **View menu.** Click **Tab Order** to display the Tab Order dialog box in Figure 2.9g. (Click the double arrow at the bottom of the menu if you don't see the Tab Order command.)

➤ Click the **AutoOrder command button** so that the tab key will move to fields in left-to-right, top-to-bottom order as you enter data in the form. Click **OK** to close the Tab Order dialog box.

➤ Check the form one more time in order to make any last-minute changes.

➤ Save the form.

CHANGE THE TAB ORDER

The Tab key provides a shortcut in the finished form to move from one field to the next; that is, you press Tab to move forward to the next field and Shift+Tab to return to the previous field. The order in which fields are selected corresponds to the sequence in which the controls were entered onto the form, and need not correspond to the physical appearance of the actual form. To restore a left-to-right, top-to-bottom sequence, pull down the View menu, click Tab Order, then select AutoOrder. Alternatively, you can specify a custom sequence by clicking the selector for the various controls within the Tab Order dialog box, then moving the row up or down within the list.

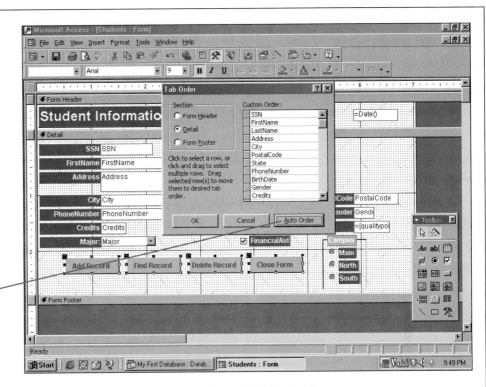

Click Auto Order button

(g) Modify the Tab Order (step 8)

FIGURE 2.9   Hands-on Exercise 3 (continued)

STEP 9: The Page Setup Command

➤ Point to any blank area in the Detail section of the form. Click the **right mouse button** to display a shortcut menu, then click **Properties** to display the Properties dialog box for the Detail section. Click the **All tab.**

➤ Click the text box for **Height.** Enter **3.5** to change the height of the Detail section to three and one-half inches. Close the Properties dialog box.

➤ If necessary, click and drag the **right border** of the form so that all controls are fully visible. Do *not* exceed a width of 7 inches for the entire form.

➤ Pull down the **File menu.** Click **Page Setup** to display the Page Setup dialog box. If necessary, click the **Margins tab.**

➤ Change the left and right margins to **.75** inch. Click **OK** to accept the settings and close the Page Setup dialog box.

CHECK YOUR NUMBERS

The width of the form, plus the left and right margins, cannot exceed the width of the printed page. Thus increasing the width of a form may require a corresponding decrease in the left and right margins or a change to landscape (rather than portrait) orientation. Pull down the File menu and choose the Page Setup command to modify the dimensions of the form prior to printing.

STEP 10: The Completed Form

➤ Click the **View button** to switch to the Form view and display the first record in the table.

➤ Complete the record by adding appropriate data (choose any values you like) for the Major, FinancialAid, and Campus fields that were added to the form in this exercise.

➤ Click the **Add Record command button** to create a new record. Click the text box for **Social Security Number.** Add the record shown in Figure 2.9h. The record selector changes to a pencil as soon as you begin to enter data to indicate the record has not been saved.

➤ Press the **Tab key** or the **enter key** to move from field to field within the record. Click the **arrow** on the drop-down list box to display the list of majors, then click the desired major.

➤ Complete all of the information in the form. Press **enter** to move to the next record.

➤ Click the **selection area** (the thin vertical column to the left of the form) to select only the current record. The record selector changes from a pencil to an arrow. The selection area is shaded to indicate that the record has been selected.

➤ Pull down the **File menu.** Click **Print** to display the Print dialog box. Click the option button to print **Selected Record**—that is, to print only the one record. Click **OK.**

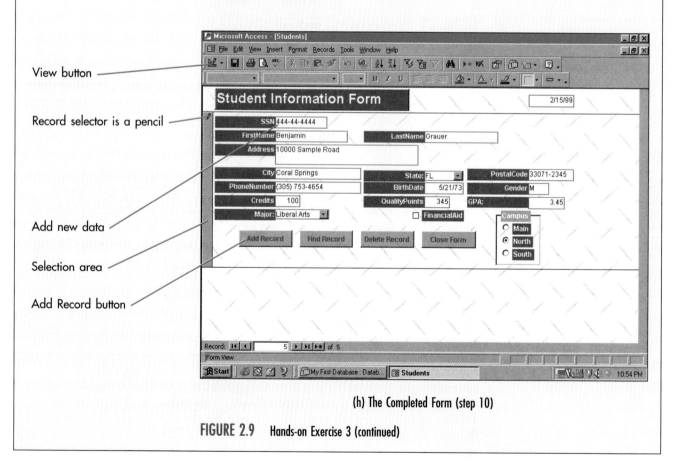

(h) The Completed Form (step 10)

FIGURE 2.9   Hands-on Exercise 3 (continued)

KEYBOARD SHORTCUTS

Press Tab to move from one field to the next in a finished form. Press Shift+Tab to return to the previous field. Type the first letter of an item's name to select the first item in a drop-down list beginning with that letter; for example, type "B" to select the first item in Major beginning with that letter. Type the first two letters quickly—for example, Bu—and you will go directly to Business. Press the space bar to toggle a check box on and off. Press the down arrow key to move from one option to the next within an option group.

STEP 11: Exit Access

➤ Examine your printed output to be sure that the form fits on a single page.

➤ It if doesn't, you need to adjust the margins of the form itself and/or change the margins using the Page Setup command in the File menu, then print the form a second time.

➤ Click the **Close Form command button** on the form after you have printed the record for your instructor.

➤ Click **Yes** if you see a message asking to save changes to the form design.

➤ Pull down the **File menu.** Click **Exit** to leave Access. Congratulations on a job well done.

SUMMARY

The information produced by a system depends entirely on the underlying data. The design of the database is of critical importance and must be done correctly. Three guidelines were suggested. These are to include the necessary data, to store data in its smallest parts, and to avoid the use of calculated fields in a table.

The Table Wizard is the easiest way to create a table. It lets you choose from a series of business or personal tables, asks you questions about the fields you want, then creates the table for you.

A table has two views—the Design view and the Datasheet view. The Design view is used to create the table and determine the fields within the table, as well as the data type and properties of each field. The Datasheet view is used after the table has been created to add, edit, and delete records.

A form provides a user-friendly way to enter and display data, in that it can be made to resemble a paper form. The Form Wizard is the easiest way to create a form. The Design view enables you to modify an existing form.

A form consists of objects called controls. A bound control has a data source such as a field in the underlying table. An unbound control has no data source. A calculated control contains an expression. Controls are selected, moved, and sized the same way as any other Windows object.

A property is a characteristic or attribute of an object that determines how the object looks and behaves. Every Access object (e.g., tables, fields, forms, and controls) has a set of properties that determine the behavior of that object. The properties for an object are displayed in a property sheet.

Allow Zero Length
   property
AutoNumber field
AutoOrder
Bound control
Calculated control
Calculated field
Caption property
Check box
Combo box
Command button
Control
Currency field
Data type
Datasheet view
Date/Time field
Default Value property
Design view

Drop-down list box
Expression
Field name
Field Size property
Form
Form view
Form Wizard
Format property
Hyperlink field
Indexed property
Inheritance
Input Mask property
Label
Lookup Wizard
Memo field
Number field
OLE Object field
Option group

Page Setup
Primary key
Print Preview
Property
Property sheet
Required property
Selection area
Tab Order
Table Wizard
Text box
Text field
Toolbox toolbar
Unbound control
Validation Rule
   property
Validation Text
   property
Yes/No field

MULTIPLE CHOICE

1. Which of the following is true?
  (a) The Table Wizard must be used to create a table
  (b) The Form Wizard must be used to create a form
  (c) Both (a) and (b)
  (d) Neither (a) nor (b)

2. Which of the following is implemented automatically by Access?
  (a) Rejection of a record with a duplicate value of the primary key
  (b) Rejection of numbers in a text field
  (c) Both (a) and (b)
  (d) Neither (a) nor (b)

3. Social security number, phone number, and zip code should be designated as:
  (a) Number fields
  (b) Text fields
  (c) Yes/No fields
  (d) Any of the above depending on the application

4. Which of the following is true of the primary key?
  (a) Its values must be unique
  (b) It must be defined as a text field
  (c) It must be the first field in a table
  (d) It can never be changed

5. Social security number rather than name is used as a primary key because:
   - (a) The social security number is numeric, whereas the name is not
   - (b) The social security number is unique, whereas the name is not
   - (c) The social security number is a shorter field
   - (d) All of the above

6. Which of the following is true regarding buttons within the Form Wizard?
   - (a) The > button copies a selected field from a table onto a form
   - (b) The < button removes a selected field from a form
   - (c) Both (a) and (b)
   - (d) Neither (a) nor (b)

7. Which of the following was *not* a suggested guideline for designing a table?
   - (a) Include all necessary data
   - (b) Store data in its smallest parts
   - (c) Avoid calculated fields
   - (d) Designate at least two primary keys

8. Which of the following are valid parameters for use with a form?
   - (a) Portrait orientation, a width of 6 inches, left and right margins of 1¼ inch
   - (b) Landscape orientation, a width of 9 inches, left and right margins of 1 inch
   - (c) Both (a) and (b)
   - (d) Neither (a) nor (b)

9. Which view is used to add, edit, or delete records in a table?
   - (a) The Datasheet view
   - (b) The Form view
   - (c) Both (a) and (b)
   - (d) Neither (a) nor (b)

10. Which of the following is true?
    - (a) Any field added to a table after a form has been created is automatically added to the form as a bound control
    - (b) Any calculated control that appears in a form is automatically inserted into the underlying table
    - (c) Every bound and unbound control in a form has an underlying property sheet
    - (d) All of the above

11. In which view will you see the record selector symbols of a pencil and a triangle?
    - (a) Only the Datasheet view
    - (b) Only the Form view
    - (c) The Datasheet view and the Form view
    - (d) The Form view, the Design view, and the Datasheet view

12. To move a control (in the Design view), you select the control, then:
    - (a) Point to a border (the pointer changes to an arrow) and click and drag the border to the new position
    - (b) Point to a border (the pointer changes to a hand) and click and drag the border to the new position

(c) Point to a sizing handle (the pointer changes to an arrow) and click and drag the sizing handle to the new position

(d) Point to a sizing handle (the pointer changes to a hand) and click and drag the sizing handle to the new position

13. Which fields are commonly defined with an input mask?

(a) Social security number and phone number

(b) First name, middle name, and last name

(c) City, state, and zip code

(d) All of the above

14. Which data type appears as a check box in a form?

(a) Text field

(b) Number field

(c) Yes/No field

(d) All of the above

15. Which properties would you use to limit a user's response to two characters, and automatically convert the response to uppercase?

(a) Field Size and Format

(b) Input Mask, Validation Rule, and Default Value

(c) Input Mask and Required

(d) Field Size, Validation Rule, Validation Text, and Required

Answers

1. d	**6.** c	**11.** c
2. a	**7.** d	**12.** b
3. b	**8.** c	**13.** a
4. a	**9.** c	**14.** c
5. b	**10.** c	**15.** a

PRACTICE WITH ACCESS 2000

1. A Modified Student Form: Modify the Student form created in the hands-on exercises to match the form in Figure 2.10. (The form contains three additional controls that must be added to the Students table.)

a. Add the DateAdmitted and EmailAddress as a date and a text field, respectively, in the Students table. Add a Yes/No field to indicate whether or not the student is an International student.

b. Add controls for the additional fields as shown in Figure 2.10.

c. Modify the State field in the underlying Students table to use the Lookup Wizard, and set CA, FL, NJ, and NY as the values for the list box. (These are the most common states in the Student population.) The control in the form will not, however, inherit the list box because it was added to the table after the form was created. Hence you have to delete the existing control in the form, display the field list, then click and drag the State field from the field list to the form.

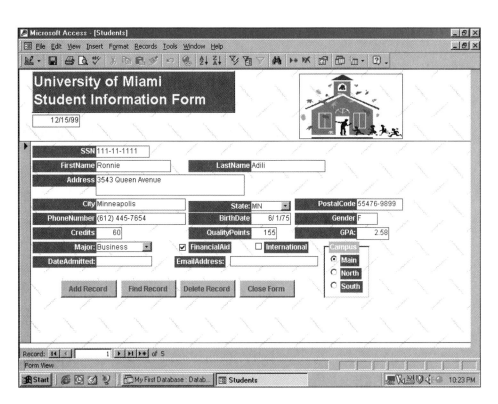

FIGURE 2.10 A Modified Student Form (Exercises 1 and 2)

d. Resize the control in the Form Header so that *University of Miami Student Information Form* takes two lines. Press Ctrl+Enter to force a line break within the control. Resize the Form Header.

e. Change the tab order to reflect the new fields in the form.

f. Add a graphic as described in problem 2.

2. Object Linking and Embedding: This exercise is a continuation of problem 1 and describes how to insert a graphic created by another application onto an Access form.

a. Open the Students form in My First Database in the Design view. Move the date in the header under the label.

b. Click the Unbound Object Frame tool on the toolbox. (If you are unsure as to which tool to click, just point to the tool to display the name of the tool.)

c. Click and drag in the Form Header to size the frame, then release the mouse to display an Insert Object dialog box.

d. Click the Create New option button. Select the Microsoft Clip Gallery as the object type. Click OK.

e. Click the Pictures tab in the Microsoft Clip Gallery dialog box. Choose the category and picture you want from within the Clip Gallery. Click the Insert Clip icon to insert the picture into the Access form and simultaneously close the Clip Gallery dialog box. Do *not* be concerned if only a portion of the picture appears on the form.

f. Right click the newly inserted object to display a shortcut menu, then click Properties to display the Properties dialog box. Select (click) the Size Mode property and select Stretch from the associated list. If necessary, change the Back Style property to Transparent, the Special Effect property to Flat, and the Border Style property to Transparent. Close the Properties dialog box.

g. You should see the entire clip art image, although it may be distorted because the size and shape of the frame you inserted in steps (b) and (c) do not match the image you selected. Click and drag the sizing handles on the frame to size the object so that its proportions are correct. Click anywhere in the middle of the frame (the mouse pointer changes to a hand) to move the frame elsewhere in the form.

h. If you want to display a different object, double click the clip art image to return to the Clip Gallery in order to select another object.

3. The Employee Database: Open the Employee database in the Exploring Access folder to create a form similar to the one in Figure 2.11. (This is the same database that was referenced in problem 1 in Chapter 1.)

a. The form was created using the Form Wizard and Standard style. The various controls were then moved and sized to match the arrangement in the figure.

b. The label in the Form Header, date of execution, and command buttons were added after the form was created, using the techniques in the third hands-on exercise.

c. To add lines to the form, click the Line tool in the toolbox, then click and drag on the form to draw the line. To draw a straight line, press and hold the Shift key as you draw the line.

d. You need not match our form exactly, and we encourage you to experiment with a different design.

e. Use the command buttons on the form to test the indicated operations. Add a record for yourself (if you have not already done so in Chapter 1), then print the form containing your data. Submit the printed form to your instructor as proof you did this exercise.

f. Click the close button on the form to close the form.

g. Exit Access.

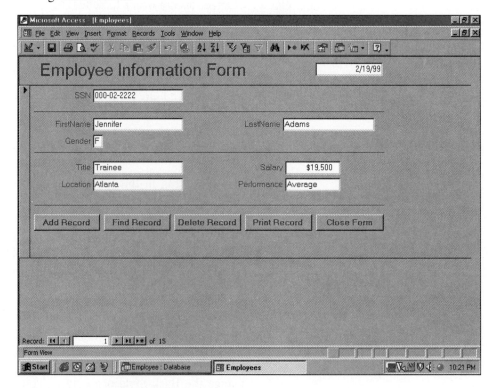

FIGURE 2.11   The Employee Database (Exercise 3)

4. The United States Database: Open the USA database found in the Exploring Access folder to create a form similar to the one in Figure 2.12.
   a. The form was created using the Form Wizard and Blends style. The controls were moved and sized to match the arrangement in the figure.
   b. Population density is a calculated control and is computed by dividing the population by the area. Format the density to two decimal places.
   c. You need not match our form exactly, and we encourage you to experiment with different designs.
   d. Add the graphic, following the steps in the second exercise.
   e. Print the form of your favorite state and submit it to your instructor. Be sure to choose the option to print only the selected record.

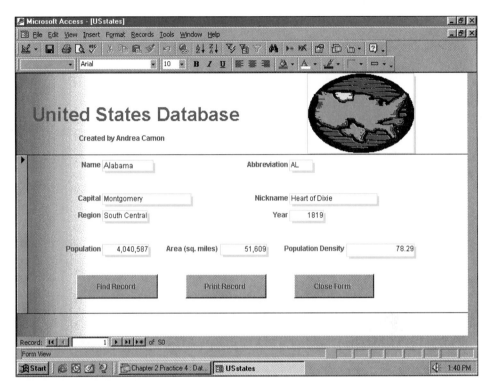

FIGURE 2.12 The United States Database (Exercise 4)

5. The Address Book: Figure 2.13 displays the Design view of a form to maintain an address book of friends and acquaintances. The picture requires you to obtain pictures of your friends in machine-readable form. Each picture is stored initially in its own file (in GIF or JPEG format). The form and underlying table build upon the information in the chapter.
   a. Create an Address Book database containing a table and associated form, using Figure 2.13 as a guide. You can add or delete fields as appropriate with the exception of the FriendID field, which is designated as the primary key. The FriendID should be defined as an AutoNumber field whose value is created automatically each time a record is added to the table.
   b. Include a logical field (e.g., SendCard) in the underlying table. This will enable you to create a report of those people who are to receive a birthday card (or season's greetings card) once the data have been entered.
   c. Include an OLE field in the table, regardless of whether or not you actually have a picture, and be sure to leave space in the form for the picture. Those records that have an associated picture will display the picture in the form. Those records without a picture will display a blank space.

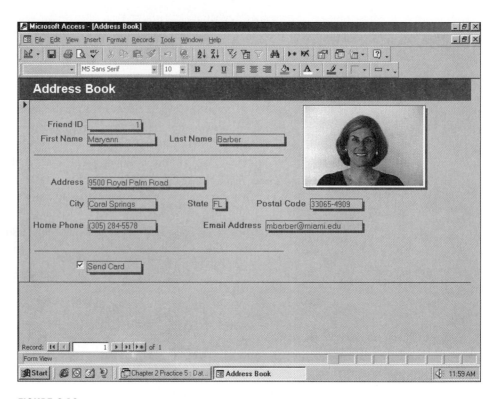

FIGURE 2.13 The Address Book (Exercise 5)

d. To insert a picture into the database, open the table, click in the OLE field, pull down the Insert menu, and click the Object command. Click the Create from File option button, click the Browse button in the associated dialog box, then select the appropriate file name and location.

e. Enter data for yourself in the completed form, then print the associated form to submit to your instructor as proof you did this exercise.

6. The NBA: The potential of Access is limited only by your imagination. Figure 2.14, for example, shows a (partially completed) table to hold statistics for players in the National Basketball Association. The decision on which fields to include is up to you; e.g., you can include statistics for the player's career and/or the current year. We suggest, however, the inclusion of a memo field to add descriptive notes (e.g., career highlights) about each player. You can also include an optional picture field provided you can obtain the player's picture. Design the table, create the associated form, then go the home page of the NBA to obtain statistics for your favorite player. Print the completed form for your player as proof you did this exercise.

7. Help for Your Users: Figure 2.15 shows the Design view of a form that we create for all of our databases. The form is designed to display information about the system such as a version number or product serial number, and hence is not based on a table or query. The default properties of the form have been changed and are set to suppress the scroll bars, record selector, and navigation buttons.

To change the properties of a form, go to the Design view and right click the Form Select button (the tiny square in the upper-left corner) to display a context-sensitive menu. Choose Properties to display the Property sheet for the form, and then look for the appropriate property. Note, too, that the dimensions of the form are also smaller than the typical form. Create the form in Figure 2.15, add your name as indicated, then print the completed form and submit it to your instructor.

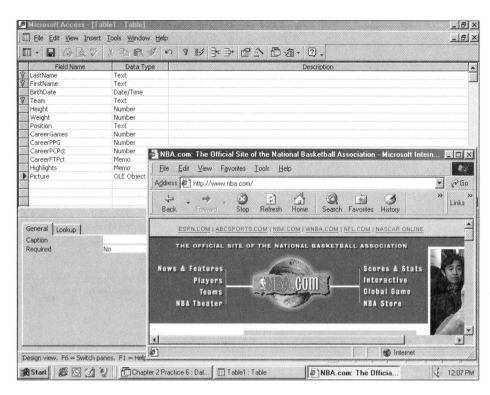

FIGURE 2.14   The NBA (Exercise 6)

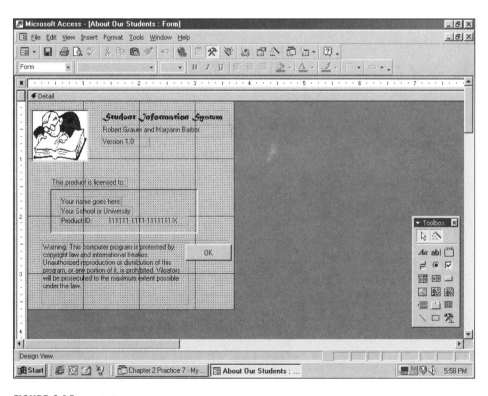

FIGURE 2.15   Help for Your Users (Exercise 7)

8. **Add a Hyperlink:** Figure 2.16 displays a modified version of the form that was created for the United States database in problem 4. We have added an additional field that is defined as a hyperlink. The new field enables you to click the hyperlink from within Access to start your Web browser and display the associated Web page provided you have an Internet connection. Do the following:

   a. Open the United States database, select the USStates table, add a new field called WebPage, and specify hyperlink as the field type.

   b. Open the existing form, pull down the View menu, and click Field List. Drag the newly added WebPage field onto the form. Size and align the controls as shown in Figure 2.16.

   c. Pull down the View menu a second time. Click the Tab Order command and click the AutoOrder command button. Save the form.

   d. Go to the Form view, select the state (e.g., California), and enter the address http://www.yahoo.com/Regional/U_S_States/California, substituting the appropriate name of the state. (This is the address returned by the Yahoo Search engine and it provides generalized information about all fifty states.)

   e. Click the newly created link to start your browser and go to the appropriate site provided you have an Internet connection. Explore the site, then print one or two pages about your state using the Print command in the browser.

   f. Click the Access button on the taskbar to return to the Access database. Choose a second state, then repeat steps (a) through (e) for that state. Can you appreciate the utility of including hyperlinks within a database? Do you see the advantages of multitasking within the Windows environment?

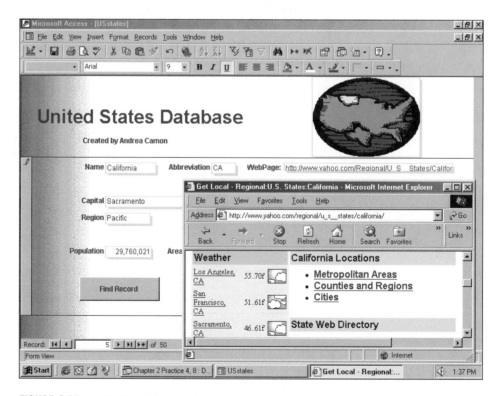

FIGURE 2.16   Add a Hyperlink (Exercise 8)

Personnel Management

You have been hired as the Personnel Director for a medium-sized firm (500 employees) and are expected to implement a system to track employee compensation. You want to be able to calculate the age of every employee as well as the length of service. You want to know each employee's most recent performance evaluation. You want to be able to calculate the amount of the most recent salary increase, both in dollars and as a percentage of the previous salary. You also want to know how long the employee had to wait for that increase—that is, how much time elapsed between the present and previous salary. Design a table capable of providing this information. Create a supporting form, then use that form to enter data for two employees.

The Stockbroker

A good friend has come to you for help. He is a new stockbroker whose firm provides computer support for existing clients, but does nothing in the way of data management for prospective clients. Your friend wants to use a PC to track the clients he is pursuing. He wants to know when he last contacted a person, how the contact was made (by phone or through the mail), and how interested the person was. He also wants to store the investment goals of each prospect, such as growth or income, and whether a person is interested in stocks, bonds, and/or a retirement account. And finally, he wants to record the amount of money the person has to invest. Design a table suitable for the information requirements. Create a supporting form, then use that form to enter data for two clients.

Metro Zoo

Your job as Director of Special Programs at the Metro Zoo has put you in charge of this year's fund-raising effort. You have decided to run an "Adopt an Animal" campaign and are looking for contributions on three levels: $25 for a reptile, $50 for a bird, and $100 for a mammal. Adopting "parents" will receive a personalized adoption certificate, a picture of their animal, and educational information about the zoo. You already have a great mailing list—the guest book that is maintained at the zoo entrance. Your main job is to computerize that information and to store additional information about contributions that are received. Design a table that will be suitable for this project.

Form Design

Collect several examples of such real forms as a magazine subscription, auto registration, or employment application. Choose the form you like best and implement the design in Access. Start by creating the underlying table (with some degree of validation), then use the Form Wizard to create the form. How closely does the form you create resemble the paper form with which you began? To what extent does the data validation ensure the accuracy of the data?

File Compression

Photographs add significantly to the value of a database, but they also add to its size. Accordingly, you might want to consider acquisition of a file compression program to facilitate copying large documents to a floppy disk in order to transport your documents to and from school, home, or work. You can download an evaluation copy of the popular WinZip program at www.winzip.com. Investigate the subject of file compression, then submit a summary of your findings to your instructor.

Copyright Infringement

It's fun to download images from the Web for inclusion into a database, but is it legal? Copyright protection (infringement) is one of the most pressing legal issues on the Web. Search the Web for sites that provide information on current copyright law. One excellent site is the copyright page at the Institute for Learning Technologies at www.ilt.columbia.edu/projects/copyright. Another excellent reference is the page at www.benedict.com. Research these and other sites, then summarize your findings in a short note to your instructor.

The Digital Camera

The art of photography is undergoing profound changes with the introduction of the digital camera. The images are stored on disk rather than traditional film and are available instantly. Search the Internet for the latest information on digital cameras and report back to the class with the results of your research. Perhaps one of your classmates has access to a digital camera, in which case you can take pictures of the class for inclusion in an Access database.

chapter 3

INFORMATION FROM THE DATABASE: REPORTS AND QUERIES

OBJECTIVES

After reading this chapter you will be able to:

1. Describe the various types of reports available through the Report Wizard.
2. Describe the various views in the Report Window and the purpose of each.
3. Describe the similarities between forms and reports with respect to bound, unbound, and calculated controls.
4. List the sections that may be present in a report and explain the purpose of each.
5. Differentiate between a query and a table; explain how the objects in an Access database (tables, forms, queries, and reports) interact with one another.
6. Use the design grid to create and modify a select query.
7. Explain the use of multiple criteria rows within the design grid to implement AND and OR conditions in a query.
8. Define an action query; list the different types of action queries that are available and explain how they are used to update a table.
9. Create a crosstab query.

OVERVIEW

Data and information are not synonymous. Data refers to a fact or facts about a specific record, such as a student's name, major, quality points, or number of completed credits. Information can be defined as data that has been rearranged into a more useful format. The individual fields within a student record are considered data. A list of students on the Dean's List, however, is information that has been produced from the data about the individual students.

Chapters 1 and 2 described how to enter and maintain data through the use of tables and forms. This chapter shows how to convert the data to information through queries and reports. Queries enable you to ask questions about the database. A special type of query, known as an action query, allows you to update a database by changing multiple records in a single operation. Reports provide presentation quality output and display detail as well as summary information about the records in a database.

As you read the chapter, you will see that the objects in an Access database (tables, forms, reports and queries) have many similar characteristics. We use these similarities to build on what you have learned in previous chapters. You already know, for example, that the controls in a form inherit their properties from the corresponding fields in a table. The same concept applies to the controls in a report. And since you know how to move and size controls within a form, you also know how to move and size the controls in a report. As you read the chapter, look for these similarities to apply your existing knowledge to new material.

REPORTS

A *report* is a printed document that displays information from a database. Figure 3.1 shows several sample reports, each of which will be created in this chapter. The reports were created with the Report Wizard and are based on the Students table that was presented in Chapter 2. (The table has been expanded to 24 records.) As you view each report, ask yourself how the data in the table was rearranged to produce the information in the report.

The *columnar (vertical) report* in Figure 3.1a is the simplest type of report. It lists every field for every record in a single column (one record per page) and typically runs for many pages. The records in this report are displayed in the same sequence (by social security number) as the records in the table on which the report is based.

The *tabular report* in Figure 3.1b displays fields in a row rather than in a column. Each record in the underlying table is printed in its own row. Unlike the previous report, only selected fields are displayed, so the tabular report is more concise than the columnar report of Figure 3.1a. Note, too, that the records in the report are listed in alphabetical order rather than by social security number.

The report in Figure 3.1c is also a tabular report, but it is very different from the report in Figure 3.1b. The report in Figure 3.1c lists only a selected set of students (those students with a GPA of 3.50 or higher), as opposed to the earlier reports, which listed every student. The students are listed in descending order according to their GPA.

The report in Figure 3.1d displays the students in groups, according to their major, then computes the average GPA for each group. The report also contains summary information (not visible in Figure 3.1d) for the report as a whole, which computes the average GPA for all students.

DATA VERSUS INFORMATION

Data and information are not synonymous although the terms are often interchanged. Data is the raw material and consists of the table (or tables) that compose a database. Information is the finished product. Data is converted to information by selecting records, performing calculations on those records, and/or changing the sequence in which the records are displayed. Decisions in an organization are made on the basis of information rather than raw data.

Student Roster

SSN	111-11-1111
FirstName	Jared
LastName	Berlin
Address	900 Main Highway
City	Charleston
State	SC
PostalCode	29410-0560
PhoneNumber	(803) 223-7868
BirthDate	1/15/72
Gender	M
Credits	100
QualityPoints	250
FinancialAid	Yes
Campus	1
Major	Engineering

(a) Columnar Report

Student Master List

Last Name	First Name	Phone Number	Major
Adili	Ronnie	(612) 445-7654	Business
Berlin	Jared	(803) 223-7868	Engineering
Camejo	Oscar	(716) 433-3321	Liberal Arts
Coe	Bradley	(415) 235-6543	Undecided
Cornell	Ryan	(404) 755-4490	Undecided
DiGiacomo	Kevin	(305) 531-7652	Business
Faulkner	Eileen	(305) 489-8876	Communications
Frazier	Steven	(410) 995-8755	Undecided
Gibson	Christopher	(305) 235-4563	Business
Heltzer	Peter	(305) 753-4533	Engineering
Huerta	Carlos	(212) 344-5654	Undecided
Joseph	Cedric	(404) 667-8955	Communications
Korba	Nickolas	(415) 664-0900	Education
Ortiz	Frances	(303) 575-3211	Communications
Parulis	Christa	(410) 877-6565	Liberal Arts
Price	Lori	(310) 961-2323	Communications
Ramsay	Robert	(212) 223-9889	Business
Slater	Erica	(312) 545-6978	Communications
Solomon	Wendy	(305) 666-4532	Engineering
Watson	Ana	(305) 595-7877	Liberal Arts
Watson	Ana	(305) 561-2334	Business
Weissman	Kimberly	(904) 388-8605	Liberal Arts
Zacco	Michelle	(617) 884-3434	Undecided
Zimmerman	Kimberly	(713) 225-3434	Education

(b) Tabular Report

Dean's List

First Name	Last Name	Major	Credits	Quality Points	GPA
Peter	Heltzer	Engineering	25	100	4.00
Cedric	Joseph	Communications	45	170	3.78
Erica	Slater	Communications	105	390	3.71
Kevin	DiGiacomo	Business	105	375	3.57
Wendy	Solomon	Engineering	50	175	3.50

(c) Dean's List

GPA by Major

Major	Last Name	First Name	GPA
Business			
	Adili	Ronnie	2.58
	Cornell	Ryan	1.78
	DiGiacomo	Kevin	3.57
	Gibson	Christopher	1.71
	Ramsay	Robert	3.24
	Watson	Ana	2.50
	Average GPA for Major		**2.56**
Communications			
	Faulkner	Eileen	2.67
	Joseph	Cedric	3.78
	Ortiz	Frances	2.14
	Price	Lori	1.75
	Slater	Erica	3.71
	Average GPA for Major		**2.81**
Education			
	Korba	Nickolas	1.66
	Zimmerman	Kimberly	3.29
	Average GPA for Major		**2.48**
Engineering			
	Berlin	Jared	2.50
	Heltzer	Peter	4.00
	Solomon	Wendy	3.50
	Average GPA for Major		**3.33**
Liberal Arts			
	Camejo	Oscar	2.80
	Parulis	Christa	1.80
	Watson	Ana	2.79
	Weissman	Kimberly	2.63
	Average GPA for Major		**2.51**

(d) Summary Report

FIGURE 3.1   Report Types

Anatomy of a Report

All reports are based on an underlying table or query within the database. (Queries are discussed later in the chapter, beginning on page 102.) A report, however, displays the data or information in a more attractive fashion because it contains various headings and/or other decorative items that are not present in either a table or a query.

The easiest way to learn about reports is to compare a printed report with its underlying design. Consider, for example, Figure 3.2a, which displays the tabular report, and Figure 3.2b, which shows the underlying design. The latter shows how a report is divided into sections, which appear at designated places when the report is printed. There are seven types of sections, but a report need not contain all seven.

The *report header* appears once, at the beginning of a report. It typically contains information describing the report, such as its title and the date the report was printed. (The report header appears above the page header on the first page of the report.) The *report footer* appears once at the end of the report, above the page footer on the last page of the report, and displays summary information for the report as a whole.

The *page header* appears at the top of every page in a report and can be used to display page numbers, column headings, and other descriptive information. The *page footer* appears at the bottom of every page and may contain page numbers (when they are not in the page header) or other descriptive information.

A *group header* appears at the beginning of a group of records to identify the group. A *group footer* appears after the last record in a group and contains summary information about the group. Group headers and footers are used only when the records in a report are sorted (grouped) according to a common value in a specific field. These sections do not appear in the report of Figure 3.2, but were shown earlier in the report of Figure 3.1d.

The *detail section* appears in the main body of a report and is printed once for every record in the underlying table (or query). It displays one or more fields for each record in columnar or tabular fashion, according to the design of the report.

The Report Wizard

The *Report Wizard* is the easiest way to create a report, just as the Form Wizard is the easiest way to create a form. The Report Wizard asks you questions about the report you want, then builds the report for you. You can accept the report as is, or you can customize it to better suit your needs.

Figure 3.3a displays the New Report dialog box, from which you can select the Report Wizard. The Report Wizard, in turn, requires you to specify the table or query on which the report will be based. The report in this example will be based on an expanded version of the Students table that was created in Chapter 2.

After you specify the underlying table, you select one or more fields from that table, as shown in Figure 3.3b. The Report Wizard then asks you to select a layout (e.g., Tabular in Figure 3.3c.) and a style (e.g., Soft Gray in Figure 3.3d). This is all the information the Report Wizard requires, and it proceeds to create the report for you. The controls on the report correspond to the fields you selected and are displayed in accordance with the specified layout.

Apply What You Know

The Report Wizard provides an excellent starting point, but typically does not create the report exactly as you would like it to be. Accordingly, you can modify a

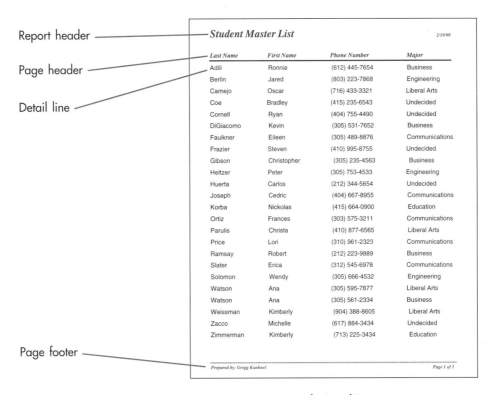

(a) The Printed Report

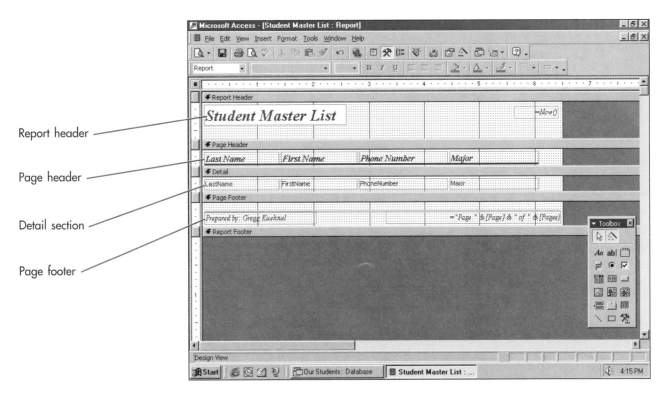

(b) Design View

FIGURE 3.2   Anatomy of a Report

Click to select table/query on which report will be based

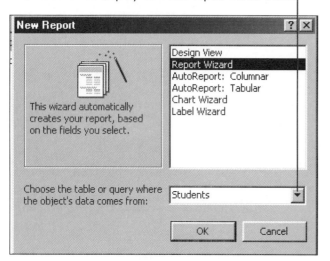

(a) Select the Underlying Table

Underlying table   Available fields   Selected fields

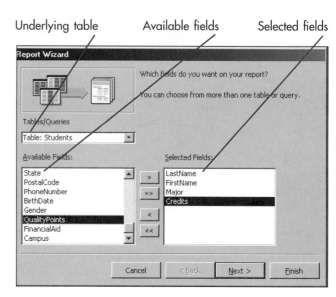

(b) Select the Fields

Selected layout

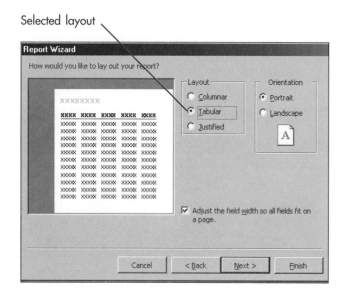

(c) Choose the Layout

Selected style

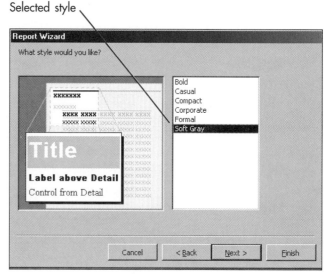

(d) Choose the Style

FIGURE 3.3   The Report Wizard

report created by the Report Wizard, just as you can modify a form created by the Form Wizard. The techniques are the same, and you should look for similarities between forms and reports so that you can apply what you already know. Knowledge of one is helpful in understanding the other.

Controls appear in a report just as they do in a form, and the same definitions apply. A **_bound control_** has as its data source a field in the underlying table. An **_unbound control_** has no data source and is used to display titles, labels, lines, rectangles, and graphics. A **_calculated control_** has as its data source an expression rather than a field. A student's Grade Point Average is an example of a calculated control since it is computed by dividing the number of quality points by the number of credits. The means for selecting, sizing, moving, aligning, and deleting controls are the same, regardless of whether you are working on a form or a report. Thus:

- To select a control, click anywhere on the control. To select multiple controls, press and hold the Shift key as you click each successive control.
- To size a control, click the control to select it, then drag the sizing handles. Drag the handles on the top or bottom to size the box vertically. Drag the handles on the left or right side to size the box horizontally. Drag the handles in the corner to size both horizontally and vertically.
- To move a control, point to any border, but not to a sizing handle (the mouse pointer changes to a hand), then click the mouse and drag the control to its new position.
- To change the properties of a control, point to the control, click the right mouse button to display a shortcut menu, then click Properties to display the property sheet. Click the text box for the desired property, make the necessary change, then close the property sheet.

INHERITANCE

A bound control inherits the same property settings as the associated field in the underlying table. Changing the property setting for a field after the report has been created does *not*, however, change the property of the corresponding control in the report. In similar fashion, changing the property setting of a control in a report does *not* change the property setting of the field in the underlying table.

HANDS-ON EXERCISE 1

The Report Wizard

Objective: To use the Report Wizard to create a new report; to modify an existing report by adding, deleting, and/or modifying its controls. Use Figure 3.4 as a guide in the exercise.

STEP 1: Open the Our Students Database

➤ Start Access. You should see the Microsoft Access dialog box with the option button to **Open an existing file** already selected.

➤ Double click the **More Files** selection to display the Open dialog box. Click the **drop-down arrow** on the Look In list box, click the drive containing the **Exploring Access folder,** then open that folder.

THE OUR STUDENTS DATABASE

The Our Students database has the identical design as the database you created in Chapter 2. We have, however, expanded the Students table so that it contains 24 records. The larger table enables you to create more meaningful reports and to obtain the same results as we do in the hands-on exercise.

➤ Click the **down scroll arrow,** if necessary, and select the **Our Students** database. Click the **Open command button** to open the database.
➤ Click the **Reports button** in the Database window, then click the **New command button** to display the New Report dialog box in Figure 3.4a. Select the **Report Wizard** as the means of creating the report.
➤ Click the **drop-down arrow** to display the tables and queries in the database in order to select the one on which the report will be based. Click **Students,** then click **OK** to start the Report Wizard.

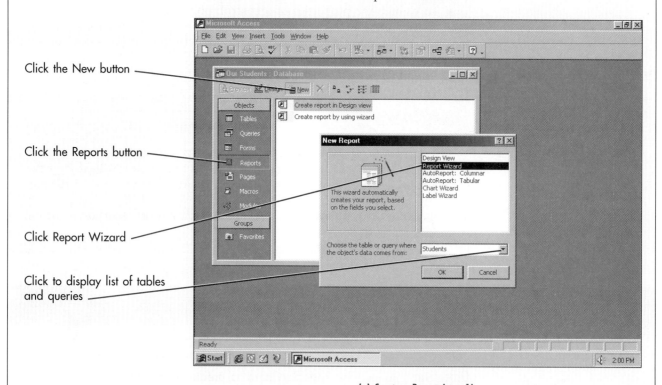

Click the New button

Click the Reports button

Click Report Wizard

Click to display list of tables and queries

(a) Create a Report (step 1)

FIGURE 3.4   Hands-on Exercise 1

STEP 2: The Report Wizard

➤ You should see the dialog box in Figure 3.4b, which displays all of the fields in the Students table. Click the **LastName field** in the Available Fields list box, then click the **> button** to enter this field in the Selected Fields list, as shown in Figure 3.4b.
➤ Enter the remaining fields (FirstName, PhoneNumber, and Major) one at a time, by selecting the field name, then clicking the **> button.** Click the **Next command button** when you have entered the four fields.

WHAT THE REPORT WIZARD DOESN'T TELL YOU

The fastest way to select a field is by double clicking; that is, double click a field in the Available Fields list box, and it is automatically moved to the Selected Fields list for inclusion in the report. The process also works in reverse; that is, you can double click a field in the Selected Fields list to remove it from the report.

Underlying table ——————

Click > to add field to selected fields list ——————

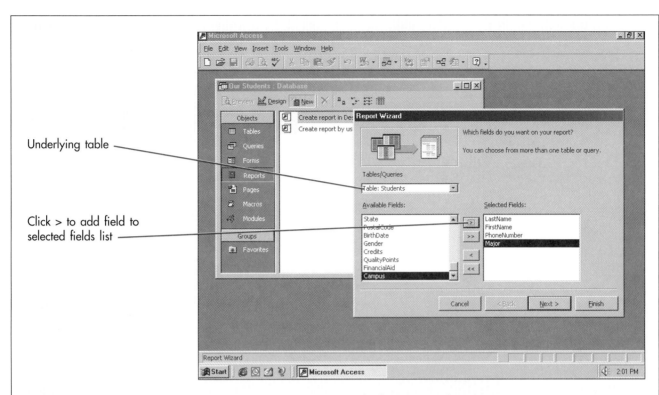

(b) The Report Wizard (step 2)

FIGURE 3.4   Hands-on Exercise 1 (continued)

STEP 3: The Report Wizard (continued)

➤ The Report Wizard displays several additional screens asking about the report you want to create. The first screen asks whether you want to choose any grouping levels. Click **Next** without specifying a grouping level.

➤ The next screen asks whether you want to sort the records. Click the **drop-down arrow** to display the available fields, then select **LastName.** Click **Next.**

➤ The **Tabular layout** is selected, as is **Portrait orientation.** Be sure the box is checked to **Adjust field width so all fields fit on a page.** Click **Next.**

➤ Choose **Corporate** as the style. Click **Next.**

➤ Enter **Student Master List** as the title for your report. The option button to **Preview the Report** is already selected. Click the **Finish command button** to exit the Report Wizard and view the report.

AUTOMATIC SAVING

The Report Wizard automatically saves a report under the name you supply for the title of the report. To verify that a report has been saved, change to the Database window by pulling down the Window menu or by clicking the Database Window button that appears on every toolbar. Once you are in the Database window, click the Reports tab to see the list of existing reports. Note, however, that any subsequent changes must be saved explicitly by clicking the Save button in the Report Design view, or by clicking Yes in response to the warning prompt should you attempt to close the report without saving the changes.

STEP 4: Preview the Report

➤ Click the **Maximize button** so the report takes the entire window as shown in Figure 3.4c. Note the report header at the beginning of the report, the page header (column headings) at the top of the page, and the page footer at the bottom of the page.

➤ Click the **drop-down arrow** on the Zoom Control box so that you can view the report at **75%.** Click the **scroll arrows** on the vertical scroll bar to view the names of additional students.

➤ Click the **Close button** to close the Print Preview window and change to the Report Design view.

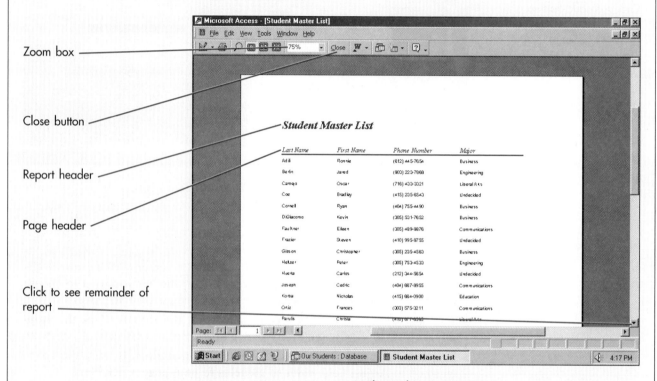

Zoom box

Close button

Report header

Page header

Click to see remainder of report

(c) The Initial Report (step 4)

FIGURE 3.4   Hands-on Exercise 1 (continued)

THE PRINT PREVIEW WINDOW

The Print Preview window enables you to preview a report in various ways. Click the One Page, Two Pages, or Multiple Pages buttons for different views of a report. Use the Zoom button to toggle between the full page and zoom (magnified) views, or use the Zoom Control box to choose a specific magnification. The Navigation buttons at the bottom of the Print Preview window enable you to preview a specific page, while the vertical scroll bar at the right side of the window lets you scroll within a page.

STEP 5: Modify an Existing Control

➤ Click and drag the border of control containing the **Now function** from the report footer to the report header as shown in Figure 3.4d.

➤ Size the control as necessary, then check that the control is still selected and click the **Align Right button** on the Formatting toolbar.

➤ Point to the control, then click the **right mouse button** to display a shortcut menu and click **Properties** to display the Properties sheet.

➤ Click the **Format tab** in the Properties sheet, click the **Format property,** then click the **drop-down arrow** to display the available formats. Click **Short Date,** then close the Properties sheet.

➤ Pull down the **File menu** and click **Save** (or click the **Save button**) to save the modified design.

Click and drag control to the Report header

Point to control and click right mouse button to display shortcut menu

Click and drag in Page Footer where label is to be placed

Label tool

Click in Font Size box

Click to display font sizes

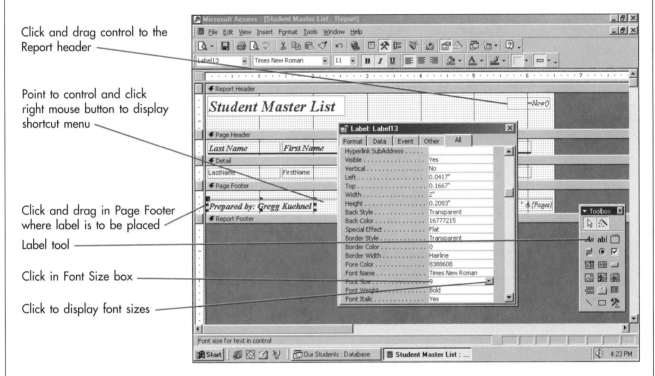

(d) Modify the Report (steps 5 & 6)

FIGURE 3.4   Hands-on Exercise 1 (continued)

ACCESS FUNCTIONS

Access contains many built-in functions, each of which returns a specific value or the result of a calculation. The Now function, for example, returns the current date and time. The Page and Pages functions return the specific page number and total number of pages, respectively. The Report Wizard automatically adds these functions at appropriate places in a report. You can also add these (or other) functions explicitly, by creating a text box, then replacing the default unbound control by an equal sign, followed by the function name (and associated arguments if any)—for example, =Now( ) to insert the current date and time.

STEP 6: Add an Unbound Control

➤ Click the **Label tool** on the Toolbox toolbar, then click and drag in the report footer where you want the label to go and release the mouse. You should see a flashing insertion point inside the label control. (If you see the word *Unbound* instead of the insertion point, it means you selected the Text box tool rather than the Label tool; delete the text box and begin again.)

➤ Type **Prepared by** followed by your name as shown in Figure 3.4d. Press **enter** to complete the entry and also select the control. Point to the control, click the **right mouse button** to display the shortcut menu, then click **Properties** to display the Properties dialog box.

➤ Click the **down arrow** on the scroll bar, then scroll until you see the Font Size property. Click in the **Font Size box,** click the **drop-down arrow,** then scroll until you can change the font size to **9.** Close the Property sheet.

MISSING TOOLBARS

The Report Design, Formatting, and Toolbox toolbars appear by default in the Report Design view, but any (or all) of these toolbars may be hidden at the discretion of the user. If any of these toolbars do not appear, point to any visible toolbar, click the right mouse button to display a shortcut menu, then click the name of the toolbar you want to display. You can also click the Toolbox button on the Report Design toolbar to display (hide) the Toolbox toolbar.

STEP 7: Change the Sort Order

➤ Pull down the **View menu.** Click **Sorting and Grouping** to display the Sorting and Grouping dialog box. The students are currently sorted by last name.

➤ Click the **drop-down arrow** in the Field Expression box. Click **Major.** (The ascending sequence is selected automatically.)

➤ Click on the next line in the Field Expression box, click the **drop-down arrow** to display the available fields, then click **LastName** to sort the students alphabetically within major as shown in Figure 3.4e.

➤ Close the Sorting and Grouping dialog box. Save the report.

STEP 8: View the Modified Report

➤ Click the **Print Preview button** to preview the finished report. If necessary, click the **Zoom button** on the Print Preview toolbar so that the display on your monitor matches Figure 3.4f. The report has changed so that:

• The date appears in the report header (as opposed to the report footer). The format of the date has changed to a numbered month, and the day of the week has been eliminated.

• The students are listed by major and, within each major, alphabetically according to last name.

• Your name appears in the Report Footer. Click the **down arrow** on the vertical scroll bar to move to the bottom of the page to see your name.

➤ Click the **Print button** to print the report and submit it to your instructor. Click the **Close button** to exit the Print Preview window.

➤ Click the **Close button** in the Report Design window. Click **Yes** if asked whether to save the changes to the Student Master List report.

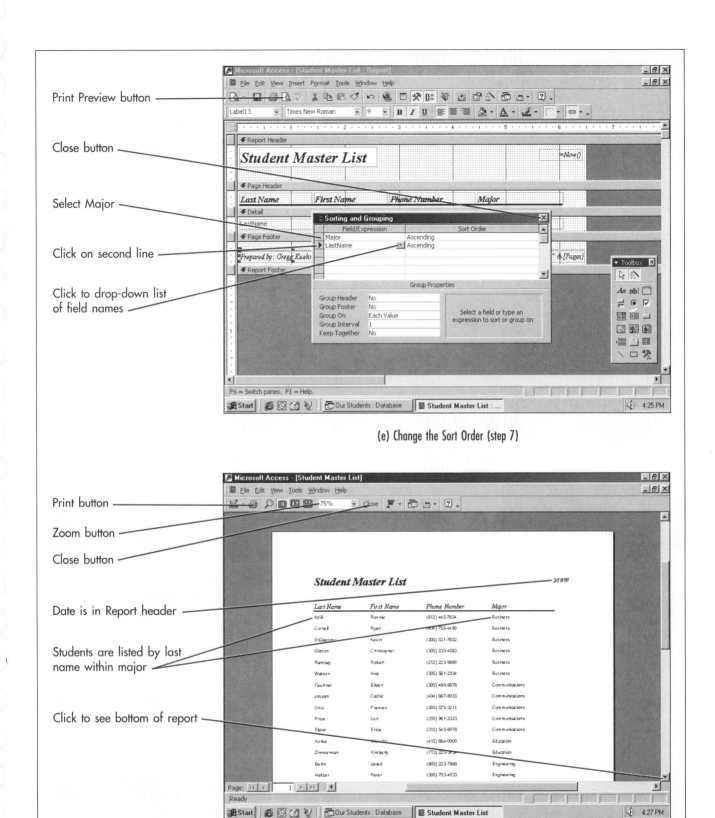

Print Preview button

Close button

Select Major

Click on second line

Click to drop-down list
of field names

(e) Change the Sort Order (step 7)

Print button

Zoom button

Close button

Date is in Report header

Students are listed by last
name within major

Click to see bottom of report

(f) The Completed Report (step 8)

FIGURE 3.4   Hands-on Exercise 1 (continued)

STEP 9: Report Properties

➤ The Database window for the Our Students database should be displayed on the screen as shown in Figure 3.4g. Click the **Restore button** to restore the window to its earlier size.

➤ The **Reports button** is already selected. Point to the **Student Master List**, click the **right mouse button** to display a shortcut menu, then click **Properties** to display the Properties dialog box as shown in Figure 3.4g.

➤ Click the **Description text box,** then enter the description shown in the figure. Click **OK** to close the Properties dialog box.

➤ Close the database. Exit Access if you do not wish to continue with the next exercise at this time.

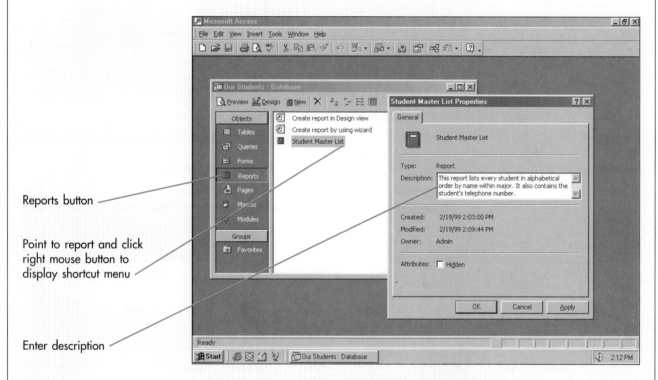

Reports button

Point to report and click right mouse button to display shortcut menu

Enter description

(g) Report Properties (step 9)

FIGURE 3.4   Hands-on Exercise 1 (continued)

DESCRIBE YOUR OBJECTS

A working database will contain many different objects of the same type, making it all too easy to forget the purpose of the individual objects. It is important, therefore, to use meaningful names for the objects themselves, and further to take advantage of the Description property to enter additional information about the object. Once a description has been created, you can right click any object in the Database window, then click the Properties command from the shortcut menu to display the Properties dialog box with the description of the object.

The report you just created displayed every student in the underlying table. What if, however, we wanted to see just the students who are majoring in Business? Or the students who are receiving financial aid? Or the students who are majoring in Business *and* receiving financial aid? The ability to ask questions such as these, and to see the answers to those questions, is provided through a query. Queries represent the real power of a database.

A *query* lets you see the data you want in the sequence that you want it. It lets you select specific records from a table (or from several tables) and show some or all of the fields for the selected records. It also lets you perform calculations to display data that is not explicitly stored in the underlying table(s), such as a student's GPA.

A query represents a question and an answer. The question is developed by using a graphical tool known as the *design grid.* The answer is displayed in a *dynaset,* which contains the records that satisfy the criteria specified in the query.

A dynaset looks and acts like a table, but it isn't a table; it is a *dyna*mic *subset* of a table that selects and sorts records as specified in the query. A dynaset is similar to a table in appearance and, like a table, it enables you to enter a new record or modify or delete an existing record. Any changes made in the dynaset are automatically reflected in the underlying table.

Figure 3.5a displays the Students table we have been using throughout the chapter. (We omit some of the fields for ease of illustration.) Figure 3.5b contains the design grid used to select students whose major is "Undecided" and further, to list those students in alphabetical order. (The design grid is explained in the next section.) Figure 3.5c displays the answer to the query in the form of a dynaset.

The table in Figure 3.5a contains 24 records. The dynaset in Figure 3.5c has only five records, corresponding to the students who are undecided about their major. The table in Figure 3.5a has 15 fields for each record (some of the fields are hidden). The dynaset in Figure 3.5c has only four fields. The records in the table are in social security number order (the primary key), whereas the records in the dynaset are in alphabetical order by last name.

The query in Figure 3.5 is an example of a *select query,* which is the most common type of query. A select query searches the underlying table (Figure 3.5a in the example) to retrieve the data that satisfies the query. The data is displayed in a dynaset (Figure 3.5c), which you can modify to update the data in the underlying table(s). The specifications for selecting records and determining which fields will be displayed for the selected records, as well as the sequence of the selected records, are established within the design grid of Figure 3.5b.

The design grid consists of columns and rows. Each field in the query has its own column and contains multiple rows. The *Field row* displays the field name. The *Sort row* enables you to sort in *ascending* or *descending sequence.* The *Show row* controls whether or not the field will be displayed in the dynaset. The *Criteria row(s)* determine the records that will be selected, such as students with an undecided major.

REPORTS, QUERIES, AND TABLES

Every report is based on either a table or a query. The design of the report may be the same with respect to the fields that are included, but the actual reports will be very different. A report based on a table contains every record in the table. A report based on a query contains only the records that satisfy the criteria in the query.

Records are in order by SSN (primary key)

Total of 24 records

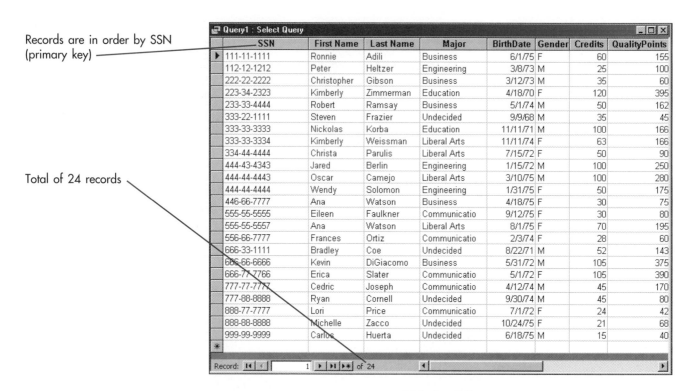

(a) Students Table

Sort order

Criteria

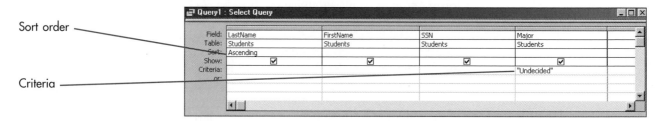

(b) Design Grid

Records are in alphabetical order by last name

Total of 5 records

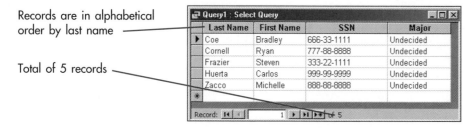

(c) Dynaset

FIGURE 3.5   Queries

Query Window

The **Query window** has three views. The **Design view** is displayed by default and is used to create (or modify) a select query. The **Datasheet view** displays the resulting dynaset. The **SQL view** enables you to use SQL (Structured Query Language) statements to modify the query and is beyond the scope of the present

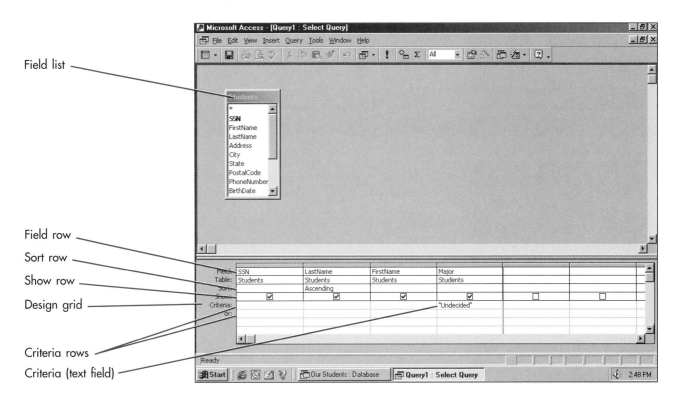

Field list

Field row
Sort row
Show row
Design grid

Criteria rows
Criteria (text field)

FIGURE 3.6   Query Design View

discussion. The View button on the Query Design toolbar lets you display all three views.

A select query is created in the Design view as shown in Figure 3.6a. The upper portion of the Design view window contains the field list for the table(s) on which the query is based (the Students table in this example). The lower portion of the window displays the design grid, which is where the specifications for the select query are entered. A field is added to the design grid by dragging it from the field list.

The data type of a field determines the way in which the criteria are specified for that field. The criterion for a text field is enclosed in quotation marks. The criteria for number, currency, and counter fields are shown as digits with or without a decimal point. (Commas and dollar signs are not allowed.) Dates are enclosed in pound signs and are entered in the mm/dd/yy format. The criterion for a Yes/No field is entered as Yes (or True) or No (or False).

CONVERSION TO STANDARD FORMAT

Access accepts values for text and date fields in the design grid in multiple formats. The value for a text field can be entered with or without quotation marks (Undecided or "Undecided"). A date can be entered with or without pound signs (1/1/97 or #1/1/97#). Access converts your entries to standard format as soon as you move to the next cell in the design grid. Thus, text entries are always shown in quotation marks, and dates are enclosed in pound signs.

Selection Criteria

To specify selection criteria in the design grid, enter a value or expression in the Criteria row of the appropriate column. Figure 3.7 contains several examples of simple criteria and provides a basic introduction to select queries.

The criterion in Figure 3.7a selects the students majoring in Business. The criteria for text fields are case-insensitive. Thus, *"Business"* is the same as *"business"* or *"BUSINESS"*.

Values entered in multiple columns of the same Criteria row implement an **AND condition** in which the selected records must meet *all* of the specified criteria. The criteria in Figure 3.7b select students who are majoring in Business *and* who are from the state of Florida. The criteria in Figure 3.7c select Communications majors who are receiving financial aid.

Values entered in different Criteria rows are connected by an **OR condition** in which the selected records may satisfy *any* of the indicated criteria. The criteria in Figure 3.7d select students who are majoring in Business *or* who are from Florida or both.

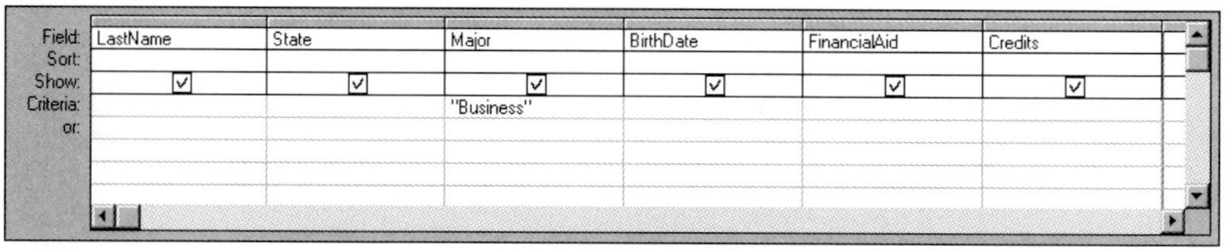

(a) Business Majors

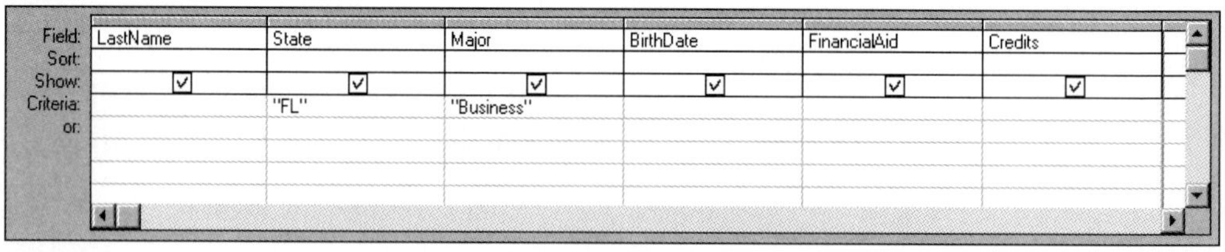

(b) Business Majors from Florida

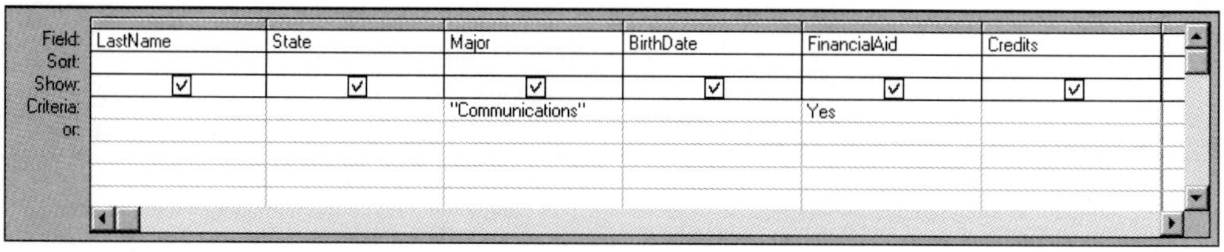

(c) Communications Majors Receiving Financial Aid

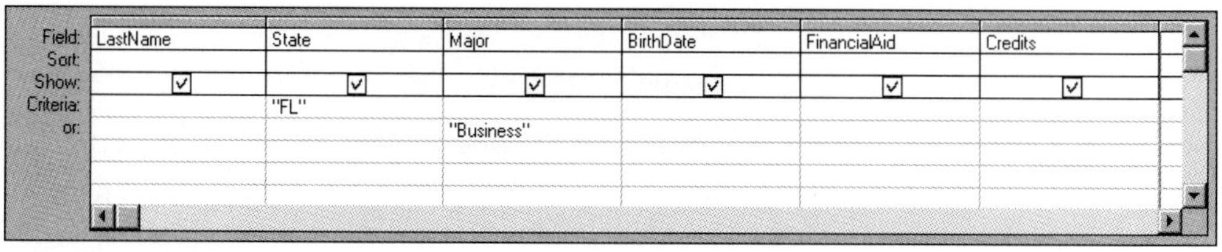

(d) Business Majors or Students from Florida

FIGURE 3.7 Criteria

Relational operators (>, <, >=, <=, =, and <>) are used with date or number fields to return records within a designated range. The criteria in Figure 3.7e select Engineering majors with fewer than 60 credits. The criteria in Figure 3.7f select Communications majors who were born on or after April 1, 1974.

	LastName	State	Major	BirthDate	FinancialAid	Credits
Field:	LastName	State	Major	BirthDate	FinancialAid	Credits
Sort:						
Show:	☑	☑	☑	☑	☑	☑
Criteria:			"Engineering"			<60
or:						

(e) Engineering Majors with Fewer than 60 Credits

	LastName	State	Major	BirthDate	FinancialAid	Credits
Field:	LastName	State	Major	BirthDate	FinancialAid	Credits
Sort:						
Show:	☑	☑	☑	☑	☑	☑
Criteria:			"Communications"	>=#4/1/74#		
or:						

(f) Communications Majors Born on or after April 1, 1974

	LastName	State	Major	BirthDate	FinancialAid	Credits
Field:	LastName	State	Major	BirthDate	FinancialAid	Credits
Sort:						
Show:	☑	☑	☑	☑	☑	☑
Criteria:			"Engineering"			<60
or:			Communications	>=#4/1/74#		

(g) Engineering Majors with Fewer than 60 Credits or Communications Majors Born on or after April 1, 1974

	LastName	State	Major	BirthDate	FinancialAid	Credits
Field:	LastName	State	Major	BirthDate	FinancialAid	Credits
Sort:						
Show:	☑	☑	☑	☑	☑	☑
Criteria:						Between 60 and 90
or:						

(h) Students with between 60 and 90 Credits

	LastName	State	Major	BirthDate	FinancialAid	Credits
Field:	LastName	State	Major	BirthDate	FinancialAid	Credits
Sort:						
Show:	☑	☑	☑	☑	☑	☑
Criteria:			Not "Liberal Arts"			
or:						

(i) Students with Majors Other Than Liberal Arts

FIGURE 3.7 Criteria (continued)

Criteria can grow more complex by combining multiple AND and OR conditions. The criteria in Figure 3.7g select Engineering majors with fewer than 60 credits *or* Communications majors who were born on or after April 1, 1974.

Other functions enable you to impose still other criteria. The **Between function** selects records that fall within a range of values. The criterion in Figure 3.7h selects students who have between 60 and 90 credits. The **NOT function** selects records that do not contain the designated value. The criterion in Figure 3.7i selects students with majors other than Liberal Arts.

WILD CARDS

Select queries recognize the question mark and asterisk wild cards that enable you to search for a pattern within a text field. A question mark stands for a single character in the same position as the question mark; thus H?ll will return Hall, Hill, and Hull. An asterisk stands for any number of characters in the same position as the asterisk; for example, S*nd will return Sand, Stand, and Strand.

HANDS-ON EXERCISE 2

Creating a Select Query

Objective: To create a select query using the design grid; to show how changing values in a dynaset changes the values in the underlying table; to create a report based on a query. Use Figure 3.8 as a guide in the exercise.

STEP 1: Open the Existing Database

➤ Start Access as you did in the previous exercise. Our Students (the database you used in the previous exercise) should appear within the list of recently opened databases.

➤ Select (click) **Our Students,** then click **OK** (or simply double click the name of the database) to open the database and display the database window.

➤ Click the **Queries button** in the Database window. Click the **New command button** to display the New Query dialog box as shown in Figure 3.8a.

➤ **Design View** is already selected as the means of creating a query. Click **OK** to begin creating the query.

THE SIMPLE QUERY WIZARD

The Simple Query Wizard is exactly what its name implies—simple. It lets you select fields from an underlying table, but it does not let you enter values or a sort sequence. We prefer, therefore, to bypass the Wizard and to create the query entirely from the Query Design window.

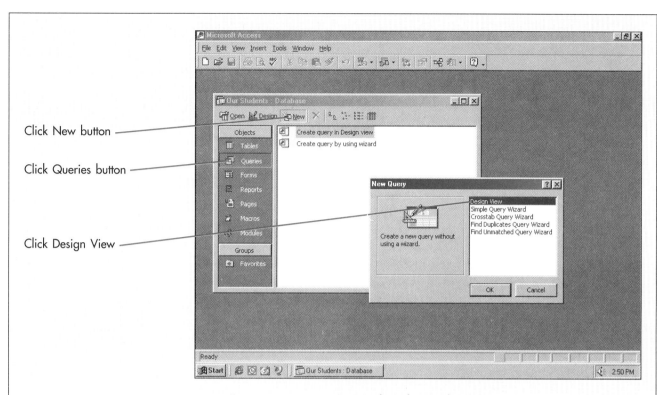

Click New button

Click Queries button

Click Design View

(a) Open the Students Database (step 1)

FIGURE 3.8   Hands-on Exercise 2

STEP 2: Add the Students Table

➤ The Show Table dialog box appears as shown in Figure 3.8b, with the **Tables tab** already selected.

➤ Select the **Students table,** then click the **Add button** to add the Students table to the query. (You can also double click the Students table.)

➤ The field list should appear within the Query Design window. Click **Close** to close the Show Table dialog box.

➤ Click the **Maximize button** so that the Query Design window takes up the entire screen.

➤ Drag the border between the upper and lower portions of the window to give yourself more room in the upper portion. Make the field list larger to display more fields at one time.

CUSTOMIZE THE QUERY WINDOW

The Query window displays the field list and design grid in its upper and lower halves, respectively. To increase (decrease) the size of either portion of the window, drag the line dividing the upper and lower sections. Drag the title bar to move a field list. You can also size a field list by dragging a border just as you would size any other window. Press the F6 key to toggle between the upper and lower halves of the Design window.

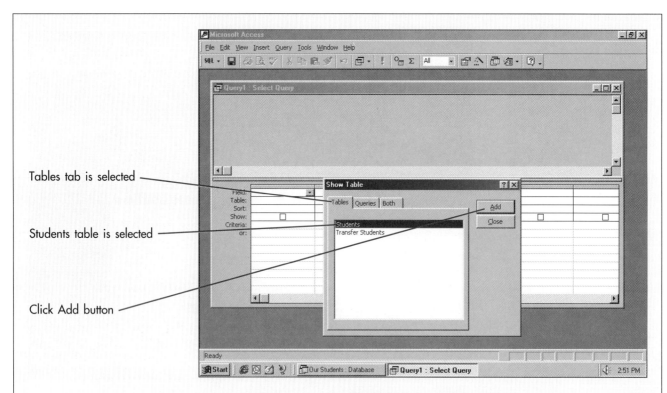

Tables tab is selected

Students table is selected

Click Add button

(b) Add the Students Table (step 2)

FIGURE 3.8   Hands-on Exercise 2 (continued)

STEP 3: Create the Query

➤ Click and drag the **LastName field** from the Students field list to the Field row in the first column of the QBE grid as shown in Figure 3.8c.

➤ Click and drag the **FirstName, PhoneNumber, Major,** and **Credits fields** (in that order) in similar fashion, dragging each field to the next available column in the Field row.

➤ A check appears in the Show row under each field name to indicate that the field will be displayed in the dynaset. (The show box functions as a toggle switch; thus, you can click the box to clear the check and hide the field in the dynaset. Click the box a second time to display the check and show the field.)

ADDING AND DELETING FIELDS

The fastest way to add a field to the design grid is to double click the field name in the field list. To add more than one field at a time, press and hold the Ctrl key as you click the fields within the field list, then drag the group to a cell in the Field row. To delete a field, click the column selector above the field name to select the column, then press the Del key.

STEP 4: Specify the Criteria

➤ Click the **Criteria row** for Major. Type **Undecided.**

➤ Click the **Sort row** under the LastName field, click the **drop-down arrow,** then select **Ascending** as the sort sequence.

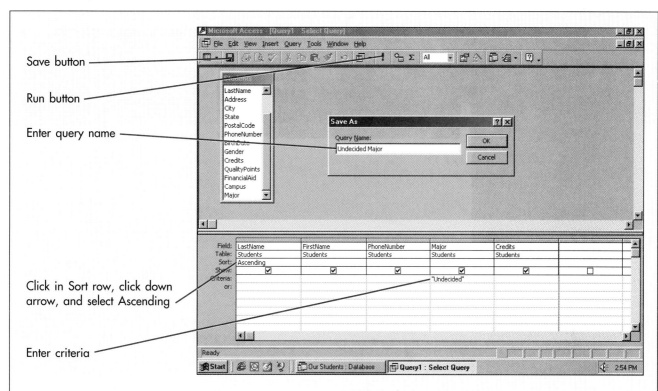

Save button

Run button

Enter query name

Click in Sort row, click down arrow, and select Ascending

Enter criteria

(c) Create the Query (steps 3 & 4)

FIGURE 3.8   Hands-on Exercise 2 (continued)

➤ Pull down the **File menu** and click **Save** (or click the **Save button**) to display the dialog box in Figure 3.8c.

➤ Type **Undecided Major** as the query name. Click **OK.**

FLEXIBLE CRITERIA

Access offers a great deal of flexibility in the way you enter the criteria for a text field. Quotation marks and/or an equal sign are optional. Thus "Undecided", Undecided, =Undecided, or ="Undecided" are all valid, and you may choose any of these formats. Access will convert your entry to standard format ("Undecided" in this example) after you have moved to the next cell.

STEP 5: Run the Query

➤ Pull down the **Query menu** and click **Run** (or click the **Run button**) to run the query and change to the Datasheet view.

➤ You should see the five records in the dynaset of Figure 3.8d. Change Ryan Cornell's major to Business by clicking in the **Major field,** clicking the **drop-down arrow,** then choosing **Business** from the drop-down list.

➤ Click the **View button** to change the query.

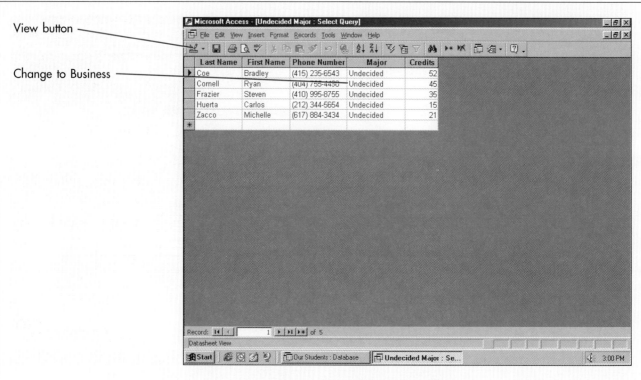

View button

Change to Business

(d) Run the Query (step 5)

FIGURE 3.8 Hands-on Exercise 2 (continued)

STEP 6: Modify the Query

➤ Click the **Show check box** in the Major field to remove the check as shown in Figure 3.8e.

➤ Click the **Criteria row** under credits. Type **>30** to select only the Undecided majors with more than 30 credits.

➤ Click the **Save button** to save the revised query. Click the **Run button** to run the revised query. This time there are only two records (Bradley Coe and Steven Frazier) in the dynaset, and the major is no longer displayed.

 • Ryan Cornell does not appear because he has changed his major.

 • Carlos Huerta and Michelle Zacco do not appear because they do not have more than 30 credits.

STEP 7: Create a Report

➤ Pull down the **Window menu** and click **1 Our Students: Database** (or click the **Database window button** on the toolbar). You will see the Database window in Figure 3.8f.

➤ Double click the icon next to **Create report by using Wizard.**

➤ Click the **drop-down arrow** on the **Tables/Queries** list box and select **Query:Undecided Major.** All of the visible fields (major has been hidden) are displayed. Click the **>>button** to select all of the fields in the query for the report. Click **Next.**

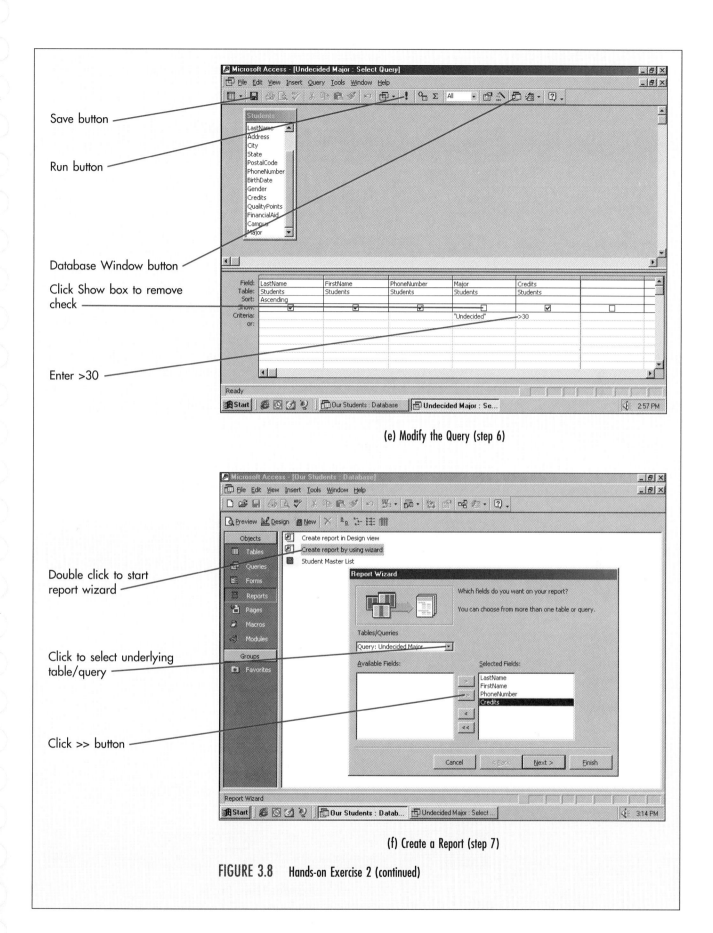

Save button

Run button

Database Window button

Click Show box to remove
check

Enter >30

(e) Modify the Query (step 6)

Double click to start
report wizard

Click to select underlying
table/query

Click >> button

(f) Create a Report (step 7)

FIGURE 3.8   Hands-on Exercise 2 (continued)

- ➤ You do not want to choose additional grouping levels. Click **Next** to move to the next screen.
- ➤ There is no need to specify a sort sequence. Click **Next.**
- ➤ The **Tabular layout** is selected, as is **Portrait orientation.** Be sure the box is checked to **Adjust field width so all fields fit on a page.** Click **Next.**
- ➤ Choose **Soft Gray** as the style. Click **Next.**
- ➤ If necessary, enter **Undecided Major** as the title for your report. The option button to **Preview the Report** is already selected. Click the **Finish command button** to exit the Report Wizard and view the report.

THE BACK BUTTON

The Back button is present on every screen within the Report Wizard and enables you to recover from mistakes or simply to change your mind about how you want the report to look. Click the Back button at any time to return to the previous screen, then click it again if you want to return to the screen before that, and continue, if necessary, all the way back to the beginning.

STEP 8: View the Report
- ➤ If necessary, click the **Maximize button** to see the completed report as shown in Figure 3.8g. Click the **down arrow** on the **Zoom box** to see the full page.

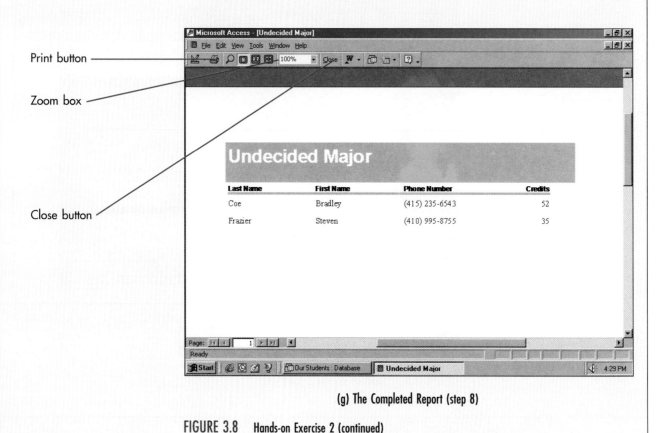

(g) The Completed Report (step 8)

FIGURE 3.8   Hands-on Exercise 2 (continued)

➤ Click the **Print button** to print the report and submit it to your instructor. Click the **Close button** to exit the Print Preview window.

➤ Switch to the Query window, then close the Query window.

➤ If necessary, click the **Database Window button** on the toolbar to return to the Database window. Click the **Maximize button**:

- Click the **Queries tab** to display the names of the queries in the Our Students database. You should see the *Undecided Major* query created in this exercise.

- Click the **Reports tab.** You should see two reports: *Student Master List* (created in the previous exercise) and *Undecided Major* (created in this exercise).

- Click the **Forms tab.** You should see the *Students* form corresponding to the form you created in Chapter 2.

- Click the **Tables tab.** You should see the *Students* table that is the basis of the report and query you just created. The *Transfer Students* table will be used later in the chapter.

➤ Close the **Our Students database** and exit Access if you do not wish to continue with the next exercise. Click **Yes** if asked to save changes to any of the objects in the database.

THE BORDER PROPERTY

The Border property enables you to display a border around any type of control. Point to the control (in the Design view), click the right mouse button to display a shortcut menu, then click Properties to display the Properties dialog box. Select the Format tab, click the Border Style property, then choose the type of border you want (e.g., solid to display a border or transparent to suppress a border). Use the Border Color and Border Width properties to change the appearance of the border.

GROUPING RECORDS

The records in a report are often grouped according to the value of a specific field. The report in Figure 3.9a, for example, groups students according to their major, sorts them alphabetically according to last name within each major, then calculates the average GPA for all students in each major. A group header appears before each group of students to identify the group and display the major. A group footer appears at the end of each group and displays the average GPA for students in that major

Figure 3.9b displays the Design view of the report in Figure 3.9a, which determines the appearance of the printed report. Look carefully at the design to relate each section to the corresponding portion of the printed report:

- The report header contains the title of the report and appears once, at the beginning of the printed report.

- The page header contains the column headings that appear at the top of each page. The column headings are labels (or unbound controls) and are formatted in bold.

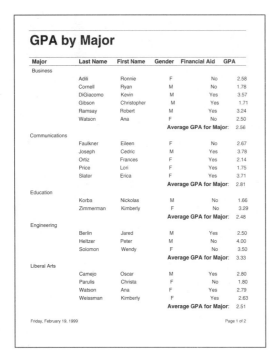

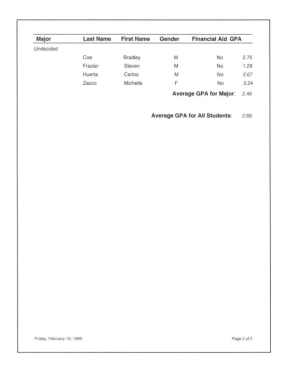

(a) The Printed Columnar Report

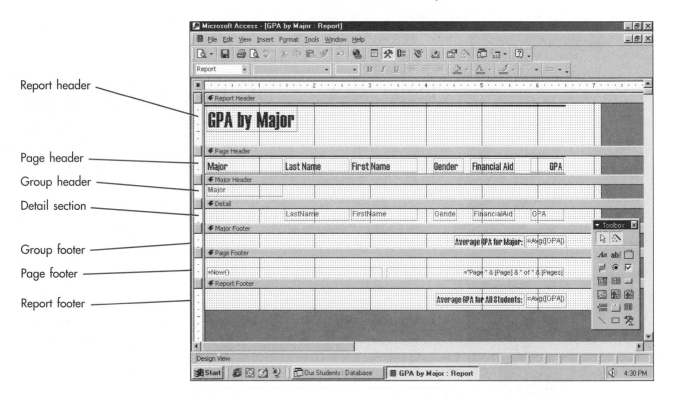

Report header

Page header

Group header

Detail section

Group footer

Page footer

Report footer

(b) Design View

FIGURE 3.9   Summary Reports

■ The group header consists of a single bound control that displays the value of the major field prior to each group of detail records.

■ The detail section consists of bound controls that appear directly under the corresponding heading in the page header. The detail section is printed once for each record in each group.

- The group footer appears after each group of detail records. It consists of an unbound control (Average GPA for Major:) followed by a calculated control that computes the average GPA for each group of students.
- The page footer appears at the bottom of each page and contains the date, page number, and total number of pages in the report.
- The report footer appears at the end of the report. It consists of an unbound control (Average GPA for All Students:) followed by a calculated control that computes the average GPA for all students.

Grouping records within a report enables you to perform calculations on each group, as was done in the group footer of Figure 3.9. The calculations in our example made use of the *Avg function,* but other types of calculations are possible:

- The *Sum function* computes the total for a specific field for all records in the group.
- The *Min function* determines the minimum value for all records in the group.
- The *Max function* determines the maximum value for all records in the group.
- The *Count function* counts the number of records in the group.

The following exercise has you create the report in Figure 3.9. The report is based on a query containing a calculated control, GPA, which is computed by dividing the QualityPoints field by the Credits field. The Report Wizard is used to design the basic report, but additional modifications are necessary to create the group header and group footer.

HANDS-ON EXERCISE 3

Grouping Records

Objective: To create a query containing a calculated control, then create a report based on that query; to use the Sorting and Grouping command to add a group header and group footer to a report. Use Figure 3.10 as a guide.

STEP 1: Create the Query

➤ Start Access and open the **Our Students database** from the previous exercise.

➤ Click the **Queries button** in the Database window. Double click **Create query in Design view** to display the Query Design window.

➤ The Show Table dialog box appears; the **Tables tab** is already selected, as is the **Students table.** Click the **Add button** to add the table to the query (the field list should appear within the Query window). Click **Close** to close the Show Table dialog box.

➤ Click the **Maximize button** so that the window takes up the entire screen as shown in Figure 3.10a. Drag the border between the upper and lower portions of the window to give yourself more room in the upper portion. Make the field list larger, to display more fields at one time.

➤ Scroll (if necessary) within the field list, then click and drag the **Major field** from the field list to the query. Click and drag the **LastName, FirstName, Gender, FinancialAid, QualityPoints,** and **Credits fields** (in that order) in similar fashion.

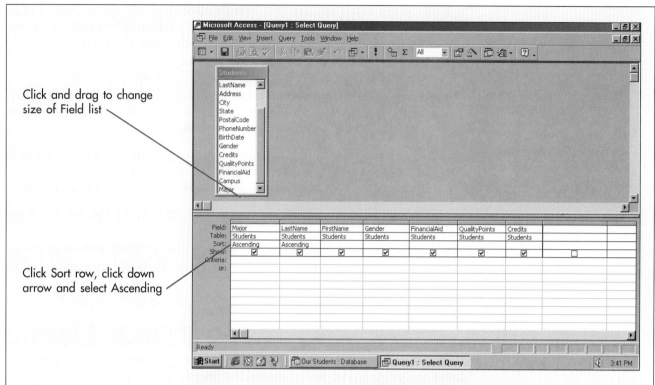

Click and drag to change size of Field list

Click Sort row, click down arrow and select Ascending

(a) Create the Query (step 1)

FIGURE 3.10   Hands-on Exercise 3

➤ Click the **Sort row** for the Major field. Click the **down arrow** to open the drop-down list box. Click **Ascending.**

➤ Click the **Sort row** for the LastName field. Click the **down arrow** to open the drop-down list box. Click **Ascending.**

SORTING ON MULTIPLE FIELDS

You can sort a query on more than one field, but you must be certain that the fields are in the proper order within the design grid. Access sorts from left to right (the leftmost field is the primary sort key), so the fields must be arranged in the desired sort sequence. To move a field within the design grid, click the column selector above the field name to select the column, then drag the column to its new position.

STEP 2: Add a Calculated Control

➤ Click in the first blank column in the Field row. Enter the expression **=[QualityPoints]/[Credits].** Do not be concerned if you cannot see the entire expression.

➤ Press **enter.** Access has substituted Expr1: for the equal sign you typed initially. Drag the **column selector boundary** so that the entire expression is visible as in Figure 3.10b. (You may have to make some of the columns narrower to see all of the fields in the design grid.)

➤ Pull down the **File menu** and click **Save** (or click the **Save button**) to display the dialog box in Figure 3.10b. Enter **GPA By Major** for the Query Name. Click **OK.**

USE DESCRIPTIVE NAMES

An Access database contains multiple objects—tables, forms, queries, and reports. It is important, therefore, that the name assigned to each object be descriptive of its function so that you can select the proper object from the Database window. The name of an object can contain up to 64 characters and can include any combination of letters, numbers, and spaces. (Names may not, however, include leading spaces, a period, an exclamation mark, or brackets ([ ]).)

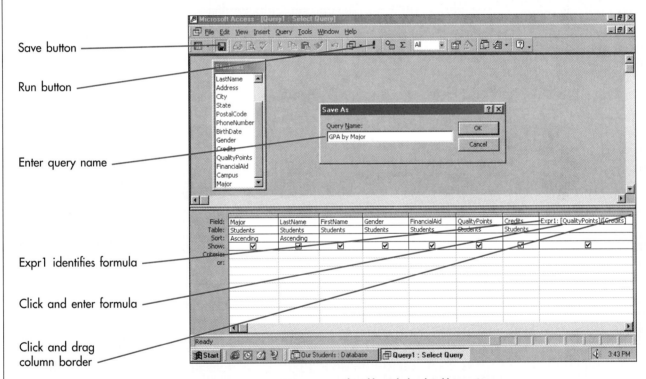

Save button

Run button

Enter query name

Expr1 identifies formula

Click and enter formula

Click and drag
column border

(b) Add a Calculated Field (step 2)

FIGURE 3.10   Hands-on Exercise 3 (continued)

STEP 3: Run the Query

➤ Pull down the **Query menu** and click **Run** (or click the **Run button** on the Query Design toolbar). You will see the dynaset in Figure 3.10c:

• Students are listed by major and alphabetically by last name within major.

• The GPA is calculated to several places and appears in the Expr1 field.

➤ Click the **View button** in order to modify the query.

View button

Field name is Exprl1

GPA has too many decimal places

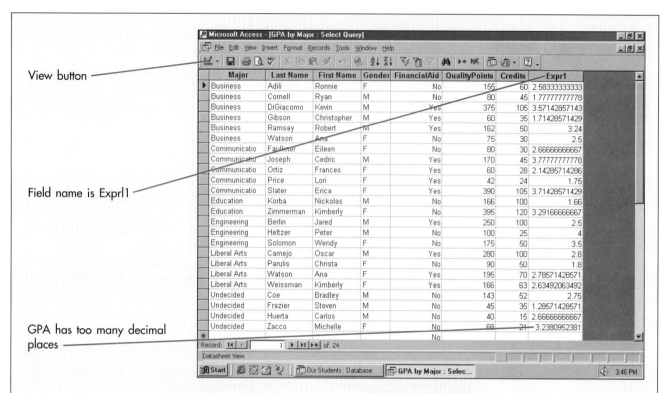

(c) Run the Query (step 3)

FIGURE 3.10   Hands-on Exercise 3 (continued)

ADJUST THE COLUMN WIDTH

Point to the right edge of the column you want to resize, then drag the mouse in the direction you want to go; drag to the right to make the column wider or to the left to make it narrower. Alternatively, you can double click the column selector line (right edge) to fit the longest entry in that column. Adjusting the column width in the Design view does not affect the column width in the Datasheet view, but you can use the same technique in both views.

STEP 4: Modify the Query

➤ Click and drag to select **Expr1** in the Field row for the calculated field. (Do not select the colon). Type **GPA** to substitute a more meaningful field name.

➤ Point to the column and click the **right mouse button** to display a shortcut menu. Click **Properties** to display the Field Properties dialog box in Figure 3.10d. Click the **General tab** if necessary:

• Click the **Description text box.** Enter **GPA** as shown in Figure 3.10d.

• Click the **Format text box.** Click the **drop-down arrow** to display the available formats. Click **Fixed.** Set Decimals to 2.

• Close the Field Properties dialog box.

➤ Click the **Save button** to save the modified query.

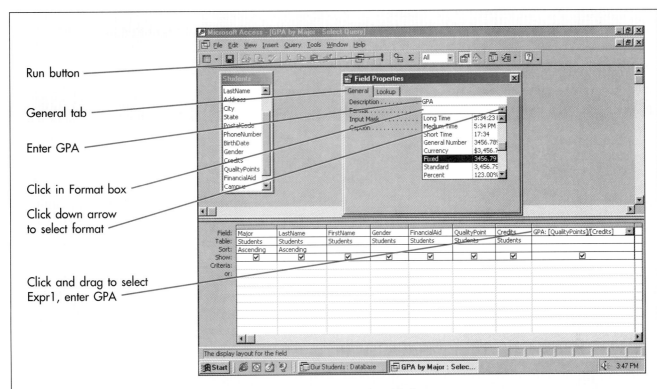

Run button

General tab

Enter GPA

Click in Format box

Click down arrow
to select format

Click and drag to select
Expr1, enter GPA

(d) Modify the Query (step 4)

FIGURE 3.10   Hands-on Exercise 3 (continued)

THE TOP VALUES PROPERTY

Can you create a query that lists only the five students with the highest or lowest GPA? It's easy, if you know about the Top Values property. First, sort the query according to the desired sequence—such as students in descending order by GPA to see the students with the highest GPA. (Remove all other sort keys within the query.) Point anywhere in the gray area in the upper portion of the Query window, click the right mouse button to display a shortcut menu, then click Properties to display the Query Properties sheet. Click the Top Values box and enter the desired number of students (e.g., 5 for five students, or 5% for the top five percent). When you run the query you will see only the top five students. (You can see the bottom five instead if you specify ascending rather than descending as the sort sequence.)

STEP 5: Rerun the Query

➤ Click the **Run button** to run the modified query. You will see a new dynaset corresponding to the modified query as shown in Figure 3.10e. Resize the column widths (as necessary) within the dynaset.

• Students are still listed by major and alphabetically within major.

• The GPA is calculated to two decimal places and appears under the GPA field.

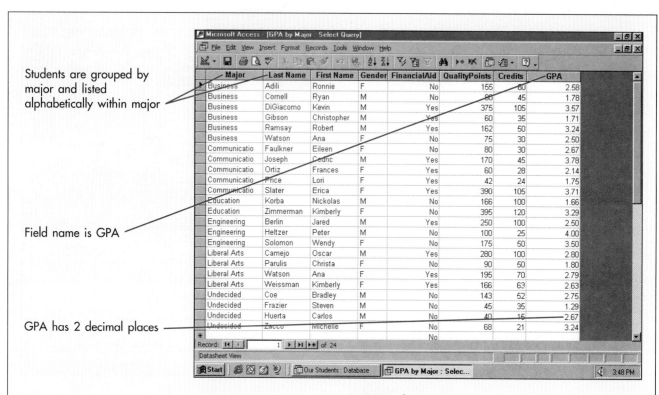

Students are grouped by major and listed alphabetically within major

Field name is GPA

GPA has 2 decimal places

(e) Rerun the Query (step 5)

FIGURE 3.10 Hands-on Exercise 3 (continued)

➤ Click the **QualityPoints field** for Christopher Gibson. Replace 60 with **70.** Press **enter.** The GPA changes automatically to 2.

➤ Pull down the **Edit menu** and click **Undo Current Field/Record** (or click the **Undo button** on the Query toolbar). The GPA returns to its previous value.

➤ Tab to the **GPA field** for Christopher Gibson. Type **2.** Access will beep and prevent you from changing the GPA because it is a calculated field as indicated on the status bar.

➤ Click the **Close button** to close the query and return to the Database window. Click **Yes** if asked whether to save the changes.

THE DYNASET

A query represents a question and an answer. The question is developed by using the design grid in the Query Design view. The answer is displayed in a dynaset that contains the records that satisfy the criteria specified in the query. A dynaset looks and acts like a table but it isn't a table; it is a dynamic subset of a table that selects and sorts records as specified in the query. A dynaset is like a table in that you can enter a new record or modify or delete an existing record. It is dynamic because the changes made to the dynaset are automatically reflected in the underlying table.

STEP 6: The Report Wizard

➤ You should see the Database window. Click the **Reports button,** then double click **Create report by using Wizard** to start the Report Wizard.

➤ Select **GPA By Major** from the Tables/Queries drop-down list. The Available fields list displays all of the fields in the GPA by Major query.

- Click the **Major field** in the Available fields list box. Click the **> button.**
- Add the **LastName, FirstName, Gender, FinancialAid,** and **GPA fields** one at a time.
- Do not include the QualityPoints or Credits fields. Click **Next.**

➤ You should see the screen asking whether you want to group the fields. Click (select) the **Major field,** then click the **> button** to display the screen in Figure 3.10f. The Major field appears above the other fields to indicate that the records will be grouped according to the value of the Major field. Click **Next.**

➤ The next screen asks you to specify the order for the detail records. Click the **drop-down arrow** on the list box for the first field. Click **LastName** to sort the records alphabetically by last name within each major. Click **Next.**

➤ The **Stepped Option button** is already selected for the report layout, as is **Portrait orientation.** Be sure the box is checked to **Adjust field width so all fields fit on a page.** Click **Next.**

➤ Choose **Compact** as the style. Click **Next.**

➤ **GPA By Major** (which corresponds to the name of the underlying query) is already entered as the name of the report. Click the Option button to **Modify the report's design.** Click **Finish** to exit the Report Wizard.

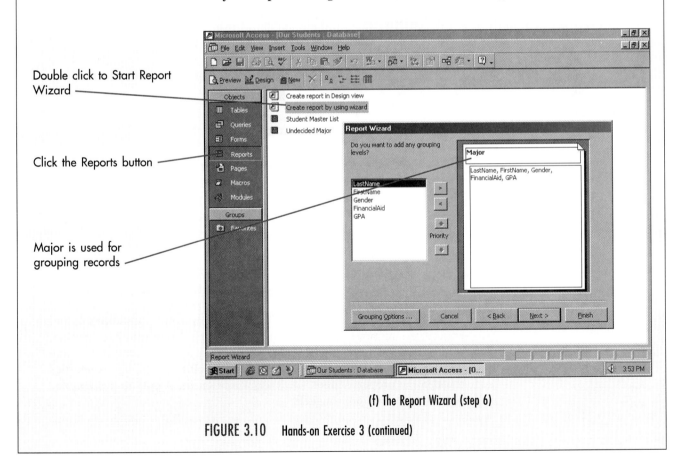

Double click to Start Report Wizard

Click the Reports button

Major is used for grouping records

(f) The Report Wizard (step 6)

FIGURE 3.10 Hands-on Exercise 3 (continued)

STEP 7: Sorting and Grouping

➤ You should see the Report Design view as shown in Figure 3.10g. (The Sorting and Grouping dialog box is not yet visible.)

➤ Maximize the Report window (if necessary) so that you have more room in which to work.

➤ Move, size, and align the column headings and bound controls as shown in Figure 3.10g. We made GPA (label and bound control) smaller. We also moved **Gender** and **FinancialAid** (label and bound control) to the right.

➤ Pull down the **View menu.** Click **Sorting and Grouping** to display the Sorting and Grouping dialog box.

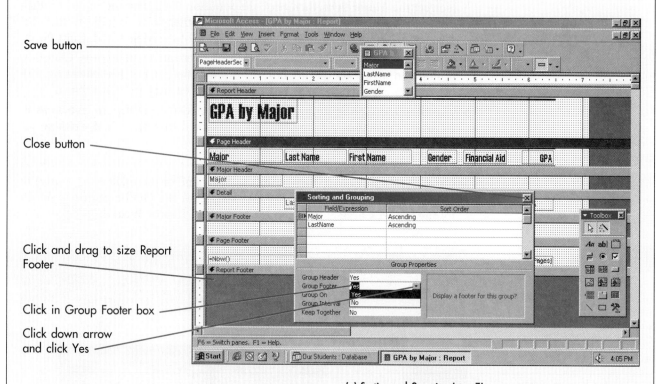

(g) Sorting and Grouping (step 7)

FIGURE 3.10   Hands-on Exercise 3 (continued)

SELECTING MULTIPLE CONTROLS

Select (click) a column heading in the page header, then press and hold the Shift key as you select the corresponding bound control in the Detail section. This selects both the column heading and the bound control and enables you to move and size the objects in conjunction with one another. Continue to work with both objects selected as you apply formatting through various buttons on the Formatting toolbar, or change properties through the property sheet. Click anywhere on the report to deselect the objects when you are finished.

➤ The **Major field** should already be selected. Click the **Group Footer** property, click the **drop-down arrow,** then click **Yes** to create a group footer for the Major field.

➤ Close the dialog box. The Major footer has been added to the report. Click the Save button to save the modified report.

STEP 8: Create the Group Footer

➤ Click the **Text Box button** on the Toolbox toolbar. The mouse pointer changes to a tiny crosshair with a text box attached.

➤ Click and drag in the group footer where you want the text box (which will contain the average GPA) to go. Release the mouse.

➤ You will see an Unbound control and an attached label containing a field number (e.g., Text 19).

➤ Click in the **text box** of the control (Unbound will disappear). Enter **=Avg(GPA)** to calculate the average of the GPA for all students in this group as shown in Figure 3.10h.

➤ Click in the attached unbound control, click and drag to select the text (Text19), then type **Average GPA for Major** as the label for this control. Size, move, and align the label as shown in the figure. (See the boxed tip on sizing or moving a control and its label.)

➤ Point to the **Average GPA control,** click the **right mouse button** to display a shortcut menu, then click **Properties** to display the Properties dialog box. If necessary, click the **All tab,** then scroll to the top of the list to view and/or modify the existing properties:

Print Preview button

Click and drag to create control, enter calculation

Enter new text for label

Enter label and calculated control in Report Footer

Text box button

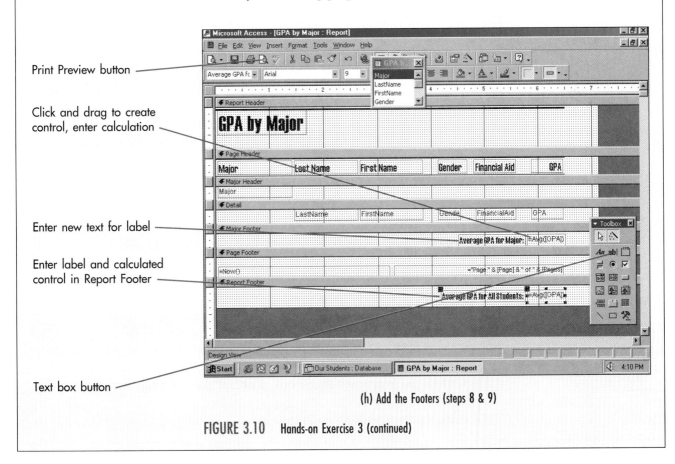

(h) Add the Footers (steps 8 & 9)

FIGURE 3.10   Hands-on Exercise 3 (continued)

- The Control Source text box contains the entry =Avg([GPA]) from the preceding step.
- Click the **Name text box.** Replace the original name (e.g., Text19) with **Average GPA for Major.**
- Click the **Format box.** Click the **drop-down arrow** and select **Fixed.**
- Click the box for the **Decimal places.** Click the **drop-down arrow** and select (click) **2.**
- Close the Properties dialog box to accept these settings and return to the report.
➤ Click the **Save button** on the toolbar.

SIZING OR MOVING A BOUND CONTROL AND ITS LABEL

A bound control is created with an attached label. Select (click) the control, and the control has sizing handles and a move handle, but the label has only a move handle. Select the label (instead of the control), and the opposite occurs: the control has only a move handle, but the label will have both sizing handles and a move handle. To move a control and its label, click and drag the border of either object. To move either the control or its label (but not both), click and drag the move handle (a tiny square in the upper left corner) of the appropriate object. (Use the Undo command if the result is not what you expect; then try again.)

STEP 9: Create the Report Footer

➤ The report footer is created in similar fashion to the group footer. Click and drag the bottom of the report footer to extend the size of the footer as shown in Figure 3.10h.

➤ Click the **Text Box button** on the Toolbox toolbar, then click and drag in the report footer where you want the text box to go. Release the mouse. You will see an Unbound control and an attached label containing a field number (e.g., Text21).

➤ Click in the **text box** of the control (Unbound will disappear). Enter **=Avg(GPA)** to calculate the average of the grade point averages for all students in the report.

➤ Click in the attached label, click and drag to select the text (Text21), then type **Average GPA for All Students** as the label for this control. Move, size, and align the label appropriately.

➤ Size the text box, then format the control:

- Point to the control, click the **right mouse button** to display a shortcut menu, then click **Properties** to display the Properties dialog box. Change the properties to **Fixed Format** with **2 decimal places.** Change the name to **Average GPA for All Students.**
- Close the Properties dialog box to accept these settings and return to the report.

➤ Click the **Save button** on the toolbar.

SECTION PROPERTIES

Each section in a report has properties that control its appearance and behavior. Point to the section header, click the right mouse button to display a shortcut menu, then click Properties to display the property sheet and set the properties. You can hide the section by changing the Visible property to No. You can also change the Special Effect property to Raised or Sunken.

STEP 10: View the Report

➤ Click the **Print Preview button** to view the completed report as shown in Figure 3.10i. The status bar shows you are on page 1 of the report.

➤ Click the **Zoom button** to see the entire page. Click the **Zoom button** a second time to return to the higher magnification, which lets you read the report.

➤ Be sure that you are satisfied with the appearance of the report and that all controls align properly with their associated labels. If necessary, return to the Design view to modify the report.

➤ Pull down the **File menu** and click **Print** (or click the **Print button**) to display the Print dialog box. The **All option button** is already selected under Print Range. Click **OK** to print the report.

➤ Pull down the **File menu** and click **Close** to close the GPA by Major report. Click **Yes** if asked to save design changes to the report.

➤ Close the **Our Students database** and exit Access.

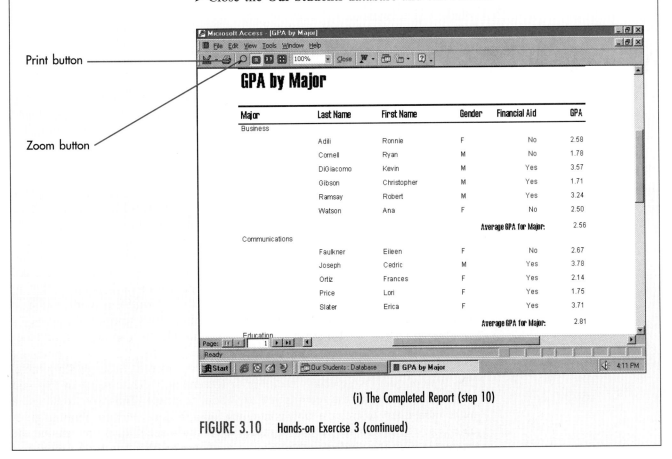

(i) The Completed Report (step 10)

FIGURE 3.10   Hands-on Exercise 3 (continued)

CROSSTAB QUERIES

We continue the earlier discussion on queries to include more powerful types of queries. A *crosstab query* consolidates data from an Access table and presents the information in a row and column format (similar to a pivot table in Excel). Figure 3.11 shows a crosstab query that displays the average GPA for all students by major and gender. A crosstab query aggregates (sums, counts, or averages) the values of one field (e.g., GPA), then groups the results according to the values of another field listed down the left side of the table (major), and a set of values listed across the top of the table (gender).

A crosstab query can be created in the Query Design view but it is easier to use the Crosstab Query Wizard, as you will see in the hands-on exercise. The Wizard allows you to choose the table (or query) on which the crosstab query is based, then prompts you for the fields to be used for the row and column values (major and gender in our example). You then select the field that will be summarized (GPA), and chose the desired calculation (average). It's easy and you get a chance to practice in the hands-on exercise that follows shortly.

Major is in rows

Gender is in columns

Query1 : Crosstab Query

Major	F	M
Business	2.54	2.58
Communications	2.57	3.78
Education	3.29	1.66
Engineering	3.50	3.25
Liberal Arts	2.41	2.80
Undecided	3.24	2.23

Record: 1 of 6

FIGURE 3.11   Crosstab Query

ACTION QUERIES

Queries are generally used to extract information from a database. A special type of query, however, known as an *action query,* enables you to update the database by changing multiple records in a single operation. There are four types of action queries: update, append, delete, and make-table.

An *update query* changes multiple records within a table. You could, for example, create an update query to raise the salary of every employee by 10 percent. You can also use criteria in the update query; for example, you can increase the salaries of only those employees with a specified performance rating.

An *append query* adds records from one table to the end of another table. It could be used in the context of the student database to add transfer students to the Students table, given that the transfer records were stored originally in a separate table. An append query can include criteria, so that it adds only selected records from the other table, such as those students with a designated GPA.

A *delete query* deletes one or more records from a table according to designated criteria. You could, for example, use a delete query to remove employees who are no longer working for a company, students who have graduated, or products that are no longer kept in inventory.

A *make-table query* creates a new table from records in an existing table. This type of query is especially useful prior to running a delete query in that you can back up (archive) the records you are about to delete. Thus, you could use a make-table query to create a table containing those students who are about to graduate (e.g., those with 120 credits or more), then run a delete query to remove the graduates from the Students table. You're ready for another hands-on exercise.

Crosstab and Action Queries

Objective: To use action queries to modify a database; to create a crosstab query to display summarized values from a table. Use Figure 3.12 as a guide.

STEP 1: Create the Make-Table Query

➤ Start Access and open the **Our Students database.** Click the **Queries button** in the Database window, then double click **Create query in Design view.**

➤ The Show Table dialog box appears automatically with the Tables tab already selected. If necessary, select the **Students table,** then click the **Add button** to add the table to the query as shown in Figure 3.12a. Close the Show Table dialog box. Maximize the query window.

➤ Click the **SSN** (the first field) in the Students table. Press and hold the **Shift key,** then scroll (if necessary) until you can click **Major** (the last field) in the table. Click and drag the selected fields (i.e., every field in the table) from the field list to the design grid in Figure 3.12a.

➤ Scroll in the design grid until you can see the Credits field. Click in the Criteria row for the Credits field and enter **>=120.**

➤ Click the **drop-down arrow** next to the **Query Type button** on the toolbar and select (click) the **make-table query** as shown in Figure 3.12a. Enter **Graduating Seniors** as the name of the table you will create.

➤ Verify that the option button for Current Database is selected then click **OK.**

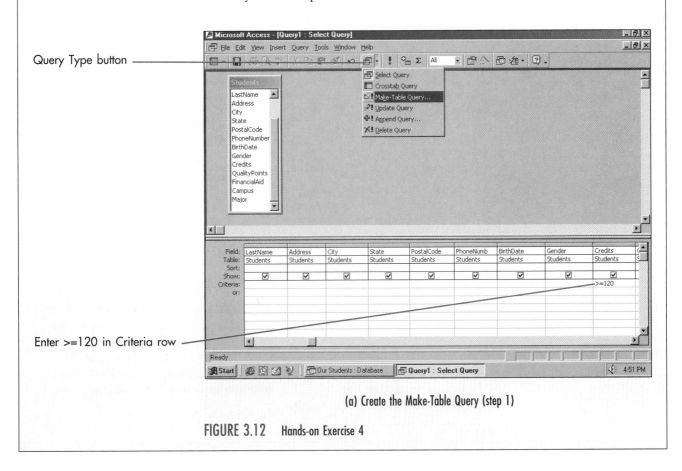

(a) Create the Make-Table Query (step 1)

FIGURE 3.12   Hands-on Exercise 4

STEP 2: Run the Make-Table Query

➤ Click the **Run button** to run the make-table query. Click **Yes** in response to the message in Figure 3.12b indicating that you are about to paste one record (for the graduating seniors) into a new table.

➤ Do not be concerned if you do not see the Graduating Seniors table at this time; i.e., unlike a select query, you remain in the Design view after executing the make-table query. Close the make-table query. Save the query as **Archive Graduating Seniors.**

➤ Click the **Tables button** in the Database window, then open the **Graduating Seniors** table you just created. The table should contain one record (for Kim Zimmerman) with 120 or more credits. Close the table.

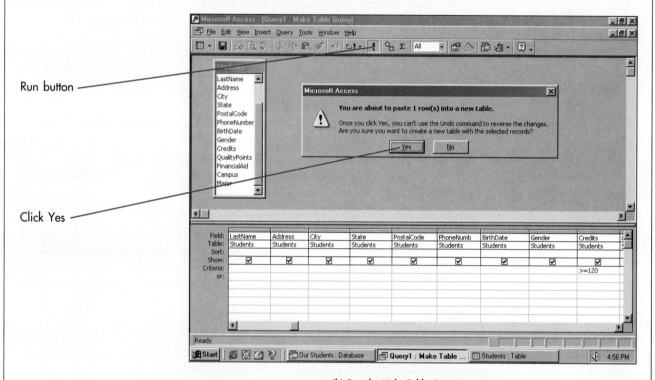

(b) Run the Make-Table Query (step 2)

FIGURE 3.12   Hands-on Exercise 4 (continued)

LOOK BEFORE YOU LEAP

The result of an action query is irreversible; that is, once you click Yes in the dialog box displayed by the query, you cannot undo the action. You can, however, preview the result before creating the query by clicking the View button at the left of the Query design toolbar. Click the button and you see the results of the query displayed in a dynaset, then click the View button a second time to return to the Design view. Click the Run Query button to execute the query, but now you can click Yes with confidence since you have seen the result.

STEP 3: Create the Delete Table Query

➤ Click the **Queries button** in the Database window, then click the **Archive Graduating Seniors** query to select the query. Pull down the **Edit menu.** Click **Copy** to copy the query to the clipboard.

➤ Pull down the **Edit menu** a second time, then click the **Paste command** to display the Paste As dialog box in Figure 3.12c. Type **Purge Graduating Seniors** as the name of the query, then click **OK.**

➤ The Database window contains the original query (Archive Graduating Seniors) as well as the copied version (Purge Graduating Seniors) you just created.

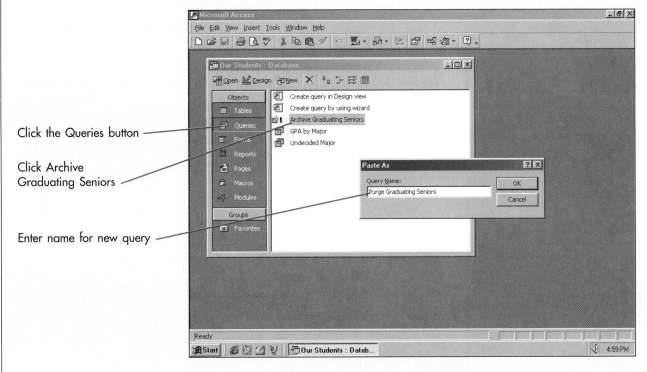

Click the Queries button

Click Archive
Graduating Seniors

Enter name for new query

(c) Create the Delete Table Query (step 3)

FIGURE 3.12   Hands-on Exercise 4 (continued)

COPY, RENAME, OR DELETE AN ACCESS OBJECT

Use the Copy and Paste commands in the Database window to copy any object in an Access database. To copy an object, select the object, pull down the Edit menu and click Copy (or use the Ctrl+C keyboard shortcut). Pull down the Edit menu a second time and select the Paste command (or use the Ctrl+V shortcut), then enter a name for the copied object. To delete or rename an object, point to the object then click the right mouse button to display a shortcut menu and select the desired operation.

STEP 4: Complete and Run the Delete Table Query

➤ Open the newly created query in the Design view. Maximize the window. Click the **drop-down arrow** next to the **Query Type button** on the toolbar and select (click) the **Delete Query.**

➤ Click and drag the box on the horizontal scroll bar until you can see the Credits field as shown in Figure 3.12d. The criteria, >= 120, is already entered because the Delete query was copied originally from Make Table query and the criteria are identical.

➤ Click the **Run button** to execute the query. Click **Yes** when warned that you are about to delete one record from the specified table. Once again, you remain in the design view after the query has been executed. Close the query window. Click **Yes** if asked to save the changes.

➤ Open the **Students table.** The record for Kim Zimmerman is no longer there. Close the Students table.

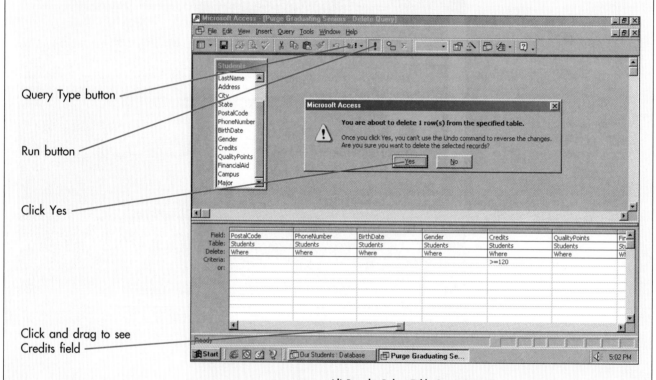

Query Type button

Run button

Click Yes

Click and drag to see Credits field

(d) Run the Delete Table Query (step 4)

FIGURE 3.12   Hands-on Exercise 4 (continued)

PLAN FOR THE UNEXPECTED

Deleting records is cause for concern in that once the records are removed from a table, they cannot be restored. This may not be a problem, but it is comforting to have some means of recovery. Accordingly, we always execute a Make Table query, with the identical criteria as in the delete query, prior to running the latter. The records in the newly created table can be restored through an append query should it be necessary.

STEP 5: Create the Append Table Query

➤ Click the **Queries button** then double click **Create query in Design view.** The Show Tables dialog box opens and contains the following tables:

- The Students table that you have used throughout the chapter.
- The Graduating Seniors table that you just created.
- The Transfer Students table that will be appended to the Students table.

➤ Select the **Transfer Students** table then click the **Add button** to add this table to the query. Close the Show Table dialog box. Maximize the window. Click and drag the **asterisk** from the field list to the query design grid.

➤ Click the **drop-down arrow** next to the **Query Type button** on the toolbar and select (click) **Append Query** to display the Append dialog box. Click the **drop-down arrow** on the Append to Table name list box and select the **Students table** as shown in Figure 3.12e. Click **OK.**

➤ Click the **Run button.** Click **Yes** when warned that you are about to add 4 rows (from the Transfer Students table to the Students table).

➤ Save the query as **Append Transfer Students.** Close the query window.

➤ Open the **Students table.** Four records have been added (Liquer, Thomas, Rudolph, Milgrom). Close the table.

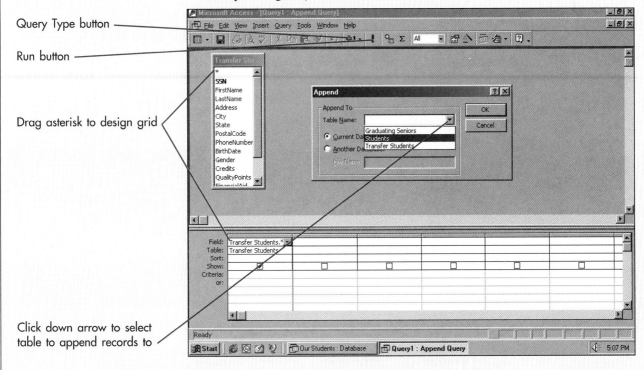

Query Type button

Run button

Drag asterisk to design grid

Click down arrow to select table to append records to

(e) Create the Append Table Query (step 5)

FIGURE 3.12   Hands-on Exercise 4 (continued)

THE ASTERISK VERSUS INDIVIDUAL FIELDS

Click and drag the asterisk in the field list to the design grid to add every field in the underlying table to the query. The advantage to this approach is that it is quicker than selecting the fields individually. The disadvantage is that you cannot sort or specify criteria for individual fields.

STEP 6: Create an Update Query

➤ Click the **Query button** in the Database window. Select (click) the **GPA by Major query,** press **Ctrl+C** to copy the query, then press **Ctrl+V** to display the Paste as dialog box. Enter **Update Financial Aid.** Click **OK.**

➤ Open the newly created query in the Design view as shown in Figure 3.12f. Click the **drop-down arrow** next to the **Query Type button** on the toolbar and select (click) **Update Query.** The query grid changes to include an Update To:row and the Sort row disappears.

➤ Click in the Criteria row for the **GPA field** and enter **>=3.** Click in the Update To row for the FinancialAid field and enter **Yes.** The combination of these entries will change the value of the Financial Aid field to "yes" for all students with a GPA of 3.00 or higher.

➤ Click the **Run button** to execute the query. Click **Yes** when warned that you are about to update nine records. Close the query window. Click **Yes** if asked whether to save the changes.

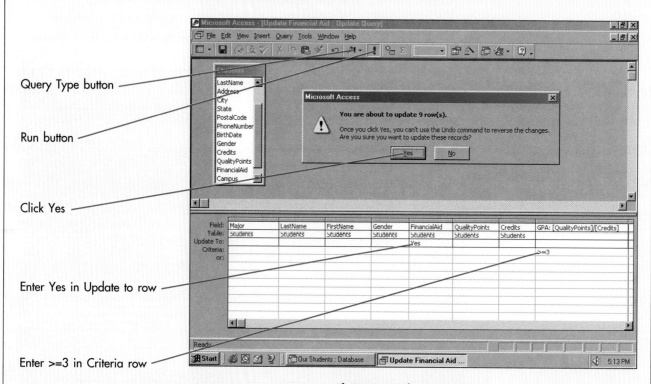

Query Type button

Run button

Click Yes

Enter Yes in Update to row

Enter >=3 in Criteria row

(f) Create an Update Query (step 6)

FIGURE 3.12 Hands-on Exercise 4 (continued)

VERIFY THE RESULTS OF THE UPDATE QUERY

You have run the Update Query, but are you sure it worked correctly? Press the F11 key to return to the Database window, click the Queries button, and rerun the GPA by Major query that was created earlier. Click in the GPA field for the first student, then click the Sort Descending button to display the students in descending order by GPA. Every student with a GPA of 3.00 or higher should be receiving financial aid.

STEP 7: Check Your Progress

➤ Click the **Tables button** in the Database window. Open (double click) the Students, Graduating Seniors, and Transfer Students tables one after another. You have to return to the Database window each time you open a table.

➤ Pull down the **Window menu** and click the **Tile Vertically command** to display the tables as shown in Figure 3.12g. The arrangement of your tables may be different from ours.

➤ Check your progress by comparing the tables to one another:

- Check the first record in the Transfer Students table, Lindsey Liquer, and note that it has been added to the Students table via the Append Transfer Students query.

- Check the record in the Graduating Senior table, Kim Zimmerman, and note that it has been removed from the Students table via the Purge Graduating Seniors query.

- The Students table reflects the current student database. The other two tables function as back up.

➤ Close the Students, Transfer Students, and Graduating Seniors tables.

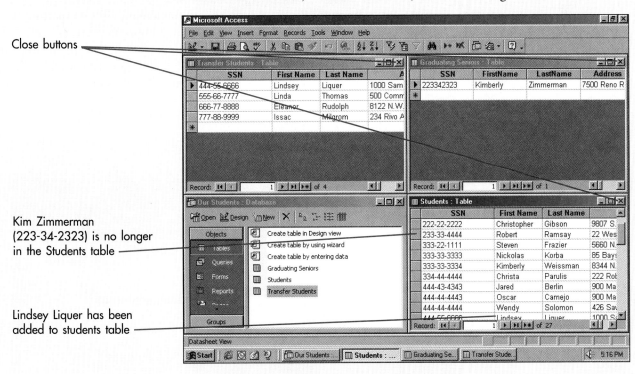

Close buttons

Kim Zimmerman (223-34-2323) is no longer in the Students table

Lindsey Liquer has been added to students table

(g) Check Results of the Action Queries (step 7)

FIGURE 3.12   Hands-on Exercise 4 (continued)

DATABASE PROPERTIES

The buttons within the Database window display the objects within a database, but show only one type of object at a time. You can, for example, see all of the reports or all of the queries, but you cannot see the reports and queries at the same time. There is another way. Pull down the File menu, click Database Properties, then click the Contents tab to display the contents (objects) in the database.

STEP 8: Create a Crosstab Query

➤ Click the **Queries button** in the Database window, click **New,** click the **Crosstab Query Wizard** in the New Query dialog box and click **OK** to start the wizard.

➤ Click the **Queries option button** and select the **GPA by Major query.** Click **Next.**

- Click **Major** in the available field list, then click **>** to place it in the selected fields list. Click **Next.**

- Click **Gender** as the field for column headings. Click **Next.**

- Click **GPA** as the field to calculate and select the **Avg function** as shown in Figure 3.12h. Clear the check box to include row sums. Click **Next.**

- The name of the query is suggested for you, as is the option button to view the query. Click **Finish.**

➤ The results of the crosstab query are shown. The query lists the average GPA for each combination of major and gender. The display is awkward, however, in that the GPA is calculated to an unnecessary number of decimal places.

➤ Click the **View button** to display the Design view for this query. Right click in the **GPA column** to display a context-sensitive menu, click **Properties** to display the Field Properties dialog box, click in the **Format row,** and select **Fixed.** Set the number of decimals to **two.**

➤ Click the **Run button** to re-execute the query. This time the GPA is displayed to two decimal places. Save the query. Close the Query window.

➤ Close the Our Students database. Exit Access.

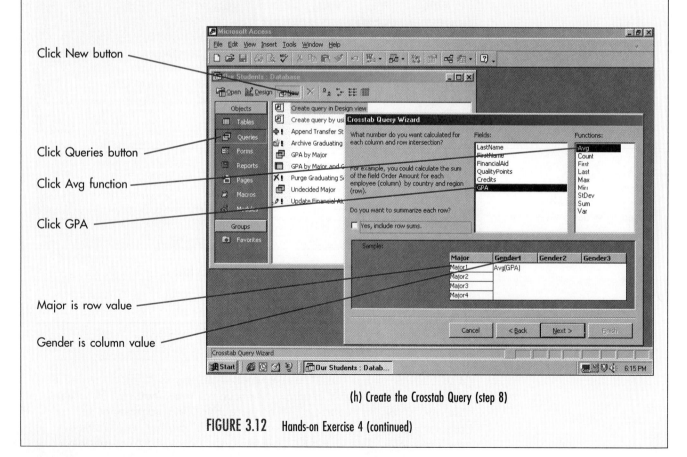

Click New button

Click Queries button

Click Avg function

Click GPA

Major is row value

Gender is column value

(h) Create the Crosstab Query (step 8)

FIGURE 3.12   Hands-on Exercise 4 (continued)

Data and information are not synonymous. Data refers to a fact or facts about a specific record. Information is data that has been rearranged into a more useful format. Data may be viewed as the raw material, whereas information is the finished product.

A report is a printed document that displays information from the database. Reports are created through the Report Wizard, then modified as necessary in the Design view. A report is divided into sections. The report header (footer) occurs at the beginning (end) of the report. The page header (footer) appears at the top (bottom) of each page. The detail section is found in the main body of the report and is printed once for each record in the report.

Each section is comprised of objects known as controls. A bound control has a data source such as a field in the underlying table. An unbound control has no data source. A calculated control contains an expression. Controls are selected, moved, and sized the same way as any other Windows object.

Every report is based on either a table or a query. A report based on a table contains every record in that table. A report based on a query contains only the records satisfying the criteria in the query.

A query enables you to select records from a table (or from several tables), display the selected records in any order, and perform calculations on fields within the query. A select query is the most common type of query and is created using the design grid. A select query displays its output in a dynaset that can be used to update the data in the underlying table(s).

The records in a report are often grouped according to the value of a specific field within the record. A group header appears before each group to identify the group. A group footer appears at the end of each group and can be used to display the summary information about the group.

An action query modifies one or more records in a single operation. There are four types of action queries: update, append, delete, and make-table. An update query changes multiple records within a table. An append query adds records from one table to the end of another table. A delete query deletes one or more records from a table according to designated criteria. A make-table query creates a new table from records in an existing table.

A crosstab query displays aggregated information as opposed to individual records. It can be created directly in the Query Design view, but is created more easily through the Crosstab Query Wizard.

KEY WORDS AND CONCEPTS

Action query	Crosstab query	Inheritance
AND condition	Database Properties	Label tool
Append query	Datasheet view	Make-table query
Ascending sequence	Delete query	Max function
Avg function	Descending sequence	Min function
Between function	Design grid	NOT function
Bound control	Design view	Now function
Calculated control	Detail section	OR condition
Columnar report	Dynaset	Page footer
Compacting	Field row	Page header
Count function	Group footer	Print Preview
Criteria row	Group header	Query

Query window	Select query	Text box tool
Relational operators	Show row	Top Values property
Report	Sort row	Unbound control
Report footer	Sorting and Grouping	Update query
Report header	Sum function	Wild card
Report Wizard	Tabular report	

MULTIPLE CHOICE

1. Which of the following is a reason for basing a report on a query rather than a table?
   (a) To limit the report to selected records
   (b) To include a calculated field in the report
   (c) Both (a) and (b)
   (d) Neither (a) nor (b)

2. An Access database may contain:
   (a) One or more tables
   (b) One or more queries
   (c) One or more reports
   (d) All of the above

3. Which of the following is true regarding the names of objects within an Access database?
   (a) A form or report may have the same name as the underlying table
   (b) A form or report may have the same name as the underlying query
   (c) Both (a) and (b)
   (d) Neither (a) nor (b)

4. The dynaset created by a query may contain:
   (a) A subset of records from the associated table but must contain all of the fields for the selected records
   (b) A subset of fields from the associated table but must contain all of the records
   (c) Both (a) and (b)
   (d) Neither (a) nor (b)

5. Which toolbar contains a button to display the properties of a selected object?
   (a) The Query Design toolbar
   (b) The Report Design toolbar
   (c) Both (a) and (b)
   (d) Neither (a) nor (b)

6. Which of the following does *not* have both a Design view and a Datasheet view?
   (a) Tables
   (b) Forms
   (c) Queries
   (d) Reports

7. Which of the following is true regarding the wild card character within Access?
   (a) A question mark stands for a single character in the same position as the question mark
   (b) An asterisk stands for any number of characters in the same position as the asterisk
   (c) Both (a) and (b)
   (d) Neither (a) nor (b)

8. Which of the following will print at the top of every page?
   (a) Report header
   (b) Group header
   (c) Both (a) and (b)
   (d) Neither (a) nor (b)

9. A query, based on the Our Students database within the chapter, contains two fields from the Student table (QualityPoints and Credits) as well as a calculated field (GPA). Which of the following is true?
   (a) Changing the value of Credits or QualityPoints in the query's dynaset automatically changes these values in the underlying table
   (b) Changing the value of GPA automatically changes its value in the underlying table
   (c) Both (a) and (b)
   (d) Neither (a) nor (b)

10. Which of the following must be present in every report?
    (a) A report header and a report footer
    (b) A page header and a page footer
    (c) Both (a) and (b)
    (d) Neither (a) nor (b)

11. Which of the following may be included in a report as well as in a form?
    (a) Bound control
    (b) Unbound control
    (c) Calculated control
    (d) All of the above

12. The navigation buttons ▶ and ◀ will:
    (a) Move to the next or previous record in a table
    (b) Move to the next or previous page in a report
    (c) Both (a) and (b)
    (d) Neither (a) nor (b)

13. Assume that you created a query based on an Employee table, and that the query contains fields for Location and Title. Assume further that there is a single criteria row and that New York and Manager have been entered under the Location and Title fields, respectively. The dynaset will contain:
    (a) All employees in New York
    (b) All managers
    (c) Only the managers in New York
    (d) All employees in New York and all managers

14. You have decided to modify the query from the previous question to include a second criteria row. The Location and Title fields are still in the query, but this time New York and Manager appear in *different* criteria rows. The dynaset will contain:

(a) All employees in New York

(b) All managers

(c) Only the managers in New York

(d) All employees in New York and all managers

15. Which of the following is true about a query that lists employees by city and alphabetically within city?

(a) The design grid should specify a descending sort on both city and employee name

(b) The City field should appear to the left of the employee name in the design grid

(c) Both (a) and (b)

(d) Neither (a) nor (b)

Answers

1. c	**6.** d	**11.** d
2. d	**7.** c	**12.** c
3. c	**8.** d	**13.** c
4. d	**9.** a	**14.** d
5. d	**10.** d	**15.** b

PRACTICE WITH MICROSOFT ACCESS 2000

1. The Our Students Database: Use the Our Students database as the basis for the following queries and reports:

a. Create a select query for students on the Dean's List (GPA >= 3.50). Include the student's name, major, quality points, credits, and GPA. List the students alphabetically.

b. Use the Report Wizard to prepare a tabular report based on the query in part a. Include your name in the report header as the academic advisor.

c. Create a select query for students on academic probation (GPA < 2.00). Include the same fields as the query in part a. List the students in alphabetical order.

d. Use the Report Wizard to prepare a tabular report similar to the report in part b.

e. Print both reports and submit them to your instructor as proof that you did this exercise.

2. The Employee Database: Use the Employee database in the Exploring Access folder to create the reports listed in parts (a) and (b). (This is the same database that was used earlier in Chapters 1 and 2.)

a. A report containing all employees in sequence by location and alphabetically within location. Show the employee's last name, first name, location, title, and salary. Include summary statistics to display the total salaries in each location as well as for the company as a whole.

b. A report containing all employees in sequence by title and alphabetically within title. Show the employee's last name, first name, location, title, and salary. Include summary statistics to show the average salary for each title as well as the average salary in the company.

c. Add your name to the report header in the report so that your instructor will know the reports came from you. Print both reports and submit them to your instructor.

3. The United States Database: Use the United States database in the Exploring Access folder to create the report shown in Figure 3.13 on page 154. (This is the same database that was used in Chapters 1 and 2.) The report lists states by geographic region, and alphabetically within region. It includes a calculated field, Population Density, which is computed by dividing a state's population by its area. Summary statistics are also required as shown in the report.

   Note that the report header contains a map of the United States that was taken from the Microsoft Clip Gallery. The instructions for inserting an object can be found on page 100 in conjunction with an earlier problem. Be sure to include your name in the report footer so that your instructor will know that the report comes from you.

4. The Bookstore Database: Use the Bookstore database in the Exploring Access folder to create the report shown in Figure 3.14 on page 155. (This is the same database that was used in the hands-on exercises in Chapter 1.)

   The report header in Figure 3.14 contains a graphic object that was taken from the Microsoft Clip Gallery. You are not required to use this specific image, but you are required to insert a graphic. The instructions for inserting an object can be found on page 100 in conjunction with an earlier problem. Be sure to include your name in the report header so that your instructor will know that the report comes from you.

5. Use the Super Bowl database in the Exploring Access folder to create the report in Figure 3.15 on page 156, which lists the participants and scores in every game played to date. It also displays the Super Bowl logo, which we downloaded from the home page of the NFL (www.nfl.com). Be sure to include your name in the report footer so that your instructor will know that the report comes from you. (See the Super Bowl case study for suggestions on additional reports or queries that you can create from this database.)

6. Database Properties: Do the four hands-on exercises in the chapter, then prove to your instructor that you have completed the exercises by capturing the screen in Figure 3.16 on page 157. Proceed as follows:

   a. Complete the exercises, then pull down the File menu and select Database Properties to display the Properties dialog box in Figure 3.16. Click the Contents tab to list all of the objects in the database.

   b. Press the Alt+PrintScreen key to copy the screen to the clipboard (an area of memory that is available to every Windows application).

   c. Click the Start button, click Programs, click Accessories, then click Paint to open the Paint accessory. If necessary, click the maximize button so that the Paint window takes the entire desktop.

   d. Pull down the Edit menu. Click Paste to copy the screen from the clipboard to the drawing. Click Yes if you are asked to enlarge the bitmap.

   e. Click the text tool (the capital A), then click and drag in the drawing area to create a dotted rectangle that will contain the message to your instructor. Type the text indicating that you did the exercises. (If necessary, pull down the View menu and check the command for the Text toolbar. This enables you to change the font and/or point size.) Click outside the text to deselect it.

United States by Region

Prepared by Gregg Kuehnel

Region	Name	Capital	Population	Area	Population Density
Middle Atlantic					
	Delaware	Dover	666,168	2,057	323.85
	Maryland	Annapolis	4,781,468	10,577	452.06
	New Jersey	Trenton	7,730,188	7,836	986.50
	New York	Albany	17,990,455	49,576	362.89
	Pennsylvania	Harrisburg	11,881,643	45,333	262.10
	Total for Region		**43,049,922**	**115,379**	
	Average for Region		**8,609,984**	**23,076**	**477.48**
Mountain					
	Arizona	Phoenix	3,665,228	113,909	32.18
	Colorado	Denver	3,294,394	104,247	31.60
	Idaho	Boise	1,006,749	83,557	12.05
	Montana	Helena	799,065	147,138	5.43
	Nevada	Carson City	1,201,833	110,540	10.87
	New Mexico	Santa Fe	1,515,069	121,666	12.45
	Utah	Salt Lake City	1,722,850	84,916	20.29
	Wyoming	Cheyenne	453,588	97,914	4.63
	Total for Region		**13,658,776**	**863,887**	
	Average for Region		**1,707,347**	**107,986**	**16.19**
New England					
	Connecticut	Hartford	3,287,116	5,009	656.24
	Maine	Augusta	1,227,928	33,215	36.97
	Massachusetts	Boston	6,016,425	8,257	728.65
	New	Concord	1,109,252	9,304	119.22
	Rhode Island	Providence	1,003,464	1,214	826.58
	Vermont	Montpelier	562,758	9,609	58.57
	Total for Region		**13,206,943**	**66,608**	
	Average for Region		**2,201,157**	**11,101**	**404.37**
North Central					
	Illinois	Springfield	11,430,602	56,400	202.67
	Indiana	Indianapolis	5,544,159	36,291	152.77
	Iowa	Des Moines	2,776,755	56,290	49.33
	Kansas	Topeka	2,477,574	82,264	30.12

FIGURE 3.13   The United States Database (Exercise 3)

University of Miami
Book Store

Prepared by Gregg Kuehnel

Publisher	ISBN	Author	Title	ListPrice
Macmillan Publishing				
	1-56686-127-6	Rosch	The Hardware Bible	$35.00
			Number of Books:	1
			Average List Price:	$35.00
McGraw Hill				
	0-07-029387-2	Hofstetter	Internet Literacy	$45.00
	0-07-041127-1	Martinez	Getting Ahead by Getting	$39.95
	0-07-054048-9	Rothstein	Ace the Technical Interview	$24.95
	0-07-070318-3	Willard	The Cybernetics Reader	$15.75
			Number of Books:	4
			Average List Price:	$31.41
Prentice Hall				
	013-011100-7	Grauer/Barber	Exploring Microsoft Office 2000	$45.00
	0-13-011108-2	Grauer/Barber	Exploring Excel 2000	$28.95
	0-13-011190-0	Grauer/Barber	Exploring Microsoft Office 2000	$45.00
	0-13-011816-8	Grauer/Barber	Exploring PowerPoint 2000	$28.95
	0-13-020476-5	Grauer/Barber	Exploring Access 2000	$28.95
	0-13-020489-7	Grauer/Barber	Exploring Word 2000	$28.95
	0-13-065541-4	Grauer/Barber	Exploring Windows 3.1	$24.95
	0-13-504077-9	Grauer/Barber	Exploring Windows 95	$28.95
	0-13-754193-7	Grauer/Barber	Exploring Windows 98	$28.95
	0-13-754201-1	Grauer/Barber	Exploring Word 97	$30.95
	0-13-754219-1	Grauer/Barber	Exploring Excel 97	$30.95
	0-13-754227-5	Grauer/Barber	Exploring Access 97	$30.95
	0-13-754235-6	Grauer/Barber	Exploring PowerPoint 97	$30.95
	0-13-790817-2	Grauer/ Villar	COBOL: From Micro to Mainframe	$52.95
			Number of Books:	14
			Average List Price:	$33.24

Friday, February 19, 1999   **Page 1 of 2**

FIGURE 3.14   The Bookstore Database (Exercise 4)

Super Bowl

Year	AFC Team	AFC Score	NFC Team	NFC Score
1999	Denver	34	Atlanta	19
1998	Denver	31	Green Bay	24
1997	New England	21	Green Bay	35
1996	Pittsburgh	17	Dallas	27
1995	San Diego	26	San Francisco	49
1994	Buffalo	13	Dallas	30
1993	Buffalo	17	Dallas	52
1992	Buffalo	24	Washington	37
1991	Buffalo	19	Giants	20
1990	Denver	10	San Francisco	55
1989	Cincinnati	16	San Francisco	20
1988	Denver	10	Washington	42
1987	Denver	20	Giants	39
1986	New England	10	Chicago	46
1985	Miami	16	San Francisco	38
1984	Los Angeles Raiders	38	Washington	9
1983	Miami	17	Washington	27
1982	Cincinnati	21	San Francisco	26
1981	Oakland	27	Philadelphia	10
1980	Pittsburgh	31	Los Angeles	19
1979	Pittsburgh	35	Dallas	31
1978	Denver	10	Dallas	27
1977	Oakland	32	Minnesota	14
1976	Pittsburgh	21	Dallas	17
1975	Pittsburgh	16	Minnesota	6
1974	Miami	24	Minnesota	7
1973	Miami	14	Washington	7
1972	Miami	3	Dallas	24
1971	Baltimore	16	Dallas	13
1970	Kansas City	23	Minnesota	7

Friday, February 19, 1999   Page 1 of 2

FIGURE 3.15 The Super Bowl Database (Exercise 5)

f. Pull down the File menu and click the Page Setup command to display the Page Setup dialog box. Click the Landscape option button. Change the margins to one inch all around. Click OK.

g. Pull down the File menu a second time. Click Print. Click OK.

h. Exit Paint. Submit the document to your instructor.

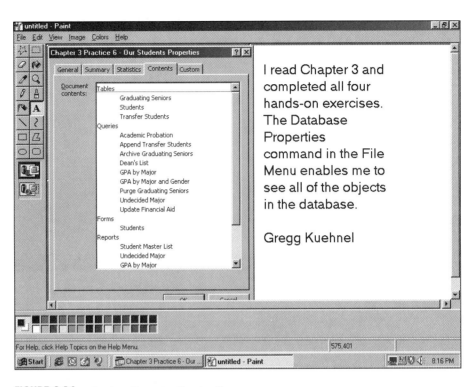

FIGURE 3.16 Database Properties (Exercise 6)

7. Action Queries: Open the Employees database that has been referenced throughout the text. The table in Figure 3.17 reflects the results of the earlier exercises in Chapters 1 and 2. If necessary, modify the data in your table so that it matches ours, then create and run the following action queries:

a. A make-table query containing the complete records for all employees with poor performance.

b. A Delete query to remove the employees with poor performance from the Employee table.

c. An Update query to award a 10% increase to all employees with a good performance rating. (Use Salary*1.1 as the entry in the Update to column.) Be sure to run this query only once.

d. Print the Employees table after all of the queries have been run.

8. The Switchboard Manager: The Switchboard Manager was not covered in the chapter, but it is worth exploring, especially if you want to develop a database that is easy to use. A switchboard is a user interface that enables a nontechnical person to access the various objects in an Access database by clicking the appropriate command button. The switchboard in Figure 3.18 enables the user to click any button to display the indicated form or report. Use the Help command to learn about the Switchboard Manager, then try your hand at creating your own switchboard. It's much easier than you might think. Note, too, you can modify the design of the Switchboard form (just as you can change the design of any form) to include your name and/or a graphic image as in Figure 3.18.

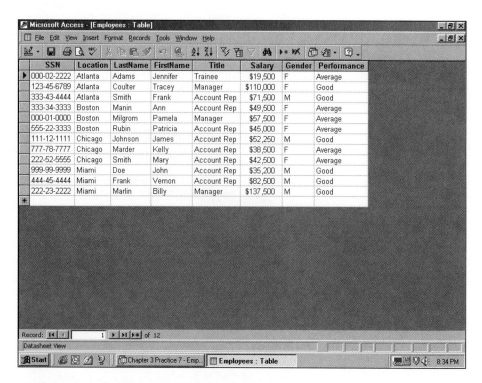

FIGURE 3.17   Action Queries (Exercise 7)

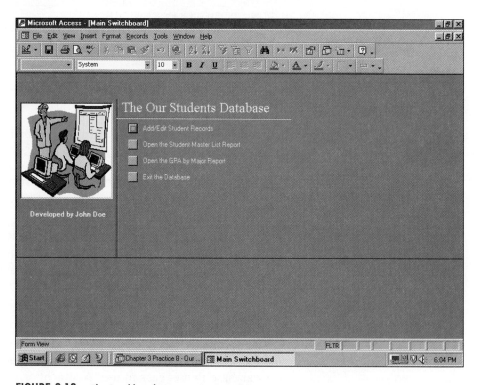

FIGURE 3.18   The Switchboard Manager (Exercise 8)

CASE STUDIES

The United States of America

What is the total population of the United States? What is its area? Can you name the 13 original states or the last five states admitted to the Union? Do you know the 10 states with the highest population or the five largest states in terms of area? Which states have the highest population density (people per square mile)?

   The answers to these and other questions can be obtained from the United States database that is available on the data disk. The key to the assignment is to use the Top Values property within a query that limits the number of records returned in the dynaset. Use the database to create several reports that you think will be of interest to the class.

The Super Bowl

How many times has the NFC won the Super Bowl? When was the last time the AFC won? What was the largest margin of victory? What was the closest game? What is the most points scored by two teams in one game? How many times have the Miami Dolphins appeared? How many times did they win? Use the data in the Super Bowl database to create a trivia sheet on the Super Bowl, then incorporate your analysis into a letter addressed to NBC Sports. Convince them you are a super fan and that you merit two tickets to next year's game. Go to the home page of the National Football League (www.nfl.com) to obtain score(s) from the most recent game(s) to update our table if necessary.

Mail Merge

A mail merge takes the tedium out of sending form letters, as it creates the same letter many times, changing the name, address, and other information as appropriate from letter to letter. The form letter is created in a word processor (e.g., Microsoft Word), but the data file may be taken from an Access table or query. Use the Our Students database as the basis for two different form letters sent to two different groups of students. The first letter is to congratulate students on the Dean's list (GPA of 3.50 or higher). The second letter is a warning to students on academic probation (GPA of less than 2.00).

Compacting versus Compressing

An Access database becomes fragmented, and thus unnecessarily large, as objects (e.g., reports and forms) are modified or deleted. It is important, therefore, to periodically compact a database to reduce its size (enabling you to back it up on a floppy disk). Choose a database with multiple objects; e.g., the Our Students database used in this chapter. Use the Windows Explorer to record the file size of the database as it presently exists. Start Access, open the database, pull down the Tools menu and select Database Utilities to compact the database, then record the size of the database after compacting. You can also compress a compacted database (using a standard Windows utility such as WinZip) to further reduce the requirement for disk storage. Summarize your findings in a short report to your instructor. Try compacting and compressing at least two different databases to better appreciate these techniques.

chapter 1

INTRODUCTION TO POWERPOINT: PRESENTATIONS MADE EASY

OBJECTIVES

After reading this chapter you will be able to:

1. Describe the common user interface; give several examples of how PowerPoint follows the same conventions as other Office applications.
2. Start PowerPoint; open, modify, and view an existing presentation.
3. Describe the different ways to print a presentation.
4. List the different views in PowerPoint; describe the unique features of each view.
5. Use the Outline view to create and edit a presentation; display and hide text within the Outline view.
6. Add a new slide to a presentation; explain how to change the layout of the objects on an existing slide.
7. Use the Microsoft Clip Gallery to add and/or change the clip art on a slide.
8. Apply a design template to a new presentation; change the template in an existing presentation.
9. Add transition effects to the slides in a presentation; apply build effects to the bullets and graphical objects in a specific slide.

OVERVIEW

This chapter introduces you to PowerPoint, one of the four major applications in the Professional version of Microsoft Office (Microsoft Word, Microsoft Excel, and Microsoft Access are the other three). PowerPoint enables you to create a professional presentation without relying on others, then it lets you deliver that presentation in a variety of ways. You can show the presentation on the computer, on the World Wide Web, or via 35-mm slides or overhead transparencies.

PowerPoint is easy to learn because it is a Windows application and follows the conventions associated with the common user interface. Thus, if you already know one Windows application, it is that much easier to learn PowerPoint because you can apply what you know. It's even easier if you use Word, Excel, or Access since there are over 100 commands that are common to Microsoft Office.

The chapter begins by showing you an existing PowerPoint presentation so that you can better appreciate what PowerPoint is all about. We discuss the various views within PowerPoint and the advantages of each. We describe how to modify an existing presentation and how to view a presentation on the computer. You are then ready to create your own presentation, a process that requires you to focus on the content and the message you want to deliver. We show you how to enter the text of the presentation, how to add and/or change the format of a slide, and how to apply a design template. We also explain how to animate the presentation to create additional interest.

As always, learning is best accomplished by doing, so we include three hands-on exercises that enable you to apply these concepts at the computer. One final point before we begin, is that while PowerPoint can help you create attractive presentations, the content and delivery are still up to you.

A POWERPOINT PRESENTATION

A PowerPoint presentation consists of a series of slides such as those in Figure 1.1. The various slides contain different elements (such as text, clip art, and WordArt), yet the presentation has a consistent look with respect to its overall design and color scheme. You might think that creating this type of presentation is difficult, but it isn't. It is remarkably easy, and that is the beauty of PowerPoint. In essence, PowerPoint allows you to concentrate on the content of a presentation without worrying about its appearance. You supply the text and supporting elements and leave the formatting to PowerPoint.

In addition to helping you create the presentation, PowerPoint provides a variety of ways to deliver it. You can show the presentation on a computer using animated transition effects as you move from one slide to the next. You can include sound and/or video in the presentation, provided your system has a sound card and speakers. You can also automate the presentation and distribute it on a disk for display at a convention booth or kiosk. If you cannot show the presentation on a computer, you can convert it to 35-mm slides or overhead transparencies.

PowerPoint also gives you the ability to print the presentation in various ways to distribute to your audience. You can print one slide per page, or you can print miniature versions of each slide and choose between two, three, four, six, or even nine slides per page. You can prepare speaker notes for yourself consisting of a picture of each slide together with notes about the slide. You can also print the text of the presentation in outline form. Giving the audience a copy of the presentation (in any format) enables them to follow it more closely, and to take it home when the session is over.

POLISH YOUR DELIVERY

The speaker is still the most important part of any presentation and a poor delivery will kill even the best presentation. Look at the audience as you speak to open communication and gain credibility. Don't read from a prepared script. Speak slowly and clearly and try to vary your delivery. Pause to emphasize key points and be sure the person in the last row can hear you.

Introduction to PowerPoint

Robert Grauer and Maryann Barber

(a) Title Slide

The Essence of PowerPoint

- You focus on content
  - Enter your thoughts in an outline or directly on the individual slides
- PowerPoint takes care of the design
  - Professionally designed templates
  - Preformatted slide layouts

(b) Bullet Slide

Add Other Objects for Interest

- Clipart, WordArt, and organization charts
- Charts from Microsoft Excel
- Photographs from the Web
- Animation and sound

(c) Clip Art

Flexibility in Output

- Computer presentations
- Overhead transparencies
- Presentation on the Web
- 35mm slides
- Audience handouts
- Speaker notes

(d) Clip Art

PowerPoint is Easy To Learn

- It follows the same conventions as every Windows application
- It uses the same menus and command structure as other Office applications
- Keyboard shortcuts also apply, such as **Ctrl+B** for boldface
- Help is only a mouse click away

(e) Animated Text

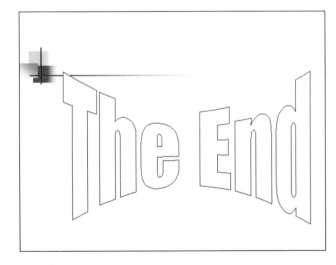

(f) Word Art

FIGURE 1.1 A PowerPoint Presentation

The desktop in Figure 1.2 should look somewhat familiar, even if you have never used PowerPoint, because PowerPoint shares the common user interface that is present in every Windows application. You should recognize, therefore, the two open windows in Figure 1.2—the application window for PowerPoint and the document window for the current presentation.

Each window has its own Minimize, Maximize (or Restore), and Close buttons. Both windows have been maximized and thus the title bars have been merged into a single title bar that appears at the top of the application window. The title bar indicates the application (Microsoft PowerPoint) as well as the name of the presentation on which you are working (Introduction to PowerPoint). The *menu bar* appears immediately below the title bar and it provides access to the pull-down menus within the application.

The Standard and Formatting toolbars are displayed below the menu bar and are similar to those in Word and Excel. Hence, you may recognize several buttons from those applications. The *Standard toolbar* contains buttons for the most basic commands in PowerPoint such as opening, saving, and printing a presentation. The *Formatting toolbar,* under the Standard toolbar, provides access to formatting operations such as boldface, italics, and underlining.

The vertical *scroll bar* is seen at the right of the document window and indicates that the presentation contains additional slides that are not visible. This is consistent with the *status bar* at the bottom of the window that indicates you are working on slide 1 of 6. The *Drawing toolbar* appears above the status bar and contains additional tools for working on the slide. The view buttons above the Drawing toolbar are used to switch between the different views of a presentation. PowerPoint views are discussed in the next section. The Windows 95/98 taskbar appears at the bottom of the screen and shows you the open applications.

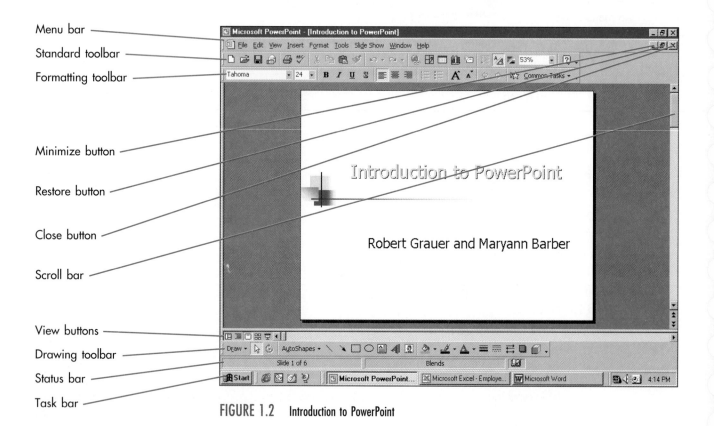

FIGURE 1.2   Introduction to PowerPoint

Six Different Views

PowerPoint offers six different views in which to create, modify, and/or show a presentation, as shown in Figure 1.3. Each view represents a different way of looking at the presentation, and each view has unique capabilities. Some views display only a single slide whereas others show multiple slides, making it easy to organize the presentation. You can switch back and forth between the views by clicking the appropriate view button at the bottom of the presentation window.

The *Slide view* in Figure 1.3a displays one slide at a time and enables all operations for that slide. You can enter, delete, or format text. You can also add other objects such as a graph, clip art, or organization chart, or even sound and video. The Drawing toolbar is displayed by default in this view.

The *Slide Sorter view* in Figure 1.3b displays multiple slides on the screen (each slide is in miniature) and lets you see the overall flow of the presentation. You can change the order of a presentation by clicking and dragging a slide from one position to another. You can delete a slide by clicking the slide and pressing the Del key. You can also set transition (animation) effects on each slide to add interest to the presentation. The Slide Sorter view has its own toolbar, which is discussed in conjunction with creating transition effects.

The *Outline view* in Figure 1.3c shows the presentation in outline form (in conjunction with a miniature slide and notes page). You can also delete a slide by clicking its icon and pressing the Del key. The Outline view is the fastest way to enter or edit text, in that you type directly into the outline. You can copy and/or move text from one slide to another. You can also rearrange the order of the slides within the presentation. The Outline view has its own toolbar that is displayed at the left of the slide.

The *Notes Page view* in Figure 1.3d lets you create speaker's notes for some or all of the slides in a presentation. These notes do not appear when you show the presentation, but can be printed for use during the presentation to help you remember the key points about each slide.

The *Normal view* in Figure 1.3e displays the Slide, Outline, and Notes Page views in a single window, with each view in its own pane. Anything that you do in one view is automatically reflected in the other views. If, for example, you add or format text in the Outline view, the changes are also made in the Slide view. Note, too, that the size of panes can be changed as necessary within the Normal view.

The *Slide Show view* in Figure 1.3f displays the slides one at a time as an electronic presentation on the computer. The show may be presented manually where you click the mouse to move from one slide to the next. The presentation can also be shown automatically, where each slide stays on the screen for a predetermined amount of time, after which the next slide appears automatically. Either way, the slide show may contain transition effects from one slide to the next, as you will see in the hands-on exercise that follows shortly.

THE MENUS CHANGE

PowerPoint 2000 displays abbreviated menus that contain only basic commands, so as to simplify the application for a new user. There is also a double arrow at the bottom of each menu that you can click to display the remaining commands. In addition, each time you execute a command it is added to the menu, and conversely, less frequently used commands are removed from the menu. You can choose, however, to display the full menus through the Customize command in the Tools menu.

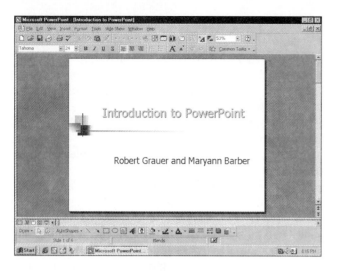

(a) Slide View

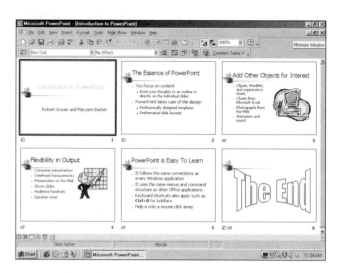

(b) Slide Sorter View

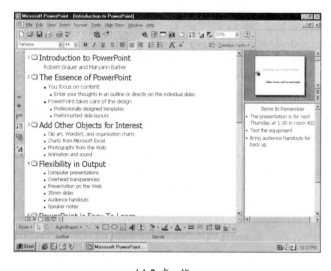

(c) Outline View

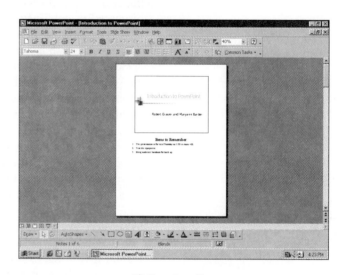

(d) Notes Page View

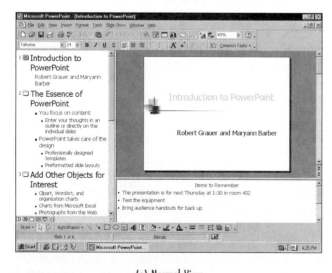

(e) Normal View

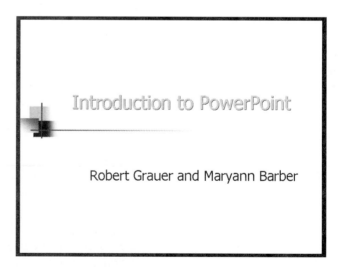

(f) Slide Show View

FIGURE 1.3 Six Different Views

The File Menu

The *File menu* is a critically important menu in virtually every Windows application. It contains the Save and Open commands to save a presentation on disk, then subsequently retrieve (open) that presentation at a later time. The File Menu also contains the *Print command* to print a presentation, the *Close command* to close the current presentation but continue working in the application, and the *Exit command* to quit the application altogether.

The *Save command* copies the presentation that you are working on (i.e., the presentation that is currently in memory) to disk. The command functions differently the first time it is executed for a new presentation, in that it displays the Save As dialog box as shown in Figure 1.4a. The dialog box requires you to specify the name of the presentation, the drive (and an optional folder) in which the presentation is to be stored, and its file type. All subsequent executions of the command save the presentation under the assigned name, replacing the previously saved version with the new version.

The *file name* (e.g., My First Presentation) can contain up to 255 characters including spaces, commas, and/or periods. (Periods are discouraged, however, since they are too easily confused with DOS extensions.) The Save In list box is used to select the drive (which is not visible in Figure 1.4a) and the folder (e.g., Exploring PowerPoint) in which the file will be saved. The *Places bar* provides shortcuts to frequently used folders without having to search through the Save In list box. Click the Desktop icon, for example, and the file is saved on the Windows desktop. The *file type* defaults to a PowerPoint 2000 presentation. You can, however, choose a different format, such as PowerPoint 95, to maintain compatibility with earlier versions of PowerPoint. You can also save any PowerPoint presentation as a Web page (or HTML document).

The *Open command* is the opposite of the Save command as it brings a copy of an existing presentation into memory, enabling you to work with that presentation. The Open command displays the Open dialog box in which you specify the file name, the drive (and optionally the folder) that contains the file, and the file type. PowerPoint will then list all files of that type on the designated drive (and folder), enabling you to open the file you want. The Save and Open commands work in conjunction with one another. The Save As dialog box in Figure 1.4a, for example, saves the file My First Presentation in the Exploring PowerPoint folder. The Open dialog box in Figure 1.4b loads that file into memory so that you can work with the file, after which you can save the revised file for use at a later time.

The toolbars in the Save As and Open dialog boxes have several buttons in common that facilitate the execution of either command. The Views button lets you display the files in one of four different views. The Details view (in Figure 1.4a) shows the file size as well as the date and time that the file was last modified. The Preview view (in Figure 1.4b) shows the first slide in a presentation, without having to open the presentation. The List view displays only the file names, and thus lets you see more files at one time. The Properties view shows information about the presentation including the date of creation and number of revisions.

SORT BY NAME, DATE, OR FILE SIZE

The files in the Save As and Open dialog boxes can be displayed in ascending or descending sequence by name, date modified, or size. Change to the Details view, then click the heading of the desired column; e.g., click the Modified column to list the files according to the date they were last changed. Click the column heading a second time to reverse the sequence; that is, to switch from ascending to descending, and vice versa.

Select drive and folder
in which to save file

Views button

Places bar

File name

File type

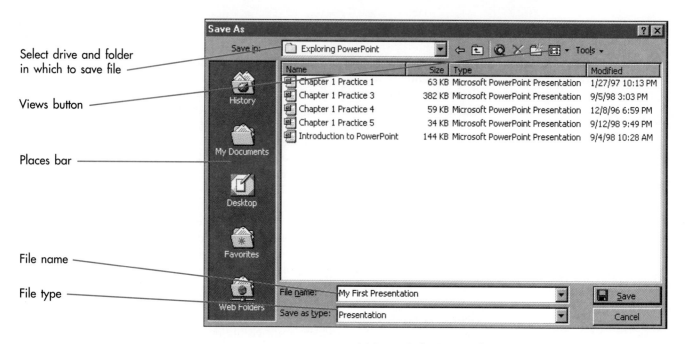

(a) Save as Dialog Box (Details View)

Select drive and folder
from which to open file

Search the Web button

Delete button

Select file to be opened

File type

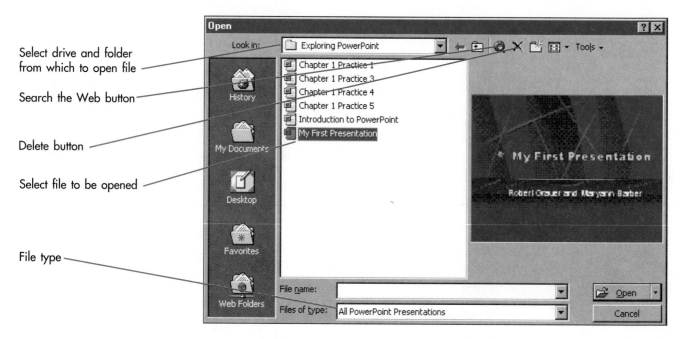

(b) Open Dialog Box (Preview View)

FIGURE 1.4   The Save and Open Commands

Introduction to PowerPoint

Objective: To start PowerPoint, open an existing presentation, and modify the text on an existing slide; to show an existing presentation and print handouts of its slides. Use Figure 1.5 as a guide in the exercise.

STEP 1: Welcome to Windows

➤ Turn on the computer and all of its peripherals. The floppy drive should be empty prior to starting your machine. This ensures that the system starts by reading from the hard disk, which contains the Windows files, as opposed to a floppy disk, which does not.

➤ Your system will take a minute or so to get started, after which you should see the desktop in Figure 1.5a. Do not be concerned if the appearance of your desktop is different from ours.

➤ You may see additional objects on the desktop in Windows 95 and/or the active desktop in Windows 98. It doesn't matter which operating system you are using because Office 2000 runs equally well under both Windows 95 and Windows 98, as well as Windows NT.

➤ You may also see a Welcome to Windows dialog box with commands to take a tour of the operating system. If so, click the appropriate button(s) or close the dialog box.

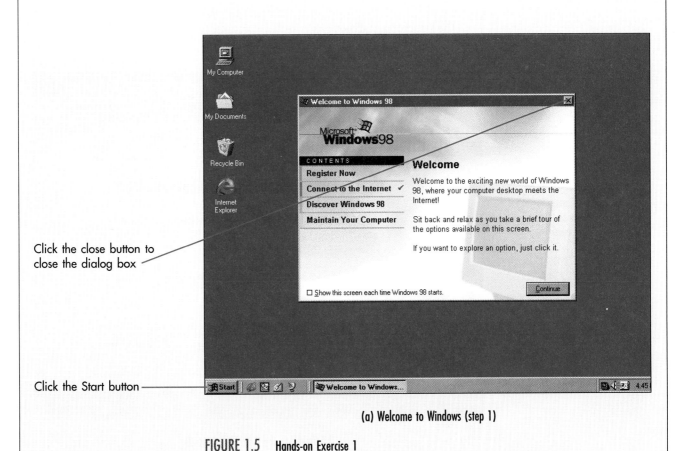

Click the close button to close the dialog box

Click the Start button

(a) Welcome to Windows (step 1)

FIGURE 1.5 Hands-on Exercise 1

STEP 2: Obtain the Practice Files

➤ We have created a series of practice files (also called a "data disk") for you to use throughout the text. Your instructor will make these files available to you in a variety of ways:

• The files may be on a network drive, in which case you use Windows Explorer to copy the files from the network to a floppy disk.

• There may be an actual "data disk" that you are to check out from the lab in order to use the Copy Disk command to duplicate the disk.

➤ You can also download the files from our Web site provided you have an Internet connection. Start Internet Explorer, then go to the Exploring Windows home page at **www.prenhall.com/grauer.**

• Click the book for **Office 2000,** which takes you to the Office 2000 home page. Click the **Student Resources tab** (at the top of the window) to go to the Student Resources page as shown in Figure 1.5b.

• Click the link to **Student Data Disk** (in the left frame), then scroll down the page until you can select PowerPoint 2000. Click the link to download the student data disk.

• You will see the File Download dialog box asking what you want to do. The option button to save this program to disk is selected. Click **OK.** The Save As dialog box appears.

• Click the down arrow in the Save In list box to enter the drive and folder where you want to save the file. It's best to save the file to the Windows desktop or to a temporary folder on drive C

• Double click the file after it has been downloaded to your PC, then follow the onscreen instructions.

➤ Check with your instructor for additional information.

Click here for student data disk

Click here for Companion Web site (see problem 8 at the end of the chapter)

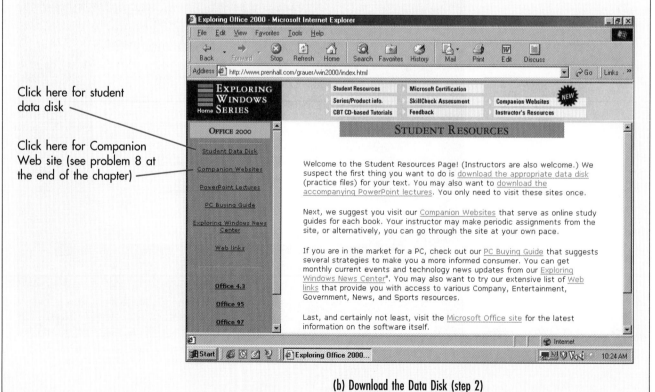

(b) Download the Data Disk (step 2)

FIGURE 1.5   Hands-on Exercise 1 (continued)

STEP 3: Start PowerPoint

➤ Click the **Start button** to display the Start menu. Slide the mouse pointer over the various menu options and notice that each time you point to a submenu, its items are displayed; i.e., you can point rather than click a submenu.

➤ Point to (or click) the **Programs menu,** then click **Microsoft PowerPoint 2000** to start the program and display the screen in Figure 1.5c. Right click the **Office Assistant** if it appears, then click the command to hide it. We return to the Assistant in step 7.

➤ Click the option button to **Open an Existing Presentation,** click **More Files** in the open list box, then click **OK.** (If you do *not* see the PowerPoint dialog box, pull down the **File menu** and click **Open** or click the **Open button** on the Standard toolbar.)

Right click the Office Assistant ——

Click the option button to
open an existing presentation ——

Click More Files ——

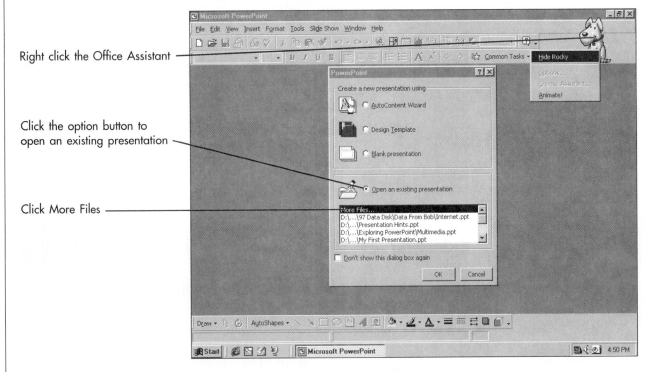

(c) Start PowerPoint (step 3)

FIGURE 1.5 Hands-on Exercise 1 (continued)

ABOUT THE ASSISTANT

The Assistant is very powerful and hence you want to experiment with various ways to use it. To ask a question, click the Assistant's icon to toggle its balloon on or off. To change the way in which the Assistant works, click the Options button within this balloon and experiment with the various check boxes to see their effects. If you find the Assistant distracting, click and drag the character out of the way or hide it altogether by pulling down the Help menu and clicking the Hide the Office Assistant command. Pull down the Help menu and click the Show the Office Assistant command to return to the Assistant.

STEP 4: Open a Presentation

➤ You should see an Open dialog box similar to the one in Figure 1.5d. Click the **drop-down arrow** on the Look In list box. Click the appropriate drive, drive C or drive A, depending on the location of your data.

➤ Double click the **Exploring PowerPoint folder** to make it the active folder. This is the folder from which you will retrieve and into which you will save the presentation.

➤ Click the **Views button** repeatedly to cycle through the different views. We selected the Preview view in Figure 1.5d.

➤ Double click **Introduction to PowerPoint** to open the presentation and begin the exercise.

Toolbars have been placed on separate rows

Click to display available drives

Double click Introduction to PowerPoint

Views button

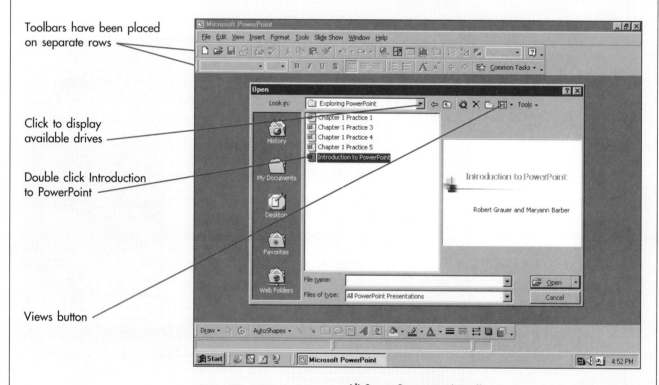

(d) Open a Presentation (step 4)

FIGURE 1.5   Hands-on Exercise 1 (continued)

SEPARATE THE TOOLBARS

Office 2000 displays the Standard and Formatting toolbars on the same row to save space within the application window. The result is that only a limited number of buttons are visible on each toolbar, and hence you may need to click the double arrow (More Buttons) tool at the end of the toolbar to view additional buttons. You can, however, separate the toolbars. Pull down the Tools menu, click the Customize command, click the Options tab, then clear the check box that has the Standard and Formatting toolbars share one row.

STEP 5: The Save As Command

➤ If necessary, click the maximize button in the application window so that PowerPoint takes the entire desktop. Click the maximize button in the document window (if necessary) so that the document window is as large as possible.

➤ Pull down the **File menu.** Click **Save As** to display the dialog box shown in Figure 1.5e. Enter **Finished Introduction** as the name of the new presentation. Click the **Save button.**

➤ There are now two identical copies of the file on disk, "Introduction to PowerPoint" which is the original presentation that we supplied, and "Finished Introduction" which you just created. The title bar shows the latter name, as it is the presentation currently in memory.

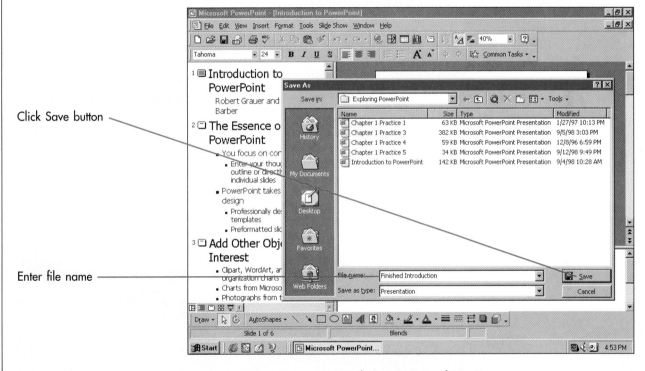

Click Save button

Enter file name

(e) The Save As Command (step 5)

FIGURE 1.5   Hands-on Exercise 1 (continued)

DIFFERENT FILE TYPES

The file format for PowerPoint 2000 is compatible with PowerPoint 97, but incompatible with earlier versions such as PowerPoint 95. The newer releases can open a presentation that was created using the older program (PowerPoint 95), but the reverse is not true; that is, you cannot open a presentation that was created in PowerPoint 2000 in PowerPoint 95 unless you change the file type. Pull down the File menu, click the Save As command, then specify the earlier (PowerPoint 6.0/PowerPoint 95) file type. You will be able to read the file in PowerPoint 95, but will lose any commands that are unique to the newer release.

STEP 6: Modify a Slide

➤ Press and hold the left mouse button as you drag the mouse over the presenters' names, **Robert Grauer and Maryann Barber.** You can select the text in either the outline or the slide pane.

➤ Release the mouse. The names should be highlighted (selected) as shown in Figure 1.5f. The selected text is the text that will be affected by the next command.

➤ Type your name, which automatically replaces the selected text in both the outline and the slide pane. Press **enter.**

➤ Type your class on the next line and note that the entry is made in both the slide and the outline pane.

➤ Pull down the **File menu** and click **Save** (or click the **Save button** on the Standard toolbar).

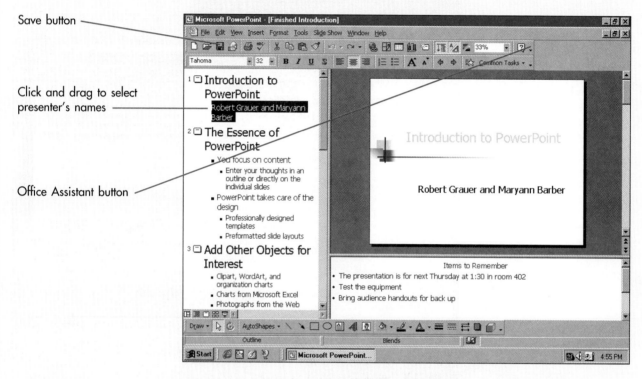

(f) Modify a Slide (step 6)

FIGURE 1.5   Hands-on Exercise 1 (continued)

THE AUTOMATIC SPELL CHECK

A red wavy line under a word indicates that the word is misspelled, or in the case of a proper name, that the word is spelled correctly, but that it is not in the dictionary. In either event, point to the underlined word and click the right mouse button to display a shortcut menu. Select the appropriate spelling from the list of suggestions or add the word to the supplementary dictionary. To enable (disable) the automatic spell check, pull down the Tools menu, click the Options command, click the Spelling and Style tab, then check (clear) the option to check spelling as you type.

STEP 7: The Office Assistant

➤ You can display the Assistant in one of three ways—press the **F1 key,** click the **Microsoft PowerPoint Help** button on the Standard toolbar, or pull down the **Help menu** and click the **Show the Office Assistant command.**

➤ If necessary, click the Assistant to display a balloon, then enter your question, for example, **How do I show a presentation?** Click the **Search button** within the balloon.

➤ The Assistant will return a list of topics that it considers potential answers to your question. Click the first topic, **Start a slide show,** to display the Help window in Figure 1.5g.

➤ Click the second topic in the Help window, **Start a slide show from within PowerPoint,** which displays steps that show the commands you need. You can print the contents by clicking the **Print button** in the Help window. Close the Help window.

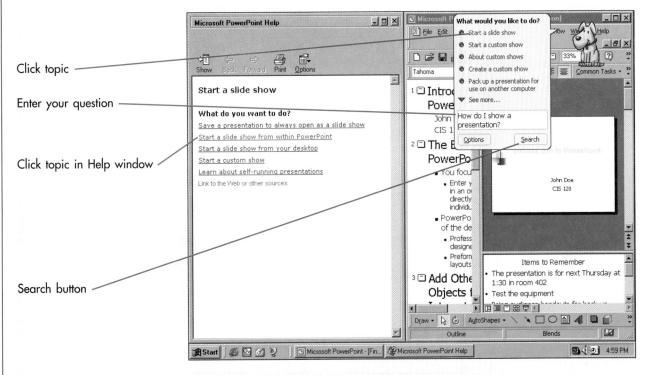

(g) The Office Assistant (step 7)

FIGURE 1.5   Hands-on Exercise 1 (continued)

CHOOSE YOUR OWN ASSISTANT

You can choose your own personal assistant from one of several available candidates. If necessary, press the F1 key to display the Assistant, click the Options button to display the Office Assistant dialog box, then click the Gallery tab where you choose your character. (The Office 2000 CD is required in order to select some of the other characters.) Some assistants are more animated (distracting) than others. The Office logo is the most passive, while Rocky is quite animated. Experiment with the various check boxes on the Options tab to see the effects on the Assistant.

STEP 8: Show the Presentation

➤ Click the **Slide Show button** above the status bar, or pull down the **View menu** and click **Slide Show.** The presentation will begin with the first slide as shown in Figure 1.5h. You should see your name on the slide because of the modification you made in the previous step.

➤ Click the mouse to move to the second slide, which comes into the presentation from the right side of your monitor. (This is one of several transition effects used to add interest to a presentation.)

➤ Click the mouse to the next (third) slide, which illustrates a build effect that requires you to click the mouse to display each succeeding bullet.

➤ Continue to view the show until you come to the end of the presentation. (You can press the **Esc key** at any time to cancel the show and return to the PowerPoint window.) Note the transition effects and the use of sound (provided you have speakers on your system) to enhance the presentation.

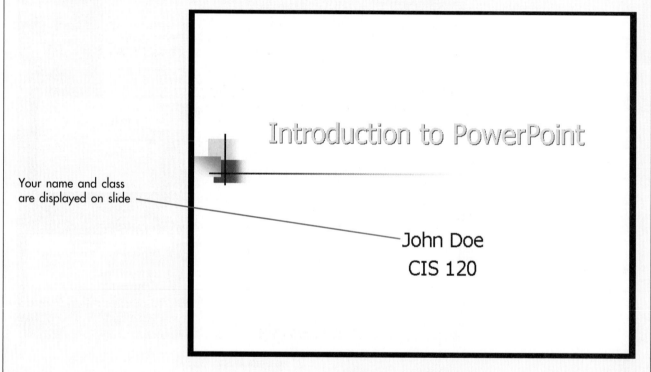

Your name and class are displayed on slide

Introduction to PowerPoint

John Doe
CIS 120

(h) Show the Presentation (step 8)

TIP OF THE DAY

You can set the Office Assistant to greet you with a "tip of the day" each time you start PowerPoint. Click the Microsoft PowerPoint Help button (or press the F1 key) to display the Assistant, then click the Options button to display the Office Assistant dialog box. Click the Options tab, check the Show the Tip of the Day at Startup box, then click OK. The next time you start PowerPoint, you will be greeted by the Assistant, who will offer you the tip of the day.

STEP 9: Print the Presentation

➤ Pull down the **File menu.** Click **Print** to display the Print dialog box in Figure 1.5i. (Clicking the Print button on the Standard toolbar does not display the Print dialog box.)

➤ Click the **down arrow** in the **Print What** drop-down list box, click **Handouts,** and specify 6 slides per page as shown in Figure 1.5i.

➤ Check the box to **Frame Slides.** Check that the **All option button** is selected under Print range. Click the **OK command button** to print the handouts for the presentation.

➤ Pull down the **File menu.** Click **Close** to close the presentation but remain in PowerPoint. Click **Yes** when asked whether to save the changes.

➤ Pull down the **File menu.** Click **Exit** to exit PowerPoint if you do not want to continue with the next exercise at this time.

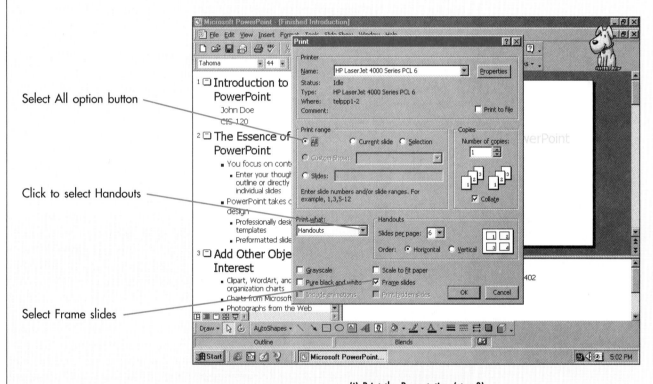

Select All option button

Click to select Handouts

Select Frame slides

(i) Print the Presentation (step 9)

FIGURE 1.5   Hands-on Exercise 1 (continued)

SHOW THE KEYBOARD SHORTCUT IN A SCREENTIP

You can expand the ScreenTip associated with any toolbar button to include the equivalent keyboard shortcut. Pull down the View menu, click Toolbars, then click Customize to display the Customize dialog box. Click the Options tab and check the box to show the shortcut keys in the Screen-Tips. Close the dialog box, then point to any toolbar button and you should see the name of the button as well as the equivalent keyboard shortcut.

You are ready to create your own presentation, a process that requires you to develop its content and apply the formatting through the use of a template or design specification. You can do the steps in either order, but we suggest you start with the content. Both steps are iterative in nature and you are likely to go back and forth many times before you are finished.

You will also find yourself switching from one view to another as you develop the presentation. It doesn't matter which view you use, as long as you can accomplish what you set out to do. You can, for example, enter text one slide at a time in the Slide view. You can also use the Outline view as shown in Figure 1.6, to view the text of many slides at the same time and thus gain a better sense of the overall presentation.

Each slide in the outline contains a title, followed by bulleted items, which are indented one to five levels, corresponding to the importance of the item. The main points appear on level one. Subsidiary items are indented below the main point to which they apply. Any item can be promoted to a higher level or demoted to a lower level, either before or after the text is entered. Each slide in the outline is numbered and the numbers adjust automatically for the insertion or deletion of slides as you edit the presentation.

Consider, for example, slide 4 in Figure 1.6a. The title of the slide, *Develop the Content,* appears immediately after the slide number and icon. The first bullet, *Use the Outline view,* is indented one level under the title, and it in turn has two subsidiary bullets. The next main bullet, *Review the flow of ideas,* is moved back to level one, and it, too, has two subsidiary bullets.

The outline is (to us) the ideal way to create and edit the presentation. The *insertion point* marks the place where new text is entered and is established by clicking anywhere in the outline. (The insertion point is automatically placed at the title of the first slide in a new presentation.) Press enter after typing the title or after entering the text of a bulleted item, which starts a new slide or bullet, respectively. The new item may then be promoted or demoted as necessary.

Editing is accomplished through the same techniques used in other Windows applications. For example, you can use the Cut, Copy, and Paste commands in the Edit menu (or the corresponding buttons on the Standard toolbar) to move and copy selected text or you can simply drag and drop text from one place to another. You can also use the Find and Replace commands that are found in every Office application.

Note, too, that you can format text in the outline by using the *select-then-do* approach common to all Office applications; that is, you select the text, then you execute the appropriate command or click the appropriate button. The selected text remains highlighted and is affected by all subsequent commands until you click elsewhere in the outline.

Figure 1.6b displays a collapsed view of the outline, which displays only the title of each slide. The advantage to this view is that you see more slides on the screen at the same time, making it easier to move slides within the presentation. The slides are expanded or collapsed using tools on the Outlining toolbar.

CRYSTALLIZE YOUR MESSAGE

Every presentation exists to deliver a message, whether it's to sell a product, present an idea, or provide instruction. Decide on the message you want to deliver, then write the text for the presentation. Edit the text to be sure it is consistent with your objective. Then, and only then, should you think about formatting, but always keep the message foremost in your mind.

1 ☐ **A Guide to Successful Presentations**
    Robert Grauer and Maryann Barber
2 ☐ **Define the Audience**
    • Who is in the audience
        • Managers
        • Coworkers
        • Clients
    • What are their expectations
3 ☐ **Create the Presentation**
    • Develop the content
    • Format the presentation
    • Animate the slide show
4 ☐ **Develop the Content**
    • Use the Outline view
        • Demote items (Tab)
        • Promote items (Shift+Tab)
    • Review the flow of ideas
        • Cut, copy, and paste text
        • Drag and drop
5 ☐ **Format the Presentation**
    • Choose a design template
    • Customize the template
        • Change the color scheme
        • Change the background shading
    • Modify the slide masters
6 ☐ **Animate the Slide Show**
    • Transitions
    • Animations
    • Hidden slides
7 ☐ **Tips for Delivery**
    • Rehearse timings
    • Arrive early
    • Maintain eye contact
    • Know your audience

(a) The Expanded Outline

1 ☐ <u>**A Guide to Successful Presentations**</u>
2 ☐ <u>**Define the Audience**</u>
3 ☐ <u>**Create the Presentation**</u>
4 ☐ <u>**Develop the Content**</u>
5 ☐ <u>**Format the Presentation**</u>
6 ☐ <u>**Animate the Slide Show**</u>
7 ☐ <u>**Tips for Delivery**</u>

(b) The Collapsed Outline

FIGURE 1.6   The Outline View

Slide Layouts

All slides that are created in the Outline view are formatted as "bullet slides" that consist of a slide title and a single column of bullets. What if, however, you want to add clip art or another object, and/or display a double column of bullets? In other words you are satisfied with the text that is on the slide, but you want to add interest by including additional objects. You can add and/or arrange the objects manually in the Slide view, but it is often easier to change the slide layout and have PowerPoint do it for you.

PowerPoint provides a total of 24 predefined slide formats known as *Slide Layouts* that determine the position of the objects on a slide. To change the layout of a slide, click anywhere in the slide, pull down the Format menu, and click the Slide Layout command to display the Slide Layout dialog box. Select the type of slide you want and click the button to apply that layout. You can also insert a new slide in similar fashion. Pull down the Insert menu and click the New Slide command to display the slide layouts, then click OK. The slide will be added to the presentation immediately after the current slide. Either way, you are presented with a dialog box in which you choose the slide layout.

Figure 1.7 illustrates the creation of a bulleted slide with clip art after this slide layout was selected. The resulting slide has three *placeholders* that determine the position of each object. Just follow the directions on the slide by clicking the appropriate placeholder to add the title or text, or by double clicking to add the clip art. (The text that appears within a placeholder is there to guide the user and will not appear on the actual slide unless you click in the area and enter text as directed.) It's easy, as you will see in the exercise that follows shortly.

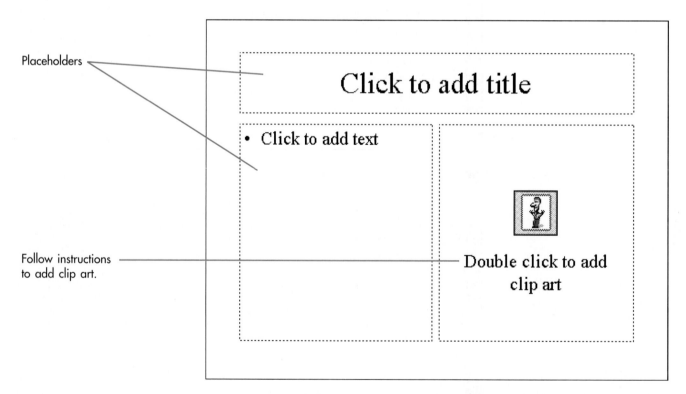

FIGURE 1.7   Slide Layouts

PowerPoint enables you to concentrate on the content of a presentation without concern for its appearance. You focus on what you are going to say, and trust in PowerPoint to format the presentation attractively. The formatting is implemented automatically by selecting one of the many templates that are supplied with PowerPoint.

A *template* is a design specification that controls every element in a presentation. It specifies the color scheme for the slides and the arrangement of the different elements (placeholders) on each slide. It determines the formatting of the text, the fonts that are used, and the size and placement of the bulleted text.

Figure 1.8 displays the title slide of a presentation in four different templates. Just choose the template you like, and PowerPoint formats the entire presentation according to that template. And don't be afraid to change your mind. You can use the Format menu at any time to select a different template and change the look of your presentation.

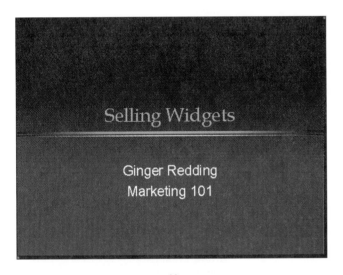

(a) Double Lines

(b) Sparkle

(c) Coins

(d) Bevel

FIGURE 1.8   Templates

Creating a Presentation

Objective: To create a presentation by entering text in the Outline view; to apply a design template to a presentation. Use Figure 1.9 as a guide.

STEP 1: Create a New Presentation

➤ Start PowerPoint. Hide the Office Assistant if it appears. (You can unhide the Assistant at any time by clicking its button on the Standard toolbar.)

➤ Click the **option button** to create a new presentation using a **Blank Presentation.** Click **OK.**

➤ You should see the **New Slide** dialog box in Figure 1.9a with the AutoLayout for the title slide already selected. Click **OK** to create a title slide.

➤ If necessary, click the **Maximize buttons** in both the application and document windows so that PowerPoint takes the entire desktop.

Click OK

Title slide is selected

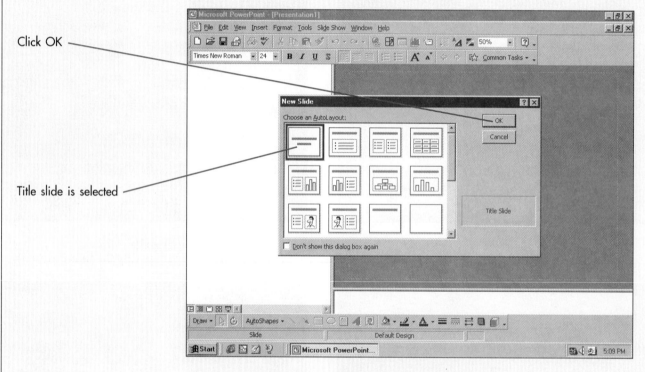

(a) Create a New Presentation (step 1)

FIGURE 1.9   Hands-on Exercise 2

CONTENT, CONTENT, AND CONTENT

It is much more important to focus on the content of the presentation than to worry about how it will look. Start with the AutoContent Wizard (described later in the chapter) or with a blank presentation in the Outline view. Save the formatting for last. Otherwise you will spend too much time changing templates and too little time developing the text.

STEP 2: Create the Title Slide

➤ Click anywhere in the box containing **Click to add title,** then type the title, **A Guide to Successful Presentations** as shown in Figure 1.9b. The title will automatically wrap to a second line.

➤ Click anywhere in the box containing **Click to add subtitle** and enter your name. Click outside the subtitle placeholder when you have entered your name.

➤ Click in the Notes pane and enter a speaker's note that pertains to the title slide; for example, the date and time that the presentation is scheduled.

➤ You may see a lightbulb indicating that the Office Assistant has a suggestion for you. The Assistant may suggest that you add clip art, apply a design template, or change the style (capitalization) on your slide.

➤ The suggestions are interesting, but we suggest you ignore them initially and focus on entering the content of your presentation.

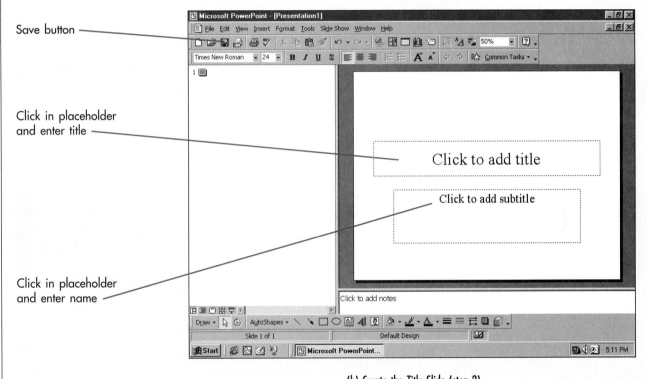

Save button

Click in placeholder and enter title

Click in placeholder and enter name

(b) Create the Title Slide (step 2)

FIGURE 1.9   Hands-on Exercise 2 (continued)

THE DEFAULT PRESENTATION

PowerPoint supplies a default presentation containing the specifications for color (a plain white background with black text), formatting, and AutoLayouts. The default presentation is selected automatically when you work on a blank presentation, and it remains in effect until you choose a different template.

STEP 3: Save the Presentation

➤ Pull down the **File menu** and click **Save** (or click the **Save button** on the Standard toolbar). You should see the Save dialog box in Figure 1.9c. If necessary, click the **down arrow** on the **Views button** and click **Details.**

➤ To save the file:

- Click the **drop-down arrow** on the Save In list box.

- Click the appropriate drive, drive C or drive A, depending on whether or not you installed the data disk on your hard drive.

- Double click the **Exploring PowerPoint folder** to make it the active folder (the folder in which you will save the document).

- Enter **My First Presentation** as the name of the presentation.

- Click **Save** or press the **enter key.** Click **Cancel** or press the **Esc key** if you see the Properties dialog box. The title bar changes to reflect the name of the presentation.

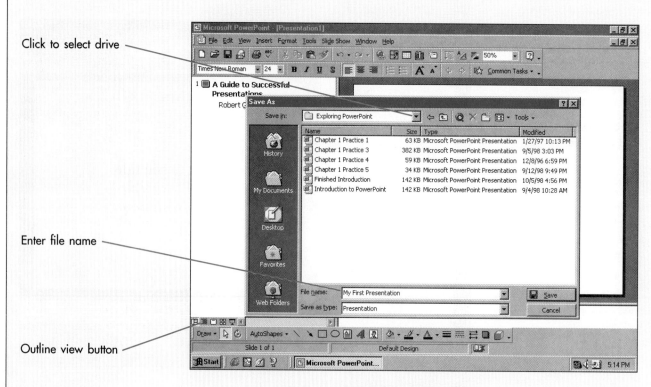

Click to select drive

Enter file name

Outline view button

(c) Save the Presentation (step 3)

FIGURE 1.9   Hands-on Exercise 2 (continued)

STEP 4: Create the Presentation

➤ Click the **Outline View button** above the status bar so that the Outline pane is made larger within the Normal view.

➤ Click after your name in the Outline pane. Press **enter** to begin a new item, then press **Shift+Tab** to promote the item and create slide 2. Type **Define the Audience.** Press **enter.**

➤ Press the **Tab key** (or click the **Demote button** on the Outline toolbar) to enter the first bullet. Type **Who is in the audience** and press **enter.**

➤ Press the **Tab key** (or click the **Demote button** on the Outline toolbar) to enter the second-level bullets.

- Type **Managers.** Press **enter.**
- Type **Coworkers.** Press **enter.**
- Type **Clients.** Press **enter.**

➤ Press **Shift+Tab** (or click the **Promote button** on the Outline toolbar) to return to the first-level bullets.

- Type **What are their expectations.** Press **enter.**

➤ Press **Shift+Tab** to enter the title of the third slide. Type **Tips for Delivery.** Press **enter,** then press **Tab key** to create the first bullet.

➤ Add the remaining text for this slide and for slide 4 as shown in Figure 1.9d. Save the presentation.

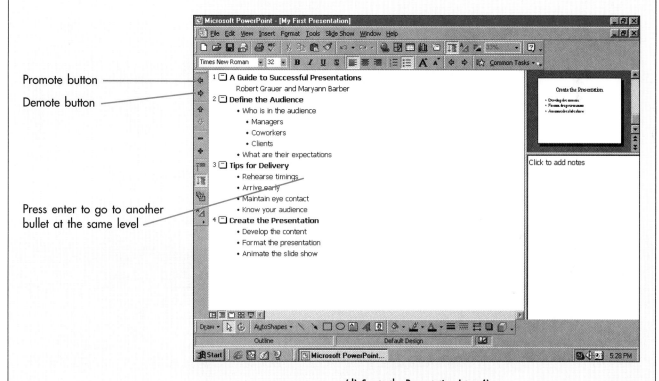

Promote button

Demote button

Press enter to go to another bullet at the same level

(d) Create the Presentation (step 4)

FIGURE 1.9   Hands-on Exercise 2 (continued)

JUST KEEP TYPING

The easiest way to enter the text for a presentation is to type continually in the Outline view. Just type an item, then press enter to move to the next item. You will be automatically positioned at the next item on the same level, where you can type the next entry. Continue to enter text in this manner. Press the Tab key as necessary to demote an item (move it to the next lower level). Press Shift+Tab to promote an item (move it to the next higher level).

STEP 5: The Spell Check

➤ Enter the text of the remaining slides as shown in Figure 1.9e. Do *not* press enter after entering the last bullet on the last slide or else you will add a blank bullet.

➤ Click the **Spelling button** on the Standard toolbar to check the presentation for spelling:

- The result of the Spell Check will depend on how accurately you entered the text of the presentation. We deliberately misspelled the word *Transitions* in the last slide.

- Continue to check the document for spelling errors. Click **OK** when PowerPoint indicates it has checked the entire presentation.

➤ Click the **Save button** on the Standard toolbar to save the presentation.

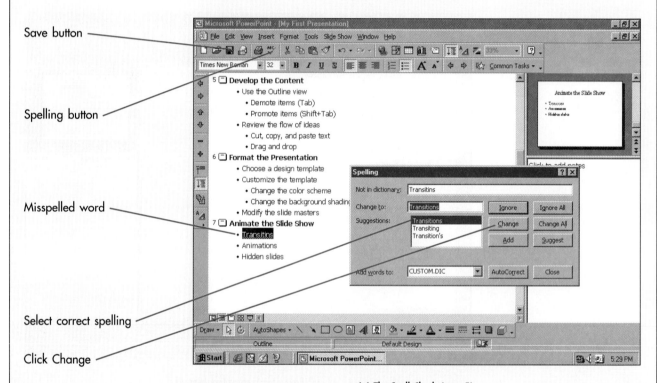

Save button

Spelling button

Misspelled word

Select correct spelling

Click Change

(e) The Spell Check (step 5)

FIGURE 1.9   Hands-on Exercise 2 (continued)

CREATE YOUR OWN SHORTHAND

Use the AutoCorrect feature, which is common to all Office applications, to expand abbreviations such as "usa" for United States of America. Pull down the Tools menu, click AutoCorrect, then type the abbreviation in the Replace text box and the expanded entry in the With text box. Click the Add command button, then click OK to exit the dialog box and return to the document. The next time you type usa in a presentation, it will automatically be expanded to United States of America.

STEP 6: Drag and Drop

➤ Press **Ctrl+Home** to move to the beginning of the presentation. If you don't see the Outlining toolbar, pull down the **View menu,** click the **Toolbars command,** and check **Outlining** to display the toolbar.

➤ Click the **Collapse All button** on the Outline toolbar to collapse the outline as shown in Figure 1.9f.

➤ Click the **icon** for **slide 3** (Tips for Delivery) to select the slide. Point to the **slide icon** (the mouse pointer changes to a four-headed arrow), then click and drag to move the slide to the end of the presentation.

➤ All of the slides have been renumbered. The slide titled Tips for Delivery has been moved to the end of the presentation and appears as slide 7. Click the **Expand All button** to display the contents of each slide. Click anywhere in the presentation to deselect the last slide.

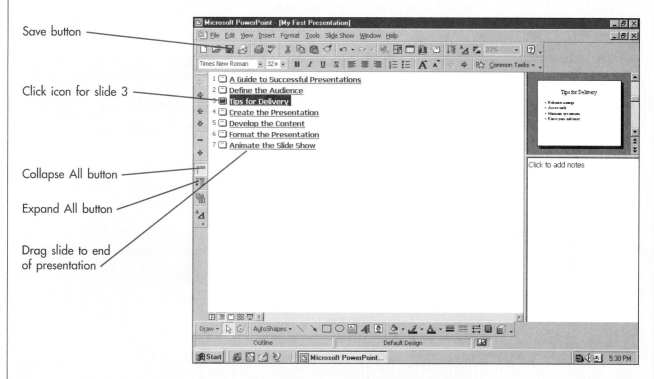

Save button

Click icon for slide 3

Collapse All button

Expand All button

Drag slide to end of presentation

(f) Drag and Drop (step 6)

FIGURE 1.9   Hands-on Exercise 2 (continued)

SELECTING SLIDES IN THE OUTLINE VIEW

Click the slide icon or the slide number next to the slide title to select the slide. PowerPoint will select the entire slide (including its title, text, and any other objects that are not visible in the Outline view). Click the first slide, then press and hold the Shift key as you click the ending slide to select a group of sequential slides. Press Ctrl+A to select the entire outline. You can use these techniques to select multiple slides regardless of whether the outline is collapsed or expanded. The selected slides can be copied, moved, expanded, collapsed, or deleted as a unit.

STEP 7: Choose a Design Template

➤ Pull down the **Format menu** and click **Apply Design Template** to display the dialog box in Figure 1.9g:

➤ The **Presentation Designs folder** should appear automatically in the List box. If it doesn't, change to this folder which is contained within the Templates folder within the Microsoft Office Folder, which in turn is in the Program Files Folder on drive C.

➤ **Design Templates** should be selected in the Files of Type list box. If it isn't, click the **drop-down arrow** to change to this file type.

➤ The **Preview view** should be selected. If it isn't, click the **Views button** until you toggle to the Preview view where you can preview the selected template.

➤ Scroll through the available designs to select (click) the **Soaring template** as shown in Figure 1.9g. Click **Apply** to close the dialog box.

➤ The appearance of the slide changes in the Normal view. Save the presentation.

Presentation Designs folder

Select Soaring template

File Type is Design Templates

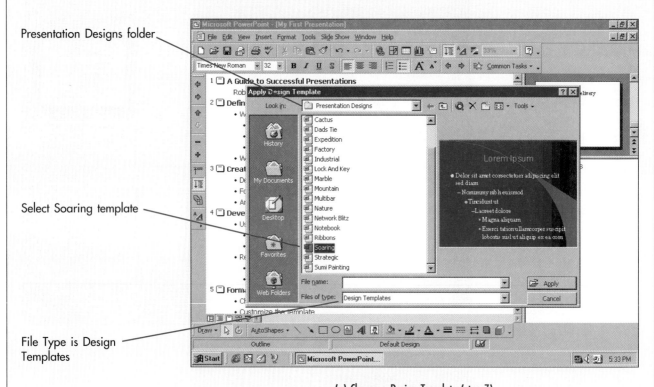

(g) Choose a Design Template (step 7)

FIGURE 1.9   Hands-on Exercise 2 (continued)

THE UNDO AND REDO COMMANDS

Click the drop-down arrow next to the Undo button to display a list of your previous actions, then click the action you want to undo which also undoes all of the preceding commands. Undoing the fifth command in the list, for example, will also undo the preceding four commands. The Redo command works in reverse and cancels the last Undo command.

STEP 8: View the Presentation

➤ **Press Ctrl+Home** to move to the beginning of the presentation. Click the **Slide Show button** on the status bar to view the presentation as shown in Figure 1.9h.

  • To move to the next slide: Click the **left mouse button,** type the letter **N,** or press the **PgDn key.**

  • To move to the previous slide: Type the letter **P,** or press the **PgUp key.**

➤ Continue to move from one slide to the next until you come to the end of the presentation and are returned to the Normal view.

➤ Save the presentation. Exit PowerPoint if you do not want to continue with the next exercise at this time.

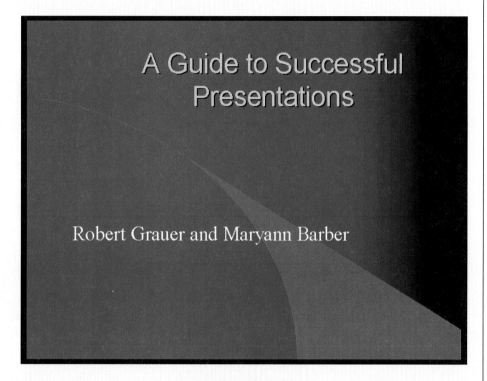

(h) View the Presentation (step 8)

FIGURE 1.9   Hands-on Exercise 2 (continued)

ADVICE FROM THE OFFICE ASSISTANT

The Office Assistant indicates it has a suggestion by displaying a lightbulb. Click the lightbulb to display the tip, then click the OK button to close the balloon and continue working. The Assistant will not, however, repeat a tip from an earlier session unless you reset it at the start of a new session. This is especially important in a laboratory situation where you are sharing a computer with many students. To reset the tips, click the Assistant to display the balloon, click the Options button in the balloon, click the Options tab, then click the Reset My Tips button.

You develop the content of a presentation, then you format it attractively using a PowerPoint template. The most important step is yet to come—the delivery of the presentation to an audience, which is best accomplished through a computerized slide show (as opposed to using overhead transparencies or 35-mm slides). The computer becomes the equivalent of a slide projector, and the presentation is called a slide show.

PowerPoint can help you add interest to the slide show in two ways, transitions and animation effects. *Transitions* control the way in which one slide moves off the screen and the next slide appears. *Animation effects* vary the way in which objects on a slide appear during the presentation.

Transitions are created through the Slide Transition command in the Slide Show menu, which displays the dialog box in Figure 1.10a. The drop-down list box enables you to choose the transition effect. Slides may move on to the screen from the left or right, be uncovered by horizontal or vertical blinds, fade, dissolve, and so on. The dialog box also enables you to set the speed of the transition and/or to preview the effect.

Animation enables the bulleted items to appear one at a time with each successive mouse click. The effect is created through the Custom Animation command in the Slide Show menu, which displays the dialog box of Figure 1.10b. Each bullet can appear with its own transition effect. You can make the bullets appear one word or one letter at a time. You can specify that the bullets appear in reverse order (i.e., the bottom bullet first), and you can dim each bullet as the next one appears. You can even add sound and make the bullets appear in conjunction with a round of applause.

Transitions and animation effects can also be created from the Slide Sorter toolbar as shown in Figure 1.10c. As with the other toolbars, a ScreenTip is displayed when you point to a button on the toolbar.

Delivering the Presentation

PowerPoint can help you to create attractive presentations, but the content and delivery are still up to you. You have worked hard to gain the opportunity to present your ideas and you want to be well prepared for the session. Practice aloud several times, preferably under the same conditions as the actual presentation. Time your delivery to be sure that you do not exceed your allotted time. Everyone is nervous, but the more you practice the more confident you will be.

Arrive early. You need time to gather your thoughts as well as to set up the presentation. Start PowerPoint and open your presentation prior to addressing the audience. Be sure that your notes are with you and check that water is available for you during the presentation. Look at the audience to open communication and gain credibility. Speak clearly and vary your delivery. Try to relax. You'll be great!

QUESTIONS AND ANSWERS (Q & A)

Indicate at the beginning of your talk whether you will take questions during the presentation or collectively at the end. Announce the length of time that will be allocated to questions. Rephrase all questions so the audience can hear. If you do receive a hostile question, rephrase it in a neutral way and try to disarm the challenger by paying a compliment. If you don't know the answer, say so.

Preview transition effect

Click to choose
transition effect

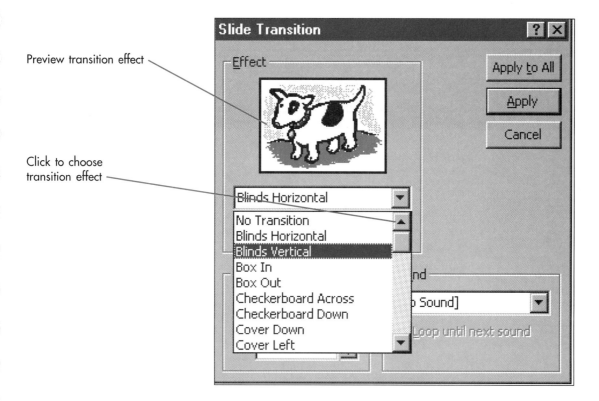

(a) Transitions

Object for which animation is
being created

Bullet transition effect

Sound options

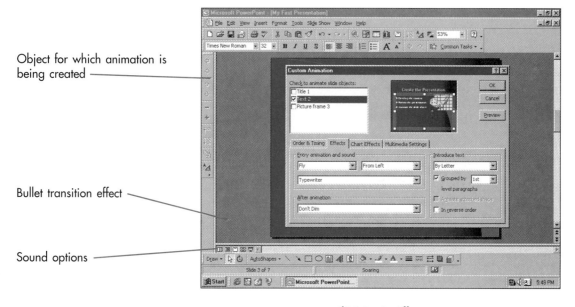

(b) Animation Effects

Hide Slide   Rehearse Timings

Slide Transition Effects   Preset Animations   Animation Preview   Summary Slide

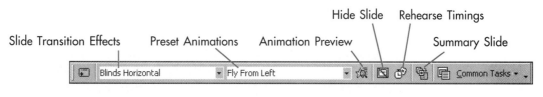

(c) Slide Sorter Toolbar

FIGURE 1.10   Transitions and Animation Effects

Animating the Presentation

Objective: To change the layout of an existing slide; to establish transition and animation effects. Use Figure 1.11 as a guide in the exercise.

STEP 1: Change the Slide Layout

➤ Start PowerPoint and open **My First Presentation** from the previous exercise. If necessary, switch to the **Slide view.** Press **Ctrl+End** to move to the last slide as shown in Figure 1.11a, which is currently a bulleted list.

➤ Pull down the **Format menu** and click **Slide Layout.**

➤ Choose the **Text and Clip Art layout** as shown in Figure 1.11a. Click the **Apply command button** to change the slide layout.

Select Text and Clip Art layout

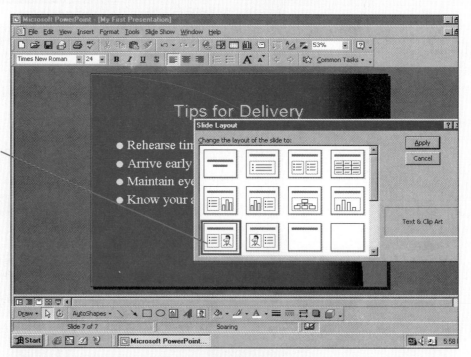

(a) Change the AutoLayout (step 1)

FIGURE 1.11   Hands-on Exercise 3

THE MOST RECENTLY OPENED FILE LIST

The easiest way to open a recently used presentation is to select the presentation directly from the File menu. Pull down the File menu, but instead of clicking the Open command, check to see if the presentation appears on the list of the most recently opened presentations located at the bottom of the menu. If so, you can click the presentation name rather than having to make the appropriate selections through the Open dialog box.

STEP 2: Add the Clip Art

➤ Double click the **placeholder** on the slide to add the clip art. You will see the Microsoft Clip Gallery dialog box as shown in Figure 1.11b (although you may not see all of the categories listed in the figure).

➤ Select (click) the **Academic category,** choose any image, then click the **Insert Clip button** on the Shortcut menu. The clip art should appear on the slide within the placeholder.

➤ Click outside the clip art to deselect the picture so that you can continue working on the presentation.

➤ The clip art is sized automatically to fit the existing place holder. You can, however, move and size the clip art just like any other Windows object.

➤ Save the presentation.

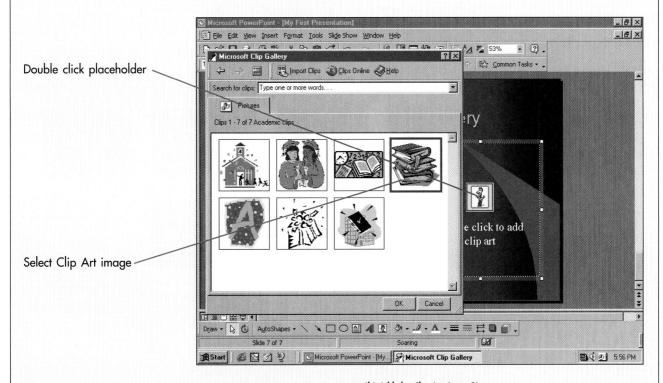

(b) Add the Clip Art (step 2)

FIGURE 1.11   Hands-on Exercise 3 (continued)

ROTATE AND FLIP AN OBJECT

Change the appearance of any clip art object by rotating it left or right, or flipping it horizontally or vertically. Right click the clip art to display a context sensitive menu, click the Grouping command, and click Ungroup. Click Yes if asked whether to convert the clip art to a Power-Point object. Right click the ungrouped objects immediately (you must select all the objects), click the Grouping command, and click the group. Click the down arrow on the Draw menu, click the Rotate or Flip command, then experiment with the different options

STEP 3: Add Transition Effects

➤ Click the **Slide Sorter View button** to change to the Slide Sorter view as shown in Figure 1.11c. The number of slides you see at one time depends on the resolution of your monitor and the zoom percentage.

➤ Press **Ctrl+Home** to select the first slide. Pull down the **Slide Show menu,** then click **Slide Transition** to display the dialog box in Figure 1.11c. Click the **down arrow** on the Effect list box, then click the **Blinds Vertical** effect. You will see the effect displayed on the sample slide (dog) in the effect preview area. If you miss the effect, click the **dog** (or the **key**) to repeat the effect.

➤ Click **Apply** to accept the transition and close the dialog box. A slide icon appears under slide 1, indicating a transition effect.

➤ Point to slide 2, click the **right mouse button** to display a shortcut menu, then click the **Slide Transition command.** Choose **Checkerboard Across.** Click the **Slow option button.** Click **Apply** to close the dialog box.

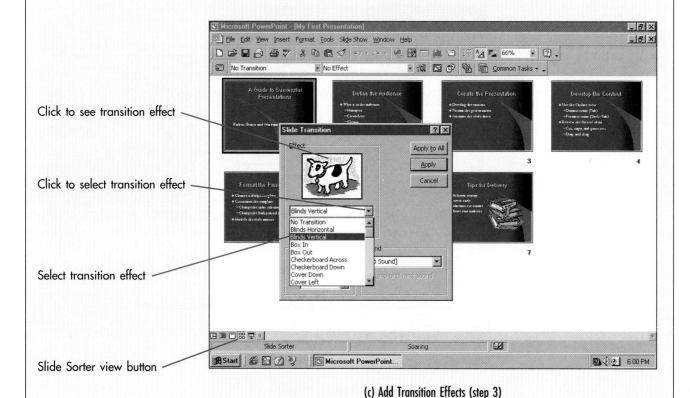

Click to see transition effect

Click to select transition effect

Select transition effect

Slide Sorter view button

(c) Add Transition Effects (step 3)

FIGURE 1.11   Hands-on Exercise 3 (continued)

CHANGE THE MAGNIFICATION

Click the down arrow on the Zoom box to change the display magnification, which in turn controls the size of individual slides. The higher the magnification, the easier it is to read the text of an individual slide, but the fewer slides you see at one time. Conversely, changing to a smaller magnification decreases the size of the individual slides, but enables you to see more of the presentation.

STEP 4: Create a Summary Slide

➤ Pull down the **Edit menu** and press **Select All** to select every slide in the presentation. (Alternatively, you can also press and hold the **Shift key** as you click each slide in succession.)

➤ Click the **Summary Slide button** on the Slide Sorter toolbar to create a summary slide containing a bullet with the title of each selected slide. The new slide appears at the beginning of the presentation as shown in Figure 1.11d.

➤ Click and drag the **Summary Slide** to the end of the presentation. (As you drag the slide, the mouse pointer changes to include the outline of a miniature slide and a vertical line appears to indicate the new position of the slide.)

➤ Release the mouse. The Summary Slide has been moved to the end of the presentation and the slides are renumbered automatically.

➤ Save the presentation.

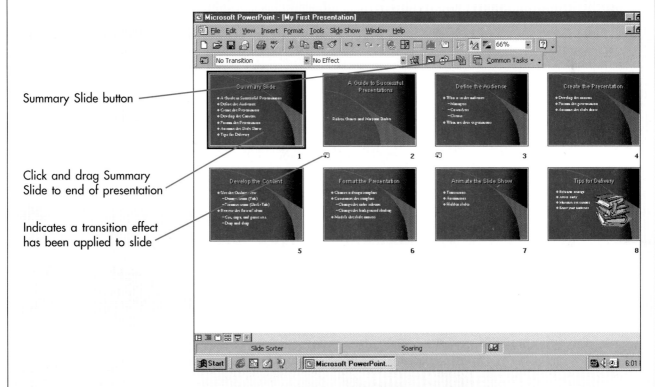

Summary Slide button

Click and drag Summary Slide to end of presentation

Indicates a transition effect has been applied to slide

(d) Create a Summary Slide (step 4)

FIGURE 1.11   Hands-on Exercise 3 (continued)

SELECTING MULTIPLE SLIDES

You can apply the same transition or animation effect to multiple slides with a single command. Change to the Slide Sorter view, then select the slides by pressing and holding the Shift key as you click the slides. Use the Slide Show menu or the Slide Sorter toolbar to choose the desired transition or preset animation effect when all the slides have been selected. Click anywhere in the Slide Sorter view to deselect the slides and continue working.

STEP 5: Create Animation Effects

➤ Double click the Summary slide to select the slide and simultaneously change to the Slide view. Click anywhere within the title to select the title.

➤ Pull down the **Slide Show menu,** click **Preset Animation** to display a cascade menu, then click **Typewriter** to display the title with this effect during the slide show.

➤ Click anywhere within the bulleted text to select the bulleted text (and deselect the title). Pull down the **Slide Show menu** and select **Custom Animation** to display the dialog box in Figure 1.11e.

➤ Click the **Effects tab.** Click the first **drop-down arrow** under Entry animation and sound to display the entry transitions. Click **Fly.** Click the second drop-down arrow and select **From Left.**

➤ Click the **drop-down arrow** to show the Introduce Text effects and select **All at Once.** Click the **drop-down arrow** for sound effects, then scroll until you can select **Screeching Brakes.**

➤ Click the **Order & Timing tab.** Check that the title appears first within the animation order. If not, select the title, then click the **up arrow** to move it ahead of the text. Click **OK** to close the dialog box. Click outside the place-holder to deselect it.

➤ Pull down the **Slide Show menu** a second time. Click **Animation Preview** to display the slide miniature window to see (and hear) the animation effect. If you don't see the command, click the **double arrow** to see more commands.

➤ Close the miniature window. Save the presentation.

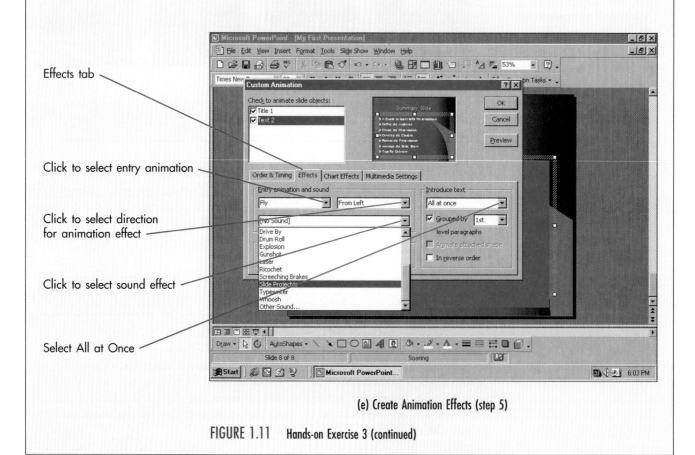

Effects tab

Click to select entry animation

Click to select direction for animation effect

Click to select sound effect

Select All at Once

(e) Create Animation Effects (step 5)

FIGURE 1.11   Hands-on Exercise 3 (continued)

STEP 6: Show the Presentation

➤ Press **Ctrl+Home** to return to the first slide, then click the **Slide Show button** above the status bar to view the presentation. You should see the opening slide in Figure 1.11f.

➤ Click the **left mouse button** to move to the next slide (or to the next bullet on the current slide when animation is in effect).

➤ Click the **right mouse button** to display the Shortcut menu and return to the previous slide (or to the previous bullet on the current slide when a build is in effect).

➤ Continue to view the presentation until you come to the end. Click the **left mouse button** a final time to return to the regular PowerPoint window.

➤ Exit PowerPoint.

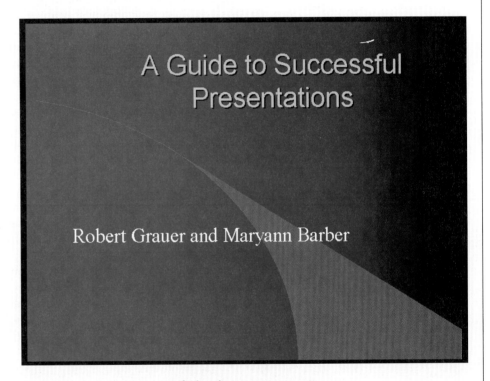

(f) Show the Presentation (step 6)

FIGURE 1.11   Hands-on Exercise 3 (continued)

ANNOTATE A SLIDE

You can annotate a slide just like the sports announcers on television. Click the Slide Show button to begin your presentation, press Ctrl+P to change the mouse pointer to a pen, then click and drag to draw on the slide. The effect is temporary and lasts only while the slide is on the screen. Use the PgDn and PgUp keys to move forward and back in the presentation when the drawing tool is in effect. Press Ctrl+A at any time to change the mouse pointer back to an arrow.

SUMMARY

Microsoft PowerPoint enables you to focus on the content of a presentation without worrying about its appearance. You supply the text and supporting elements and leave the formatting to PowerPoint. The resulting presentation consists of a series of slides with a consistent design and color scheme. You can deliver it in a variety of ways such as a computer slide show, the World Wide Web, or via overhead transparencies or 35-mm slides. You can also print the presentation in a variety of formats.

PowerPoint is easy to learn because it follows the conventions of every Windows application. The benefits of the common user interface are magnified further if you already know another application in Microsoft Office such as Word or Excel. PowerPoint is designed for a mouse but it provides keyboard equivalents for almost every command. Toolbars provide still another way to execute the most frequent operations.

PowerPoint has six different views, each with unique capabilities. The Slide view displays one slide at a time and enables all operations on that slide. The Slide Sorter view displays multiple slides on one screen (each slide is in miniature) and lets you see the overall flow of the presentation. The Outline view shows the presentation text in outline form and is the fastest way to enter or edit text. The Notes Page view enables you to create speaker's notes for use in giving the presentation. The Normal view displays the Slide, Outline, and Notes Page views in a single window, with each view in its own pane. The Slide Show view displays the slides one at a time with transition effects for added interest.

The easiest way to enter the text of a presentation is in the Outline view. You see the entire presentation and can change the order of the slides and/or move text from one slide to another as necessary. Text can be entered continually in the outline, then promoted or demoted so that it appears on the proper level in the slide.

Slides are added to a presentation using one of 24 predefined slide formats known as Slide Layouts. Each Slide Layout contains placeholders for the different objects on the slide. A slide may be deleted from a presentation in any view except the Slide Show view.

A template is a design specification that controls every aspect of a presentation. It specifies the formatting of the text, the fonts and colors that are used, and the design, size, and placement of the bullets.

Transitions and animations can be added to a presentation for additional interest. Transitions control the way in which one slide moves off the screen and the next slide appears. Animation effects are used to display the individual elements on a single slide.

KEY WORDS AND CONCEPTS

Animation effects	Formatting toolbar	Places bar
AutoCorrect	Insertion point	Print command
Clip art	Menu bar	Promote
Close command	Normal view	Redo command
Demote	Notes Page view	Save As command
Drawing toolbar	Open command	Save command
Exit command	Outline view	ScreenTip
File name	Outlining toolbar	Scroll bar
File type	Placeholders	Slide Layout

Slide Show view   Spell check   Template
Slide Sorter toolbar   Standard toolbar   Transition effect
Slide Sorter view   Status bar   Undo command
Slide view   Taskbar

MULTIPLE CHOICE

1. How do you save changes to a PowerPoint presentation?
   (a) Pull down the File menu and click the Save command
   (b) Click the Save button on the Standard toolbar
   (c) Both (a) and (b)
   (d) Neither (a) nor (b)

2. Which of the following can be printed in support of a PowerPoint presentation?
   (a) Audience handouts
   (b) Speaker's Notes
   (c) An outline
   (d) All of the above

3. Which menu contains the Undo command?
   (a) File menu
   (b) Edit menu
   (c) Tools menu
   (d) Format menu

4. Ctrl+Home and Ctrl+End are keyboard shortcuts that move to the beginning or end of the presentation in the:
   (a) Outline view
   (b) Slide Sorter view
   (c) Slide view
   (d) All of the above

5. The predefined slide formats in PowerPoint are known as:
   (a) View
   (b) Slide Layouts
   (c) Audience handouts
   (d) Speaker notes

6. Which menu contains the commands to save the current presentation, or to open a previously saved presentation?
   (a) The Tools menu
   (b) The File menu
   (c) The View menu
   (d) The Edit menu

7. The Open command:
   (a) Brings a presentation from disk into memory
   (b) Brings a presentation from disk into memory, then erases the presentation on disk
   (c) Stores the presentation in memory on disk
   (d) Stores the presentation in memory on disk, then erases the presentation from memory

8. The Save command:
   (a) Brings a presentation from disk into memory
   (b) Brings a presentation from disk into memory, then erases the presentation on disk
   (c) Stores the presentation in memory on disk
   (d) Stores the presentation in memory on disk, then erases the presentation from memory

9. Which view displays multiple slides while letting you change the text in a slide?
   (a) Outline view
   (b) Slide Sorter view
   (c) Both (a) and (b)
   (d) Neither (a) nor (b)

10. Where will the insertion point be after you complete the text for a bullet in the Outline view and press the enter key?
    (a) On the next bullet at the same level of indentation
    (b) On the next bullet at a higher level of indentation
    (c) On the next bullet at a lower level of indentation
    (d) It is impossible to determine

11. Which of the following is true?
    (a) Shift+Tab promotes an item to the next higher level
    (b) Tab demotes an item to the next lower level
    (c) Both (a) and (b)
    (d) Neither (a) nor (b)

12. What advantage, if any, is there to collapsing the Outline view so that only the slide titles are visible?
    (a) More slides are displayed at one time, making it easier to rearrange the slides in the presentation
    (b) Transition and build effects can be added
    (c) Graphic objects become visible
    (d) All of the above

13. Which of the following is true regarding transition and build effects?
    (a) Every slide must have the same transition effect
    (b) Every bullet must have the same build effect
    (c) Both (a) and (b)
    (d) Neither (a) nor (b)

14. Which of the following is true?
    (a) Slides can be added to a presentation after a template has been chosen
    (b) The template can be changed after all of the slides have been created
    (c) Both (a) and (b)
    (d) Neither (a) nor (b)

15. Which of the following can be changed after a slide has been created?
    (a) Its layout and transition effect
    (b) Its position within the presentation
    (c) Both (a) and (b)
    (d) Neither (a) nor (b)

ANSWERS

1. c	**4.** d	**7.** a	**10.** a	**13.** d
2. d	**5.** b	**8.** c	**11.** c	**14.** c
3. b	**6.** b	**9.** a	**12.** a	**15.** c

PRACTICE WITH POWERPOINT 2000

1. Looking for a Job: Figure 1.12 displays the Normal view of a presentation that was created by one of our students in a successful job search. Open the *Chapter 1 Practice 1* presentation, as it exists on the data disk (it is found in the Exploring PowerPoint folder), then modify the presentation to reflect your personal data. Print the revised Audience Handouts (six per page) and submit them to your instructor as proof you did this exercise.

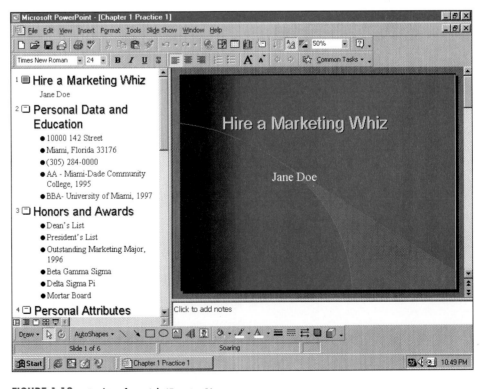

FIGURE 1.12   Looking for a Job (Exercise 1)

2. Ready-Made Presentations: The most difficult part of a presentation is getting started. PowerPoint anticipates the problem and provides general outlines on a variety of topics as shown in Figure 1.13.

   a. Pull down the File menu, click New, click the Presentations tab (if necessary), then click the Details button so that your screen matches Figure 1.13.

   b. Select Recommending a Strategy as shown in Figure 1.13. Click OK to open the presentation.

   c. Change to the Outline view so that you can see the text of the overall presentation, which is general in nature and intended for any type of strategy. Modify the presentation to develop a strategy for doing well in this class.

   d. Add your name to the title page. Print the presentation in miniature and submit it to your instructor.

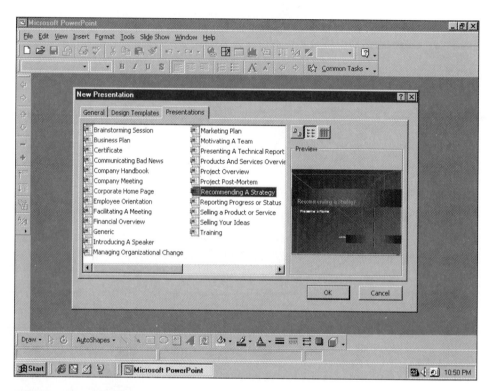

FIGURE 1.13   Ready-Made Presentations (Exercise 2)

3. The Purchase of a PC: Figure 1.14 displays the title slide of a presentation that can be found in the Exploring PowerPoint folder on the data disk. Much of the presentation has been created for you, but there are several finishing touches that need to be made:

   a. Open the existing presentation titled *Chapter 1 Practice 3*, then save it as *Chapter 1 Practice 3 Solution* so that you can return to the original presentation, if necessary.

   b. Replace our name with your name on the title slide.

   c. Move the slide on Modems after the one on Multimedia Requirements.

   d. Delete the slide on The PC, Then and Now.

   e. Add a slide at the end of the presentation on additional software that should be considered in addition to Windows and Microsoft Office.

f. Create a new slide that suggests several sources for a computer purchase. You can list computer magazines, vendor Web sites, and/or the campus bookstore.

g. Change the layout of slide 7 to a Two-column Text slide. Modify the text as necessary for the new layout.

h. Select a different design template.

i. Print the completed presentation in both outline and handout form. Submit both to your instructor.

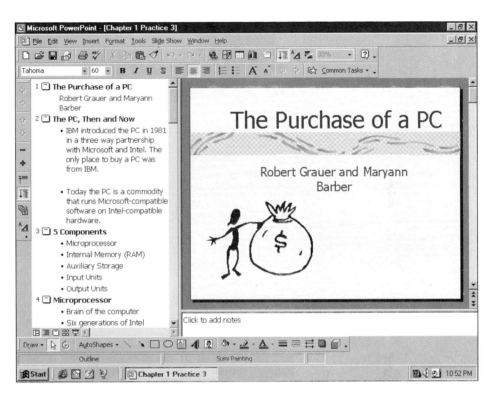

FIGURE 1.14   The Purchase of a PC (Exercise 3)

4. The Internet and the World Wide Web: A partially completed version of the presentation in Figure 1.15 can be found in the file *Chapter 1 Practice 4.* Open the presentation, then make the following changes:

a. Add your name and e-mail address on the title page.

b. Boldface and italicize the terms, *server, client,* and *browser* on slide 4. Boldface and italicize the acronyms, HTTP, HTTPS, HTML, and TCP/IP on slide 5.

c. Use Internet Explorer to go to your favorite Web page. Press the Print Screen key to capture the screen image of that page and copy it to the clipboard, then use the Windows taskbar to switch to PowerPoint. Click the Paste button on the Standard toolbar to paste the screen into the Power-Point presentation. Size the image as appropriate.

d. Double click the WordArt image on the last slide to open the WordArt application. Change the words *Thank You* to *The End.* Change the style of the WordArt in any other way you see fit.

e. Print the presentation in different ways. Print the outline of the entire presentation. Next, print the entire presentation to display six slides per page. Finally, select the first slide and print it as a slide to use as a cover page.

f. Submit your output to your instructor as proof you did this exercise.

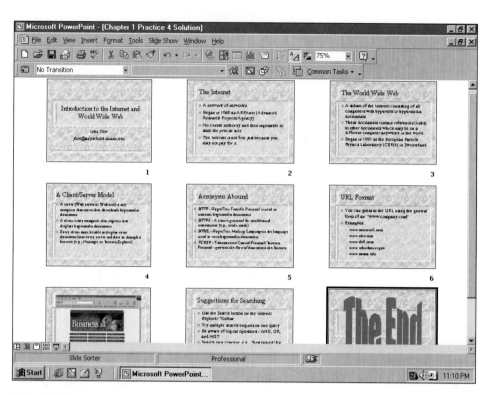

FIGURE 1.15 The Internet and the World Wide Web (Exercise 4)

5. **Visit the White House:** Create a presentation similar to the one in Figure 1.16. We have started the presentation for you and have saved it as *Chapter 1 Practice 5.* This presentation consists of three slides, a title slide, and two slides containing an object and text.

   a. Go to the White House Web site (www.whitehouse.gov). Click the link to White House History & Tours, then click the link to Presidents of the USA and select your favorite presidents. Point to the picture of the president, click the right mouse button to display a shortcut menu, then save the picture on your PC. Be sure you remember the location of the file when you save it on your local machine.

   b. You should still be at the White House Web site. Click the link to a familiar quotation from your president, then click and drag to select the text of that quotation. Pull down the Edit menu and click the Copy command to copy the selected text to the Windows clipboard (an area of memory that is available to every Windows application).

   c. Use the Windows taskbar to switch to PowerPoint. Select slide 2, the first slide containing bulleted text. Click in the text area, then click the Paste command on the Standard toolbar to paste the quotation into the slide. Click and drag the sizing handles that surround the text to make the box narrower in order to allow room for the president's picture. Click and drag a border of the text area to the right of the slide, again to make room for the president's picture.

   d. Click in the title area of the slide and add the president's name and years in office. Save the presentation.

   e. Click outside the text area. Pull down the Insert menu, click the Picture command, then click From File to display the Insert Picture dialog box. Enter the folder where you saved the file in step (a), then click the Insert button to insert the picture onto the slide. Move and size the picture as appropriate. Save the presentation.

f. Repeat these steps for a second president.

g. Create a title slide for the presentation with your name somewhere on the slide. Print all three slides and submit them to your instructor as proof you did this exercise.

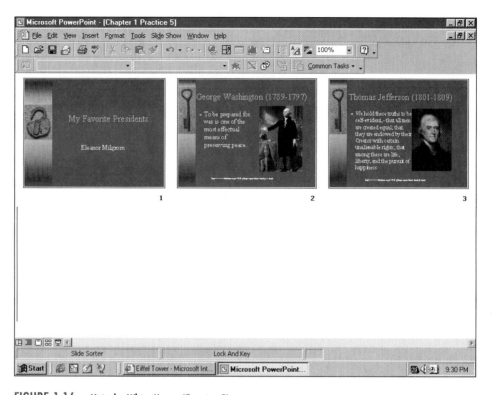

FIGURE 1.16   Visit the White House (Exercise 5)

6. The Travel Agent: Search the Web to select three different landmarks, download the picture of each, then create a short presentation consisting of a title slide plus three additional slides similar to the one in Figure 1.17. Be sure to include a reference to the Web page where you obtained each picture. Print the completed presentation for your instructor as proof you did this exercise.

7. Your Favorite Performer: The subject of a PowerPoint presentation is limited only by your imagination. Use any Internet search engine to locate information about your favorite singer or recording group, then download information about that person or group to create a presentation such as the one in Figure 1.18.

8. Companion Web Sites: Each book in the *Exploring Microsoft Office 2000* series is accompanied by an online study guide or Companion Web site. Start Internet Explorer and go to the Exploring Windows home page at www.prenhall.com/grauer. Click the book for Office 2000, click the link to student resources, click the Companion Web site tab at the top of the screen, then choose the appropriate text *(Exploring PowerPoint 2000)* and the chapter within the text (e.g., Chapter 1).

Each study guide contains a series of short-answer exercises (multiple-choice, true/false, and matching) to review the material in the chapter. You can take practice quizzes by yourself and/or e-mail the results to your instructor. You can try the essay questions for additional practice and engage in online chat sessions. We hope you will find the online guide to be a valuable resource.

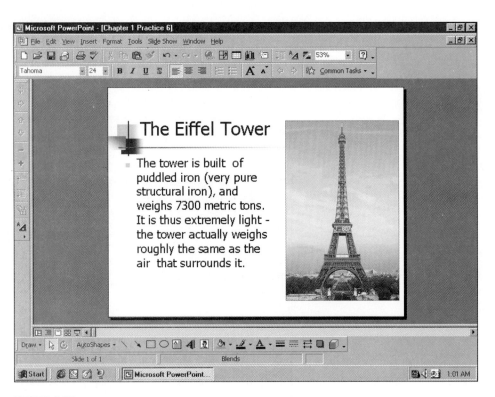

FIGURE 1.17   The Travel Agent (Exercise 6)

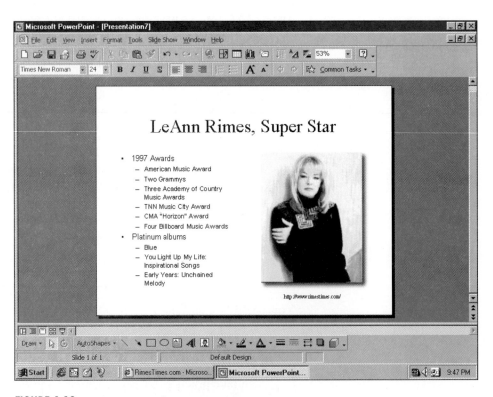

FIGURE 1.18   Your Favorite Performer (Exercise 7)

Planning for Disaster

This case has nothing to do with presentations per se, but it is perhaps the most important case of all, as it deals with the question of backup. Do you have a backup strategy? Do you even know what a backup strategy is? This is a good time to learn, because sooner or later you will need to recover a file. The problem always seems to occur the night before an assignment is due. You accidentally erased a file, are unable to read from a floppy disk, or worse yet suffer a hardware failure in which you are unable to access the hard drive. The ultimate disaster is the disappearance of your computer, by theft or natural disaster. Describe in 250 words or less the backup strategy you plan to implement in conjunction with your work in this class.

Changing Menus and Toolbars

Office 2000 implements one very significant change over previous versions of Office in that it displays a series of short menus that contain only basic commands. The additional commands are made visible by clicking the double arrow that appears at the bottom of the menu. New commands are added to the menu as they are used, and conversely, other commands are removed if they are not used. A similar strategy is followed for the Standard and Formatting toolbars which are displayed on a single row, and thus do not show all of the buttons at one time. The intent is to simplify Office 2000 for the new user by limiting the number of commands that are visible. The consequence, however, is that the individual is not exposed to new commands, and hence may not use Office to its full potential. Which set of menus do you prefer? How do you switch from one set to the other?

Microsoft Online

Help for Microsoft PowerPoint is available from two primary sources, the Office Assistant, and the Microsoft Web site at www.microsoft.com/powerpoint. The latter enables you to obtain more recent, and often more detailed information. You will find the answer to the most frequently asked questions and you can access the same knowledge base used by Microsoft support engineers. Experiment with both sources of help, then submit a summary of your findings to your instructor.

Be Creative

One interesting way of exploring the potential of presentation graphics is to imagine it might have been used by historical figures had it been available. Choose any historical figure or current personality and create at least a six-slide presentation. You could, for example, show how Columbus might have used PowerPoint to request funding from Queen Isabella, or how Elvis Presley might have pleaded for his first recording contract. The content of your presentation should be reasonable but you don't have to spend an inordinate amount of time on research. Just be creative and use your imagination. Use clip art as appropriate, but don't overdo it. Place your name on the title slide as technical adviser.

chapter 1

WELCOME TO CYBERSPACE: THE INTERNET AND WORLD WIDE WEB

OBJECTIVES

After reading this chapter you will be able to:

1. Describe the Internet and its history; explain how to access the Internet in your campus computing environment.

2. Describe the World Wide Web in the context of hypertext and hypermedia; distinguish between a Web server and a Web client.

3. Use Internet Explorer to access the World Wide Web; describe several similarities between Internet Explorer and other Windows applications.

4. Define a URL and give several specific examples; describe how to enter a Web address in Internet Explorer.

5. Define a hyperlink; explain why hyperlinks within the same document appear in different colors.

6. Describe the various buttons on the Internet Explorer toolbar.

7. Explain how to save the address of a favorite Web site and return to it later.

OVERVIEW

The Internet. You see the word on the cover of half the magazines on the newsstand. The media make continual reference to the Information Superhighway. Movie ads provide Internet addresses so you can download and view movie clips. Your friends at other colleges want to know your Internet e-mail address. But what exactly is the Internet, and how do you use it? Is the World Wide Web part of the Internet, or is it a separate entity? This chapter will answer these and other questions as you begin your journey through *cyberspace,* the term used to describe the invisible realm of the Internet.

We begin with a brief history of the Internet and World Wide Web. We describe how Web documents are accessed and created, and define basic terms such as HTTP (HyperText Transfer Protocol) and HTML (HyperText Markup Language).

The World Wide Web cannot be appreciated, however, until you visit it yourself. Thus, the chapter also introduces Internet Explorer, the browser that was developed by Microsoft. As always, learning is best accomplished by doing, and so we include two hands-on exercises and provide our own guided tour so that you can experience firsthand what the excitement is all about.

THE INTERNET

The *Internet* is a network of networks that connects computers across the country and around the world. It grew out of a U.S. Department of Defense (DOD) experimental project begun in 1969 to test the feasibility of a wide area (long distance) computer network over which scientists and military personnel could share messages and data. The country was in the midst of the Cold War, and the military imposed the additional requirement that the network be able to function with partial outages in times of national emergency (e.g., a nuclear disaster), when one or more computers in the network might be down.

The proposed solution was to create a network with no central authority. Each node (computer attached to the network) would be equal to all other nodes, with the ability to originate, pass, and receive messages. The path that a particular message took in getting to its destination would be insignificant. Only the final result was important, as the message would be passed from node to node until it arrived at its destination.

The experiment was (to say the least) enormously successful. Known originally as the *ARPAnet (Advanced Research Projects Agency network),* the original network of four computers has grown exponentially to include tens of millions of computers at virtually every major university and government agency, and an ever increasing number of private corporations and international sites. To say that the Internet is large is a gross understatement, but by its very nature, it's impossible to determine just how large it really is. How many networks there are, and how many users are connected to those networks, is of no importance as long as you yourself have access.

The Internet is a network of networks, but if that were all it were, there would hardly be so much commotion. It's what you can do on the Internet, coupled with the ease of access, that makes the Internet so exciting. In essence, the Internet provides two basic capabilities, information retrieval and worldwide communication, functions that are already provided by libraries and print media, the postal system and the telephone, television, and other types of long-distance media. The difference, however, is that the Internet is interactive in nature, and more importantly, it is both global and immediate.

TCP/IP

Data is transmitted from one computer to another across the Internet through a series of protocols known collectively as *TCP/IP* (Transmission Control Protocol/Internet Protocol). You can progress quite nicely through our text without knowing anything more about TCP/IP. We do, however, provide an appendix in case you are curious about the internal workings of the Internet.

The Internet enables you to request a document from virtually anywhere in the world, and to begin to receive that document almost instantly. No other medium lets you do that. Television, for example, has the capability to send information globally and in real time (while events are unfolding), but it is not interactive in that you cannot request a specific program. Federal Express promises overnight delivery, but that is hardly immediate. The books in a library provide access to the information that is physically in that library, but that is not global access. Indeed, the Internet, and in particular, the World Wide Web is truly unique.

THE WORLD WIDE WEB

The original language of the Internet was uninviting and difficult to use. The potential was exciting, but you had to use a variety of esoteric programs (such as Telnet, FTP, Archie, and Gopher) to locate and download data. The programs were based on the Unix operating system, and you had to know the precise syntax of the commands within each program. There was no common user interface to speed learning. And, even if you were able to find what you wanted, everything was communicated in plain text, as graphics and sound were not available. All of this changed in 1991 with the introduction of the World Wide Web.

The *World Wide Web* (WWW or, simply, the Web) can be thought of as a very large subset of the Internet, consisting of hypertext and/or hypermedia documents. A *hypertext document* is a document that contains a *hyperlink* (link) to another hypertext document, which may be on the same computer or even on a different computer, with the latter located anywhere in the world. *Hypermedia* is similar in concept, except that it provides links to graphic, sound, and video files in addition to text files.

Either type of document enables you to move effortlessly from one document (or computer) to another. Therein lies the fascination of the Web, in that you simply click on link after link to go effortlessly from one document to the next. You can start your journey at your professor's home page in New York, for example, which may link to a document in the Library of Congress, which in turn may take you to a different document, and so on. So, off you go to Washington DC, and from there to a reference across the country or perhaps around the world.

Any computer that stores a hypermedia document anywhere on the Web, and further, makes that document available to other computers, is known as a *server* (or *Web server*). Any computer that is connected to the Web, and requests a document from a server, is known as a *client.* In other words, you work on a client computer (e.g., a node on a local area network or your PC at home) and by clicking a link in a hypermedia document, you are requesting a document from a Web server.

HyperText Transfer Protocol (HTTP)

In order for the Web to work, every client (be it a PC or a Mac) must be able to display every document from every server. This is accomplished by imposing a set of standards known as a protocol to govern the way data is transmitted across the Web. Thus, data travels from client to server, and back, through a protocol known as the *HyperText Transfer Protocol* (or *http* for short). In addition, in order to access the documents that are transmitted through this protocol, you need a special type of program known as a *browser.* Indeed, a browser is aptly named because it enables you to inspect the Web in a leisurely and casual way (the dictionary definition of the word "browse"). *Internet Explorer 5.0* (IE5) is the browser we use throughout the text.

Consider, for example, the hypermedia documents in Figure 1.1. To display these documents on your computer, you would need to be connected to the Internet and you would need to know the address of the first document, in this case, www.refdesk.com. (Yes, it helps to know the addresses of interesting Web pages, and we suggest several sites to explore in Appendix B.) We describe the structure of Internet addresses later in the chapter, but for the time being, suffice it to say that every server, and every document on every server, has a unique address. The "http" that precedes the address indicates that the document is being transferred according to the hypertext transfer protocol we discussed earlier.

The first document displayed by a Web site is its *home page;* thus the document in Figure 1.1a is the home page of My Virtual Reference Desk and it is one of our favorite sites on the Web. Not only does it demonstrate the concept of hypertext, but by its very nature it elegantly shows the global nature of the World Wide Web. Once you arrive at a Web page, you can click any link that interests you.

Consider, for example, our path through Figure 1.1. We began by scrolling down the home page of My Virtual Reference Desk in Figure 1.1a until we could click the link to Fast Facts 1998, which in turn displayed the document in Figure 1.1b. Note how the address changes automatically in the address bar. Indeed, that is what the Web is all about as you move effortlessly from one document to another. We then clicked the link to CarPoint, which took us to an entirely different site in Figure 1.1c. Next, we clicked the link to Sports Cars to display the list of cars in Figure 1.1d. (The CarPoint home page provides graphical links as well as underlined text links; that is, each of the buttons on the left side of the page is a link to the respective category.) We clicked Corvette from the list of sports cars in Figure 1.1d then clicked an additional link to display the specific information about the new car in Figure 1.1e. We explored the various links on this page, and then ended with the Buying Service in Figure 1.1f.

The underlined links that appear in Figure 1.1 are displayed in one of two colors, blue or magenta, depending on whether or not the link has been previously selected. Any link in blue (the majority of links) indicates the document has not yet been viewed. Links in magenta, however (such as Fast Facts 1998 in Figure 1.1a), imply the associated document has been retrieved earlier in that session or in a previous session. Note, too, the presence of advertising on the Web in the CarPoint screens of Figures 1.1d and e. The vendors (1-800-FLOWERS and Barnes and Noble) pay the host of the site for advertising space in the hope of enticing the visitor to click the advertisement.

Think for a moment of what we have just accomplished. We started with a general reference page and in a matter of minutes were in the process of purchasing a new car. There is no beginning (other than the starting point or home page) and no end. You simply read a Web document in any way that makes sense to you, jumping to explore whatever topic you want to see next. All of this is accomplished with a graphical browser such as Internet Explorer and a connection between your computer and the Internet.

SEARCH ENGINES—A LOOK AHEAD

There are two very general ways to navigate through the Web. You can start by entering the address of a specific site such as www.refdesk.com, then once you arrive at the site, you can go leisurely from link to link. Browsing in this manner is interesting and enjoyable, but it is not always efficient. Hence, when searching for specific information, you often need a special tool called a search engine, with which you conduct a keyword search of the Web, much as you search a card catalog or online database in the library. Search engines are discussed in Chapter 2.

Address of document

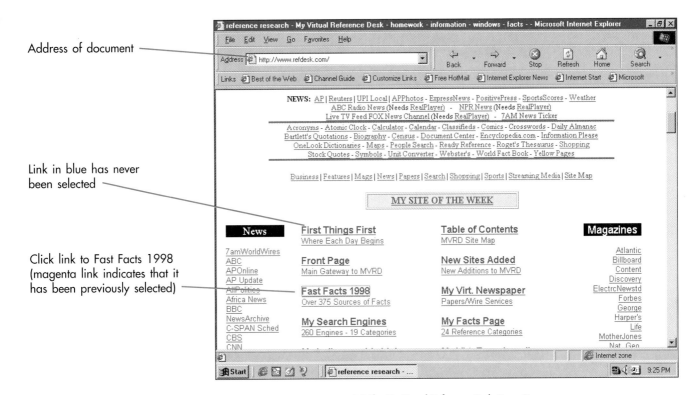

Link in blue has never been selected

Click link to Fast Facts 1998 (magenta link indicates that it has been previously selected)

(a) The My Virtual Reference Desk Home Page

Address has changed

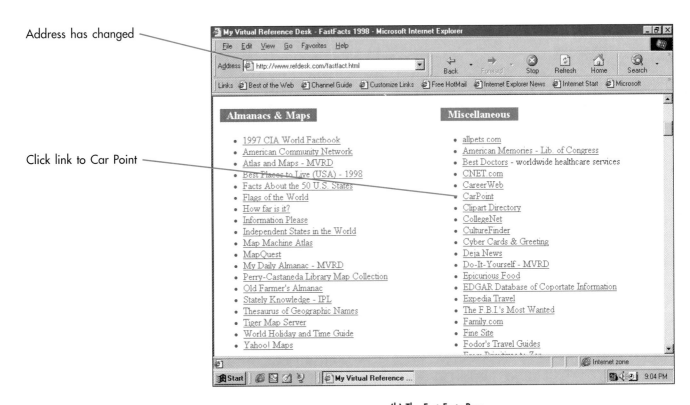

Click link to Car Point

(b) The Fast Facts Page

FIGURE 1.1   The World Wide Web

Address has changed

Click link to Sports Cars

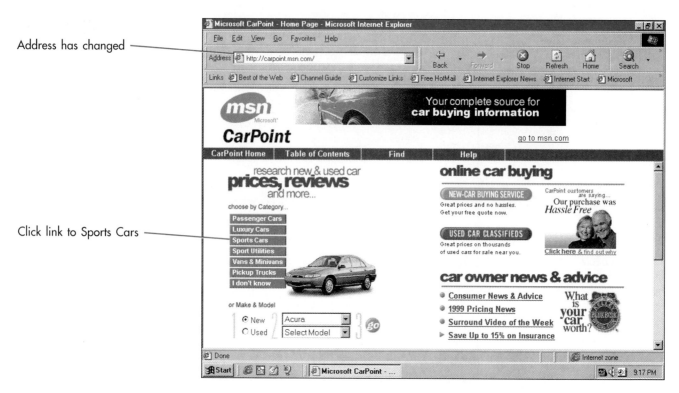

(c) The CarPoint Home Page

Ad from 1–800–FLOWERS

Click link to Corvette

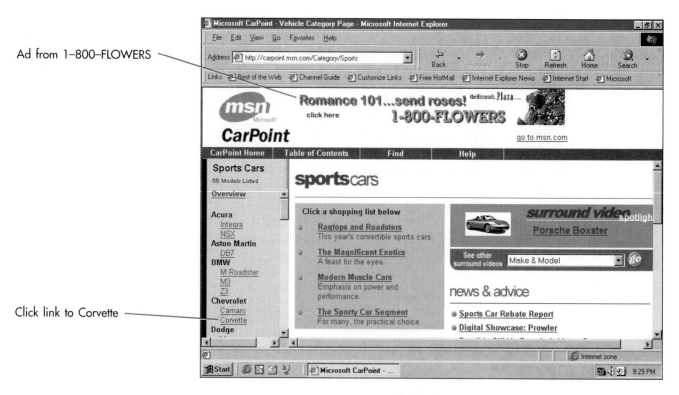

(d) Sports Cars

FIGURE 1.1   The World Wide Web (continued)

Ad from Barnes and Noble

Click link to Buying Service

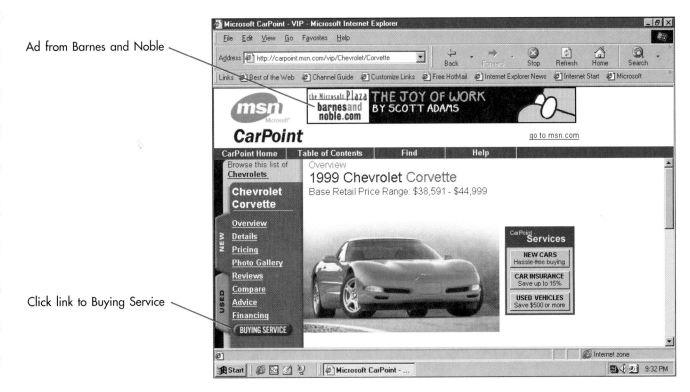

(e) The Chevrolet Corvette

Select the car

Choose the options

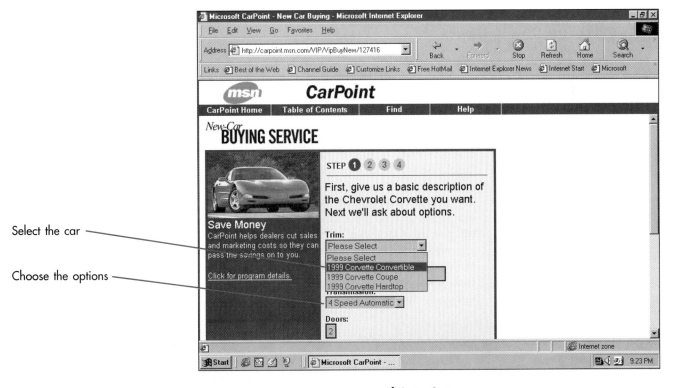

(f) Buying Service

FIGURE 1.1   The World Wide Web (continued)

Internet Explorer is easy to use because it shares the common user interface and consistent command structure present in every Windows application. Look, for example, at any of the screens in Figure 1.1 and you will see several familiar elements. These include the title bar, minimize, maximize (or restore), and close buttons. Commands are executed from pull-down menus or from command buttons that appear on a toolbar under the menu bar. A vertical and/or horizontal scroll bar appears if the entire document is not visible at one time. The title bar displays the name of the document you are currently viewing.

The Uniform Resource Locator (URL)

The location (or address) of the document appears in the *Address bar* and is known as a *Uniform Resource Locator* (URL), or more simply as a Web address. The URL is the primary means of navigating the Web, as it indicates the address of the Web server (computer) from which you have requested a document. Change the URL (e.g., by clicking a link or by entering a new address in the Address bar) and you jump to a different document, and possibly a different server.

A URL consists of several parts: the method of access, the Internet address of the Web server, an optional path in the directory (folder) structure on the Web server to the document, and finally the document name. (Some URLs do not include the document name, in which case the browser displays a default document, typically called index.html.) Each time you click a link, you are effectively entering a new address with which to connect. The general format of a Web address is:

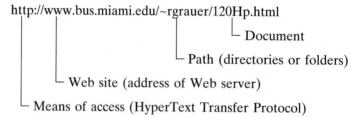

The components in the address can be read from right to left. In other words, the preceding address references the document 120Hp.html (the document name is case-sensitive) in the ~rgrauer directory on the Web server www.bus.miami.edu according to the http protocol. (This document is the home page for Bob's introductory computer course at the University of Miami.)

To go to a particular site, enter its address through the *Open command* in the File menu or type the address directly in the Address bar, press the enter key, and off you go. Once you arrive at a site, click the *hyperlinks* (underlined items or graphical icons) that interest you, which in turn will take you to other documents at that site or even at a different site. The resources on the Web are connected in such a way that you need not be concerned with where (on which computer) the linked document is located.

WHAT IS HTML?

All hypertext and hypermedia documents are written in HTML (HyperText Markup Language) and display the extension html at the end of the document name in the Web address. You will, however, see an extension of htm (rather than html) when a document is stored on a server that does not support long file names. Unix-based systems, which constitute the majority of Web servers, support long file names, and so html is the more common extension.

CONNECTING TO THE INTERNET

There are two basic ways to connect to the Internet—from a *local area network (LAN)* or by dialing in. It's much easier if you connect from a LAN (typically at school or work) since the installation and setup has been done for you, and all you have to do is follow the instructions provided by your professor. If you intend to dial in from home, however, you will need a modem and an Internet Service Provider. A *modem* is the hardware interface between your computer and the telephone. In essence you instruct the modem, via the appropriate software, to dial the phone number of your ISP, which in turn lets you access the Internet.

An *Internet Service Provider (ISP)* is a company or organization that maintains a computer with permanent access to the Internet. Typically, you have to pay for this service, but you may be able to dial into your school or university at no charge. If not, you need to sign up with a commercial vendor such as America Online (AOL). Not only does AOL provide access to the Internet, but it also offers a proprietary interface and other services such as local chat rooms. The Microsoft Network (MSN) is a direct competitor to AOL, and it, too, offers a proprietary interface and extra services. Alternatively, you can choose from a host of other vendors who provide Internet access without the proprietary interface of AOL or MSN.

Regardless of whom you choose as an ISP, be sure you understand the fee structure. The monthly fee may entitle you to a set number of hours per month (after which you pay an additional fee), or it may give you unlimited access. The terms vary widely, and we suggest you shop around for the best possible deal. In addition, be sure you are given a local access number (i.e., that you are not making a long-distance call), or else your telephone bill will be outrageous. Check that the facilities of your provider are adequate and that you can obtain access whenever you want. Few things are more frustrating than to receive continual busy signals when you are trying to log on.

DISABLE CALL WAITING

Your friend may understand if you excuse yourself in the middle of a conversation to answer another incoming call. A computer, however, is not so tolerant and will often break the current connection if another call comes in. Accordingly, check the settings of your communications program to disable call waiting prior to connecting to the Internet (typically by entering *70 in front of the access number). Your friends may complain of a busy signal, but you will be able to work without interruption.

LEARNING BY DOING

The Web cannot be appreciated until you experience it for yourself, and so we come to our first hands-on exercise, which takes you to the Web site of the national newspaper *USA Today*. You are accustomed to reading a newspaper in conventional fashion, perhaps with a morning cup of coffee. Now you can read that paper (and countless others) in an entirely different way. We suggest a specific starting point (the home page of *USA Today*) and a progression through that document. You will not, however, see the exact figures in our exercise because the Web is changing continually. Note, too, that you can start with any other home page and choose any set of links to capture the spirit of the exercise. Going from one document or link to the next is what the World Wide Web is all about. Enjoy.

Introduction to the World Wide Web

Objective: To access the Internet and World Wide Web and to practice basic commands in Internet Explorer. Use Figure 1.2 as a guide in the exercise.

STEP 1: Start Internet Explorer

➤ Click the **Start button,** click (or point to) **Programs,** click or point to **Internet Explorer** to display a cascaded menu listing various programs within Internet Explorer, then click **Internet Explorer.**

➤ If you do this exercise at school, you will most likely see the home page of your college or university. It does not matter which page you see initially as long as you are able to start Internet Explorer and connect to the Internet.

➤ If necessary, click the **maximize button** so that Internet Explorer takes the entire desktop. Enter the address of the *USA Today* site:

- Pull down the **File menu** and click the **Open command** to display the **Open** dialog box in Figure 1.2a. Enter the address of the Web site you want to explore—in this case, **www.usatoday.com** (you don't have to enter http:// as it is assumed). Click **OK.**

- *Or,* click in the **Address bar,** which automatically selects the current address. Enter **www.usatoday.com** (the http:// is assumed). Press **Enter.**

➤ Be sure you enter the address correctly.

University of Miami is the home page at our school

Enter address of Web site

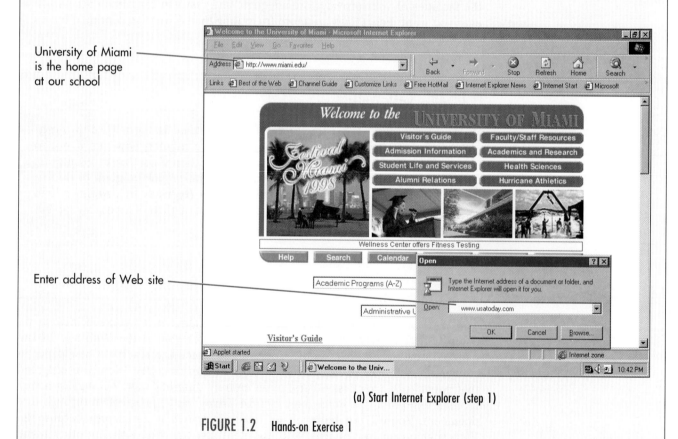

(a) Start Internet Explorer (step 1)

FIGURE 1.2   Hands-on Exercise 1

STEP 2: *USA Today*

➤ You should see the home page of *USA Today*, as shown in Figure 1.2b, although the content will surely be different. Note how the address you entered in the previous step appears in the Address bar.

➤ If you are unable to get to the *USA Today* site, pull down the **File menu,** click **Open,** and re-enter the address shown in the Address bar in Figure 1.2b. Press **Enter.**

➤ If you are still unable to get to the site, it may be because it is not available due to technical problems at the site. Enter the address of any other site you wish to explore. You will not be able to duplicate the remainder of the exercise exactly, but you will still be able to practice with Internet Explorer.

Address you entered in step 1 appears

Click link to Nationline

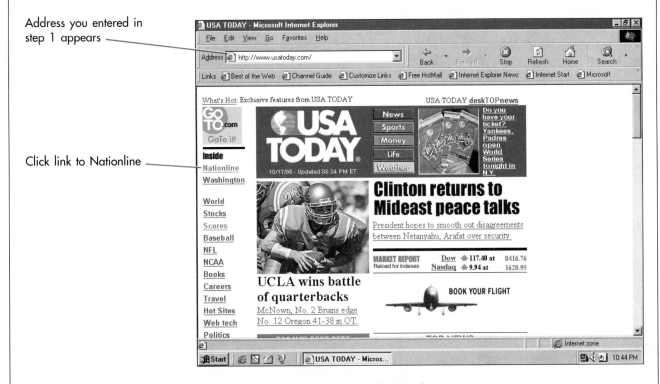

(b) USA Today (step 2)

FIGURE 1.2   Hands-on Exercise 1 (continued)

DIAL-UP NETWORKING

Connecting to the Internet can be frustrating, especially from home when you are using a dial-up connection. Starting Internet Explorer is supposed to activate your modem and initiate the Internet connection automatically. Occasionally, however, this does not happen and you have to create the connection manually. Open My Computer, open the Dial-Up Networking folder, then open the icon corresponding to your Internet Service Provider, which displays the Connect To dialog box. Click the Connect command button to dial the ISP and establish the connection.

STEP 3: Read the News

➤ This step assumes that you were able to connect to the *USA Today* site. Click the link to **Nationline** to displays today's national news. Scroll down the page to view the news.

➤ You should see a page similar to Figure 1.2c, which displays the top national news stories, each of which in turn has additional links.

➤ Choose a story to read, click the link to **Full Story** to read the full article, then click the **Back button** to return to the original page. The link to the document you just selected has changed color (e.g., from blue to magenta on our page) to indicate that you have viewed the associated page.

➤ Continue to browse through the newspaper to view the day's events. Note how the address changes each time you go to a different page, and further how the colors of various links change to reflect pages that have been visited.

Back button

Click link to Full story

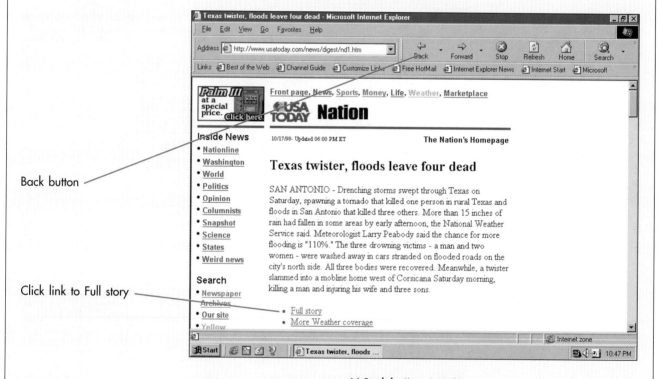

(c) Read the News (step 3)

FIGURE 1.2   Hands-on Exercise 1 (continued)

CHANGE THE FONT

The Web designer selects the font size he or she deems most appropriate. You can, however, change the font size of the displayed page to display more or less information as you see fit. Pull down the View menu and click the Fonts command to display a menu with five different sizes. The sizes are relative (from smallest to largest) as opposed to a specific point size. Click the size you prefer, and the display changes automatically.

STEP 4: Print a Web Page

➤ If necessary, pull down the **View menu,** click the **Toolbars command,** and check the **Standard buttons, Address Bar,** and **Links** commands so that your toolbars match ours.

➤ Return to the *USA Today* home page. You can click the **Back button** repeatedly until you are back to the desired page. It's easier, however, to click the **down arrow** on the **Back button** and select the desired page directly from the list of pages that were visited this session.

➤ Pull down the **File menu** and click the **Print command** to display the **Print** dialog box common to all Windows applications. Click the **All option button** as shown in Figure 1.2d to print all of the pages, then click the **OK button** to print the document and submit it to your instructor as proof you did this exercise.

Click All option button

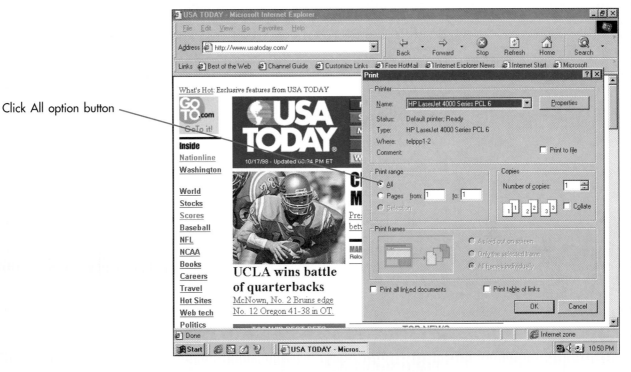

(d) Print a Web Page (step 4)

FIGURE 1.2   Hands-on Exercise 1 (continued)

THE BACK AND FORWARD BUTTONS

The Back and Forward buttons track your progress through any given session of Internet Explorer. Click the Back button at any time to return to the previous page or click the Forward button to move in the other direction. Click the down arrow on either button to see the complete set of pages that were accessed in that session.

STEP 5: View the Source Code

➤ Pull down the **View menu** and click **Source** to display the underlying HTML for the page you are viewing. You will see a document similar to that in Figure 1.2e. Maximize the window.

➤ You need not understand the syntax of the HTML document. Indeed, that is the beauty of Internet Explorer as it interprets the HTML statements for you. Click the **Close button** to close the source document and return to the normal view.

HTML Code

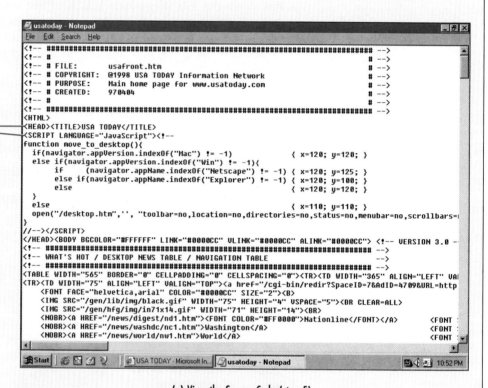

(e) View the Source Code (step 5)

FIGURE 1.2 Hands-on Exercise 1 (continued)

STEP 6: Surf the Net

➤ You've done what we have asked and have gotten a taste of what the World Wide Web has to offer.

➤ Now it's time to explore on your own by going to new and different sites. Accordingly, pull down the **Favorites menu,** click **Links,** then click **Best of the Web** to display the screen in Figure 1.2f.

➤ We don't know what you will find, but you can expect something interesting. Click the hyperlinks that interest you and off you go. Use the **Print command** to print an additional page from a second site to prove to your instructor that you did the exercise.

➤ Set a time limit for yourself, as the Web is addicting and you have other work to do. Close Internet Explorer when you are finished exploring. Shut down your computer if you do not wish to do the next exercise at this time.

Best of the Web button ——

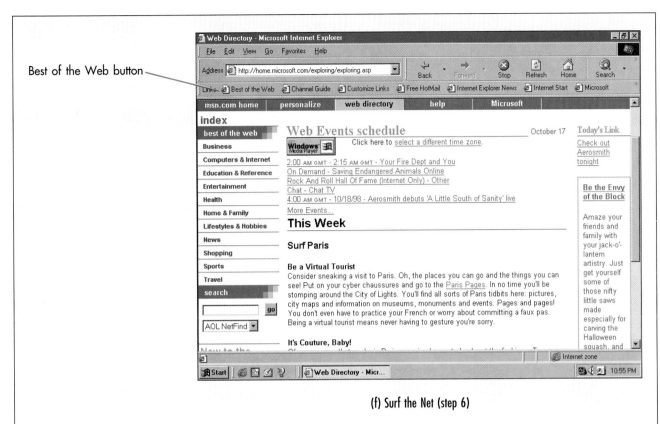

(f) Surf the Net (step 6)

FIGURE 1.2   Hands-on Exercise 1 (continued)

GUESS THE URL

You can often guess the address of a site according to a consistent addressing scheme—www.company.com. The address of the Lycos and Yahoo search engines (www.lycos.com and www.yahoo.com) both follow this pattern. So do the home pages of many companies—for example, www.netscape.com and www.microsoft.com for Netscape and Microsoft, respectively. And if you are in the mood for sports, try www.nfl.com or www.nba.com to go to the home page of the National Football League or National Basketball Association.

INTERNET EXPLORER 5.0

We trust that you enjoyed the hands-on exercise and that you completed it without difficulty. Our objective was to get you up and running as quickly as possible so that you could experience the Web and appreciate its potential. Internet Explorer 5.0 (IE5) is easy to use because it is a Windows-based program that follows the common user interface. The next several pages examine Internet Explorer in more detail to help you use the program effectively.

Figure 1.3a displays the home page of Microsoft Corporation as it appears with the default settings of Internet Explorer. Figure 1.3b displays a different view of the same page (the address is the same in both figures) in order to illustrate additional features within Internet Explorer. The most obvious difference between

Menu bar

Address bar

Links toobar

Hot Spot

Link

Status bar

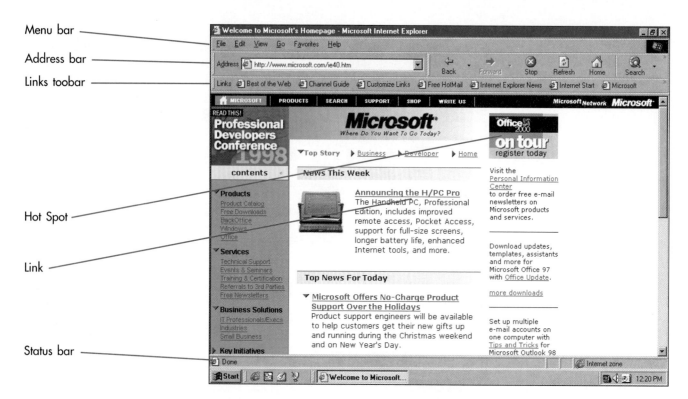

(a) Default Options

Menu bar

Address bar

Standard Buttons toolbar
(graphic icons only)

No graphics are displayed

Status bar

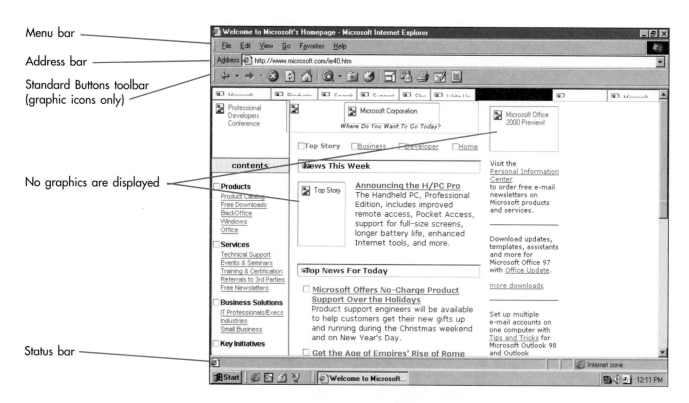

(b) Custom Options

FIGURE 1.3   Internet Explorer

the two is the display or omission of the graphics, which enhance the appearance of a page, but increase the time it takes to download the page and display it on your PC. The presence or absence of the graphics is controlled through the *Internet Options command* in the *Tools menu,* one of several pull-down menus within Internet Explorer.

The *menu bar* provides access to all commands within Internet Explorer. Some menus (File, Edit, View, and Help) are common to most Windows applications, whereas others (Go and Favorites) are unique to Internet Explorer. The *Favorites menu* is especially important, as it enables you to store the addresses of your favorite pages in order to return to those pages at a later date.

The *Help menu* in Internet Explorer is similar to that of other applications. The Contents and Index command presents a tabbed dialog box with three tabs—Contents, Index, and Search. The Help menu also provides a link to online support, which takes you to the Microsoft Web site that contains up-to-the-minute information. Help is illustrated in detail in the hands-on exercise that follows shortly.

The *toolbars* offer an alternate way to execute the most common commands. The *Standard Buttons toolbar* in Figure 1.3a displays both text and graphic icons. The Standard Buttons toolbar in Figure 1.3b, however, displays only the graphic icons and thus provides additional space within the Internet Explorer window to view the actual document. The appearance of the toolbar is controlled through the Toolbars command in the View menu.

The *Address bar* displays the address of the page you are currently viewing (http://www.microsoft.com in both Figure 1.3a and 1.3b), and its contents change automatically whenever you click a hyperlink to a different page. You can also click in the Address bar to enter an address manually, after which you press the Enter key to access that page.

Links (short for hyperlinks) and *hot spots* provide connections to other documents. A link appears as underlined text. Hot spots are hyperlinks that have been embedded within a graphic (e.g., Office 2000 on Tour in Figure 1.3a) as opposed to appearing as underlined text. The mouse pointer changes to a hand when pointing to a link or hot spot.

The *status bar* at the bottom of the window displays information about the current operation. If, for example, Internet Explorer is in the process of retrieving a document, the status bar will show the progress of the file transfer, such as "Done" in Figure 1.3a. Alternatively, the status bar will display the underlying address whenever you are pointing to a link or hot spot.

Returning to a Previous Site

Internet Explorer enables you to move effortlessly from one Web document to another. As you browse through the Web, it's all too easy to forget how you arrived at a particular site, making it difficult to return to that site at a later time. You could click the *Back button* repeatedly, but that is somewhat tedious, and further, it works only for the particular session. What if you wanted to return to a site you visited last Monday? Internet Explorer anticipates the problem and provides two different sets of links, the Favorites list and the History list.

The *Favorites list* in Figure 1.4a consists of sites that you save with the expectation of returning to those sites at a future time. Once you arrive at a site that you consider special, just pull down the Favorites menu and click the Add to Favorites command. Internet Explorer then creates a link to that site within the Favorites list. The links can be stored individually (e.g., NTSB - Home Page), or they can be stored with related links in a folder (e.g., Microsoft Links). The typical user starts by creating individual links, then eventually opts for folders to organize the links more efficiently.

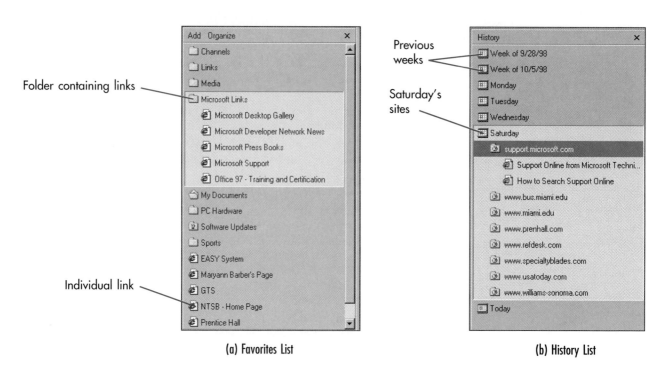

Folder containing links

Individual link

Previous weeks

Saturday's sites

(a) Favorites List

(b) History List

FIGURE 1.4 Returning to a Previous Site

The **History list** in Figure 1.4b is even easier to use in that the links are created automatically and consist of all sites that were visited during a specified time span. (The default is 20 days.) The links in the History list are organized automatically into subfolders, one for today, one for each day of the current week, then a separate folder for previous weeks. The links are further divided to show the site (e.g., www.microsoft.com), then the pages at that site.

Either list can be displayed by clicking the appropriate button on the Standard Buttons toolbar. The lists can also be accessed via the **Explorer bar command** in the View menu. In either case, the browser window is divided into two panes. The left pane displays the links in a specific list (such as History or Favorites). The right pane displays the selected Web page. The Explorer bar is illustrated in our next exercise.

SET A TIME LIMIT

The exercise you are about to do has you browse continually, looking for interesting sites on which to hone your skills. We warn you that the Web is addictive, and that once you start surfing, it is difficult to stop. We suggest, therefore, that you set a time limit before you begin, and that you stick to it when the time has expired. Tomorrow is another day, with new places to explore.

Finer Points of Internet Explorer

Objective: Practice the basic commands in Internet Explorer as you surf the Internet and World Wide Web. Use Figure 1.5 as a guide in the exercise.

STEP 1: Customize Internet Explorer

➤ Start Internet Explorer as you did in the first exercise. It doesn't matter which page you see initially (our figure displays the home page for our school) as long as you are able to connect to the Internet and start Internet Explorer.

➤ Pull down the **View menu,** click (or point to) the **Toolbar command,** then verify that the **Standard buttons** and **Address bar** commands are toggled on (have a check), and that the Links command is off (does not have a check).

- Each command functions as a toggle switch; that is, click the command and a check appears. Click the command a second time and the check disappears. You have to pull down the **View menu** once for each command.

- Click and drag the **move handle** at the left of the **Standard buttons** toolbar so that the toolbar appears below the address bar.

➤ Your screen should match Figure 1.5a (although you will be looking at a different Web site).

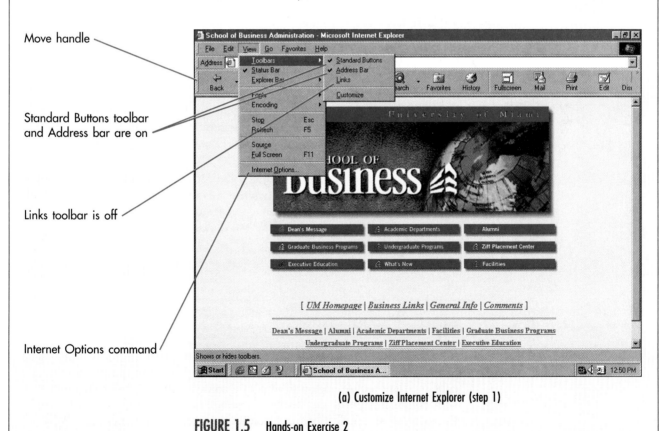

Move handle

Standard Buttons toolbar and Address bar are on

Links toolbar is off

Internet Options command

(a) Customize Internet Explorer (step 1)

FIGURE 1.5   Hands-on Exercise 2

➤ Pull down the **Tools menu** a final time, click the **Internet Options command** to display the **Internet Options** dialog box, and click the **Advanced tab.**

➤ Scroll until you can clear the **Show pictures** check box (in the Multimedia section), then click **OK** to accept the new setting and close the dialog box.

➤ The graphic images on the displayed page are still visible because the page was displayed prior to changing the settings. Click the **Refresh button** on the toolbar to reload the page.

➤ Graphic icons replace the graphic images. The page is not as attractive as before, but subsequent pages will display faster because the graphics do not have to be downloaded.

THE LINKS BAR

The Links bar provides shortcuts to interesting Web sites as selected by Microsoft. The Best of the Web page is an excellent starting point as it takes you to a generalized page with additional links in a variety of categories. Pull down the View menu, click (or point to) the Toolbars command, then toggle the Links toolbar on. Click and drag the move handle to position the Links toolbar as you see fit.

STEP 2: Restore the Pictures

➤ Click in the **Address bar** and enter **www.refdesk.com** (the http:// is assumed) as shown in Figure 1.5b. The page displays with graphic icons, rather than the graphic images, but it is displayed more quickly than if the pictures were included.

➤ Point to any icon, click the **right mouse button** to display a context-sensitive menu, then click the **Show Picture command** to display this image. You can display individual images in this fashion, or you can reset the options to display all graphics automatically. We opt for the latter.

➤ Pull down the **Tools menu,** click the **Internet Options command** to display the **Internet Options** dialog box, click the **Advanced tab,** then check the **Show Pictures** check box to display graphic images on subsequent pages. Click **OK** to accept the new settings and close the dialog box.

➤ Click the **Refresh button** (or press the **F5 key**) to reload the current page from the Web site. The graphic icons are replaced by graphic images.

THE RIGHT MOUSE BUTTON

The right mouse button is one of the most powerful shortcuts in all of Windows. Point to any object in (virtually) any Windows application then click the right mouse button to display a context-sensitive (shortcut) menu with commands pertaining to that object. The button works in Internet Explorer, in all applications in Microsoft Office, and in many other Windows applications.

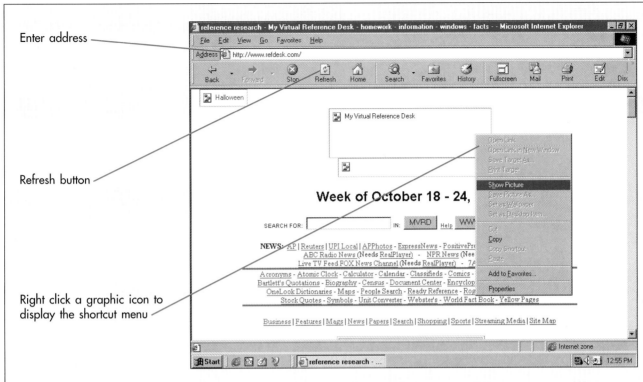

Enter address

Refresh button

Right click a graphic icon to display the shortcut menu

(b) Restore the Pictures (step 2)

FIGURE 1.5   Hands-on Exercise 2 (continued)

HIDE THE TASKBAR

You can hide the Windows taskbar to gain additional space within the Internet Explorer window. Right click an empty area of the taskbar to display a context-sensitive menu, click Properties to display the Taskbar properties dialog box, and, if necessary, click the Taskbar Options tab. Check the box to Auto Hide the taskbar, then click OK to accept the change and close the dialog box. The taskbar disappears from the screen but will reappear automatically as you point to the bottom edge of the window. You can cancel the command to Auto Hide the taskbar by reversing the steps just described.

STEP 3: Add a Favorite

➤ Pull down the **Favorites menu** and click the **Add to Favorites command** to display the dialog box in Figure 1.5c. Internet Explorer provides a default name for the page, but you can enter a more descriptive name if you prefer.

➤ Click **OK** to close the dialog box and add the page to your list of favorite sites.

➤ Visit one or two additional sites, then add those sites to your list of favorites in similar fashion. We went to **encyclopedia.com** (which we reached from the Reference Desk home page), **www.nfl.com** (the home page of the National Football League), and **thomas.loc.gov** (the Congressional Web site).

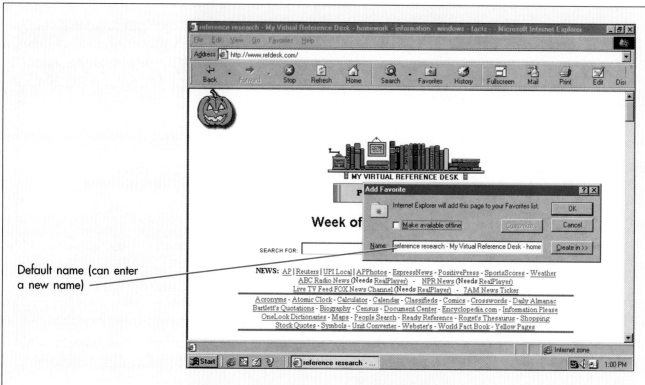

Default name (can enter a new name)

(c) Add a Favorite (step 3)

FIGURE 1.5   Hands-on Exercise 2 (continued)

ORGANIZE YOUR FAVORITES

It doesn't take long before the Favorites menu becomes cluttered with multiple entries, making it difficult to move quickly to a specific site. Pull down the Favorites menu and click the Organize Favorites command to display the Organize Favorites dialog box. From here, you can delete entries you no longer use or rename entries so that they are more meaningful. You can also create folders to organize sites into categories and then move entries into these folders. Use the Help menu for additional information.

STEP 4: The Favorites List

➤ Pull down the **View menu,** click (or point to) the **Explorer Bar command,** then click **Favorites** (or click the **Favorites button** on the toolbar).

➤ The Explorer bar opens at the left side of the browser window, displaying the Favorites list, as shown in Figure 1.5d. Click any of the listed favorites (those sites you added in step 3) to return to the site.

➤ Click and drag the vertical line that separates the Explorer bar from the Web page as appropriate. Click the **Close button** in the Favorites list to close the Explorer bar.

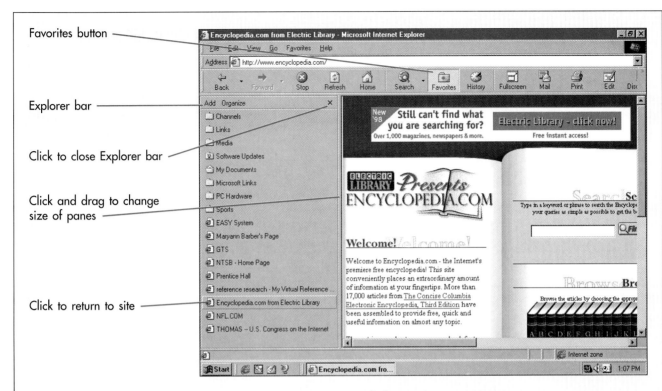

Favorites button

Explorer bar

Click to close Explorer bar

Click and drag to change size of panes

Click to return to site

(d) The Favorites List (step 4)

FIGURE 1.5   Hands-on Exercise 2 (continued)

CHANGE THE START PAGE

You can set Internet Explorer to display a specific page whenever the program is started initially. Pull down the Tools menu, click the Internet Options command, then click the General tab. Click in the Address text box and enter the address of the desired page (e.g., www.usatoday.com to display the home page for the newspaper). Click OK to close the dialog box. The next time you start Internet Explorer, it will display the indicated page.

STEP 5: The Help Menu

➤ Pull down the **Help menu** and click the **Contents and Index command** to display the Help window. If necessary, click the **Contents tab** to see a list of major help topics, each of which is represented by a book. Maximize the window.

➤ Click the icon next to **Finding the Web Sites You Want,** then click the topic **Find pages you've recently visited** to display this information in the right pane as in Figure 1.5e. (You can also click an open book to close it.)

➤ Click the **Index tab,** click in the text box, then enter the first several letters of the topic you want, such as "History" if you are searching for information on the Explorer bar.

➤ The index represents an alternate way to find the information. Click the **Close button** to exit Help.

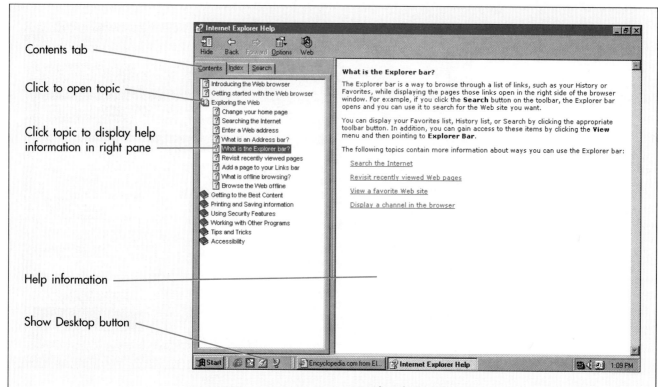

Contents tab

Click to open topic

Click topic to display help information in right pane

Help information

Show Desktop button

(e) The Help Menu (step 5)

FIGURE 1.5   Hands-on Exercise 2 (continued)

THE SHOW DESKTOP BUTTON

Windows 98 introduced the Show Desktop button that minimizes all open windows with a single click. The button functions as a toggle switch. Click it once, and all windows are minimized. Click it a second time, and the open windows are restored. If you do not see the Show Desktop button, right click a blank area of the taskbar to display a context-sensitive menu, click Toolbars, then check the Quick Launch toolbar, which contains the Show Desktop button.

STEP 6: Online Support

➤ Internet Explorer takes help to a new level by providing current information online via a Web site. Pull down the **Help menu** and click **Online Support** to display a screen similar to Figure 1.5f. You will not see the exact screen because Microsoft is continually changing its site.

➤ This page allows you to search the Microsoft Knowledge Base for information on any Microsoft product. Add this page to your list of favorites because it is invaluable.

➤ Select a product. Click the **option button** to **Ask a question using Natural Language Search.** (Click **example** to see additional information on how to conduct a search.)

➤ Enter a question about that product. Click the links that are presented to see if your question is answered. Visit the site for a few minutes, then continue with the next step when you are ready.

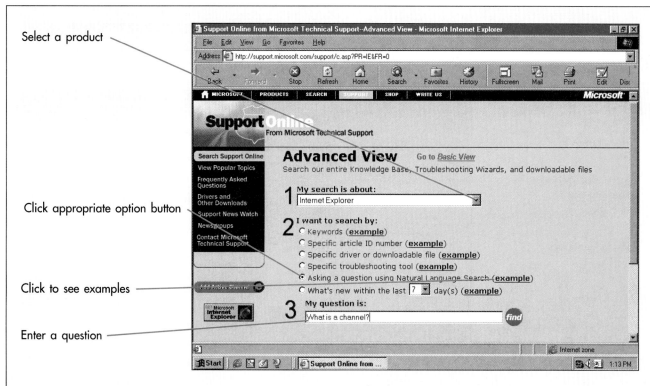

Select a product

Click appropriate option button

Click to see examples

Enter a question

(f) Online Support (step 6)

FIGURE 1.5   Hands-on Exercise 2 (continued)

PUT A WEB SHORTCUT ON THE DESKTOP

A shortcut is a Windows tool that takes you directly to a Web page or other object. Point to an empty area on the Windows desktop, click the right mouse button to display a shortcut menu, click the New command, then click Shortcut to display the Shortcut dialog box. Enter a Web address (e.g., www.nba.com), enter a name for the shortcut, then click Finish to close the dialog box and display a shortcut icon on the desktop. You can also create a shortcut from within Internet Explorer by pulling down the File menu, clicking the Send command, then clicking Shortcut to Desktop. Either way, you can open the shortcut (an icon with a "jump" arrow) to start Internet Explorer and display the indicated Web page.

STEP 7: The History List

➤ Click the **History button** on the toolbar to display the History list in Figure 1.5g. The dates and sites you see will be different from ours, but you should see all of the sites you visited in this session.

➤ Click the icon next to any site, such as support.microsoft.com, to display the pages you viewed at the site. Click the link to any page and it is displayed on your monitor.

➤ Click the **Close button** to close the Explorer bar. Close Internet Explorer when you have finished browsing.

➤ Welcome to cyberspace!

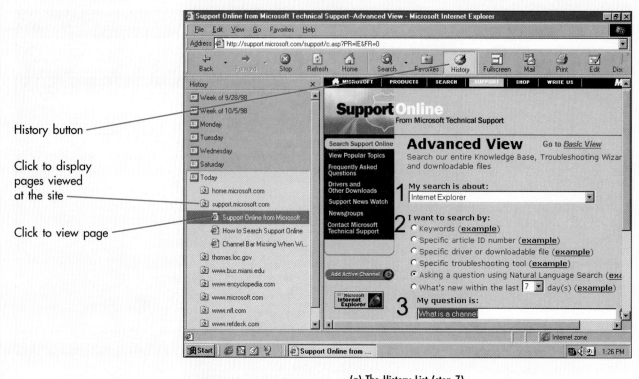

History button

Click to display
pages viewed
at the site

Click to view page

(g) The History List (step 7)

FIGURE 1.5   Hands-on Exercise 2 (continued)

WHAT IS CACHE?

A cache stores the Web pages you have accessed on your PC in an attempt
to improve performance. The pages are stored in two phases—in RAM
and on the hard drive. The first time you request a page, it is downloaded
from a Web server, which, depending on the size of the page and the traffic on the Internet, can take considerable time. The next time you request
the page, Internet Explorer checks to see if it is already in cache (in memory, then disk), and if so, displays it from there. This explains why it takes
several seconds (or longer) to display a page initially, and why the same
page appears almost instantly if you return to it later in the session.

SUMMARY

The Internet is a network of networks. The World Wide Web (WWW or simply
the Web) is a very large subset of the Internet, consisting of hypertext and/or
hypermedia documents.

A hypertext document is a document that contains a link to another document, which may be on the same computer or a different computer, with the latter located anywhere in the world. Hypermedia provides links to graphic, sound,
and video files in addition to text files. All hypertext and hypermedia documents
are written in HyperText Markup Language (HTML).

The Web uses a client/server model in which every client must be able to display every document from every server. A computer that stores (and provides access to) a hypermedia document is called a server. A computer that requests a document is called a client. Data travels from server to client and back through a protocol known as the HyperText Transfer Protocol (or HTTP for short).

A program known as a browser is required to view documents transmitted through the HTTP protocol. Internet Explorer 5.0 is the browser included in Microsoft Office 2000.

Internet Explorer is easy to use because it shares the common user interface and consistent command structure present in every Windows application. Commands are executed from pull-down menus or from command buttons that appear on a toolbar under the menu bar.

The location (or address) of the Web page appears in the Address bar and is known as a Uniform Resource Locator (URL). A URL consists of several parts: the method of access, the Internet address of the Web server, the path in the directory (folder) structure on the Web server to that document, and the name of the document.

There are two basic ways to connect to the Internet—from a local area network (LAN), or by dialing in. To dial in—for example, to connect from home—you need an Internet Service Provider, a company or information service that enables you to access the Internet via a modem.

Your exploration of the World Wide Web is limited only by your imagination. You can obtain a list of interesting sites to visit by clicking various links on the Links toolbar. Alternatively, you can enter the address of a specific site directly in the Address bar.

Internet Explorer provides two different ways to return to previous sites—the Favorites list and the History list. The links in the Favorites list are added by the user through the Favorites menu. The links in the History list are created automatically by IE4 and are organized into folders—one folder for today's sites, one folder for each day of the current week, then a separate folder for previous weeks. Either list can be displayed by clicking the appropriate button on the standard toolbar.

KEY WORDS AND CONCEPTS

Address bar
Advanced Research
    Projects Agency
    network (ARPAnet)
Back button
Browser
Cache
Client
Cyberspace
Dial-up networking
Explorer bar
Favorites list
Favorites menu
Forward button
Help menu
History list
Home page

Hot spot
Hyperlink
Hypermedia
Hypertext
HyperText Markup
    Language (HTML)
HyperText Transfer
    Protocol (HTTP)
IE4
Internet
Internet Explorer
Internet Service
    Provider (ISP)
Link
Links bar
Local area network
    (LAN)

Menu bar
Modem
Open command
Protocol
Search engine
Server
Status bar
TCP/IP
Toolbar
Uniform Resource
    Locator (URL)
Web server
World Wide Web
    (WWW)

1. Which of the following statements about the Internet is true?
   (a) The Internet and World Wide Web are one and the same
   (b) The Internet is accessed by millions of people, the exact number of which is impossible to determine
   (c) The Internet is maintained and administered by the federal government
   (d) All of the above

2. Which of the following is the central authority of the Internet?
   (a) The Department of Defense
   (b) The Advanced Research Projects Agency
   (c) The Central Intelligence Agency
   (d) None of the above

3. All Web documents are created in
   (a) HyperText Transfer Protocol (HTTP)
   (b) HyperText Markup Language (HTML)
   (c) Transmission Control Protocol (TCP)
   (d) Internet Protocol (IP)

4. Which of the following statements about the World Wide Web is true?
   (a) It has been in existence since the beginning of the Internet
   (b) It is a subset of the Internet consisting of hypertext and hypermedia documents
   (c) It can be accessed only through Internet Explorer
   (d) All of the above

5. Which of the following are found in the Internet Explorer window?
   (a) The minimize, close, and maximize (or restore) buttons
   (b) Vertical and horizontal scroll bars
   (c) A title bar
   (d) All of the above

6. Which of the following best describes the links in a typical Web document?
   (a) All of the links on a given page will always appear in one color
   (b) They are in capital letters
   (c) They are restricted to accessing documents on the same Web server as the current page
   (d) None of the above

7. Which of the following best describes the links in a typical Web document?
   (a) They are in different colors depending on whether or not they have been previously accessed
   (b) They are underlined and/or embedded within a graphic
   (c) They may access documents on different computers
   (d) All of the above

8. Which of the following indicates the address of the current Web document?
   (a) The title bar
   (b) The URL in the Address bar
   (c) The status bar at the bottom of the Internet Explorer window
   (d) All of the above

9. Which of the following were suggested in conjunction with connecting to the Internet through a dial-up connection?
   (a) Enabling call waiting so that you can still speak to anyone trying to call you as you work at the computer
   (b) Having a monthly service plan with multiple ISPs to maximize your chance of getting through
   (c) Ensuring that you have a local number to avoid long-distance charges
   (d) All of the above

10. When, if ever, would you want to suppress the display of images within a Web document?
    (a) To enhance the effectiveness of a search
    (b) To protect yourself against copyright infringement
    (c) To save time when the document is downloaded
    (d) None of the above

11. What is the likeliest address of IBM's home page?
    (a) ibm@internet.com
    (b) www.ibm.com
    (c) www.ibm.edu
    (d) internet.ibm.com

12. What is the best way to save the address of a page you want to visit in a future session of Internet Explorer?
    (a) Use the Go menu to return to the site
    (b) Use the Favorites menu to create a permanent record of the address
    (c) Enter the address in the Address bar near the top of the Internet Explorer window, then click the Save button on the toolbar
    (d) Pull down the File menu, select the Open command, then specify the address in the resulting dialog box

13. Which of the following is generally the first document displayed at a Web site?
    (a) The home page
    (b) The root
    (c) The search form
    (d) The gopher server

14. Which of the following is true about the links in the History and Favorites list?
    (a) Links are added automatically by IE4 to the History list
    (b) Links are added automatically by IE4 to the Favorites list
    (c) Both (a) and (b) above
    (d) Neither (a) nor (b) above

15. A hyperlink may point to
(a) A sound file
(b) A text file
(c) A video file
(d) Any of the above

ANSWERS

1. b	**6.** d	**11.** b
2. d	**7.** d	**12.** b
3. b	**8.** b	**13.** a
4. b	**9.** c	**14.** a
5. d	**10.** c	**15.** d

PRACTICE WITH THE INTERNET

1. Visit a National Park: Go to the National Parks Service (www.nps.gov/) as shown in Figure 1.6 and plan a (hypothetical) trip. Browse through the site until you come to a park you want to visit, then print one or more pages with the information you need. (Please limit the number of printed pages to two in respect for our nation's forests.) Add a cover page with your name, class, and today's date, then submit all of the material to your instructor as proof that you did this exercise.

2. News on the Net: Online publishing is becoming a very competitive area on the Web, as almost every major magazine and newspaper has its own Web site. One easy way to access a host of these sites is through the Pathfinder service provided by Time Warner (www.pathfinder.com) as shown in Figure 1.7. Explore the site of your favorite magazine, then summarize your findings in a brief note to your instructor. You can extend the exercise to your local newspaper. Do you think that online news will replace the morning newspaper or printed magazine?

3. Sports on the Web: The NBA home page in Figure 1.8 is one of our favorite sites and one we visit frequently throughout the course of the season. Every sport, and indeed every team, has its own home page. Football and soccer fans should visit the National Football League and FIFA at www.nfl.com and www.fifa.com, respectively. ESPN (the television network) maintains a site at espnet.sportszone.com. You can also try the site at www.cnnsi.com, which is a joint effort by CNN and *Sports Illustrated*. Choose any of these sites, or find your own, then summarize your findings in a one-page note to your instructor.

4. The Census Bureau: What is the current population of the United States? You can find the answer to this and many other questions at the official Web site of the U. S. Census Bureau as shown in Figure 1.9. Go to this site, answer our question, then explore the site to see what additional information is available. You can also visit the Congressional Web site at thomas.loc.gov. (The site is named for Thomas Jefferson, the third president of the United States.) Summarize your findings in a brief note to your instructor.

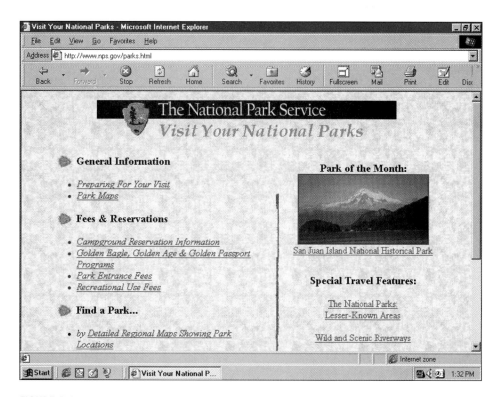

FIGURE 1.6   Visit a National Park (Exercise 1)

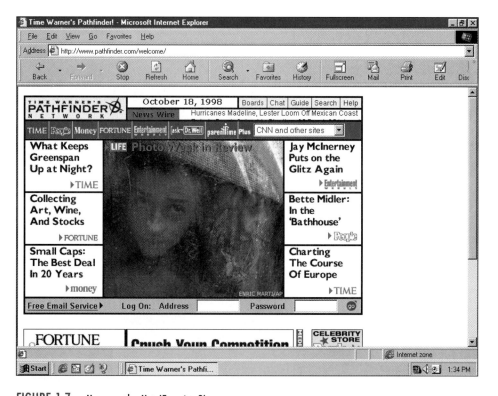

FIGURE 1.7   News on the Net (Exercise 2)

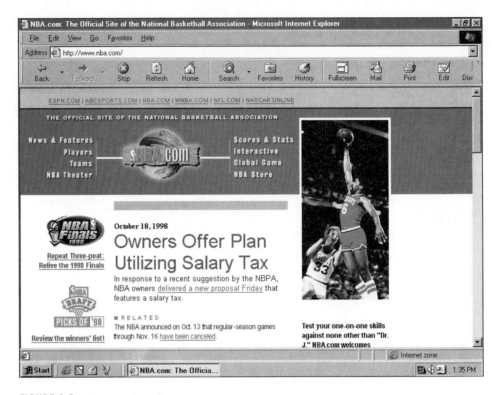

FIGURE 1.8   Sports on the Web (Exercise 3)

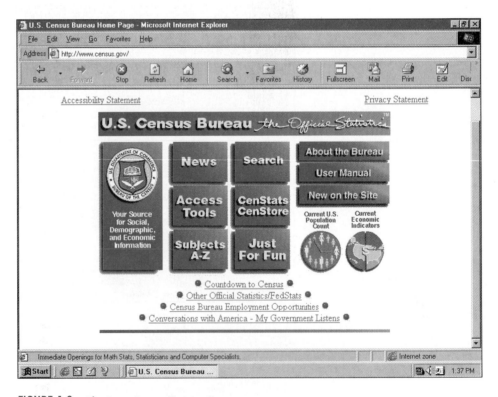

FIGURE 1.9   The Census Bureau (Exercise 4)

5. The Top 100: There are so many excellent sites on the Web that it is impossible to track them all. One site we visit frequently is that of *PC Magazine*, (www.pcmagazine.com) which provides a link to its list of the top 100 sites as shown in Figure 1.10. Another excellent list of suggested sites is found by clicking the Best of the Web button on the Internet Explorer Links bar. Visit at least three sites suggested by the magazine or Internet Explorer, then summarize your findings in a brief note to your instructor. Set a time limit for this assignment because surfing can become quite addictive.

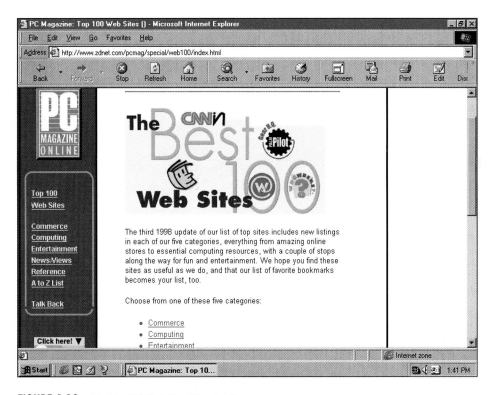

FIGURE 1.10   The Top 100 Web Sites (Exercise 5)

6. Buying a PC: There are many sites on the Web where you can obtain the latest information on price and configuration and/or order a machine online. (The Gateway 2000 site is shown in Figure 1.11 as one example.) Give yourself a budget of $2,000, choose two different vendors, then determine the best configuration for your money. Don't forget to include the cost of software and a printer. Go to two different vendors and submit the results to your instructor as proof you did this exercise. And, if you do purchase a machine, be sure to insist on an unconditional 30-day money back guarantee with price protection.

7. Movies on the Web: You can check the movie listings in your local newspaper, but it's more fun to use the Web as shown in Figure 1.12. The Movie Link home page (www.777film.com) allows you to search for a theater, title, star, type, or time. You can also view the MovieLink Top Ten and/or browse through the new releases. Another movie site to consider is Cinemania (cinemania.msn.com). It has everything but the popcorn.

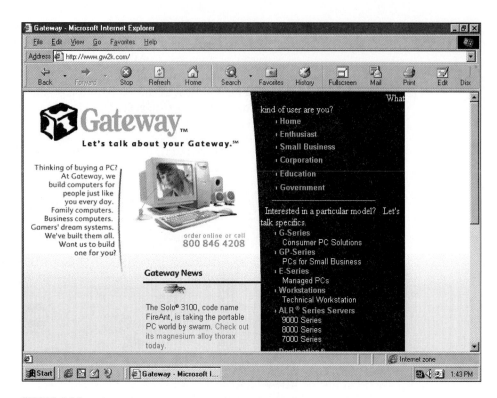

FIGURE 1.11   Buying a PC (Exercise 6)

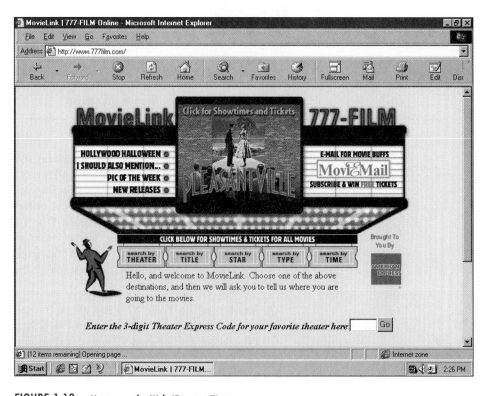

FIGURE 1.12   Movies on the Web (Exercise 7)

Access to the Internet

The easiest way to access the Internet is from a local area network on campus. But which students are given access, and what if anything do you have to do to open an account? Does the university provide an e-mail account? If so, what is your username and password? What is your e-mail address? Does your e-mail account expire at the end of the semester, or does it continue throughout your stay at the university? And finally, do you have dial-in access to your campus network? If so, can you use a graphical browser such as Internet Explorer from home? You don't have to put the answers to these questions in writing; you do, however, have to determine what resources are available to you in order to do the exercises in our text. Check with your instructor, then go to the Help desk for additional information.

It's the URL, Not the Browser

Our text focuses on Internet Explorer, but the concepts apply equally well to any other browser. Choose a different browser (Netscape Communicator) and use it to display several pages that were referenced in this chapter. What difference (if any) do you see in a given page when it is viewed in Netscape rather than Internet Explorer? Which browser is better from a developer's point of view? From a user's point of view?

The Concept of Cache

The concept of cache was referenced briefly in the second hands-on exercise, but the topic merits additional study if you are to use Internet Explorer efficiently. Use the Help menu or Microsoft Knowledge Base to study the topic, then write a short summary of that information and submit it to your instructor. Be sure you address the following issues: What is a cache, and how does it improve performance? What is the difference between a cache in memory versus one on disk? What is the default size of each, and how can you change these parameters? When, if ever, would you want to retrieve a page from the Internet if it is already in cache?

Is a Picture Worth a Thousand Words?

Much has been made of the World Wide Web and its ability to retrieve and display documents with embedded graphics. Go back through this chapter and cover the illustrations and screens with a piece of paper, reading just the text. What value do graphics add to these documents? Do graphics ever detract from a document? Summarize your findings in a brief report to your instructor in which you describe how to download documents with and without the graphics.

Our Favorite Bookstore

Amazon Books (www.amazon.com) is one of our favorite sites on the Web. The site is a perfect illustration of how a small company with an innovative idea can compete on an equal footing with large corporations. Amazon Books provides access to more than three million titles. You order from Amazon, and Amazon in turn orders the book from the publisher for you at a discount. You can search by author, subject, or title, read reviews written by other Amazon visitors, or contribute your own review. Go to the site, find a book that you are interested in, then compare Amazon's price with that of your local bookstore.

Security on the Web

You can purchase almost anything on the Web (e.g., a book from Amazon Books as in the previous case study). How you pay for the item is another issue. Is it safe to transmit your credit card number over the Internet? What protection, if any, does the vendor provide, to maintain the privacy of your credit card? How is the https protocol different from the http protocol that we have referenced throughout the chapter? What is the Secure Sockets layer? The answers to these questions are important, especially if you intend to actually buy an item over the Internet.

Visit Microsoft

The Microsoft site (www.microsoft.com) is an invaluable resource for individuals at every level of computer expertise. We value the site for its online support. You can choose any application and consult a variety of technical resources. You can also download free software and be brought up to date on current events. Go to the site for a short visit, then summarize your impression in a brief note to your instructor.

chapter 2

SEARCH ENGINES: FINDING INFORMATION ON THE WEB

OBJECTIVES

After reading this chapter you will be able to:

1. Name three different search engines; explain why it is often necessary to use multiple search engines with a single query.
2. Distinguish among the Boolean operations And, Or, and Not; explain why it is important to qualify a search.
3. Explain why searching the Web is often a process of trial and error; discuss several techniques you can use to improve your chances for success.
4. Distinguish between a Web search and a site search; explain why it is often necessary to do both.
5. Describe the structure of a Web address; explain why backing up within the address may lead to other relevant documents.
6. Explain the use of the Edit Find command within a Web document.
7. Download a graphic from the Web, then incorporate that graphic into a word processing document.

OVERVIEW

The Internet contains a wealth of information that is readily available. That's the good news. The bad news is that the Internet contains so much information that it is often difficult to find what you are looking for. Browsing, while interesting and enjoyable, is not a very efficient way to locate specific information. This chapter introduces the concept of a search engine, a program that systematically searches the Web for documents on a specific topic.

We begin with an explanation of how search engines work and why they are essential. You will learn that many search engines are available and that the same query can return different documents via different engines.

You will find that a search often yields too many documents (hits) that are only marginally relevant to your query. You will also learn that a search that is too specific may not yield any documents at all, making it necessary for you to use multiple engines for the same query.

Suffice it to say, therefore, that searching is a trial and error process. Accordingly, the chapter describes a variety of search techniques to maximize your chance for success. We explain why it is important to use several different search engines. We introduce the concept of Boolean operations and describe how to qualify a search using different logical operators. We also distinguish between searching the Web versus searching a specific site; for example, you may search the Web to locate an online bookstore, then search the resulting site to find a specific book. As always, the chapter gives you the opportunity to apply the conceptual information through hands-on exercises at the computer.

AVOID TRAFFIC JAMS

Rush hour traffic is always tedious, whether you are on the city streets or the Information Superhighway. Sometimes it can't be helped, in that you have to go to work at a certain time or use the computer lab when it's open. Try, however, to avoid the peak hours during the middle of the day when traffic on the Web is busiest and response time is very slow. Go to the lab early in the morning or late at night. Not only will you (almost certainly) be guaranteed a computer, but you will avoid rush hour on the Internet as well.

SEARCH ENGINES

The same techniques apply to effective research, regardless of whether it is done in the library or on the World Wide Web (although the Web has made the task much easier). If, for example, you were using the library to do research for a term paper, you wouldn't do very well by randomly strolling through the stacks from floor to floor until you found what you wanted. It's equally inefficient to just browse through the Web, going from one link to another until you stumble onto a relevant document.

It's obvious that you would do much better in both cases to conduct a *key word search,* in which you look for documents on a specific topic. In yesterday's library you would look up the topic in the card catalog; in today's library you would use an online database, and on the Web you would use a *search engine,* the Web's equivalent of the library's card catalog or database.

A search engine is a program that systematically searches the Web for documents on a specific topic. You enter a *query* (a key word or phrase) into a *search form,* and the search engine scans its database to see which documents (if any) are related to the key word you requested. The search engine will list the titles of the documents it finds, together with a link to each document. Some search engines also display an abstract of each document to help you determine its relevancy to your query.

Many search engines are available, each of which uses its own database of Web documents. Each database stores information about each document it contains, typically the document's *URL* (i.e., its Web address), key words that describe the document, and selected information from the document. Some databases store only the document's title, others contain the first few lines of text, and still others contain every word in the document. Each engine uses its own version of a special program known as a *spider* to automatically search the Web on a periodic basis, looking for new pages to add to its database.

Some search engines are better than others, but there is no consensus on the "best" engine. In any event, a search engine is only as good as its database and the algorithm it uses to search that database for relevant documents. The larger the database, the greater the number of *hits* (documents matching your query) that are returned.

A large number of hits, however, does not necessarily guarantee a successful search, because you also need to be concerned with the relevancy of those hits. In other words, the mere fact that a document contains a key word or phrase does not mean the document is useful to you. If, for example, you were searching for information on airline reservations, you might not be interested in the home page of a specific travel agent. And while you might be interested in the home page of a specific airline, you might be better served by a document that lets you access the flight schedule of several airlines.

Assume, for example, that you are planning a trip and that you want the cheapest and/or most convenient flight from Fort Lauderdale to San Francisco. Any query that specific, however, would be unlikely to return any hits at all. You might begin, therefore, by searching the Web for a site that lets you make an airline reservation, then once you found such a site, search for the specific flight. The process is illustrated in Figure 2.1.

The easiest way to initiate a search is to click the Search button on the Standard Buttons toolbar. This opens the Explorer bar and displays the Search pane that is visible in Figures 2.1a and 2.1b. The latter contains a text box in which you enter the search criteria, after which you see the results of the search. We selected the *Lycos* and *Infoseek* engines in Figures 2.1a and 2.1b, respectively, and used the same query, "airline reservations," for both.

The results of the search are displayed as a series of links underneath the list box. The results are different because each engine uses a different database, as well as a different search algorithm. In other words, the same query produces different results with different engines, and thus it is important to use multiple engines for the most complete results. Note, too, that you can click any link in the left pane to display the corresponding document in the right pane.

The document in Figure 2.1b looked promising, so we decided to explore it further. We were required to enter a personal profile, obtain a username and password, but there was no charge to do so. We were then able to enter the parameters of our desired flight in Figure 2.1c, after which we were presented with a series of flights that met our requirements in Figure 2.1d. There was no obligation, whatsoever. We could make the reservation online through the Travelocity site, we could call the airline to make the reservation directly, or we could contact a travel agent to do it for us.

The point of this example is not to make an actual reservation, but to illustrate the mechanics of searching the Web. Think for a minute about what was accomplished. You were looking for information on a flight from Fort Lauderdale to San Francisco. You used a search engine to look through millions of Web documents for information on airline reservations, which in turn led you to a site that let you search for a specific flight. All of this was accomplished in minutes, and the information you retrieved is as complete as that provided by any airline or travel agent.

This example also illustrates the difference between a generalized *Web search* versus a specific *site search.* This two-step approach is very common and is used in a variety of instances. The following exercise has you look for the e-mail address of one of the authors. In so doing, you will search the Web for the University of Miami (the author's place of employment), then search the UM site for information about the author himself. Note, too, that the UM site, like many other universities, provides links to a host of campus information. Hence, you can also use the exercise as a guide to learn more about your own college or university.

Search button

Lycos Search Engine
was selected

Enter query

Series of links

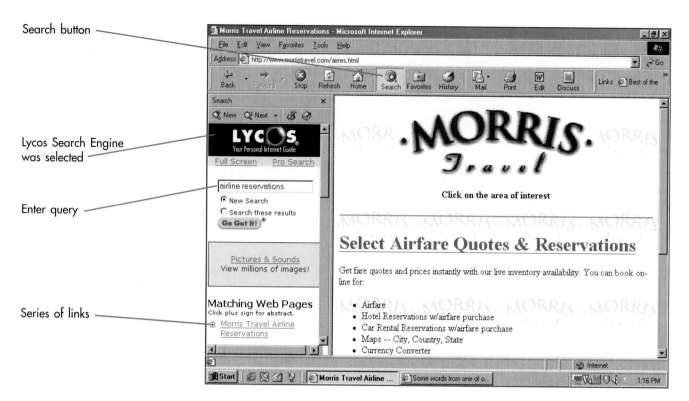

(a) Lycos

Click to close Explorer bar

Infoseek Search Engine
was selected

Click link to Travelocity

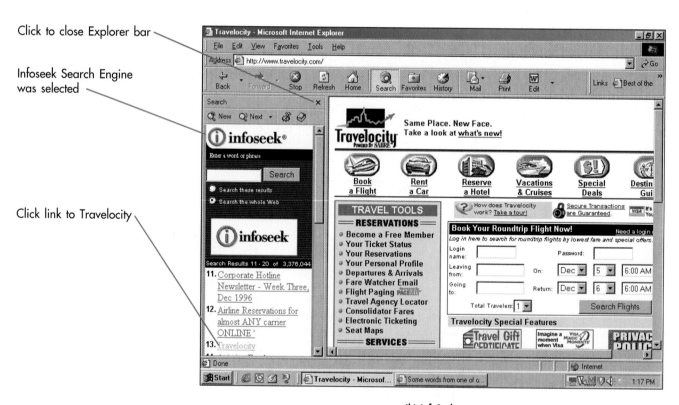

(b) InfoSeek

FIGURE 2.1   Searching the Web

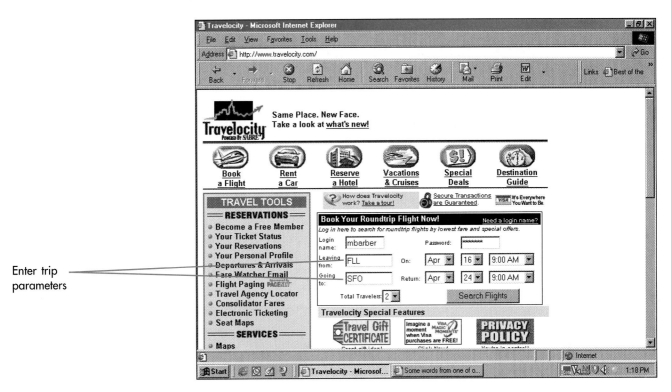

Enter trip
parameters

(c) Create a Flight Plan

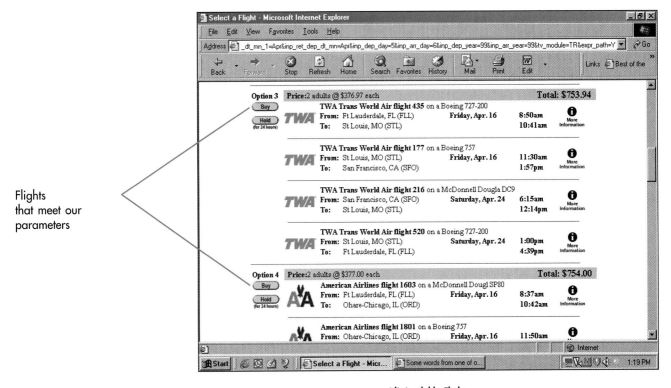

Flights
that meet our
parameters

(d) Available Flights

FIGURE 2.1   Searching the Web (continued)

Searching the Web

Objective: To use a search engine to find the University of Miami home page, then search for a specific e-mail address at the UM site. Use Figure 2.2.

STEP 1: Choose a Search Engine

➤ Start Internet Explorer as you did in Chapter 1. Click the **Search button** on the toolbar to display a screen similar to Figure 2.2a.

➤ The option button to find a Web page is selected by default. Enter **University of Miami** in the Find a Web page text box, then click the **Search button.** The results of the search are displayed in the left pane. You can follow any of these links, or you can attempt to duplicate our results using Yahoo. Click the **down arrow** next to the **Next button** and choose **Yahoo.**

Search button —

Click to choose a
search engine —

Enter query —

Click Search —

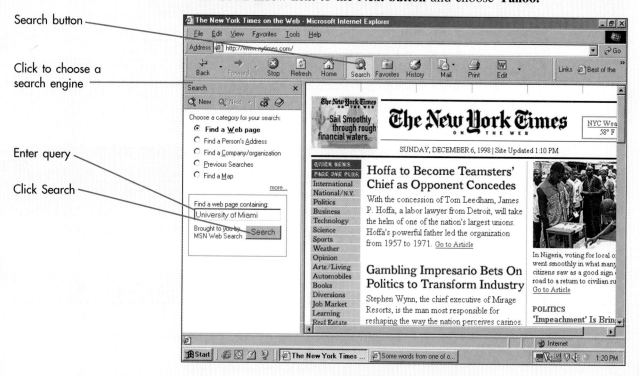

(a) Choose a Search Engine (step 1)

FIGURE 2.2   Hands-on Exercise 1

CUSTOMIZE THE SEARCH ASSISTANT

You can customize the Search Assistant to change the categories that appear and/or the providers in each category. Start Internet Explorer and click the Search button on the Standard toolbar to open the Search pane, then click the Customize tool to display the custom Search Settings page. Check or clear the category boxes to determine the categories that appear. Check or clear the check boxes to select or eliminate the providers in each category. Click the Update button to record your changes.

STEP 2: Yahoo Results

> ➤ The results of the search are displayed underneath the Search text box as shown in Figure 2.2b. You may see a different set of documents or categories from those in our figure.

> ➤ Select (click) the first category in the left pane for the **University of Miami.** You should see a page with links to various categories (such as Athletics or Libraries and Museums) at the University.

> ➤ Click **University of Miami,** the first link on the page, to display the University of Miami home page as shown in Figure 2.2b.

> ➤ Click the **Close button** for the Explorer bar to give yourself more viewing space for the document. (You can also click the **Search button** on the Internet Explorer toolbar to toggle the Explorer bar on or off.)

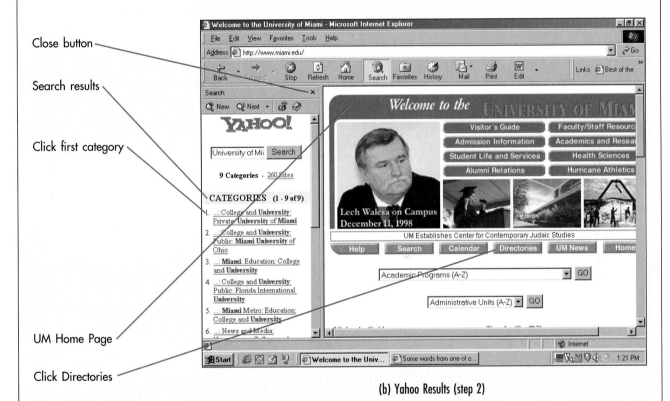

Close button

Search results

Click first category

UM Home Page

Click Directories

(b) Yahoo Results (step 2)

FIGURE 2.2   Hands-on Exercise 1 (continued)

ABOUT YAHOO—CATEGORIES VERSUS DOCUMENTS

Yahoo (www.yahoo.com) is one of the oldest and best-known search tools on the Web. It provides a search engine in which you can enter the text of a specific query. It also organizes its database into categories (a list of sites) that let you search in a more leisurely way. Click any category (e.g., Computers and Internet) and you are taken to a list of subcategories (e.g., Personal Computers), which in turn take you to other categories, which lead eventually to specific documents. You can browse leisurely through the listed categories, which often suggest related sites that you might not have considered initially.

STEP 3: Search the UM Site

➤ You should see the University of Miami home page (www.miami.edu), where you will search for specific information. Every site is different, and there are many ways to proceed. It is up to you to view the links at the site and determine the appropriate path to follow.

➤ You are looking for Robert Grauer's e-mail address. Click the **Directories button,** then click the link to **Faculty and Staff Listing** to display the form in Figure 2.2c.

➤ Click in the first text box, enter **Grauer,** then, if necessary, click in the **Field** list box and select the **Last Name** field. Click in the second text box, enter **Robert,** then, if necessary, click in the **Field** list box and select the **First Name** field.

➤ Click the **Submit button.** Click **Yes** if you see the Security Information dialog box and are asked whether you want to continue.

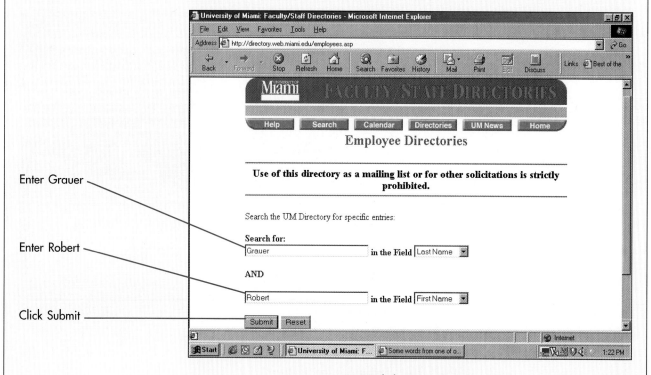

(c) Search the UM Site (step 3)

FIGURE 2.2   Hands-on Exercise 1 (continued)

THE AUTOSEARCH FEATURE

The fastest way to initiate a search is to click in the Address box, enter the key word "go" followed by the topic you are searching for (e.g., go University of Miami), then press the Enter key. Internet Explorer automatically invokes the Yahoo search engine and returns the relevant documents.

STEP 4: Retrace Your Steps

➤ You should see a screen with the information on Robert Grauer as shown in Figure 2.2d. Click the **down arrow** on the Back button to display a list of the sites you have visited.

➤ Your sites may differ from ours, but even so, the list reviews the steps you took to find the information on Robert Grauer:

- Your session began with the display of a home page.
- You selected the Yahoo Search Engine.
- You selected the University of Miami.
- You selected the University of Miami Directories page.
- You selected the Faculty and Staff Listings page.

➤ Click the link to **Welcome to the University of Miami** to return to the University's home page. Print one or two relevant documents to prove to your instructor that you have visited the UM site.

Click down arrow on
Back button

List of sites visited this session

Click Welcome to the
University of Miami

Grauer's information

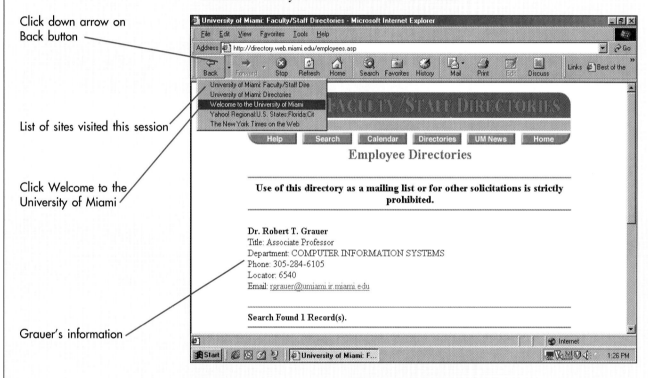

(d) Retrace Your Steps (step 4)

FIGURE 2.2   Hands-on Exercise 1 (continued)

TOGGLE THE EXPLORER BAR ON OR OFF

Use the Search button on the Internet Explorer toolbar to open (close) the Explorer bar. Click the button, and you can access links to various search engines in the left pane of the browser window. Click the button a second time, and the left pane is closed. The History and Favorites buttons function in similar fashion to display (hide) the History and Favorites lists, respectively. If these buttons are not displayed, pull down the View menu, click the Toolbar command, and click the Standard Buttons command.

STEP 5: The Internet White Pages

➤ The steps you just completed had you search for an e-mail address starting from the individual's school or organization. You may also be able to find the information from an Internet directory, provided the individual you are searching for is listed.

➤ Click in the **Address bar,** type **www.whowhere.com** and press the **enter key.** You should see the WhoWhere page as shown in Figure 2.2e.

➤ Enter your name and other information as appropriate, then click the **Go Get It button** to see whether you are listed. (You can add yourself to the directory by clicking the link to **Add Your Listing.** As with all directories, however, there are advantages/disadvantages to an unlisted number.)

➤ Close Internet Explorer if you do not want to continue with the next exercise at this time.

Enter address
www.whowhere.com

Click to add yourself to the
WhoWhere directory

Enter your name

Click Email option button

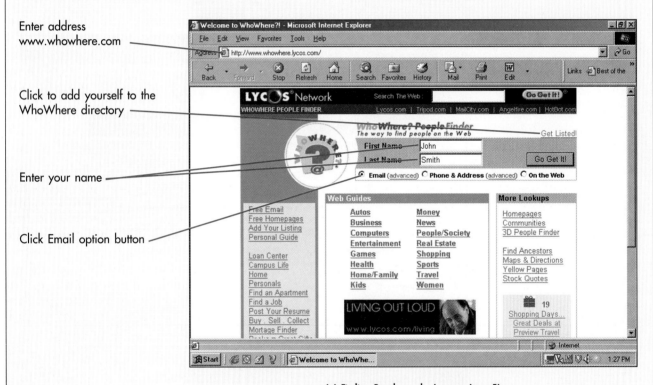

(e) Finding People on the Internet (step 5)

FIGURE 2.2   Hands-on Exercise 1 (continued)

LOOK IN OTHER DIRECTORIES

The Search Assistant in Internet Explorer provides direct links to additional directories to search for an individual's e-mail or regular address. Click the Search button on the Internet Explorer toolbar, click the option button to find a person's address, then click the down arrow on the Search for list box to choose the type of address you are looking for. Enter the individual's name and state if you know it, then compare the results to those obtained in the WhoWhere directory.

We trust that you completed the hands-on exercise without difficulty and that you have a better appreciation for the research potential of the Web. Searching for information is a trial-and-error process in that there is no guaranteed method for success. The Web may or may not contain the documents you need, and even if it does, there is no assurance that you will be able to find them. Nevertheless, we have been successful more often than not, and patience and common sense will usually prevail.

As we have already indicated, there is no single best search engine. Each engine uses its own database and its own search algorithm, so that the same query will return different results with different engines. Yahoo, for example, may provide the best results with one type of query, whereas a different search engine, such as Excite or Infoseek, will provide better results on a different query. Hence, it is good practice to use at least two different engines on the same query in order to obtain a sufficient number of relevant documents.

Note, too, that any given query can return hundreds (even thousands) of documents, so it is essential to structure queries in such a way as to return only the most relevant hits. In general, the more specific your query, the better. A search on "movies," for example, would be unnecessarily broad if your real interest was "science fiction movies." Conversely, a query that is too specific may not return any documents at all. Thus, as we have said throughout, searching is an iterative process during which you continually refine your search criteria.

Logical (Boolean) Operators

All queries are, in essence, a combination of the *logical (Boolean) operators And, Or,* and *Not.* The And operator requires that every key word must be present. Searching for "President" and "Clinton," for example, will return documents about Mr. Clinton's presidency. The Or operator, however, requires that only one of the terms be present, so that searching for "President" or "Clinton" will return documents about presidents (any president) and Clinton (any Clinton). Some search engines also enable you to use Not. Searching for "Bill" and "Clinton," but specifying "Not President," will return documents about other aspects of Mr. Clinton's life and other Bill Clintons. The way in which you specify the Boolean operators depends on the search engine and is described in its online help.

Figure 2.3 illustrates the use of the Yahoo search engine to look for information about Leonardo da Vinci and the Mona Lisa. Figure 2.3a shows the Search pane of the Explorer bar in which we entered the parameters of the search using the Yahoo engine. Yahoo uses the Boolean And operation by default and returns those documents that contain references to both Leonardo and da Vinci. The results of the search are displayed below the query. The contents of the selected document (the category in this example) are displayed in the right pane.

The Find and Save Commands

The Explorer bar is closed in Figures 2.3b, c, and d to provide more room in which to examine the various documents in detail. Figure 2.3b displays a portion of the Leonardo Web Museum document that was listed as a link in Figure 2.3a. Figure 2.3b also illustrates the *Find command* to search for a specific character string within a document. (The Find command is contained in the Edit menu.) In other words, the document in Figure 2.3b describes da Vinci's life in detail, and the Find command represents the fastest way to locate a reference to the Mona Lisa. Alternatively, you could scroll through the document manually, until you came to the Mona Lisa.

Click down arrow
to try other
search engines

Enter key words for the search

Search results

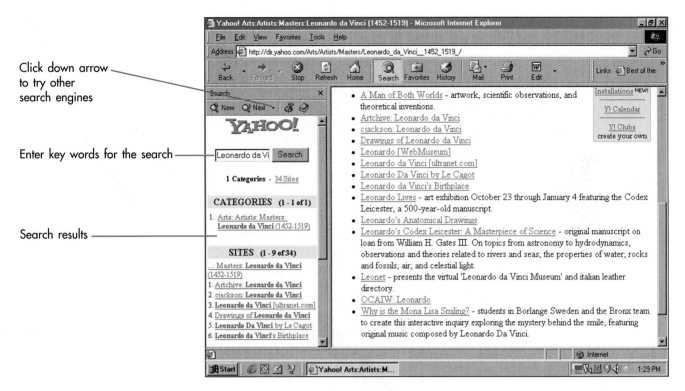

(a) Yahoo Search Form

Search string is found
in document

Thumbnail image

Enter search string

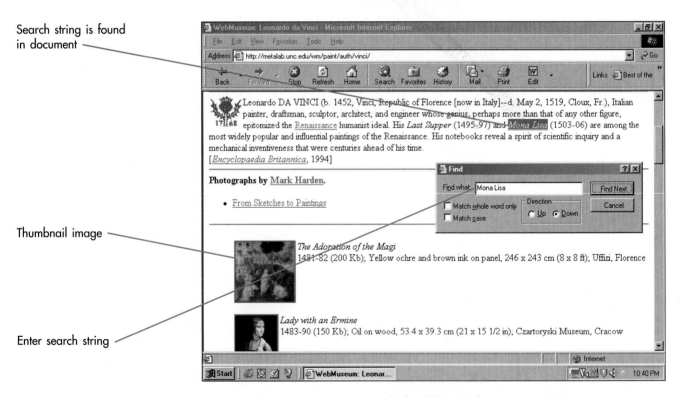

(b) The Find Command

FIGURE 2.3   Research on the Web

Right click on graphic to display
shortcut menu

Click Save Picture As

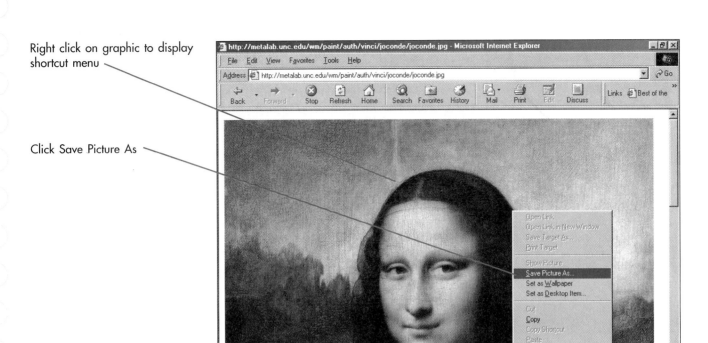

(c) Save Picture As Command

URL of document

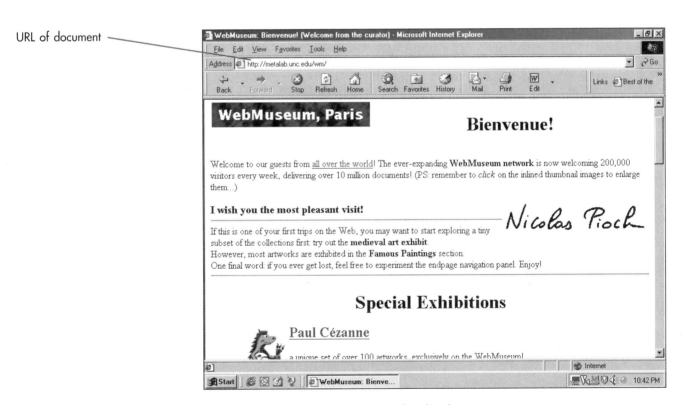

(d) Explore the URL

FIGURE 2.3   Research on the Web (continued)

Note, too, the *thumbnail images* (graphic icons or small versions of a larger image) in Figure 2.3b that appear in the document rather than the actual drawings. This is a nice touch used by many Web designers who want to include a graphic, but who are considerate enough not to force the visitor to wait for a large image to be displayed each time the page is loaded. Thus, they include a thumbnail image that a visitor can click to bring up the larger graphic as shown in Figure 2.3c.

Once you locate the Mona Lisa, you can download the graphic to your PC in order to include the picture in a document of your own. The easiest way to do this is to right click the graphic to display a context-sensitive menu, as shown in Figure 2.3c. Select the *Save Picture As command,* which in turn displays a dialog box in which you specify the drive and folder in which to save the graphic.

After the picture has been downloaded to your machine, you can use the *Insert Picture command* in Microsoft Word to include the picture in a document of your own, perhaps on the cover page of your paper about Leonardo da Vinci. The Insert Picture Command is not part of Internet Explorer per se, but we think you will find the suggestion very helpful. You can use a similar technique to download graphic images for inclusion in a PowerPoint presentation or Excel workbook.

Explore the URL

In searching the Web, there is no substitute for common sense and imagination on the part of the researcher. You will find, for example, that a server (Web site) often contains additional documents that may be relevant to your search if only you take the time to look. Consider, for example, the URL of the document in Figure 2.3c:

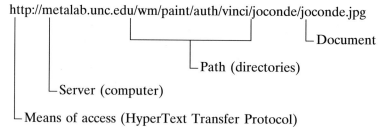

A URL consists of several components in the following sequence: the means of access (typically http), the server (computer on which the document is located), the path on that computer (if any) to travel to the document, and finally the document itself. In other words, we found a specific server (whose address is sunsite.unc.edu) that contained a picture of the Mona Lisa. It's logical to think that the same computer may contain other pictures or information in which we would be interested.

On a hunch (born out of experience) we backed up one level at a time within the address for the Mona Lisa, until we came to the document shown in Figure 2.3d. This proved to be a bonanza as it placed us in the Web museum, from where we had access to all types of art by a host of other artists. We suggest you take a few minutes to visit the museum.

Aside from being a wonderful way to browse, it may also be a boon to your research, because you are often searching for a concept rather than a specific term. You might, for example, be interested in Renaissance artists in general, rather than just da Vinci, and you have just discovered an invaluable resource.

Use Specialized Engines

There are many ways to search for information. Typically, you begin with a generalized search of the entire Web, which often leads to a specific site that you search in depth. The flight reservation example at the beginning of the chapter fell into this pattern. We began by searching for information about "airline reservations," which led to a specific site that contained a database with information about flights from many airlines. The latter site was what we really wanted, and would be a logical starting point for all future searches on flight availability.

Many specialized databases are available. One such site is My Virtual Reference Desk (www.refdesk.com) that was introduced in Chapter 1. You can go to this site, then explore its links to arrive at a host of specialized searches. Try, for example, the link to acronyms, to access a specialized database that lets you enter an acronym and determine its meaning. You can also enter a word and request a list of all acronyms containing that word.

Figure 2.4 displays another favorite page in which you search by category as opposed to entering the text of a specific query. Enter the address of the Web site (www.looksmart.com), and then scroll down the left pane until you find the category that you want to explore (Entertainment and Media). Click the subcategory (Movies), click the next subcategory (Movies by Genre), then select the specific movie type.

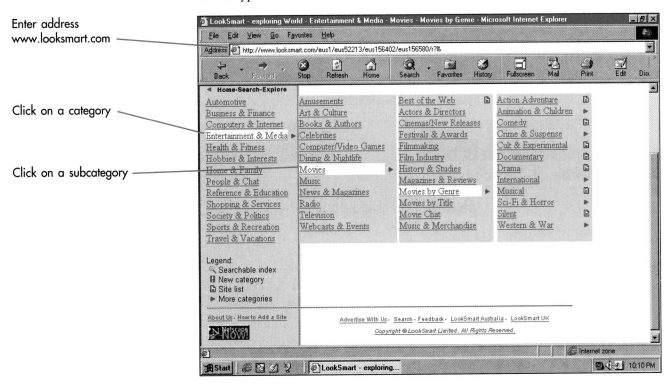

Enter address
www.looksmart.com

Click on a category

Click on a subcategory

FIGURE 2.4 Specialized Searches

BOOKS ONLINE

The Internet Public Library at www.ipl.org/reading contains various links to various books and texts that are freely available over the Internet. The electronic version is fully searchable and thus enables you to research the text as never before. Many of the texts are available as a result of Project Gutenberg (promo.net/pg). These are two sites you don't want to miss.

Copyright Protection

A *copyright* provides legal protection to a written or artistic work, giving the author exclusive rights to its use and reproduction, except as governed under the *fair use exclusion* as explained below. Anything on the Internet or World Wide Web should be considered copyrighted unless the document specifically says it is in the *public domain,* in which case the author is giving everyone the right to freely reproduce and distribute the material.

Does this mean you cannot quote statistics and other facts that you found on the Web in your term papers? Does it mean you cannot download an image to include in your report? The answer to both questions depends on the amount of the material and on your intended use of the information. It is considered fair use, and thus not an infringement of copyright, to use a portion of the work for educational or nonprofit purposes, or for the purpose of critical review or commentary. In other words, you can use a quote, downloaded image, or other information from the Web, provided you cite the original work in your footnotes and/or bibliography. Facts themselves are not covered by copyright, so you can use statistical and other data without fear of infringement. Be sure, however, to always cite the original source in your document.

COPYING LICENSED SOFTWARE IS BREAKING THE LAW!

The fair-use doctrine does not extend to licensed software, even if you intend your copy to be used for educational use only. You can, however, legally copy licensed software to create a backup copy in case the original is damaged, but that's it. Any other copies are illegal.

HANDS-ON EXERCISE 2

Finer Points of Searching

Objective: To illustrate finer points of searching; to download a graphic image and include it in a Word document. Use Figure 2.5 as a guide in the exercise.

STEP 1: Choose a Search Engine

➤ Start Internet Explorer as you did in the previous exercise. Click the **Search button** on the toolbar to display the Search pane.

➤ The option button to find a Web page is selected by default. Enter **Eleanor Roosevelt Photographs** in the Find a Web page text box, then click the **Search button**. The results of the search are displayed in the left pane as shown in Figure 2.5a.

➤ The Alta Vista engine is typically the first engine that is used in a search; if not, click the **down arrow** on the Next button and choose **Alta Vista** so that you can try to duplicate our search.

➤ The results of the search are displayed underneath the Search text box. You may see a different set of documents or categories from those in our figure, in which case you can select a different link.

➤ Select (click) the sixth link, **Eleanor Roosevelt Links,** then click **Eleanor Roosevelt—American First Lady and Humanitarian** to display the page as shown in Figure 2.5a. (Do not be concerned if you do not see our exact document. You will, however, need a document containing a picture of Mrs. Roosevelt.)

Search button

Click to close Explorer bar

Enter query

List of search results

Click link to Eleanor Roosevelt Links

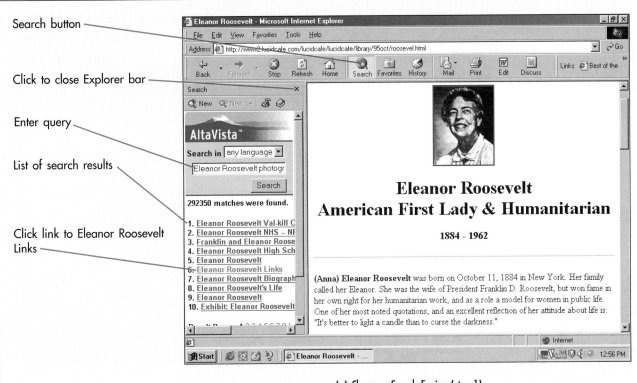

(a) Choose a Search Engine (step 1)

FIGURE 2.5   Hands-on Exercise 2

SEARCH LANGUAGE HELP

Every search engine has a different syntax and a different set of guidelines for efficient use. Scroll down in the Search pane until you come to the bottom of the Alta Vista window where you can click Help to learn about subtleties in using the search engine. Look closely at the links at the bottom of the search pane and note the link to Add a Page. Click the link, then follow the instructions and your home page will be in the Alta Vista database.

STEP 2: The Print Command

➤ Click the **Search button** on the toolbar to close the Explorer bar. The Search button functions as a toggle switch. Click the button and the Explorer bar opens to display the Search pane. Click the button a second time and the Explorer bar is closed.

➤ Pull down the **File menu** and click the **Print command** to display the Print dialog box in Figure 2.5b. You must execute the Print command from the File menu in order to display the Print dialog box. Check the box to Print table of links. Click **OK** to print the page.

➤ Examine the printed copy of the document, which contains the text corresponding to the document you see on the screen. In addition, there is a table at the bottom of the document that contains the Internet address of every link on the page.

Click check box to print table of links

Click OK to print

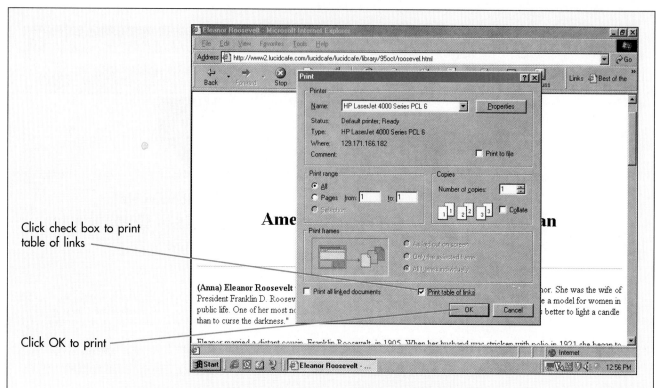

(b) The Print Command (step 2)

FIGURE 2.5   Hands-on Exercise 2 (continued)

THE PAGE SETUP COMMAND

Look closely at any document printed from Internet Explorer. The header displays the title of the document and the number of pages. The footer contains the URL and the date the document was printed. This information appears through parameters entered in the Page Setup command. Pull down the File menu and click the Page Setup command to display the Page Setup dialog box to view or change this information. Click the Help button (the question mark at the right of the title bar), then point to the Header or Footer text boxes for an explanation.

STEP 3: The Save Picture Command

➤ Point to the picture of Mrs. Roosevelt, click the **right mouse button** to display a shortcut menu, then click the **Save Picture As command** to display the Save Picture dialog box as shown in Figure 2.5c.

➤ Click the **drop-down arrow** in the **Save in** list box to specify the drive and folder in which you want to save the graphic (e.g., the My Documents folder on drive C).

➤ The file name and file type are entered automatically by Internet Explorer. (You may change the name, but don't change the file type.) Click the **Save button** to download the image. Remember the file name and location, as you will need to access the file in the next step.

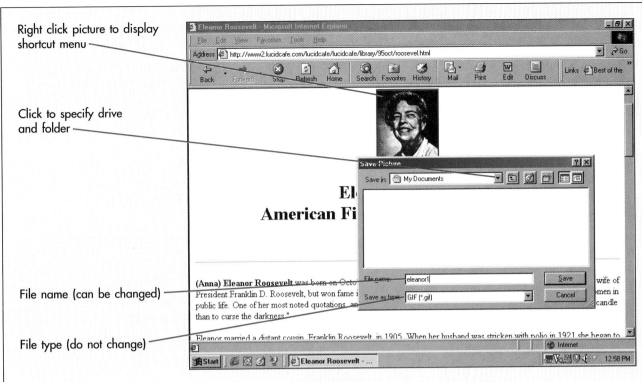

Right click picture to display shortcut menu

Click to specify drive and folder

File name (can be changed)

File type (do not change)

(c) The Save Picture Command (step 3)

FIGURE 2.5   Hands-on Exercise 2 (continued)

THE HOVER COLOR

Hyperlinks are displayed in two colors to indicate links that have or have not been visited. Internet Explorer also provides for a third color, the hover color, to highlight the link you are pointing to. Pull down the View menu, click Internet Options to display the Internet Options dialog box, click the General tab, then click the Colors button. Check the box to use the hover color, then click the Hover box to select a color. Click OK to close the Colors box, then click OK a second time to close the Internet Options dialog box. Point to (hover over) any link, and it is highlighted in the color you selected.

STEP 4: The Insert Picture Command

➤ Start Microsoft Word and, if necessary, maximize the application window. (Our instructions are for Word 2000 and will vary slightly in earlier versions of the program.) If necessary, click the **New button** on the Standard toolbar to start a new document.

➤ Pull down the **View menu** and click the **Print Layout command.** Pull down the **View menu** a second time, click the **Zoom command,** select the **Page Width option button,** and click **OK.**

➤ Enter the title for your paper in an appropriate font and point size as shown in Figure 2.5d. (The Insert Picture dialog box is not yet visible.)

➤ Type your name under the title, press the **Enter key,** then enter any additional information required by your instructor. Press the **Enter key** to begin a new line.

➤ Pull down the **Insert menu,** click **Picture,** then click **From File** to display the Insert Picture dialog box. Select the drive and folder in which you saved the picture (e.g., My Documents on drive C).

➤ Select (click) the picture (e.g., Eleanor), then click **Insert,** and the picture is inserted into the Word document. Do not worry about its size or position at this time. Save the document as Eleanor Roosevelt.

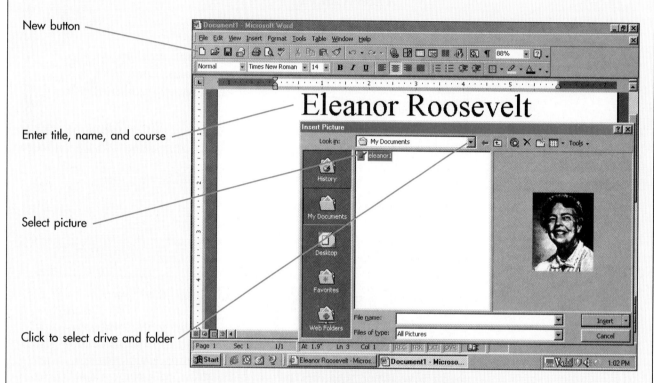

New button

Enter title, name, and course

Select picture

Click to select drive and folder

(d) The Insert Picture Command (step 4)

FIGURE 2.5   Hands-on Exercise 2 (continued)

MULTITASKING

Multitasking, the ability to run multiple applications at the same time, is one of the primary advantages of the Windows environment. Switching from one application to another is easy—just click the appropriate button on the Windows taskbar. (If the taskbar is not visible on your screen, it is because the Auto Hide feature is in effect—just point to the bottom edge of the window, and the taskbar will come into view.) You can also use the classic Alt+Tab shortcut. Press and hold the Alt key as you click the Tab key repeatedly to display icons for the open applications, then release the Tab key when the desired application icon is selected.

STEP 5: Move and Size the Picture

➤ Pull down the **View menu,** click **Zoom,** then click the option button to zoom to **Whole Page.** Click **OK.** Click on the picture of Mrs. Roosevelt to display the sizing handles as shown in Figure 2.5e.

- To size the picture, drag a corner handle (the mouse pointer changes to a double arrow) to keep the graphic in proportion.

- To move the picture, right click the picture to display a context-sensitive menu, then click the Format Picture command to display the Format Picture dialog box. Click the Layout tab, then choose any wrapping style other than In line with text. Now point to any part of the picture except a sizing handle (the mouse pointer changes to a four-sided arrow), then click and drag the picture to position it in the document.

➤ Save the document. Check that the picture is still selected. Click the **Line Style button** on the Picture toolbar to display a drop-down list of line styles. Click the **1 pt line** to place a one point border around the picture.

Sizing handles

Crop button

Line Style button

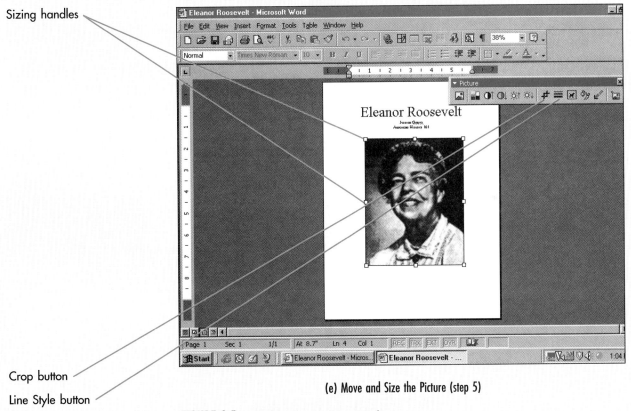

(e) Move and Size the Picture (step 5)

FIGURE 2.5   Hands-on Exercise 2 (continued)

CROPPING A PICTURE

The Crop tool is one of the most useful tools when dealing with a photograph as it lets you eliminate (crop) part of a picture. Select (click) the picture to display the picture toolbar and sizing handles. (If you do not see the Picture toolbar, pull down the View menu, click the Toolbars command, then select the Picture toolbar.) Click the Crop tool (the Screen-Tip will display the name of the tool), then click and drag a sizing handle to crop the part of the picture you want to eliminate.

STEP 6: Insert a Footnote

➤ Click after the word Roosevelt (the point at which you will insert the footnote) in the title of the document. The picture of Mrs. Roosevelt is deselected and the sizing handles disappear.

➤ Pull down the **Insert menu.** Click **Footnote** to display the Footnote and Endnote dialog box in Figure 2.5f. Check that the option buttons for **Footnote** and **AutoNumber** are selected, then click **OK.**

➤ Word inserts a new footnote and simultaneously moves the insertion point to the bottom of the page to add the actual note. Zoom to **Page Width.** Enter the address of the Web page from where you took the picture together with an appropriate reference. Save the document. Exit Word.

Zoom button

Click after Roosevelt

Click OK

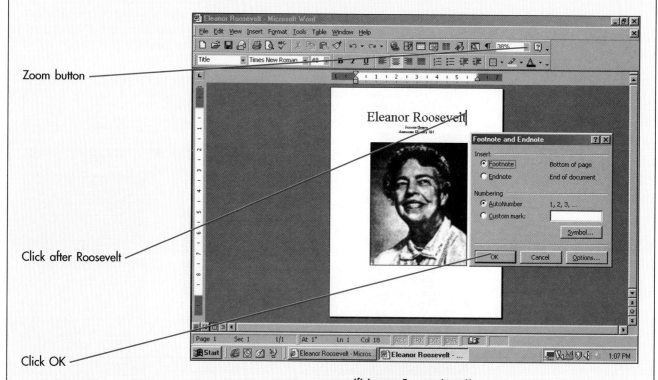

(f) Insert a Footnote (step 6)

FIGURE 2.5 Hands-on Exercise 2 (continued)

ENTER THE URL AUTOMATICALLY

Use the Copy command to enter the URL into a footnote. Not only do you save time by not having to type the address yourself, but you also ensure that it is entered correctly. Click in the address bar of Internet Explorer to select the URL, then pull down the Edit menu and click the Copy command (or use the Ctrl+C shortcut). Switch to the Word document, click at the place in the document where you want to insert the URL, then pull down the Edit menu and click Paste (or press Ctrl+V).

STEP 7: Use Multiple Search Engines

➤ If necessary, point to the bottom of the screen to display the taskbar, then click the button for **Internet Explorer.** Click the **Search button** on the toolbar to reopen the Search pane.

➤ Click the **New button** to start a new search, enter **Eleanor Roosevelt Photographs** in the Find a Web page text box, then click the **Search button.** If necessary, click the **down arrow** next to the **Next button,** then choose **Yahoo** from the list of available search engines.

➤ The results of our search are shown in Figure 2.5g, but you will most likely get a different set of documents from ours. Browse through these documents for a few minutes, then refine the search as necessary. Review the information you have collected in preparation for the term paper (which you don't really have to write).

➤ Exit Internet Explorer. Congratulations on a job well done.

Search button

Click to select a
search engine

Enter query

List of search results

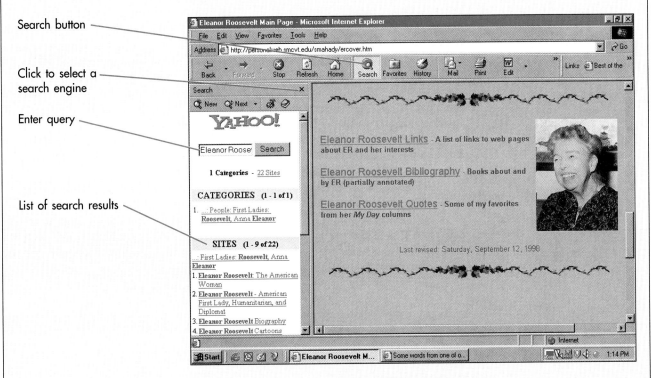

(g) Use Multiple Search Engines (step 7)

FIGURE 2.5   Hands-on Exercise 2 (continued)

SEARCH FOR A CONCEPT

You can extend the reach of a search engine by thinking in terms of a concept rather than a key word; for example, search on "Franklin Roosevelt" or "first ladies" to find additional documents on Mrs. Roosevelt. In similar fashion, you might try searching on "Renaissance painting" to gain background information for a paper on Leonardo da Vinci or Michelangelo. See practice exercise 3 at the end of the chapter.

SUMMARY

Search engines provide an efficient way to look for information on the World Wide Web. You enter a query consisting of the key words you are searching for, and the search engine responds with a number of "hits," or Web documents that meet the search criteria. Searching is, however, a trial and error process with no guarantee for success.

Many different search engines are available, each of which uses a different database and different search algorithm. Each database stores information about its collection of Web documents (running into the millions) and consists of the document's URL (i.e., its Web address) and information (key words) about what is contained in each document. It is important, therefore, to try different engines with the same query, and further, to continually refine a query during the course of a search.

Any given query (request to a search engine) can return hundreds (even thousands) of documents, so it is essential to structure queries in such a way as to return only the most relevant hits. All queries are, in essence, combinations of the logical operations And, Or, and Not. In general, the more specific your query, the better.

Specialty search engines are also available and enable in-depth searches on a specific topic. Specialty engines can be found through a generalized Web search for a specific topic such as "airline reservations," which in turn leads to several databases with flight information. One can also click the Search button on the Internet toolbar to display a list of specialty engines.

Images can be downloaded from the Web and saved onto a local drive for subsequent inclusion in a document. The Insert Picture command inserts a graphic image into a Word document or PowerPoint presentation.

A copyright provides legal protection to a written or artistic work, giving the author exclusive rights to its use and reproduction. Anything on the Internet or World Wide Web should be considered copyrighted unless the document specifically says it is in the public domain. The fair use exclusion, however, lets you use a portion of the work for educational, nonprofit purposes, provided you cite the original work in your footnotes and/or bibliography.

KEY WORDS AND CONCEPTS

And
Boolean operator
Copyright
Excite search engine
Explorer bar
Fair use exclusion
Find command
Hit
Infoseek search engine
Insert Picture command
Internet White Pages

Key word search
Logical operators
Lycos search engine
Not
Or
Public domain
Query
Save command
Save Picture As
   command
Search engine

Search form
Site search
Spider
Thumbnail image
URL
Web search
Yahoo search engine

1. Which of the following is a true statement regarding search engines?
   (a) Different search engines can return different results for the same query
   (b) The same search engine can return different results for the same query at different times (e.g., a month apart)
   (c) Both (a) and (b)
   (d) Neither (a) nor (b)

2. What happens when you click the Search button on the Internet Explorer toolbar?
   (a) The Explorer bar is opened and displays a search window in the left pane
   (b) The Explorer bar is closed
   (c) The Explorer bar opens or closes depending on its state prior to clicking the Search button
   (d) The Yahoo search engine is invoked by default

3. Which of the following is a *false* statement about search engines?
   (a) Every search engine has a unique syntax
   (b) Every search engine uses a unique database
   (c) Every search engine permits the use of the And, Or, and Not operations
   (d) Every search engine can be accessed through its URL

4. Which of the following is *not* a search engine?
   (a) Internet Explorer
   (b) Lycos
   (c) Infoseek
   (d) Excite

5. Which of the following is considered the best search engine, and thus the only engine you need to use?
   (a) Yahoo
   (b) Lycos
   (c) Excite
   (d) There is no agreement on the best search engine

6. Yahoo, Lycos, and Infoseek are examples of
   (a) URL addresses
   (b) Boolean operations
   (c) Web browsers
   (d) Search engines

7. Which of the following operators should you use between the key words "American" and "Revolution" to implement the most restrictive search?
   (a) And
   (b) Or
   (c) Not
   (d) And, Or, or Not, depending on the search engine

8. Which of the following operators should you use between the key words "American" and "Revolution" to implement the least restrictive search and return the greatest number of documents?
   (a) And
   (b) Or
   (c) Not
   (d) And, Or, or Not, depending on the search engine

9. Which of the following will return the largest number of documents regardless of the search engine in use?
   (a) "Marlins" and "Baseball"
   (b) "Marlins" or "Baseball"
   (c) "Marlins" not "Baseball"
   (d) Impossible to determine

10. A spider is a program that
    (a) Displays HTML documents that are downloaded from the Web
    (b) Automatically crawls through the Web searching for new pages to add to the database of a search engine
    (c) Searches the Web for specific documents according to the entries in a search form
    (d) Protects a computer against infection from viruses

11. Which part of the URL http://www.microsoft.com/ie/iedl.htm identifies the Internet address of the Web site (server)?
    (a) http://
    (b) www.microsoft.com
    (c) ie
    (d) iedl.htm

12. Which part of the URL http://www.microsoft.com/ie/iedl.htm identifies the actual Web document?
    (a) http://
    (b) www.microsoft.com
    (c) ie
    (d) iedl.htm

13. A thumbnail image is used
    (a) As a graphic placeholder in a Web document to prevent the graphic from being downloaded initially
    (b) As a placeholder for text within an HTML document to indicate the contents of a Web page in the output of a search engine query
    (c) In a home page to indicate the author's interests
    (d) As a favorite whenever a page contains a graphic image

14. What is the general rule regarding the use of information that was downloaded from the Internet?
    (a) It should be assumed that the material is under copyright protection unless the author states that the document is in the public domain
    (b) Factual material may be cited even if the material has been copyrighted
    (c) A limited portion of copyrighted material may be used for noncommercial purposes under the fair use exclusion, provided the source is cited
    (d) All of the above

15. What is the purpose of the Find command within the Edit menu?
    (a) It provides access to a list of common search engines
    (b) It initiates a search on the Web for all documents containing a designated set of key words
    (c) It enables the user to search within a document for a specific character string
    (d) All of the above

ANSWERS

1. c	**6.** d	**11.** b
2. c	**7.** a	**12.** d
3. c	**8.** b	**13.** a
4. a	**9.** b	**14.** d
5. d	**10.** b	**15.** c

PRACTICE WITH THE WORLD WIDE WEB

1. A More Powerful Search Form: The search form in Figure 2.6 is intended to locate documents about Chelsea Clinton that omit information about either of her parents. The easiest way to display this form is by going directly to the Excite home page (www.excite.com) where you can click the Power Search link. Try a search using the parameters in Figure 2.6, then summarize the results in a short note to your instructor.

2. Your Favorite Movie Star: Figure 2.7 is taken from one of many sites on the Web that provide detailed information about movie stars. Choose your favorite star, then try finding information about that person via a generalized search. Alternatively, you can browse through the directories at www.looksmart.com, as described in the chapter. Go to the site, select the Entertainment and Media category, choose celebrities, choose actors, then find your star. Try expanding your search to locate a database of movies that are currently playing. Can you find a theater in your neighborhood that is showing a movie with your favorite star? What time does the movie start?

3. Searching on a Concept: We were pleased with the results of our search on Eleanor Roosevelt using the Alta Vista search engine in the second hands-on exercise. Lots of other information is available, however, especially if you search on a related concept. Choose any engine you like and search on "First Ladies" to see if you can find the photograph in Figure 2.8. Download the graphic image, then print a one-page note to your instructor containing the photograph and describing how you found the picture.

4. Found Money: Our favorite database is the Found Money database shown in Figure 2.9. It's not a gag, and you really do have a chance at finding money in your name, or the name of a relative. In essence, the site stores public records of abandoned money—bank accounts, utility deposits, tax refunds, and so on. There is no charge to search the database to see whether there is an account in your name; there is, however, a $10 charge for detailed information on any hits that you receive if you elect to pursue that information. Try it, and let us know if you find any money. We actually found some!

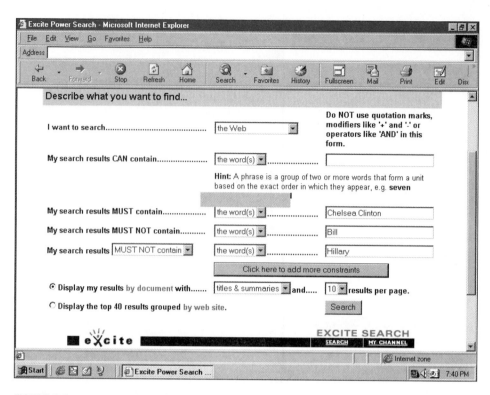

FIGURE 2.6   A More Powerful Search Form (Exercise 1)

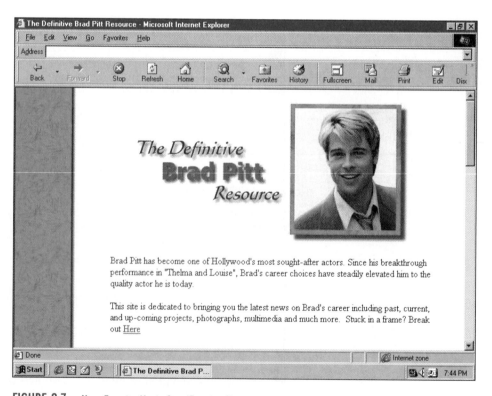

FIGURE 2.7   Your Favorite Movie Star (Exercise 2)

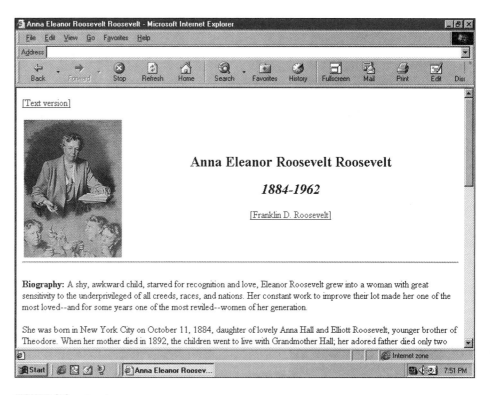

FIGURE 2.8   Searching on a Concept (Exercise 3)

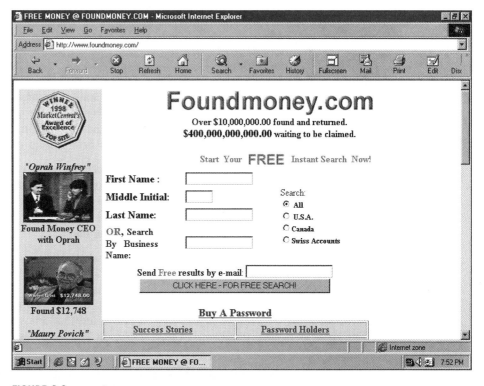

FIGURE 2.9   Found Money (Exercise 4)

5. **Search Microsoft:** It's not as good as finding money, but the Microsoft site contains valuable information, especially if you are encountering a technical problem. Go to the Microsoft site (www.microsoft.com), click the Support button, then click the link to Support Online to display a screen similar to Figure 2.10. Choose any application, submit one or two questions, then summarize the result of your research in a short note to your instructor.

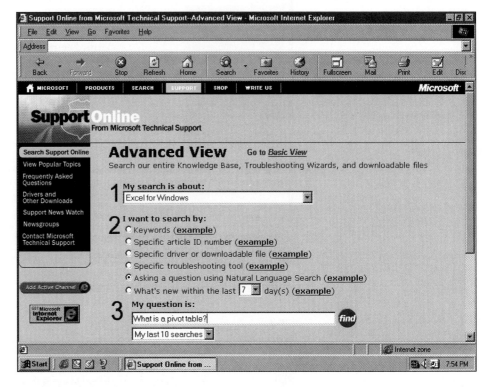

FIGURE 2.10   Search Microsoft (Exercise 5)

6. **Driving Directions:** A form similar to the one in Figure 2.11 is available from multiple databases on the Web. Choose your school as a starting point and a favorite vacation spot as the destination, then search the Web to see if you can get directions. Can you print a map in addition to written directions?

7. **Shakespeare Online:** There are many Shakespearean sites on the Web, but the site in Figure 2.12 is our favorite. (We have erased the URL, or else this problem would be too easy.) See if you can search the Web to identify the Shakespearean character who said, *"This above all, to thine ownself be true."* From which play was the quotation taken?

8. **Your Favorite Recording Artist:** The site in Figure 2.13 is one of many sites on the Web that provide detailed information about musicians and their music. Choose any recording artist, then search the Web to see what information is available. Do any of the sites enable you to listen to music or a music clip? Can you find a site that lets you purchase a CD?

9. **The iCOMP Index:** Intel developed the iCOMP Index to compare the speed of various microprocessors to one another. We want you to search the Web and find a chart showing values in the current iCOMP Index. (The chart you find need not be the same as the one in Figure 2.14.) Once you find the chart, download the graphic and incorporate it into a memo to your instructor. Add a paragraph or two describing the purpose of the index.

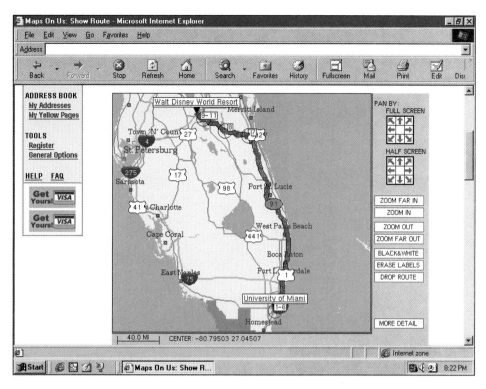

FIGURE 2.11 Driving Directions (Exercise 6)

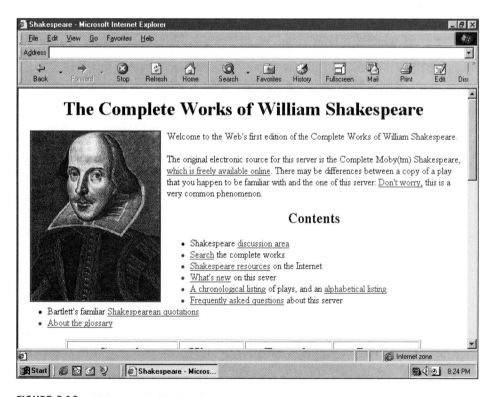

FIGURE 2.12 Shakespeare Online (Exercise 7)

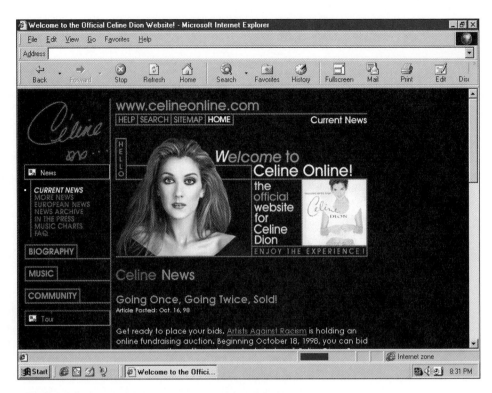

FIGURE 2.13 Your Favorite Recording Artist (Exercise 8)

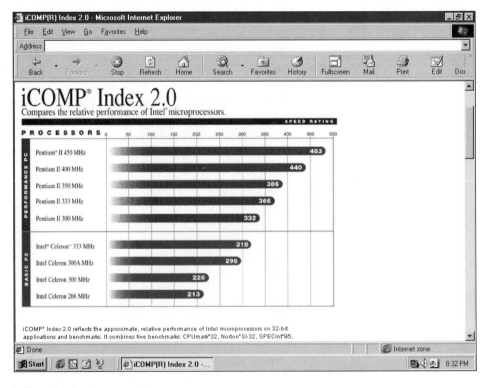

FIGURE 2.14 The iComp Index (Exercise 9)

CASE STUDIES

A Collection of Trivia

This exercise asks you to find the answer to a variety of unrelated questions. Some of the answers are contained in a specialized directory whereas others may require a general search. Good luck. What is the toll-free number for Federal Express? What is the zip code for the address 580 Fifth Avenue in New York City? What is today's price of Microsoft stock? What is the value of $1 in British pounds? What does PCMCIA (associated with laptop computers) stand for? When is Barbra Streisand's birthday?

On Your Own

This loosely structured case study asks you to experiment with different search engines and search parameters. Select any topic in which you are interested, then choose a search engine, construct an initial query, then record the number of hits the engine returns. Choose a different engine, enter the identical query, and record the number of hits you get with that engine. Select the more promising result, then submit a new query that limits your search through inclusion of additional key words or other logical operators. Summarize the results in a one- or two-page Word document that you will submit to the instructor. The document should contain all the information you recorded manually in the preceding steps.

File Compression

Photographs add significantly to the appearance of a document, but they also add to its size. Accordingly, you might want to consider the acquisition of a file compression program to facilitate copying large documents to a floppy disk in order to transport your documents to and from school, home, or work. You can download an evaluation copy of the popular WinZip program at www.winzip.com. Investigate the subject of file compression, then submit a summary of your findings to your instructor.

Copyright Infringement

It's fun to download images from the Web for inclusion in a document, but is it legal? Copyright protection and infringement is one of the most pressing legal issues on the Web. Search the Web for sites that provide information on current copyright law. One excellent site is the copyright page at the Institute for Learning Technologies at www.ilt.columbia.edu/projects/copyright. Another excellent reference is the page at www.benedict.com. Research these and other sites, then summarize your findings in a short note to your instructor.

Frequently Asked Questions (FAQs)

All the information you need to understand the Web is on the Web! General information about popular subjects is often kept in files titled Frequently Asked Questions (FAQs). Compose a search to find out more about the World Wide Web; something like WWW FAQS should work. Follow the hyperlinks until you feel comfortable with the terms you're reading. Summarize your results in a one-page memo to your instructor.

The Annual Report

America's public corporations spend a small fortune creating annual reports to report on the status of a company to its shareholders. You can write to a corporation and request a traditional printed report, or you can go online to view the report on the Web if it is available. Choose any public corporation, search the Web for its home page, then see if you can find the annual report. Another way to search for the same information is to structure a query to look for the words "annual report." Summarize what you find in a report to your instructor.

Going Abroad

Congratulations! You have just won a scholarship to spend your junior year abroad. You need a passport, and you need it quickly. Search the Web to learn how to apply for a passport. You should be able to find a site that enables you to download an actual passport application with specific instructions on where to apply, that is, an address in the city in which you live or attend school. What additional software, if any, do you need to print the application?

Tax Time

April 15 is just around the corner and you have yet to file your income tax. Search the Web to download the necessary tax forms to file your federal income tax. What other information regarding your income taxes is available from this site? What additional software, if any, do you need to print the form on your PC? Extend your search to the necessary forms for state income taxes if you live in a state that has an income tax.

appendix a

HOW THE INTERNET WORKS: THE BASICS OF TCP/IP

OVERVIEW

Data is transmitted across the Internet through a series of protocols known collectively as *TCP/IP (Transmission Control Protocol/Internet Protocol).* A *protocol* is an agreed-upon set of conventions that define the rules of communication. You follow a protocol in class; for example, you raise your hand and wait to be acknowledged by your professor. In similar fashion, the sending and receiving computers on the Internet follow the TCP/IP protocol to ensure that data is transmitted correctly.

The postal system provides a good analogy of how (but certainly not how fast) TCP/IP is implemented. (The post office analogy was suggested by Ed Krol in his excellent book, *The Whole Internet*, published by O'Reilly and Associates, Sebastopol, CA, in 1992.) When you mail a regular letter, you drop it into a mailbox, where it is picked up along with a lot of other letters and delivered to the local post office. The letters are sorted and sent on their way to a larger post office, where the letters are sorted again, until eventually each letter reaches the post office closest to its destination, where it is delivered to the addressee by the local mail carrier. If, for example, you sent a letter from Coral Springs, Florida, to Upper Saddle River, New Jersey, the letter would not travel directly from Coral Springs to Upper Saddle River. Instead, the Postal Service would forward the letter from one substation to the next, making a new decision at each substation as to the best (most efficient) route; for example, from Coral Springs, to Miami, to Newark, and finally, to Upper Saddle River.

Each postal substation considers all of the routes it has available to the next substation and makes the best possible decision according to the prevailing conditions. This means that the next time you mail a letter from Coral Springs to Upper Saddle River, the letter may travel a completely different path. If the mail truck from Coral Springs to Miami had already left or was full to capacity, the letter could be routed through Fort Lauderdale to New York City, and then to Upper Saddle River. The actual route taken by the letter is not important. All that matters is that the letter arrives at its destination.

The Internet works the same way, as data travels across the Internet through several levels of networks until it gets to its destination. E-mail messages arrive at the local post office (the mail server) from a remote PC connected by modem, or from a node on a local area network. The messages then leave the local post office and pass through a special-purpose computer known as a *router,* that ensures each message is sent to its correct destination.

A message may pass through several networks to get to its destination. Each network has its own router that determines how best to move the message closer to its destination, taking into account the traffic on the network. A message passes from one network to the next, until it arrives at the destination network, from where it can be sent to the recipient, who has a mailbox on that network. The process is depicted graphically in Figure A.1.

THE WINDOWS TRACERT COMMAND

The TCP/IP protocol may sound like science fiction, but it works, and you can see it in action if you know how to look. Click the Start button, click the Programs command, then click the MS-DOS prompt to open a DOS window. Enter the command TRACERT followed by the name of a server—for example, TRACERT WWW.MICROSOFT.COM to connect to the Microsoft server. You will see the actual path traveled, together with the minimum, average, and maximum time for each hop. Type Exit at the C prompt to close the DOS window, then log off from your Internet provider.

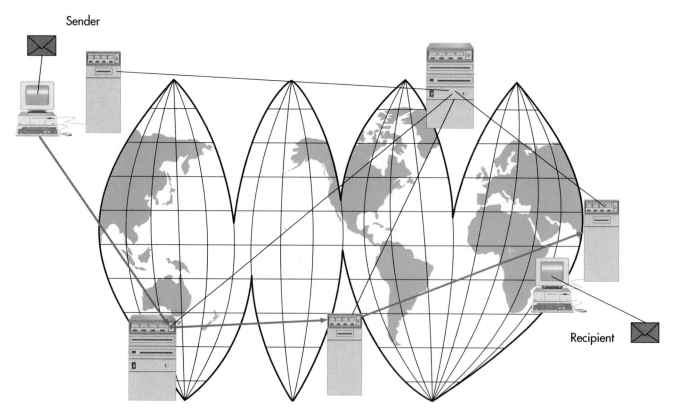

FIGURE A.1   A Message Travels the Internet

The TCP/IP protocol is more complex than what we have indicated, and it applies to all types of data, not just e-mail. To continue with the post office analogy, let's assume that you are sending a book, rather than a letter, and that the Post Office (for whatever reason) does not accept large packages. One alternative would be to rip the pages out of the book, mail each page individually by placing it into its own envelope, then trust that all of the envelopes arrive at the destination and finally, that the person on the other end would be able to reassemble the individual pages. That may sound awkward, but it is a truer picture of how the Internet works.

Data (whether it is an e-mail message or a Web page) is sent across the Internet in *packets,* with each packet limited in size. The rules for creating, addressing, and sending the packets are specified by TCP/IP, which is actually two separate protocols. The TCP portion divides the file that you want to send into packets, then numbers each packet so that the message can be reconstructed at the other end. The IP portion sends each packet on its way by specifying the addresses of the sending and receiving computers so that the routers will be able to do their job.

The TCP/IP protocol may seem unnecessarily complicated, but it is actually very clever. Dividing large files into smaller pieces ensures that no single file monopolizes the network. A second advantage has to do with ensuring that the data arrives correctly. Static or noise on a telephone line is merely annoying to people having a conversation, but devastating when a file (especially a computer program) is transmitted and a byte or two is lost or corrupted. The larger the file being sent, the greater the chance that noise will be introduced and that the file will be corrupted. Sending the data in smaller pieces (packets), and verifying that the packets were received correctly, helps ensure the integrity of the data. If one packet is received incorrectly, the entire file does not have to be sent again, only the corrupted packet.

A university or corporation can justify the high cost of a permanent TCP/IP connection to the Internet. This type of connection is very expensive and is reasonable only when multiple users on a LAN (Local Area Network) need to access the Internet simultaneously. A standalone PC, however (e.g., a home computer), will access the Internet through a dial-up connection via a modem. This provides a temporary connection known as a *SLIP* (Single Line Internet Protocol) or *PPP* (Point to Point Protocol) *connection,* but it enables full access to the Internet as long as you maintain the telephone connection.

WHAT IS ISDN?

ISDN (Integrated Services Digital Network) is a high-speed digital telephone service that speeds the transfer of data over the Internet for a dial-up connection. ISDN operates at speeds up to 128K bytes per second, or more than four times faster than a 28.8 modem. The disadvantage is cost. ISDN is expensive to install, and its monthly fee is more expensive than a standard telephone line. You also need specialized equipment and an Internet provider that supports ISDN connectivity. The march of technology assures us, however, that ISDN will become increasingly common and cost effective as time goes on.

Internet Architecture Layers

The Internet is built in layers that revolve around the TCP/IP protocol, as shown in Figure A.2. At the sending computer, the ***application layer*** creates the message and passes it to the ***transport layer,*** where the message is divided into packets. The packets are addressed at the ***Internet layer,*** then sent across the Internet using the ***network access layer,*** which traverses the various networks through which the data passes to get to its destination. The process is reversed at the receiving computer. The Internet layer receives the individual packets from the network access layer, then passes the packets to the transport layer, where they are reassembled in sequence and sent to the application layer to display the message.

Each computer on the Internet, whether dialing in or attached via a local area network, must have the necessary software (called TCP/IP drivers or stacks) to accomplish the task of the four layers. (The software is built into Windows 95/98.) Each computer also requires a unique ***IP address*** that identifies the computer as a node on the Internet. If you are connected to the Internet via a LAN, your workstation has a permanent IP address, which remains constant. A dial-up SLIP or PPP connection, however, provides you with only a temporary address, which changes from session to session.

The IP address is analogous to the street address on a letter. It is composed of four numbers, each less than 256, each separated by a period; for example, 192.25.13.01. (Fortunately, however, you can use a mnemonic address rather than the numeric IP address, as will be explained shortly.) Each site on the Internet must apply for a specific block of IP addresses from its Internet provider. Each PC, Mac, router, server, and other device on the network is then assigned an IP address by the network administrator, just as someone in your town has designated a number for every house or building on your street.

Let's consider the example shown in Figure A.2, in which Bob, at the University of Miami, composes and sends an e-mail message to Gretchen at Saint

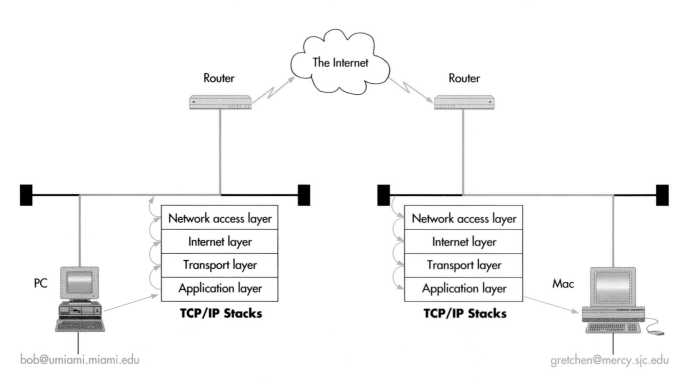

bob@umiami.miami.edu   gretchen@mercy.sjc.edu

FIGURE A.2   The Internet Architecture

Joseph College. The application layer (Bob's e-mail program) creates the message and passes it to the transport layer, which divides the message into packets. The transport layer also records how many bytes are in each packet so that it can verify that the data was transmitted successfully. The transport layer then passes the packets to the Internet layer, where they are addressed and sent to the network access layer.

The network access layer, in turn, sends the individual packets out through the router onto the Internet. From there they are passed to another router, which examines the destination address and passes each packet on to another router. Each router contains a routing table, which determines where (to which network router) to send the packet next, based on the IP address of the message. This process continues until the destination router is reached and the TCP/IP software on the receiving computer delivers the message.

The Internet layer on the receiving end passes the individual packets to the transport layer, which sends an acknowledgment to the transport layer of the sending computer. The latter verifies that the data have been sent correctly, and automatically resends any erroneous packets. The transport layer on the receiving end then reassembles the packets, and delivers them to the application layer, which signals the arrival of Bob's message on Gretchen's computer. All of this happens in a matter of seconds, in a network that spans the globe.

The protocols that govern each layer are hardware independent, enabling the sender and recipient to use different types of computers, yet receive the messages without problems. In our diagram we show Bob working on a Windows 95 PC and Gretchen on a Mac. In addition, the networks themselves may be different—that is, use different types of wiring—in which case the Internet layer will change the size of the packets to that required for the specific network.

Think of the post office analogy. Some mail routes are handled by mail truck, others on foot. If the mail carrier is on a walking route, he or she must remove the mail from the plastic mail tub and place it in the mail shoulder bag. Not all of the mail will fit, so some pieces will wait for the carrier to return and load up for the second round. In a similar way, some Internet messages must be broken into different-sized packets for different parts of the physical network. The information about the type of protocols used is contained in the header information attached to the packets.

Fortunately, most, if not all of these functions are transparent to the user. You simply send an e-mail message, download a data file or program from a remote computer, or request a Web page, and off it goes, aided by the various software protocols installed on your system.

The Domain Name System

A numeric IP address is easily processed by a computer, but not so easily by a person. What's easier to remember, the IP address 123.201.85.244, or its mnemonic equivalent, www.myschool.edu? The *Domain Name System (DNS)* provides the mnemonic equivalent of a numeric IP address, and further, ensures that every site on the Internet has a unique address.

The DNS divides the Internet into a series of component networks called *domains* that enable e-mail (and other files) to be sent across the entire Internet. Each site attached to the Internet belongs to one of these domains. Universities, for example, belong to the EDU domain. Government agencies are in the GOV domain. Commercial organizations (companies) are in the COM domain. Large domains are in turn divided into smaller domains, with each domain responsible for maintaining unique addresses in the next lower-level domain, or subdomain. Table A.1 lists the six original Internet domains. Several other domains have been added since.

Table A.1   Internet Domains

Domain	Description	Example Subdomain
edu	Educational institutions	Your college or university
gov	Federal, state, and local government entities	NASA, the CIA, the U.S. Senate, the Library of Congress, the National Archives
mil	Military organizations	U.S. Navy
com	Commercial entities	Microsoft, Prentice Hall, Prodigy
net	Network service providers	The National Science Foundation's Internet Network Information Center
org	Nonprofit organizations	The Internet Town Hall

The mnemonic names you enter, either explicitly or implicitly, must be continually translated to the numeric addresses used by the TCP/IP protocol. This takes place automatically and is completely transparent to you. The host computer to which you are connected looks up the numeric IP address corresponding to the mnemonic DNS address by querying the nearest ***domain root server,*** one of several special computers on the Internet, which keeps information about IP addresses in its domain. This is similar to your going to the post office to look up a zip code for a letter you wish to send. You can keep the zip code handy in case you want to send a letter to that address again. In a similar fashion, the Internet host can keep a numeric IP address in memory, so it will not have to look it up again the next time a message is sent to that Internet address.

SUMMARY

Data is transmitted across the Internet through a series of protocols known collectively as TCP/IP (Transmission Control Protocol/Internet Protocol). The data are transmitted in packets, with each packet limited in size. The path that a particular message takes in getting to its destination is not important. All that matters is that the data arrives at its destination.

The Internet is built in layers that revolve around the TCP/IP protocol. The application layer at the sending computer creates a message and passes it to the transport layer where the message is divided into packets. The packets are addressed at the Internet layer, then sent across the Internet using the network access layer, which interacts with the various networks through which the data must travel to get to its destination. The process is reversed at the receiving computer.

Each computer connected to the Internet, whether dialing in or attached on a local area network (LAN), must have the software necessary to accomplish the task of the four layers. TCP/IP protocol drivers, or stacks as they are called, must be installed on each computer. Each computer must also have an IP address, a unique Internet address that identifies the computer as a node on the Internet. The IP address is composed of four numbers, each less than 256, each separated by a period—for example, 192.25.13.01.

The Domain Name System (DNS) provides the mnemonic equivalent of the numeric IP address and ensures that every site on the Internet has a unique address. The DNS divides the Internet into a series of component networks called domains. Large domains are in turn divided into smaller domains, with each domain responsible for maintaining unique addresses in the next lower-level domain, or subdomain.

appendix b

HOT WEB SITES

OVERVIEW

This appendix lists approximately 100 Web sites in various categories for you to explore. By its very nature, however, the Web is changing daily and it is impossible for any printed list to be completely current. It is helpful, therefore, to suggest ways to explore the Web in addition to going to a specific site.

One very useful technique is to guess the address of a site according to a consistent addressing scheme, such as www.company.com. The addresses of Netscape (www.netscape.com) and Microsoft (www.microsoft.com) follow this pattern. So do the home pages of many search engines, such as www.lycos.com or www.yahoo.com that take you to the home page of the Lycos and Yahoo engines, respectively. Some magazines also follow this pattern—for example, www.businessweek.com.

It helps to look for lists of sites, such as www.nba.com or www.nfl.com that take you to the home pages of the National Basketball Association and National Football League, respectively, which provide links to every team. Other lists of sites are not as obvious, but are equally valuable; for example, www.pathfinder.com takes you to the home page of Time Warner Communications, which provides links to multiple magazines including *Time, Fortune, Sports Illustrated, Money,* and *People.* The home page of Ziff-Davis publications (www.zdnet.com) directs you to multiple computer publications, many of which have their own list of "hot" sites. And finally, remember our address at Prentice Hall, www.prenhall.com/grauer, a site that we maintain to provide you with current information about the Internet.

Government, Political, and Nonprofit Organizations

Site Name	URL	Description
Campaign Central	**www.clark.net/ccentral**	Links to the Democratic and Republican National Committees, House leadership, and more.
Concord Coalition	**www.concordcoalition.org**	Learn more about the national debt—what you don't know could hurt you.
Director of Central Intelligence	**www.odci.gov**	The CIA, Directorate of Science & Technology, and more.
Electronic Frontier Foundation	**www2.eff.org**	A nonprofit civil liberties organization working to protect privacy, free expression, and access to public resources.
EPA	**www.epa.gov**	A searchable guide to the Environmental Protection Agency.
FBI	**www.fbi.gov**	Contains the FBI's 10-most-wanted list and other law enforcement information.
Federal Information Exchange	**www.fie.com/www/us_gov.htm**	List of US Gov't WWW servers with links to hundreds of other government sites.

Government, Political, and Nonprofit Organizations (continued)

Site Name	URL	Description
FedWorld	www.fedworld.gov	Searchable links to 120 government agencies.
IRS	www.irs.ustreas.gov	Thousands of tax forms, advice, and information to help you file your taxes.
Library of Congress	lcweb.loc.gov	A national treasure. Start with the American History Project, and browse for hours.
NASA	www.nasa.gov	Find out about the latest space shuttle launch and other vital NASA information.
National Park Service	www.nps.gov	Information on more than 350 sites in the National Park System.
Right Side of Web	www.rtside.com	Find out more about conservative hot topics.
Small Business Administration	www.sbaonline.sba.gov	Thinking of starting a business? Here's the place to start.
Social Security Administration	www.ssa.gov	Everything you need to know about the Social Security Administration.
Space Shuttle Site	liftoff.msfc.nasa.gov	Daily schedule of mission events, including video and virtual reality clips.
U.S. Census	www.census.gov	Contains a wealth of demographic information about the US.
U.S. Congress	thomas.loc.gov	Searchable information from the last two congressional sessions.
U.S. Geological Service	edcwww.cr.usgs.gov	The USGS declassified satellite photos—find your home or college from 50,000 feet.
U.S. House of Representatives	www.house.gov	Send a message to wired House members.
U.S. Patent and Trademark Office	www.uspto.gov	Check here to see if someone already has a patent on your invention.
White House	www.whitehouse.gov	Obtain the text of the president's speeches, or tour the White House.

Fun, Education, Entertainment, Shopping, and Sports

Site Name	URL	Description
100 Hot Sites	www.100hot.com	A constantly changing list of fun sites to explore.
America's Cup	www.ac2000.org	Follow the progress of the race to win the cup back from the Kiwis.
Bob Grauer's Home Page	www.bus.miami.edu/~rgrauer	Bob's home page at the University of Miami.
Branch Mall	branch.com	Shop at the Web's first mall without leaving your house.
Games Domain	www.gamesdomain.com	Contains links to computer and online games.
Homeopathy Home Page	www.dungeon.com/home/cam	Find out alternatives to mainstream medicine.
Hostel's Europe Pages	www.eurotrip.com	The home page for budget travel in Europe.
Interactive Frog Dissection	teach.virginia.edu/go/frog	Dissection without the formaldehyde.
Interactive Geometry	www.geom.umn.edu	Math on the Net.
Internet Movie Database	www.yahoo.com/Entertainment/ Movies_and_Films	Searchable guide to all the movies there ever were. Provides links to filmography on actors.
Internet Plaza	plaza.xor.com	A great cybermall organized by type of merchandise.
Internet Shopkeeper	shops.net	Another great place to shop.
Internet Shopping Network	www.internet.net	Shop for computers and peripherals here.
Lego Home Page	www.lego.com	Find out what's up in Legoland.
Medical Matrix	www.kumc.edu	Links to online medical resources.
National Basketball Association	www.nba.com	The home page for the NBA with links to individual teams.
National Football League	www.nfl.com	The home page for the NFL with links to individual teams.
MTV Online	www.mtv.com	Your favorite channel does it on the Net.

Fun, Education, Entertainment, Shopping, and Sports (continued)

Site Name	URL	Description
National Organization for Women	now.org	Women's rights are still an issue—check out this page to see why.
Tennis Server	www.tennisserver.com	Tennis anyone?
The Movie Link	www.movielink.com	A link to all sorts of movie information, including local show times.
Ultimate TV List	tvnet.com	Everything you want to know about TV.
Virtual Tourist	www.city.net	An online map with links around the world.
Warner Bros. Records	www.wbr.com	Information on Warner Bros. artists.
Women on the Net	www.cybergrrl.com	Links to many online resources for women, including information about domestic violence.
WWW of Sports	www.tns.lcs.mit.edu/cgi-bin/sports	Sports home page, with links to many other

Internet Information/Web News

Site Name	URL	Description
Georgia Institute of Technology	www.cc.gatech.edu/gvu	Links to Georgia Tech's graphics lab and survey of Web users.
Publicly Accessible Mailing Lists	www.neonoft.com:/internet/paml	Alphabetical list of mailing lists on lots of interesting topics.
The Scout Report	scout.cs.wisc.edu/report	Subscribe to receive a weekly e-mail update on what's new and interesting on the Net.
University of North Carolina/ Sun Microsystems, Inc.	sunsite.unc.edu	An award-winning site with lots of information about the Internet.
World Wide Web Consortium	www.w3.org	Home page of the World Wide Web Consortium.

Software Sites

Site Name	URL	Description
Cybersource	www.software.net	The Internet software store.
Internet Phone	www.vocaltec.com	Download software to send voice over the Internet.
RealAudio	www.realaudio.com	Audio over the Internet, uses compression methods to reduce audio files to 8% of original size.
Sun Microsystems, Inc.	java.sun.com	Check out Java software for the Web.

Online News, Newspapers, and Magazines

Site Name	URL	Description
ABC	www.abc.com	Home page of the ABC network.
Business Week	www.businessweek.com	Home page of *Business Week* magazine.
CBS	www.cbs.com	Home page of the CBS network.
CNN	www.cnn.com	Home page of the CNN network.
Fox	www.fox.com	Home page of the Fox network.
NBC	www.nbc.com	Home page of the NBC network.
New York Times	www.nytimes.com	"All the news that's fit to print."
Pathfinder	www.pathfinder.com	Access to many magazines including *People, Money, Fortune,* and *Time.*
PC Magazine	www.pcmag.com	Software downloads and *PC Magazine's* top 100 Web site list.
Public Broadcasting Service	www.cpb.org	Home Page of the Corporation for Public Broadcasting.

Online News, Newspapers, and Magazines (continued)

Site Name	URL	Description
San Jose Mercury News	**www.sjmercury.com**	The newspaper of Silicon Valley.
Slate	**www.slate.com**	Microsoft's online magazine.
The Wall Street Journal	**www.wsj.com**	Read today's paper online.
USA Today	**www.usatoday.com**	Read today's paper online.
Washington Post	**www.newsservice.com**	Access to the *Los Angeles Times* and *Washington Post* news service.
Ziff-Davis Publishing	**www.zdnet.com**	Scroll down the page for links to multiple computer magazines.

Commercial Sites

Site Name	URL	Description
American Airlines	**www.americanair.com**	You can now make reservations for ticketless travel at American's Web site.
AOL	**www.aol.com**	Subscribe to AOL here.
AT&T	**www.tollfree.att.net**	AT&T 800 number directory.
AutoByTel	**www.autobytel.com**	Find your model, get the best price, and buy your car online.
CarPoint	**www.carpoint.com**	Microsoft's answer to AutoByTel.
Chase Manhattan	**www.chase.com/loans/Sharewa.html**	Download software to help you analyze your finances.
CNN Financial Network	**cnnfn.com/**	Get daily information about markets, money management, and more.
CompuServe	**www.compuserve.com**	Information about the largest commercial online service in the US.
Dow Jones Quote Server	**www.secapl.com/cgi-bin/qs**	Find out the latest stock prices.
Dun & Bradstreet	**www.dbisna.com/dbis/dnbhome.htm**	The D&B home page.
Federal Reserve Bank of New York	**www.ny.frb.org/**	All sorts of banking and US Treasury information.
Fidelity Investments	**www.fidelity.com**	Monitor your investment online.
Godiva On-line	**www.godiva.com/**	Chocolate anyone?
IBM	**www.ibm.com**	Find out about IBM products.
Intel	**www.intel.com**	Get a technology briefing and find out about Intel's PC plans.
InterSoft Solution's, Inc.	**financehub.com**	The Finance Hub, with loads of information about stocks, bonds, venture capital, etc.
Microsoft	**www.microsoft.com/**	The best place to go for information about any Microsoft product.
Netscape	**www.netscape.com**	Stay up to date with Netscape.
Prodigy	**www.prodigy.com**	Home page for online commercial service provider
Travelocity	**www.travelocity.com**	Make reservations, order travel merchandise, and more.
Wall Street Journal Research Net	**www.wsrn.com/**	Find important financial information and read carefully before investing.

Searchable Lists and Directories

Site Name	URL	Description
Argus Clearinghouse	**www.clearinghouse.net**	A list of educational Web sites by category.
EINet Galaxy	**www.einet.net/galaxy.html**	A searchable directory of Internet resources.
InterNIC Directory	**ds.internic.net**	A searchable directory of Internet resources.
List of American Universities	**www.clas.ufl.edu/CLAS/ american-universities.html**	Contains links to over 200 college and university home pages.

Getting Started
ESSENTIAL COMPUTING CONCEPTS

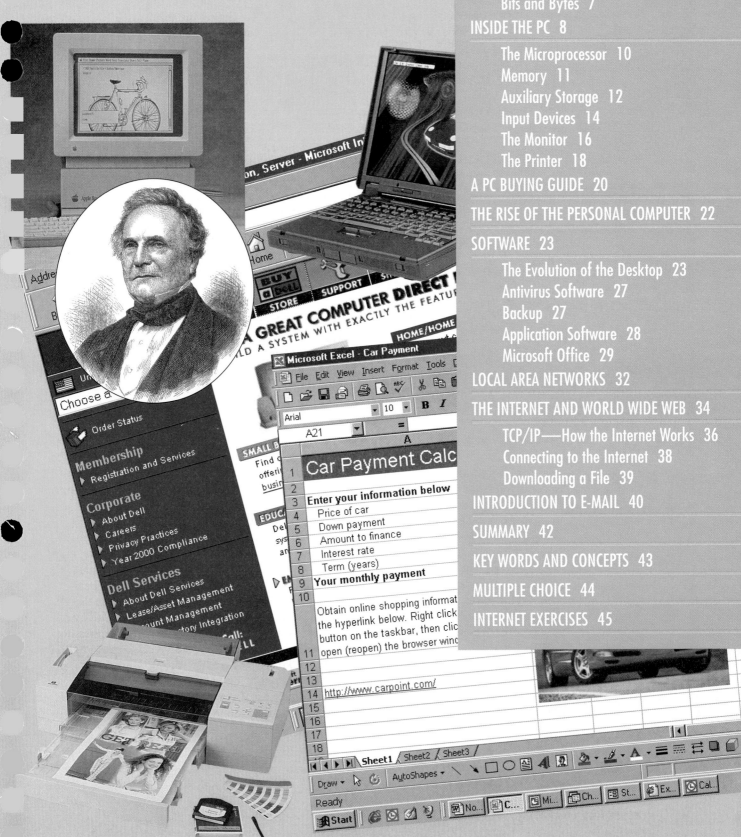

CONTENTS

OVERVIEW

Objectives

After reading this supplement you will be able to:

1. Describe components of a computer system; define the terms used to measure the capacity and speed of a microprocessor, memory, and auxiliary storage.

2. Describe the contribution of IBM, Microsoft, and Intel in the evolution of the PC; discuss several considerations in the purchase of a computer system.

3. Distinguish between system software and application software; describe the applications in Microsoft Office 2000 Professional.

4. Describe how to safeguard a system through acquisition of an antivirus program and through systematic backup.

5. Define a local area network; distinguish between a server and a workstation.

6. Define the Internet and the World Wide Web; explain how to access the Internet via a local area network or by dialing in through an Internet Service Provider.

7. Define a browser; distinguish between Internet Explorer and Netscape Communicator.

8. Describe e-mail; distinguish between a mail server and a mail client.

Overview

Computer literacy is the buzzword as we approach the year 2000. Corporations want their employees to be computer literate, parents expect their children to become computer literate, and you are probably taking this course in order to fulfill the computer literacy requirement at your school or university. We hope, therefore, that when you finish, you will feel comfortable with the computer and be able to use it effectively in a world of rapidly changing technology.

This supplement introduces you to the essential computer concepts you will need to achieve this goal. It is divided into three main sections—hardware, software, and the Internet. We begin with a discussion of hardware in which we describe the basic components in any computer system. We differentiate between the various types of computers, such as mainframes and PCs, but focus on the latter since it is the type of computer you will use in this course.

We continue with a discussion of software, which effectively determines how successful a computer system will be in satisfying your needs. Our presentation distinguishes between system software such as Windows 95 and application software such as Microsoft Office. No discussion of essential computing concepts would be complete, however, without mention of computer networks, the Internet, and the World Wide Web, the topics that are addressed in the last portion of this supplement.

A *computer* is an electronic device that accepts data (input), then manipulates or processes that data to produce information (output). It operates under the control of a *program* (or set of instructions) that is stored internally within the computer's memory. A *computer system* consists of the computer and its memory, peripheral devices such as a keyboard, disk, monitor, and printer, and the various programs that enable it to perform its intended function.

The idea of a general-purpose machine to solve mathematical problems was first proposed over 150 years ago by an Englishman named *Charles Babbage.* Babbage's machine would have been the world's first computer, but the technology of his day was incapable of producing the mechanical components to the required precision. Babbage died alone and penniless, having lost a personal fortune in a vain attempt to build his computer.

AHEAD OF THEIR TIME

Charles Babbage (1792–1871) went broke trying to build a general-purpose computing device he called the Analytical Engine. Babbage worked closely with Ada Lovelace (Lord Byron's daughter), who realized the potential of the machine and formulated basic programming principles. She is credited with being history's first programmer.

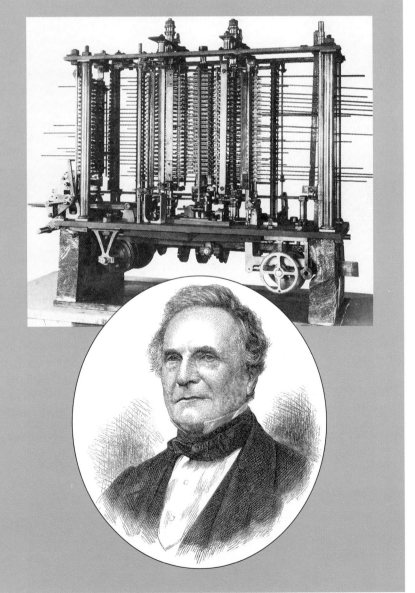

As happens so often with geniuses who are ahead of their time, Babbage's theory was validated a century after his death, since all modern computers are designed along the lines he proposed. Thus, every computer system, from Babbage's dream (called the Analytical Engine) to today's PC, includes the following components:

- The *central processing unit (CPU)* is the "brain" of the computer and performs the actual calculations.

- *Memory* (also known as *r*andom *a*ccess *m*emory or *RAM*) temporarily stores any program being executed by the computer, as well as the data on which the program operates.

- *Auxiliary storage* (also called secondary storage or external storage) provides a place where data can be permanently stored, and then transferred to and from main memory. A floppy disk, hard disk, CD-ROM, high-capacity removable media, and tape backup unit are the primary types of auxiliary storage used with a PC.

- *Input devices* accept data from an external source and convert it to electric signals, which are sent to the CPU. Virtually every PC is configured with a keyboard and mouse as its input devices. A joystick, scanner, and microphone are other common input devices. Auxiliary storage is also considered an input device.

- *Output devices* accept electric signals from the CPU and convert them to a form suitable for output. The monitor and printer are common output devices. Speakers are an output device necessary in order to hear sound from a PC. Auxiliary storage is also considered an output device.

The relationship between the components in a computer system is shown graphically in Figure 1. In essence, the CPU accepts data from an input device or auxiliary storage, stores it temporarily in memory while it computes an answer, then sends the results to an output device or auxiliary storage. All of this happens under the control of the *operating system,* a computer program (actually many programs) that links the various hardware components to one another. The operating system is stored on the hard disk, and it is loaded into memory when the computer is turned on. Once in memory, the operating system takes over, and it manages the system throughout the session.

Think for a moment about what happens when you sit down at the PC. You turn on the computer, which automatically loads the operating system from the hard disk (auxiliary storage) into memory (RAM) where its instructions are processed by the CPU. The initial commands in the operating system direct the monitor (an output device) to display the Windows desktop. You react to the output displayed on the screen by using the mouse (an input device) to click an icon such as the Start button, then follow with subsequent clicks to start a program. The operating system processes your commands, then determines it needs to load an application program (such as Microsoft Word) from auxiliary storage (the hard disk) into memory.

Figure 1 Components of a Computer System

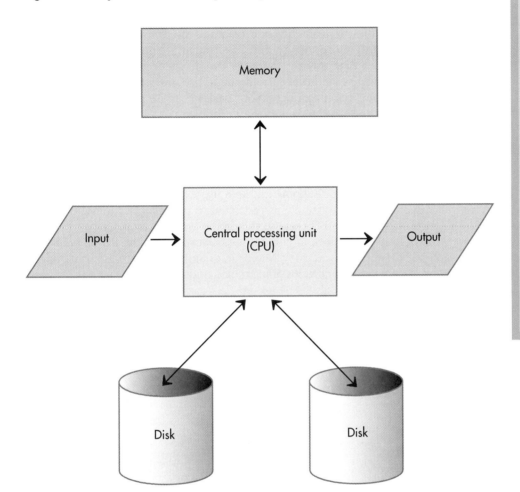

Every computer functions the same way. The CPU accepts data from an input device or auxiliary storage, stores it temporarily in memory while it computes an answer, then sends the result to an output device or auxiliary storage. All of this happens under the control of an operating system, a computer program (actually many programs) that links the various components of a computer to one another.

Now you are ready to go to work. You type at the keyboard (an input device) and enter the text of your document, which is stored in the computer's memory and simultaneously displayed on the monitor (an output device). When you're finished with the document, you execute a Print command to transfer the contents of memory to the printer (an alternate output device). And, of course, you will save the document, which copies the contents of memory to a disk (auxiliary storage). The next time you want to access the document, you execute the Open command, which copies the document from disk into memory, at which point you can further edit the document.

As you gain proficiency, you will take these operations for granted. It helps, however, if you reflect on the components of a computer system and how they interact with one another. And remember these principles apply to every computer system, from a PC to a mainframe.

Traditionally, computers have been divided into three broad classes—*mainframes, minicomputers* (called servers in today's environment), and *microcomputers* (PCs). The classification is primarily one of scale. Mainframes are much larger, faster, cost significantly more money, and have much greater memory and auxiliary storage capacities than other computers. The distinction is becoming increasingly difficult, however, as mainframes continue to become smaller while PCs grow more powerful. Indeed, the machine on your desk has more processing power and storage capability than the mainframe of a decade ago.

Another way to distinguish among the different types of computers is by the number of users who can access the machine at one time. A mainframe supports hundreds (or even thousands) of users simultaneously and is at the core of national and global networks supported by large corporations and other organizations. Minicomputers (servers) also support multiple users, but a smaller number than a mainframe. A microcomputer or PC is restricted to one user at a time.

Our text focuses on the PC because that is the type of computer you see most frequently. There is much more to computing, however, than the PC on your desk or the notebook computer you carry. Mainframes and servers are the backbone of information systems in corporations, universities, and other organizations. Figure 2 illustrates an IBM mainframe.

Figure 2   IBM Mainframe

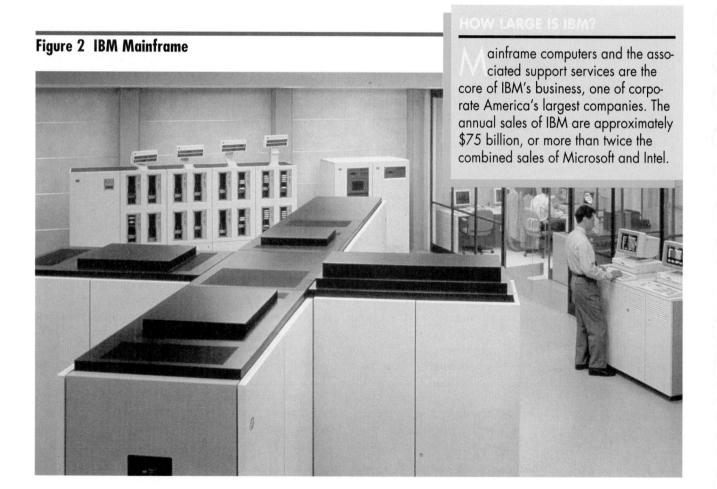

HOW LARGE IS IBM?

Mainframe computers and the associated support services are the core of IBM's business, one of corporate America's largest companies. The annual sales of IBM are approximately $75 billion, or more than twice the combined sales of Microsoft and Intel.

Bits and Bytes

A computer is first and foremost a numerical machine. It is designed to perform mathematical calculations, and it does so very efficiently. It also works with text, graphics, and multimedia files such as sound and video, all of which are converted to a numeric equivalent. You need not be concerned with precisely how this is accomplished. What is important is that you realize that computers work exclusively with numerical data.

In addition, computers use binary numbers (zeros and ones) rather than decimal numbers. Why binary, and not decimal? The answer is that a binary machine is easy to build, as only two values are required. A current may be on or off, or a switch may be up or down. A decimal computer would be far more difficult.

The binary system is described in terms of bits and bytes. A **bit** (binary digit) has two values, zero and one. Individual bits do not, however, convey meaningful information, and so computer storage is divided into bytes, where one **byte** consists of eight bits. In other words, a byte is the smallest addressable unit of memory, and any reference to the size of a computer's memory or to the capacity of its disk drive is in terms of bytes.

As indicated, a byte consists of eight bits, each of which can be either a zero or a one. Thus, there are 2^8 (or 256) possible combinations of zeros and ones that can be stored in a byte. We need, however, a way to make sense of the bits and bytes that are processed by the computer. Accordingly, a code was developed in which each combination of eight bits (one byte) represents a different character. It is known as the American Standard Code for Information Interchange (**ASCII** for short and pronounced as "as key").

The ASCII code provides for 256 different characters, which is more than enough to represent the 26 letters of the alphabet (both upper- and lowercase), the digits 0 through 9, the punctuation marks, and various special keys you find on the typical keyboard. The ASCII codes for the uppercase letters are shown in Figure 3a. Can you see how those representations are used to create the message in Figure 3b, which represents the contents of five contiguous (adjacent) bytes in memory?

Figure 3 ASCII

ASCII CODES	
Character	**ASCII Code**
A	01000001
B	01000010
C	01000011
D	01000100
E	01000101
F	01000110
G	01000111
H	01001000
I	01001001
J	01001010
K	01001011
L	01001100
M	01001101
N	01001110
O	01001111
P	01010000
Q	01010001
R	01010010
S	01010011
T	01010100
U	01010101
V	01010110
W	01010111
X	01011000
Y	01011001
Z	01011010
space	00000000

(a) ASCII Codes

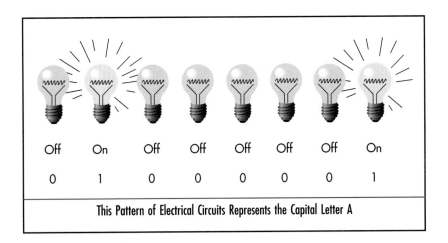

Off	On	Off	Off	Off	Off	Off	On
0	1	0	0	0	0	0	1

This Pattern of Electrical Circuits Represents the Capital Letter A

01001000 01000101 01001100 01001100 01001111

H   **E**   **L**   **L**   **O**

(b) "Hello" in ASCII

Thus far, we have spoken of computers in general. And while you encounter mainframes when you deal with a large organization in making a plane reservation or checking an account balance, you will use a PC in this course. Accordingly, the remainder of our discussion focuses exclusively on the PC.

IBM announced its version of the personal computer (PC) in 1981 and broke a longstanding corporate tradition by going to external sources for supporting hardware and software. *Intel* designed the microprocessor. *Microsoft* developed the operating system. The decision to go outside the corporation was motivated in part because IBM was playing "catch up." The Apple II and the Radio Shack TRS-80 had each been available for three years. More to the point, IBM was a mainframe company and simply did not believe in the future of the PC, a decision that the company would regret.

The IBM PC was an instant success, in large part because of its open design that let independent vendors offer supporting products to enhance the functionality of the machine. This was accomplished by creating *expansion slots* on the *motherboard* (the main system board inside the PC) that could accommodate *adapter cards* from sources outside IBM. The motherboard contains the circuitry that connects the components of the PC to one another, and thus plugging in an adapter card is the equivalent of adding another device to the machine. IBM made public the necessary technical information to create the adapter cards, enabling other companies to build peripheral devices for the PC and enhance its overall capability.

The open design of the PC was a mixed blessing for IBM, in that PC-compatibles based on the same microprocessor and able to run the same software, began to appear as early as 1982 and offered superior performance for less money. Companies and individuals that were once willing to pay a premium for the IBM name began ordering the "same" machine from other vendors. IBM today has less than ten percent of the market it was so instrumental in creating, as the personal computer has become a commodity. "PC" is now a generic term for any computer based on Intel-compatible microprocessors that are capable of running Microsoft Windows.

Figure 4 illustrates a typical Windows workstation as it exists today. We view the system from the front (Figure 4a), the rear (Figure 4b), and from inside the system unit (Figure 4c). Your system will be different from ours, but you should be able to recognize the various components regardless of whether you use a desktop, tower, or notebook computer. We continue with a discussion of each component.

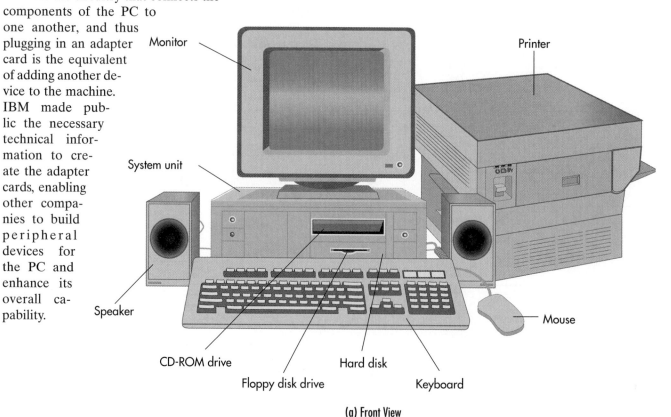

(a) Front View

Figure 4 A Windows Workstation

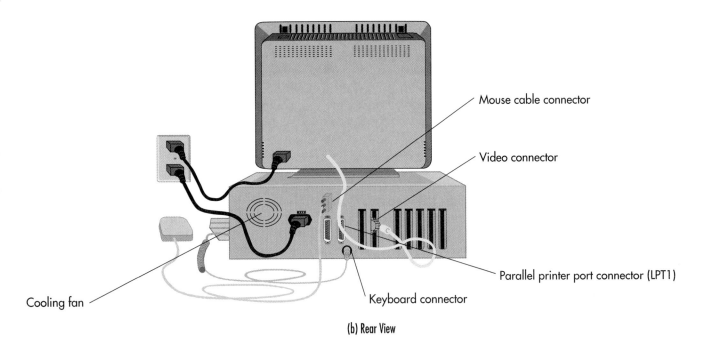

Mouse cable connector

Video connector

Parallel printer port connector (LPT1)

Cooling fan

Keyboard connector

(b) Rear View

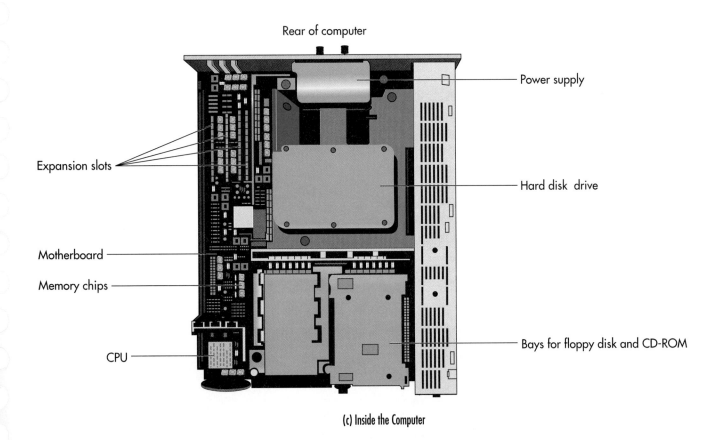

Rear of computer

Power supply

Expansion slots

Hard disk drive

Motherboard

Memory chips

CPU

Bays for floppy disk and CD-ROM

(c) Inside the Computer

The PC, like any microcomputer, is characterized by the fact that its entire CPU is contained on a single silicon chip known as a ***microprocessor.*** Intel has continually improved its microprocessor so that today's PC is significantly more powerful than any of its predecessors. The earlier Intel chips were referenced by number such as 286, 386, or 486, all of which are obsolete. Rather than continuing to number its microprocessors Intel trademarked the names ***Pentium, Pentium II, Pentium III*** and ***Celeron*** to differentiate its chips from the competition. (You can purchase Intel-compatible chips from other vendors, such as AMD or Cyrix, but only Intel has the various Pentium chips, which has become a highly recognized brand name.)

Not all Pentiums are created equal, as the chips are further differentiated by ***clock speed,*** an indication of how fast instructions are executed. The clock speed is measured in ***megahertz (MHz),*** and the higher the clock speed the faster the microprocessor (e.g., a Pentium II running at 450MHz is faster than a Pentium II running at 400MHz.). To facilitate the comparison of one microprocessor to another, Intel has created the ***Intel CPU performance (iCOMP) index*** as shown in Figure 5. The index consists of a single number to indicate the relative performance of a microprocessor; the higher the number the faster the processor.

Figure 5 The Microprocessor

You can obtain the most current version of the iCOMP index
by going to the Intel Web site at www.intel.com

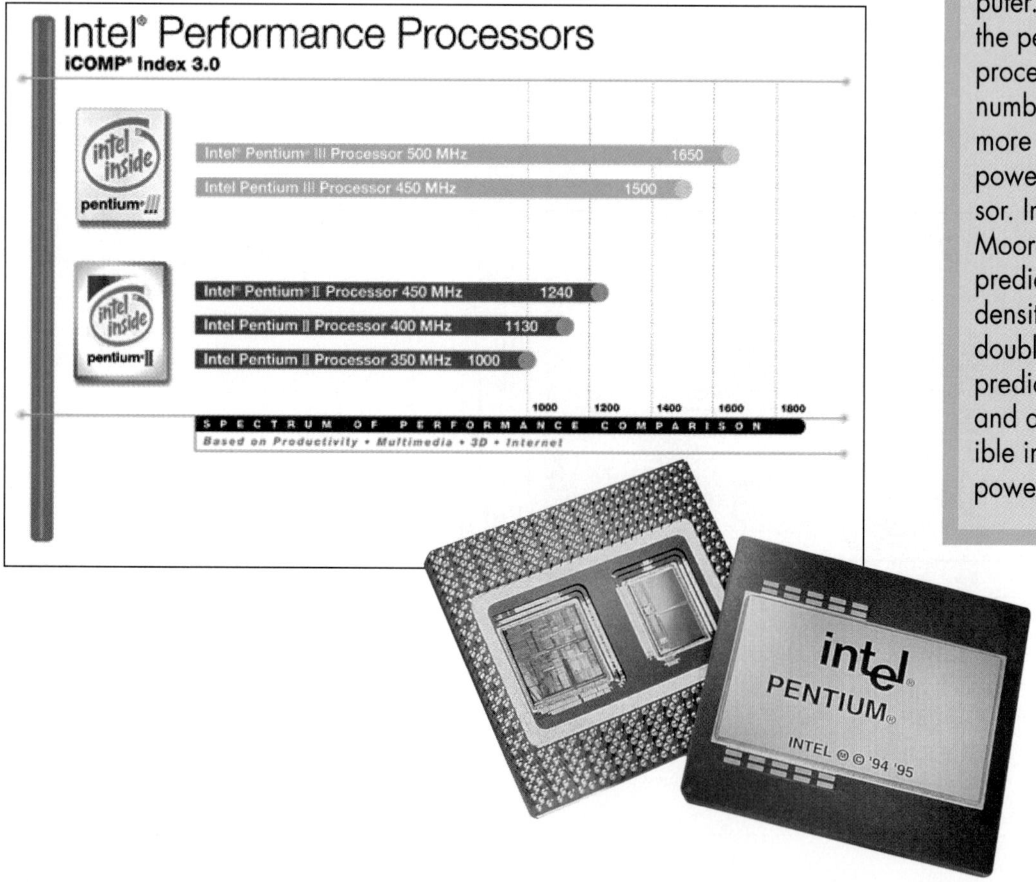

Intel® Performance Processors
iCOMP® Index 3.0

Processor	iCOMP Index
Intel® Pentium® III Processor 500 MHz	1650
Intel Pentium III Processor 450 MHz	1500
Intel® Pentium® II Processor 450 MHz	1240
Intel Pentium II Processor 400 MHz	1130
Intel Pentium II Processor 350 MHz	1000

Scale: 1000 1200 1400 1600 1800

SPECTRUM OF PERFORMANCE COMPARISON
Based on Productivity • Multimedia • 3D • Internet

MOORE'S LAW

The fundamental unit of the microprocessor is the transistor—the on/off, zero/one switch that is at the heart of the digital computer. The key to improving the performance of a microprocessor is to increase the number of transistors; the more transistors, the more powerful the microprocessor. In 1965 Gordon Moore, the founder of Intel, predicted that transistor densities would continue to double every 18 months, a prediction that has held, and accounts for the incredible increase in computer power.

Memory

The microprocessor is the brain of the PC, but it needs instructions that tell it what to do, data on which to work, and a place to store the result of its calculations. All of this takes place in *memory,* a temporary storage area that holds data, instructions, and results, and passes everything back and forth to the CPU. The amount of memory a system has is important because the larger the memory, the more sophisticated the programs are that the computer is capable of executing, and further, the more programs and data that can remain in memory at the same time.

As depicted in Figure 6, the memory of a computer (also known as random access memory or RAM) is divided into individual storage locations, each of which holds one byte. In the early days of the PC, memory was measured in *kilobytes (KB).* Today RAM is measured in *megabytes (MB).* One KB and one MB are equal to approximately one thousand and one million characters, respectively. (In actuality 1KB equals 1024 bytes, or 2^{10} bytes whereas 1MB is 1,048,576 bytes, or 2^{20} bytes.) A Windows workstation typically has 32MB (or even 64MB) of memory in today's environment.

The microprocessor also reads data from a second type of memory known as *read-only memory (ROM).* Read-only memory is accessed only when the computer is first turned on, as it contains the instructions telling the computer to check itself, and then to load the essential portion of the operating system into memory. The contents of ROM are established at the factory and cannot be altered by application programs, hence the name "read only."

The size of a computer's memory refers only to the amount of RAM available. The contents of RAM, however, are volatile and change constantly as different programs are executed, or every time the same program is executed with different data. RAM is also transient, which means that shutting off (or losing) the power to the system erases the contents of memory. Auxiliary storage devices, however, retain their contents even when there is no power.

HOW LARGE IS 16 MB?

magine that you have been assigned the task of checking the contents of each byte, and that it takes you one second per byte. At that rate, it would take approximately 6 months to view the contents of every location. And if the system received a memory upgrade to 32MB, it would take a full year!

Figure 6 Memory

01001101	01000101	01001101	01001111	01010010	01011001

A computer's memory can be thought of as a large grid, with each cell corresponding to a single memory location, capable of holding a single ASCII character. It's known as RAM (random access memory) because it takes the same amount of time to access any memory location, and further because the assignment of specific locations is arbitrary. The contents of RAM depend on a power source and are erased when the power is shut off. Can you decipher the word that is stored in the first six memory locations?

Figure 7 depicts several types of auxiliary storage devices. Disks are the most common and fall into two categories—floppy disks and hard disks. The *floppy disk* gets its name because it is made of a flexible plastic (although it is enclosed in a hard plastic case). The *hard disk* uses rigid metal platters. A hard disk is also called a fixed disk because it remains permanently inside the system unit. A hard disk holds significantly more data than a floppy disk, and it accesses that data much faster.

The PC of today has standardized on the 3½-inch high-density floppy disk with a capacity of 1.44MB. (The 5¼-inch floppy disk is obsolete, as is the double-density floppy disk, which had a capacity of 720KB. Thus, all references to a floppy disk will be to the 3½-inch high-density disk.) The capacity of a hard disk is much greater and is measured in *gigabytes (GB),* where 1GB is approximately one billion ($2^{30} = 1,073,741,824$) bytes. There is no such item as a standard hard disk, as each system is configured independently, but disks with 2GB or more are typical. (Older hard disks had capacities that were measured in megabytes.)

All disks are also characterized by *access time,* which is the average time required to locate a specific item on the disk. Access time is measured in milliseconds (ms) where one millisecond equals one thousandth of a second. The shorter the access time, the faster the disk. The floppy disk has an average time of 175 ms. By contrast, the typical hard disk has an access time of only 10 ms.

As indicated, there are many types of auxiliary storage. The *CD-ROM,* once a high-priced optional device, has become a virtual standard on today's PC. CD-ROM stands for Compact Disk, Read-Only Memory, meaning that you can read from the CD but you cannot write to the CD. A CD-ROM is characterized by its access time just as a disk. The original standard was 600 milliseconds (ms), but as with all technology, that has improved significantly over time, giving rise to today's 12X (12-speed) and 24X (24-speed) devices.

All CDs, regardless of speed, have a storage capacity of 650MB (compared to 1.44MB on a floppy disk). The large capacity, coupled with the relatively modest cost of duplicating a CD ($1.00 or less in large quantities) makes the CD an ideal way to distribute large amounts of data. Most computer games and programs, for example, are distributed on a single CD as opposed to multiple floppy disks of years past. Reference material, such as an encyclopedia, is also distributed via a CD. A new type of compact disk known as *DVD* holds up to 17GB, enabling a full-length movie to be distributed via a single disk.

Two other auxiliary storage devices of which you should be aware are the *tape backup unit* and *high-capacity removable media.* Both enable you to record data, and further, to take that data with you. Thus, either is suitable to back up the data from a hard drive. The Iomega Zip drive is an example of a removable media device and is fast becoming a standard on today's PC. It has a capacity of 100MB, and functions as a very large floppy disk. Other vendors manufacture other types of removable media.

WHAT IS DRIVE C?

The CPU needs to differentiate one auxiliary storage device from another and does so by designating each device with a letter. The floppy drive is always drive A. (A second floppy drive, if it were present, would be drive B.) The hard disk is always drive C with other auxiliary devices assigned letters from D on. Thus, a system with one floppy drive, a hard disk, and a CD-ROM (today's most common configuration) would have as devices, A, C, D, corresponding to the floppy disk, hard disk, and CD-ROM, respectively.

Figure 7 Auxiliary Storage

HOW DISK STORAGE WORKS

Computer disks—both floppy and hard—are flat dishes coated on both sides with a magnetic film. When a disk is formatted, magnetic codes are embedded in the film to divide the surface of the disk into sectors (pie-slice wedges) and tracks (concentric circles). They organize the disk so that data can be recorded in a logical manner and accessed quickly by the read/write heads that move back and forth over the disk as it spins. The number of sectors and tracks that fit on a disk determine its capacity.

(a) Floppy Disks

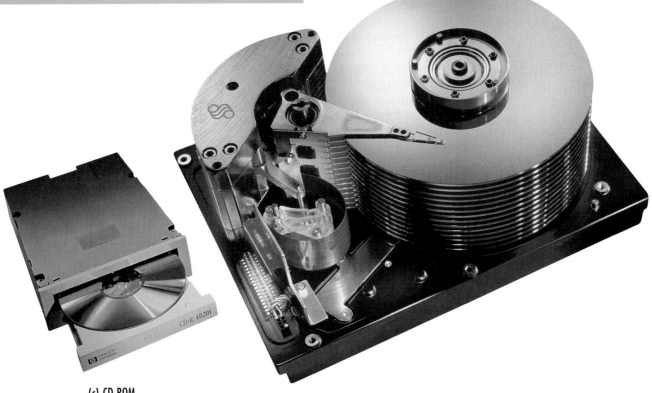

(c) CD-ROM

(b) Hard Disk

(d) Tape Backup

(e) ZIP Drive

The *keyboard* and the mouse are the primary input devices for the PC. The keys on the keyboard are arranged much like those of a typewriter, in the standard QWERTY pattern (named for the first six characters in the third row). In addition, there are several special keys that are unique to the PC as shown in Figure 8.

The *Caps Lock key* eliminates the need to continually press the shift key to enter uppercase letters. The Caps Lock key functions as a toggle switch; that is, pressing it once causes all uppercase letters to be entered; pressing it a second time returns to lowercase; pressing it again returns to uppercase, and so on. The *Num Lock key* is similar in concept and activates the numeric keypad at the right side of the keyboard.

Function keys (F1 through F12) are special-purpose keys, used by various application programs to execute specific commands and/or save keystrokes. The exact purpose of a particular function key varies from program to program. The *Ctrl* and *Alt keys* work in similar fashion and are used with other keys to execute a specific command.

Cursor keys [the four arrow keys, up (↑), down (↓), right (→), and left (←)] control movement of the cursor (the blinking line or box), which shows where on the monitor the data will be entered. The *Home, End, PgUp,* and *PgDn* keys also serve to move the cursor.

The *Enter* (return) *key* signals the completion of an entry and correspondingly causes the characters typed on the keyboard to be transmitted to the CPU. Other special keys include the *Insert (Ins)* and *Delete (Del) keys* that insert and/or delete characters, respectively. The *Escape (Esc) key* is used by many programs to cancel (or escape from) current actions. The *Print Screen key* copies the image on the monitor into memory from where it can be inserted into a document. And finally, the *Windows key* (found only on newer keyboards) is equivalent to clicking the Start button on the taskbar in Windows 95 or Windows 98.

The standard *mouse* has two buttons and recognizes four basic operations with which you must become familiar:

- To *point* to an object, move the mouse pointer onto the object.

- To *click* an object, point to it, then press and release the left mouse button; to *right click* an object, point to the object, then press and release the right mouse button.

- To *double click* an object, point to it, then quickly click the left button twice in succession.

- To *drag* an object, move the pointer to the object, then press and hold the left button while you move the mouse to a new position.

The keyboard and mouse are the primary input devices for the PC, but there are others. A *microphone* is required to record your own sound files, which can then be played through the sound card and speakers. A *scanner* enables you to convert a graphic image into its digital equivalent for subsequent inclusion in a document. A scanner also enables you to convert text into a form suitable for word processing. And don't forget a *joystick,* which is an essential component of many computer games.

Figure 8 Input Devices

Joystick

Mouse

Keyboard

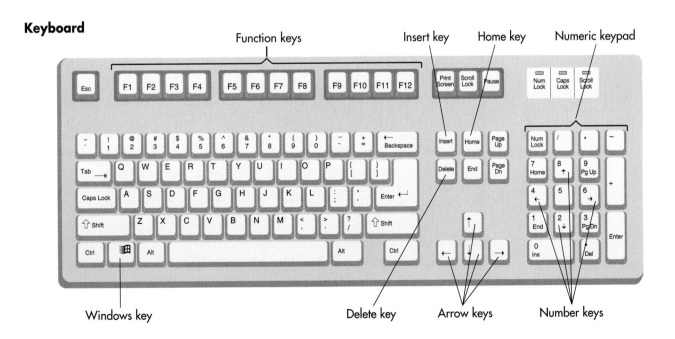

Function keys

Insert key   Home key   Numeric keypad

Windows key   Delete key   Arrow keys   Number keys

The **monitor** (or video display) is an output device. The monitor of a typical desktop configuration uses CRT (cathode ray tube) technology, the same technology that is in a television. Notebook computers, however, use a flat-panel display known as a liquid crystal display (LCD). Either way, the image that is displayed consists of **pixels** (the tiny dots or *pic*ture *el*ements).

The quality of a monitor is determined by its dot pitch, a measure of how close adjacent pixels are to one another. The smaller the dot pitch, the crisper the image; conversely the larger the dot pitch the more grainy the picture. You should reject any monitor with a dot pitch larger than .28.

The **resolution** of a monitor is defined as the number of pixels that are displayed at one time. Several resolutions are possible, but you are most likely to see either 640 × 480 (640 pixels across by 480 pixels down) or 800 × 600 (800 pixels across by 600 pixels down). The advantage of the higher resolution is that more pixels are displayed on the screen and hence you see more of the document—for example, more columns in a spreadsheet or more pages in a word processing document. Realize, however, that the higher the resolution, the larger the monitor should be, or else the image will be too difficult to read. Today's standard monitor sizes of 15 and 17 inches work well with resolutions of 640 × 480 and 800 × 600, respectively. Higher resolutions are also possible (e.g., 1024 × 728, 1280 × 1024 or 1600 × 1200), but require larger and (considerably) more expensive monitors. Figure 9 displays the same spreadsheet at different resolutions.

The processing requirements imposed on the monitor are enormous. The CPU has to send approximately 300,000 bytes of data for each screen (given that each pixel requires one byte and that there are 640 × 480 pixels per screen). That is only the beginning. The screen has to be refreshed approximately 70 times a second. Each pixel can require two or even three bytes of data if color palettes with more than 256 characters are specified. The requirements become even more demanding at higher resolutions. To keep the entire system from grinding to a halt, the PC is equipped with a **video (display) adapter** (or graphics card) to facilitate the display of output on a monitor. The graphics card has its own memory, which is known as **video memory.** A minimum of 2MB is suggested.

CHOOSING A MONITOR

Do some monitors produce a sharper, crisper picture than others, even at the same resolution? Does the image on one monitor appear to flicker while the image on another remains constant? The differences are due to information that is often buried in the fine print of an advertisement.

The dot pitch is the distance between adjacent pixels. The smaller the dot pitch the crisper the image, or conversely, the larger the dot pitch the more grainy the picture. Choose a monitor with a dot pitch of .28 or less.

The vertical refresh rate determines how frequently the screen is repainted from top to bottom. A rate that is too slow causes the screen to flicker because it is not being redrawn fast enough to fool the eye into seeing a constant pattern. A rate of 70Hz (70 cycles per second) is the minimum you should accept.

Figure 9 Monitor Size and Resolution

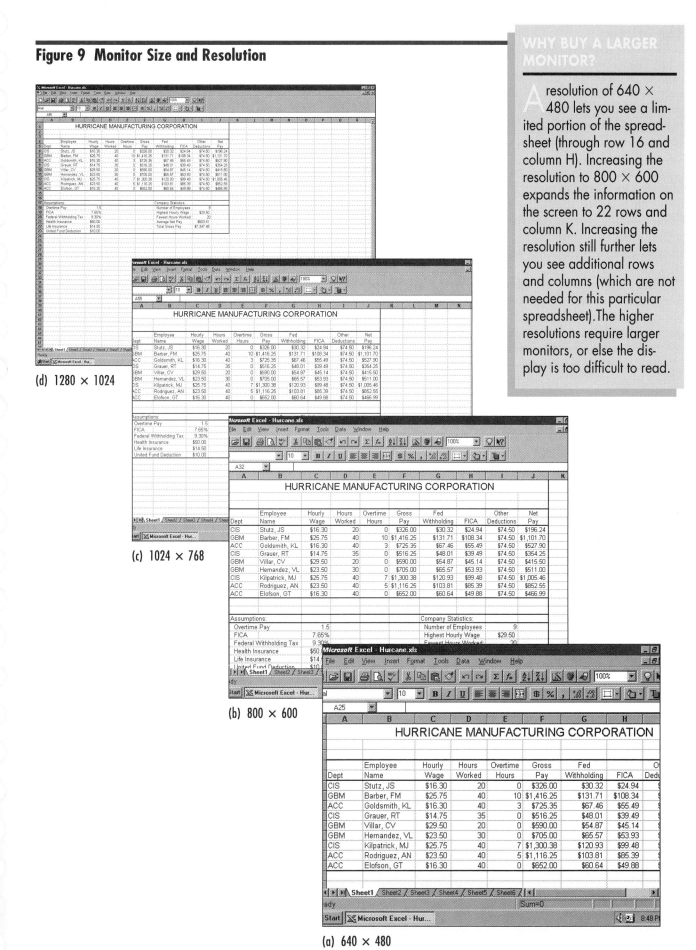

A resolution of 640 × 480 lets you see a limited portion of the spreadsheet (through row 16 and column H). Increasing the resolution to 800 × 600 expands the information on the screen to 22 rows and column K. Increasing the resolution still further lets you see additional rows and columns (which are not needed for this particular spreadsheet). The higher resolutions require larger monitors, or else the display is too difficult to read.

(d) 1280 × 1024

(c) 1024 × 768

(b) 800 × 600

(a) 640 × 480

The Printer

A *printer* produces output on paper or acetate transparencies. The output is referred to as *hard copy* because it is more tangible than the files written to a disk or other electronic devices. Printers vary greatly in terms of design, price, and capability as can be seen in Figure 10.

The *dot matrix printer* was the entry-level printer of choice for many years, but it has passed into obsolescence in favor of the inkjet printer. The dot matrix printer was inexpensive and versatile, but it had two major drawbacks—noise and a less-than-perfect print quality since each character was created with a pattern of dots.

The *inkjet printer* has become today's entry-level printer, and it offers a significant improvement in both areas—it's quieter than a dot matrix printer, and its print quality is much better. Best of all, it costs only a few hundred dollars, with color a very affordable option.

The *laser printer* is the top-of-the-line device and it offers speed and quality superior to that of an inkjet. The resolution of a laser printer is measured in dots per inch (e.g., 600 dpi), and its speed is measured in pages per minute (e.g., 8 ppm). *Network printers* are significantly faster.

Regardless of the printer you choose, you will need to learn about typography when you begin to create your own documents. *Typography* is the process of selecting typefaces, type styles, and type sizes. It is a critical, often subtle element in the success of a document. Good typography goes almost unnoticed, whereas poor typography calls attention to itself and detracts from a document.

A *typeface* (or *font*) is a complete set of characters (upper- and lowercase letters, numbers, punctuation marks, and special symbols). Typefaces are divided into two general categories, serif and sans serif. A *serif typeface* (e.g., Times New Roman) has tiny cross lines at the ends of the characters to help the eye connect one letter with the next. A *sans serif typeface* (e.g., Arial) does not have these lines. A commonly accepted practice is to use serif typefaces with large amounts of text and sans serif typefaces for smaller amounts

Type size is a vertical measurement and is specified in points. One *point* is equal to $1/72$ of an inch. The text in most documents is set in 10 or 12 point type. (The book you are reading is set in 10-point.) Different elements in the same document are often set in different type sizes to provide suitable emphasis.

This is Times New Roman 10 point
This is Times New Roman 12 point
This is Times New Roman 18 point
This is Times New Roman 24 point
This is Times New Roman 30 point

This is Arial 10 point
This is Arial 12 point
This is Arial 18 point
This is Arial 24 point
This is Arial 30 point

Basics of Typography—Typefaces and Point Sizes

Figure 10 Printers

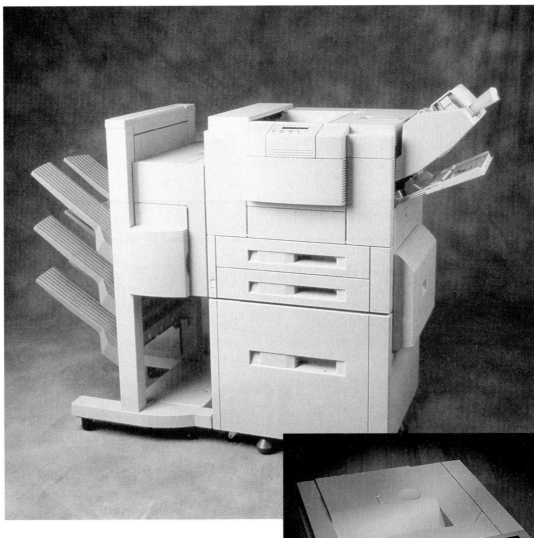

(a) Network Printer

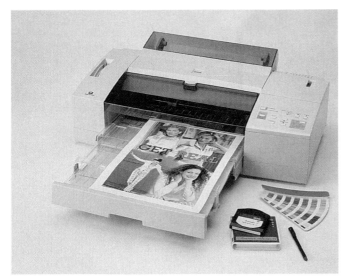

(b) Inkjet Printer

(c) Laser Printer

Are you confused about all the ads for personal computers? You can buy from hundreds of companies, retail or through the mail, with no such thing as a standard configuration. The PC has, in effect, become a commodity where the consumer is able to select each component. We suggest you approach the purchase of a PC just as you would the purchase of any big-ticket item, with research and planning. Be sure you know your hardware requirements before you walk into a computer store, or else you will spend too much money or buy the wrong system. Stick to your requirements and don't be swayed to a different item if the vendor is out of stock. You've waited this long to buy a computer, and another week or two won't matter.

Figure 11 Working in Comfort

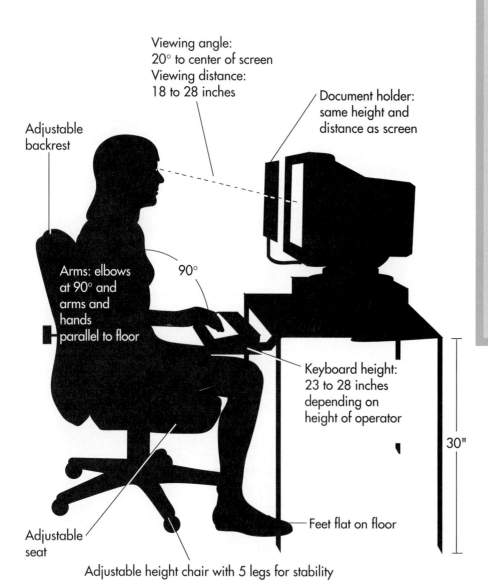

Viewing angle:
20° to center of screen
Viewing distance:
18 to 28 inches

Document holder:
same height and
distance as screen

Adjustable
backrest

Arms: elbows
at 90° and
arms and
hands
parallel to floor

90°

Keyboard height:
23 to 28 inches
depending on
height of operator

30"

Feet flat on floor

Adjustable
seat

Adjustable height chair with 5 legs for stability

BE KIND TO YOURSELF

Are you the type of person who will spend thousands on a new computer, only to set it up on your regular desk and sit on a $10 bridge chair? Don't. A conventional desk (or the dining room table) is 30 inches high, but the recommended typing height is 27 inches. The difference accounts for the stiff neck, tight shoulders, and aching backs reported by many people who sit at a computer over an extended period of time. Be kind to yourself and include a computer table with lots of room as well as a comfortable chair in your budget (Figure 11).

Mail order will almost always offer better prices than a retail establishment, but price should not be the sole consideration. Local service and support are also important, especially if you are a nontechnical new user. A little research, however, and you can purchase through the mail with confidence, and save yourself money in the process. If you do purchase by mail, confirm the order in writing, stating exactly what you are expecting to receive and when. Include the specific brands and/or model numbers and the agreed-upon price, including shipping and handling, to have documentation in the event of a dispute.

Our experience has been that the vast majority of dealers, both retail and mail order, are reputable, but as with any purchase, *caveat emptor*. Good luck, good shopping, and keep the following in mind.

Don't forget the software. Any machine you buy will come with Windows 95 (or in the near future, Windows 98), but that is only the beginning since you must also purchase the application software you intend to run. Many first-time buyers are surprised that they have to pay extra for software, but you had better allow for software in your budget. Ideally, Microsoft Office will be bundled with your machine, but if not, the university bookstore is generally your best bet as it offers a substantial educational discount.

Don't skimp on memory. The more memory a system has the better its overall performance. Windows 95 and its associated applications are powerful, but they require adequate resources to run efficiently. 32MB of RAM is the minimum you should consider in today's environment. You should also be sure that your system can accommodate additional memory easily and cheaply.

Buy more disk space than you think you need. We purchased our first hard disk as an upgrade to the original PC in 1984. It was a "whopping" 10MB, and our biggest concern was that we would never fill it all. The storage requirements of application programs have increased significantly. Microsoft Office, for example, requires 150MB for a complete installation. A 6GB drive is the minimum you should consider in today's environment, but for an additional $100 (or less) you can add another gigabyte or more. It is money well spent.

Let your fingers do the walking. A single issue of a computer magazine contains advertisements from many vendors, making it possible to comparison-shop from multiple mail-order vendors from the convenience of home. You can also shop online and can visit a vendor's web site to obtain the latest information. Go to the Exploring Windows home page at www.prenhall.com/grauer, click the link to student resources, then click the link to a PC Buying Guide to visit some suggested sites.

Look for 30-day price protection. An unconditional 30-day money-back guarantee is an industry standard. Insist on this guarantee and be sure you have it in writing. A reputable vendor will also refund the amount of any price reduction that occurs during the first 30 days, but it is incumbent on you to contact the vendor and request a refund. Don't forget to do so.

Use a credit card. You can double the warranty of any system (up to one additional year) by using a major credit card provided it offers a "buyer's protection" policy. (Check with your credit card company to see whether it has this feature, and if not, you may want to consider getting a different credit card.) The extended warranty is free and it goes into effect automatically when you charge your computer. The use of a credit card also gives you additional leverage if you are dissatisfied with an item.

Don't forget the extras. The standard PC comes with a simple speaker that is capable of little more than the beep you hear when you press the wrong key. True sound requires the installation of a sound card and the availability of speakers. A microphone is required if you want to record your own sound. A modem is also extra. Any vendor will gladly sell you these components. Just remember to ask.

Don't be frustrated when prices drop. The system you buy today will invariably cost less tomorrow, and further, tomorrow's machine will run circles around today's most powerful system. The IBM/XT, for example, sold for approximately $5,000 and was configured with an 8088 microprocessor, a 10MB hard disk, 128KB of RAM, and monochrome monitor, but it was the best system you could buy in 1983. The point of this example is that you enjoy the machine you buy today without concern for future technology. Indeed, if you wait until prices come down, you will never buy anything, because there will always be something better for less.

THE RISE OF THE PERSONAL COMPUTER

The development of the PC has been absolutely astounding. Its capabilities dwarf those of earlier mainframes at a fraction of the cost. To appreciate how far and fast we've come, consider four of its immediate predecessors.

Altair 8800 (1975): The January 1975 issue of *Popular Electronics* featured the Altair 8800 on its cover: The world's first PC had to be built from a kit that cost $439. It had no keyboard or monitor, no software, and was programmed by switches on the front panel.

Apple II (1977): The Apple II was a fully assembled home computer in an attractive case, complete with keyboard, connection to a TV screen, color, memory to 64Kb, and BASIC interpreter. The machine was to launch the personal computer revolution and vault its founders, Steve Wozniak and Steve Jobs, from garage to glory.

IBM PC (1981): IBM was neither first nor technologically innovative, but their announcement put the personal computer on the desks of America's businesspeople, just as Apple had put the computer in the home. By 1985 IBM had manufactured its three millionth PC, and had spawned an entire industry in the process.

Apple Macintosh (1984): The Macintosh was far from an instant success, but once Apple got the bugs out and added an internal hard disk, laser printer, and expanded memory, the machine took off. Its ease of use and graphical interface offered an entirely different perspective on computing.

The PC Today (1999): Today's PC runs rings around its predecessor. You can buy a Pentium II processor with 128MB of RAM, an 8GB hard drive, a 17-inch monitor, a high-speed CD-ROM, a sound card and speakers, and an ink-jet color printer for approximately $2,000. The software is equally advanced, as Windows and Microsoft Office empower the end user in ways that were unforeseen just a decade ago.

Altair 8800

Apple II

The PC Today

Macintosh

The most advanced computer system is useless without appropriate software. Indeed, it is the availability of software that justifies the purchase of hardware and dictates how the computer will be used. Without software, the computer is just an expensive paperweight. Thus, to truly understand the computer, you need to learn about the types of programs that it can run.

All software is divided broadly into two classes—**system software** (referred to as the operating system) and **application software.** Perhaps you are familiar with applications such as word processing or computer games. If so, you realize that the wonderful thing about application software is that replacing one application with another completely changes the personality of the computer. The same computer that is used for word processing can also be used to surf the Internet, prepare long-range financial forecasts using spreadsheet models, compose music, play a computer game, or perform hundreds of other chores merely by changing the application program being used.

The application programs depend, however, on the operating system, a program (actually many programs) that links the hardware components to one another. Thus, it is the operating system that lets you enter text at a keyboard, have that text displayed on a monitor, stored permanently on disk, then appear as hard copy on the printer. An application program (such as Microsoft Word) simply forwards your commands to the operating system, which does its work unobtrusively behind the scenes. A portion of the operating system is loaded into memory at the time the computer is turned on, and it remains there throughout the session, enabling you to do the work that you want to do.

The operating system determines the types of applications you can run. Microsoft Office 2000 is a powerful suite of application programs, but it requires at least the Windows 95 operating system. In other words, you cannot run Office 2000 with an operating system prior to Windows 95, such as Windows 3.1 or MS-DOS. It is important, therefore, that you recognize the different operating systems that are available for the PC and the capabilities and requirements of each.

The Evolution of the Desktop

The operating system for the PC has improved continually over time. As new hardware became available, new versions of the operating system were written to take advantage of the increased performance. Each improvement in hardware brought with it a new and better operating system, which in turn demanded faster hardware with more storage capability. Figure 12 displays a screen from each of four operating systems—MS-DOS 1.0, Windows 3.1, Windows 95, and Windows 98.

MS-DOS 1.0 was announced with the PC in 1981. The hardware was primitive by today's standards as a fully loaded PC came with 64KB of RAM, two 5¼ floppy drives (a hard disk was not yet available), and a monochrome monitor that displayed only text (not graphics). The operating system was equally basic and required only 20KB of disk storage, but it was perfectly matched to the available hardware.

MS-DOS would improve significantly over the years (eventually ending with MS-DOS 6.0), but it was always a text-based system. The flashing cursor and cryptic A:\> or C:\> prompt that was displayed on the screen was intimidating to the new user who had to know which commands to enter. The applications were also limited in that they were text-based and totally unrelated to one another. WordPerfect and Lotus, for example, were the dominant applications of their day, but each had a completely different interface so that knowledge of one did not help you to learn the other. And even if you knew both applications, you could run only one application at a time.

Figure 12 Evolution of Desktop

WINDOWS 3.1

Windows 3.1 (1991) introduced the graphical user interface as well as a common user interface and consistent command structure for all applications. It also provided multi-tasking and Object Linking and Embedding.

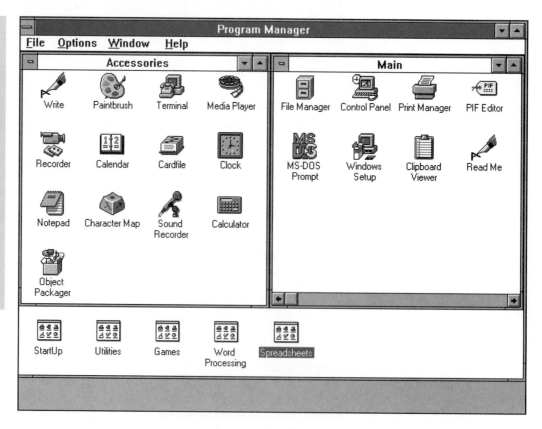

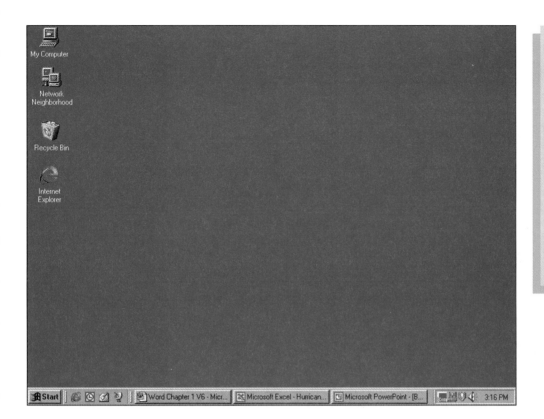

All of this changed with the introduction of **Windows 3.1** in 1991, which introduced the **graphical user interface** (**GUI** and pronounced "gooey") that let you use a mouse to point and click icons instead of having to enter text-based commands. Windows 3.1 also provided a **WYSIWYG** (pronounced "wizzywig" and standing for What You See Is What You Get) interface in which text and graphic elements appeared on the screen exactly as they appeared on the printer. Boldface and Italics were displayed in different point sizes and different typefaces. We take it for granted today, but it was a very big deal at the time.

Windows 3.1 was much more than just a pretty facelift as it introduced three other significant innovations. First and foremost is the **common user interface** whereby all applications adhere to the same conventions and work basically the same way. This means that once you learn one Windows application, it is that much easier to learn the next because all applications follow a consistent command structure. The second innovation is **multitasking,** which lets you run more than one program at a time. This enables you to go back and forth between tasks, putting down a word processing document, for example, to read an e-mail message. The third innovation **Object Linking and Embedding** (abbreviated **OLE** and pronounced "olay") enables you to share data between applications. Using OLE you can create a document with data (objects) from multiple applications— for example, a Word document that contains an Excel spreadsheet and chart.

Four years later Microsoft announced **Windows 95,** which sought to make the PC even easier to use. The simpler desktop in Windows 95 lets the user click the Start button to begin. Multitasking is implemented by clicking a button on the Windows 95 taskbar (as opposed to having to use the Alt+Tab shortcut in Windows

3.1). File management is made more intuitive in Windows 95 through introduction of the My Computer icon on the desktop. Windows 95 also introduced long filenames (up to 255 characters) as opposed to the eight-character filenames that existed under MS-DOS and carried over to Windows 3.1.

No sooner did Windows 95 come out, than the Internet, and more specifically, the World Wide Web exploded into the public consciousness. Microsoft, for once, was caught unaware as the Netscape Corporation introduced its Web browser, which thoroughly eclipsed anything Microsoft had to offer. Not to be outdone, Microsoft refocused its efforts on the Internet, which resulted in **Windows 98.**

There are two key changes to the Windows 98 desktop. First, the user has the option of clicking, rather than double clicking, the desktop icons. Look carefully at the My Computer icon, for example, in both Figures 12c and 12d. It is underlined in the latter figure where it functions in the same way as a hyperlink in a Web browser; that is, you click an icon in Windows 98 to open the object as opposed to having to double click it in Windows 95.

Windows 98 also introduced the **Active Desktop,** whereby Web content is displayed on the desktop without specific action on the part of the user (other than subscribing to the site initially). Look carefully at Figure 12d, for example, and note the presence of two resizable windows, one for *USA Today* and one for the *ESPN SportsZone.* The taskbar does not show any open applications, however, because the Web content has been delivered to the desktop automatically, without the user having to go to the associated Web sites.

Antivirus Software

Windows 95—and its successors—each consume at least 100MB of space on a hard disk. No version of Windows, however, will protect your system from a **computer virus**, an actively infectious program that attaches itself to other programs and thus alters the way your computer works. Some viruses do nothing more than display an annoying message at an inopportune time. Other viruses are more harmful and infect memory, the files on a hard disk, and in extreme instances can erase every file on your system. What makes a virus even more dangerous is that it can copy itself to a floppy disk and thus infect other systems through the contaminated disk. In other words, should a friend or colleague give you an infected floppy disk, your PC would be exposed to every virus with which that disk had come into contact.

The threat of contaminating your system with a virus is very real. The only way to eliminate all exposure is to never copy anything from a floppy disk, and further to never download anything from the Web. A less extreme but still effective approach is the acquisition of an **antivirus program** that can automatically detect a virus should it threaten your system. Many such programs are available, but their effectiveness depends on constant updating because new viruses appear all the time. Most vendors maintain a Web site through which the updates are delivered. Forewarned is forearmed.

Backup

The bulk of your time at the computer will be spent using different applications to create a variety of documents. Take it from us, however, it's not a question of *if* it will happen, but *when*—hard disks die and files are lost, and further, it always seems to happen the day before a major assignment or project is due. We urge you, therefore, to prepare for the inevitable by creating adequate **backup** (duplicate copies of important files) before the problem occurs. The essence of a backup strategy is to decide which files to back up, how often to do the backup, and where to keep the backup. Once you decide on a strategy, follow it, and follow it faithfully!

Our strategy is very simple—back up what you can't afford to lose, do so on a daily basis, and store the backup away from your computer. You need not copy every file, every day. Instead copy just the files that changed during the current session. Realize, too, that it is much more important to back up your data files than your program files. You can always reinstall the application from the original CD or floppy disks, or if necessary, go to the vendor for another copy of an application. You, however, are the only one who has a copy of the term paper that is due tomorrow.

BACK UP YOUR DATA

How much would you pay to have another copy of your term paper or company project that just disappeared from your hard drive? It has happened to us, and it will happen to you. We urge you, therefore, to take a few minutes at the end of every session to back up the files you cannot afford to lose. You need not copy every file, only the data files that were changed during that session. It takes only a few minutes, but one day, you will thank us.

The ultimate goal of computer literacy is the ability to do useful work, which is accomplished through application software. ***Word processing*** was the first major business application of microcomputers. A novelty in the 1970s, it is now commonplace. With a word processor you enter a document into the computer using the keyboard, then save the document on disk. You can return to the document at a later time to insert new text and/or delete superfluous material. A powerful set of editing commands lets you move words, sentences, or even paragraphs from one place to another, and/or alter the appearance of your document by changing margins or line spacing. Additional features check spelling and grammar, provide access to a thesaurus, and prepare form letters. And like all Windows applications, the WYSIWYG nature of today's word processing software enables you to create the document in a variety of typefaces, sizes, and styles, and/or combine a document with graphical images such as clip art or photographs.

Spreadsheets are the application most widely used by business managers. A spreadsheet is the electronic equivalent of an accountant's ledger. Anything that lends itself to expression in row and column format is a potential spreadsheet (for example, a professor's grade book or a financial forecast). The advantages of the spreadsheet are that changes are far easier to make than with pad and pencil, and further, that the necessary calculations and recalculations are made instantly, accurately, and automatically.

Data management software allows you to maintain records electronically, be they student records in a university, customer records in a business, or inventory records in a warehouse. Data management software provides for the addition of new records as well as the modification or deletion of existing data. You can retrieve your data in any order that you like—for example, alphabetically or by identification number. You can display all the information or only a selected portion. For example, you could see only those customers with delinquent accounts, or only those inventory items that need reordering.

Presentation software helps you to communicate your ideas to others in an effective way. It lets you focus on the content of your presentation without concern for its appearance. Then, when you have decided what you want to say, the software takes care of the formatting and creates an attractive presentation based on one of many professionally designed templates. The color scheme and graphic design are applied automatically. You also have the option of delivering the presentation in a variety of formats, such as on a computer screen or transparencies displayed on an overhead projector.

The emergence of the Internet and World Wide Web has created an entirely new type of application known as a ***browser*** that enables you to display pages from the Web on a PC. Internet Explorer and Netscape Communicator are the two most popular browsers and are discussed in more detail later in this supplement.

GARBAGE IN, GARBAGE OUT (GIGO)

A computer does exactly what you tell it to do, which is not necessarily what you want it to do. It is absolutely critical, therefore, that you validate the data that goes into a system, or else the associated information will not be correct. No system, no matter how sophisticated, can produce valid output from invalid input. The financial projections in a spreadsheet, for example, will produce erroneous results if they are based on invalid assumptions. In other words, garbage in—garbage out.

Microsoft Office 2000 Professional contains four individual applications— ***Microsoft Word, Excel, Access,*** and ***PowerPoint,*** corresponding to the application areas just discussed. This section describes the similarities between the various applications in Office 2000, where you will find the same commands in the same menus, you will see the same toolbar buttons from one application to the next, and you will be able to take advantage of the same keyboard shortcuts.

Figure 13 displays a screen from each major application in the Microsoft Office. (Microsoft Outlook is part of Office 2000, but is not shown.) Look closely at Figure 13, and realize that each screen contains both an application window and a document window, and that each document window has been maximized within the application window. The title bars of the application and document windows have been merged into a single title bar that appears at the top of the application window. The title bar displays the application (e.g., Microsoft Word in Figure 13a) as well as the name of the document (Note from Bob and Maryann) on which you are working.

All four screens in Figure 13 are similar in appearance even though the applications accomplish very different tasks. Each application window has an identifying icon, a menu bar, a title bar, and a minimize, maximize or restore, and a close button. The Windows taskbar appears at the bottom of each application window and shows the open applications. The status bar appears above the taskbar and displays information relevant to the window or selected object.

The applications in Microsoft Office have a consistent command structure in which the same basic menus (the File, Edit, View, Insert, Tools, Window, and Help menus) are present in each application. In addition, the same commands are found in the same menus. The Save, Open, Print, and Exit commands, for example, are contained in the File menu. The Cut, Copy, Paste, and Undo commands are found in the Edit menu.

The means for accessing the pull-down menus are consistent from one application to the next. Click the menu name on the menu bar, or press the Alt key plus the underlined letter of the menu name; for example, press Alt+F to pull down the File menu. If you already know some keyboard shortcuts in one application, there is a good chance that the shortcuts will work in another application. Ctrl+Home and Ctrl+End, for example, move to the beginning and end of a document, respectively.

All four applications use consistent (and often identical) dialog boxes. The dialog boxes to open and close a file, for example, are identical in every application. All four applications also share a common dictionary that is accessed whenever a spell check is executed.

There are, of course, differences between the applications. Each application has its own unique menus and associated toolbars. Nevertheless, the Standard and Formatting toolbars in all applications contain many of the same tools (especially the first several tools on the left of each toolbar). The ***Standard toolbar*** contains buttons for basic commands such as open, save, or print. It also contains buttons to cut, copy, and paste, and all of these buttons are identical in all four applications. The ***Formatting toolbar*** provides access to common formatting operations such as boldface, italics, or underlining, or changing the font or point size, and again, these buttons are identical in all four applications. ScreenTips that identify the purpose of a tool are present in all applications. Suffice it to say, therefore, that once you know one Office application, you have a tremendous head start in learning another.

Figure 13 Microsoft Office 2000

Menu bar
Standard toolbar
Formatting toolbar

Minimize button
Restore button
Close button

Status bar
Taskbar

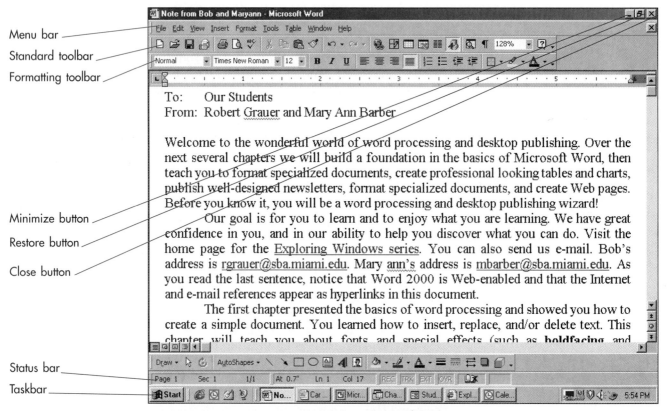

(a) Microsoft Word

Menu bar
Standard toolbar
Formatting toolbar

Minimize button
Restore button
Close button

Status bar
Taskbar

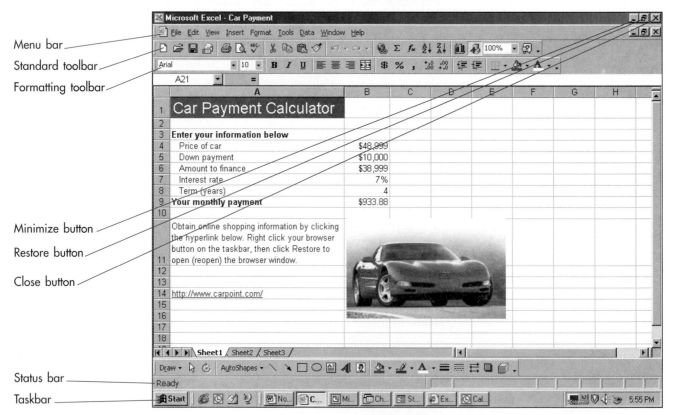

(b) Microsoft Excel

Menu bar

Standard toolbar

Formatting toolbar

Minimize button

Restore button

Close button

Status bar

Taskbar

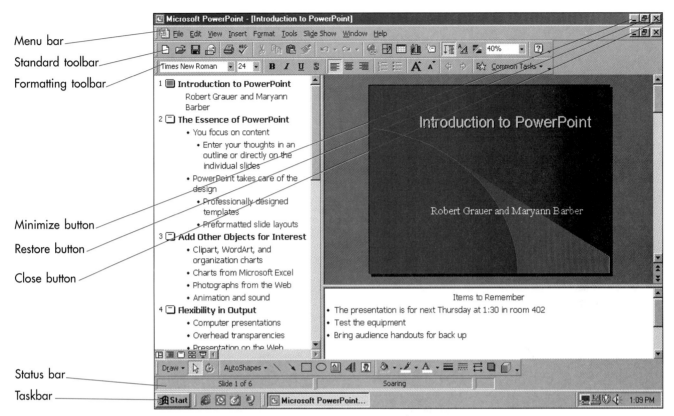

(c) Microsoft PowerPoint

Menu bar

Standard toolbar

Formatting toolbar

Minimize button

Restore button

Close button

Status bar

Taskbar

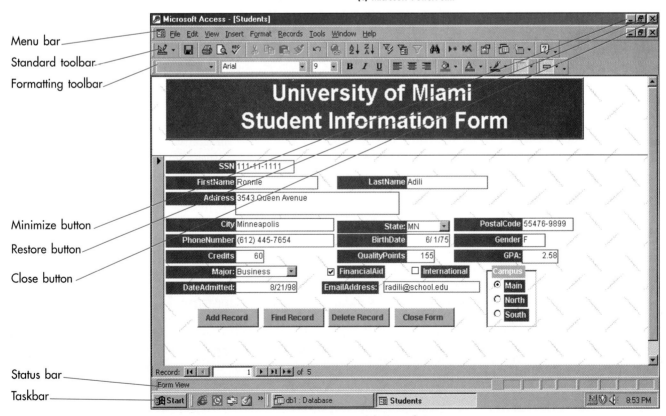

(d) Microsoft Access

A **network** is a combination of hardware and software that enables the connected computers to share resources and communicate with one another. It may be large enough to encompass computers around the world or it may be limited to the computers on one floor of a building. The latter is known as a **local area network** or **LAN,** and it is very likely that the computer you use at school or work is connected to a local area network.

Local area networks are common today, but that was not always true. Without a LAN, you often created a file on one computer, then carried the disk to another machine in order to use the laser printer. Or you might have had to run down the hall to borrow a disk that contained a specific file in order to load the file on your computer. Or you might have left a message for a friend or colleague in his or her inbox, only to have it get lost under a pile of paper.

All of these situations are examples of network applications, implemented informally in a "sneaker net," whereby you transferred a file to a floppy disk, put on your sneakers, and ran down the hall to deliver the disk to someone else. A local area network automates the process, and while sneaker net may not sound very impressive, it does illustrate the concept rather effectively.

The idea behind a LAN is very simple—to enable the connected computers, called workstations or nodes, to share network resources such as application software, hardware, and data. One printer, for example, can support multiple workstations, because not everyone needs to print at the same time. The network is managed by a more powerful computer called a **file server** that provides a common place to store data and programs. Another major function of the local area network is to provide Internet access for its workstations. This is typically done via a separate network computer known as an **Internet server.**

Figure 14 represents a conceptual view of three different LANs that are connected to one another, which is typical on a university campus. Each network consists of multiple workstations, a file server, and a laser printer. Each workstation on the network has access to the disk storage on the server and thus has access to its programs and/or data. Different types of workstations (PCs and Macs) can be connected to the same local area network. One of the LANs also has an Internet server to provide Internet access to the connected workstations on both networks.

Application programs are typically stored on a server rather than on individual machines. To use a network application on your workstation, you click the icon to load the program, which issues a request to the server. The server in turn verifies that you are permitted access to the program, then it loads the application into your PC's memory and the application appears on your screen. The document used with the application may be stored on either a local or a network drive. If the document is stored locally, the network does not come into play. If, however, the document is kept on the network, the server will check that you are permitted access to the document and that it is not already in use, then it will open the document for you. The server will then prevent other users from gaining access to that document as long as it is open on your machine.

While you're working, other people on the network may load the word processor, but no one else can access your particular document. Anyone attempting to do so receives a message saying the file is in use, because the network locks out everyone else from that file. You finish editing and save the file. Then you execute the print command, and the network prints the document on a network printer.

PROTECT YOUR PASSWORD

Almost all computer break-ins occur because of a poorly chosen password. A four-letter password, for example, has fewer than 500,000 combinations, and can be broken by a hacker in only 30 seconds of computer time. Opting for eight letters increases the number of combinations to more than 200 billion, which makes the intruder's job much more difficult. And if you include numbers in addition to letters, an eight-character password (letters and numbers) has more than 2 trillion combinations. Protect your password!

Figure 14 A Local Area Network

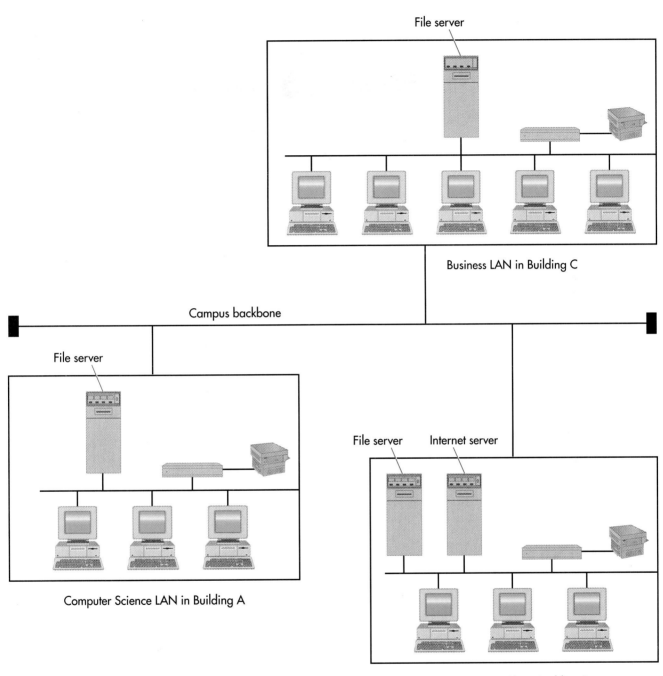

File server

Business LAN in Building C

Campus backbone

File server

Computer Science LAN in Building A

File server   Internet server

Engineering LAN in Building B

The **Internet** is a network of networks that spans the globe. It grew out of a government project that began in 1969 to test the feasibility of a network where scientists and military personnel could share messages and data no matter where they were. There was no central computer and every node was equal. The only thing that mattered was the origin and destination of a message. The original network consisted of only four computers. Today, there are literally millions of computers with an Internet connection (the exact number is impossible to determine) and tens of millions of people with Internet access.

The **World Wide Web** (**WWW** or simply the Web) is a very large subset of the Internet, consisting of those computers that store hypertext and hypermedia documents. Unlike a traditional document, which is read sequentially from top to bottom, a hypertext document includes links to other documents, which may be located on other computers that can be viewed (or not) at the reader's discretion. Hypermedia is similar in concept except that it provides links to graphic, sound, and video files in addition to text files.

Either type of document enables you to move effortlessly from one document (or computer) to another. And therein lies the fascination of the Web, in that you simply click on link after link to go effortlessly from one document to the next. You can start your journey at your professor's home page in New York, for example, which may link to a document in the Library of Congress, which in turn may take you to a different document, and so on. So, off you go to Washington DC, and from there to a reference across the country or perhaps around the world.

Any computer that stores a hypermedia document anywhere on the Web, and further, makes that document available to other computers, is known as a server (or Web server). Any computer that is connected to the Web, and requests a document from a server, is known as a client. In other words, you work on a client computer (e.g., a node on a local area network or your PC at home) and by clicking a link in a hypermedia document, you are requesting information from a Web server.

In order for the Web to work, every client (be it a PC or a Mac) must be able to display every document from every server. This is accomplished by imposing a set of standards known as a protocol to govern the way data is transmitted across the Web. Thus, data travels from client to server and back through a protocol known as the **HyperText Transfer Protocol** (or http for short). In addition, in order to access the documents that are transmitted through this protocol, you need a special type of program known as a **browser**. Indeed, a browser is aptly named because it enables you to inspect the Web in a leisurely and casual way (the dictionary definition of the word "browse").

Internet Explorer is the browser provided by Microsoft. **Netscape Navigator** (or the more recent **Netscape Communicator**) is a competing product. Microsoft and Netscape are constantly trying to outdo one another, but both programs are incredibly good. Figures 15a and 15b display the Exploring Windows home page (www.prenhall.com/grauer) in Internet Explorer 4.0 and Netscape Communicator, respectively. The toolbars and menu bars are different, but both programs have similar capabilities and share the common user interface common to all Windows applications. Either program will suffice. Your main concern is gaining access to the Internet.

IT'S THE URL, NOT THE BROWSER

Microsoft and Netscape argue vehemently about which is the superior browser. In actuality, however, both products are so feature rich that it doesn't really matter which one you choose. To see for yourself, try viewing the same Web page in both browsers. What difference (if any) do you see when a page is viewed in Netscape rather than Internet Explorer? Do you agree with our statement, that it is the URL (Web address) that is important, rather than the actual browser?

Figure 15 Internet Browsers

Menu bar

Toolbar

Address of displayed page

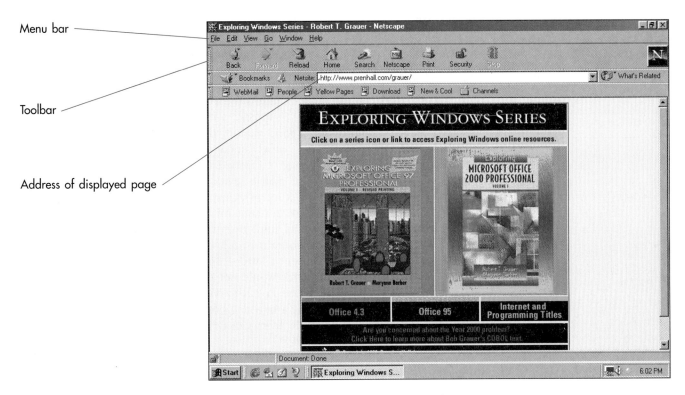

(a) Netscape Communicator

Menu bar

Address of displayed page

Toolbar

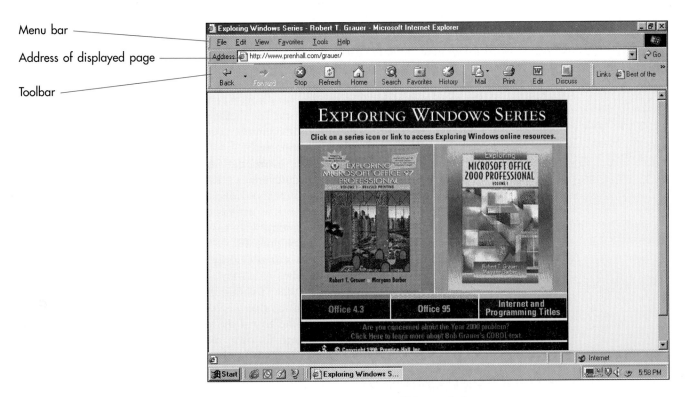

(b) Internet Explorer

Data is transmitted across the Internet through a series of protocols known collectively as **TCP/IP** (Transmission Control Protocol/Internet Protocol). A **protocol** is an agreed-upon set of conventions that define the rules of communication. You follow a protocol in class; for example, you raise your hand and wait to be acknowledged by your professor. In similar fashion, the sending and receiving computers on the Internet follow the TCP/IP protocol to ensure that data is transmitted correctly.

The postal system provides a good analogy of how (but certainly not how fast) TCP/IP is implemented. (The post office analogy was suggested by Ed Krol in his excellent book *The Whole Internet,* published by O'Reilly and Associates, Inc., Sebastopol, CA, 1992.) When you mail a regular letter, you drop it in a mailbox where it is picked up along with a lot of other letters and delivered to the local post office. The letters are sorted and sent on their way to a larger post office, where the letters are sorted again, until eventually each letter reaches the post office closest to its destination, where it is delivered to the addressee by the local mail carrier. If, for example, you sent a letter from Coral Springs, Florida, to Upper Saddle River, New Jersey, the letter would not travel directly from Coral Springs to Upper Saddle River. Instead, the Postal Service would forward the letter from one substation to the next, making a new decision at each substation as to the best (most efficient) route; for example, from Coral Springs, to Miami, to Newark, and finally, to Upper Saddle River.

Each postal substation considers all of the routes it has available to the next substation and makes the best possible decision according to the prevailing conditions. This means that the next time you mail a letter from Coral Springs to Upper Saddle River, the letter may travel a completely different path. If the mail truck from Coral Springs to Miami had already left or was full to capacity, the letter could be routed through Fort Lauderdale to New York City, and then to Upper Saddle River. The actual route taken by the letter is not important. All that matters is that the letter arrives at its destination.

The Internet works the same way, as data travels across the Internet through several levels of networks until it gets to its destination. E-mail messages arrive at the local post office (the mail server) from a remote PC connected by modem, or from a node on a local area network. The messages then leave the local post office and pass through a special-purpose computer known as a **router,** that ensures each message is sent to its correct destination.

A message may pass through several networks to get to its destination. Each network has its own router that determines how best to move the message closer to its destination, taking into account the traffic on the network. A message passes from one network to the next until it arrives at the destination network, from where it can be sent to the recipient, who has a mailbox on that network. The process is depicted graphically in Figure 16.

In actuality, the TCP/IP protocol is slightly more complicated than what we have been portraying, and it applies to all types of data, not just e-mail. To continue with the post office analogy, let's assume that you are sending a book, rather than a letter, and that the Post Office (for whatever reason) does not accept large packages. One alternative would be to rip the pages out of the book, mail each page individually by placing it into its own envelope, then trust that all of the envelopes arrive at the destination, and finally, that the person on the other end would be able to reassemble the individual pages. That may sound awkward, but it is a truer picture of how the Internet works.

Data (whether it is an e-mail message or a Web page) is sent across the Internet in *packets,* with each packet limited in size. The rules for creating, addressing, and sending the packets are specified by TCP/IP, which is actually two separate protocols. The TCP portion divides the file that you want to send into packets, then numbers each packet so that the message can be reconstructed at the other end. The IP portion sends each packet on its way by specifying the address of the sending and receiving computer so that the routers will be able to do their job.

The TCP/IP protocol may seem unnecessarily complicated, but it is actually very clever. Dividing large files into smaller pieces ensures that no single file monopolizes the network. A second advantage has to do with ensuring that the data arrives correctly. Static or noise on a telephone line is merely annoying to people having a conversation, but devastating when a file (especially a computer program) is transmitted and a byte or two is lost or corrupted. The larger the file being sent, the greater the chance that noise will be introduced and that the file will be corrupted. Sending the data in smaller pieces (packets), and verifying that the packets were received correctly, helps ensure the integrity of the data. If one packet is received incorrectly, the entire file does not have to be sent again, only the corrupted pocket.

Figure 16 A Message Travels the Internet

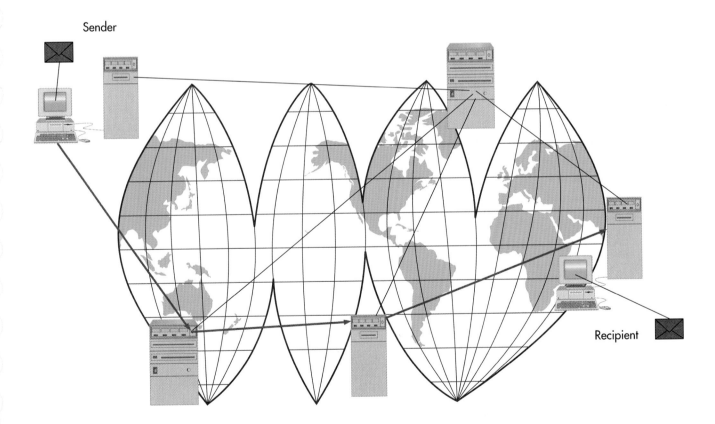

Many people are under the false impression that just because they have Netscape or Internet Explorer, they automatically have Internet access. Obtaining a browser is the first step as it provides the necessary software. You must also establish a physical connection, which is done through a local area network (LAN) at school or work, or by using a modem to dial into an Internet Service Provider (ISP).

A *modem* is the interface between your computer and the telephone system. In essence you instruct the modem, via the appropriate software, to dial the phone number of your ISP, which in turn lets you access the Internet. Most people acquire a modem when they purchase a PC, but it can be added or upgraded at any time. The faster your modem, the faster the data will pass back and forth, and it is well worth your investment to purchase the fastest modem available. Figure 17 provides a conceptual view of a connection to the Internet via modem.

Figure 17 Connecting to the Internet via Modem

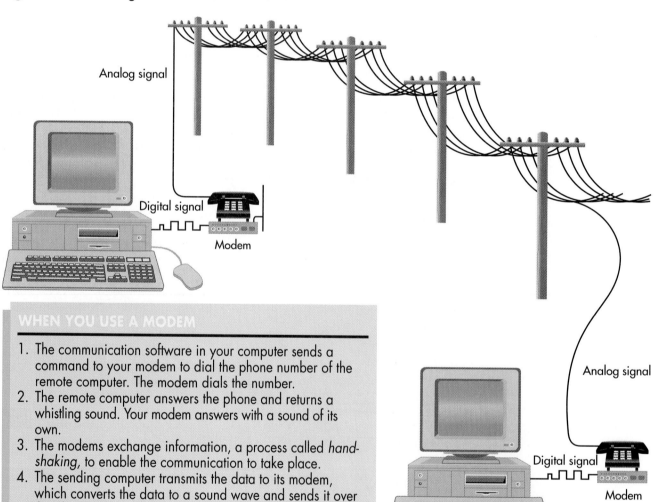

WHEN YOU USE A MODEM

1. The communication software in your computer sends a command to your modem to dial the phone number of the remote computer. The modem dials the number.
2. The remote computer answers the phone and returns a whistling sound. Your modem answers with a sound of its own.
3. The modems exchange information, a process called *handshaking*, to enable the communication to take place.
4. The sending computer transmits the data to its modem, which converts the data to a sound wave and sends it over the phone line.
5. The receiving modem converts the sound wave to a digital signal for the receiving computer which processes the data and sends a reply.
6. Communications continue back and forth until eventually one of the computers instructs its modem to end the session.

An Internet Service Provider (ISP) is a company or organization that maintains a computer with permanent access to the Internet. Typically, you have to pay for this service, but you may be able to dial into your school or university at no charge. If not, you need to sign up with a commercial vendor such as America Online (AOL). Not only does AOL provide access to the Internet, but it also offers a proprietary interface and other services such as local chat rooms. The Microsoft Network (MSN) is a direct competitor to AOL and it, too, offers a proprietary interface and extra services. Alternatively, you can choose from a host of other vendors who provide Internet Access without the proprietary interface of AOL or MSN.

Regardless of which ISP you choose, be sure you understand the fee structure. The monthly fee may entitle you to a set number of hours per month (after which you pay an additional fee), or it may give you unlimited access. The terms vary widely, and we suggest you shop around for the best possible deal. In addition, be sure you are given a local access number (so that you do not have to make a long distance call), or else your telephone bill will be outrageous. Check that the facilities of your provider are adequate and that you can obtain access whenever you want. Few things are more frustrating than to receive continual busy signals when you are trying to log on.

Downloading a File

The ability to download a file from the Internet is one of its most important capabilities. It enables a vendor to post the latest version of a file on its Web site and to make that file available to its clients or end users. The cost saving is significant, as the vendor does not have to manufacture disks or CDs, and further, saves on postage and handling costs. The end user benefits as well, as he or she gains access to a file immediately, and often without cost.

Downloading a file is a straightforward process, but it can be confusing for the novice. Software and other files are typically compressed (made smaller) to reduce the amount of storage space the files require on disk and/or the time it takes to download the files. In essence, you download a *compressed file* (which may contain multiple individual files), then you uncompress the file on your local drive in order to access the individual files. Compression algorithms are very sophisticated, and the details of how they work are beyond the scope of this discussion. Realize, however, that compression algorithms are very efficient and effect significant savings, as much as 90 percent for certain types of files.

DISABLE CALL WAITING

Your friend may understand if you excuse yourself in the middle of a conversation to answer another incoming call. A computer, however, is not so tolerant and will often break the current connection if another call comes in. Accordingly, check the settings of your communications program to disable call waiting prior to connecting to the Internet (typically by entering *70 in front of the access number). Your friends may complain of a busy signal, but you will be able to work without interruption.

Electronic mail, or *e-mail*, is the most widely used Internet service. E-mail is conceptually the same as writing a letter and sending it through the U.S. Postal Service, with one very significant advantage—e-mail messages are delivered almost instantly as opposed to regular (snail) mail, which requires several days. E-mail was unknown to the general public only a few years ago, but it has become an integral part of American culture.

All Windows-based e-mail systems work basically the same way. You need access to a *mail server* (a computer with an Internet connection) to receive your incoming messages and to deliver the messages you send. You also need a *mail client,* a program such as *Outlook Express,* in order to read and compose e-mail messages, and to transfer mail back and forth to the server.

The mail server functions as a central post office and provides private mailboxes to persons authorized to use its services. It receives mail around the clock and will hold it for you until you sign on to retrieve it. You gain access to your mailbox via a *username* and a *password.* The username identifies you to the server. The password protects your account from unauthorized use by others. Once you log on to the server, incoming mail is downloaded from the server and stored in the inbox on your PC. Outgoing mail is uploaded from your PC to the server, where it is sent on its way across a local area network to another person within your organization or across the Internet to the world at large.

Figure 18a displays the inbox as it appears in Outlook Express. The inbox lists all incoming messages, the person who sent the message, the subject of the message, and the date and time the message was received. The messages are listed in the order they were received (the most recent message is listed at the top of the list).The inbox is one of several folders that are used in conjunction with Internet mail. Click a different icon on the Outlook bar, and its contents will be displayed in the right pane.

The purpose of the other folders can be inferred from their names. The Outbox folder contains all of the messages you have written that have not yet been sent (uploaded) to the server. Once a message has been sent, it is moved automatically to the Sent Items folder. Messages will remain indefinitely in both the Inbox and Sent Items folders unless you delete them, in which case they are moved to the Deleted Items folder.

All e-mail systems provide the same basic commands, which are accessed via pull-down menus or by toolbar icons. Thus, you can compose a new message, or reply to or forward an existing message. You can also use an address book to look up the e-mail address of the intended recipient. Figure 18b displays the Compose Message window in which you create a new message or reply to an existing message.

As you begin to use e-mail, you should realize that one of the most significant differences between e-mail and regular mail is privacy or the lack thereof. When you receive a sealed letter through the mail, you can assume that no one else has read the letter. Not so with e-mail. The network administrator can read the messages in your inbox, and indeed, many employers maintain they have the legal right to read their employees' e-mail. And don't assume that deleting a message protects its privacy, since most organizations maintain extensive backup and can recover a deleted message. In other words, never put anything in an e-mail message that you would be uncomfortable seeing in tomorrow's newspaper.

NO MORE TELEPHONE TAG

E-mail has changed the way we communicate and in many ways is superior to the telephone. You send a message when it is convenient for you. The recipient reads the message when it is convenient to do so. Neither person has to be online for the other to access his or her e-mail system. You can send the same message to many people as opposed to having to call them individually. And best of all, e-mail is a lot cheaper than a long-distance phone call.

Figure 18 Introduction to E-mail

The Inbox folder is selected

Text of selected message

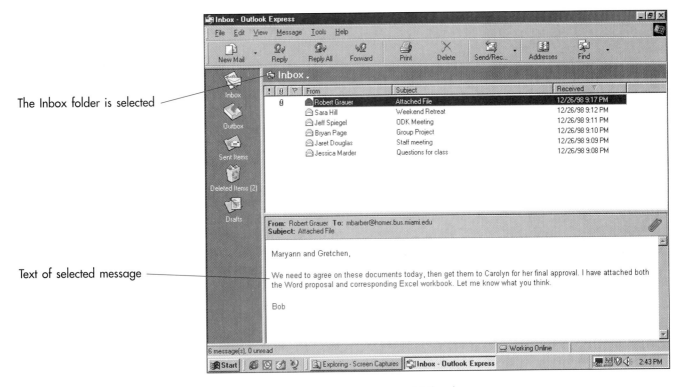

(a) The Inbox

Address of recipient

Subject of message

Text of message

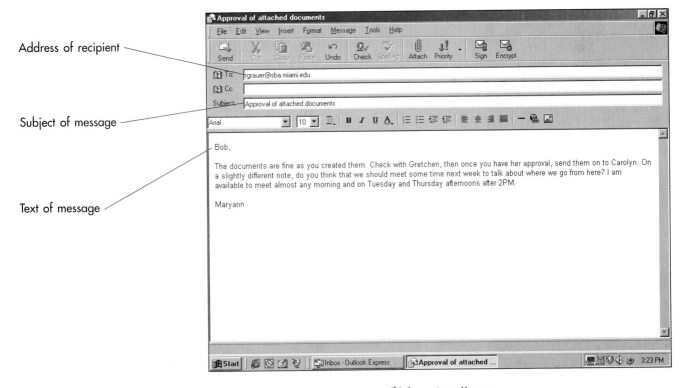

(b) Composing a Message

A computer is an electronic device that accepts data (input), then manipulates or processes that data to produce information (output). A computer system consists of the computer and its memory, peripheral devices such as a keyboard, disk, monitor, and printer, and the various programs that enable it to perform its intended function.

Traditionally, computers have been divided into three broad classes—mainframes, minicomputers (called servers in today's environment), and microcomputers (PCs). The classification is primarily one of scale. Mainframes are much larger, faster, cost significantly more money, and have much greater memory and auxiliary storage capacities than other computers. Mainframes and servers also permit multiple users.

IBM announced its version of the personal computer (PC) in 1981 and broke a longstanding corporate tradition by going to external sources for supporting hardware and software. Intel designed the microprocessor. Microsoft developed the operating system. The success of the PC was due in large part to its open design that let independent vendors offer supporting products to enhance the functionality of the machine.

Computer memory and storage capacity are described in bytes. Each byte holds 8 bits (binary digits) or one ASCII character. A kilobyte, megabyte, and gigabyte are approximately one thousand, one million, and one billion bytes, respectively.

There are several types of auxiliary storage devices. Disks are the most common and fall into two categories—floppy disks and hard disks. A hard disk holds significantly more data than a floppy disk, and it accesses that data much faster. The CD-ROM is also a standard auxiliary storage device on today's PC. A tape backup unit and/or high-capacity removable storage media are used to back up the data on a hard disk.

The keyboard and the mouse are the primary input devices for the PC. The keys on the keyboard are arranged much like those of a typewriter, in the standard QWERTY pattern (named for the first six characters in the third row). The standard mouse has two buttons and recognizes four basic operations: point, click (with either button), double click, and drag.

The monitor (or video display) is an output device. The resolution of a monitor is defined as the number of pixels (picture elements) that are displayed at one time; for example, 640×480 or 800×600. The higher the resolution, the larger the monitor that is needed to display the image. The quality of a monitor is measured by its dot pitch; the smaller the dot pitch, the crisper the image.

A printer produces output on paper or acetate transparencies. The output is referred to as hard copy because it is more tangible than the files written to a disk or other electronic device. Printers vary greatly in terms of design, price, and capability. Inkjet and laser printers are today's common technologies.

Software is divided broadly into two classes—system software (referred to as the operating system) and application software. The operating system determines the types of applications the system can run. MS-DOS 1.1 was the first version of the PC operating system. Windows 3.1 introduced several improvements including the graphical user interface, common user interface and consistent command structure for all applications, multitasking, and object linking and embedding. Windows 95 simplified the desktop and made the power of the operating system more apparent to the user. Windows 98 integrated the Internet and the desktop.

Microsoft Office 2000 Professional contains four separate applications—Microsoft Word, Excel, Access, and PowerPoint—for word processing, spreadsheets, database, and presentations, respectively. Office 2000 requires at least the Windows 95 operating system.

A computer system should be protected through the acquisition of antivirus software. Adequate backup should also be created for all essential files on a regular basis and stored offsite.

A network is a combination of hardware and software that enables the connected computers to share resources and communicate with one another. It may be large enough to encompass computers around the world, or it may be limited to the computers on one floor of a building. The latter is known as a local area network or LAN.

The Internet is a network of networks. The World Wide Web (or simply the Web) is a very large subset of the Internet, consisting of those computers that store hypertext and hypermedia documents. A browser such as Internet Explorer or Netscape Navigator is required to view documents from the Web. A connection to the Internet is established through a local area network (LAN) or by connecting to an Internet Service Provider (ISP) via a modem. Electronic mail, or e-mail, is the most widely used Internet service.

Key Words and Concepts

Multiple Choice

1. How many bytes are in 1KB?
   - (a) 1,000
   - (b) 1,024
   - (c) 1,000,000
   - (d) 1,024,000

2. The size of a computer's memory refers to
   - (a) The capacity of its hard disk
   - (b) The capacity of its floppy disk
   - (c) The amount of ROM available
   - (d) The amount of RAM available

3. Hard copy refers to
   - (a) The difficulty of duplicating a disk
   - (b) Information stored on a hard drive
   - (c) Written material that is difficult to read
   - (d) None of the above

4. Which of the following was the first major application of microcomputers?
   - (a) Word processing
   - (b) Spreadsheets
   - (c) Presentations
   - (d) Data management

5. The contents of ROM
   - (a) Are constantly changed as different programs are executed
   - (b) Contain information to start the system
   - (c) Can be easily changed by the user
   - (d) All of the above

6. Which of the following is best suited as a backup device?
   - (a) A floppy disk
   - (b) A hard disk
   - (c) A CD-ROM
   - (d) An Iomega Zip drive

7. Which of the following is true?
   - (a) A byte is the smallest addressable unit of memory
   - (b) The capacity of a disk is measured in bytes
   - (c) The ASCII system equates the various bit combinations in a byte to a specific character
   - (d) All of the above

8. Which of the following displays capacities from largest to smallest?
   - (a) KB, MB, GB
   - (b) GB, MB, KB
   - (c) GB, KB, MB
   - (d) MB, KB, GB

9. Which of the following best describes the memory and hard disk in a PC you would buy today?
   - (a) The capacity of RAM is measured in megabytes, the capacity of a hard disk is measured in gigabytes
   - (b) The capacity of RAM is measured in gigabytes, the capacity of a hard disk is measured in megabytes
   - (c) The capacities of RAM and a hard disk are both measured in gigabytes
   - (d) The capacities of RAM and a hard disk are both measured in megabytes

10. A local area network is intended to
    - (a) Share data among connected computers
    - (b) Share peripheral devices among computers
    - (c) Share programs among connected computers
    - (d) All of the above

11. A virus can be transmitted to your computer when you
    - (a) Download files from the Internet
    - (b) Copy files from a floppy disk to your hard drive
    - (c) Both (a) and (b)
    - (d) Neither (a) nor (b)

12. Which of the following is not included in Microsoft Office 2000?
    - (a) Microsoft Excel
    - (b) Microsoft Word
    - (c) Windows 2000
    - (d) Microsoft PowerPoint

13. Which version of Windows is (was) not intended for the typical home user?
    - (a) Windows 98
    - (b) Windows 95
    - (c) Windows NT
    - (d) Windows 3.1

14. Which operating system introduced the common user interface, multitasking, and Object Linking and Embedding?
    - (a) MS-DOS 6.0
    - (b) Windows 3.1
    - (c) Windows 95
    - (d) Windows 98

15. Which operating system was the first to support Microsoft Office 2000?
    - (a) Windows 3.1
    - (b) Windows 95
    - (c) Windows 2000
    - (d) Windows 98

Answers

1. b	**6.** d	**11.** c
2. d	**7.** d	**12.** c
3. d	**8.** b	**13.** c
4. a	**9.** a	**14.** b
5. b	**10.** d	**15.** b

The Internet provides an infinite variety of places to explore. We have selected six sites and created a set of mini-exercises that relate to various topics covered in this supplement.

You're in the market for a PC and have a $2,000 budget. Go to the Dell site and select a configuration that will fit into your budget. Go to two other vendors to obtain competitive prices, then summarize your findings in a note to your instructor.

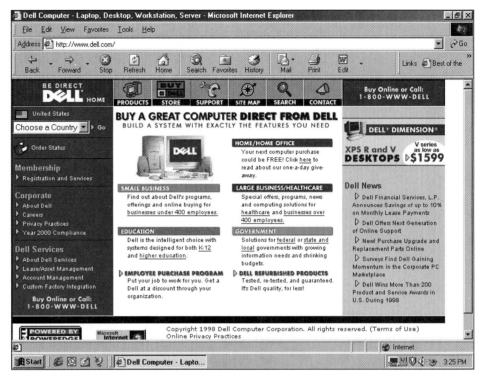

(a) Dell Computer (www.dell.com)

There are so many excellent sites on the Web that it's hard to know where to begin. We like the *PC Magazine* Top 100, which groups sites into categories and is updated continually. Write a brief report of a favorite site for your instructor.

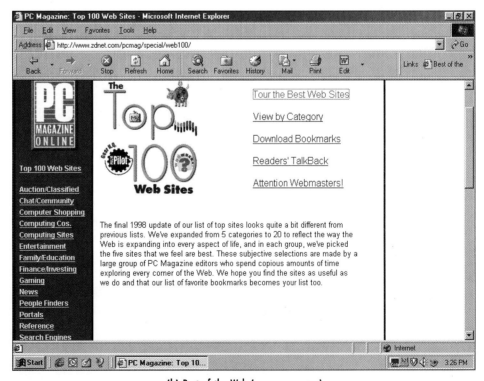

(b) Best of the Web (www.pcmag.com)

The Microsoft site provides free downloads plus technical support on any of its products. Choose a program you are using, then explore the support that is available for that program. Does the site provide useful information?

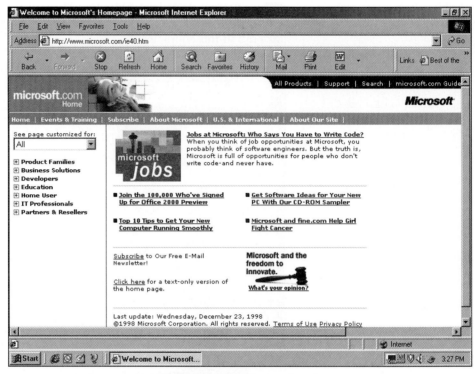

(c) Visit Microsoft (www.microsoft.com)

Visit the home page of your school or university to see what type of information is available. We're sure you will find items you never knew existed. Share your discoveries with your classmates.

(d) Visit Your School (supply your own address)

Visit the American Computer Museum (or another museum of your choice) to learn about the history of computers. See if you can find a picture of the ENIAC, one of the first commerical computers. Are you surprised about its size or cost?

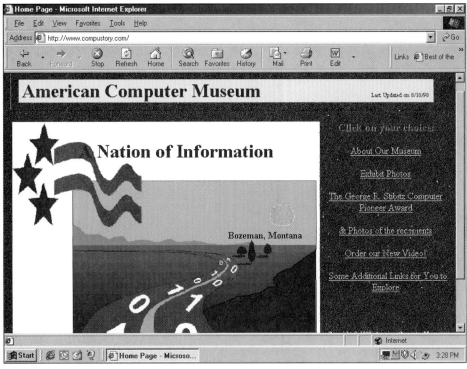

(e) History of Computers (www.compustory.com)

Visit the home page of the Fortune 500 to learn more about IBM, Microsoft, and Intel. Which is the largest company in terms of annual sales? In terms of profits? Which company is growing the fastest?

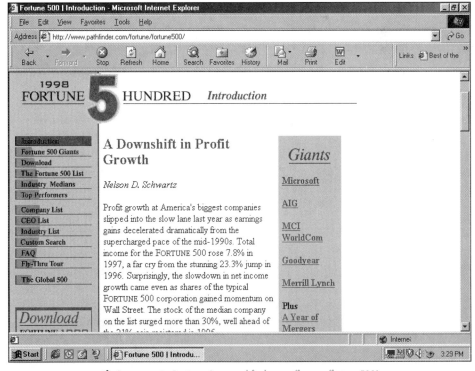

(f) Computers in Business (www.pathfinder.com/fortune/fortune500)

The *Miami Herald* is typical of most major newspapers in that it publishes an online version in addition to the traditional format. Choose any newspaper and see if it has a Web page. How does the paper make money if the online version is available at no charge? Which format do you prefer to read—the online version or the hard copy?

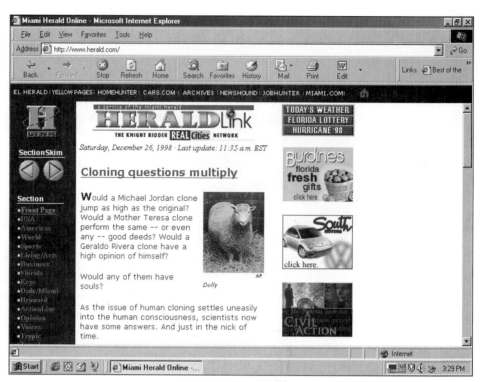

(g) Miami Herald (www.herald.com)

Photo Credits

Page 3	Stock Montage, Inc.
Page 6	Courtesy of International Business Machines Corporation. Unauthorized use not permitted.
Page 10	Courtesy of Intel Corporation/C & I Photography.
Page 13	(a) Courtesy of International Business Machines Corporation. Unauthorized use not permitted. (b) Courtesy of Seagate Technology/C & I Photography; (c) Courtesy of Hewlett-Packard Company; (d) Courtesy of International Business Machines Corporation. Unauthorized use not permitted. (e) Courtesy of Gateway 2000, Inc.
Page 15	Joystick: Courtesy of Microsoft Corporation; Mouse: Courtesy of International Business Machines Corporation. Unauthorized use not permitted.
Page 19	(a) Courtesy of International Business Machines Corporation. Unauthorized use not permitted. (b) Courtesy of Epson America, Inc. (c) Courtesy of Hewlett-Packard Company.
Page 22	(a) Courtesy of the Computer Museum History Center. (b) Courtesy of Apple Computer, Inc. (c) Courtesy of Apple Computer, Inc. (d) Courtesy of Gateway 2000, Inc.

INDEX